Temples and Sanctuaries from the Early Iron Age Levant

HISTORY, ARCHAEOLOGY, AND CULTURE OF THE LEVANT

Edited by

JEFFREY A. BLAKELY   *University of Wisconsin, Madison*
K. LAWSON YOUNGER   *Trinity Evangelical Divinity School*

Temples and Sanctuaries from the Early Iron Age Levant

Recovery after Collapse

WILLIAM E. MIERSE

WINONA LAKE, INDIANA
EISENBRAUNS
2012

www.eisenbrauns.com

Library of Congress Cataloging-in-Publication Data

Mierse, William E.
  Temples and sanctuaries from the early Iron Age Levant : recovery after collapse / William E.
  Mierse.
      pages   cm — (History, archaeology, and culture of the Levant ; 4)
  Includes bibliographical references and index.
  ISBN 978-1-57506-246-4 (hardback : alk. paper)
      1. Temples—Middle East.   2. Architecture, Ancient—Middle East.   3. Iron Age—Middle
East.   I. Title.
  NA212.M54 2012
    726'.109394—dc23
                                                                      2012028630

To my parents
for all their love and support

Contents

Preface

A book like this is never the result of one person's effort alone. There are many people who need to be thanked for their assistance over the years. Though it is common to thank one's spouse at the end, I wish first of all to acknowledge my wife, Helen. She, more than anyone other than me has been forced to adapt to the requirements of writing a book that has taken too many years, and I want to thank her publicly for all her patience and good humor. Helen accompanied me on all of the many site excursions, trudging through fields and barren wastes to find the remains of overgrown temples. She has ridden buses and broken-down taxis throughout much of the Middle East and has never complained. I certainly could not have kept up my own spirits without her good company. Moreover, she has patiently waited, given up weekend autumn trips in New England or holiday getaways so that I could produce yet another version of the manuscript. While I may have written the book, she certainly has lived it alongside me.

Three colleagues must be singled out for having willingly undertaken the task of reading earlier versions of this book. Without the insightful criticisms and suggestions of Martha Joukowsky, Greg McMahon, and Aaron Brody, much of what is valuable in this manuscript would not be here. The anonymous reader for Eisenbrauns also provided important corrective information. Obviously, he or she could not spot all the weaknesses in the manuscript, and I take complete credit for what remains.

The research began at the American Center for Oriental Research in Amman, where the then-director and co-director, Pierre and Patricia Bikai, created a warm and stimulating environment in which I was able to explore many avenues of investigation as I began the project. The discussions that I had with them at this early stage helped me to refine the project over the ensuing years. The staff of ACOR during the fall of 1996 was particularly helpful and contributed to making our stay there one of our fondest memories.

Over the years, many other individuals have helped me to complete this work. I want to acknowledge and thank the staff of the library of the Albright Institute in Jerusalem and the photographic researchers at the British Museum, Walters Museum, and Israel Museum. In my home institution, the University of Vermont, I must single out the staff of the interlibrary loan department of the Bailey-Howe Library, who have always found for me the obscure items that I seek. I would never have been able to complete the work on the drawings without the patient help and technical advice of computer technician Walker Blackwell of my department, the Department of Art and Art History. All drawings are mine. The original published drawings were copied and redrawn to achieve visual uniformity.

I thank Jim Eisenbraun for taking a chance with a book such as this, written by someone outside the field of ancient Near Eastern studies; and Beverly McCoy for her excellent work editing the manuscript.

Funding came from the American Center for Oriental Research in the form of a NEMERTA grant, with which I was able to begin my research. The University of Vermont provided assistance that allowed me to spend a summer working at the Albright Institute Library and to make a third trip to Lebanon, Syria, and Turkey.

Finally I want to thank all of the people throughout Turkey, Syria, Lebanon, Jordan, the Palestinian Territories, Israel, and Egypt who looked after my wife and me as we wandered through their countries. The legendary hospitality of the Middle East was always on view, and never did either of us feel unwelcomed or concerned about our situation. People always helped us and were generous in their interactions. It is the memories of the travels and of the personal engagements that will stay with me long after the details of the research have drifted away.

WILLIAM E. MIERSE
Burlington, VT
Fall 2010

Abbreviations

General

AO	registration number of tablet in the collections of the Louvre
AT	Alalakh text registration number
chap(s).	chapter(s)
cm	centimeter(s)
col(s).	column(s)
EB(A)	Early Bronze (Age)
fig(s).	figure(s)
ft.	foot/feet
IAA	Israel Antiquities Authority registration number
ill(s).	illustration(s)
in.	inch(es)
J	Jordan, Archaeological Museum in Amman, inventory number
LBA	Late Bronze Age
LC	Late Cypriot
LH	Late Helladic
LM	Late Mycenean
m	meter(s)
MB(A)	Middle Bronze Age
NEB	New English Bible
NJPS	New Jewish Publication Society version of the Bible
no(s).	number(s)
pl(s).	plate(s)
RS	Ras Shamra text registration number
RSV	Revised Standard Version
vol(s).	volume(s)

Reference Works

AA	*Archäologischer Anzeiger*
AAAS	*Les Annales Archéologiques Arabes Syriennes*
AASOR	*Annual of the American Schools of Oriental Research*
ABD	Freedman, D. N., ed. *Anchor Bible Dictionary*. 6 vols. New York: Doubleday, 1992
ADAJ	*Annual of the Department of Antiquities of Jordan*
AF	*Altorientalische Forschungen*

AfO	*Archiv für Orientforschung*
AJ	Homès-Frederiq, D., and Hennessy, J. B., eds. *Archaeology of of Jordan*, vol. 2/1–2: *Field Reports: Surveys and Sites A–K and L–Z.* Leuven: Peters, 1989
AJA	*American Journal of Archaeology*
ANE Anth.	Pritchard, J. B., ed. *The Ancient Near East: An Anthology of Texts and Pictures.* Princeton: Princeton University Press, 1958
AoF	*Altorientalische Forschungen*
ARM	Archives Royales de Mari 1–3 (1950), 4 (1951), 5 (1952), 6 (1954), 10 (1967; 1978), 13 (1964), 14 (1974; 1976), 18 (1976; 1977)
AnSt	*Anatolian Studies*
ASTI	*Annual of the Swedish Theological Institute*
AUSS	*Andrews University Seminary Studies*
BA	*Biblical Archaeology*
BAR	*Biblical Archaeology Review*
BASOR	*Bulletin of the American Schools of Oriental Research*
BCH	*Bulletin de correspondance hellénique*
BO	*Bibliotheca Orientalis*
BSOAS	*Bulletin of the School of Oriental and African Studies*
CAH	*Cambridge Ancient History.* 3rd ed. London: Cambridge University Press, 1970–
CBQ	*Catholic Biblical Quarterly*
CTA	Herdner, A., ed. *Corpus des tablettes en cunéiformes alphabétiques.* Paris: Imprimerie Nationale, 1963
ErIsr	*Eretz-Israel*
ESI	*Excavations and Surveys in Israel*
HSM	Harvard Semitic Monographs
HUCA	*Hebrew Union College Annual*
IEJ	*Israel Exploration Journal*
IEQ	*Israel Exploration Quarterly*
JACF	*Journal of Ancient Chronology Forum*
JANES(CU)	*Journal of the Ancient Near Eastern Society (of Columbia University)*
JBL	*Journal of Biblical Literature*
JMA	*Journal of Mediterranean Archaeology*
JNES	*Journal of Near Eastern Studies*
JSOT	*Journal for the Study of the Old Testament*
JSOTSup	Journal for the Study of the Old Testament Supplements
JSS	*Journal of Semitic Studies*
KAI	Donner, H., and Röllig, W. *Kanaanäische und aramäische Inschriften.* 3 vols. Wiesbaden: Harrassowitz, 1962–64
KTU	Dietrich, M.; Loretz, O.; and Sanmartín, J., eds. *Die Keilalphabetischen Texte aus Ugarit.* Alter Orient und Altes Testament 24. Kevelaer: Butzon & Bercker / Neukirchen-Vluyn: Neukirchener Verlag, 1976
KUB	Keilschrifturkunden aus Boghazköi
NEA	*Near Eastern Archaeology*
NEAEHL	Stern, E., ed. *New Encyclopedia of Archaeological Excavations in the Holy Land.* 4 vols. Jerusalem: Israel Exploration Society and Carta / New York: Simon & Schuster, 1993

OEANE	Meyers, E., ed. *The Oxford Encyclopedia of Archaeology in the Near East.* 5 vols. New York: Oxford University Press, 1997
OIP	Oriental Institute Publications
OJA	*Oxford Journal of Archaeology*
OLA	*Orientalia Lovaniensia Analecta*
Or	*Orientalia*
PEFQS	*Palestine Exploration Fund Quarterly*
PEQ	*Palestine Exploration Quarterly*
QDAP	*Quarterly of the Department of Antiquities in Palestine*
RAr	*Revue archéologique*
RB	*Revue Biblique*
TA	*Tel Aviv*
TAPS	Transactions of the American Philosophical Society
UF	*Ugarit-Forschungen*
VT	*Vetus Testamentum*
VTSup	Vetus Testamentum Supplements
ZAW	*Zeitschrift für die alttestamentliche Wissenschaft*
ZDPV	*Zeitschrift des Deutschen Palästina-Vereins*

Chapter 1

Another Study of Levantine Temples?

Introduction

The research that culminated in the writing of this volume began as a response to frustration. I had been working on Roman temple designs on the Iberian Peninsula (Mierse 1999), and as my research progressed I was constantly finding references to Semitic influences on the designs of sanctuaries both on the Peninsula and in North Africa. It was assumed that Phoenician colonization had brought with it the full flowering of Levantine architectural forms. Thus, I began to search for relevant material on the ancient Levant. Here, I discovered that no overall synthesis had ever been written. There was an excellent encyclopedic work on ancient building in much of the Levant that covered all types of structures from the prehistoric through the Iron Age periods but in which it was difficult to locate my particular area of interest. There were specialized studies but no systematic discussions of the developments, making it virtually impossible to recognize and isolate Semitic elements in architectural forms in North Africa and southern Iberia. This book addresses this void.

My concern is with the sanctuary architecture that took shape in the half millennium of the early Iron Age, from 1200 B.C.E. to 700 B.C.E., the period between the collapse of the Late Bronze Age societies of the Levant and the domination of the region by Assyria (Lipschits 2005: 3–11).[1] This was a time when no outside cultural force from Egypt, Anatolia, or Mesopotamia dominated the developments within the Levant. During these centuries, the new societies of the Levant revived older forms and created new building types. It was from this repertoire of forms that architects working in the Western outposts of the Phoenician colonies drew their inspiration.

---

1. I have concentrated attention on the temples that can be argued to reflect the local responses to the changes brought about with the collapse of the Late Bronze Age world and the subsequent development of the Iron Age in the region. Temples that have been identified as resulting from the presence of outside forces in the region in the seventh century—Ekron's Assyrian-influenced Complex 650, the Greek temple at period G Tell Sukas in Syria, and the Persian period sanctuary at Eshmun outside Sidon in Lebanon—are not covered here because they are really constituents of a different architectural history.

1

Earlier Work[2]

G. R. H. Wright (1985) produced the first encyclopedic study of many of the architectural remains in southern Syria and the Levant, and the work remains the most complete study of Levantine architecture. It is not the equivalent of William Dinsmoor's monumental study of Greek architecture (Dinsmoor 1975) or John Ward-Perkins's equally magisterial overview of Roman Imperial architecture (Ward-Perkins 1981), and this is partly because so much of the Levantine architectural material is in a fragmentary state. Few structures exist aboveground to be studied in situ as many ruined Greek and Roman buildings can be studied (Wright 1985: 1–2). Many remains are only known from archaeological reports because the buildings themselves were destroyed partly or fully in the process of excavation. However, limitations aside, much has been written about Levantine architecture. Since the sixteenth century, scholars have been attempting to reconstruct the temple of Solomon, which has been lost since the sixth century B.C.E. (Zwickel 1999: fig. 1). The nineteenth century was especially rich in these reconstructions based on interpretations of the relevant texts in 1 Kings, 2 Chronicles, and Ezekiel (Busink 1970: 44–47), and interest has not waned, though the nature of the study changed in the twentieth century because of the use of archaeological evidence to flesh out the information in the biblical passages (Zwickel 1999; Busink 1970: 51–52). Excavated sites began to yield remains of structures that were identified as temples, some dating back to the Chalcolithic period and Early Bronze Age. Particularly significant were the finds of major temples of the Middle Bronze and Late Bronze Ages as well as Iron Ages 1 and 2. The German excavations at Shechem uncovered the remains of a Middle Bronze Age temple that appeared to operate into Iron Age I (Sellin 1932). At Carchemish, the British excavations undertaken by Hogarth on the eve of the First World War revealed an important Iron Age II structure identified as a Neo-Hittite temple integrated into a massive sculptural program (Woolley 1953). The years between the First and Second World Wars were rich in temple finds. Schaeffer's French excavations at Ugarit unearthed two major Late Bronze Age temple structures early in the work (Schaeffer 1931). Farther down the coast at Megiddo, the American team found evidence for sacred structures stretching back to the Early Bronze Age but with significant structures in the Late Bronze Age, as well as important early Iron Age nonreligious constructions (May 1939). At the same time, another American team under Rowe (1940) uncovered a sequence of Late Bronze Age–early Iron Age temples on the acropolis at Beth-shean, and McEwan's (1937) group from the University of Chicago found a short-lived but major Iron Age II temple at Tell Taʿyinat (1937). Not far away, Woolley (1955) excavated a long-lived

---

2. The new publication by Dominik Elkowicz, *Tempel und Kultplätze der Philister und der Völker des Ostjordanlandes: Eine Untersuchung zur Bau- und zur Kultgeschichte während der Eisenzeit I–II* (Alter Orient und Altes Testament 378; Münster: Ugarit-Verlag, 2012) appeared too late to be included in this study.

temple-palace complex at the site of ancient Alalakh (Tell Atchana). Far to the east, at the very edge of what might be considered the Levant, German excavators (Langenegger et al. 1950) found the remains of a most unusual temple at Guzana (Tell Halaf). An English team led by Tufnell (Tufnell et al. 1940) revealed two major Late Bronze Age temples and a humble Iron Age I shrine at Lachish. The years following the end of the Second World War have been no less rich. Yadin's Israeli group discovered the impressive Late Bronze Age temple at Hazor as well as a small early Iron Age shrine (Yadin et al. 1975). F. James and McGovern with a University of Pennsylvania crew recovered more-complete information about the temples and their history at Beth-shean (F. James 1966; James and McGovern 1993). A. Mazar with an Israeli expedition isolated the Philistine temple at Tell Qasile (A. Mazar 1980), and this was followed by the work of the Dothans at Ashdod and Ekron (Tell Miqne), both of which have yielded Philistine sanctuaries (Dothan and Dothan 1992). Though Phoenician temples at the great cities of Tyre and Sidon have proved elusive, Pritchard's group succeeded in liberating a small, village-level sanctuary at Sarepta (Pritchard 1978), while excavations at the site of Kition near Larnaka on Cyprus resulted in exposing a series of superimposed temples dating back to the Late Bronze Age and continuing well into Iron Age II (Karageorghis 1982). The Israeli excavations at Tell Arad in southern Israel unearthed a sanctuary embedded within a fortress from the period of the divided kingdom (Herzog et al. 1984). During the same period, the Syrian excavations led by Abu ʿAssāf published the major Iron Age II temple from ʿAin Dara (Abu ʿAssāf 1990). Most recently, a German-Syrian excavation led by Kohlmeyer unearthed a Late Bronze Age temple that continued into the Iron Age on the citadel of Aleppo (Kohl-meyer 2000). These temple finds and several more that form the excavated data for this study should have provided more than adequate material for a major synthesis.

Frankfort did make a survey of Levantine architecture that included temple material in his massive study of the art and architecture of the ancient Near East (Frankfort 1985). The Levantine material was not his major concern, and temple designs received only limited coverage. Naumann (1955) offered a fine comparative architectural study of the temples of the region but focused on the Anatolian material and whatever could be related to it, with most of the attention devoted to Bronze Age finds. Mazar presented a synthetic overview of temple designs of the Middle Bronze Age, Late Bronze Age, and the early Iron Age in Kempinski and Reich's architectural survey of ancient Israelite architecture (A. Mazar 1992b), but the survey was limited to material within the modern nation of Israel, which thereby artificially restricted the discussion. Busink's massive work on Near Eastern temples was by far the most complete overview of the material because he considered all temple construction in the Levant, much in Anatolia, and many examples in Mesopotamia as well (Busink 1970). Busink was directed in his quest to understand the possible influences on the designs of the temples that had stood in Jerusalem, beginning with the temple of Solomon and ending with that of Herod. He presented a comprehensive survey but always focused on

explaining aspects of the Jerusalem temples. The temple of Solomon has had a significant role in many considerations of the architecture of the region, but this is less a
result of the importance of the temple in its own period than the role that the temple
has played in later developments (Hamblin and Seely 2007). Most recently, Zwickel
(1999) has again undertaken a study that reconstructs the temple of Solomon based
on the textual evidence and comparative investigations of the existing archaeological
evidence. As part of the massive publication on the fifth season of work at Hazor,
Bonfil (1997) presented a large-scale review of excavated temples from the Levant as
they could be related to the Hazor material. A little-known review of Levantine Late
Bronze Age and early Iron Age architecture in general and its influence on Phoenician
and Iberian architecture developments was published in Spanish by Diés Cusí (2001).

All of the synthetic studies are limited, either by arbitrary geographical constraints or by the focus of the investigation. While they all acknowledge the break
between the Late Bronze Age and the Iron Age I–II periods, they also tend to favor
notions of architectural continuity, often treating the buildings from Iron Age I and
II as responses to Late Bronze Age forms. There is good reason to doubt that the
Levantine region suffered the kind of sharp division in material culture that marks the
change from Late Bronze Age to early Iron Age in the Aegean area. Here, the lines of
architectural continuity between the last great flourish of building under the Myceneans and first major examples of the Geometric period are hard to trace. While the
temples of the Geometric period may have some type of association with older Late
Bronze Age forms, these older forms were clearly not temples. This is not the case in
the Levant, where some temples, such as those at Shechem, Megiddo, and Pella may
well have remained in continuous operation from the Middle Bronze Age to Iron
Age II. A sense of the past must always have been present. The entire Levantine region
shows signs of major recovery within two centuries of the disruption. Recent work
in ʿAmuq Plain shows that probably no real break occurred there (Hawkins 2009:
172; T. Harrison 2007: 91), as it did along the Levantine coast south of Ugarit (P. M.
Bikai 1978b). Continuity was also maintained by the simple fact that two of the great
outside cultural forces that had been impinging on the region since the Early Bronze
Age, Mesopotamia and Egypt, both recovered quickly and began to re-exert cultural
and eventually political influence and control in the area. Neither Egypt nor the reemergent Assyria had lost a sense of their pre-1200 historical identity, and this must
also have been the case at least for some of the Levantine regions in recovery, such as
the Neo-Hittite centers of the north. However, the Iron Age I and particularly Iron
Age II periods did see new architectural developments that must have resulted from
the changed situation in the region due to major demographic shifts, alterations in
the political landscape, and significant adaptations of religious belief. The centuries
encompassed by Iron Age I and II were a time of architectural exploration, and the
remains of the temples from this period suggest that, while memories of earlier Late
Bronze Age forms were still alive and well, many new forms were also being devel-

oped. Although the past was never very distant in the Levant, the new architectural forms reveal that the recovery in the region did cause a break with the past to some extent. The social structures, political forms, and emerging religious concepts were the products of new societies that were quite different from their Late Bronze Age predecessors and required temple architecture that responded to their needs. What T. Harrison (2009: 187) has described for the Orontes region is actually applicable to all of the Levant. It was a Balkanized region with remnants of older cultural forces competing with strong new cultural constructs that were the product of the changed demography of the whole region. It is worth remembering that buildings often survive major cultural disasters and even total changes in population. They can be altered dramatically in their usage; the fact that a structure still exists and is in use several centuries after it was built does not mean that the way it functions in its final stages of operation has anything to do with its original intent. One need only note the number of buildings that were previously churches in the United States and Europe but today have become arts centers, cultural complexes, upscale condominiums, or housing for the elderly. A building that was a temple in earlier centuries need not have been a temple in its final form. This is important to our understanding of Mediterranean architecture, because the Phoenicians carried Levantine architectural forms with them westward as they established colonies in Sicily, Africa, and on the Iberian Peninsula. The remains at many of these sites come from later contexts, after the establishment of the Carthaginian Empire,with strong influence from Greece, but it is still possible in some places to isolate the earlier forms and see what the Phoenicians were introducing. What has emerged in the excavations of these western sites is the fact that, as Levantine peoples moved west, they were quite selective about what they carried. The archaeological evidence does not demonstrate a wholesale transfer of Levantine architectural forms to the West. Rather, these emigrants brought particular architectural forms with them—forms that could easily be adapted.

Type of Study

In this book, I do not attempt to provide the Levantine region with coverage similar to Dinsmoor's coverage of Greece or Ward-Perkins's coverage of the Imperial Roman world. The remains of Levantine temples are far less extensive and do not permit the type of highly refined measurement and proportion that marks Dinsmoor's work; neither have the superstructures survived well enough to analyze the stylistic changes to ornamentation that occupies much of Ward-Perkins's work. Moreover, the historical context for the extant remains is usually far less informative than the context for Greek temples by the late sixth century B.C.E. or Roman temples throughout much of the history of the Empire. In many instances, Levantine temples can be, at best, roughly dated to a century. The analysis presented here is comparative and follows the methodology most commonly employed by architectural historians throughout the twentieth century. It is a formalist approach and permits the isolation of lines of continuity and the detection of discontinuity, though it does not necessarily explain them. While I rely heavily on this traditional method, I also introduce some approaches from the postprocessual school of archaeology in its attempts to discern an appropriate way for cult to be investigated by archaeology (Renfrew 1994; Renfrew et al. 1985). As much as possible, I focus my attention on the structures identified as temples by their excavators because of several diagnostic features: (1) the unusual nature of the structure compared with others at the site in the treatment of architecture, the prestige of the materials or building techniques, and the internal furnishings that have no obvious practical function, such as platforms or benches; (2) the discovery of objects that seem out of place, either because they are too precious or too abundant; and (3) objects found that appear to have cultic significance or to have been used in ritual. Although there are buildings in this study that do not meet these criteria, I focus the analytical discussions on the structures that provide ample justification for the identification of the structure as a temple. I avoid the identification of a building as a temple merely because it does not fit into another category. The structures that this study comprises were erected between the end of the Late Bronze Age (conventionally assigned the date of 1200 B.C.E.) and the annexation of the Levantine region into the Assyrian Empire (when Mesopotamia again became highly influential in the region). I am interested in what was produced during the period when the Levant was its own entity and politically independent of Egypt, Mesopotamia, or Anatolia. During this period, designs must reflect local choices rather than resulting from imposed outside concepts. Missing from this study are Levantine temples that are technically Iron Age but that were initially constructed after the Assyrian conquest.[3] Though some of the discussions include what is technically the Iron Age IIC phase (seventh–sixth centuries B.C.E.), these are limited to the temples that continued into this last phase but were built before it.

When a temple building can be securely isolated from the archaeological record, then one is beginning to treat the issue of the "archaeology of cult" (Renfrew et al. 1985: 1126). Religious belief systems do leave evidence of their existence in the archaeological record, and temples form one part of this material evidence. By the early Iron Age, belief systems were well established in the Levant, though they were clearly undergoing a major shift during these centuries, at least as evidenced by the primary textual documents that we possess. New gods were coming onto the scene as part of new governmental structures. Temple remains can be traced back to the Chalcolithic in some areas; and by the Middle Bronze Age, temples (following diagnostic stylistic forms) were a well-established type of architecture in Levantine centers. This continued to be true for the Late Bronze Age, even though the independence of the region

---

3. The most noticeable absences are: Temple Complex 650 and the Temple Auxiliary Complex at Ekron (T. Dothan and Gitin 2005); *NEAEHL* 5, s.v. "Miqne, Tel (Ekron)"; the Temple of Eshmun outside Sidon and the complex at Omm el-Amed, both of which are of Persian date (Markoe 2000: 127).

was severely curtailed by Egyptian and Hittite political ambitions. Reemerging temples in Iron Age I and II followed a well-established pattern throughout the region.

Levantine temples of all periods were most often independent structures. When they stood in cities or towns, they were physically somewhat separated from the urban fabric that surrounded them. Temples were the most impressive physical manifestations of religious belief. One of their purposes was to operate on a symbolic level, to designate a special place set aside for some type of reverence, and most often tied to prescribed ritual (Renfrew 1994: 51). In the Late Bronze Age, they were clearly understood to be the houses of the god to which they were dedicated. The Late Bronze Age story preserved in Ugarit of Baʿal's palace presented the palace and the temple as interchangeable. The association of the temple building with the residence of the named god was a well-established feature of Mesopotamian belief as early as the third millennium and probably obtained in the Levant at an early stage as well. There is little reason not to assume that this belief continued into Iron Age I and II.

Unlike the Late Bronze Age, from which some of the cult statue bases survived,[4] from the early Iron Age no temple cult statue bases survived, and therefore the location of the the cult statues within the inner chambers of temples is not clear. Some of them were designed in such a way that a cult statue could have been visible from outside, but several of the temples were not. In these instances, the object of the cult was neither accessible nor visible. This sort of arrangement communicated in no uncertain terms the privileged nature of human and divine contact. Only a select few individuals could engage the divine. The temple also had a social role. It offered a strong physical presence testifying to the belief system that built it. Early Iron Age Levantine temples required a certain degree of community resources to erect. In most instances, though not all, the remains reveal structures that were bigger than the average house and were often constructed with better materials. In some cases, the temples were quite clearly associated with royal prerogative. As such, their building, maintenance, and access were connected with the ruler and perhaps the incipient state. The temple was a symbolic and physical manifestation of the hegemony of the ruler—what Gramsci might recognize as a statement of the ruler's moral and ethical right to rule (P. Anderson 1976–77: 20–32). The temples were also, I argue, intellectual products and, in the emerging states of the early Iron Age Levant, the most apparent representation of intellectual achievement. B. Routledge (2004: 31) has suggested that a separate category of society that can be isolated as an intellectual group was operating in early Iron Age Levantine society, and its role was to serve the state by educating the general populace and articulating the hegemonic structure. Its job was to manipulate society through consensual or coercive means to fulfill the desires of the ruler/emerging state. The priests and functionaries who served the temple were the most

4. Temple I at Hattuša (Boğazköy) does have a surviving cult statue base against the back wall, with windows on either side (private communication with Gregory McMahon).

obvious and easily recognizable representatives of this intellectual group. The temples were a focus for the actions of this group just as they could be a representation of the political order. Because so much of the cultic activity was hidden from view and was considered an aspect of the mysteries of the god, the exterior of the temple and the space surrounding must have been the locus for presenting the temple's roles to the general population. The surrounding space functioned as a sort of "stage setting" for the public. The interior, on the other hand, was visible only to a select few but was important as the space for the epiphany of the god. Exterior rituals could be grand in their devising, but interior rituals needed to respond within the limits of an enclosed space and thus were intimate by nature.

Textual Material

The Middle Bronze and Late Bronze eras provide ample primary texts in the form of archives of clay tablets for us to reconstruct (however vaguely) enough beliefs, rituals, and temple practices to explain certain aspects of temple architecture. The same is not true for the early Iron Age. The undisputed primary texts for the Levant are limited at best and offer no real information about rituals to permit an architectural historian to understand how spaces were used. On the other hand, the period provides what must be considered the most controversial surviving text from the ancient Near East, the Hebrew Bible. Nothing substantial of the older forms of this text exists prior to the Hebrew scrolls found at Qumran (Hoffman 2004: 121–48), the oldest of which dates back to the middle third century B.C.E. (Gottwald 1989: 116). However, only fragments of the books that cover Iron Age I and II—that is, 1–2 Samuel and 1–2 Kings—were found among the texts. There is no agreement on when much of the text was composed or when it was written down. The *Temple Scroll* from Qumran offers general statements that may be informative regarding the role of the temple in the setting of Iron Age II, but it was not written during the period, and it is not clear how it can be used (Yadin 1967). Because I am in no position to offer a critical reading of these highly problematic texts, I have used them with great care and have based none of my analyses or arguments on them. However, one major portion of the biblical text must be examined in some detail: the description of the temple of Solomon; the biblical record of this "lost temple" overshadows all discussions of existing remains.

Temple of Solomon

The biblical passages that describe the temple of Solomon are 1 Kgs 6:1–9:25 and 2 Chronicles 2–4, and often Ezekiel's dream (Ezekiel 40–48) is included. The section from Kings purports to describe the situation in the court of Solomon, dating the events presented to the tenth–ninth centuries B.C.E., but there is general agreement that the text was redacted by the Deuteronomist sometime in the later seventh century or even during the late period of the exile (van der Toorn 2007; Stager and King

2001: 331; Hölscher 1923; Busink 1970: 22). An antimonarchic bias has been has been noted, in part to explain the destruction of the temple and the defeats of Israel and Judah (Friedman 1987: introduction). The book of the prophet Ezekiel was probably written in the final decades of the exile. Ezekiel might have known Solomon's temple in its final state before the destruction of 587 B.C.E., but how much this influenced his vision and how much the vision is reflective of a concept of a new beginning and, therefore, a new temple can be debated (Howie 1950; Irwin 1943; Busink 1970: 701). It has been argued that the image of the restored temple was part of a larger structural element in the book, "the vision of God's glory," and therefore was a type of literary conceit rather than a reflection of any type of reality; furthermore, the initial description may well have been embellished by later writers who added information about cultic personnel and rituals (Gottwald 1989: 484, 488–89) and even carefully structured the presentation of the description (Talmon and Fishbane 1976).

The reliability of the biblical textual descriptions is further compromised by the reality of the transmission over 3000 years. The two oldest extant versions of the Hebrew Bible, both of which are products of the Masoretic tradition, are the almost complete Aleppo Codex of the tenth century C.E. and the Leningrad Codex of the eleventh century C.E. (Goshen-Gottstein 1979; Beck, Sanders, and Freedman 1998). Though the Masoretic scribal tradition probably dates back to the fifth century C.E., several hundred years separate the surviving Hebrew texts of Qumran and the earliest Masoretic work. That an intervening Hebrew text or texts existed is undisputed (Taylor 1997: 8), but how trustworthy these are from the point of view of maintaining consistency in the description of a nonexistent temple and of features that no longer would have made sense to the scribes is a different question.[5]

The versions of the Septuagint cannot be used without care because there was a degree of Hellenistic cultural influence that informed certain aspects of its translation (Lefebvre 1991). When scholars analyze the Greek for textual clarity of descriptive information, it becomes apparent that the translators often did have difficulties understanding what architectural features were being described in the Vorlage that they were using (Ouellette 1972: 187). A comparison of the description of the temple in the LXX and the Masoretic description shows that specific features are often quite differently treated, making it hard to determine which version, if either, should be accepted as being more reflective of the original text (Polak 2001; Gooding 1965; 1967). If we introduce the Latin translations, the matter becomes more complicated still (Fernández Marcos 1995). For the student of architecture, the problems of the textual transmission are twofold. First, as has already been discussed, there is the question of whether architectural terminology and descriptions of structural features that no longer stand and have no current equivalents are maintained correctly in the various recensions

---

5. For a more complete discussion of the relationship of the Masoretic texts to ancient Hebrew, see Hoffman 2004: 49–80.

of the original text or are glossed properly in translations. A scribe is neither an architect nor a builder and cannot necessarily be expected to understand a building term, especially an archaic term. The second problem concerns the initial reason for the description. The biblical text is not a neutral document. It is not a straightforward chronicle of the yearly aspects of a reign like a medieval monastic chronicle. It is also not a royal listing of achievements and notable events of a reign dictated to a scribe, such as may be found in the Mesopotamian royal archives. It is a composed work, the result of several authors, several redactors, and several centuries of composition. The texts are parts of larger programs, and certainly this is the case with the sections in Kings, Chronicles, and Ezekiel that treat the temple. While there are problems with the actual text that we possess, there are also problems with the nature of the original creation of the text. The architectural historian who is going to use the text needs to understand why it was composed, understand what its models were, and decide how trustworthy as an architectural document it is.

Most commentators treat the narrative in Chronicles as a redaction of the account in Kings. The two accounts do not agree on all points, and where there are differences, Kings is treated as the more authentic (Hurowitz 1992: 25–27). Because the author of Kings lived several centuries after the events described, one needs to consider how he manipulated the description. It is obvious that he was not merely relating a firsthand account, and we must question what sources he consulted. The temple section can be subdivided into several ancient literary genres[6] (Hurowitz 1992: 107; Long 1984): contracts and treaties (5:15–23), archival administrative records (5:27–31; 6:1; 7:2–8), architectural description (chaps. 6–7), speeches (8:15–21, 54–61), prayers (8:22–53), a poem (8:12–13), a description of ritual (8:1–11; 62–65), and divine oracles (6:11–13; 9:1–9). The text is best treated as a composite work with Deuteronomistic elements (5:17–19; 8:1–11, 14–61; 9:1–9), Priestly expansion (8:1–11), and pentateuchal material from the J and E sources. Of all the literary forms, only the poem is considered by some to be of tenth-century date—that is, contemporaneous with the actual building. If indeed the original behind the text that we possess today was redacted or even composed in the sixth century B.C.E., then it could well have been written by an author completely unfamiliar with the actual structure, since it was destroyed in 587 B.C.E. However the raw data used by the writer, the archival material, and the architectural description could have been produced coeval with the building of the temple.

Hurowitz (1992: 110) notes that Kings resembles Assyrian and Neo-Babylonian building accounts; this supports the notion that the author produced it within the context of the exile. If Chronicles indeed rests on the support of Kings, then Chronicles is from a still-later date, probably the Persian period (Gottwald 1989: 301). Hu-

---

6. For the citations in this discussion, I use *The Tanakh* (NJPS; see Pelikan 1985). For other biblical citations, I use the *Oxford Bible* (NEB, 1962).

rowitz wonders whether Chronicles was written expressly to link the building of the Second Temple back to the building of the first and to stress the popular contribution. Chronicles emphasizes certain aspects of the story: enhancing David's role in the temple even as it explains more fully why he did not build it; explaining that Solomon knew David's desire and was divinely sanctioned as David's heir; revealing how the tabernacle is linked to the temple (Hurowitz 1992: 25–27).

The placement of the narrative concerning the temple in Kings is interesting. It appears in the center of Solomon's reign, and the construction of the temple becomes the chronological marker for the historical account. Specific events are recorded as having occurred before the building of the temple. The description of the temple structure is also located in the middle of the account of the building process, all of which suggests a careful crafting of the story. Hurowitz points out that in both Mesopotamia and the Levant there existed a tradition of building inscriptions that often included the divine command to build a temple—for example, the Amman Citadel inscription (Horn 1969); thus, the biblical narrative fits comfortably within this tradition. However, the lengthy and quite detailed description of the temple that appears in Kings and is repeated in Chronicles is a unique text, quite different from the building accounts known in Mesopotamia or even in the Egyptian *Königsnovelle* (A. Hermann 1938; S. Hermann 1953–54). Montgomery argued that the very precise nature of the description suggests that the author used archival materials that dated to the building period itself (Montgomery 1934). On the other hand, nothing has been found in any of the surviving archives in the Middle East or Egypt that has yielded a parallel text, suggesting that this was not the type of building information that was normally placed in archives. Although there are dedication texts, they do not contain specific information of this sort about the buildings themselves (Van Seters 1983).

The description in Kings is carefully constructed. It begins with the outside of the structure (6:2–9) and then describes the interior (6:14–31). The whole unit of the building description is formally set off from the surrounding text by the use of chronological statements that serve as bookends (6:1, 37). The author moves from the physical features of the building to an inventory of the temple furnishings, first the bronze implements (7:15–47), then the gold items (7:48–51). The bronze pieces are credited to the coppersmith Hiram of Tyre (7:13–14). The gold work is Solomon's gift to the temple (7:48). Separating the descriptions of the temple building and the temple furnishings is a quite different section that recounts other building activities that Solomon undertook (7:1–12).

Although the level of detail provided about the temple's appearance and its furnishings in Kings differs from the few other known building accounts, Hurowitz has argued that the general structure of the story matches the structure known from other ancient Near Eastern accounts. According the temple "pride of place" among the building activities of a ruler is a standard feature of Mesopotamian narratives as are the use of formulaic language, presentation of stereotypical refrains, and description of the parts as a means of presenting the whole (Hurowitz 1992: 110, 224–44).

Though the precision of the details about the temple in Kings cannot be paralleled by descriptions elsewhere in the ancient Near East or Egypt, it can be found in other biblical narratives. The tabernacle in Exodus (Exod 26:1–36) and the temple in Ezekiel's vision (Ezekiel 40–48) are described in a similar manner. It may be that there was a special Israelite or Judean literary topos for describing important structures that was modeled loosely on Mesopotamian prototypes but that placed greater stress on specifics. However, this still would not explain where the author of Kings was able to obtain his primary information. Was it a written description produced at the time of the construction, stored in the palace archives, and somehow retrieved and preserved after the 587 destruction (Eissfeldt 1965)? Was it a lost building plan of the sort that seems to be shown on one of the seated Gudea statues (Montgomery and Gehman 1951: 48)? Was it a tradition of oral instructions given to the builders and somehow kept alive for later generations (Noth 1968: 105)? Van Seters has noted that no material such as these descriptions of Solomon's temple, the tabernacle, and the temple in Ezekiel's vision is found in surviving archives. Moreover, the distinctly visual nature of these descriptions prompts him to argue that these were attempts to give form to items that were lost, to describe what no longer existed, and were probably more conjectural than real (Van Seters 1983: 310 n. 68).

The description of the temple of Solomon in Kings is best understood to be a composition of the sixth century, very likely postdating the destruction of the actual temple, and using several different literary genres to form a composite whole. It may have been written for propaganda purposes, as has been argued regarding Ezekiel's vision (Bentzen 1952; Zimmerli 1965; Vogelstein 1950–51). Under these circumstances, can any part of the account be trusted for its architectural information?

Many scholars (among them Albright 1968; M. S. Smith 1990), though fully aware of the problems of the transmission of the text, have accepted the description as being largely valid. Monson (2000: 26) has argued for the validity of the measurements (1 Kgs 6:2–3): 60 cubits long by 20 cubits broad (1 : 3) and 30 cubits high (1 : 2) with a separate vestibule 20 cubits broad by 10 cubits long (1 : 6). If the royal cubit being used was 52.5 cm, then the temple's dimensions were 120 ft. by 34 ft., which he thinks is close to the measurements for the temple remains at ʿAin Dara (98 ft. by 6 ft.). G. R. H. Wright (1985: 1.260) noted that the proportions form a simple arithmetical ratio of 1 : 2 : 3, and for him, this is unusual because, in later ancient building, proportions are geometrical rather than arithmetical. Wright goes further to show that, if one follows the biblical description, the ʾûlām would be 10 cubits deep, 20 wide, and 30 high—1 : 2 : 3. The main structure would be 60 cubits long by 20 cubits wide. Of the length, 20 cubits at the rear defined the dĕbîr, a structure 20 cubits by 20 cubits, leaving the hêkāl 40 cubits by 20 cubits. The proportions of the plan would be 1:1, 1:2, and 1 : 3. If the height of the main structure was 30 cubits, then it was half the length of the unit, or 1 : 2. If the *děbîr* had a height of 20 cubits, allowing it to fit into the bigger structure, then it formed a cube, 20 by 20 by 20 cubits. In Wright's view, this begins to have the quality of mysticism tinged with intellectualism rather than real building information. I too am inclined to dismiss the measurements. The connection with ʿAin Dara seems weak to me. The measurement 98 ft. by 65 ft. does not seem very close to 120 ft. by 34 ft. The measurements given for Solomon's temple are too formulaic.[7] They appear to be driven by a concern for numerology and working around the use of 60, a number with a long Mesopotamian pedigree.

This is not unlike the description of Marduk's Temple, the Esagil, preserved on a fragmentary tablet from Babylon known as the "Esagil Tablet," for which George has argued that the recorded measurements were not based on reality but were motivated by mathematics (George 2008a: 63). Few of the surviving temple ruins appear to possess this sort of proportional relationship between the parts and the whole. The excavators of the Middle Bronze Age temple in the Aleppo Citadel tried to analyze the remains in this way, but only a portion of the main cult room has survived, throwing into doubt the validity of the analysis (Gonnella, Khayyata, and Kohlmeyer 2005: 89). The proportional relationships in the biblical description seem more likely to be a literary conceit than a formal reality.

It is worth noting that the description of the ark that Noah built (Gen 6:15–16) reads in a somewhat similar manner. Certainly, builders must have worked using standardized measurements and often with some type of proportional associations regarding the relationship of structural parts. The temple of Solomon could have been dependent on a sexagesimal system as the guiding unit. After all, the Hebrew vocabulary for palace, temple, throne, and scribe are ultimately of Mesopotamian origin (Ellenbogen 1962: 67, 78, 89; Metzger and Coogan 1993: s.v. "Temple"; Dalley et al. 1998: 61), and so a Mesopotamian aspect to the design is not improbable. However, the sexagesimal element might also have been introduced when the text was redacted, if the redaction occurred in Babylon.

Clearly, there are statements buried within the account that warrant attention from the perspective of an architectural historian. First, there is the building itself, a self-contained structure, longer than it is wide, with a clearly demarcated vestibule area. This is not a common Mesopotamian temple type, not a structure that an author writing in Babylon would probably have seen. What is described is, however, a standard Levantine form dating back to the third millennium (Fritz 1987b), a long-room type. Since its discovery in 1937, the long-room temple at Tell Taʿyinat in western Syria

---

7. Hurowitz (2011: 48) thinks that the continuity of proportional relationships among the desert tabernacle, Solomon's temple, and Ezekiel's envisioned temple (Ezek 40:49–41:4) is evidence of the validity of the measurements. I think it is evidence of a consistent literary concern, not necessarily an architectural issue.

has been considered the closest model for the temple of Solomon (McEwan 1937: 9, fig. 4). Nevertheless, it is recognized to be an eighth-century B.C.E. building and could not have been the prototype for Solomon's structure. But it does have the tripartite division of the longitudinal axis that seems to match with the divisions recorded for the temple of Solomon—*'ûlām, hêkāl, dĕbîr*—indicating that the standard reconstruction of the temple of Solomon as a long-room form divided into three discrete units is probably correct. More recently, the temple at ʿAin Dara, which in its earliest form dates to the Late Bronze Age, has been put forward as a closer parallel to the temple of Solomon.

The three terms that seem to label portions of the temple come to us through the Masoretic textual tradition, and so it is reasonable to question whether they are indeed ancient terms. The word *'ûlām*, which appears one more time, in Ezek 40:7, probably relates to Akkadian *ellamu*, a term used to designate a throne hall (Busink 1970: 166). In both the description of Solomon's temple and in Ezra 40, it is used to designate the front space, the vestibule of the building. It was not a term for which the translators of the Septuagint could find a Greek gloss. In the LXX, it is transcribed into Greek as *ailam* (*kai to ailam kata prosopon tou naos*), which suggests that indeed *'ûlām* was the term used, though it must have changed meaning from its Akkadian root; and because the Greek translators were not comfortable assigning it the gloss of *pronaos*, which is the expected word for the vestibule area of a long-room Greek temple, it is worth considering whether the normal association of the term with the first room in a tripartite division of a long-room form is really correct. *Hêkāl* is used to identify the main chamber of the temple, and for the Greek translators this posed no problem. They rendered it *naos* (Busink 1970: 166 n. 15). But it was not the cult chamber of the temple, and so it was not really functioning as the *naos* of a Greek temple. Like *'ûlām*, *hêkāl* has a good Akkadian root, *ekallu*, but also *é-gal* in Sumerian and *hkl* in Ugaritic. Sumerian uses of *é-gal* can refer to temples,[8] but in the Nuzi texts *é-gal* describes the main room of a house. In Akkadian, *ekallu tapsuhti* refers to the royal tomb associated with the palace; on the other hand, Marduk's Temple in Babylon is called *Ésagil ekallu šamê u erṣeti* ('Ésagil, palace of heaven and of earth';[9] Busink 1970: 180). *Hêkāl* is employed in 1 Sam 1:9 for the sanctuary in Shiloh and in Jer 50:28 again for the temple in Jerusalem, perhaps in some manner associating a house with a temple. *Dĕbîr* presented the Greek translators the same problem as *'ûlām*; they could not gloss it, and so they transliterated it. It appears as *dabir* in the LXX, though Josephus (*J. W.* 5.5.7) refers to the innermost chamber of Herod's temple as *to aduton* rather than *dĕbîr*. The root is not very clear. Gordon argued for an Ugaritic root, *dbr*, meaning 'shrine' (Gordon

---

8. Ultimately, this is coming from a Sumerian root: É = 'house', *GAL* = 'large or great'. *Égal* is most often used for 'palace'.

9. Or 'the House whose top is high' (George 2008b: 54).

1955: 254 no. 458; Busink 1970: 197). The Greek translators may have been perplexed if our understanding of the placement of the feature is correct: a deeper space or more likely a specially built unit within the cult chamber itself. This could be the Greek *adyton*, often the most sacred region of a temple (Hollinshead 1999). The term would not have been an inappropriate gloss, and so it is surprising that the translators did not use it, since Josephus was obviously comfortable with it. *Dbr* was obviously a specialized term within the context of Israelite religious architecture; moreover, it may have been a unique term because it does not appear elsewhere in the Hebrew Bible, unlike *'ûlām* and *hêkāl,* which seem to have had a wider currency. The nature of the space that it designated, the space in which the ark was housed, may have rendered it a word with no other possible context—the ultimate shrine.

Waterman saw the textual problem with *děbîr as* something deeper, an intentional change to the function of the building that the Deuteronomistic author was himself trying to understand (Waterman 1943: 290–94). He noted that *děbîr,* while normally rendered 'holy of holies' in translation, was actually only referring to the rear part of a room or space. Although 1 Kgs 6:16 suggests a separate structure, a perfect cube of 20 cubits, this aspect is missing in Ezekiel's vision, suggesting that it is a later addition. Waterman was concerned with showing that the original structure that is now known as the temple of Solomon was in reality built to house Solomon's treasury and that the whole notion that the structure was designed to architecturally focus attention on the place where the ark was placed in the *děbîr* was a much later change to the building that the author attempted to explain by means of the description. Originally, Waterman argued, the *hêkāl* was in reality the main space of the building, and it gave access to side chambers, each protected by a colossal statue of a cherubim.

A major part of Waterman's argument rests on the unusual element of the side chambers of the structure. which clearly caused problems for all the later translators and copyists. This feature of some type of corridor of chambers that wrapped around three sides of the temple core and that was probably entered somewhere in the front—Waterman believed from within the *hêkāl* itself—had no known architectural counterpart (Ouellette 1972; Waterman 1947). Waterman thought that, because in actual floor space the corridor was larger than the temple proper, initially the structure was designed to house the treasury (since more space was devoted to storage than to ritual). As a ritual space, the *hêkāl* might have served as a kind of royal chapel but with no major focus on the *děbîr*. However, the excavations of the temple at ʿAin Dara in northwest Syria have produced a temple structure with precisely this sort of corridor that encloses three sides of the temple core; thus an archaeological parallel for the description in Kings has been found (Monson 2000: 33–34).

The question remains whether the glossing of *děbîr* caused the Greek translators a problem because of a lack of vocabulary or because they had a better understanding of the spaces. *Naos* is a clear term in Greek. It is the dwelling place of the god (Homer,

Iliad 1.39), or it is the space in which the cult statue is placed (Herodotus 1.83; 6.19; Xenophon, *Apol.* 15). It had not changed its meaning when the Alexandrian translators were at work. When they designated the *hêkāl* as the *naos,* they certainly must have understood what they were implying. If the Greek translators somehow knew of this original architectural sense of the main chamber that Waterman has proposed, then their gloss of *naos* is perfectly reasonable. Similarly, they may have known that the *'ûlām* did not function as a *pronaos* but was some type of structure unlabeled in Greek.

Aharoni has noted the ambiguous quality of the description of the temple building. It opens with the general measurements for *habbayit,* which must include the *hêkāl* and the *děbîr* but not the *'ûlām.* The *'ûlām* seems to be a separate unit with its own distinct measurements that is somehow appended to the main building (Aharoni 1973: 1–3)—a formal entrance into the temple of some sort (Ouellette 1969). If this were the arrangement, then the confusion of the Greek translators becomes much clearer. What was built for Solomon may well have been a rectangular structure aligned on the longitudinal axis and preceded by a separate unit that housed the entrance. Three sides of the main building were enclosed by a corridor that was perhaps entered from the main building. The main building may have initially been a single, unified space that only later was divided and arranged into a hierarchical coupling. A single, unified cult chamber had a well-established pedigree in the Levant, and the separate architectural embellishment of the entrance unit is not unknown in either Late Bronze Age Egyptian or Hittite temple-building. Therefore, such a reconstruction is not at all at odds with what is known archaeologically, but whether it is the reality of the building is a different question.

The architecture of the temple of Solomon remains elusive because the main source, the biblical description, is fraught with problems. The actual building description does not help to explain any other remains; quite the contrary, the remains, if anything, help to clarify aspects of the description. The temple of Solomon cannot be ignored in any study of temple architecture in the early Iron Age Levant, but its shadowy existence renders it useless for trying to understand actual buildings, and its role in a quite independent historical narrative that was very likely composed in a later historical setting also renders much of the contextual material highly suspect. Throughout this book, the temple of Solomon will reappear when it seems to offer an element of explanation for some aspect of temple-building, but the reader must always remember that, regarding the temple of Solomon, nothing is certain.

Design of the Book

The Mediterranean Levant has a long architectural history stretching back to the Neolithic period. Certainly, important architectural developments occurred during both the Early and the Middle Bronze Ages. The Late Bronze Age was probably one of the least significant periods because the region was so heavily dominated by outside forces. However, the architecture that emerged in the wake of the downfall of the Late Bronze Age and the subsequent reemergence of social cohesiveness manifested significant changes in form and function. The five centuries under review reveal exciting developments in sacred architecture and show that, although the architects of the first millennium B.C.E. maintained important lines of continuity with the developments of the previous two millennia, they were also capable of creating novel forms to meet new needs. As in all preindustrial societies, architects worked within the constraints of the physical environment in which they created. They exploited resources that were available to them. It was only possible to overcome limitations if political, social, and economic forces could be brought to bear and if trade networks existed that allowed resources to be used that were not on hand locally.

While the region of the Levant has a long history of settlement, it is also true that, during the first centuries of the Iron Age, new patterns of settlement emerged that differed from those of the Late Bronze Age, and new trade routes were exploited. In chap. 2 below, I consider the geographical and environmental settings of the Levant. I also examine the demographic continuities and changes that mark the settlement patterns of the early Iron Age as being distinct from the settlement patterns of the Late Bronze Age. The descriptions and discussions of the archaeological remains of structures that have been identified as sanctuaries along with associated finds are presented in chap. 3, and formal analyses of the building techniques and plans constitute chaps. 4 and 5. In chap. 4, I consider the lines of design continuity that join early Iron Age structures to their Late Bronze Age predecessors. In chap. 5, I look at the design elements that mark the early Iron Age temples as distinct, new forms for the region.

Many of the societal structures of the early Iron Age contrasted with those of the Late Bronze Age. There had been a degree of linguistic and cultural homogeneity, and political fragmentation into city-states was often controlled by outside forces. Now, however, the region was characterized by cultural heterogeneity with several new local cultural manifestations but a limited number of powerful nation-states that competed for hegemony. The emergence of the new states in the area was accompanied by a promotion of new gods, often associated with ruling dynasties. This was a time that witnessed changes to intellectual life in the cities, and temples played an important role in the intellectual development of early Iron Age society. The societal and political complexity of the early Iron Age and the way that these forces informed temple-building is the topic of chap. 6. In chap. 7, I investigate the ways that a great deal of the Levantine sacral architecture was carried to the far West in the colonial expansion of the Levant.

This is first and foremost an architectural study. The primary source material is the archaeological record itself as it is presented in the reports of the sites. Where ancient literary testimonia shed light on the architecture, they have been considered; this is most significant for the lost temple of Solomon. Conclusions are based on the actual finds of structures. Not every one of the temples discussed still exists, but in most instances, I have seen the remains of the temples that do.

Like most similar studies, this investigation is about categorization and classification. My goal has been to group the various sanctuaries into appropriate categories, to offer some idea of how the structures of the early Iron Age link or do not link with each other and with Levantine sanctuaries of the Late Bronze Age, to isolate the lines of continuity and the points of discontinuity, and then to consider the various factors that may have influenced the design choices made by architects throughout the region.

The role of the ancient Levantine architect is not at all clear to us. However, sanctuaries did not build themselves, and decisions needed to be made. Moreover, the fact that not all sanctuaries look the same, and not every element can be related to what came before should indicate that, no matter how strong the force of conservatism was in sanctuary designs, there was also space for choice. Whether the architect or the patron made the choice is impossible to tell. However, it is probably safe to assume that, when a building became the least bit structurally complicated, it was because the architect and the contractor (very likely the same person) somehow needed to comply with a patron's request. It is my hope that, in the process of classifying and categorizing the remains, I may also convey the excitement about architectural investigation and discovery that marks the centuries of the early Iron Age in the Levant.

Chapter 2

Geography and People

The modern states of Turkey, Syria, Lebanon, Israel, the Palestinian Authority, and Jordan constitute the geographical area covered in this volume: the region comprehended by the traditional term *Levant* as understood for the ancient Near East (Tubb 1998: 13). The region also more or less conforms to the Greek Coele-Syria at its most extensive. Southern Turkey is included because some of the Neo-Hittite and Aramean sites are located there, and the landscape itself is a natural extension of northern Syria. Most people would not include eastern Syria under the term *Levant*, but again, the Arameans came from the east and occupied especially the Khabur area, and their culture thus influenced all of eastern Syria. Ancient Transjordan faced west, and the states that developed in that region—Ammon, Moab, and Edom—were regularly engaged with the emerging state of Israel. They form part of the cultural story, and so their land must be considered in the survey.

This region of the Near East can be defined by a few physical features. It was bounded on the north by the great limestone massif of Northern Syria and southeastern Anatolia. To the east was the Syrian Desert that really begins as the steppeland around Aleppo and continues east to form the Hamada, or the 'Waterless Desert'. As Gertrude Bell noted, from the top of the citadel in Aleppo, it would be possible to see Baghdad were it not for the curvature of the earth, because there is no physical obstruction on the flat plain (Bell 1987: 262). The south is formed by the deserts of Jordan and the Negev, which together define the outlet at the Red Sea. Finally, the west is bounded by the Mediterranean Sea. At the heart of the region is a massive mountain range, the Anti-Lebanon (*al-Jebel ash-Sharqi*), which stretches 230 km on a diagonal from the steppeland of the northeast to the Golan Heights in the southwest and is 30 km at its widest point. It rises to 2,400 m in several places and to 2,800 m at its southern extension, Mount Hermon, which is the tallest mountain in the region (Millar 1993: 17). The mountains are opposed by a great valley system that slashes through the region. The Jordan River Valley (the Ghor*)*, the Baq'ah Valley in the Lebanon Mountains, and the 'Amuq Plain or valley that now straddles the northwest border of Syria and Turkey are all part of the northern extension of the east Great African Rift.

The landscape presents a series of opposing pairs: plains and mountains, well-watered land and desert, cultivated areas inhabited by sedentary peoples and steppe and desert land best exploited by nomadic or seminomadic peoples. Moreover, the juxtapositions are never far from one another. Reading through travel accounts of nineteenth century visitors to the areas, one is constantly aware of how quickly one sort of landscape gives way to another. Often no more than a few hours' mule ride will result in a major change (Bell 1987; Effendi 2001; Stephens 1991). Four great rivers flow through the land: the Orontes in the northwest, the Euphrates in the north and east, the Khabur (Nahr al Khabur) in the northeast, and the Jordan which flows south from Mount Hermon through the Sea of Galilee and into the Dead Sea. The Jordan River provides the major resource for the exploitation of the Ghor. The Orontes waters one of the most fertile and productive plains in the Middle East. The Euphrates and Khabur rivers provide strips of arable land in the middle of steppe and desert.

The geography of the Levant cannot be made the causative agent for developments in the region to the degree that can be claimed for Egypt or Mesopotamia. There is no single feature in the landscape to equal the power of the great rivers to determine cultural responses. If anything, the Levant offers a variety of microenvironments that can be argued to have played some role in local cultural formations.[1] Although climate and environmental studies for the Levant during the Late Bronze Age and Iron Age are still limited, basic information has appeared in the last few years that needs to be considered. The Iron Age seems to have coincided with a gradual rise in temperature, an increase in sea levels (Markoe 2000: 23), and a regional shift in rainfall. Samplings following the Rift Valley from the Dead Sea through the Sea of Galilee, up the Baqʿah Valley onto the ʿAmuq Plain show an increasing amount of annual rainfall, reaching its highest level during the Roman period but probably beginning sometime in Iron Age I. This pattern for the Rift Valley is confirmed by samplings in eastern Syria at Lake Khatinniye. There is evidence from Ugarit showing that by the city's end the region had become drier and hotter (Kaniewski et al. 2010), and the Negev witnessed a change in vegetation from a Mediterranean type to more drought resistant Saharan types around 1200 B.C.E. (Neumann and Parpola 1987: 163–65). A climatic shift to drier and warmer beginning as early as the eighteenth century B.C.E. and perhaps climaxing around 1200 B.C.E. has been argued for Mesopotamia (Neumann and Parpola 1987: 177; Neumann and Sigrist 1978: 249) and for Egypt (Butzer 1984: 111). The climatic deterioration must have forced human communities to adapt. Aristotle, in the *Meteorologica,* describes a major drought in Mycene that has been argued to have occurred about 1200 B.C.E. (Neumann 1985: 441–47), and the Hittite heartland of Anatolia was probably suffering from droughts as well. It has been suggested that

---

1. For example, the Nusayriyah Mountains in northwestern Syria effectively divide the coast from the inland, resulting in two quite different climates next to each other (Kaniewski et al. 2008: 13941–46).

part of the peace treaty between Ramesses II and Hattusilis III in 1259 B.C.E. was an arrangement by which Egypt provided a steady supply of grain to the Hittites (Bryce 2005) because, beginning as early as King Amuwanda III's father, they had been having to contend with a major drought followed by famine (Warburton 2003: 75–100). These anecdotes suggest that the problem may partly have been caused by the stress placed on the environment by an increase in population. There is growing evidence that human activity after more than 5,000 years of occupation in the Levant was affecting the land, and these effects were probably exacerbated by the climate changes (B. Weiss 1982: 173–98). There are signs of human-caused deforestation in the Amanus Mountains in the northwest and deforestation resulting from increased agricultural developments on the hills along the Orontes River in the west. As the climate shifted to a wetter regime after approximately 900 B.C.E., the Iron Age witnessed an increase in flooding, which was exacerbated by the deforestation that caused more runoff. This problem peaked later during the Roman period (Yener et al. 2000: 178–79). A similar scenario was no doubt occurring in other places but has not yet been documented.

The Levantine region is not very large. Coastal movement was clearly an important feature of the Late Bronze Age, and this was firmly reestablished by Iron Age II. The interior can also be traversed. Nineteenth-century travelers on mule or horseback could move from the far south to the north or from east to west in several days of travel and were rarely out of reach of settled populations if they stayed west of the great deserts. This was not necessarily easy travel. Once the Roman roads were no longer functioning, which would have been a situation similar to the period of the Late Bronze Age and early Iron Age, it was often difficult to pick one's way through the mountains or over what to a visitor appeared to be featureless steppes, and obviously crossing rivers without bridges posed challenges. However, travelers' accounts make clear that movement was possible and often easy (Bell 1987; Effendi 2001; Stephens 1991). This sort of movement in the Late Bronze Age and early Iron Age means that overcoming the limitations of one microenvironment within the region was possible. Moreover, the communities within the Levant were isolated neither from one another nor from Egypt, Mesopotamia, Anatolia, or the Aegean. The restrictions imposed by one setting could be mediated through contact with another.

It is also worth keeping in mind that the two basic modes of survival, sedentary farming and pastoral nomadism, were never far from one another. The Levant is framed on the east and south by great deserts, which were largely devoid of sedentary populations. It is not clear how much these regions were being used by nomadic populations before the end of the Late Bronze Age, since the archaeological record for these groups is difficult to discern (Saidel 2001). Moreover, the fully mature Bedouin lifestyle required the camel in order to access the full potential of the region, and the dromedary was only domesticated at the very end of the Late Bronze Age (Finkelstein 1988a: 247). However, it was probably during the Iron Age that nomadic desert pastoral life began to take shape. It is natural for the desert nomads of the area to enter the steppelands and even the settled regions. Nineteenth-century travelers often encountered desert nomads in the mountainous regions of the coast during certain seasons (Bell 1987). It must have been during the Iron Age that the symbiotic relationship that still exists between the desert nomads (whose area of wandering extends out into the great desert regions) and the settled folk of the agricultural areas began to form (Khazanov 1984: 203–27).

This being said, the fact remains that no ancient society escaped the influence of the environment in which it existed. Architecture is certainly one of the manifestations of material culture that must respond immediately to environmental factors. The choice of materials used for a building is significant. The materials are either a local product and reflect a concern for economic resources, or they are imported and identify a building as being worthy of special treatment and greater economic expense. The design of a building either fits the environmental factors and adjusts to them, or it demonstrates a lack of concern for environmental and economic limitations and a determination not to be constrained by them. On the other hand, the Iron Age societies of the Levant were not developing in some type of environmental vacuum. The Levant had already witnessed more than 5,000 years of continuous settled life, and as is now abundantly clear, landscapes and environments are as much a result of human actions as they are the product of natural events (Kouchoukos 2001: 84). Humanity had already substantially altered the landscape of the ancient Levant by establishing settled communities and by producing agriculture. The large-scale urbanization of the Middle Bronze Age had profoundly affected local environments, and the international trade routes and foreign conquests of the Late Bronze Age had influenced the ways in which human interaction with the landscape had proceeded. The Iron Age societies continued to use niches already created by earlier human activities in the region and developed new ones, as previously ignored areas were now exploited.

The peoples responsible for erecting temples and sanctuaries in the Levant during the early Iron Age were not all from the region. Evidence for the arrival of new peoples who brought cultural forms adapted to other environments is conclusive. To understand the designs and the structural features of the temples of the Iron Age Levant, it is often necessary to look beyond the geographical boundaries of the region. The introduction by new arrivals of outside architectural forms was augmented by novel architectural ideas borrowed from commercial contacts. The geography of the Levant invites outside trade through a series routes running north to south and west to east. Furthermore, the past was probably still visible in the landscape. Human activity during the previous millennia had modified most of the Levantine landscape and, although there were shifts in settlement patterns and communication networks, older structures probably still dotted the landscape, as they do throughout the region today, and could be seen by individuals living nearby or traveling through the region.

The Physical Geography

The Anti-Lebanon Mountains can be used to split the Levant into two parts, a northern sector and a southern sector.[2] The northern limit of the region under consideration is defined by the Taurus Mountains of southern Anatolia, in front of which sits a coastal area known as the Cilician triangle formed by a bend in the Taurus Mountains. This fertile plain is watered by the southward drainage of the Çeyhan and Şeyhan rivers. To the west is the plain of Adana within which appears the site of Tarsus (Effendi 2001: 63–66). From the Cilician Plain, the central Anatolian Plateau and the heartland of Late Bronze Age Hittite culture could be accessed at Göksün via the Akyol ("White Road"), which crosses the Çeyhan River and then runs alongside Karatepe (Winter 1979: 134–35). Rising to the east is Mount Amanus, a north–south running mountain range that is crossed by a principal east–west pass at Bahçe (Schloen and Fink 2009: 204). East of Mount Amanus is a rugged upland limestone massif that, on its western end, is hilly and largely barren and treeless (Bell 1987: 272) but has spots of arable land and has at times supported significant sedentary populations. This was the area of the site of ʿAin Dara. The massif continues east and merges with the similar landscape of northern Iraq and western Iran (Mostyn and Hourani 1988: 19–20).

The Euphrates River heads south through this region from modern Turkey, and it was here that the Neo-Hittite kingdoms of Carchemish and Kumuhu were located (Akurgal 1985: 346–47). As it turns east, the Euphrates forms an arc through the northeastern part of modern Syria, and on this arc rose the ancient site of Emar. The available rainwater (250–500 mm per year) and the presence of the river and its tributaries have turned this region into a large grain-producing plain of brown and chestnut soils (Mostyn and Hourani 1988: 10–17). To the northeast is the Jezireh, defined by several small tributaries of the Euphrates and one large tributary, the Khabur River. This increase in river water and the existence of an aquifer that bubbles up as springs on the north flank of the Jebel ʿAbd el Aziz, a low range of mountains on an east–west line that extends through the area, provide pockets of rich agricultural land; however, to sustain a major sedentary population, pastoralism also needed to be exploited. This significant region after the Early Bronze Age and during Iron Age II was controlled by ancient Guzana (Tell Halaf). South and east, the land becomes desert and semidesert.

West of the bend in the Euphrates is the wide plain around modern Aleppo, bounded on the west by two parallel ranges, the smaller Jebel Zawiyah (*Jebel ez-Zawiye*) and Jebel Ansariyah (*Jabal al-Salawiyih*; Effendi 2001: 54) that together form the Jebel Nusayriyah. Between the two mountain groups is the Ghab depression through which the Orontes River flows, making the area a fertile though marshy zone (Akkermans and Schwartz 2003: 4). Along with Mount Amanus in the north and the

---

2. See maps 1–3, pp. 373–374, at the end of the volume.

Lebanon range to the south, Jebel Nusayriyah forms a mountainous barrier separating the inland plains from the coastal band in the northern sector of the Levant. In the north, this mountain wall is penetrated between Mount Amanus and Jebel Nusayriyah by the ʿAmuq Plain, part of the Hatay region of modern southwestern Turkey, where the site of the Bronze Age city of Alalakh (Tell Atchana) is located. This is the fertile, well-watered region (Effendi 2001: 83–84) that became important for its coastal associations with the cities of Antioch and Seleucia Pieria during the Hellenistic and Roman periods; in the Late Bronze Age and Iron Age I, it was an inland-looking region. This probably began to change in Iron Age II, with the establishment of the trading station at Al Mina[3] at the mouth of the Orontes and the development of the inland site of Tell Taʿyinat on the plain itself. The ʿAmuq Plain spreads out south and east of Mount Amanus, which itself serves to seal off the Gulf of Iskenderun and the coastal route north to Cilicia. The plain itself is watered by the Orontes, the Afrin, and the Kara Su rivers. The plain is blessed with a temperate climate and is suitable for agriculture, particularly grain, olives, and grapes (Kondoleon 2000: 3). The Orontes (*Nahr al-Asi*) begins in the Lebanon Mountains and flows north, watering the plains that spread from the eastern flanks of this discontinuous mountain chain. The chain breaks again at the Homs Gap, an opening that allows Mediterranean climatic influences into the interior (Fortin 1999: 31–32) and makes for green and lush vegetation in parts of the mountains (Bell 1987: 197). To the east, the watered plains change to steppe and then desert dotted with occasional oases such as at El Kown and ancient Palmyra (also known as Tadmor; Fortin 1999: 33).

The entire Levant is on the edge of the eastern Mediterranean, with a shoreline stretching from the Cilician triangle on the Gulf of Iskenderun (Scanderon, Issus) to Gaza. There is a major difference between the north and south coasts. The best harbors are all on the northern portion, beginning with the modern port of Iskenderun (Alexandretta); continuing south through ancient Antioch's port of Seleucia (Samanda); and ancient Ugarit's harbor of Ras Shamra; and on to Tripoli; and the ancient Late Bronze and early Iron Age ports of Byblos, Beirut, Sidon, Tyre, and Haifa Bay, on which the site of Abu Hawam is found. South of Mount Carmel, the coast has no good harbors, only small coves and tidal river outlets. The coast north of Ras en Naqura (*Rosh Haniqrah*), the modern border between Lebanon and Israel, is a band defined by the Lebanon, Jebel Nusayriyah, and Mount Amanus ranges. Farther north on the west of the ʿAmuq Plain is Mount Kasios (Mount Cassios, Cassius). The mountain wall effectively keeps the moisture on the (consequently) humid coast (Akkermans and Schwartz 2003: 4). This northern coast is narrow and is easily crossed in a few hours by horse, mule, or foot (Effendi 2001: 15).

---

3. The ethnic identity of the founders or of the majority population at Al Mina remains a point of serious debate; see the recent articles by Boardman 2002 and Niemeyer 2004 for a review of the issues.

To the east of the Lebanon Mountains rise the taller Anti-Lebanon, and between them is the high valley of the Baqʿah in which was located the Late Bronze Age site of Kamid el-Loz. In the eastern shadow of the Anti-Lebanon Mountains is the great oasis of al-Ghutah, home of the city of Damascus. The mountains serve to halt the movement of any residual moisture from the coast and render the land north and east of Damascus dry steppe. In the nineteenth and early twentieth century c.e., it was possible to ride out of Damascus into the mountains via the fertile valley of the Baraba River, cross the Anti-Lebanon, and arrive at the northern end of the Baqʿah in two days' time (Bell 1987: 159). Another long day of riding would take one down to the coast at Tripoli (Effendi 2001: 102). The Lebanon and Anti-Lebanon Mountains also could be crossed at a point near the ancient site of Kamid el-Loz. This was the road that led from the south coast of ancient Phoenicia to Damascus. The Baqʿah could also be approached directly from the south through the Upper Galilee (Hachmann 1983: 25–26).

Groves of cedar trees—which today can be found only above Tripoli and in the highest parts of the Chouf (Fisk 2002: 160–62)—covered the upper slopes of Mount Amanus and the Lebanon range and began to be exploited as an important export item in the Early Bronze Age, when Egyptian Old Kingdom rulers coveted the timber, and by southern Mesopotamians according to the *Epic of Gilgamesh* (Schloen and Fink 2009: 205). Because large cedar beams made the finest roofing material in the ancient Near East and allowed for the covering of large interior spaces, the timber continued to be an important export into the period of Assyrian domination in the seventh century, when it was among the tribute items sent to the Assyrian kings. All of the mountain ranges of this northern portion of the Levant shared in common the ability to house and protect isolated groups of people who for one reason or another needed or wanted to be separated from those who controlled the plains and coastal areas. Although all of the mountains could be entered and navigated, they offered (and still do offer) a degree of sanctuary (Fisk 2002: 56–58; Bell 1987: 85–279) during the Late Bronze Age and early Iron Age.

South and east of the Anti-Lebanon is the basalt Hauran (*Hawran*) Plateau, a fertile land of lava outcrops and decomposing volcanic rock. This eventually bleeds into the Hamada, the Great Syrian desert (Bell 1987: 108). At the southern end of the Anti-Lebanon is the Jawlan or Golan Heights, in which are the springs that provide one of the sources for the River Jordan and where Tel Dan is positioned. The Jordan drops down into the Huleh Valley then continues to the Sea of Galilee and finally forms the Ghor (the Jordan Valley) on its way to the Dead Sea. To the east of the Ghor rise the Transjordanian highlands, which contained the early Iron Age kingdoms of Ammon, Moab, and Edom. The Ghor is a deep cleft, 394 m below sea level, between two sets of highlands (Ibrahim [1987] 39–51). It is a fertile, riparian region with a tropical climate that was once more-densely covered in natural vegetation than it is today. It is a distinct microclimate from the climates on either side (Ben-Avraham and Hough 2003: 44–49). Deir ʿAlla was located in this region. To the east rise the steep and rugged scarps of granite and sandstone that are cut through by east–west-tending canyons, including Wadi Mujib and the Wadi Hasa, coming from the hill country of Transjordan. This is a stony region (consisting of basalt in the north), the continuation of the Syrian Hauran Plateau. The Yarmuk River defines the northern border of this landscape. It then becomes an agriculturally rich area, the ʿAijlun highlands. The region ends at the Wadi Zarqa. Next is a rolling limestone landscape cut through by the Wadi Mujib. The Wadi Hasa marks the end of this section, and the far south becomes an arid zone of richly colored sandstone, sculpted by water and wind, that continues to the Red Sea (Bloch-Smith and Nakhai 1999: 105). Though large tracts of the land are barren, agriculture is possible in some parts of the region, allowing for permanent settlement, particularly the Baqʿah Valley and the ʿAijlun highlands of central Transjordan. The eastern rim of the Ghor, the highlands, lies in the "rain shadow" of the western plateau. The northern area has a Mediterranean climate and once had pine forest. Going south, the land becomes increasingly more arid (Mountfort 1965: 23–24). The Transjordanian highlands were joined together from south to north by a natural highland that developed into the main artery moving parallel to the Ghor up to Syria and was called the King's Highway. It became important for trade after the domestication of the camel (Amiet 1987: 15). Farther east from the Transjordanian highlands stretches the northern extension of the Arabian Desert. In the north, this is a limestone strip overlaid with basalt, a continuation of the Syrian Hauran. It becomes the great depression of the Azraq Oasis and then a flint chip desert, the Hamada, which gives way, finally, farther east to the Syro-Arabian Desert (Montfort 1965: 24).

On the west side of the Jordan River between the Ghor and the steep cliffs of mountains to the west is the Judean Desert, a band roughly 20 km in width (A. Mazar 1992a: 4–7). To the west of the desert strip is a mountainous region, with many fertile areas suitable for farming. The northern section, the Upper Galilee, includes high steep mountains and is the location of the site of Hazor. South of this area, the Lower Galilee contains a number of east–west valleys (A. Mazar 1992a: 3–4). The most important is the system of the Jezreel and Beth-shean valleys that connect the Ghor with the coast at Haifa Bay. The site of Beth-shean is located in the valley of the same name. The mountains continue to the south to the region of Shechem (where the ancient site of Shechem is located), and south of this rise is a steeper range of mountains that are not crossed by east–west valleys. Instead, there exists the north–south watershed that connects the sites of Shechem, Jerusalem, and Hebron. The saddle at Jerusalem is the one major east–west route connecting the central coastal plain with Jericho in the Ghor. The mountainous area around Hebron was heavily forested in antiquity. Hebron was the first major hill town and the point at which travelers coming from the south on their way to Jerusalem entered the Judean hills (Dunn 1988: 55; Stephens 1991: 311). To the south and west begins the Negev Desert.

The Negev and the Arabian Desert of southern Jordan (ancient Edom) are separated by the barren Wadi Arabah (Stephens 1991: 283–98), which is the continuation of the Ghor south to the Gulf of Aqaba. Wadi Arabah was an important source for copper in the Late Bronze Age and early Iron Age. The mining site of Timna was established at its southern end. On the west side, the Wadi Arabah joins with the Beersheba Valley, which cuts west through the northern Negev and continues to the coast, providing access to Gaza. Near the boundary of the Beersheba Valley are the sites of Tell Arad and Horvat Qitmit. To the east of the Wadi Arabah appear the Transjordanian highlands and the King's Highway. In the southern sector of the Negev, along the border with the Sinai Peninsula rise highlands; this is where the site of Teman (Kuntillet ʿAjrud) developed.

The coastal region running north from Gaza to Mount Carmel, although it had no good ports, did offer anchorages in small coves at Jaffa and ʿAtlit and in the estuaries of tidal rivers that also worked as highways into the interior. Tell Qasile is located in just such a spot on the Yarkon River (Dothan and Dothan 1992: 99–100). The coast is wide and dune covered from Gaza to the mouth of the Yarkon River. From the Yarkon to Mount Carmel, the coast becomes narrower and forms the Plain of Sharon. This narrow coast tends to be split into *kurkar* (calcareous aeolianite) ridges and troughs that block the streams flowing down from the mountains towards the sea and caused the area to be marshy in antiquity. This is a fertile land of red loamy *hamra* and *rendzina* soils, the result of the breakdown of the limestone bedrock. These two distinct coastal zones were to become the Philistine region (Bloch-Smith and Nakhai 1999: 88) with important temple remains at the coastal sites of Tell Qasile and Ashdod. The coastal plain is bounded by a range of foothills, the Shephelah, in which Lachish was settled, and Ekron straddles the coastal plain and the Shephelah.

There are differences between the northern and southern coastlines. The best natural harbors are in the north. Those in the south are small in comparison, though port cities existed in both the Late Bronze Age and the Iron Age all along the coast. The entire coastal region receives sufficient water to be agriculturally productive throughout most of its length. While coastal foothills in the south and mountains in the north do offer some degree of separation between coast and interior, none of these forms a serious impediment to communication and the movement of people. On the other hand, the nearness of the mountains to the Phoenician coast limits the actual arable land available to support the cities on the coast.

The Levantine landscape presents a varied enough geology to offer several types of building problems and options. The low-lying areas of the southern coastal plain, the riparian plains, and the Ghor do not have abundant stone. Mud and mud-brick construction were natural in these regions, particularly where rainfall was limited (Akkermans and Schwartz 2003: 6–7).[4] And, while wood is available, most commonly

---

4. Jericho (Tell es-Sultan) in the Ghor has produced perhaps the earliest evidence for mud building,

it is used to reinforce buildings rather than as the main material for building. The north coast and the massif have more abundant stone and easy access to good timber sources including the famed cedar trees. Stone is common for prestige building, and the cedars were often used for the roofing systems. Wood was also an important item in the building of the North Syrian region. It was incorporated with mud brick and stone at Guzana. Cedar beams were a tribute item that Carchemish paid to the Assyrian King Tiglath-pileser (Ikeda 1982: 232). Stone combined with mud brick was used in the highlands of Israel and in the region of the Transjordanian highlands. The highlands on the west side of the Jordan receive more rain than those on the Transjordanian side. The southern sector, ancient Edom, and the Negev are deserts. Stone architecture is found at Tell Arad and Horvat Qitmit. However, in the latter case, the buildings are of unworked fieldstones.

The Levant is not protected from assaults from outside by any natural barrier; quite to the contrary it is positioned in such a manner as to be open to forces from all sides. However, the landscape does dictate how those forces move. Mesopotamian elements tended to come through the Syrian region and then filtered elsewhere into the Levant. The Jezireh was actually within the orbit of northern Mesopotamia. Aegean notions entered through the ʿAmuq Plain and through the ports and anchorages of the coast. There was a natural land bridge to Egypt across the Sinai. This has resulted in southern Palestine often being within the sphere of Egypt's direct or indirect control. Nothing in the landscape would stop an aggressive Egyptian force from exerting itself all the way into Syria and south Anatolia except for another power. The Egyptian influences moved easily either via the coast road (the Via Maris/Way of Horus) or through the Beersheba Valley to the Wadi Arabah and up the King's Highway.

The Levant was a series of distinct small scale ecological niches requiring a variety of strategies for survival and exploitation. If one takes the Braudelian approach and looks at the cycles of settlement over a long stretch of time, then one can see the patterns of settlement into which the early Iron Age developments need to be placed. The coastal region along the north from the Cilician triangle to the ʿAmuq Plain was fertile and always offered good agricultural potential though parts must have been potentially marshy and disease ridden (Effendi 2001: 71). The areas watered by the Orontes, Euphrates, and Khabur also have usually supported large sedentary populations. North Syria and southern Anatolia supported large cities in the Iron Age. This

---

dating to the Natufian period of the Mesolithic, tenth millennium B.C.E. The first handmade, rectangular mud bricks are found in the Pre-pottery Neolithic B level of the eighth–sixth millennia B.C.E. During this same period, handmade mud-brick buildings show up in Turkish sites (Aşikli Hüyük and Haçilar) and Iranian sites (Ganj Dareh and Ali Kosh). By 5000 B.C.E., handmade mud bricks were in use at Choga Mami and Tell es-Sawaam in Mesopotamia. The earliest mold-made mud bricks appeared in Egypt and Palestine about 3200 B.C.E. or the beginning of the Early Bronze Age, and perhaps a bit earlier in Mesopotamia (Van Beek and Van Beek 2008: 7–10).

was also the case of the fertile Jezreel and Beth-shean valleys. The limestone hills to the west of the ʿAmuq Plain have tended to be more of a peripheral area. During the Iron Age clearly there was some settlement here. The coastal band beginning west of Mount Kasios provided several good harbors south to Haifa Bay, but the Lebanon Mountain impinged on the coast, providing a small region for agricultural development. If the region was to prosper, it needed to gain access to the fertile regions of the interior or look to the Mediterranean and overseas expansion, which was its chosen route by Iron Age IIA. The coast south of Haifa Bay was capable of supporting small urban settlements, which had been true since the Middle Bronze Age. Beginning in Iron Age I there was short distance coastal traffic from sites like Tell Qasile near the mouth of the Yarkon River which connected the Shephelah coast to Cyprus and some of the ports slightly to the north. Of the oases in the Syrian steppelands to the east of the Lebanon Mountains, only Damascus was of major importance in the Iron Age. Its history of settlement stretches back into the Early Bronze Age, and its location on trade routes that could be plied by donkey caravans made it possible for it to prosper before the domestication of the camel. The Arabian Desert and its northern extensions into the great Syrian Desert effectively formed the eastern boundary of the Levant, and covered a great swath of land between the end of the settled world of the Syrian Hauran and the Transjordanian highlands and the Euphrates River. The domestication of the dromedary some time around 1200 B.C.E. finally allowed for the exploitation of the deep interior steppelands which were too dry for donkey caravans: the Syrian steppe as well as the steppelands east of the region of Transjordan and the Negev. Domesticated camels permitted the most efficient exploitation of this region by nomads, and the camel is included in the repertoire of figures from the carved reliefs at Guzana in the Khabur (Bulliet 1990: 57–86, fig. 33). The Lebanon and Anti-Lebanon mountains have historically supported small, village size populations and were perhaps inhabited during the Iron Age, but there is no archaeological support. The same is true for the Hauran. The tropical depression formed by the Ghor is suitable for sedentary life and has been so used since the Chalcolithic; interestingly it seems to have been somewhat under utilized during the Late Bronze Age and Iron Age I. The Late Bronze Age Deir ʿAlla sanctuary operated here, but not as part of a large settlement. Nearby were Tell el-Mazar and Tell es-Saʾidiyeh, and all show evidence for occupation in both the Late Bronze Age and the Iron Age I. However, compared to the much more extensive settlement of the earlier periods, the region shows depopulation and may have reverted to much greater nomadic and seminomadic use. This was also the case for the Transjordanian highlands during the Late Bronze Age. The village level occupations that had begun during the prepottery Neolithic disappeared by the Late Bronze Age, and the region continued to be pastoral until the Iron Age I. A similar pattern emerged for the hill country to the west. The landscape here divides between the northern region of Samaria with large, fertile intermontane valleys, and moderate topography, a fertile steppeland which was somewhat settled in Late Bronze Age, and the southern region of Judea with a much harsher topography of rocky outcrops, small mountain valleys, and desert steppeland to the east and south. This was a region largely unpopulated by sedentary peoples until the Iron Age I. The steppelands of the southern Transjordan region and the Negev are frontier zones that were largely lacking in population (probably of any sort), except for a small area on the fringe of Judea, until the domestication of the camel. In the Iron Age there is evidence for exploitation by both nomadic groups and sedentary people. The fertile Shephelah and Sharon have a long history of continuous agricultural exploitation, and this was true in both the Late Bronze Age and the Iron Age.

Regions were never totally isolated in the Levant. Communication was possible in all areas. However, the differences in natural resources, in life-style responses, and in movements of outside influences did result in cultural variations. Big cities were most likely to prosper in areas that provided a good agricultural base and easy access to trade. These tended to be areas that were located either in flat lands or near flat lands. The less-advantaged coastal land and the various highland regions, although they may have offered some agricultural opportunity, usually had only limited farmland and tended to support only village-level development. In the highland settings and in areas that bordered the steppelands, farming needed to be augmented with limited herding. This could not be the nomadic type of herding with large numbers of sheep but was, rather, small-scale transhumance. Desert and semiarid regions offered no possibility for urban development and settled life but could be effectively exploited for large-scale herding.

Temple-building reflects each of the above aspects of the landscape. The materials employed were determined by location and natural availability. Temples in prestigious locations often reveal this fact by consisting of trade-construction materials— most commonly, containing cedar from the Lebanese Mts. of the north coast. Temple plans reflect the presence and persistence of outside influences as well as exhibiting the local traditions. The size and nature of the temple building itself are a direct result of the economic status of the community unless the temple is actually serving a group beyond the immediate community. Temples, because they were the most significant building projects for most Iron Age communities, cannot be separated from the landscape context. The landscape provided the materials, influenced the nature of the design, and ultimately underwrote the economy that took on the project.

The Human Geography

The Levant suffered a series of destructive events sometime in the late thirteenth century and early twelfth century B.C.E. Conventionally, 1200 B.C.E. is regarded as the time when the Late Bronze Age gave way to the early Iron Age (Aharoni 1982: 157). How these events might have been associated has yet to be determined, but among the important changes were two that concern this volume. First, several of the major cities of the Late Bronze Age were destroyed, never to be reoccupied. Second, there was a significant demographic shift throughout the region. New peoples from the Mesopotamian and Aegean areas infiltrated, either partially causing the collapse of the Late Bronze Age cultures or taking advantage of it to move into the region. The disruption of the Late Bronze Age social structures permitted societal inversions as peoples who had previously been nomadic began to settle down as agriculturalists, and others who had lived in one area were forced to seek refuge or search for opportunities in new places. The demographic changes resulted in shifts in residential and landscape use patterns. Areas that had been underexploited in the Late Bronze Age became significant in the early Iron Age. Secondary and tertiary urban sites in the Late Bronze Age emerged as primary centers in the early Iron Age, while many of the primary Late Bronze Age urban sites were not reestablished. During the 300 years of the Late Bronze Age (1500–1200 b.c.e.), the Levantine cultures, as opposed to the conquering peoples in the region, seem to have had more similarities than regional variations. The society that developed in the early Iron Age, however, was not the same. Pockets of older Late Bronze Age culture survived and probably affected early Iron Age developments in certain spots, but on a large scale, the human landscape of the early Iron Age appears to have been quite different from that of the Late Bronze Age. The new arrivals changed the demographic makeup and subsumed the older cultures in most areas. The outside imperial forces of the Late Bronze Age were removed and played no role in the early Iron Age but were replaced by new forces coming in from the east. The changed human landscape becomes visible quite early—soon into Iron Age I—but the full extent of the new environment does not manifest itself until Iron Age II.

The Levant at 1200 b.c.e. and the Lines of Demographic Continuity

The Canaanites, born out of the confused demographic state of the early Middle Bronze Age (Finegan 1979: 253; Killebrew 2005; Negev 1986: 27), were the dominant people of the southern Levant in 1200 and perhaps ranged as far north as Byblos on the coast (Negev 1986: 70–81). Even in places where now they may only be recognized as neighbors, such as at Ugarit (Ras Shamra) and Alalakh (Tell Atchana) (Naʾaman 1999: 32), their culture may have been dominant then (Amiran 1970: 167). Elsewhere the Amorites, a people related linguistically and culturally to the Canaanites, who had been dominant in the north in the Middle Bronze Age and had established the Old Babylonian Kingdom (which was destroyed by the Hittite king Muršili I in the sixteenth century b.c.e.) may still have existed in pockets but had been displaced politically by the kingdom created by the Mitanni as early as the fifteenth century b.c.e.

The Mitanni controlled a band of territory stretching from Cilicia in the west to the foothills of the Zagros Mountains in the east. Unlike Canaanites and Amorites who were speakers of West Semitic languages, the Mitanni were speakers of Hurrian and probably originated in the Anatolian region (Finegan 1979: 90; Akkermans and Schwartz 2003: 327). The Canaanites and Amorites had developed cultures based on city-state units, with petty kings controlling primary centers. A similar situation may have prevailed among the early Hurrian arrivals, but by the fifteenth century B.C.E. the individual units had joined together. The independence of these three groups was curtailed in the later Late Bronze Age by the forceful emergence into the region of the empires of Egypt and the Hittites, and important urban centers were regularly put into a vassalage arrangement with either of the two powers or were conquered and ruled directly.

The significant Late Bronze Age cities of Alalakh on the ʿAmuq Plain and Ugarit on the coast succumbed to some crisis around 1200 B.C.E. and were destroyed, never to be rebuilt. Their destructions marked a change in the balance of power in the north. Elsewhere, some of the Canaanite cities in the hill country in the south seem to have been able to weather the initial disruptions to survive if not flourish for awhile into the twelfth century B.C.E. (A. Mazar 1994b: 247). The major Late Bronze Age Canaanite center at Megiddo remained important, and it displays evidence of surviving Late Bronze Age material culture well into the twelfth century B.C.E. (A. Mazar 1992a: 297), but the other great center, Hazor, was probably already destroyed in the early thirteenth century B.C.E. (Rabinovich and Silberman 1998: 53–54).[5] Whether the Canaanite cities of the coast with good harbors in the stretch between Ugarit and Haifa Bay suffered in the depredations at the end of the Late Bronze Age is not known from either literary or archaeological records. There is some evidence to suggest that, while they may have been damaged somewhat, these cities–which were to emerge as the Phoenician centers in Iron Age II—were able to recover quickly after the Late Bronze Age collapse elsewhere and to begin to exploit the economic vacuum created by the demise of Ugarit, which had been the strongest force in their area of the coast during the Late Bronze Age.[6] Their populations may have changed somewhat because of the need to integrate new peoples from elsewhere who were driven into the area by the general mayhem that seems to have marked the end of the Late Bronze Age (Röllig 1983: 79–80). Justin (*Epitoma* 18.3.2–5) records a telling episode of how Tyre was founded by Sidonians escaping from the Ashkelonians in the year before the fall of Troy. While the reality of the event is dubious, it has been interpreted by some as indicating that the Phoenician coast was under attack from people from the south, possibly one of the newcomers known collectively as "Peoples of the Sea" (Gilboa 2005: 50).

No doubt there was some population mixing as a result of such raids. The Egyptian story of Wen-Amon's trip to Lebanon's coast in search of cedar, a story normally

---

5. This is the new date of destruction based on A. Ben-Tor's excavations at Hazor. Ben-Tor disagrees with Yadin, who dated the destruction between 1230 and 1220 B.C.E.

6. Tyre, in the one place where deep excavations have been conducted, shows no evidence of interruption (P. M. Bikai 1978b: 73; 1992b: 133). The same situation applies to Sarepta (Anderson 1988: 423).

dated to the eleventh century B.C.E., the middle of Iron Age I, describes little that hints at destruction or confusion. At the end of the twelfth century B.C.E., the Assyrian king Tiglath-pileser I (1115–1077 B.C.E.) marched to the coast and demanded tribute from Byblos, Sidon, and Arwad, suggesting that these were functioning cities at that point in time (Muhly 1985: 264). By Iron Age II, the Phoenician cities appeared as significant forces in the political and cultural firmament of the eastern Aegean. They now can be recognized in the archaeological record by their material culture, language, script (Lebrun 1987), and their appearance in the literary sources (P. M. Bikai 1978a: 48–56). If the Phoenician coast did indeed witness undisturbed continuity of settlement between Late Bronze Age and early Iron Age, then the early Iron Age Phoenician cities must have preserved some elements of Late Bronze Age Canaanite culture. However, it is important to note that, while some of the major coastal centers in the early Iron Age were flourishing earlier in the Late Bronze Age, this was not the case for all the settlements. Several of the Late Bronze Age sites in the region never recovered after 1200 B.C.E., and many of the significant sites of the early Iron Age were not standing in the Late Bronze Age (Röllig 1983: 85). Moreover, the language and religion of the early Iron Age Phoenicians may have been different from those of the Late Bronze Age (Röllig 1983: 88–91: for an alternative view, see Brody 2002 and Bikai 1994b).

By the last century of the Late Bronze Age, much of the northern Levant was under the thumb of the Hittite Empire, which had moved into northern Syria from central Anatolia and had destroyed the Mitanni. The conquered cities of Carchemish and Aleppo were rechristened Hittite viceregal capitals governed by cadet branches of the royal family, and Emar was refounded as a new city. The Hittite Empire extended its sphere of influence to form vassal states of the cities of Ugarit and Alalakh. The Hittite Empire collapsed and disappeared with the troubles of 1200 B.C.E. Some communities of Hittites who were resident throughout the Levantine region must have survived, and Na'aman (1994: 239–43) has argued that there was a migration of peoples from the former Hittite Empire into southern Canaan, to be recognized in the names of the nations dispossessed by the Israelites: the Hittites, Hivites, Jebusites, Girgashites, and Perizzites. However, when the epithet *Hittite* appears in the other biblical contexts, it seems to have carried no more meaning than being a marker of foreignness (McMahon 1989: 71–75).

By Iron Age II in North Syria and southeast Anatolia, several sites (some with older Hittite levels) revived, and elements of their culture, particularly their language, look to be Hittite in origin. This may have been the result of a movement of Anatolian people from the central plateau down to the southern regions in the wake of the fall of the Hittite Empire and its capital Hattuša (Sandars 1987: 143). They found refuge here, and as they recovered, they restored a semblance of the Hittite world that had been lost (Kohlmeyer 1985a: 248–49). This has been dramatically demonstrated in the finds from the excavations of the temple of the Weather God in the Aleppo Citadel.

The Iron Age IA reliefs that decorated the interior of the temple, dated to the eleventh century B.C.E., show strong stylistic and iconographic connections with the reliefs at the late Hittite sanctuary of Yazılıkaya outside the Hittite capital at Hattuša (Gonnella, Khayyata, and Kohlmeyer 2005). The early rulers of Iron Age Carchemish maintained the older connection to the defunct Late Bronze Age Hittite ruling house (Hawkins 1988). These revived centers are collectively referred to as Neo-Hittite kingdoms, and instead of a Neo-Hittite Empire on the Late Bronze Age model, the Iron Age II arrangement was of a group of independent competing city-states. On the other hand, the residents of these cities spoke Luwian, which, while not the old Late Bronze Age official Hittite language, was one of the languages in use in the Late Bronze Age Hittite Empire. Several of the rulers of these cities put up inscriptions in which their names emulated those of the Late Bronze Age Hittite rulers (Akkermans and Schwartz 2003: 366–67), but they were written in a new form, not the old Hittite cuneiform. All of this suggests that there are lines of continuity between Late Bronze Age Hittite culture and Iron Age II Neo-Hittite culture, though clearly the new culture that emerged was not a mere revival of the older culture.

In the Late Bronze Age, the Hittite Empire did have a rival in the northeast, the Middle Assyrian Empire, which finished off the Mitanni and took over the Jezireh. The Assyrians governed this territory as a provincial region, with a governor installed in the city of Dur-Katlimmu (Sheikh Hamad) on the Khabur River, well located for easy communication with the imperial capital of Assur. There is evidence for additional Assyrian governmental outposts elsewhere in the Jezireh in the Late Bronze Age. Unlike the Hittite Empire which fell rapidly, the Middle Assyrian Empire was able to hold onto power perhaps until the mid-eleventh century B.C.E. (Akkermans and Schwartz 2003: 348–51, 358–59). In the eleventh century B.C.E., if not earlier, northern Mesopotamia and northeastern Syria had become destabilized by the arrival of the nomadic Arameans (Hagens 2002: 62–64). By the late tenth century B.C.E., the Neo-Assyrian Empire had come into being and was pushing back into the Jezireh to retake control, which it succeeded in doing in the ninth century B.C.E.; and by the end of the eighth century B.C.E., most of the Levant was either directly controlled by the Neo-Assyrian rulers or under their influence (Lipschits 2005: 3–11; Akkermans and Schwartz 2003: 377–79).

The expansion of the Hittite Empire into the northern Levant was preceded in the south by the New Kingdom Egyptian Empire, which controlled much of the Canaanite territory in the south throughout the Late Bronze Age. While it has been suggested that Egyptian control had begun to weaken in this region early in the thirteenth century B.C.E. (Malamat 1954: 231–42),[7] realistically the native Canaanite cities were ei-

---

7. Certainly the discovery of a stela of Ramesses II near Damascus and dated to his 52nd regnal year suggests that Egyptian involvement with the region was still strong into the thirteenth century B.C.E. (Kitchen 1999: 133–38).

ther governed by resident Egyptian governors with their garrisons at Beth-shean and Lachish or were in a vassal relationship to the pharaohs of the New Kingdom dynasties. These Canaanite cities were but shadows of their former Middle Bronze Age grandeur. The Amarna letters make clear that the region was divided among several petty city-states, and the archaeological evidence shows that there was a steady process of deurbanization paralleled by increased rural growth—both processes perhaps aided by Egyptian imperial policies toward the Canaanite polities (Falconer 1994: 326–30). There were conflicts between the Canaanite cities, probably exacerbated by the different settlement patterns determined by responses to the landscape (Savage and Falconer 2003: 31–45). Along the coast south of Haifa Bay were a number of settlement clusters with large capital cities that dominated the other nearby communities. The highlands were less sedentary and less densely populated, with little integration among the settlements and few prominent urban centers. Even Jerusalem and Shechem controlled limited secondary centers around them. The exception seems to be Gezer, which may have followed the pattern of the coast. The northern portion of the Jordan Valley had a number of smaller, well integrated groupings along with a couple of major settlement clusters dominated by the cities of Hazor and Pella.

Egyptian presence in the region seems to have been shifting before 1200 B.C.E. and was surely compromised with the troubles of 1200 B.C.E. However, Egyptian forces remained a feature of the region for at least another half century, though they were probably confined to the areas in which resident garrisons could be maintained (A. Mazar 1992a: 296–300). Aspects of Egyptian culture were still be found at Lachish and Beth-shean and in the Jordan Valley and the Transjordanian highlands. However, the story of Wen-Amon's trip to the coastal area of Byblos in the eleventh century B.C.E. suggests that in this region Egyptians no longer commanded respect or fear. The retraction of Egyptian power after 1200 B.C.E. opened the way for some of the old Canaanite cities to revive, and for a time remnants of Late Bronze Age Canaanite culture could still be found at Megiddo, even as the human landscape around them was changing because of the influx of new peoples.

New Arrivals

Although the Neo-Hittite Luwian-speaking population in northern Syria may well have been a continuation of the older population of the region, the other demographic force, the Arameans, was new—a people who first appear in the twelfth century B.C.E. The earliest mention of *Ahlamu Aramaya* (Lipiński 2000: 25–54) is in the Assyrian campaign reports of Tiglath-pileser I (1115–1077 B.C.E.), in which they are described as pastoral nomadic people who moved into the sedentary regions of Syria as far west as Lebanon from the steppeland of the Syro-Arabian desert. They came in two waves: one to the north through upper Mesopotamia, and the other to the south through Syria (Hawkins 1982: 379–80). They were speakers of a West Semitic language and therefore are quite distinct from the Indo-European Luwian speakers, among whom they settled in the North Syrian region. Evidence for their presence can be found in the regions of modern Iraq, Jordan, and Lebanon, as well as Syria. It is certainly possible that in the Aramean group were refugees from the destroyed urban centers who were able to find a place with these newcomers (Naʾaman 1994: 237). The Aramean nomadic life-style may have led them naturally into international, long-distance land trade; certainly the domestication of the camel assisted in this advancement because it permitted travel across the Syrian and Arabian deserts. Both the Arameans and the Arabs, who first appear as an identifiable group at this time (probably living in the Hauran Plateau and southern Syrian areas), seem to have been engaged in the early stages of camel-borne, caravan trade (Strommenger 1985: 324). Arameans lacked any type of unified or cohesive political unit. There were a few significant cities: Hamath (modern Hamas), Damascus, and Arpad (north of modern Aleppo), each of which controlled hinterlands and smaller cities and villages. These units formed coalitions with smaller nearby centers for the benefit of defensive or offensive strategies (Snell 1985: 326–29). The Neo-Hittite cities and the new Aramean centers fought for control of the areas where they overlapped. Carchemish and the Aramean city of Til Barsib contested the nearby crossing point on the Euphrates. Farther east, the Jezireh and the Khabur plains came under the domination of the Aramean city of Guzana by Iron Age II (Fortin 1999: 65–72).

The Arameans vied with the Neo-Hittites for domination of western and northern Syria and initially with the remnants of the Middle Assyrian Empire for control of the Jezireh. By the late ninth century in the east, the Arameans were fighting a losing battle to remain independent of the reinvigorated Assyrian Empire—a contest that was to engulf most of the Levant over the course of the next century. During the ascendancy of the Neo-Hittites and the Arameans, the former controlled the ʿAmuq Plain with a kingdom identified as Unqi. This was the region of the Iron Age II site of Tell Taʿyinat which succeeded the nearby Bronze Age Alalakh. ʿAin Dara may also have been part of this Neo-Hittite kingdom. North and east of this kingdom was an Aramean kingdom or confederation centered on Samʾal (Zincirli), which seems to have been surrounded by Neo-Hittite territory of which the Neo-Hittite Kingdom of Carchemish to the south was the most important. However, south of ʿAin Dara and just north of Aleppo was the Aramean center of Arpad, which controlled the Aleppo region (Hawkins 1982: 372–82). Thus ʿAin Dara was really on the edge of Aramean territory.

The division of the northern region into Neo-Hittite and Aramean camps may be doing an injustice to the reality of the situation. The analysis of the later ninth-century B.C.E. relief sculptures from the temple of the Weather God in the Aleppo Citadel has suggested to the excavators that the iconographic program combined older Hittite motifs with Mesopotamian forms (Kohlmeyer 2000: 35–39). These could have existed as part of the general repertoire of forms available in this region, which had long-standing connections with Mesopotamia stretching back to the Early Bronze and Middle Bronze ages, but they could also have been brought west by the Arameans or at least been revived by the catalyst of the arrival of this fresh Semitic people in the area. It is also possible that they entered with Assyrian influences, because the Assyrian kings led their troops into the region several times: Tiglath-pileser I in the late twelfth century B.C.E., Aššur-nasirpal II in the early ninth century B.C.E., and Šalmanassar III in 853 B.C.E. However, the sculptural display at the Aleppo Citadel temple predates anything from the Assyrian palaces. As a mixture of Hittite and Mesopotamian forms in the service of a local ruler, it seems likely to have been invented on the spot and perhaps is best explained as the earliest mixing of Neo-Hittite and Aramean influences here in the new kingdoms of the north.

The most confusing new group of people to emerge during the time of troubles at the end of the Late Bronze Age, the "Peoples of the Sea," may well have been a destructive, migrating force that moved by both sea and land. The "Peoples of the Sea" have long been recognized as a mix of Late Bronze Age Aegean peoples, including populations from the Greek and Anatolian mainlands as well as from the Aegean islands of Crete and Cyprus (Dothan and Dothan 1992: 168–69; Killebrew 2005). A series of droughts and famines appear to have destroyed parts of Anatolia and the Aegean during the thirteenth century B.C.E. and set in motion this large-scale human emigration (Bloch-Smith and Nakhai 1999: 63). The social disruptions of the late thirteenth century B.C.E. that contributed to the fall of the Hittite Empire, the end of several cities, and the diminishing of the power of the pharaohs of the New Kingdom Egyptian Empire (Redford 1992: 253–56) provided an opening for the "Peoples of the Sea" to enter the Levant, in many cases unopposed, and allowed them to play some part in the general destruction of the period.

The "Peoples of the Sea" are known because the texts of the pharaohs Merneptah (1213–1203) and Ramesses III (1182–1151) give them the collective name. Both pharaohs confronted confederations of foreign peoples that tried to invade the delta region during their reigns (Redford 1992: 247–56). Merneptah fought Libyans and their allies, the Meshwesh, Sherden (or Shardana), Lukka, Ekwesh (ʿIkws), Teresh (*Trs*), and Shekelesh (*Skrs*), in his 5th year on the throne (1208 B.C.E.?) and recorded his victory on a stele. A generation later, Ramesses III (in his 8th regnal year, 1186 B.C.E.?) fought off the Peleset, Tjeker, Shekelesh, Denyen, and Weshesh (Edgerton and Wilson 1936: pl. 46, p. 53) and celebrated his success with inscriptions and reliefs at Medinet Habu; these are augmented with an inscribed stele from Deir el Medineh and Papyrus Harris (Sandars 1987: 164–65).

Alt (1953: 227–28) proposed that after Ramesses III defeated the coalition of "Peoples of the Sea" he settled them along the coast of southern Palestine. In particular, three of the peoples seem to have established their homes here, the Sherden/Shardana

(*SHRDN*), the Tjeker (or Sikila or Shekelesh—*SKL*), and the Philistines. They are listed in this order on the Onomasticon of Amenemope, an Egyptian document of the Twenty-First or Twenty-Second Dynasty (Gilboa 2005: 47 n. 2; A. Mazar 1992a: 305).[8] Bietak argued that the newcomers to the coastal region of southern Palestine actually arrived as conquering invaders and not as resettled defeated peoples (Bietak 1985: 216–19). Finds of new domestic units built over the ramparts of some sites, evidence of purple dye production, and fragments of Aegean-style pottery from Abu Hawam, Dor, and other sites in the area of the Bay of Haifa reveal a demographic change in process already during the late thirteenth century (Bloch-Smith and Nakhai 1999: 88), and these people have been identified as Sherden/Shardana. They were already employed as mercenaries by Ramesses II and fought at the Battle of Kadesh for the Egyptians (Negev 1986: 294), indicating that settlement of a new group was already taking place before the defeats by the Egyptian pharaohs. The name Sherden/Shardana has been used to link them to Sardinia, though Sandars is certain that the group that invaded Egypt came from somewhere around the Syrian coast (Sandars 1987: 106–7, 160–61). Sandars has interpreted a description in a Hittite letter found at Ugarit of a people, the "Šikala," "who live in ships," as a reference to the Shekelesh. These people have also been linked to Sicily, because their name resembles that of the Sikels of southeastern Sicily, who were first encountered by Greek colonists in the eighth century and were supposedly immigrants from the disruptions following the Trojan War. The discovery at Ugarit of a sword blade recognized as an Italian Monza type may strengthen the connection of the Shekelesh with Sicily (Sandars 1987: 111–12, 157–58).

The Tjeker have been connected to the later Greek hero Teucer, the founder of Salamis following the Trojan War, and with the Teucri of the Troad (Sandars 1987: 158). Sandars has identified the Peleset with a specific group of figures represented on the reliefs at Medinet Habu. These reliefs show people moving with oxcarts. The oxen are the humped zebu known from Anatolia and Mesopotamia but not Palestine or the Aegean. These are slow-moving animals that can cover about ten miles a day. The people represented with the oxcarts must have come to the delta overland and on a long, slow migration. Moreover, the images show four oxen per cart, suggesting that each cart was accompanied by two spare oxen. If Sandars's association of the images specifically with the Peleset is correct, then it is reasonable to assume that they were an agricultural people who migrated perhaps out of eastern Anatolia or northern Syria—perhaps the Caucasus region (Sandars 1987: 121–24, 169, ills. 76–78).

Yasur-Landau has read the images more broadly and argued that they represent a massive population shift from the north Aegean down into Canaan, a movement

---

8. Bimson (1990–91) suggested that there were actually two invasions of people that would come to be known as Philistines: the first occurred in the Middle Bronze Age, long before the arrival of the "Peoples of the Sea." This is not a widely accepted view.

including men, women, and children comprising several of the groups of the "Peoples of the Sea," who migrated after the collapse of the Late Bronze Age societies of the northern Aegean and Anatolia (Barako and Yasur-Landau 2003: 39). The Philistines have been identified with the people called the Peleset (*PLST*) in the inscription of Ramesses III (Negev 1986: 294). The association is not without problems. If the Peleset are the later Philistines, then they are just one group of many who formed the confederation of peoples moving around the eastern Mediterranean. However, they alone survive into the early Iron Age to become a distinct people in the Hebrew Bible. The separation between the Egyptian references and the first mention in the Bible is at least 400 years. Sandars has concluded that there is no good evidence for identifying the Peleset as being the specific ancestors of the biblical Philistines. She argues for an amalgam of Peleset with Tjeker, Shekelesh, and Denyen in the initial foreign population of southern Palestine that later emerged as Philistines (Sandars 1987: 167). This matches with the generally accepted view that the pottery commonly called Philistine is really a regional variant of Mycenean IIIC:1b (Muhly 1984: 39–56; Furumark 1941: 118) and not the marker of a specific subgroup of the "Peoples of the Sea." More recently, Hawkins has proposed that a toponym "the Land of the Palistin," which appears in two Luwian inscriptions from the Aleppo Citadel, shares an etymology with Peleset; and there are three other Luwian inscriptions that use a variant—Walistin instead of Palistin. Hawkins has argued for an Iron Age I kingdom on the ʿAmuq Plain of Syria. It may have been from this region in the twelfth century b.c.e. that the group of "Peoples of the Sea" known as the *prst* in the Egyptian sources departed (Hawkins 2009: 169–72; Harrison 2007: 83–84).

Independent of whether the Peleset were indeed one of the early groups to form the Philistines, the fact remains that the Philistines have come to be recognized as a distinct folk from within the larger complex of "Peoples of the Sea." Their presence on the southern coast of Palestine is identified by a specific material cultural assemblage (Naʾaman 2000), and this people has been linked to the biblical Philistines, even though the textual references and the actual material finds are separated by four centuries. The practice of labeling people by pots is always highly suspect (Amiran 1970: 266–67), and exactly how the Philistine subgroup differed from the others in the large grouping of "Peoples of the Sea" is not clear, nor is it at all certain that they completely eradicated the existing Late Bronze Age Canaanite culture of the south coast (Bunimovitz 1990: 210–22). However, T. Dothan and Zukerman (2004) argue that the assemblages of Mycenean IIIC:1b ceramics found in the area in Philistine strata at Ekron and Ashdod are local products and are evidence of new cultural forces that arrived in the area, bringing with them Aegean cultural traits that continued to influence their local production. They see no chronological overlap between these new local products and the earlier Mycenean IIIA–B wares that represent the importation of Aegean works into the Late Bronze Age Canaanite setting.

These newcomers of Iron Age I brought with them a taste for Aegean-style food preparation and serving that could only be satisfied by making local versions of the pots that they knew, though the finds from the Levantine contexts reveal fewer shapes than are known from contemporary Cypriot and Aegean sites. At the same time, the assemblages in the Philistine setting show enough features in common with those from Cypriot and Aegean sites to posit a continuation of contact between all these regions into the first half of the twelfth century B.C.E. (Dothan and Zukerman 2004: 43–47). The strong similarity between the Mycenean LH IIIC:1b found in the lowest strata of Ashdod and Ekron and that from Cyprus might well point to a strong Mycenean element in the new population. The Cypriot examples are regarded as having been created by refugees from the older Mycenean settlements of the Greek mainland, and there could be a direct connection between them and what was produced near the southern coast of Palestine (A. Mazar 1992a: 307; Sandars 1987: 166–67).

However, the Peleset may have formed an important subgroup within the mix of peoples later to emerge as Philistines. There is nothing in the later biblical text or in the archaeological record to support the idea that the Philistines were sea-faring folk in particular. Of the cities that later came to form the Philistine pentapolis, two—Ekron and Gath—were far inland and were centers for agricultural production. The coastal cities of Gaza, Ashkelon, and Ashdod were situated slightly inland along the swampy coast, with dunes and swamp between them and the sea. This portion of the coast does not have good natural harbors; instead, these towns depended on river estuaries. This may support the notion that the main body of the population was not a coastal people but were inland farmers—as they also seem to be represented on the reliefs at Medinet Habu according to Sandars's reading.

Many of the groups identified as forming part of the loose confederation known as the "Peoples of the Sea" have been associated with peoples described in Hittite texts as occupying coastal areas of the western and southern Anatolian Peninsula—groups with whom the Hittites were engaged politically and diplomatically in the thirteenth century (Singer 1983: 205–17). The Lukka and the Ekwesh have been assigned to Anatolia: the former to the Carian coast (they may be the later Lycians of the region) and the latter to the west coast and the Mycenean region of Miletus (Millawanda; Sandars 1987: 107–11, 137). Mellaart argued (1968: 87–190) that in the Late Bronze Age the Anatolian coastal regions of Lycia and Pamphylia were populated mainly by seminomadic people; this is a view that is still borne out by the most recent archaeological work in the region (Greaves and Helwing 2003: 71–103; Gates 1996: 277–335).

The Lukka, who seem to be attested in Hittite documents as fighting as mercenaries on the Hittite side at the Battle of Kadesh (Singer 1983: 206, 208), were probably not a real state entity but, rather, a seminomadic tribal group living somewhere in the region of Lycia. Singer (1983: 214), using Hittite texts, has argued for the existence of the Kingdom of Tarhuntašša in western Cilicia in the thirteenth century, though archaeological evidence for significant Late Bronze Age settlement in the area is still lacking. Sandars has proposed that the Teresh were the same as the Taruiša referred to in a Hittite text and whom the Hittites located near the Troad. The origin of the Weshesh in Ramesses' inscriptions has not been located, though northwest Anatolia has been proposed because of the possible association with Wiluša or Wilušiya in Hittite texts.

The land from which the Denyen came may be that referred to as the "land of Danuna" in Amarna correspondence, which seems to have been north of Ugarit and the Orontes, perhaps the Hatay region (Sandars 1987: 162). The "Land of Danuna" survived into the eighth century B.C.E., when it occupied the Cilician triangle and the Plain of Adana, with its capital at Adana and its ruler holding sway over Karatepe. These were Luwian speakers. Because one of the later kings, Asitawandas, describes himself as "of the House of Mps" Sandars has posited an association between the early Denyon and the Greek legend of Mopsus, who supposedly led his people out of the Troad south through Anatolian Pamphylia and Cilicia after the Trojan War, only to die, ultimately, at Ashkelon in southern Palestine. According to this hypothesis, the Denyon would ultimately have migrated from farther west, possibly overrun the Lukka lands, and then settled in the region around Adana. Some may have continued farther south to form part of the group that was harassing Egypt. It was these people who were settled in southern Palestine after being rebuffed by the Egyptians—hence Mopsus's death at Ashkelon.

In turn, this may tie the Denyon into the story of the biblical tribe of Dan, who in their earliest appearance belong not in the Golan and the site of Tel Dan, which according to Judg 18:28 was under Sidonian hegemony, but on the southern Palestinian coast. As Sandars and others have pointed out, the Danites are a problematic group among the early Israelites. The reference to them in the story of Deborah places them on the coast with ships (Judg 5:17), making them distinct from all other tribes. It has been suggested that Dan was not among the original tribes of Israel (Gen 49:16–17), but was allowed to join the Covenant like the other tribes (Raban and Stieglitz 1991: 41; Sandars 1987: 161–63). This particular reconstruction of the migration of one of the "Peoples of the Sea" relates to specific localities of significance in the development of the early Iron Age culture. The Denyon would perhaps have been settled initially in the region of ancient Jaffa, not too far from Tell Qasile.

Whether the Denyon really belong settled on the southern coast of Palestine can be debated. The generally accepted view of the coast and coastal plain of Palestine in Iron Age I is that the territory became the home to three groups from the "Peoples of the Sea": the Sherden/Shardana, the Shekelesh/Tjerker, and the Philistines (Gilboa 2005: 47; Bloch-Smith and Nakhai 1999: 88–89). They ranged along the coast from the Bay of Haifa south. They represented a new influx of Aegean peoples, who carried with them debased versions of the Late Bronze Age Aegean culture (Brody 2002).[9] The

9. Also personal communication from Aaron Brody regarding his work on Iron Age Akko.

Sherden/Shardana became the occupiers of Tell Abu Hawam and may have spread to the northern plains and valleys, including Tell Akko (Raban and Stieglitz 1991: 41). Recently, Zertal has attempted to assign an ethnic identity to the site of El-Ahwat at the southern end of the ʿAruna Pass that linked the Mediterranean coast to the Jezreel Valley. He argues that it was settled by the Sherden/Shardana (Zertal 2002: 18–31). The site sits atop a crest and overlooks the Sharon Plain. The plain was probably held by the Shekelesh/Tjeker, who seem to have been settled around Dor and south of Mount Carmel. This appears to be confirmed by the Tale of Wen-Amon, in which they operate as pirates (Sandars 1987: 170). Farther south emerged the best known of the newcomers, the Philistines, who occupied the region from Gaza to modern Tel Aviv (Wood 1991: 44). The Onomasticon of Amenope also mentions three of the Philistine cities: Ashkelon, Ashdod, and Gaza (A. Mazar 1992a: 305).

While some of the "Peoples of the Sea" may have been settled on the southern Canaanite coast by Ramessses III, the actual evidence supports the notion that many of these peoples arrived of their own volition as early as the final decades of the Late Bronze Age, establishing themselves in the land before the abortive attempts to take the Egyptian Delta. In this latter scenario, the "Peoples of the Sea" who entered into southern Canaan came as a violent force, and they must have helped to overturn the Late Bronze Age structure of Canaanite cities under Egyptian hegemony; these cities themselves became a new competing demographic feature in the landscape of Iron Age I (Bunimovitz and Faust 2001: 6).

The last demographic shift that needs consideration is the arrival on the scene of the Israelites and the peoples of the region of Transjordan. The literature on early Israelites has become enormous and recently quite politicized. The various hypotheses can be placed in three basic groups: the scholars who follow the work of Albright and who argue for a physical invasion of Canaan by outside forces, perhaps somewhat connected to the story of Exodus; scholars who prefer Mendenhall's and, later, Gottwald's theories of an internal disruption of the Late Bronze Age Canaanite social structure—a peasant revolt or a shift in the relative power of the townsfolk and the marginalized and nomadic peoples; and scholars who favor Alt's and Aharoni's notions of a peaceful infiltration. More recently, Naʾaman (1994: 246–47) has criticized all previous theories for being too limited geographically. He has proposed that the emergence of the Israelites was part of the larger demographic disruption and movement that marked the end of the Late Bronze Age.

In reality, the southern Levant felt the impact of several different invading groups: some moving peacefully into sparsely inhabited areas of the hill country and others forcibly settling in territory that had belonged to strong Canaanite cities in the period before the collapse. The Israelites were one of the new entities to emerge from this variegated population. There is no reason to rehearse here all the details of these hypotheses (Bloch-Smith and Nakhai 1999: 66–70; Isserlin 1998: 48–64). Whatever their origin, the Israelites appear as a recognizable entity in Iron Age I first in the central hill country (Killebrew 2005; Miller 2005), and from there they spread north into the Galilee and south into Judah (Isserlin 1998: 62; A. Mazar 1992a: 334–37). Zertal, based on his work in the Manasseh highlands, has proposed that the entrance of distinctly Israelite communities was through the northern part of the Jordan Valley, probably the Damiyeh Pass and south of the Beth-shean Valley, opposite Shechem (Zertal 1991: 37). The settlements that serve to mark the new Israelite occupation are usually found in areas that were peripheral and without previous settlements. The communities were small, under three acres, with populations of a few dozen people (Fritz 2002: 30) and are often identified by the presence of the "collared-rim pithos" and the four-room, pillared house type (A. Mazar 1992a: 340–47). Raban and Stieglitz (1991: 41) have disputed the Israelite origin of the "collared-rim" pithos, instead suggesting that it was a by-product of the arrival of the "Peoples of the Sea." The four-room, pillared house form has been excavated at sites outside of the area normally associated with the early Israelite presence (Bunimovitz and Faust 2002: 33–41). The settlements were themselves small villages of a few dozen people.

The region of Transjordan was within the sphere of Egyptian interest during the Late Bronze Age, and the biblical tradition has Moses leading the Hebrews through Transjordan on their way to Israel. In the texts of Ramesses II at the temple of Luxor, there is mention of a military campaign in the area later identified as Moab, and several cities are listed, suggesting some degree of settlement in the region in the Late Bronze Age. However, most of the Egyptian textual evidence describes a nomadic population (Bloch-Smith and Nakhai 1999: 105–6). The Baqʿah Valley (the biblical Gilead) and the ʿAijlun highlands may have had small-scale permanent settlements in LBA II that continued uninterrupted into Iron Age I. Central Transjordan communicates naturally with the Jordan Valley via the Yarmuk River and the Wadi Zarqa. In the Late Bronze Age, the northern half of the Jordan Valley was populated on the east side of the river by a number of small settlements arranged in clusters around the principal centers of Pella (Tabaqat Fahil) and Anaharath (Savage and Falconer 2003: 40–43). Pella is mentioned in the Amarna letters (Negbi 1991: 205) and has yielded quite rich finds, suggesting that it was important and tied into the major high-value commerce network in the Late Bronze Age (Balensi et al. 1987: 93). A little farther south, the sites at Tell es-Saʾidiyeh, Tell Deir ʿAlla, and Tell Mazar were all physically close to one another; some of these had already existed in the Middle Bronze Age (Ibrahim and Kafafi 1987: 86–87). Both Deir ʿAlla and the site of the old Ammon airport in the upland region of Transjordan have yielded remains of buildings identified as Late Bronze Age sanctuaries, though they probably served the needs of a pastoral population rather than large sedentary groups. The site of Deir ʿAlla was reoccupied in Iron Age I, although there is no evidence that the sanctuary continued to operate. The eighth-century B.C.E. Aramaic inscription of Putz from the site records the vision of the prophet Bileam, son of Beor, which may be related in some manner to the vision of Balaam (Numbers 22–36; MacDonald 1994: 28–29; Millard 1991: 144; Zayadine and Bordreuil 1987: 150–52). A structure found at Tell es-Saʾidiyeh has been recognized as a possible Iron Age II sanctuary (Bloch-Smith and Nakhai 1999: 107)

The region south of the Wadi Zarqa and extending south to the Plain of Moab was the area of the Iron Age II Kingdom of Ammon. At times, its land seems to have extended south all the way to the Wadi Mujib. The kingdom included the Baqʿah Valley and thus probably had a core sedentary population living in small settlements. Other portions of the land are suitable for agriculture, which must have invited development during the Iron Age. These communities were probably centered on the more important site of Ammon (MacDonald 1994: 58). At present, it seems best to assume that the pastoral population of the Late Bronze Age began to settle down during the early Iron Age (Hopkins 1993: 200–211). Based on the evidence from graves and the study of the ceramic types, the region shows signs of continuity between the Late Bronze Age and Iron Age I, and there is no reason to posit the arrival of a major new population into the area. The presence of collared-rim jars at some sites may indicate the presence of an element of the hill country folk, who perhaps had migrated from west to east but not in large numbers. This has been tied to the biblical story of the wandering tribes of Gad and Reuben (Bloch-Smith and Nakhai 1999: 111). While the evidence for sacred architecture is admittedly limited, the citadel at Amman has yielded some impressive wall fragments. These sit beneath the later Roman temple. Also from the citadel, though not in association with the possible temple walls, were found important examples of Iron Age II stone statuary that could have originally played some part in a sacred setting (Zayadine 1991: 38–51; Zayadine and Bordreuil 1987: nos. 129 and 130). The stylistic treatment of the two statues and details of dress suggest that Phoenicio-Syrian influence was present even this far east.

Moab emerged as a distinct kingdom in Iron Age II, situated on the high plateau east of the Jordan Valley (B. Routledge 2004: 44–53). The northern boundary was contested by Ammon and Moab, but the Wadi Hasa fixed the kingdom's southern boundary. The highlands of Moab do receive adequate rainfall for agriculture. The region may be one of those listed as being plundered by Ramesses II in his inscription on the east wall of the inner courtyard at Luxor. From Baluʾa, to the north of Karak (Kerak), comes a stele found in 1930. It seems to show a local ruler receiving his scepter from an Egyptian god. The stele has been variously dated from the thirteenth century to the tenth century B.C.E. (Bloch-Smith and Nakhai 1999: 106; Zayadine and Bordreuil 1987: 117–18). It shows possible Egyptian involvement with the region and may also indicate the existence of some type of political structure and sedentary population during the Late Bronze Age, although this is not supported by the archaeological work to date. There is little to suggest more than sparse settlement during the Late Bronze Age. As in Ammon, there is reason to see the local population as changing from pastoralism to sedentary life during the Iron Age I and reaching its peak during Iron Age II, when the kingdom was established. At present, the archaeological evidence suggests that settlement was heaviest in the northern plain, particularly along the Wadi Mujib. There was some settlement in the Karak region, but south of that, very little (Bloch-Smith and Nakhai 1999: 111–14; MacDonald 1994: 60–63). What has been excavated seems to indicate that the bulk of Moab's population was never sedentary, and the land may always have been best exploited by pastoralists (Dearman 1992: 73). Only one site has yielded a structure recognized to be a temple—Khirbat al-Mudayna on the Wadi ath-Thamad, which connects with the Wadi Mujib. Nearby, there may also have stood a small wayside shrine.

The southernmost Iron Age II kingdom was Edom, named after the red sandstone of the region. It contained the area from the Wadi Hasa south to the Gulf of Aqaba. There is no archaeological evidence for settlement in the Late Bronze Age. This was a region best suited to nomadic existence. These may have been the *shasu* mentioned in Papyrus Anastasi VI 51–61, which is dated to Merneptah's eighth year of reign (1204 B.C.E.?). Ramesses III destroyed the people, property, and livestock of the *shasu* according to Papyrus Harris (Bloch-Smith and Nakhai 1999: 105). This would suggest that these nomadic peoples were causing Egypt problems on the eastern front at the same time as the "Peoples of the Sea" were disrupting life along the north. There is no reason to see any association between the two peoples. Archaeological survey work (MacDonald 1994: 64–67) has revealed the development of sedentary life along the Wadi Hasa during Iron Age I—small-scale village settlements along the southern bank, where the best land for agriculture is found.

The other area of concentrated settlement seems to have been the Wadi al-Ghuweib, which is part of the Wadi Arabah. Here the population density was probably not due to agricultural development so much as mining operations, which extended into Timna. These had begun under the Nineteenth-Dynasty Egyptian domination and continued into Iron Age I. The products of these mining and smelting operations may well have moved north through the Wadi Arabah and along the east side of the Jordan River, since they appear to show up in sites such as Tell es-Sa'idiyeh and Tell Mazar (Bloch-Smith and Nakhai 1999: 114). One sanctuary from the region has been identified at the Late Bronze Age Egyptian controlled copper mining center at Timna. An Iron Age II Edomite cult site in the Arabah at ʿEn Hatzeva has yielded cult paraphernalia but no substantial architecture.

The Wadi Arabah, extending north from the Gulf of Aqaba, borders the Negev to the west. Trade connecting the Mediterranean to southern Transjordan moved from the southern coast of Palestine across the northern Negev via the Beersheba Valley and into Transjordan using the incense and copper route that developed in early Iron Age I (Bienkowski and van der Steen 2001; Finkelstein 1988a). There is no trace of sedentary life during the Late Bronze Age (Bienkowski and van der Steen 2001: 35–41).

The Negev offered little possibility for agricultural settlement except in the northwest at Gaza and Besor brooks and in the Beersheba Valley and at Arad, so long as irrigation was used. The highlands show evidence for the establishment of small-scale sedentary outposts in Iron Age I, probably occupied by people who had previously been nomadic pastoralists in the region (Finkelstein 1988a: 245–46). Elsewhere the region remained the home of nomadic peoples. Egyptian interest in the mining concerns may have stimulated trade, and this may have increased with the establishment of the Philistines in the southwestern area of Palestine. The Iron Age settlements that have been identified in the northern Negev probably existed on a mixed economy of herding and farming, augmented by the trade moving to or from the coast either through the Beersheba Valley or along the foot of the highlands. One Iron Age II Edomite shrine has been identified for the region of the Beersheba Valley at Horvat Qitmit. The Iron Age II Judahite fort at Arad had an important sanctuary, and there may have been a small shrine at the site of Kuntillet ʿAjrud along the line of the highlands.

Identifying Ethnicity

Providing names for the various groups that lived in the Early Iron Age Levant makes discussing the region much easier. For the purposes of this book, the peoples have been assigned to the areas with which they have generally come to be associated during Iron Age II. Nevertheless, one must bear in mind that these names are problematic. The various peoples who occupied the Levant in the Late Bronze Age and in the early Iron Age are known in three ways. (1) First there are ancient literary sources in which the authoring group mentions another group, providing a name and some reference to a topographical location. These sources include the Bible, the Late Bronze Age archives at Ugarit, Emar, and Alalakh, the Middle and Neo-Assyrian imperial archival records, and the New Kingdom diplomatic correspondence and victory texts. To this can be added another ancient source that is somewhat more removed: the writings of later historians, mostly Greek and mostly, but not completely, of the Roman imperial period, who often claim to have made use of earlier sources, now lost. These authors include Herodotus, Pliny, Philo of Byblos, Strabo, Josephus, Porphyry, Justin, and Ammianus Marcellinus. (2) The second major item used is epigraphic material, including inscriptions and graffiti—usually inscribed or painted items made by the people themselves. These items include royal and imperial inscriptions as well as more mundane things such as writing inscribed on stone whorls or scratched into or painted on pots or potsherds. They can provide specific information about how a group identified itself, but they also attest to the existence of a group due to its distinct language or script. It is a generally held view of cultural geographers and ethnographers that "language is strongly implicated in the transmission of culture and is thus linked to many nonlinguistic cultural traits, such as folklore, religion, and music"

(Knapp 1988: 223); if a language can be isolated, it is reasonable to assume that it is evidence of a distinct group. However, one must bear in mind that writing in the first centuries of the Iron Age probably had a very distinct political role; this fact renders writing a less reliable tool for identifying specific ethnicities (Byrne 2007; and see further in the discussion that follows). (3) The third element is "material culture," which is a term that refers to things produced by specific groups that are regarded as being associated with them. The most common item used in this way is pottery, which can be examined from the standpoints of fabric, shape, and exterior decoration.

Over the last century, these three approaches, often in combination, have allowed scholars to identify and locate the peoples of the Late Bronze Age and early Iron Age Levant. The need to classify and categorize the various demographic units in terms of identity and location is obvious; this descriptive nomenclature allows for easier discussion. However, the problem with systems of this sort is that they impose on the Late Bronze Age and early Iron Age peoples constructs that more and more seem to have little or nothing to do with their worlds.

The initial problem is the duration of time involved: 500 years separate the thirteenth century B.C.E. from the eighth century B.C.E. The various primary sources belong to different epochs within this half-millennium stretch and often do not overlap. This is even more troublesome when one uses the later ancient sources. Josephus provides identities for many of the peoples of the Levant based on the biblical genealogies (*Ant.* 1.6.2.130–38; 1.6.4.143–45; 1.12.4.22–221), and he does attempt some anthropological observations (Millar 1993: 12), but how much is applicable to Late Bronze Age and early Iron Age settings? The primary archival material is mostly Late Bronze Age or Iron Age II, and so it is of little use in trying to understand the situation in Iron Age I. The biblical descriptions of the Philistine world were written in Iron Age II, causing problems for us in reconstructing the situation in coastal Palestine in Iron Age I or in correlating the information from the contemporary Egyptian sources. The Phoenicians exist because Greek sources gave the collective name to the people with whom they competed in establishing trade networks in the eighth century B.C.E. The Levantine sources know them by their city names—Sidonians, Tyrians, and so on—and these are either Late Bronze Age or Iron Age II texts, which leaves the Iron Age I with little coverage. Furthermore, it is not clear that these people of the coast saw themselves as a single unit, Phoenicia, rather than as residents of specific cities.

The epigraphic material poses a similar problem. It is mostly Iron Age II, and moreover, it is most abundant in the North Syrian region. Royal inscriptions were erected in several of the Neo-Hittite and Aramean cities. These provide evidence of languages in use but in the setting of Iron Age II. There is some epigraphic evidence for the Phoenician region and, when it is combined with epigraphic evidence from the Neo-Hittite and Aramean sites, the picture of linguistic differentiation in the northern

Levant of Iron Age II becomes clearer. Different languages suggest different people, a point reinforced by the textual material that actually mentions other peoples in these areas.

For the south, there are smaller pieces of epigraphic interest that testify to a new language by Iron Age II—Hebrew—and a new script, again dating to Iron Age II (Shanks 2010: 51–54). However, nothing from Iron Age I of the written language of the Philistines or any of the "Peoples of the Sea" has been found (Negev 1986: 296).[10] It is not until the seventh century B.C.E., Iron Age IIC in Herr's classification, that languages and scripts may well have functioned as consciously employed markers used by specific people who lived in particular places in the southern Levant (Herr 1997c: 151–76).

The northern areas seem to have begun this process earlier. Some of the Neo-Hittite and Aramean cities erected inscribed monuments using either Luwian or Aramaic, but the choice of language may have reflected the ruler's identity rather than the makeup of the population of the city. The Syrian region was probably multiethnic, because the material culture finds from both Neo-Hittite and Aramean areas suggest more commonality than difference (Akkermans and Schwartz 2003: 367–68). In the tenth century B.C.E., the beginning of Iron Age IIB, the Northwest Semitic alphabet in its Phoenician script began to be widely used throughout the area under investigation, and thus, script styles do not indicate peoples during this period (Byrne 2007: 1). Even later, in the seventh century, the Phoenician language and script were used for some official inscriptions installed by non-Phoenician rulers in Cilicia (Lebrun 1987: 24).

In order to reconstruct the demographic situation of Iron Age I, scholars have most frequently used the evidence of specific features of material culture found in excavated contexts. This is often referred to as the "pots = people approach." Distinctive types of pottery are thought to be the product of specific people, and the presence of pots in some quantity at a site generates the argument that the site belonged to these people or housed a group of these people or was at least in economic contact with these people (Gilboa 2005). In the last decade, this approach has been shown to be seriously flawed (Bunimovitz and Faust 2001). Although some aspects of the material culture—certain symbols used for decoration, a select group of pot shapes, or a specific type of architecture that is not easily reproduced by accident—may well be valid as markers of a particular group of people, these items must certainly be used with care. What they actually testify to may not be ethnicity.

However, it is important to note that some of the pottery made during the Iron Age was produced in specific locations, but the presence of this pottery at a site does not mean that the people who manufactured it were necessarily resident at the site or

---

10. There is a substantial seventh-century B.C.E. inscription from Ekron, but this is quite late and does not help with understanding the situation in Iron Age I (Demsky 1998).

were even the means by which the pots arrived at the site. However, the specific pots can point to particular places of production. This is true for the locally manufactured Mycenean IIIC:1b wares; Philistine monochrome and bichrome pottery; and the Ashdod wares (Dothan and Zukerman 2004; Ben-Shlomo et al. 2004; Bloch-Smith and Nakhai 1999: 90; Amiran 1970: 266–67). All of these come from the region of the southern Shephelah, and all were produced in Philistine settings. Similarly, Phoenician pottery was produced in a specific geographical region but had a wide area of distribution (Amiran 1970: 272–73: Bikai 1978a; 1978b; Anderson 1988; Herr 1997c: 166), and it followed a distinctive chronological sequence from Achziv and Metropolitan fine wares to distinctive hybrids of Assyrian form produced in the seventh century B.C.E. The collared-rim storage jars, often used to identify Israelite or proto-Israelite settlements from Iron Age I, have proved to be less useful as an ethnic marker. They may identify such a people in the southern highlands, but the situation is not as clear in the Upper Galilee (Bloch-Smith and Nakhai 1999: 74, 80–81; Faust 2006).

The whole problem stems from modern discussions of ethnicity (Killebrew 2005; Miller 2005). Did the various peoples of the ancient Levant see themselves as ethnic units in the way that ethnicity has come to be understood in the twentieth and twenty-first centuries C.E.? Ethnographers have abandoned the construct that ethnicity has genealogical affiliations; people may describe their associations with other individuals in a group in these terms, but in reality, outside forces bring a group together. One of the alternative approaches has been to look for shared specific traits—hence the notion of specific features in the material culture as indicating an ethnic group. However, scholars who use traits of this sort may categorize together individuals who did not share any sense of ethnic affiliation (Miller 2004: 55–56).

In discussing the situation for the ancient Near East at the time of the Roman conquest, Millar (1993: 5–12) has suggested that one aspect of self-conscious identity and possibly self-recognized ethnicity was a shared historical consciousness by members of the group. This may actually be quite applicable to the situation of Iron Age I. The collapse in 1200 B.C.E. and the subsequent demographic movements must have resulted in two distinct sorts of groups. Where some sense of continuity was preserved—a few of the Canaanite cities of the south, possibly the cities of the Phoenician coast, and the Egyptian garrison towns—a notion of a shared historical past directly connected to a place probably did survive and may have been preserved into Iron Age II.

The Arameans, the "Peoples of the Sea," the Israelites, and the Transjordanian peoples could not have had a historical sense of past association with the places in which they were to settle. They would establish an identity rooted to location only in the course of Iron Age I, and this begins to appear in Iron Age II in the form of inscriptions in the new languages and contemporary accounts of peoples connected with specific geographical locations. On the other hand, even in these areas in which there is evidence for new peoples settling, there was usually an older population that must have remained on the land. The exception was probably the hill country of the south, which seems to have been minimally settled during the Late Bronze Age. How this older population was folded into the new dominant group has proved difficult to determine. If indeed the Arameans, "Peoples of the Sea," and Israelites came as conquerors, then the contention that the older populations were deprived of their autonomous identity and in due time ceased to exert a cultural influence seems to contradict the evidence of more-recent conquests and colonial enterprises, in which the conquered do play a significant role in shaping the new forms that emerge (Richter 2001; Lockhart 1992).

Aside from answering the basic question of who lived where in the early Iron Age, the issue of demography in the context of the early Iron Age Levant is important to any study of architecture because it undergirds all discussions of continuity and discontinuity with regard to architectural forms. The survival of Late Bronze Age elements in the early Iron Age context is quite different at a site with a population that remained constant during these centuries from a site that witnessed demographic change. The meaning of new forms in the region needs to be understood one way in a setting where the people using them carried them to another place as part of their cultural baggage; and they should be understood differently when the people using them had no cultural association with them. For some of the forms, it is relatively easy to make meaningful connections with specific cultural traditions. Late Bronze Age Canaanite material culture is well documented, as is the material culture of contemporary Egyptian and Hittite societies. It is possible to engage in sophisticated and meaningful comparative analyses to establish the degree of their cultural connectedness. On the other hand, the connections are nowhere near as easy to make when one is trying to establish the cultural underpinnings of the Ammonites, Moabites, and Edomites. Similarly, the Arameans have no recognizable earlier architectural traditions against which to contrast the forms that appear in the Aramean context of Iron Age II.

It has been standard practice to associate the emergent Israelite culture with the architectural form of the four-room, pillared house type. This has been most commonly interpreted as a response to the particular needs of a rural farming folk for a house type that provided spaces for food processing, small craft production, animal stabling, and storage, as well as living (Stager 1985: 17). Bunimovitz and Faust argue for a deeper cultural concept that is embedded into the form, one that stresses the egalitarianism of early Israelite society that explains both the widespread distribution of the type and its longevity (Faust 2006; Bunimovitz and Faust 2002: 33–41). Whether or not the users of the four-room, pillared house knew themselves to be Israelites, as some have argued based on the presence of the term *Israel* on the Merneptah Stele (1209 B.C.E.?)—it has been proposed that these Iron Age I highland dwellers on the west side of the Jordan Valley were proto-Israelites from whom the Israelites emerged in Iron Age II (Miller 2004: 63).

In some ways, the "Peoples of the Sea" are the most challenging group to understand regarding the cultural elements that they must have brought with them. In theory, their Aegean origins should be evident in connections with better-understood cultural developments of the Late Bronze Age in the Aegean, but these connections have proved elusive. As Yasur-Landau (Barako and Yasur-Landau 2003: 37) has rightly pointed out, the Aegean population element that formed the "Peoples of the Sea" must not have come from the Late Bronze Age palace culture that has been so well studied. There is nothing in the Iron Age I developments along the Levantine coast that suggests any direct line of continuity with the Late Bronze Age palace culture. Moreover, archaeological investigations of the south and southwest coasts of Anatolia, the regions posited as the homelands for several of the folk that formed the "Peoples of the Sea," have still to reveal major Late Bronze Age cultural forces at work in terms of producing a recognizable material culture and architecture (Greaves and Helwing 2003: 71–103; Gates 1996: 277–335). Mellaart's 1968 contention that the area was largely inhabited by seminomadic tribal groups still appears to be valid (Mellaart 1968: 187, 189).

Yet, the scholarly rehabilitation of the Philistines that has taken place over the last two decades has been followed recently by increased interest in isolating the contributions made by their progenitors. While it may not be possible to make specific associations with Anatolian and Aegean spots and the culture that was carried by the various groups forming the "Peoples of the Sea," Raban and Stieglitz have isolated evidence for a cultural development specific to the "Peoples of the Sea" (Raban and Stieglitz 1991: 35–42). They have noted new features that appear in Iron Age I contexts in old Late Bronze Age Canaanite sites that they argue are the result of the arrival of some group from the "Peoples of the Sea" who brought with them a "Peoples of the Sea" culture. While most of their evidence does not concern architecture, one important item does: ashlar masonry. The first Iron Age examples of ashlar masonry to appear on the Levantine coast are at Tell Dor, a site assumed to have been taken over by the Shekelesh and the Sherden/Shardana. Ashlar masonry was an important construction technique in the Iron Age, and if the "Peoples of the Sea" were responsible for its introduction to the Levant, then their presence did play a significant role in the history of architecture for the area.

It may actually have been the island of Cyprus, close to the northern Levantine coast, that served as the location in which the disparate cultural elements comprising the "Peoples of the Sea" were homogenized to form a real cultural entity. The island had been a major player in the international trade network of the Late Bronze Age (Late Cypriot IIC). In the late thirteenth century, several of the LC IIC cities suffered destruction, usually interpreted as the result of raiding by the "Peoples of the Sea." The destructions were then followed by new settlements. The excavations of the site of Maa-Palaeokastro on the west coast of the island suggest that the process was a bit more complicated (Karageorghis 1982: 86–88). The first settlement was on a previously unused spit of land not far from a major LC IIC city at Palaeopaphos. The group has been identified as a raiding party from the "Peoples of the Sea." These new arrivals established themselves at the site of Maa and stayed for about two decades, during which time they built a major cyclopean defensive wall and an important building of some type using ashlar masonry construction. They abandoned the site, possibly to merge with the residual population at Palaeopaphos and were quickly followed by another wave of newcomers, this time from a different source identified specifically as Achaeans, who were emigrating from the mainland of Greece. Interestingly, this new group did no ashlar building. They used rubble masonry in their construction rather than carefully cut and fitted stone. This population also abandoned the site after a short occupation, perhaps to integrate with the reemergent city at Palaeopaphos. A similar pattern has been noted at the site of Sinda near Enkomi on the island's east side.

The evidence for ashlar construction in the first phase of occupation at Maa does offer some support for Raban and Stieglitz's contention. Likewise, the architectural poverty of the second occupation by the Achaeans lends strength to Yasur-Landau's view that these migrants, or at least many of them, were not coming from the Late Bronze Age centers of palace culture. While the short durations of both occupations can be explained as the integration of the newer population with the residual older population nearby, it is wise not to overlook the possibility that both groups of newcomers abandoned Maa in order to continue their movement or raiding and plundering. Raban and Stieglitz have identified a number of items that they argue were part of the material culture of the "Peoples of the Sea," most associated with boats and sailing. The coastal Cypriot sites may have served as nothing more than staging points before a movement further south or east. However, the excavation of the small inland site of Athienou demonstrates that the presence of the "Peoples of the Sea" on Cyprus in some instances did penetrate far deeper than just the coastal land, indicating that some of these peoples intended to stay. Moreover, the evidence for extensive and sophisticated copper smelting at the site (Dothan and Dothan 1992: 194–98) may add strength to the arguments of scholars who theorize the presence of a group of the "Peoples of the Sea" in the Jordan Valley actively working in the copper and bronze industry in Iron Age I and early Iron Age II (Tubb 1988: 257; Pritchard 1968: 108–9; opposing view, Negbi 1991: 205–43).

The Cypriot evidence for a second wave of newcomers distinct from the earlier arrivals, specifically the Achaeans, may fit with the emerging picture of the mid-twelfth century as a period in which there was more demographic shifting than just the movement of the "Peoples of the Sea" into the eastern Mediterranean. Certainly the disruption of settled life in the coastal cities that is indicated in the archaeological record and in textual statements would have resulted in some type of flight by people who could leave. Canaanites and earlier settled groups of the "Peoples of the Sea" such as the Sherden/Shardana and Sikels could well have sought safety on Cyprus. Cyprus's location so close to the Levantine coast would have facilitated the rapid reestablishment of trade networks once the chaos of the initial collapse subsided. This network would have followed the same routes that the preceding generation of "Peoples of the Sea" had used in moving from Cyprus to the Levant for raids or settlement (Barako 2000: 513–30; S. Sherratt 1992: 316–47; 1998: 292–313; Sherratt and Sherratt 1991: 373–75) and also would have reestablished lines of communication between displaced Levantine populations and their homelands.

Patterns of Trade

The Levant had two great south–north trade routes: the coastal road from Egypt to Lebanon (Way of Horus or Via Maris) and the inland route from the Arabian Peninsula to Damascus along the highlands of Transjordan (the King's Highway). These two routes permitted international trade through the region probably as early as the third millennium, and donkey caravans had plied these roads, to be eventually replaced by camel traffic. The coastal road also brought Egyptian armies into the Levant beginning in the middle of the second millennium. Connecting the south–north routes was a series of west–east roads that brought the Mediterranean into communication with the interior. There was the east–west Beersheba Valley along the north of the Negev that connected with the mining operations in the Wadi Arabah and the trade coming north from the Arabian Peninsula; the east–west route from the south coast through the central highlands to Jerusalem and down to the Jordan Valley at Jericho; and the east–west route through the Jezreel and Beth-shean valleys to the Jordan Valley.

The north–south connection between the Galilee and the Baqʿah Valley allowed overland access to the major coastal port cities of the Phoenicians and connected this coastal plain with the traffic moving into the Jordan Valley. This route also continued north to the ʿAmuq Plain. The coastal belt also communicated with the Orontes Plain east of the coastal mountains through the Homs gap; and this provided contact with the region of the ʿAmuq Plain to the north as well as east toward the Neo-Hittite and Aramean city-states.

Toward the end of Iron Age II, the ʿAmuq Plain was again opened to the Aegean with the development of the port at Al Mina, with its possible resident Greek population (Niemeier 2001: 11–24; contra Akkermans and Schwartz 2003: 388), which may have provided a means by which the Neo-Hittite and Aramean city-states, now under Assyrian control, gained easy access to Cyprus and beyond. However, the involvement of the ʿAmuq Plain and Afrin Valley with the Aegean probably remained a feature of the region even immediately following the disruptions of 1200 B.C.E., to judge from the finds of locally made Aegeanizing pottery that have been documented at a number of sites in the area (Lehmann 2002a: 82; 2002b: 85). Boardman has argued that active Greek penetration into Syria must be acknowledged already by the mid-eighth century B.C.E. (Boardman 2001: 36). North of the ʿAmuq Plain, the Cilician triangle and the Plain of Adana are separated from the southeastern region of modern Turkey by Mount Amanus. Cultural connections between the two regions were maintained via east–west passes through the mountain block, while the coastal areas of Cilicia and Adana offered access to the Anatolian central plateau.

While a major portion of the trade throughout the Levant was no doubt by sea along the coast, the fact remains that, for the interior to profit from trade, the land routes had to be exploited. Some of these clearly had already existed during the Late Bronze Age, as evidenced by the large Canaanite cities that have yielded imported goods. During the second millennium, northern Syria served as the bridge between Mesopotamia and the Mediterranean. Donkey caravans plied a route from the Middle Euphrates to Emar (Maskane); and from there went south over the Aleppo Plain to Aleppo; then split, one route heading to Ugarit and the other north to Alalakh. This route seems to have been modified in the Iron Age as Emar ceased to be, and the route instead went north to Carchemish and then to the ʿAmuq Plain (Akkermans and Schwartz 2003: 376).

An alternate road went south to join Aleppo with Damascus (Marʾi 1996: 137). There is also evidence of possible traffic across the Syrian Desert. This route abandoned the Euphrates at Mari and then headed west via Palmyra and Qatna. The route is much better known from the Hellenistic period, and it must not have been a regularly used route during the Bronze Age because of the difficulty of finding good water sources for the donkeys. It was really only a viable route for camels, which began to be exploited in the Iron Age; it does seem to have existed in some form, at least based on the limited epigraphic evidence (Klengel 1996; Zayadine 1996).

The early Iron Age witnesses the development of new areas in the story. The highlands of Transjordan and the hill country of Palestine now became important players in the trade. The formation of the Transjordanian region could have some connection with the spread of camel domestication from southern Arabia northward—an event still argued to have begun in full force only after 1200 B.C.E. Certainly, the introduction of the domestic camel (first as a beast of burden in the incense trade) into the eastern area of the Levant would have permitted the development of the nomadic, camel-based Bedouin culture of that region (Bulliet 1990: 57–86) and allowed for a more efficient exploitation of the resources than had been possible during the Bronze Age. The dispersion of the camel as a major beast of burden was tied to the spread of the incense trade. This trade, which moved incense from the southern part of the Arabian Peninsula to the urbanized regions of Mesopotamia and Egypt, began in the third millennium and had extended into Syria by the second millennium.

The movement of Semitic people to the Arabian Peninsula in the second millennium, probably in two waves during the Middle Bronze Age, resulted in the trade's expanding even more. The domestication of the camel can be traced up the west side of the Syrian Desert after about 1200 B.C.E. By Iron Age II, there had developed two major caravan routes in regular use linking the northern portion of the Arabian Peninsula with the Ammonite kingdom. Both began at Yathrib (Medina). One went north and east to Tayma, then north and east again to Dumah, skirting the southwest portion of the Nafud Desert. At Dumah, the route continued west and north through the Wadi Sirhan, passing through part of the Moabite kingdom to emerge at Rabbath-Ammon (Amman), the Ammonite capital. The other route left Yathrib in a northwest direction paralleling the Red Sea. It passed through Didan and Tabak and at Ma'an (Edomite territory) turned north following the King's Highway to Rabbath-Ammon, where it and the other route joined together and continued north to Damascus. At the Rabbath-Ammon juncture, the caravans also had access, via the Beth-shean and Jezreel valleys, to the Mediterranean coast at Akko and the Bay of Haifa (Byrne 2003: 11–12).

The force that propelled the inclusion of Edom and the Negev in the emerging trade networks of Iron Age II was the reactivation and expansion of copper mining into a real industry in Edom, particularly in the Fayan area, and in the Negev at Timna (Bienkowski and van der Steen 2001: 23). The southern copper could move north through the Wadi Arabah into the Jordan Valley, and it could be moved west toward the coast across the northern Negev through the Beersheba Valley. The movement west could have taken advantage of the trade routes already opened for the Arabian incense trade. The presence of Arab materials in the Philistine region probably resulted from Arab caravans involved with copper as well as incense traveling from Elah or Ma'an to Gaza along the northern Negev. Arab caravans also moved south along the coast after exiting the Jezreel Valley (Byrne 2003: 11). The discovery of a bronze figurine of a camel and rider from Rhodes but probably the product of a Levantine workshop (Bulliet 1990: 84, fig. 37) seems to indicate that camel caravans were not an unusual sight along the coastal corridor. Iron Age I trade may have been stimulating some settlement developments in the northern Negev (Bienkowski and van der Steen 2001; Finkelstein 1988a). The site of Tel Masos has yielded a rich assortment of finds suggesting that it was involved in redistributing raw copper from the south. The presence of quantities of Israelite utility ware and the predominance of the four-room house type in stratum II has suggested to some that, in the second phase of development, Iron Age II, the settlement was Israelite, perhaps replacing an earlier, seminomadic settlement in stratum IIIA (Fritz 1983: 33–36).

A Sacred Landscape

Our thinking about the landscape of the Levant includes the physical geography and the human geography, but we must also taken into consideration a mental geography. The peoples who inhabited the region isolated and revered certain spots. The temples that were built throughout the Levant during the Iron Age were not placed in a neutral landscape. The settings had become charged with sacredness during the Middle Bronze Age and Late Bronze Age. They had been perceived as numinous landscapes, and locales had meanings beyond what appeared as mere physical features. Sacred mountains figure prominently in the Late Bronze Age Canaanite mythology, and unlike the presence of cosmic or sacred mountains in the mythology of Egypt and Mesopotamia, the mountains in Canaanite mythology reflect the reality of the Levantine landscape (Clifford 1972: 34). El's tent, where the assembly of the gods convened, stood atop a mountain, and Ba'al built his palace on a mountain. It has been argued that El's dwelling was specifically at Aphaca (modern Khirbet Afqa; see Pope 1955: 92–104). Clifford has countered that El's abode was understood, at least by the Late Bronze Age Ugaritians, to be in northwest Syria, but its location was not very specific (Clifford 1972: 50). Ba'al's mountain was named *ṣpn* in the Ugartic texts, referring to Mount Ṣaphon, and also appears in the Hebrew Bible, where it is understood to be located in the north of Palestine. It does seem, however, to be a movable locale, appearing in Exod 14:2–9 as a small hill in the Nile Delta. Mount Ṣaphon is where Ba'al battled Mot, and it was here that the Craft-God Kothar wa-Khasis built Ba'al's palace (*CTA* 4.5.116–19)

> Hurry! Let a palace be raised
> In the midst of *srrt* Zaphon!
> Let the house cover a thousand acres,
> Ten thousand hectares, the palace! (Clifford 1972: 60–61)

How much of the sacral quality of the landscape survived the demographic changes in the decades around 1200 B.C.E. is hard to say. However, the concept of the sacred mountain is also found in the setting of the Hebrew Bible. It may be no more than a survival, but it could indicate that the notion of a landscape given divine quality by the occasional presence of the deity still had meaning for early Iron Age communities.

The traditions of Sinai and Zion are built on the notion of Yahweh's residence on the mountains. The Sinai tradition tied together the exodus, the conquest, and the covenant cultus and initially located Yahweh's sacred mountain in the south, though the Sinai tradition is associated with a number of sites, probably pilgrimage sites, in the central highlands at Gilgal, Shechem, Shiloh, Bethel, and Hebron (Cross 1998: 44–45). The Zion tradition places Yahweh's residence in the stronghold of Zion, which eventually became associated with Jerusalem. Mount Zion referred to the fortified hill between the Tyropoeon and Kidron valleys, the Temple Mount (Haram al-Sharif). Clifford has argued that the Zion tradition (2 Sam 5:7; 1 Chr 11:5) ultimately derives from *ṣpn*, Ba'al's Mount Ṣaphon of the Ugaritic texts (Clifford 1972: 131–33).

The sacred mountain was a feature of Mesopotamian cosmology as well, though it lacked the physical reality that marked the conceptual form of the Levantine tradition. However, an older Mesopotamian element could well have informed notions as they developed in the early Iron Age setting of the Aramean city-states of the eastern edge of Syria in the Khabur region. Similarly, Hittite sources refer to a mountain, Hazzi, which Clifford reads as Ṣaphon. This may indicate that the construct of a holy mountain was known in Hittite contexts and continued to inform the religious ideas of the Neo-Hittite city-states (Clifford 1972: 58).

Chapter 3

Iron Age Temple Remains

Iron Age Absolute Chronology and Stratigraphy

There is not yet an absolute chronology for the eastern Mediterranean of the Late Bronze and Iron Ages. The most complete chronologies have been developed for Egypt and Mesopotamia, and when it is possible, synchronizations are made between events and monuments in the Levantine region and the better-dated material from Egypt or Mesopotamia. The process of formulating both accepted internal regional chronologies and meaningful synchronizations is an ongoing process that has been accelerated since Manfred Bietak's colloquium in 1996 (Bietak 2000b).

The chronologies for Egypt and Mesopotamia are best understood because the extensive primary written records permit many events and monuments to be given precise dates. The sequence of rulers for the second half of the second millennium and the first half of the first millennium B.C.E. in Egypt (the 17th through the 25th Dynasties) can be reconstructed and the length of reigns calculated (Kitchen 2000: 39–44). Since Egypt was deeply involved with the Levant during the 18th–20th Dynasties and again during the beginning of the Twenty-Second Dynasty, the synchronizations that can be made play a significant role in determining the dating for many aspects of Late Bronze Age and Iron Age I Levantine archaeology.

The Mesopotamian king lists have aided in the establishment of a secure chronology for the first millennium B.C.E. based on the Babylonian and Assyrian records of the sequence of kings. The records can be correlated with the mentions of astronomical observations, allowing for a relatively refined chronology. The involvement of Assyria and later Babylon in the Levantine region during the first millennium B.C.E. has tied some Levantine archaeological finds, using synchronizations, with the better-dated events in the Mesopotamian record. Although the Mesopotamian material assists with the first millennium, it is of less value for the second half of the second millennium (Hunger 2000: 60).

There are three synchronizations that are normally cited for the Egyptian sources and the Levant: the naming of specific kingdoms and rulers in the Late Bronze Age Canaanite region in the Eighteenth-Dynasty Amarna letters; the description of the

"Peoples of the Sea" and their settlement on the southern coast of Palestine during the reigns of Merneptah and Ramesses III; and invasion of the Kingdom of Judah in the 5th year of Rehoboam by Shishak (recorded in 1 Kgs 14:25–26 and 2 Chr 12:3–4), who has been equated with Shoshenq I, the founder of the Twenty-Second Dynasty (Kitchen 1989). These are regularly cited as firm synchronizations joining datable events in Egypt with events in the Levant. In a similar manner, the Assyrian accounts of the expansion of the empire to the west presented ruler by ruler, especially the actual conquest of the western regions beginning with Tiglath-pileser III in the eighth century B.C.E., are used as a means of reconstructing a chronology for the Levantine region (Lipschits 2005: 4–11) into which monuments and archaeological strata can be fitted.

These devices are not questioned in this book, because almost all the assumptions about the dates of architecture made by excavators depend on these associations. However, one should note that the synchronizations have not been accepted universally without serious reservations. Rather startling alternative chronologies for the Egyptian material have been proposed (Newgrosh, Rohl, and van der Veen 1992–93; Bimson 1990–91; and Bimson 1992–93). Similarly, objections have been raised about the validity of the Assyrian and Babylonian king lists with regard to their veracity, particularly in their coverage of the late second millennium, and an alternative chronology has been presented (Hagens 2002). If the generally accepted synchronizations were discarded and the alternative chronologies applied to this area of study, there would be serious ramifications for the relative chronology that has been used in this book. Since these newer chronologies have not yet received wide acceptance and were not used by the excavators of the temples, they have not been employed for the analysis of the material presented here.

The modern countries of the Levant have dictated distinct excavation histories for different areas. As a result, there is no agreement regarding stratigraphic treatment for the entire region. For the Syrian area, the recent synthesis by Akkermans and Schwartz (2003: 363–64) offers a scheme: Iron Age I: 1200–900; Iron Age II: 900–700; Iron Age 3: 700–550. The divisions are based on the relative chronology that can be assigned to the pottery from stratigraphic records for the sites of Tell Sukas (H2–H1 and G3–G2) on the coastal band and Tell Afis (VII–IX) on the Aleppo Plain (Mazzoni 1990). Markoe's scheme for the Phoenician area of the north coast makes use of the Tell Sukas findings, since it is technically part of the Phoenician region, along with findings from Sarepta and the deep sounding done at Tyre. Locally produced pottery has allowed for the creation of a relative chronology for the region and has permitted sites outside to be linked to the chronology by the presence of Phoenician pots in the archaeological record. A distinctive bichrome pottery identified as Phoenician emerged in the mid-eleventh century B.C.E. This was replaced by an equally distinctive burnished redware in the mid-ninth century, which was to remain a Phoenician manufacture and trade item until the sixth ccentury B.C.E. (Amiran 1970: 270–73). Markoe proposes Iron Age I: 1200–1000, Iron Age II: 1000–556, and Iron Age 3: 586–538 (Markoe 2000: 23–25, 160–61, 207).

The southern Levant has received by far the most attention and has generated several stratigraphic schemes (Bloch-Smith and Nakhai 1999: 62–69; Herr 1997c: 115–18). In this book, I use the recent syntheses for Iron Age I: 1200–1000 B.C.E., by Bloch-Smith and Nakhai.[1] For Iron Age II, I use Herr's system: Iron Age IIA: tenth century B.C.E.; Iron Age IIB: ninth–late eighth centuries B.C.E.; and Iron Age IIC: late eighth–mid-sixth centuries B.C.E. Both schemas were developed for survey articles in the journal of *Near Eastern Archaeology*. The archaeological record for the southern Levant has provided several sites with good stratigraphy, and there is a well-established pottery sequence for Shephelah sites—LM IIIC, its local imitation (Dothan and Zukerman 2004), Philistine monochrome, Philistine bichrome (Amiran 1970: 266–67), and Ashdod fine ware (Ben-Shlomo, Shai, and Maeir 2004)—that can be used to establish relative chronologies for the sites that have examples of the pottery. Ceramic traditions associated with the emerging Israelite culture have also been isolated and used as a diagnostic tool, particularly for the later Iron Age. Phoenician and Cypriot wares were imported into the region. The relative chronologies for these wares have been worked out in their respective regions of origin, and so the finds are usable for establishing relationships.

There are differences in the interpretations of the sequences worked out for the Syrian, Phoenician, and southern areas. The distinctions are in the subdivisions. Iron Age I is taken to 900 B.C.E. in the Syrian sequence but only to 1000 B.C.E. in the Phoenician and southern sequences. Markoe's Iron Age II for the Phoenician region is Herr's Iron Age IIA, B, and C. The Syrian sequence has an Iron Age 3, whereas the southern sequence has Iron Age IIC; these are the same period. For the purposes of this book, Iron Age I is treated as ending at 1000 B.C.E. rather than 900. Akkermans and Schwartz admit that the Iron Age I period in Syria is the least well understood. Thus, I consider it reasonable to conform to the period used for Phoenicia and the southern Levant, which ends at 1000 B.C.E. Herr's rather more-refined system for Iron Age II has been applied universally because the northern and Phoenician sanctuaries fit comfortably into this structure without any serious forcing, and this structure allows for more-nuanced comparisons.

The Temples

The lack of coordination between the three stratigraphic sequences poses no real problem for the study of the temples. Thirty-eight structures (buildings, complexes,

---

1. It should be noted that the 200-year span for Iron Age I is generally accepted by most archaeologists working in the region, but there are a number of scholars who argue for shortening the Iron Age I span by a century or more (Rohl 1991–92: 58; P. J. James 1991; R. Porter 1994–95a: 68).

installations) that have been identified by their excavators as early Iron Age sanctuaries constitute the core of this study.[2] Some of these were in use for one period. Several were maintained over a long span of time and witnessed multiple rebuildings, often with significant changes to the original plan. In some instances, the changes are also associated with demographic shifts and probably major modifications of cult. However, they can be fit into the general Iron Age stratigraphic sequence for the entire Levant. There is a group of sanctuaries built during Iron Age I; these were the product of either the recently settled "Peoples of the Sea" or the Arameans or were the result of recovery at older Canaanite and Hittite (Neo-Hittite) sites. This is the time described in the account of Wen-Amon's trip from Egypt to Byblos. Another small group belongs to Iron Age IIA which, until recently, was argued to be the period of the emergence of the Kingdom of Israel under David and Solomon as recorded in the Bible and in Josephus. The most abundant number of sanctuaries survived from Iron Age IIB, a period understood from the ancient historical and epigraphic sources to have been a time of several small competing states throughout the region. The sanctuaries associated with Iron Age IIC are few in number. This was a period of a strong Assyrian presence in the region, and only a couple of sites preserve structures that should be considered Levantine as opposed to provincial Assyrian.

The temple remains are spread throughout the Levantine region. Excavators have labeled these structures *temples* based usually on a combination of two factors: (1) unusual plan and building features in comparison with other structures on the site, and (2) the special nature of the material remains found in association with the building. Most of the Iron Age sanctuaries come from urban contexts. There are exceptions: the open air shrines in the hill country that came to be associated with early Israel, the small shrine outside Khirbat al-Mudayna in Moab territory, the shrine at Makmish, the two sanctuaries in the northern Negev, and the shrines in the fortress at Arad and in the gate chamber at Kuntillet ʿAjrud. Extra-urban shrines existed in the Late Bronze Age, but their locations were quite different from those in the early Iron Age. The change, no doubt, reflects the substantial shift in population and the development of new areas for human settlement and exploitation that marked the advent of the early Iron Age. For the moment, the small temple set within the fortress at Tell Arad is a unique example.

The temples are grouped together by Iron Age divisions and subdivisions. In cases of temples that operated during more than one Iron Age subdivision, the information is presented under the period of the initiation of the temple. On the other hand, sites

---

2. When a sanctuary was reconstructed and the reconstructed temple can be clearly related to what existed before, then I do not count it as a separate sanctuary; but when there is a significant change, then I treat the new structure as a separate temple. Thus the three versions of the temple at Tell Qasile are counted only once, but the two structures in level V at Beth-shean are treated as different from the temple that they replaced in level VI.

with separate temples that were built centuries apart are re-presented for each temple. Within each period, the sites are arranged according to the geographical/ethnic divisions of the Levant from north to south and west to east that are used to classify the region for each Iron Age subdivision, and then the individual entries are arranged alphabetically.

Iron Age I Sites: 1200–1000 B.C.E.

Stratigraphic Correspondences: ʿAin Dara 6 = Abu Hawam VA = Ashdod Area H stratum XII = Ekron VI–V = Tell Qasile XII–X = Beth-shean VI–V = Hazor XII–XI = Megiddo VIIA–VIA = Taʿanach I–IIA = Bull Site of the Manasseh = Mount Ebal structure.

The collapse of the Late Bronze Age system of small city-states that formed part of the palace-based economic exchange program combined with the disruption of settled life resulting from the influx of new peoples to change the settlement pattern in Iron Age I. There was a movement away from the coastal region toward the steppelands in the north and the hill country in the south. The old urban-based structure gave way to a village-based system. At the same time, the pastoral element that would later emerge as the Aramean, Israelite, and Tranjordanian states gained ground in the eastern steppes and the hill country (Markoe 2000: 23). The "Peoples of the Sea" began to coalesce into recognizable groups, of which the best known was to be the Philistines, who became the dominant force in the southern coastal region of the Iron Age. Not all of the old structure completely disappeared. The Egyptians remained a force for another half century, and some of the Canaanite cities survived, albeit in much reduced form.

North Syria and Sanctuaries of the
Emergent Neo-Hittite and Aramean Cities

North Syria had a long history of urban culture stretching back to the Early Bronze Age. It had never ceased to be a landscape of cities and, though the great seats of power moved over the millennia, with once-independent cities becoming vassals of former subject cities, the importance of the urban core as a permanent feature of the life in the region never waned. In the Late Bronze Age, North Syria served as the transitional region between the Hittite north and the Canaanite south. Into this region stormed the troops of the Hittite kings and of the pharaohs of the 18th and 19th Dynasties. Throughout the centuries of the Late Bronze Age, the region played host to competing outside powers. With the end of the Hittite Empire and the decline of Egyptian hegemony, however, the region was once again free to develop in response to local needs and pressures. Several old Late Bronze Age cities such as Alalakh and Emar (which had roots back to the Middle Bronze Age and even the Early Bronze Age) ceased to exist. Many of the important early Iron Age regional centers were new. This area from the Cilician triangle through the ʿAmuq Plain and the limestone plateau to the east all the way to the Jezireh may not have revived immediately following the destructions at the end of the Late Bronze Age, and several kingdoms do not appear as fully developed entities until Iron Age IIB. However, the appearance of a major break between Late Bronze Age and Iron Age is more the result of limited excavations than the reality of what happened. At Tell Afis on the Aleppo Plain near ancient Ebla, the stratigraphic record has been uncovered, and it shows continuity in architecture and material culture between the end of the Late Bronze Age and the first stratum of the Iron Age (Afis VII; see Akkermans and Schwartz 2003: 362–63). The inhabitants of several sites on the ʿAmuq Plain and Afrin Valley regions in this transitional period were making their own versions of Aegean LM IIIC and "Granary Style" pots (Lehmann 2002b: 84–85); these could have been products of the last years of the Late Bronze Age or the first decades of the Iron Age I, a fact that suggests continuity of settlement. At Carchemish, the Hittite vice-regal capital, there may be meaningful evidence of continuity between Late Bronze Age and Iron Age in the claims made by the Iron Age ruling dynasty regarding familial associations with the old Hittite ruling house (Hawkins 1988); however, the excavations reveal nothing for this period, and the standing remains belong to Iron Age IIB and later. On the other hand, at Aleppo there are the remains of an Iron Age I temple that originated in the Middle Bronze Age if not the Early Bronze Age, and at ʿAin Dara the Iron Age I temple rests on a Late Bronze Age structure.

ʿAin Dara

ʿAin Dara, an oasis site on the right bank of the Afrin River in northwestern Syria, was located in a region with both Aramean and Neo-Hittite cultural forces, and its specific affiliation is not certain. Abu ʿAssāf (1985: 350), the excavator of the site, has proposed that it was affiliated with Kinalua, the capital of the Aramean state of Bit Agusi. The site was probably one of the largest settlements in northern Syria in the late second and early first millennia B.C.E., with an Iron Age population of perhaps about 6,000 persons. The site does appear to have been occupied continuously from the Late Bronze Age through Iron Age I and II until it was destroyed between 742 and 740, probably by Tiglath-pileser III (Abu ʿAssāf 1985: 347; 1993: 160–61). It was most likely larger than Tell Taʿyinat, which is about 50 km farther west (Lehmann 2002b: 85; Stone and Zimansky 1999: fig. 5). The site consists of a lower town of about 20 ha, and an upper tell that was enclosed by a stone wall, which thus formed a citadel region where the temple is located (fig. 1). The temple was situated to dominate the settlement.

The temple at ʿAin Dara was built on the northwest side of the acropolis and went through three incarnations, perhaps beginning in the Late Bronze Age and continuing until the eighth-century destruction (Abu ʿAssāf 1990; 1993: 170–71). The earliest version is from stratum 6, which could be either Late Bronze Age or Iron Age I, due to the fact that the division is difficult to make at the site. The first temple was oriented northwest to southeast with the portal on the southeast side. The orientation and entrance never changed. The first design was tripartite, a portico ca. 4 m × 6 m, an antechamber ca. 15.5 m × 6 m, and a main hall ca. 16.7 m × ca. 16.8 m with a raised platform at the northwest end, occupying about one-third of the space, all aligned on the longitudinal axis. A narrow corridor separated the antechamber from the main hall. Much of the construction was of well-cut basalt blocks (Fortin 1999: 65) that sat on a 1 m–high platform of rubble and limestone surrounded with basalt slabs (Monson 2000: 27–29; Abu ʿAssāf 1982: 351; 1997: 34–35). One entered the temple by climbing four basalt stairs. The main chamber was three steps higher (fig. 2). The building's design emphasized the physical ascension, because one climbed stairs in order to move deeper into the structure.

The basic format remained the same through the next phase, probably Iron Age IIA (fig. 3). The entrance was formalized. Four basalt stairs now provided access to a portico with two basalt columns on basalt bases. This created a distyle *in antis* porch. Basalt piers were added to the façade, placed behind the columns, and built into the corridor between the porch and the antechamber. Relief sculpture was set up in the back of the main hall (Monson 2000: 24).

The third and final phase, from which come the standing remains, retained the plan of the previous two. Some modifications were made to the platform in the main chamber. A ramp now provided access to the top, heightening the ascension motif. A shallow niche was built into the wall behind the platform. A wooden screen, perhaps designed to hide the platform from the rest of the chamber, is attested by the presence of holes in the side walls, probably intended to hold the brackets. During the final phase, the structure itself—the phase 1–2 temple—was incorporated into a larger construction, for which it became the core (fig. 4). The new superstructure was an ambulatory surrounding three of the sides. This new addition was not structurally bonded to the temple core, but it did rest on the temple's old platform, which had always extended beyond the walls of the temple proper. The new ambulatory consisted of a series of connected chambers (fig. 5) that averaged 6 meters wide, and the entirety could be entered from either side of the porch. The walls of the ambulatory were punctuated by large basalt piers that created the individual chamber-like units and suggest to us that the new element may have stood at least two stories high. The upper story would have been constructed of mud brick and wood (Monson 2000: 28). At either side of the portico are wide, square projections that could have supported towers to contain the stairs.

The temple stood in a precinct, the final form of which can be ascertained from the remains. The temple was approached by a large courtyard paved with flagstones. These were large slabs of white limestone framed by narrow bands of black basalt. The courtyard held a chalkstone basin. The large complex was visible from the plain below (fig. 1). It was laid out so that one of its long walls faced toward the lower plain, an arrangement that is also seen at the Iron Age IIB Aramean site of Guzana. The entrance to the temple opened away from the view below.

The temple, in all its iterations, probably had sculpture (Kohlmeyer 2008), but it was particularly richly ornamented with relief sculpture in its final stage. Black basalt slabs, or orthostats, surrounded the podium and formed the first layer of sculpture. They were visible from the courtyard and surrounded the entire podium (fig. 6). They were carved in high relief, with figures of paired facing lions and paired facing sphinxes. The lions and the sphinxes formed a secondary pattern of adorsed pairs (fig. 7). In addition to the animal images, the exterior decoration included another creature, of which only the clawed feet survive, and human-like figures identified as mountain gods (Monson 2000: 24). The basalt stairs that formed a series of black bands ascending from the white limestone courtyard were decorated with guilloche patterns. The grand staircase was flanked on either side by a single sphinx that was part of the larger decorative pattern of the sculpture. Lions also guarded the two entrances to the ambulatory.

The interior of the temple and the ambulatory were also decorated with sculpture. The sphinx and lion motif carried into the portico, and they guarded the corridor into the antechamber. The lower walls of the antechamber were carved with a flowery ribbon pattern. Above them were the clawed feet of a creature otherwise lost (fig. 8). Monson has identified two possible faux windows in the antechamber. These are signified by carved recessed window frames. The upper portion of the frames is carved with rows of figure eights, placed on their sides, perhaps intended to represent lattices (Monson 2000: 34). The three steps up to the main hall carried a chain motif.

Lions in profile stood at each of the doorposts leading into the main hall. The podium in the main chamber and the walls of the room were sculpted with reliefs of human-like figures. These figures face forward, with arms raised to the sides of their heads. They are bearded figures, some with bull lower halves and horned heads and others wearing scaled skirts, pointy-toed shoes, and conical horned hats (Monson 2000: 27–28). Giant footprints, a meter in length, are impressed on the limestone floor slabs of the portico and the corridor between the antechamber and the main chamber (fig. 9). Two feet, a right and left, occupy the first portico slab. A single left footprint is found on the second portico slab, and a single right footprint appears on the corridor slab.

The ambulatory was richly decorated with sculpture. Eighty carved panels survive. In addition, there are 30 steles erected inside the corridor that carried more complicated images. These include an enthroned figure, a palm tree, a standing figure in a semitransparent gown, and images of offerings. Orthmann has identified the style of the reliefs as being post–Imperial Hittite but very early in the development of the local North Syrian, south Anatolian style, "späthethitisch I," providing a date of ca. 950 B.C.E. (Orthmann 1971)—that is, Iron Age IIA. This would make the final sculptural work at ʿAin Dara just a little earlier than or contemporaneous with the tenth-century B.C.E. sculptural additions to the Aleppo Citadel temple, and substantially earlier than the Neo-Hittite center at Carchemish and the Aramean city of Guzana in the Jezireh (see below).

Aleppo: Middle and Late Bonze Age Temples

Aleppo, ancient Halab, dominates the plain in the northwest of Syria, east of the Orontes River. It was already old in the Iron Age, having first emerged in the Early Bronze Age. There are references to a Sanctuary to the Storm-God Hadda at Aleppo dating back to the third millennium B.C.E. The cult was associated with the cult of nearby Ebla. There are references in the Ebla tablets to restorations made to the temple at Aleppo by the kings at Ebla (Kohlmeyer 2009: 191). The archaeological evidence shows a massive temple from MB I that dates to ca. 1700 B.C.E. and was constructed on the citadel hill, the ruins of which were discovered in recent excavations within the confines of the later Ayyubid fortress (Kohlmeyer 2000: 23, 26). This later temple probably maintained the form of the Early Bronze Age structure, and Kohlmeyer has identified the cult as that of the Middle Bronze Age Storm-God Addu. The Mari tablets describe a massive cult statue of the god at Aleppo as being seated and holding a smaller Sun God on his knee (Lawler 2009: 22). During this MB I period, Aleppo served as the capital for the Yamkhad kingdom, one of the major powers in the region (Akkermans and Schwartz 2003: 297).

Only a small portion of the MB I temple still exists, but there is enough to offer some idea of its form (fig. 10). It stood inside what is now the center of the citadel, so it must not have been visible from the terrain below, because the hill itself rises some 50 m above the plain. The remains consist of parts of the north and west walls. Kohlmeyer proposes a square structure with a broad-room cult chamber and separate entrance room. The north wall contained a large niche, 7.8 m wide, which was the focus of the room, which must have been entered from the south. The entrance has not been found. The walls were some 10 m thick at their bases, covered with limestone orthostats, and these lower walls held up a mud-brick superstructure, perhaps to a total height of 3 m. The inside measurements of the room, 26.75 m × 17.10 m, describe a large interior space, with no evidence of internal supports for a roof. Cedar beams from Lebanon must have been used. Though only a portion of the temple has survived, the excavators have argued that the temple was related to Ebla's temple P$_2$ in terms of its monumental qualities and the importance of the niche, which must have held the cult statue, but it had a different format. Instead of being a long room, it was a broad-room type (Gonnella, Khayyata, and Kohlmeyer 2005: 87–90; Kohlmeyer 2000: 22–27), and the design resembled that of the Level VII temple at Alalakh (Tell Atchana; see fig. 90). It may have been a two-story structure of the *migdāl* type (Kohlmeyer 2009: 194).

The MB I structure was destroyed by fire but was rebuilt (Lawler 2009: 23). The Late Bronze Age witnessed the Hittite conquest of the region and the introduction of the Hittite/Hurrian Weather-God Teshub, who was integrated with the older Syrian god. In the late fourteenth century B.C.E., a new temple was constructed from the older Middle Bronze Age temple. The old, plain orthostats of the Middle Bronze Age temple were retained, but the focus of the interior shifted. The niche on the north wall was hidden behind a row of carved orthostats, which resulted in a narrowing of the interior space, perhaps making it easier to roof. By hiding the old cult focus behind the new façade of orthostats, the architect of the Hittite structure was able to introduce a "bent-axis" format, placing emphasis on the center of the east wall, where a relief of Teshub—identified by a hieroglyphic Luwian inscription, standing 2 m in height, and portrayed as being in a "smiting" posture—was erected. This feature marks a departure from the earlier temple design and can be attributed to Hittite influence (Kohlmeyer 2009: 194–95). Kohlmeyer has seen in the treatment of the Aleppo temple something comparable to what Woolley argued occurred at Alalakh in the Late Bronze Age Level III temple, in which a "bent-axis" design was introduced (Woolley 1955: 78). Only a portion of the main cult room of the new temple survives. The western side and the southeast corner were destroyed by later building on the site (Gonnella, Khayyata, and Kohlmeyer 2005: 90–93).

Most of the carved orthostats in the Late Bronze Age temple showed either a "false window" or bull-men, both of which are well-known Hittite motifs. The "false window" is known from Hittite temple models and may have been used here as stand-ins for real windows, which could not be added to the older fabric of the structure. Kohlmeyer sees stylistic traits in the treatment of the tails and the lower bodies of the bull-men that recall the carvings at the Hittite Sanctuary of Yazılıkaya. A new structural element was added to the interior space, a pedestal 1.7 m × 1.8 m to the south of the new northern interior wall. This was decorated with relief sculpture showing two composite monster figures and a mountain god. Kohlmeyer identifies these as being in a regional North Syrian style with elements of Hurrian and Mitannian influences (Kohlmeyer 2009: 195). The reliefs of bull-men and "false windows" are about half the height of the relief of Teshub. There may have been a second row of reliefs placed above them. A second relief of the Teshub with *lituus* and lance was unearthed in a pit and may have belonged to a series of divine images that occupied this upper register of the interior.

The entrance into the cult chamber was indicated by limestone reliefs of a fish-man, a sphinx, and a lion. Of these, the sphinx and the lion can be related to similar Hittite sculptures at Hattuša and Alaca Höyük in Anatolia. The fish-man has no Hittite parallels, and Kohlmeyer sees influence from Babylon. The sculptor could have been Kassite. However, the strong stylistic similarity between the carving of the face of the fish-man and the carving of Teshub on the east wall lead him to suggest that the sculptor was Hittite but conversant with Babylonian mythology (Kohlmeyer 2009: 196). While there are clearly Hittite-inspired elements in the Late Bronze Age temple—the "bent axis" format, the use of bull-men, and possibly the "false window" to take the place of real windows—the design of the temple looks nothing like the great temple of the Weather God at Hattuša, with its many storerooms forming a protective ring around the small cult spaces inside the grand complex (fig. 120). Although not enough survives to reveal the plan of this new temple at Aleppo, nothing suggests that it comprised multiple spaces with courtyards and processional lanes moving through the complex, as was the case for the Hattuša temple. Whatever the actual strength of the Hittite cultural influence was, it did not lead to the complete abandonment of older forms.

Aleppo: Iron Age Temple

At some point, probably in the eleventh century B.C.E., after the collapse of the Hittite Empire, a change was made to the Aleppo temple. A section of the east wall adjacent to the south side of the relief of Teshub was removed and replaced with a new carved image of a standing man approaching the god. The treatment of the body of the man reveals an artist who was more interested in reproducing the reality of human form than was the sculptor of the image of the god. This is a stylistic feature more commonly found in post-Hittite relief sculpture. The figure wears a short tunic and conical cap, attributes that were normally associated with divinities, but it may reveal the survival of older Hittite iconography, in which rulers are often shown with divine attributes when placed in the presence of gods (Kohlmeyer 2009: 197–98). The hieroglyphic Luwian inscription that accompanies the figure identifies him as Taita, "King and Hero of the Land of Palistin." Hawkins argues that Taita was not the king of Aleppo but, instead, ruled it as one of his many centers in the eleventh century B.C.E. (Hawkins 2009: 169). Kohlmeyer suggests that the addition of the king into the scene changed the nature of the composition from a layout in which the Teshub image was the cult focus of the space to a scene that is a historical representation of Taita's dedication of a renovated temple to the god. The cult focus then reverted back to the niche on the north wall that had been hidden during the Hittite period. Moreover, the treatment of Taita's eyes as wide open and the top of the socket close to the bridge of the nose can be found on some of the sculptures at ʿAin Dara, which first took shape at this same point in time. Not only did Taita return the cult focus back to the north wall and in so doing reintroduced the direct approach via the south entrance, but he also added another lion to the entrance, perhaps replacing an older, destroyed pendant to the surviving Hittite lion. It also was inscribed with a hieroglyphic Luwian inscription referring to Carchemish and horses from Egypt (Kohlmeyer 2009: 199). This type of return to the older cult focus was noted by Woolley in the Level III temple at Alalakh (Woolley 1955: 78).

Kohlmeyer and his team think that the temple underwent a final renovation in the tenth century B.C.E. (Gonnella, Khayyata, and Kohlmeyer 2005: 94–99). This change was made solely to the sculptural program of the Late Bronze Age pedestal. The earlier three figures of the mountain god and two composite monsters were retained, but added to the composition was a long image showing the Weather God mounting his chariot ,which is being drawn by a bull. This panel was lined up so that its center intersected with the mid-point of the niche, which was no longer visible but was clearly influencing the arrangement of the reliefs. The relief sculptures of the 900 B.C.E. temple were carved on basalt slabs with an average height of 0.95 m and varying lengths. They are a series of individual units like metopes, most holding a single figure presented in profile facing right. They are arranged as though in procession. There are three exceptions. A large relief depicts two bulls facing a tree, probably a tree of life. Another relief features a figure fully facing front, with arms raised. The third relief is divided into an upper and lower portion. The upper portion contains a sphinx. The lower portion shows a lion. There are stylistic elements that connect some of these reliefs to the earlier ones and suggest the continued strength of Hittite forms, but Kohlmeyer sees stylistic connections with sculpture from Carchemish that is normally dated to the end of the tenth century B.C.E., which he uses to argue for a date of 900 B.C.E. for the last renovation.

Among the sculptures in this last group are several that in subject matter betray influences from Mesopotamia: the sphinx figure, a human-headed scorpion figure, and several winged individuals that look like early versions of the apotropaic images so prominent in the later Assyrian palace relief programs (Kohlmeyer 2000: 36). These may indicate that the influence of Assyria was beginning to be felt in the region even before the major military penetrations that started in the ninth century B.C.E. As with the earlier, 1100 B.C.E. temple, this temple is also incomplete. The work on the sculptural program was ongoing when the temple was burned down and abandoned. It is not certain that all the sculptural programs were intended to be in simultaneous use, but there is no evidence of a new relief sculpture for the east wall of the 900 B.C.E. temple to replace the sculpture of the eleventh century B.C.E.

Unlike the reliefs at ʿAin Dara, the reliefs in both versions of the Iron Age temple at Aleppo seem to have been intended to relate to sacred narratives. Taita introduced the sacred dedication image and, in so doing, changed the cultic focus of the temple. The tenth-century B.C.E. alterations retained the axial cultic force but widened the spectrum of images with individual figures that must have related either to stories or to rituals associated with the temple. The Weather God mounting his chariot may recall the Hittite spring ritual, known to have been practiced in the capital, in which the Weather God was carried in procession from his temple on a chariot pulled by two bulls (Gonnella, Khayyata, and Kohlmeyer 2005: 99).

Though the archaeological record does not demonstrate continuity at all of the major urban sites of the later Iron Age in the Syrian region (e.g. Zincirli (Schloen and Fink 2009: 207), the findings in the temples at the Aleppo Citadel, ʿAin Dara, and in the renewed work on the ʿAmuq Plain and in the north Orontes Valley (T. Harrison

2007: 91) suggest that there must have been strong continuity of settlement even after the problematic decades around 1200 B.C.E., and this must have included the continuation of cult places and political forces. Certainly for the areas that had been under the influence of the Hittites or the great Levantine cities of Ugarit and Alalakh, a return to some semblance, albeit modest, of the prosperity and monumentality of the Late Bronze Age must have been possible, and more excavations, particularly at sites such as Carchemish, will perhaps demonstrate the validity of this notion. The Arameans did represent a new force, on par with the Amorites' invasion of a millennium earlier. Their influence may be felt in the particular subjects selected for some of the reliefs in the second stage of the Iron Age temple on the Aleppo Citadel. They had a nomadic heritage and thus had no tradition of building. If the ʿAin Dara temple was indeed built for one of the new Aramean settlements, then its construction is a truly amazing architectural feat. The patrons for its three phases must have used skilled builders from the region who knew how to work with the materials, but the patron for the third phase must have also allowed the contractor/architect free reign to design the temple. There was nothing in the Aramean background that would have enabled them to comprehend and create this design. One of the reviving Neo-Hittite settlements could have provided a builder. It may be best to consider the North Syrian sites as combining Aramean and Neo-Hittite elements, at least in the highest echelons of their society.

"Peoples of the Sea" and Their Sanctuaries

Bay of Haifa and the Sharon Plain
Tell Abu Hawam

At the time of the Late Bronze Age collapse, the town at Abu Hawam (perhaps ancient Aksaph) on the rim of Haifa Bay at the delta of the River Kishon was probably a significant if small port offering access to the Mediterranean for products brought to the coast from the Beth-shean and Jezreel valleys. The original Late Bronze Age site must have been Canaanite, but as Iron Age I took shape, a resurgent Canaanite presence but now in the form of Phoenicians from the coastal cities of the north seems to have increased.[3] During the tenth and ninth centuries B.C.E., Tell Dor, farther along the coast, was under the sovereignty of Sidon (Ciasca 1999: 183–84). However, in the twelfth century B.C.E., Abu Hawam may have already become home to one of the

---

3. As discussed in chap. 2, Hawkins (2009: 169–72) has proposed that the "Land of Palistin" in the Taita inscriptions refers to a kingdom located on the ʿAmuq Plain that included ʿAin Dara, Aleppo, and Tell Taʿyinat. He has also suggested that this region may have formed the homeland from which the Philistines (*prst*) of the Egyptian sources emerged to attack the Delta and later settle in the southern Levant. For this book, however, the Philistine region remains the southern Levant, and the ʿAmuq Plain and related materials are treated as North Syrian.

groups associated with "Peoples of the Sea." The population must have been a mix of Canaanite and Sherden/Shardana. Although the Late Bronze Age town was destroyed, a new settlement arose in the eleventh century b.c.e., no doubt built by the same population. Much of the earlier Late Bronze Age layout was retained in the Iron Age I stratum, representing some degree of continuity of occupation. However, there were some significant changes in orientation for some structures, and the three-room-house type made its appearance (Markoe 2000: 192–93). The old Late Bronze Age sanctuary (Building 50; fig. 11A) was one of the structures that was rebuilt (Building 30; fig. 11B) atop the earlier remains (Dever 1997a: 9) and used the same orientation and axial symmetry, thus retaining a degree of association (Hamilton 1934: 8, pl. 4). The new structure was larger, 9 m × 14 m. Instead of the thin walls with exterior buttresses that had marked the earlier design, the new version had thicker walls and no external supports.

The older building was entered through the west side (though the entrance did not survive). The basic continuity of design suggests that the same was true for the early Iron Age version. Alas, the remains are confused here. There are two roughly parallel walls that seem to define a small corridor about one meter in width on the west side. This corridor does not clearly lead to any type of entrance into the structure itself. Inside Building 30, there are remains of stone-built constructions in the north half of the west side of the space, which would argue against any type of entrance. The south half of the west side contains traces of a pier or pillar. All of this implies that the entrance was not on the west side, as had been the case for Building 50.

Building 30 was part of a cluster of structures. There is evidence that buildings came right up to its north wall. To the southwest of the west side of the structure, the buildings became denser. However, the space immediately in front of the west side was open, suggesting that a courtyard preceded the temple on one side. This also appears to have been the case for the Late Bronze Age Building 50.

There are significant design changes between Buildings 50 and 30. The Late Bronze Age temple, Building 50, stood out from the other structures surrounding it. It physically seems to have been some distance from any neighboring buildings. The walls with their external buttresses were unlike any other walls. The interior enclosed by the walls was larger than most of the other enclosed spaces at the Late Bronze Age town. This is not the case with Iron Age I Building 30. The walls were not abnormally thick compared with the walls of other buildings on the site, and the enclosed space, although large, can be paralleled elsewhere on the site.

The finds from Building 30 have led to the conclusion that the structure was still operating as a temple. High quantities of imported wares, especially Cypriot pottery, as compared with other areas on the site suggest that it continued to be a privileged space (Hamilton 1934: 8). Moreover, the building, and the site itself, was attracting imports from both the northern and southern coastal regions. There are items from the Phoenician north and the south where another group of the "Peoples of the Sea" was emerging as a distinct group, the Philistines (Balensi et al. 1993: 11). The evidence for continuity of occupation implies that some degree of Late Bronze Age Canaanite coastal culture remained vital at the site, especially during Iron Age I, when the first rebuilding occurred. However, this sector of Haifa Bay saw early settlement by the Sherden/Shardana and Sikel peoples, already by the thirteenth century B.C.E., and the Phoenician presence was growing in the region in Iron Age I, probably associated with the Sidonian expansion. At Abu Hawam in Iron Age IA, there were several new, different cultural forces operating that would have influenced the residual local Canaanite element as it adapted to the changed cultural setting of Iron Age I (Bloch-Smith and Nakhai 1999: 88–89).

Southern Coastal Plain

The "Peoples of the Sea" who were settled in the southern Levantine area developed an independent cultural region along the south coast of Palestine which by Iron Age IIB was known as Philistia but which is already distinct in the archaeological record by Iron Age I. By the end of Iron Age I and the beginning of Iron Age IIA, the region was politically united as a confederation of five cities, the Philistine Pentapolis: Gaza, Ashkelon, Ashdod, Gath, and Ekron. Of these, Gaza, Ashkelon, and Ashdod had been important Canaanite cities in the Middle Bronze and Late Bronze Ages who must have fallen to the onslaughts of the newly arrived "Peoples of the Sea." A major Middle Bronze Age sanctuary is known from Ashkelon (Stager 1991: 24–43). Besides the five major cities, there were smaller Philistine settlements along the coast, one of which was north of modern Tell Aviv at Tell Qasile. Ashdod, Ekron, and Tell Qasile have yielded remains for Philistine sanctuaries.

Ashdod

The evidence for the earliest Philistine occupation at Tell Ashdod (fig. 12) is found in stratum XII of Area H on the acropolis (see fig. 13 here; also M. Dothan 1993: 97). This section shows remains of urban planning built over earlier structures. There are remains of two complexes of buildings separated by a street 3.5 m wide. The north complex contained an apsidal building along with a large hall and a row of rooms that opened onto paved patios. Within the hall stood two stone bases that must have supported columns. Attached to one of these bases was a rectangular installation of white plastered mud brick 1.80 m × 1.30 m. Some of the spaces seem to have been for domestic use, and in them were found decorated pottery, spinning bowls, and one finger ring (Dothan and Dothan 1992: 152–53). The apsidal structure and the hall with columns evidence the existence of two impressive buildings within the quarter.

The apsidal design marks it as different. Apsidal constructions are not common in Late Bronze Age or Iron Age I Levantine contexts. The structure was divided into two rooms, and in these were recovered fragments of Philistine pottery. There were also two dagger pommels covered in gold leaf, some other traces of gold, fragments of faience, an ivory cosmetics box, and two seals—one with a script identified as Cypro-

Minoan and best known from thirteenth- and twelfth-century B.C.E. contexts on Cyprus. These have been treated as special objects, the kind often found in sanctuary ruins. More significant may be the discovery of a small clay figurine of a seated female, what has been identified as a modified Mycenean mourner type, which was unearthed not in the apsidal building but in the complex across the street from it (Yasur-Landau 2001: 335). T. Dothan has concluded that this was a type of figurine developed at Ashdod in the twelfth century B.C.E. that continued to be manufactured until the eighth century B.C.E. She has coined the phrase "Ashdoda" type, and several of these figurines have been found at Ashdod. She argues that they were icons of the mother goddess and traced their formal origin and their cult origin back to the Late Bronze Age Mycenean world (Dothan 1982: 41, 234–37, fig. 9, pl. 19). The apsidal building and the nearby columned hall could have formed the sanctuary for the cult.

A terra-cotta cult stand decorated with figures playing double pipes and flutes (fig. 14) was uncovered in the grave of a warrior dated to the twelfth century B.C.E. Its findspot separates it from the possible sanctuary, but this type of object was used in temple rituals, and the cult stand probably belonged in some type of cult building originally. The motif of performing musicians may suggest the importance of music to religious ritual in the Iron Age I.

Ekron (Tell Miqne)

The Philistine levels at Ekron (strata VII–II) have been found in both the lower city and the acropolis (fig. 15). The earlier levels of Ekron testify to a substantial Canaanite city during the Middle Bronze and Late Bronze Ages, which seems to have witnessed a major change in the ethnic makeup of the population at the beginning of the early Iron Age (Gitin and Dothan 1987: 207). While this change can be traced in much of the Philistine region by the shift in pottery styles, at Ekron it is further evidenced by the sudden appearance of pork and beef in the diet (Dothan and Dothan 1992: 248). The sanctuary complex was unearthed in Field I (fig. 16) and was first seen in stratum VI (twelfth century B.C.E.). It continued to function through stratum V. Field I is in the upper city near an industrial sector but probably within the confines of a residential quarter. It is located next to the upper city wall (Dothan and Dothan 1992: 242).

The complex consisted of four rooms separated by narrow passageways. Within one of the rooms, a stone base for a pillar was unearthed. In the phase associated with stratum V, the floor was plastered, and benches and a platform were constructed. A pit dug into the floor of the room contained the remains of bovine scapulas. Pottery finds included kernoi, bichrome fragments, one lion-headed vessel, and a miniature pot identical to pots found at the Cypriot site of Athienou (Dothan and Dothan 1992: 242). These findings and the furnishings led the excavators to conclude that the complex of rooms had been a sanctuary. In the stratum prior to the actual building, excavations had turned up "Ashdoda" figurines, which indicate a long stretch of sanctity for the spot itself.

Far more impressive are the remains of a second sanctuary in the lower city in Field IV (fig. 17). The general nature of the finds in Field IV led to the conclusion that this was an elite district of the city. As in Field I, the sanctuary building (Building 351) first appears in stratum VI. The structure was square, 10 m per side, and was built of plastered mud brick that for most of the walls was only one row thick. The thinness of the walls argues against a two-story structure except for the area around the hearth. The entrance was through the northwest corner, where there was an outer threshold composed of five rows of stones one course high.

The interior was not a single unified square space. The entrance led into a rectangular room with walls thick enough to have supported a second story and containing a large hearth, 2.5 m in diameter (T. Dothan 1995: 42–45). Along the sides of the walls were benches coated in plaster. The floor was plaster over a pebble bedding. Behind the hearth room were additional enclosed spaces, possibly an unroofed courtyard with two small enclosed rooms. The hearth itself may predate the building, since it seems to be associated with earlier stratum VII, where the excavators found Mycenean CIII:b ware.

The importance accorded the hearth, which has no parallels elsewhere at the site, identifies the structure as significant. The walls enclosing the hearth were thicker than the other walls, and the hearth continued to exist as a feature of the building complex through at least two refurbishings (T. Dothan 1995: 45). Finds also support this reading. These finds included a miniature bone pomegranate (Artzy 1990: 48–51), a lamp with a red-banded rim bowl placed over it, and an Aegean style round ivory lid incised with battling griffins, lions, and bulls.

Building 351 was radically altered in stratum V to create Building 350 (fig. 18). Stone foundations 1–2 m high were set into the remains of Building 351. The new structure was was now part of a larger ensemble of buildings to the east including living quarters, a bath, and a colonnaded hall (Buildings 352, 353, 354). There was no direct communication between Building 350 and the grouping to the east. Placed over the stone foundations of Building 350 were mud-brick walls plastered white. These now have a width of 1.2 m. These thick, strong walls could have supported a second story. The entrance remained in the northwest corner, but the design of the interior space changed. The entrance consisted of a shallow porch defined by the antae of the exterior west wall and a buttress along the north wall. The doorway opening held two columns *in antis,* for which the bases survive. The doorway opened into a squarish space, ca. 5.5 m × 7.5 m. The door from this antechamber into the next was moved off axis to the west, where it led into a rectangular space. Three stone bases arranged on the longitudinal axis of this space may have held up columns to support the ceiling of a room or some type of partial roofing for a courtyard space. On the east side of the space and toward the north end were the remains of a hearth, about half the size of the hearth in Building 350. It is not exactly in the same place as that in the earlier building, but it may indicate some level of continuity. On the east side were three parallel rooms that open off the rectangular space. These too were rectangular rooms of about equal size, ca. 2.5 m × 4 m, but their longitudinal axes were perpendicular to the axis of the main rectangular space. The north room in this grouping had an opening in its north wall that led to yet another room. This was another rectangular space, but with the longitudinal axis again parallel to that of the large rectangle. The northern room had the same depth as the antechamber, which it paralleled but with which it had no direct communication.

The furnishings of the spaces in Building 350 were different from room to room. There was nothing in the antechamber. The main rectangular space had the hearth and possibly a colonnade. Of the four rooms on the east side, the three parallel rooms all contained some type of installation, while the northern-most room had nothing. The middle of three parallel rooms had a plastered mud-brick platform that was 1 m high and was set in the southeast corner of the space. Around its base was a bench. The room immediately to the north had a small mud-brick bench along its back wall. The south room had three superimposed floors, and into the east end of the room was a plastered, funnel-shaped installation 0.40 m deep.

The finds within this complex confirm its special status. Fish bones were recovered from the ashes of the hearth in the main rectangular room, and chicken bones were in the nearby scatter. A deposit had been made in the southeast corner of the space that included a lamp placed inside of two bowls, not unlike the lamp found with a bowl in the earlier Building 351. In the north of the three small eastern rooms were Philistine bichrome pottery fragments, an iron knife with bronze rivets, an ivory handle with ring-shaped pommel, a bronze cauldron handle, a bronze spear butt, and a double human-headed bronze chariot linchpin. The middle room with its platform contained the richest finds. On the platform in the southeast corner were two bowls and a flask decorated with red concentric circles. There were also an ivory knife handle, three small bronze eight-spoke wheels, and a fragment of a bronze frame. The wheels and frame had come from a wheeled stand. The south room of the grouping of three had different finds for each of the plaster floor levels. On the lowest were a gold-leaf object and an ivory earplug. On the middle floor were round, conical, pinch-shaped, unperforated loom weights. On the top floor was a cache of Philistine vessels with horizontal handles found stacked along the east wall.

In stratum IV, Building 350 was backfilled. This was also done to another structure in Field III. However, the plan of Building 350 seems to have been used in some way, and the finds from stratum IV continue to show cultic activity at the spot. These include a cache of ivory, faience, and stone objects, among them a rosette-decorated earplug and a finger ring depicting the Egyptian goddess Sekhmet. The pottery finds were mostly miniature red-slipped bowls, flasks, and chalices. The area was finally abandoned at the time of the city's destruction at the end of the eleventh century B.C.E. and lay unused for the next 300 years (Dothan and Dothan 1992: 251).

Tell Qasile

Tell Qasile, which is in a northern suburb of modern Tel Aviv, was probably settled in order to exploit the resources of the nearby Yarkon River. It was established some-time between the twelfth and eleventh centuries b.c.e. and, unlike Ashdod and Ekron, cannot be related to any named Philistine cities in the ancient records (A. Mazar 1980: 3–9). During the period covered by strata XII–X, the site was a Philistine town at the northern edge of the territory controlled by the Philistine pentapolis. In the following period, represented by strata IX–VII, the site was within the orbit of Israelite control, though it probably remained a Philistine town. Area C was continuously occupied during these centuries, and several superimposed buildings have been discovered, all identified as different iterations of a sanctuary that began operation in stratum XII and ceased to function in stratum VIII (A. Mazar 1980: 9–12).

Area C is near the summit on the eastern side of the mound (fig. 19). In its first manifestation, area C may have been the center of a small settlement at the top of the mound. Eventually, the town proper developed below it to the south and west. The total area encompassed by the town itself was 4 acres. The first version of the sanctuary, Temple 319 (fig. 20A), formed the main structure in stratum XII and was built above the remains of an earlier construction. Temple 319 did not stand alone. To its east and west were courtyards and subsidiary buildings, but the excavations were too limited to provide much information about these structures. Temple 319 had external dimensions of 6.40 m × 6.60 m and consisted of a single room set on a slope descending toward the north and west (A. Mazar 1980: 13–20). The corners did not form right angles. The northwest and southeast corners were acute angles, and the other two were obtuse. The mud-brick walls rested on bedrock without the benefit of stone foundations and were adjusted to the sloping ground. The walls were uneven in thickness, ranging from 0.50 m for the east wall to 1 m for the north wall. A flat stone placed above the lowest brick course in the east wall marked the entrance.

The walls defined an interior space of 4.75 m × 5.06 m. Plastered benches of beaten earth, 0.42 m wide and 0.15 m high, lined portions of the north, east, and south walls. The floor was a composite of lime and earth. The western side of the room was ap-pointed with a mud-brick platform that protruded into the room from the north wall, where it was seemingly attached to the bench. It was preserved to a height of 0.50 m above the floor but had been taller. It may have had two step-like projections on its east side. The west side of the platform is not clear. It could have been solid and attached to the west wall, or it could have defined a small space at the west, separated from the main room itself. If this latter reading is correct, then the entrance into this space was via the southwest corner of the room. The floor shows traces of fire in two places (A. Mazar 1980: 15), and it is possible that the room had a hearth (T. Dothan 1995: 44).

Temple 319 was situated in a courtyard that extended east and north, forming an L-shaped precinct, with secondary buildings to the north and south. This encompassed ca. 300 square meters and clearly created a specific space defined by a lime floor, on top of which were uncovered layers of light gray ash with a single layer of black ash. The gray ash may have resulted from a buildup of organic material in the court, while the black ash layer resulted from a burnoff of the fill. At least two levels for the courtyard could be discerned, the lower one composed of friable kurkar stone. Like the temple itself, the courtyard sloped with the bedrock.

Limited finds can be associated with Temple 319 and its courtyard. The excavators found the fragment of a kernos ring, an animal-head spout from another kernos, four miniature vessels, and a lump of iron along with an iron knife with ivory handle, a scarab of local manufacture, 15 bowls scattered around, and 3 other complete vessels (A. Mazar 1980; 1985b).

Stratum XII and Temple 319 may have been destroyed by an earthquake. The new sanctuary in Area C arose as the town was rebuilt. The sanctuary in stratum XI, Temple 200 (fig. 20B), was erected atop the stumps of the walls of Temple 319. Two features from the earlier design were retained in the new temple: the general orientation and the interior treatment of the west side as a more privileged space (A. Mazar 1980: 21–32). The new building was a larger, roughly square structure, 8.55 m × 8.20 m × 7.70 m × 7.94 m. What remains of the walls are kurkar stone blocks with a general thickness of 1 m that stand to a height of ca. 1 m. Nothing survives of a mud-brick nature, and it is possible that the entire structure was of stone. There are traces of clay plaster on the inside but nothing on the exterior.

The floor level was raised to the same height as the surviving top of the platform in the former temple. The new surface was of beaten earth and lime, 0.15–0.20 m thick. The interior floor level of Temple 200 was lower than the outside courtyard, so one needed to step down into the sanctuary proper. Benches of red hamra mud brick lined the north and east walls. A small bench occupied the southeast corner. In the western half of the interior space stood a new installation, an L-shaped wall jutting out from the west wall 2.76 m to the east. A bench ran along its north side. A second wall extended to the south toward the south wall about 2.80 m. Both of these walls were of mud brick laid directly on the floor of the sanctuary without any stone foundations. The enclosed space was small, 1.53 m × 2.85 m, and was entered from the south through a small opening. The northwestern corner of the temple was also set off by this installation. Here, a U-shape space with benches was created on the three sides. The entrance into Temple 200 remained on the east side but was moved to the northeast corner.

As had been the case with Temple 319, Temple 200 was also set into a courtyard that opened to its east and north. However, the number of surrounding structures was increased, and a wall may have closed off the south. The floor of the courtyard was of compacted earth laid on a layer of black ash that sealed stratum XII. Along the east face of Temple 200 was a paving of kurkar stone. During the course of the use of stratum XI, the courtyard was raised several times, while the interior floor of Temple 200 remained unchanged during the period.

Appended to the exterior of the west wall of Temple 200 was a second structure (Shrine 300) consisting of two parts: an entrance porch and an enclosed room. The structure was of mud brick set without stone foundations. Only the exterior dimensions for the enclosed room are clear: 3.40 m × 5.60 m with possible interior dimensions of 2.20 m × 4.18 for the main room and 1.85 m × 4.20 m for the porch area. This new construction was laid over some of the walls from stratum XII. The bedrock slopes at this point, and the floor of the porch at 0.60 m is lower than the main room of Temple 200. The south wall of Shrine 300 abuts another small building that has been identified as a house. This has led excavators to conclude that the area had a mixed-use pattern with some cultic activity and some residential functions.

The west wall of Temple 200 formed the east wall for Shrine 300. The entrance to the porch of Shrine 300 was at the northeast corner formed by the west wall of Temple 200 and the north wall of Shrine 300. A bench ran along the west wall and through the doorway into the porch space. The entrance to the inner room was set slightly farther west, and so the two entrances did not line up. The focus of the inner chamber seems to have been the southwest corner. Mud-brick benches, 0.34–0.49 m wide by 0.16–0.26 m high, lined the north, west, south, and east walls of the inner room. They were plastered with a combination of brown clay and kurkar grit. There is a gap in the benches at the southwest corner, where a raised mud-brick platform of two steps was placed, each step measuring 1 m wide and 0.42 m deep. Three projections, each 0.18 m high, stood to the east of the platform and 0.30 m in front of the bench lining the south wall.

The finds of stratum XI are richer than those from stratum XII. Within Temple 200, only a few artifacts were found scattered over the floor: some bones, a bronze arrowhead, a bowl, and a goblet. In the U-shaped niche opposite the entrance, 2 Philistine stirrup jars, a Philistine bowl, and traces of a painted textile were recovered (A. Mazar 1980: 24). The most abundant finds came from a partitioned area in the southwest corner. Vessels including small offering bowls (A. Mazar 1985b: 25, 33–35), beads, and figurines were found here. There were two unusual objects: an ivory cosmetics box (A. Mazar 1985b: 10, no. 1) of a type better known from Late Bronze Age contexts, which was a product of either Egyptian manufacture or influence; and an alabaster kohl pot (A. Mazar 1985b: 15), also of Egyptian type.

The finds from Shrine 300 were more varied in type and quantity. From the porch came a broken bowl with a bead decoration. Nearby was a large slab of worked stone (a possible *maṣṣēbâ?*). A cup-and-saucer set and a low ceramic stand were also found here. From the area of the platform in the southwest of the inner room came 3 cylindrical terra-cotta stands (A. Mazar 1980: 90–96). These are of a Near Eastern type known to have developed as early as the third millennium and to have remained in use into the Late Bronze Age. Two of them were found with cult bowls in place. A third possible cult bowl was located in the porch area. These were all wheel-made bowls, and 2 of them had applied birds' heads as decoration. One had wings and a tail as well. These were painted red and black. In a structure on the south side of the courtyard was a chalice, also decorated with applied heads (A. Mazar 1980: 96–100). The prototypes for these objects may have been Egyptian New Kingdom bowls or Canaanite metalwork. Also found were goblets, jugs, chalices, and lamps. On the north bench stood a low cylindrical stand, and on the west bench of the inner room, a bronze hook.

In the courtyard to the northwest of Temple 200 was a deposit of cult vessels and pots. The pit had been excavated down to the bedrock, and among the finds was a ceramic anthropomorphic vase of a type known from elsewhere in the Levant (A. Mazar 1980: 78–81). The figure is a female with pierced breasts through which the contents of the vessel could be poured. A second group of items consisted of terra-cotta zoomorphic masks. The fragments were large enough to show that the masks could have been worn. These are without close parallels (A. Mazar 1980: 85–86).[4] There were also decorated Philistine bowls, goblets, jugs, and lamps. The date for the digging of the pit is not clear. It probably belongs to stratum XI or to the period after the end of the stratum but before the next phase of occupation. If it is from the later period, then perhaps it was intended to preserve some of the sacred and cult objects on the site, the remnants of a ritual cleaning. Above the pit was found a layer of earth mixed with animal bones.

A. Mazar has argued for lines of continuity between stratum XII and stratum XI. The basic layout of the sacred region remained the same for both strata. The walls that were demolished in stratum XII were reused in stratum XI. However, the actual buildings were all new. The builders of Temple 200 used much more stone, which was a new technique at the site. The sacred complex was enlarged, and two quite different and unconnected spaces were created. Several new buildings were added at this point, perhaps public structures, and they created a truly urban complex. There are no real signs of destruction for the end of stratum XI. Instead, stratum XI develops into stratum X. A. Mazar (1980: 33–49) views Temple 131 (fig. 21) as a rebuilding and extension of Temple 200. Three of the older structure's stone walls were reused. The small Shrine 300 also continued in operation (fig. 22). The major change was the addition of an entrance vestibule to the east side of the temple. This unit was entered from the north side and required people to take a right-angle turn to the west to enter the main chamber of the sanctuary. The architectural change resulted in the creation of a bent-axis design. The new temple was larger, 8 m × 14.50 m, covering 116 square meters. The floor was raised, set on an artificial fill, and held in place by a frame of mud

---

4. Masks were employed in Aegean worship practice and may also have been used on Cyprus during the Late Bronze Age (Vermeule 1974: fig. 29).

brick. In constructing the terrace, the builders took care to cover the artifacts from the previous stage of the sanctuary, Temple 200. The walls of the main hall enclosed a trapezoidal space, and the corners were not exact right angles, which was also the case with the previous structures. The new entrance vestibule was different. The walls were more precisely aligned and consisted of right angles. The thickness of the east and west walls was evenly maintained at 1.20 m. The south wall, which joined with the main structure, was thinner, at 0.80 m. Stone foundations supported mud-brick walls, and the foundations were adjusted for the slope in the bedrock. The walls evidenced a bit of variety in techniques. Some bricks were laid only as headers and others only as stretchers. All the walls were plastered with brown clay mixed with kurkar grit.

The main hall (fig. 23) was an irregular rectangle with inner dimensions of 7.2 m length on the axis, 5.35 m width at the east end, and 5.80 m at the west end. The north wall was 1.25 m thick and was constructed of mud bricks laid in a header-and-stretcher pattern. The west and south walls were used from the previous structure and were of stone—the end result of which was a main chamber of mixed construction.

The new complex was entered through the northeast via a large opening, 3.23 m wide, paved with 3 large stones. The doorway was flanked by pilasters. Along the east, south, and west walls of the entrance chamber ran stepped benches of mud brick, 0.40 m wide and 0.80 m high. The preservation of the door is good, and the absence of door sockets must indicate that the doors were set into a wooden frame. The walls, benches, and floor were covered by a layer of plaster. A large kurkar stone, 1 m × 1 m, rested at the southeast corner atop the bench. The floor was covered with a layer of ash, and at points there were accumulations of organic materials 0.20 m thick. These contained traces of wood, probably from the door frame.

Pilasters also framed the entrance to the main hall from the vestibule. This was another wide doorway, of 3.30 m. Two large stones form part of the threshold. It is not clear whether an actual door existed. The main hall repeated the shape of Temple 200. Two round, chalky stone bases with diameters of 0.68 m lay along the axis of the hall and must have supported columns. These served to divide the space into two roughly equal halves with the axial line paralleling the north wall. Traces of cedar wood have been found in the main hall, thus indicating the probable material used for columns and roof. On one of the bases, impressions of a column with a diameter of 0.30 m survived and was surrounded by bricks. The floor itself was plastered.

At the west end of the hall, an L-shaped partition wall of mud brick 0.65 m thick projected from the north wall 3.08 m and effectively sealed off a small space, 1.35 m × 3.20 m, that could only be entered from the southeast. The partition wall was added after the completion of the structure and was not part of the original building. The arrangement continued the pattern of the previous two sanctuaries, with the focus for the main hall being on the west side of the room. There was a new feature, for the L-shaped projecting wall served to define a space behind it, a deeper chamber.

In essence, the main hall now consisted of a large, almost square east space to the side and a narrow west chamber entered from the south where there was a kind of entrance area. The main square space was set off by plastered benches, which lined its north and south sides. Along the east face of the L-shaped partition wall was a large, plastered mud-brick platform, 1.12 m × 1.30 m. It was not on the central axis of the room as defined by the central column, but it was clearly visible from the entrance into the hall. It survived to a height of 0.90 m but had been partially destroyed by a later foundation trench. On its south side were two steps that led up to the platform. These two mud-brick steps incorporated the second of the two columns in the room.

Temple 131 was also embedded in a complex of courtyards and buildings (fig. 22) but on a more congested scale. To the north and east, an L-shaped courtyard served to funnel visitors into the entrance. At the far north end was a structure reused from the previous stratum. In front of the entrance to Temple 131, to the northeast was a small stone foundation 1.30 m × 1.50 m that held up a platform that may have functioned as an altar. A formal entrance led into the courtyard from the street to the northwest. A second entrance off the same street led south to another entrance, this time to a courtyard flanking the northwest side of the temple and the entrance to the appended Shrine 300 which continued to function. Walls sealed each of these courtyards, rendering them isolated and defined spaces. The common south wall of Shrine 300 and Temple 131 provided the north wall for a large rectangular hall. A line of stone bases survives, suggesting that the roof for this hall was held up by an internal colonnade. A small doorway in the east wall of this structure led to 2 small chambers. Within all of this construction, Temple 131 stood out because of its thicker and more impressive construction and its special interior treatment.

As had been the case with stratum XI, the finds from stratum X were quite rich. The entrance vestibule yielded 2 small flasks and fragments of bowls. The finds from the main hall were concentrated around the platform and the entrance area in front of the small west room. Elsewhere in the main hall were 3 bowls, a pilgrim flask, an iron bracelet, and a bronze ax or adze. Elsewhere in the room were concentrations of pots, storage jars, jugs—including a bichrome strainer jug and a globular jug—kraters, bowls, lamps, and a pomegranate-shaped vessel. Several of the pots were found intentionally arranged against the walls.

The platform area provided a ceramic naos, a cylindrical cult stand decorated with human figures, and a ceramic vessel composed of a tube surrounded on the lower half by 6 elliptical hollow bodies arranged in 2 symmetrical rows of 3 (A. Mazar 1980: 104–5). The naos, which may have stood on the platform, was a fired ceramic plaque with a white slip. In an architectural frame stood 2 figures, each separately made and attached to the plaque. Additional figures had been attached as decoration. A similar piece was found at Gezer; this kind of plaque is known from Middle and New Kingdom Egyptian contexts and from Phoenicia as well (A. Mazar 1980: 82–84).

The cult stand was a wheel-made ceramic tube with 2 rows of windows, each 12 cm high. Each window contained a schematic human form. The motif of repeated marching figures is well known in the Levant and can be seen on Middle Bronze and Late Bronze Age cylinder seals from Syria and Palestine. The stand itself has been compared to the stand with musicians from the warrior's grave at Ashdod (A. Mazar 1980: 87–89). Nearby was found a second cult stand, this time decorated with 2 dog or lion figures, each separately made and attached to opposite sides of the stand (A. Mazar 1980: 89–90).

The small west room defined by the L-shaped partition wall contained more than 100 pottery vessels, most in piles at the north end. Among the finds were bowls, jugs, juglets, flasks, and decorated Philistine pieces. There was also a pot with a tubular rim and a pomegranate vessel. The pomegranate motif, also found at Ekron in Building 350 (see above), is known from Canaanite metalware (A. Mazar 1980: 116). Three storage jars and a collared-pithos rim were also found. A. Mazar has argued that the room formed by the partition was strictly for storage and that the finds represent the buildup during the course of the sanctuary's use.

Courtyards and secondary buildings provided additional finds. The small room appended to the west court may have been a kitchen for the preparation of ritual meals. The room yielded remains of storage pits. An oven was found in the area east of Temple 131. There were only a few scattered finds in the courtyards proper, mostly sherds and bones. No special finds were made in the area around the possible altar northeast of the main entrance.

Stratum X ended in a fire in which most of the buildings were burned. Whether this was destruction due to war or to an earthquake is not obvious. However, in the period following the stratum X destruction, Tell Qasile was a port city for Israel. Strata IX and VIII show evidence of two major repairs to the temple but no significant structural alterations. In stratum IX, Shrine 300, the single rooms on the courtyard, and the boundary walls defining the courtyards all went out of use, and the temple came to be situated alone on a paved plaza in which a large stone installation and 2 ovens stood (A. Mazar 1980: 47–53). New houses went up to the south. This new arrangement continued into stratum VIII.

Most of the remains of temples from the Philistine region date to Iron Age I. The three phases of the Tell Qasile temple are dated to 1150 B.C.E. (stratum XII), 1100 B.C.E. (stratum XI), and 1050 B.C.E. (stratum X; Dothan and Dothan 1992: 225); strata IX–VIII have been attributed to the period after Tell Qasile's incorporation into the new Israelite state (Nakhai 1994: 24). The apsidal structure at Ashdod is dated to the twelfth century B.C.E. Ekron's two phases for Buildings 351 and 350 were no later than the end of the eleventh century B.C.E. The sanctuary in Field I of the upper city initiated operation in the twelfth century. Only a complex in Area D at Ashdod belongs to Iron Age II, since it dates to the eighth century B.C.E. (see below). These structures are the earliest evidence of recovery after the destructions of 1200 B.C.E. This fits with the idea that the region was being settled by a newly arrived population that had not suffered from the destructions and disruptions but, rather, may have been one of their causes.

The posited sanctuaries do not evidence a common type. A hearth was clearly important to the early version of Building 351 at Ekron and retained its importance through at least one refurbishing. Whether the smaller hearth in the courtyard of the complex of Building 350 is in some way related to the earlier is hard to say. There is evidence of a hearth in the first version of the temple at Tell Qasile, Temple 319, and it also seems to have disappeared in the second version, Temple 200.

The apsidal building at Ashdod has been singled out as a cult structure because the form is thus far unique in the Levant in early Iron Age contexts. However, the actual cult object, the "Ashdoda" figurine, came not from the apsidal building complex but from the building across the street. The apsidal room does contain a built platform. The temple in Field I at Ekron in the final phase of stratum V contained a built installation, a platform in association with benches. The three parallel rooms in Building 350 at Ekron each had some type of built installation, and two of the rooms had benches. All the versions of the sacred space at Tell Qasile had installations within the main cult chamber that may have been intended to create a separate space.

The most common feature found was the courtyard. Both Buildings 350 and 351 at Ekron used internal courtyards as a means of distributing small, enclosed spaces. The area devoted to formal courtyard space defined by surrounding walls increases with each rebuilding of the sanctuary at Tell Qasile. An interesting feature at Tell Qasile is the kitchen that appears as a small room appended to the courtyard in the final version of Temple 131. No other Philistine sanctuary manifests this feature, nor do the finds from other Philistine sites suggest that ritual meals were consumed in the sanctuary precinct.

The lack of a clearly defined design form and the changing nature of the use of platforms and courtyards in the various versions of the Iron Age I sanctuaries in the Philistine region may well indicate that, just as these people were the first to engage in monumental construction following the devastation of 1200 B.C.E., they were also open to experimentation in the architectural form of their shrines in this new land.

Revived Canaanite Sanctuaries

The Upper Galilee, Beth-shean, and Jezreel Valleys
Beth-shean (Beisân, Tell el-Hosn)
Beth-shean's position made it a natural place for an Egyptian garrison town in the Late Bronze Age. It commanded access both east to the Jordan Valley and north to the Baqʿah via the Huleh Valley. The surrounding land is fertile, and the site itself is well

watered. The mound of the Late Bronze Age occupation (fig. 25) is 113 m high and was naturally defensible due to steep ravines and the confluence of the Asi and Harod rivers. The site has a long history of use stretching back to the fifth millennium, but the Egyptians may have selected it over larger nearby sites because it was not built up as a Canaanite city during MBA II and thus was not surrounded by massive fortifications (A. Mazar 1997b: 62–64). Beth-shean became an Egyptian garrison during the Late Bronze Age, and it continued this role into the first decades of Iron Age I.

The stratigraphic sequence for the Beth-shean acropolis has been one of the most contested (R. Porter 1994–95a: 55–62) in Levantine archaeology, and this is of major importance because the site contained a number of Egyptian, datable items that should have facilitated the precise dating of specific strata and finds. One of the problems emerged early in the University of Pennsylvania excavations. In 1923, they unearthed a pair of steles of Seti I and Ramesses II and a statue of Ramesses III. These all came from stratum V, and the director of the excavations, C. Fisher, dated stratum V to the thirteenth century based on synchronization with the Egyptian chronology (Fisher 1923: 231–36).

The next director of excavations, A. Rowe, found in stratum V a cylinder seal of Ramesses II and an inscribed door jamb of the Egyptian commander of the garrison, Ramesses Weser Khepesh. Using these finds, he redated stratum V to the twelfth century B.C.E. He also dug below to strata VI and VII. In strata V, VI, and VII, he unearthed a sequence of superimposed structures that he identified as temples. Rowe argued that the temple and associated buildings of stratum VII on the acropolis had all been destroyed in a great conflagration that he dated to the end of the Eighteenth Dynasty or fourteenth century B.C.E. He thought that they were rebuilt with the beginning of the Nineteenth Dynasty, when Egyptian power was again ascendant in the area, in the thirteenth century B.C.E. (Rowe 1930: 23–31).

Problems with the actual stratigraphy and the coherence of level V began to emerge in the succeeding excavations led by G. Fitzgerald (Fitzgerald 1931: 141–42). Later, F. James (1966) and F. James and McGovern (1993: 5) read the evidence differently and offered a more nuanced stratigraphy. They saw the destruction of stratum VII as occurring at the close of the Nineteenth Dynasty, thirteenth century B.C.E., and the rebuilding that is stratum VI as datable to the Twentieth Dynasty, or twelfth century B.C.E. For their dating, they depended on the finds of early Iron Age pottery in stratum VI that marked it as twelfth century rather than thirteenth century B.C.E. (A. Mazar 1997a: 307; F. James 1966: 149–50; see also A. Mazar 1997b: 68–73). The stratum VI (fig. 26) temple then belonged to Iron Age I. However, they saw continuity of occupation at the site between the 19th and 20th Dynasties, between the Late Bronze Age and the early Iron Age. James posited a late VI stratum that witnessed the departure of the Egyptians, and their replacement by a squatter settlement just a few decades after 1200 B.C.E. She argued for a long period of occupation in stratum

V that divided into a Lower (older) V and an Upper (more-recent) V. Lower V she dated to the eleventh–tenth centuries B.C.E., the period of the revived city that was interrupted by the invasion of Shishak; this was followed by the Upper V in the late tenth–ninth centuries B.C.E., the Israelite city. James did not end stratum Upper V until 815 B.C.E., when the site was attacked by Syrians during Israel's wars with Syria (R. Porter 1994–95b: 92–93).

The most-recent excavations at Beth-shean by Hebrew University have refined the reading of the stratigraphy. The director, A. Mazar (R. Porter 1994–95a: 63), has argued that the end of stratum VII, thirteenth century B.C.E., occurred with the general upheavals of ca. 1200 B.C.E. but did not mark the end of the city, which continued to flourish as an Egyptian garrison until the end of Lower VI, a few decades later, when the Egyptians departed from the site and an independent Canaanite city reemerged (A. Mazar 1997b: 70–72). The end of Upper VI saw the collapse and destruction of the Canaanite city caused by the Israelites in the early tenth century B.C.E. Lower V, the new Israelite city, was destroyed by the invasion of Shishak dated to 925 B.C.E. (Kitchen 2000: 41). However, the city recovered, and Upper V did not end until the Assyrian invasion under Tiglath-pileser III in 720 B.C.E., another standard point of synchronization (Lipschits 2005: 5–7).

All of the investigators agreed that the label *temple* should be assigned to the sequence of buildings in strata VII, VI, and V. Temple VI was built directly over the remains of the temple in stratum VII, with a separation of about one meter of earth between the two structures. The stratum Upper VI (Mazar) or stratum Lower V (James) temple is actually two separate buildings, with the south temple being built above the ruins of the Late Bronze and first early Iron Age temples (strata VII/VI [Lower VI, Mazar]) sequence. The walls of the earlier Late Bronze Age stratum VII temple (fig. 27) were reused for the new temple of stratum VI. The new sanctuary retained several fundamental features of the sanctuary beneath it: the orientation running northeast to southwest, the tripartite design of a porch area, a main hall, and a raised platform, the trapezoidal shape, and the main entrance set off-axis to the west. At the same time, certain aspects show a change. Within the main hall, the bases for two columns were pushed closer together. This may indicate that the new hall was completely roofed, while the earlier version may have had only a partial roof around the sides, creating more of a restricted courtyard than a cult hall. The mid-point between the columns marked the central axis of the room, and this led north to a small flight of stairs that mounted a narrow bench placed along the north wall; this formalized the raised area at the north end from the looser configuration of the previous temple. Similarly, low benches along the east and west walls instead of along only the east wall, as in the previous temple, gave the space a stronger sense of focus. The bench at the north end of the hall opened up to the north to form a small chamber. On its north wall was placed an installation 1 m high of two large stone slabs laid at right angles to one another and set atop a mud-brick shelf. To the east and west were two smaller rooms.

The pottery finds from the temple proper in stratum VI (Fitzgerald 1930: 8–11) included bowls, cups-and-saucers, and a variety of pots. A fragment of a cylinder seal was found in one of the rooms to the east of the small chamber at the north end of the cult hall. A high percentage of the pottery vessels were in Egyptian forms, though whether these were imported or of local manufacture has not been determined (F. James 1966: 27). Among the finds in stratum VI were the first appearances of recognizable early Iron Age ceramic types. These are mixed with Late Bronze Age items still in use. Two bronze stands (1724, 1731) of Late Bronze Age Cypriot manufacture were found in stratum VI, though not in the temple proper but in the ruins of a domestic structure north of the temple. They resemble a stand found in Iron Age I stratum XI in Area B at Hazor. The two houses, 1500 and 1700, have been identified as residences for officials of the garrison (F. James 1966: 13), but it is quite possible that similar stands were employed in the temple as well. Unfortunately, neither Rowe's original study nor Fitzgerald's pottery analysis nor James's reanalysis of the excavations explains the exact findspots for the objects recovered from stratum VI. Based on the finds, both James and Mazar date the stratum VI temple to the twelfth century, to the period after the disruptions of 1200 B.C.E. during the continued Egyptian occupation of the site.

As was the case for the earlier Late Bronze Age temple in stratum VII, the Iron Age I stratum VI temple was part of a larger complex of buildings. Open courtyards flanked the temple on its south and west sides. It was from the courtyard on the west side that one entered the vestibule that formed the entrance to the main hall. The entrance into this L-shaped courtyard surrounding the temple on the west and south sides was from the northwest. The outer west wall of the temple itself may have served to support the royal Egyptian steles, fragments of which were found in stratum VI. At the north end of the west wall of the temple are traces of a niche that could have held such a stele.

East of the temple was a congested warren of spaces that seem to have been physically attached to the temple's east side and may have been storerooms. The two domestic units, 1500 and 1700, lie north of the temple and courtyard. House 1500 is of interest because of its square, centralized plan, with rooms distributed around the four sides of the courtyard. It recalls plans of square buildings, most identified as religious structures and not residences, in the Palestinian and Transjordanian region, built during the Middle Bronze and Late Bronze Ages. F. James (1966: 150) dates the destruction of stratum VI to the end of the Twentieth Dynasty.

In Mazar's stratigraphy, stratum Upper VI continued the established sequence of occupation by being built directly atop the remains of stratum Lower VI but on a totally new plan, thus breaking with 200 years of architectural continuity that had joined together strata VIII, VII, and VI, according to the James and McGovern stratigraphy. James actually posited a stratum between VI and V, a Late VI, a squatter period following the Egyptian departure (R. Porter 1994–95a: table B). For both James's stratum Lower V and Mazar's Upper VI, the occupation marked the reestablishment of a Canaanite city (A. Mazar 1997b: 73). Moreover, F. James, James and McGovern, and Mazar agree that a new temple plan took shape during the first half of the eleventh century B.C.E. (fig. 28). This arrangement was a two-temple plan, which may explain the biblical confusion surrounding the treatment of Saul's body. 1 Sam 31:10 records that Saul's weapons were placed in the Temple of ʿAshtoroth at Beth-shean, while the author of 1 Chr 10:10 states that his body was placed in the House of Dagon. Isserlin (1998: 239) has suggested that the north temple was dedicated to ʿAshtoroth and the south temple to Dagon.

The alignments of the temples broke radically with the earlier orientation of the temple. The new temples were aligned east to west rather than north to south and were more or less parallel to each other. In the new design, the two temples formed the nucleus of stratum V. The structures were both constructed of mud-brick walls resting on rough stone foundations. The west wall of the north temple was set on debris. The north temple was rectangular, 15 m × 11 m, and enclosed a single space of 13 m × 7.5 m. The south wall extended out from the end of the west wall and terminated in a short spur wall that turned north. This extension, which must have been entered from the north, formed a kind of vestibule to lead visitors to the entrance to the cult chamber that was at the southwest corner of the building. Within the main chamber were four basalt column bases set on rectangular footings of rougher stone. On the east wall were a raised U-shaped platform and a set of stairs.

The second, or south, temple was also a rectangular structure (F. James 1966: 38–41).[5] It was the larger of the two temples, 17 m × 23 m, and consisted of a rectangular core, the main hall, which had storerooms on both of the long sides. The main hall itself was divided into three east–west running aisles. These were defined by two rows of three columns each. The columns that formed the aisles were joined together by mud-brick walls. The storerooms on the south side could be entered from the main hall of the temple. Those on the north side were entered from outside the temple's main hall, probably from a courtyard on the northwest side of the south temple, a courtyard shared by both temples. From this courtyard and in the area of the entrance to the north storeroom group was another entrance into the space between the two temples. At the west end of the south side of the north temple and the west end of the north side of the south temple are opposing niches, and these created a formal entryway on the west side of the major courtyard. These niches mark a clear space that widens to become a corridor between the temples.

---

5. Ottosson argued that the south structure was not a temple but, rather, a palace (Isserlin 1998: 239).

The two temples were conceived as a unified architectural unit. They form a dialogue with one another. However, their entrances are not close to each other. The entrance to the south temple was at the southwest corner of the temple and was not approachable directly from the west courtyard area shared by the two buildings. The large west courtyard held the statue of Ramesses III, placed near the entrance to the north temple, and the two steles of Seti I and of Ramesses II, which were both found toppled over on each other but still near their bases on a wall to the west and opposite the statue of Ramesses III (F. James 1966: 34–35). Additional bases in the area could have supported other steles that are now lost. This presents the problem of the ensemble on the acropolis of Beth-shean. Whether it belongs in stratum Upper VI or V, it looks like a royal Egyptian imperial sculptural complex with two temples. Since it is now agreed that either reading of the stratigraphy places this complex later than the Egyptian period, it seems quite out of place. It must have had an odd, archaizing quality, with imperial Egyptian monuments of the twelfth and eleventh centuries B.C.E. standing in a non-Egyptian setting (A. Mazar 1992a: 356).

Stratum V yielded a number of finds. In the interior of the north temple were stele fragments, one part of a dedication to the Canaanite goddess Anat, and a second from yet another Egyptian royal stele. There were also a cylinder encircled by a spotted serpent, fragments of shrine houses, and a sculpted dove that had been attached to a cylinder. The pottery finds included cooking pots, a juglet, several fragments of undecorated pottery, and painted sherds. The finds from the south temple were much richer. In the foundation deposits east of the two colonnades were gold and electrum ingots and a small quantity of jewelry. Also in the deposits were Iron Age red burnished pots such as have been found at Megiddo V. Two of the spaces off the northeast side of the temple and outside the main hall revealed the most numerous finds of anywhere in the temple, all coming from on the floor. Among the objects were cult cylinders, a chalice, a lamp, a serpentine cylinder depicting Ramesses II shooting Canaanite captives, and numerous red-cross bowls. The red burnished ware from this stratum has been dated to the tenth century B.C.E. and is similar to ware known from Megiddo Va. Among the imported ware was some Cypriot black-on-red. Mazar has noted that finds from stratum Upper VI of eleventh century date at Beth-shean are overwhelmingly Canaanite. The site was witnessing Canaanite survival and revival even though around it there is good evidence for massive demographic shifts, at least in the coastal area where the "Peoples of the Sea" had come to be settled.

To James, stratum V seemed to have too many buildings. She proposed that the stratum actually had two distinct phases. The temples along with the royal steles and statue of Ramesses III belonged to the lower, earlier stratum, which may have dated to the eleventh century B.C.E. The second period dated to a century later, based on the evidence of the sealed deposits with pottery. This level may have witnessed the continued operation of the temple, at least the north temple, which appears to have received a new clay floor, perhaps toward the end of the first phase. The floor was 1 m thick, and buried beneath it were the four column bases. It extended out into the courtyard, where it was placed over the statue of Ramesses III and the two royal steles. How the south temple functioned in the second phase is not clear, but the precinct did receive a gateway (F. James 1966: 151). It may be that the southern temple was incorporated into a fortress complex already in the tenth century according to Nakhai's reading of the evidence. This, she assumes, would have been an Israelite fortress, even though the pharaonic steles would have been standing, at least initially (Nakhai 1994: 24–25).

James proposes that her Stratum VI represented the height of Egyptian power in the region. During the Twentieth Dynasty, the city housed an Egyptian garrison. The religious quarter of the acropolis maintained much the same design as it had in the previous era, stratum VII. Probably the destruction of stratum VII and the building of stratum VI were not separated by many years. The date for the initiation of VI would be about 1200 B.C.E., and it operated through the reign of Ramesses III. It had two building phases, but the temple remained unchanged through both. Later stratum VI was replaced by the first phase of stratum V, which seems to have lasted for two centuries (1100–900 B.C.E.) and which marked a major break architecturally with what had preceded it. It was probably at the end of this period that the north temple received the new clay floor that also buried the steles and statue after they were decommissioned, and the Egyptian presence in all senses had ceased. The first phase of V ended in destruction, to be replaced by the second phase, the tenth century B.C.E. phase, during which time the gateway was built (F. James 1966: 133–39). Mazar's Hebrew University excavations have changed this chronology slightly. His stratum Lower V, the Israelite city of the United Monarchy, appears to have ended in a major fire sometime shortly before the end of the tenth century, probably resulting from the invasion of Shishak (A. Mazar 1997b: 73).

The discovery so early in the excavations, 1923, of the statue of Ramesses III and the two steles of Seti I and Ramesses II caused the initial problems for the stratigraphy. These are monuments that, based on the Egyptian chronology, belong to the 19th and 20th Dynasties, the thirteenth and twelfth centuries B.C.E. It was not immediately apparent to Fisher or even later to Rowe that something was wrong and that the Egyptian material did not agree with the pottery found associated with it. Only later did it become clear that some of the pottery was actually Iron Age I and had to be twelfth century B.C.E. at the earliest. F. James, McGovern, and Mazar have elected not to date stratum V based on the Egyptian statue and steles but based on the pottery, the result of which is a later date for the stratum than what Fisher and Rowe proposed. The change in date for stratum V and subsequently for strata VI and VII as well means that the historical context in which each strata operated is different from what was initially proposed. Furthermore, by subdividing strata VI and V, they have also argued for breaks in the occupation history during otherwise long periods but breaks that did not result in major changes of culture or demography during the stratum's life. Thus Mazar sees continuity of occupation in Lower and Upper VI that was interrupted by the retreat of the Egyptians which allowed the resident Canaanites to reestablish control. Similarly, the division between Lower and Upper V indicates a stress on the site but not a major shift in populations. For James and McGovern, the division between Lower and Upper V occurred around the change from the tenth to the ninth century B.C.E. and can be seen in the archaeological record by the discontinuation of reused Egyptian objects, which was followed by some major new building (F. James 1966: 58, 153, and fig. 74). Mazar saw a more specific force as causing the break: Shishak's attacks in Palestine.

Hazor

The Late Bronze Age city of Hazor was destroyed in a violent manner. Throughout the upper and lower cities, there is evidence of the destruction. In places, the burn layer is over a meter in depth. Yadin proposed a date in the late thirteenth century B.C.E. for the event, but Ben-Tor as a result of the new excavations of the site has argued for a date closer to 1300 for the destruction (Rabinovich and Silberman 1998: 53). Although a possible Egyptian campaign, either by Seti I (1300 B.C.E.) or by Ramesses II (1275 B.C.E.), could be credited with the burning, Ben-Tor has accepted Yadin's view that Hazor may have been the first victim of the destruction caused by the proto-Israelites (Ben-Tor and Rubiato 1999: 22–39).[6]

Stratum XII marks a new beginning at Hazor (Yadin 1972: 127–34). Yadin read this change as the result of a new conquering people taking over the site and establishing themselves on the remains of the Late Bronze Age Canaanite city. The new occupants confined their interests to the upper city, the top of the tell (fig. 29), and little of architectural importance was built during this first phase (Rabinovich and Silberman 1998: 54). The next stratum, XI, was also limited to an occupation on the top of the tell, but here Yadin discerned a new cult area, a possible high place, Area B (Yadin 1975: 254–57). It was partially covered by buildings from the next period, stratum X. What could be uncovered showed an enclosed space, 5 m × 4 m. The southwest portions had a bench-like structure made of large basalt slabs. Paved areas to the south and west framed the area defined by the benches.

The southwest corner, where the benches met, contained a jug filled with bronze votive objects that had been placed just under the floor. Among the objects was a seated male figure wearing a cone-shaped helmet. He may have originally held a weapon. On the paved area to the south were two broken incense stands along with beads and arrowheads. Four stone pillars delimited the paved area to the west. Here were found hematite weights, bone inlay, and bronze needles—all objects that were

---

6. Aharoni has argued for a later date for the fall of Hazor: the twelfth century B.C.E.. This goes back to the old debate between the Albright and Alt Schools regarding the real nature of the Israelite conquest (Yadin 1972b: 10 n. 4, 131).

similar to those found in the votive deposit. There are also fragments of two more incense stands found farther to the east. One of the more complete incense stands resembles stands found in stratum VI at Megiddo and at Taʿanach IIB. Yadin has argued for a chapel or high place at this spot. There is no evidence of walls or roofing. He would date this to early Iron Age I, in the twelfth–eleventh centuries B.C.E. (Ben-Tor 1997: 4).

Megiddo

Megiddo was a major Late Bronze Age center that was strategically located for controlling traffic moving toward the coast through the Jezreel and Beth-shean valley system and also traveling along the coastal road. Egyptians had long maintained an interest in the Canaanite city and very likely controlled it at the end of Late Bronze Age. There seems to be little evidence of continuity of occupation between the last Late Bronze Age stratum, VIIB, and the first Iron Age I stratum, VIIA. However, the site was not abandoned, and in fact the change in imported wares to Cypriot, Mycenean, and southern Levantine (early Philistine) wares seems to have been happening already in the thirteenth century B.C.E. Those who now lived in stratum VIIA (fig. 30) made use of the Late Bronze Age temple (Area BB, Building 2048) and rebuilt the palace (area AA)—but not directly on top of the earlier palace; instead, they began some 2 meters above it. Somewhat like Beth-shean stratum VI (James) or Upper VI (Mazar) in Iron Age I, the finds at Megiddo Iron Age I include some high-prestige items such as a hoard of ivory objects from the palace (some local, some imported, all of Late Bronze Age style) and the base for a statue of Ramesses VI. The finds and the nature of the rebuilding of the site suggest that, while there may not have been continuity of settlement between Late Bronze Age and Iron Age I, Megiddo continued to prosper and was still part of the reduced Egyptian presence in the Beth-shean and Jezreel valleys (Bloch-Smith and Nakhai 1999: 84). It also must still have been a Canaanite outpost (Silberman et al. 1999: 35). This revived Megiddo finally succumbed to destruction about the same time as and perhaps to the same force as nearby Taʿanach IB, ca. 1125 B.C.E.

Reoccupied stratum VIB shows a poor standard of living for the inhabitants of the late-twelfth-century B.C.E. village. Readings of the archaeological evidence using the biblical context have led many to argue that the city fell violently as the result of an attack by either the Israelites (Josh 12:21) or one of the "Peoples of the Sea." The extensive building at the site in the next stratum (VIA) along with the finds of luxury articles including metalwork and the presence of Philistine bichrome pottery have led some scholars to suggest that the city had not become an Israelite outpost but was still a Canaanite city with a Philistine resident group. Building 2072 from stratum VIA on the northwest side of the tell (fig. 31) was excavated by P. L. O. Guy in 1934, and the results have proved problematic to interpret. T. Harrison (2003) has recently reinvestigated Guy's material on Building 2072, which consisted of chambers A, B, and

C located on the west side of what seems to have been a courtyard. Chamber A was actually two interconnected rooms (A and A$_1$). Two additional interconnected rooms are located on the northeast side in D. Building 2072 is larger than any other structure in the area and is somewhat better built. In chamber A$_1$, a number of loom weights of a type recognized as Philistine were found. The same identification has been given to the other 2 major finds: an anchor seal and a painted vase with the image of a lyre-playing figure (fig. 32). In his reanalysis of Building 2072, Harrison has noted that the form of the structure itself resembles the design of the contemporary Building 350 at Ekron (fig. 18) with its major courtyard serving as the organizing unit for the complex. This stylistic connection is reinforced by the Philistine nature of the findings within Building 2072, and Harrison has argued that Building 2072 supports the theory of a Philistine settlement at Megiddo in the latter part of Iron Age I.

Ta'anach

The site of Ta'anach is located in the Jezreel Valley, not far from Megiddo, and it has yielded remains of a cultic installation (Rast 1978: 23) that may well have been part of a household setting during Iron Age I. The site was unoccupied during the Late Bronze Age but was settled as a fortified town throughout the twelfth century B.C.E. (strata IA–IB). The pottery from the Iron Age I strata shows continuity with the Late Bronze Age regional forms (Bloch-Smith and Nakhai 1999: 85). The cultic installation comes from the Iron Age IIA context of stratum IIB and was placed in the corner of a four-room house. There is little of architectural note to support the designation of cultic, but two terra-cotta incense burning stands of a type most commonly associated with cultic paraphernalia in Iron Age I and decorated with images of lions, winged sphinxes, trees with goats, figures holding serpents, and a possible goddess—all motifs from Canaanite religious objects—support the cultic identification for the building and suggest that it may have been operating in some way already in the Iron Age I (contra Herr 1997c: 128–29). Similar types of cult stands have been found in Hazor, stratum XI (Iron Age I), but also at Megiddo stratum VA–IV (Iron Age IIA). Moreover, among the other finds of ceramic objects, stone, loom weights, and bits of metal was a bowl containing astragali, not unlike that found at Megiddo VA–IV, locus 2081 (Master 2001: 121 n. 18). There is disagreement about the amount of metal that should actually be assigned to stratum IIB and not to IB and IIA. Frick has argued that metalworking was associated with the shrine (Frick 2002: 219–32). On the east side of the cultic space was unearthed a pressing installation. Frick thought that the installation operated for almost two centuries and during that time changed from the task of pressing olive oil in the twelfth century to some type of cultic role in the tenth century. The excavator read the findings differently, seeing only one period of operation for the press—the tenth century—as an olive press (Lapp 1967: 27–28).

In the context of Iron Age IIB, Herr notes the presence of a possible oil press in the shrine at Dan and argues that it made oil available for the ritual practices of anointing with holy oil, use in sanctuary lamps, and use as libation offerings (Herr 1997c: 141). If Frick is correct in assigning the Taꜥanach press an Iron Age I date, and if the area was already functioning as a sacred space in that same period, then the oil could have been pressed for religious rituals. The Iron Age I town was destroyed about 1125 B.C.E., and a century intervened before the site was reestablished in Iron Age IIA, which provides some reason to doubt that the Iron Age IIA cultic space actually did operate in Iron Age I (Bloch-Smith and Nakhai 1999: 86)

The Taꜥanach cultic corner can be at best treated as a secondary feature of something else, a house or an industrial building of some type. A. Mazar (1992a: 499) accepts the identification of the feature as cultic in nature and includes it in his discussion of religious material, and G. R. H. Wright (1985: 1.250) sees it as an example of the developing domestic cult (see below). On the other hand, Isserlin (1998: 246) completely rejects the cultic reading of the find and argues that the space was for gatherings and that the incense stands were used to lend distinction to the meetings.

The evidence from Beth-shean, Megiddo, and other sites in the Beth-shean and Jezreel valleys shows that, after the initial disruption around 1200 B.C.E., this area witnessed another half-century of prosperity assured by the presence of Egyptian garrisons and administrators. Beth-shean and Megiddo have yielded finds of high status goods, and the architecture suggests that life continued to be quite comfortable for individuals who were living here. No doubt, a certain degree of Canaanite culture must have survived as well. The distinction between strata VIIA and VIB at Megiddo and Lower VI and Upper VI at Beth-shean is striking. The relative poverty of Megiddo VIB and Beth-shean Late VI (James) testify to the end of the last remnants of Egyptian Late Bronze Age culture in the Levant. The widespread evidence of destruction by fire at several sites that brought an end to both Megiddo VIB and Beth-shean Late VI (James) suggests that the region finally succumbed to the general demographic forces of change that had already ended the Late Bronze Age elsewhere in the Levant. On the other hand, the sanctuary built at Beth-shean following the retreat of the Egyptians in James stratum Lower V or Mazar stratum Upper VI is a strange complex, with its public presentation of Egyptian steles and royal sculpture in the new sanctuary configuration. Under the protection of the Egyptian presence, Canaanite culture had survived in this region, as is demonstrated by the continued finds of Canaanite pottery and other crafts during the first part of the twelfth century B.C.E. (McGovern and Fleming 1993), and the new complex may have had a nostalgic element to it. Gal has argued that the Canaanite character of the valley sites of the Jezreel and Beth-shean survived even this until the end of the eleventh century B.C.E. and the beginning of Iron Age IIA (Gal 1994: 46), which would agree with Mazar's reading of the Beth-shean evidence, because he posits that stratum Upper VI ended with the Israelite attack on the city. At the same time, there is some suggestion that the emerging Philistine culture may have been spreading and establishing itself outside the southern coastal plain. Whether the little sanctuary at Megiddo 2072 represents Philistine presence or merely cultural influence cannot be determined. What is perhaps most interesting is that sites in which Egyptian presence was strong enough to protect the sites from the ravages of the changes of the late thirteenth century and early twelfth century B.C.E., Beth-shean and Megiddo, show somewhat more rapid recovery in Iron Age I and more sophisticated sanctuary building projects than what is found at the sites that seem to have suffered completely from the disruptions, Hazor and Taʿanach, where the emerging Iron Age I setting is substantially poorer than what it replaced.

Proto-Israelite Shrines

The Hill Country
The Bull Site of Manasseh and Mount Ebal

The scanty remains found at two sites in the hill country have been identified as sacred architecture (Nakhai 1994: 23). On the summit of a hill in southern Samaria, the region associated with the Israelite tribe of Manasseh, a small bronze bull statuette was recovered. In the vicinity, a fieldstone wall enclosing an elliptical area of about 22 m in diameter was also found (fig. 33B). Within the defined space was a paved region with one roughly worked single boulder that has come to be designated a *maṣṣēbâ*. The site also yielded a piece of folded bronze, some animal bones, and the fragment of a possible incense burner (A. Mazar 1982: 27–42).

In northern Samaria, there is another site on a high, exposed spot, a ridge to the side of Mount Ebal, the high point in the region, at 1,000 m (Bloch-Smith and Nakhai 1999: 77). Two strata were distinguished. Stratum II, the earlier, had the remains of a building consisting of four rooms that was perhaps a house, and then slightly above it on the slope of the hill another structure of some type with large quantities of ash and bone. The ash and bone suggest a cultic space for animal sacrifice. This stratum has been dated to the second half of the thirteenth century B.C.E., before the large-scale disruption of the region but perhaps at the time of the destruction of Hazor (stratum XIII). While the stratum already shows pottery types associated with Iron Age I, the twelfth century B.C.E., in the region, the finds of Nineteenth-Dynasty Egyptian scarabs are reminders of the nearby Egyptian presence in the thirteenth and twelfth centuries B.C.E. There is no evidence of a destruction layer between strata II and I, but stratum I evinces a major change in the form of the cultic structure (Zertal 1994: 65). Now there was a fieldstone platform ca. 8 m × 10 m and standing 3 m high, with its four corners directed to the north–south compass points (fig. 33A). A double ramp, one leading to the top and the other to the surrounding wall, provided access to the top of the platform. Exterior walls about 1.5 m thick held in place a fill of carefully laid layers of stones, earth, and ash. The platform stood within an enclosure consisting of two paved courtyards that surrounded the platform and in which were several stone installations that contained pottery and metal artifacts. West of the platform complex was a special storage area for pithoi. The whole installation was built directly on the bedrock. The stratum I complex has been dated to the first half of the twelfth century B.C.E. No evidence for destruction of the site has been unearthed. It appears to have been abandoned (Zertal 1985: 26–43; 1986: 49–53; 1987).

The identification of the remains at these two sites as being cultic in nature has not been universally accepted (Coogan 1987: 1–8; Kempinski 1986: 44–49). Neither has produced substantial architecture. These would constitute open-air sanctuaries, if indeed they are sanctuaries. Kempinski has argued that the remains on Mount Ebal were those of a watchtower and a farm.

Shiloh

The situation at Shiloh is different from the other sites because nothing structural survives. Ancient Shiloh is identified with the modern village of Seilun, an identification dating back to the fourteenth century C.E. and restated in the early nineteenth century (Kaufman 1988: 48). There may have been a cult place at the site early in LBA I intended to serve a pastoral population, but it did not survive into the later stages of the Late Bronze Age (Bunimovitz 1994: 195). The site was located on the ancient road between Shechem and Jerusalem and, according to Josh 18:1 was where the "Tent of Meeting" or "Presence" was erected. It therefore served as a regional cult center for the proto-Israelite tribes that had become established in the hill country in Iron Age I. The actual description of the "Tent of Meeting" appears in Exodus and like all the biblical descriptions of early Iron Age architecture must be treated with caution because it is an anachronistic element in the later text. What it says is that the structure was of impermanent materials, woven stuff (goat hair for part, linen for part, Exod 26:1, 7). A general description is provided in Exod 26:1–36, and the arrangement of the space is set forth in Exod 40:18–33. It is generally assumed that what is described as the "Tent of Meeting" in Exodus is what was erected at Shiloh as reported in Joshua.

Finkelstein's excavations at Shiloh in the 1980s provided no information about the "Tent of Meeting." He was unable to determine the most likely spot on which the structure might have stood (Finkelstein 1988c: 40–41). A. Kaufman has suggested that the area needed to hold the complete complex of tent and associated courtyard can be determined from the textual evidence in Exodus 26. The Tabernacle proper was 30 cubits × 10 cubits, which he interprets as 12.84 m × 4.28 m based on a cubit of 42.8 cm, or six hand lengths. Exod 27:18 places the Tabernacle, the tent itself, within an enclosure defined by some type of impermanent wall, a space of 100 cubits × 50 cubits or 42.8 m × 21.4 m. In 1 Sam 1:24, the Tabernacle is referred to as *bayit*, which Kaufman argues indicates that some aspects of the impermanent structure had been made permanent. The only spot that Kaufman believes could have held the "Tent of Meeting" was a flat area just to the north of the tell itself, a natural rock-hewn terrace (Kaufman

1988: 49–52). There is nothing archaeologically to support or to disprove Kaufman's idea. If he is correct, then a large, semipermanent cultic structure stood at Shiloh in Iron Age I that incorporated a sacred precinct defined by a wall that enclosed a courtyard and a structure containing the holy of holies. It must have been the most impressive sacred structure in the hill country in Iron Age I.

There are two questions that remain unresolved regarding the settlement of the southern Levantine hill country in Iron Age I: (1) Who were the people who settled the region? (2) What was the pattern of settlement? The hill country was unevenly exploited in the Late Bronze Age. In the northern area of Samaria was a Canaanite state—a territorial unit rather than the Canaanite city-state type of the coast—probably incorporating a mixture of agricultural and pastoralism for ecological variation. The major center was Shechem, and the state is known from the Amarna letters (Bunimovitz 1994: 190). A second smaller but similar state probably existed to the south, with Jerusalem as its center. The actual exploitation of the southern region of Judah was substantially less than the limited settlement north in Samaria and much more dependent on pastoral activities than agriculture (Finkelstein 1994: 174). This pattern changed with the appearance of much denser populations in the north in Iron Age I and in the south by the beginning of Iron Age IIA. There were no new primary centers like Shechem or Jerusalem, but the village-level settlements in Iron Age I were larger than in the Late Bronze Age. These shifts suggest new demographic forces at work (Gal 1994: 36–46; Ofer 1994: 102; Zertal 1994: 54–59).

In many instances, any one of the three competing theories for the emergence of the Israelites can be made to fit with the evidence (Frankel 1994: 29). Since several of the Canaanite cities show evidence of being destroyed violently in the thirteenth century B.C.E., Albright proposed that this resulted from the destructive arrival of an outside force into the region. There is the Alt view that a new people infiltrated the region from the steppe and desert areas and began living in tiny villages, perhaps as early as the thirteenth century B.C.E., throughout the hill country, and they coexisted in the initial stages comfortably with their Canaanite neighbors, who were still living in the large cities on the plains and in the mountain valleys—a situation that began to change in the eleventh and tenth centuries B.C.E. Conversely, the same pottery evidence can support the Mendenhall and Gottwald theory of highland villages resulting from a Canaanite peasant revolt, in which the peasants abandoned the great cities for life in hillside villages and set about destroying the Canaanite cities.

Finkelstein has argued that none of these theories fits the actual archaeological evidence (1988: 295–314) and has offered a fourth explanation. He sees the Iron Age I village settlers as the pastoralists of the Late Bronze Age who began to settle down and farm in Iron Age I. These were not the new camel herders, the ancestors of the Bedouin, who were starting to move out into the deep desert now that they could use the camel; rather, they were sheepherders already living in the area during the Late Bronze Age. Finkelstein notes that the archaeological evidence of the urban plan of the first communities in the highlands in Iron Age I resembles the nomadic tent camps of the herders (Finkelstein 1988: 337–38). They were not, however, coming as refugees from the Late Bronze Age Canaanite cities.

Zertal (1994: 64–67) has pointed out that the find of the cultic area of Mount Ebal argues against the view proposed by Mendenhall and Gottwald. The major Canaanite city of Shechem was nearby, and its great Middle Bronze Age temple was still in operation. If those who used the open-air site on Mount Ebal had come from Shechem, there should be some "echo" of the cult practices that they knew, not something quite different. Finkelstein believes that the Mount Ebal stratum I cult space was the first in a series of cult spaces designed to suit the needs of nomads who were settling down. Late Bronze Age Transjordan and the Ghor have produced two structures recognized as sanctuaries that stood with no associated settlements: one at Deir ʿAlla and the other at the old Amman airport. These have been argued to have been shrines serving the needs of nomadic herders living in the area (Finkelstein 1988: 343). The shrine at Mount Ebal could have operated in a similar manner, accommodating a number of people on a temporary basis. When the sanctuary ceased to function in the middle of the twelfth century b.c.e., its role was transferred to Shiloh, which operated until the mid-eleventh century b.c.e., when Gilgal became the cult focus. Finally, in the tenth century, Jerusalem assumed the role along with a new position as the capital of a kingdom (Finkelstein 1988: 327).

While Zertal's interpretation of the Mount Ebal's stratum I cult platform can support Finkelstein's theory, in fact Zertal sees a quite different historical reality. The platform complex at Mount Ebal, stratum I, seems to recall, in a distant manner, Mesopotamian religious architecture. The high platform that was mounted by means of ramps could be recalling ziggurat forms—a connection that Albright made early in the twentieth century (Albright 1920). This sort of connection fits more comfortably with the Alt theory that the proto-Israelites were coming from the east out of the Transjordan area—perhaps one of the nomadic groups that had existed in the region during the Late Bronze Age, who frequented shrines like that at Deir ʿAlla in the Ghor, but who may also have traced their origins back to upper Mesopotamia. They were forced into the Transjordan region in the late fourteenth and early thirteenth centuries by the actions of the Assyrian king Adad-Nirari I, who was pushing into northern Syria (Lemaire 1978 and 1984). Gal has argued that the proto-Israelite peoples who settled in the Lower and Upper Galilee included some who had abandoned the Canaanite towns of the Jezreel Valley in the late eleventh century b.c.e. However, the hill settlements for others show no association with the Canaanite cities of the northern valleys, so these people were probably not related to the Canaanite people whose cities they now destroyed. On the other hand, Kochavi has proposed that some of the highland villages in the mountainous Upper Galilee were actually settled out of Tyre, making them Phoenician in Iron Age I (Frankel 1994: 32 n. 58).

What caused the demographic shift—whether it was indeed a move from pastoralism to village life, a conquering force, a slow infiltration of neighboring peoples, or a peasant revolt followed by an abandonment of the cities—has yet to be satisfactorily answered. Both Bunimovitz (1994) and Finkelstein (1994) have argued, using a Braudelian approach, for certain cyclical patterns in the settlement and exploitation of the various ecological niches in the southern Levant. The pattern of survival that has emerged for the hill region, which is a more marginal land than the Shephelah, is one of periods with dense settlement and exploitation followed by periods of depopulation. The Middle Bronze Age had witnessed major population pressure placed on the hill country. The Late Bronze Age saw the collapse of this, and the Iron Age was to see a return to the heavy use of the region. This explanation favors the idea that the settlers themselves probably remained demographically the same, and what changed was the manner in which they used the landscape. The notion has merit, but one must remember that Iron Age I was preceded by a general systems collapse throughout much of the Levant, and one of the results or causes of the collapse was the large-scale movement of peoples around the area. This happened at a time when the introduction of the domesticated camel probably led to one whole group adapting an entirely new lifestyle. Moreover, the work of the ʿAmuq Valley survey group (Yener et al. 2000) has clearly shown that there was something changing in the climatic regime during this period. These points do not undermine Bunimovitz's and Finkelstein's arguments for large-scale patterns of use for the hill country, but they may suggest that there were quite specific short-term events that need to be considered as well.

While it is not possible to explain definitively why the changes happened, the historical sequence can be reconstructed from the archaeological surveys that have been done in the hill country over the last 15 years. Although not unpopulated, the hill country in the Late Bronze Age was certainly not heavily populated by Canaanites, a circumstance that left an opening for movement by other people. The thirteenth and twelfth centuries B.C.E. saw increasing settlement in the northern hill country, in the region that was technically under the control of Shechem. During this same period, the Beth-shean and Jezreel valleys witnessed some sort of problem, but the evidence shows that they remained Canaanite under Egyptian rule and prospered for several more decades into the twelfth century.

Hazor was the exception because it was destroyed sometime in the thirteenth century B.C.E. Yadin's view that this was one of the early conquests by the Israelites is questioned by those who do not agree with the Albright scenario of a conquering Israelite arrival. The alternative view is that the city succumbed to a joint Egyptian and Canaanite campaign, which seems reasonable in light of the ongoing strength of these two groups in the Beth-shean and Jezreel valleys. This first period of highland settlement was accompanied by the establishment of a cult center at Mount Ebal, one that recalled the older Late Bronze Age tradition of isolated cult sites in the Transjordan region and the Ghor. The site was already in use in the thirteenth century B.C.E., but the real sanctuary did not take shape until the twelfth century B.C.E. It served the needs of a people who had no affiliation with the temple and cult practices of nearby Shechem.

By the eleventh century B.C.E., the settlements had spread south into Judah and into the fringe of the Negev. At the same time, changes were happening in the Negev itself. The domestication of the camel, the movement of the incense trade along the route from the Wadi Arabah to Gaza, and the possible resurgence of mining activity at Timna all served to encourage the pastoral nomads of this steppe desert region to establish a sedentary lifestyle in the Negev highlands during the course of the eleventh century B.C.E. (Finkelstein 1988a: 245–46). The two groups, those coming south through the hill country and those moving into the Negev highlands from the desert plains were to come into confrontation in the tenth century B.C.E. The movement of proto-Israelites toward the southern hill country was followed by a change in the locus of cult activity from Mount Ebal to the site of Shiloh. In this scenario, the people involved in settling the hill country in Iron Age I seem to be a united group, at least in terms of religion, because there is no evidence for alternative cult places in the high country. The possible cultic room at Taʿanach may indicate that there was something else at play that is not yet clear from the archaeological record. Since this site really straddles the hill country and the Jezreel Valley, it is as likely to have been Canaanite as proto-Israelite.

Iron Age IIA Sites: Tenth Century B.C.E.

Stratigraphic correspondences: Tel Dan IVA = Megiddo VA–IVB = Lachish V = Makmish = Tell el-Mazar.

By 1000 B.C.E., the demographic makeup of the new Levant was an established fact. The movement of peoples that marked Iron Age I had ceased, and the states that would dominate the next 300 years of history in the Levant were beginning to take shape. In the north, the remnants of the Hittite Empire that had already coalesced into independent kingdoms in Iron Age I divided the Syrian region with the newly established Aramean states. The biblical and slightly later epigraphic records testify to the existence of kingdoms with significant force in Iron Age IIA. Other than the expansion of the temple at ʿAin Dara and the new relief program for the interior of the temple in the Aleppo Citadel, the archaeological finds do not yet manifest any other temples for this period.

The situation is much the same for the Phoenician region. During Iron Age IIA, direct control by Phoenician cities extended south as far as Haifa Bay and possibly

Dor. Phoenician influence in the form of good ashlar masonry, possibly the work of Phoenician builders, can be seen along the south coast at Dor (Markoe 2000: 81–82) and Tel Mevorakh. This is the time when Tyre replaced Sidon as the dominant Phoenician city. The biblical stories of Hiram I, king of Tyre, and his relationship with David and Solomon suggest the wide-ranging nature of Phoenician influence outside its geographical area, and this is echoed in the later descriptions of Josephus. The limited archaeological findings for Iron Age IIA in the Phoenician heartland make it impossible to confirm the two ancient historical sources. If we can trust the Bible's general information for the story of the emergence of the United Monarchy of Israel, then it was during Iron Age IIA that the hill country of the southern Levant along with parts of the coastal plain and the northern Negev were brought together as a single kingdom. The Bible ascribes this forced *synoikismos* to David, and it describes the kingdom as the dominant territorial and political power in the Levant for Iron Age IIA. However, its most significant monument, the temple built by Solomon in Jerusalem, does not survive. On the other hand, the first version of the sanctuary at Dan took shape during this period. While their territorial range was limited by the expansion of Israel, and some places including Tell Qasile passed into Israelite hegemony, the Philistines still controlled much of the southern coastal region. However, neither new temples nor still-functioning temples from Iron Age I have been found in excavations.

Shrines of the United Monarchy

> *Jezreel Valley*
> Megiddo
> The destruction of Megiddo stratum VIA by fire occurred at the end of Iron Age I. Megiddo VA in Iron Age IIA had been taken over as an Israelite center. In the early twentieth-century excavations of Megiddo in stratum IV (now read as VA/IVB), Gottlieb Schumacher dug Building 338 located at the eastern edge of the tell (fig. 34) and at the highest point in Megiddo, not far from the old MBA–LBA Temple 2048. He was struck by the objects that he found, which he thought were of a cultic nature, including 2 monolithic pillars and part of a 3rd. Seven proto-Ionic capitals had been found in a neighboring structure, and one of these must have come from a freestanding column, because it was decorated on both sides. He therefore identified the building as a temple with *maṣṣēbôt* and fortifications on the east side. He reconstructed a temple of two stories. In its first version, the temple had two main units, a northern unit which had two groups of square cells that flanked two longer units; and a southern grouping of two long rooms flush with a broad room (room 340), from which Schumacher thought most of the finds had come. He therefore identified room 340 as the real temple within the ensemble (Kempinski 1989: 164–66).

In his reassessment of Schumacher's interpretation and of the actual remains from Building 338 and room 340, Kempinski challenged Schumacher's reading (Kempinski 1989: 186–89). He argued that Building 338 was really a palace that contained a small chapel, room 340. Since Schumacher published his views, there has been much debate about the nature of the building and room 340. C. S. Fisher (1929) argued for a temple dedicated to Astarte because of an incense burner with a female figure attached, but he had confused objects in different strata—which throws into question his interpretation.

May (1939) correctly identified all of the objects in stratum IV (now stratum VA). The items of special interest were three horned incense altars and the house-shaped incense burner with a female figure attached that had attracted Fisher's attention. Kempinski argued that religious practice at Megiddo changed dramatically from the Late Bronze Age to the early Iron Age. In the early Iron Age, cultic structures were reduced to a room in otherwise domestic settings. What emerged was a household religion rather than a great state religion. This new religion had no need for massive temples, and he cited the story of Micah and his cult room (Judg 17:1–13) as the paradigm for the new status. Room 340 could have served such a purpose for the palace, Building 338. G. R. H. Wright (1985: 1.250) agreed with Kempinski that the structure might best be called a house shrine and offered a coherent description of the remains, identifying the cult element as a niche in the southwest corner of a courtyard that served as the entrance to the larger building. He also noted that similar cult paraphernalia had been found elsewhere in the residential quarters of Megiddo, supporting the notion of domestic shrines, and he saw a possible parallel in the cultic corner at Taʿanach (see above).

Ussishkin (1989: 149–72) has also reinvestigated Building 338 and room 340. He disagrees with Kempinski and Wright and supports Schumacher's original interpretation. The building should be understood to be a temple of the Israelite period.[7] He has argued that the *maṣṣēbôt* temple was built atop room 340. The room has a longitudinal axis and was oriented to the north. The shrine had two large steles that were secured to bases of field stones. There was an additional stone element consisting of two worked stones laid one over the other and placed on a monolith that Schumacher had read to be an idol. There may have been a small offering table, and there were benches, on which Schumacher had found complete vessels. On the floor was a layer of ash, mixed into which were animal bones. Ussishkin sees a relationship between the cultic paraphernalia found in room 340 and in a second building identified as a sanctuary (Building 2081; see below). Both spaces contained limestone horned altars, round limestone tables and stands, mortars with pestles, and small juglets (Nakhai 1994: 24).

The shrine, as Ussishkin reconstructed it, opened onto a courtyard. The entrance has not been found. In the courtyard, built up against the shrine wall was a base of ashlar blocks. In the center of the courtyard, opposite the entrance to the shrine was a large, round depression. The courtyard was paved with lime plaster, and the shrine

---

7. Wright hedged his bets and acknowledged that the entire structure could have been a temple with a cult focus in the courtyard.

stood at a higher level than the courtyard that fronted it. A monumental staircase led from the courtyard into the shrine through the north wall.

The actual building technique used for Building 338 has been difficult to determine. Schumacher conjectured that the superstructure was of ashlar masonry. Fisher suggested mud brick with wood columns. A fragment of burned wood, identified as Lebanese cedar, was found in the courtyard. Ussishkin maintained that the cache of proto-ionic capitals from the neighboring structure actually belong to Building 338.

When the shrine ceased to function, it was burned and then deliberately and reverentially filled. Since the walls survive to a height of 2.5 m at points, Ussishkin has argued that it was filled from the top. Other surrounding units were perhaps similarly entombed, and the whole area was left untouched until the Ottoman period. The later Israelite fortress closed off this now-defunct region behind its curtain wall.

Ussishkin's reinterpretation of Schumacher's findings regarding Building 338 has been strongly criticized by Stern (1990c: 102–7). Stern has pointed out several potential flaws in the argument, stressing that Ussishkin brought together several groups of finds from different areas in Building 338 in order to support his claim for the shrine in room 340. Stern maintains that *maṣṣēbôt* were not a common feature in small cult sites in the tenth century B.C.E. The two stone pillars here must have had structural roles rather than iconographic functions. The supposed idol was nothing more than a building stone. When found in context, proto-iconic capitals mark secular and not sacred buildings. Stern's reading returns room 340 to the secular realm, depriving it of any cultic significance, and Building 338 becomes, perhaps, just a palace (Stern 1990a: 12–30).

Megiddo had another modest domestic shrine during Iron Age IIA. In stratum VA (fig. 115), a large four-room house type was found to which had been appended side rooms and a courtyard (Building 2081; Isserlin 1998: 246). It had been furnished with two horned altars, two limestone stands, and a pottery stand, as well as a jug, a Cypro-Phoenician bowl, a chalice, and a three-legged stone bowl. There was also a round stand with fenestrated base and a bowl containing sheep/goat knuckles (astragali). The pottery and the bowl of astragali recall similar finds in the cultic corner in stratum IIB at Taʿanach. The two horned altars were found in a formal arrangement. Two projecting walls in the courtyard defined a niche into which had been placed the two altars, one larger than the other. Accompanying them were two incense burners, one of stone and one of ceramic. The door leading into the house from the courtyard was framed by two stone pillars, possibly *maṣṣēbôt,* and a flat stone in front of the door has been interpreted by some as an offering table.

High versus Low Chronology Debate

These possible sanctuaries at Megiddo have both commonly been dated to the tenth century, Iron Age IIA, and associated in some way with the development of the site as one of Solomon's district capitals (Nakhai 1994: 24). The Solomonic date for the major Iron Age IIA constructions at Megiddo has recently been challenged, with one school of thought favoring a construction date post-Solomon, either late tenth or early ninth century, after the foundation of the Northern Kingdom of Israel (Silberman et al. 1999: 38).

Most scholars of southern Levantine archaeology and history favor associating the tenth century B.C.E. with the rise of the Kingdom of Israel under the United Monarchy of David and Solomon as reported in the Bible. Of particular importance is the reference to Solomon's building activities in the cities of Megiddo, Hazor, and Gezer. Archaeological work at these sites has produced evidence of large-scale building projects that may have been the result of Solomon's activities and thus may provide an idea of the more important constructions in the capital of Jerusalem that remain unknown in terms of actual archaeological work. Stratum VA–IVB at Megiddo contains a four-chamber gate, a tripartite colonnaded structure, and a palace structure of ashlar masonry. These all seem appropriate to the notion that the city served as one of Solomon's royal cities (1 Kgs 9:15–19). This was first argued by the University of Chicago excavators in the 1920s (Guy 1931: 44–48). At Hazor, a four-chambered gate was unearthed in stratum X, and a similar gate was found in Gezer stratum VIII. The similarity in the gate structures can argue for a master designer and a political setting in which such an individual would be active in several places. This would have occurred during a period of political order and security, when an administrative force was pushing for the architectural unity of public monuments such as gates. A time of this sort was that of Solomon, at least based on the biblical account. There is no need to manipulate the stratigraphic record. At Megiddo, stratum VIIA was clearly the Late Bronze Age Egyptian city of the late twelfth century that ended sometime around 1135 B.C.E. Stratum VIB followed; then VIA, the last stratum to have clearly defined Canaanite motifs; and finally VB, a poor stratum with no monumental finds and no residual Canaanite traces. VA–IVB marks a renaissance for the city, with its impressive building program that was appropriate to the city of Solomon.

There are two problems with associating the biblical account with the excavated findings. First, Yadin showed that the tripartite columned hall belonged later, to IVA. not IVB, and more-recent excavations also assign the four-chambered gate to IVA (Ussishkin 1980), which now results in the gate's being compared with similar late gates at Lachish and Tel Ira. This shift may require a redating of the gates at Hazor and Gezer, placing all these monumental constructions after the supposed stratum of the Solomonic city.

The second problem concerns pottery. The VIA stratum has provided no Philistine bichrome wares. Megiddo was not situated in the Philistine area, and the bichrome pottery is not very common in the territory surrounding the site. However, the city was a major Egyptian administrative center with a resident Canaanite population and should have drawn some of this prevalent ware to it if it was still functioning in the eleventh century, when bichrome was widespread. Moreover, VIA is the last stratum that evidences Canaanite material. Strata VB and VA–IVB are devoid of Canaanite material.

Finkelstein (1999: 38–39) has used these discrepancies in the archaeological record to argue for a shift in the chronology. He has also provided a rationale for redating the Philistine monochrome and bichrome. In his scheme, Philistine monochrome began to be produced in the eleventh and early tenth centuries B.C.E., and bichrome replaced monochrome in the mid-tenth century B.C.E. The absence of the bichrome in Megiddo VIA means that it must postdate the bichrome, and Finkelstein has offered a new date in the late tenth century B.C.E. Since the lack of recognizable Canaanite material separates VIA from VB, Finkelstein proposes a substantial time lapse to rid the city of its residual Canaanite presence. VB was an insubstantial settlement, but VA–IVB was significant, so Finkelstein suggests an early ninth-century date. He notes that the pottery found in VA–IVB is similar to pottery found in the nearby site of Jezreel from a compound dated to the ninth century B.C.E. and the Omride Dynasty of the Northern Kingdom of Israel. This further supports his contention of a ninth-century rather than a tenth-century B.C.E. date for VA–IVB stratum at Megiddo.

Finkelstein's reinterpretation advances the monumental cities of Megiddo, Hazor, and Gezer to a century after their normally accepted dates, into Iron Age IIB instead of Iron Age IIA. This redating has not been universally accepted (Master 2001; Rainey 2001).[8] If the biblical account is still linked to stratum VA–IVB, then David and Solomon would date to the ninth, not the tenth century. If the stratum and the account are uncoupled, then the tenth-century material is poor and in no way supports the biblical descriptions of Solomon's reign. Master has argued against Finkelstein's low chronology, suggesting that there are other reasons to explain the absence of Philistine ware in the Egyptian town of stratum VIA at Megiddo. Moreover, he argues that the connection between the pottery finds of Megiddo VA–IVB and nearby Taʿanach IIB, which dates to the tenth century B.C.E., is stronger than the ceramic connections that Finkelstein tries to make with the later material from Jezreel (Master 2001: 121 nn. 17, 20).

Shephelah

Lachish

Lachish in the south had been important in the Late Bronze Age but was abandoned at the end of the Late Bronze Age. Stratum V represents a new establishment at the site and not a continuity of habitation into Iron Age IIA (Herr 1997c: 128). The settlement was an unfortified village. Finds of an altar stone, four incense stands, and pottery chalices in a space labeled Room 49 have been used to designate the area as a

---

8. See Halpern's (2001) appendix for a thoughtful review of the arguments for and against the low chronology proposed by Finkelstein.

small cult space (Isserlin 1998: 242–43; Nakhai 1994: 24). Room 49 (fig. 35) is a modest unit built against the circumference wall, but it represents the finest construction at the site during its period. It was a bench-lined, walled space enclosing a pebble-paved area. The benches were of stone plastered with clay.

The finds from within the space included domestic pottery, four incense burners, a chalice stand, a juglet, and a lamp (both the juglet and the lamp had probably stood on the stand), and a limestone, four-horned altar. Isserlin thinks that there was a *maṣṣēbâ* in the form of a stone pillar and perhaps an *asherah* (an olive tree). Nakhai sees similarities among the finds from Lachish and those from Megiddo Building 2081 and the poorly preserved and questionable cult site from Taʿanach. While the Taʿanach site may have been in existence in Iron Age I, the finds are from the Iron Age IIA context, making the comparison with Lachish and Megiddo reasonable.

Makmish (Machmish)

The small site of Makmish on the Sharon Plain near Herzliyya has revealed an extramural open-air structure that some have identified as a sanctuary. It consists of an enclosure, ca. 10 m × 10 m, defined by a mud-brick wall set on rough stone foundations inside of which stood an installation, maybe an altar, along with several flat-lying stones. These have been interpreted as spots for the preparation or eating of sacred meals (Nakhai 1994: 25) because of the finds of pottery and bones. The site has been dated to the tenth century (Isserlin 1998: 244).

The Ghor

Tell el-Mazar

Tell el-Mazar is located on the east side of the Jordan River, north of Deir ʿAlla. Mound A at the site has yielded remains of three contiguous chambers with a courtyard on the south side. Stone benches lined two walls of the eastern-most chamber, in which was also found a bell-shaped pit, a stone basin embedded in the floor, a fenestrated ceramic stand, 2 chalices, and fragments of pottery vessels datable to the tenth century B.C.E. The courtyard contained remains of several ovens (Nakhai 1994: 25). Yassine has treated this as an extramural open-court sanctuary (Yassine 1984: 108–18).

Pella

The site of Pella is situated 5 km east of the Jordan River on the edge of the Ghor and opposite the valley of Esdraelon. The site has evidence of continuous occupation beginning in 8000 B.C.E. In approximately 900 B.C.E., a small temple (fig. 24A) was built atop the ruins of a Late Bronze Age temple which in turn stood on the earlier remains of a large Middle Bronze Age temple, and still-earlier structures have been detected beneath the Middle Bronze Age structure (Bourke 2007). The Middle Bronze Age temple (fig. 24B) was by far the largest iteration, at 32 m × 24 m. The Late Bronze Age temple was about half the size, and the IA2 temple one-third the size (Churcher 2003). The successive temples seem to have been destroyed by earthquakes (Potter 2001).

The Iron Age temple rests on the back wall of the Middle Bronze Age building. It was a rectangular building aligned northeast to southwest with the entrance's southeast corner. To the east was a courtyard area. The temple consisted of a large cult chamber entered directly on the longitudinal side, and it remained unchanged for its century of operation. A storeroom for foodstuffs roughly one-third the size of the cult chamber occupied the northeast portion of the building (Bourke 2005:112). The surviving remains of the northern wall show a rough stone socle on which mid-brick walls would have stood. In the area of the temple's courtyard, a ceramic box with five clay bovine heads attached to the rim was found (Bourke 2005: 114). From within the temple itself came fragments of several ceramic jars, platters, and dipper juglets. In addition, there were basalt bowls, ladles, and stands, including several fenestrated conical stands. The southern room of the temple was probably the holy of holies, where the offerings and cult furniture were kept (Bourke 2005: 113).

Though the Iron Age temple retained the placement of the earlier Middle Bronze and Late Bronze Age temples, its orientation was different. The earlier structures were also rectangular, with entrances on the southeast side that defined the axial movement through the temples. The Iron Age temple was reoriented and was entered, not on the longitudinal axis, but from a corner. This suggests that, while the topographical setting remained hallowed through the Middle Bronze, Late Bronze, and Iron Age II periods, the form of the earlier sanctuary did not retain its significance. This change in orientation may also reflect a major shift in architectural roles. Although the Middle Bronze and Late Bronze Age temples seem to have stood by themselves, the Iron Age II temple was probably part of a larger multiroom complex, which was also built of mud brick placed on stone socles. The complex is estimated to have been some 25 m × 30 m, constructed on a grid plan, and to have gone through two phases that encompassed about two centuries (1000–800 b.c.e.). The finds within the rooms were storage vessels and the fragment of one painted vessel with a warrior figure. A sherd with a running spiral motif was identified by the excavator as possibly of Philistine origin (Bourke 2007).

Iron Age IIA was dominated by two major political forces: the emerging Phoenician federation dominated by Tyre and its kings, and the Kingdom of Israel that took shape as a territorial power under the United Monarchy. Unfortunately, the evidence for both of these political powers is derived primarily from the biblical account, and the reliability of the text is highly debated (see chap. 1). Most scholars argue that Phoenician authority stretched into the Upper Galilee and down the coast to the Bay of Haifa and perhaps the site of Dor. The extent of Israelite power is more debated, but most agree that the Ghor and parts of the Tranjordanian highlands were under some type of Israelite suzerainty.

However, the Pella temple may well indicate that there was continued Canaanite cultural strength in the Ghor well into Iron Age II, because of the hallowedness of the specific location and because of the evidence that the earlier Late Bronze Age temple appears to have been patched and to have continued to function, albeit in a dilapidated state, until the new temple was built around 900 B.C.E. On the other hand, the dramatic shift in orientation may well indicate a major cultural shift, if not demographic change. The new design with its affiliated complex, which might be a palace, also suggests that some major alteration occurred, at least within the religious sphere of the site.

Archaeology has not been able to substantiate the biblical description of the rise of the Israelite Kingdom in a way that has put the controversies to rest. What the archaeological findings do seem to show is some degree of unity in monumental building, at least at the sites of Megiddo, Hazor, and Gezer. However, it is not agreed that these constructions really belong to the tenth century or to the reign of Solomon.

If one accepts the validity of the tenth-century reigns of Hiram I of Tyre, David, and Solomon and that the tenth century B.C.E. is indeed Iron Age IIA, then the archaeological finds provide little evidence for much in the way of development in sanctuary designs. It is possible that the description of Solomon's temple in Jerusalem indicates the level of architectural sophistication that could be found in the capital of the United Monarchy. Since Hiram I supplied some of the help for the construction of the Jerusalem temple, it is probably safe to assume that his capital must have been similarly embellished, but the lack of good archaeological-architectural finds for this period from either place prevents any serious checking of the literary accounts with the reality of buildings. The sacred architecture that has been unearthed is quite unimposing. On the one hand, the presence of cultic spaces at Lachish, Makmish, and Tell el-Mazar, all sites probably under Israelite control, indicates that there was still room for local shrines to function, and this seems especially true at Megiddo, which is normally assumed to have been under Israelite administration by Iron Age IIA. On the other hand, the unpretentious nature of these shrines, especially in comparison with the Late Bronze Age sanctuaries that had been in operation at Megiddo and Lachish suggests that there was either little interest in building on a large scale or that something was hindering this type of building. Considering that the Philistines on the southern coastal plain during Iron Age I had developed quite substantial religious architecture over the course of 200 years at Tell Qasile and Ekron, it seems hard to accept that the residents at Megiddo, Lachish, or Makmish lacked the same desire or ability.

Iron Age IIB Sites: Ninth–Late Eighth Centuries B.C.E.

Stratigraphic correspondences: Beth-shean upper V–IV = Tel Dan IVB–II = Samaria I–VI = Jerusalem 13–12 = Lachish IV–III = Tell Arad XI–VIII = Ashdod VIII = Deir ʿAlla IX–VI (Balaam inscription).

The late tenth century B.C.E. saw the full flourishing of the small Neo-Hittite and Aramean states of Syria. The local dynasts built lavishly, erecting palaces and temples, and using relief sculpture as a vehicle for presenting notions of dynastic succession in a visual way. At the same time, the Phoenician cities, probably dominated if not ruled by the kings of Tyre, were fully engaged in expanding their trade network to the far west. During Iron Age IIB, Phoenician cities established daughter settlements on the coasts of North Africa and Iberia, and the United Monarchy of Israel collapsed and split into two smaller kingdoms: Israel in the north and Judah in the south. Though the east side of the Jordan may have already begun to be home to sedentary people during Iron Age IIA, it is during Iron Age IIB that major settlements appear in the archaeological record of Ammon and Moab. Edom remained largely a region of nomads. However, the Negev witnessed significant building at the fortresses of Tell Arad and the isolated fortified caravansaray at Teman (Kuntillet ʿAjrud).

Neo-Hittite and Aramean Temples

North Syria

As has already been stated, North Syria probably never witnessed a total disruption of settled life. The old Hittite centers certainly declined substantially but never completely. Aleppo may have continued with no major disruption. ʿAin Dara offers some inkling within a couple of centuries of the renewed vigor to be found in the aftermath of the collapse of the Late Bronze Age. By Iron Age IIA, the temple at ʿAin Dara had established a model of massive, compartmented architectural design with its core of sanctuary preceded by antechambers and surrounded by an ambulatory—all further embellished with sculpture. The revival continued, and by Iron Age IIB several Neo-Hittite and Aramean kingdoms were vying for control of areas. Local dynasts lavished attention on their major cities, building palace compounds with temples and erecting massive displays of relief sculpture that served visually to promote concepts of divinity and royal succession. The old vice-regal Hittite capital of Carchemish was a revived city—one that had already flourished under the Hittites and emerged as the capital of a new Neo-Hittite kingdom. Guzana was the capital of a newly developed Aramean kingdom that stood between expanding Assyria and the Neo-Hittite kingdoms farther west. Tell Taʿyinat, whose ancient name is unknown, took control of the ʿAmuq Plain from Alalakh and brought that region under Neo-Hittite control.

Carchemish

Carchemish is situated by the side of the Euphrates River. It has a long history and had already served the Hittites as the court for the cadet branch of the ruling family in the Late Bronze Age. The structure identified as the early Iron Age Temple of the Storm God is almost a square, 11.70 m × 13 m (fig. 36). It contained a single room 8 m × 7.10 m, aligned northeast to southwest, with the entrance on the southwest. The rear wall was 4 m thick, about twice the thickness of the other three walls. The slight longitudinal axis is enhanced by the building's single entrance (1.70 m wide). The entrance consisted of a shallow porch fronted by two *antae* that were the thickened ends of the side walls. The doorway was framed by two niches that Woolley maintained were designed to hold nonfunctional columns (Woolley 1952: 170). Woolley suggested that the temple had two stories, and Busink (Busink 1970: pl. 151) and Orthmann (Orthmann 1985: 414–15) restored the temple as having a tower-like format (fig. 37). Woolley and Kohlmeyer have argued that the Middle Bronze Age temples at Alalakh and Aleppo were square tower forms (Kohlmeyer 2009: 194), and Yon recently has posited tower forms for the two acropolis temples at Ugarit in the last phase of the Late Bronze Age.

The Carchemish temple was constructed of rubble stone foundations with a mud-brick superstructure. Much of the temple was revetted, because remains of limestone orthostats on both the interior and exterior were recovered. Fragments of bricks covered with a blue background on which were raised rosettes with white petals and yellow centers probably came from a decorated façade (Woolley 1952: 169). The interior floor was paved with limestone slabs. Along the interior of the back wall was a bench, 0.30 m wide. Situated on the longitudinal axis and therefore on the sightline from the door stood a basalt block 1 m × 1 m with its base below the level of the floor. It was placed 2 m from the back wall. Woolley found a single column base on the interior floor but not in its original position. Since he knew of no parallel for a single column base in an interior position and because the plan of the temple lacked only the paired columns in the entrance to be regarded as a true *bīt ḫilani* type, he suggested that the single column base was what survived of a pair that had once been elements in the entrance of the temple (Woolley 1952: 170).

The temple did not stand alone. It was an element of a larger complex that formed a quadrilateral precinct roughly 40 m × 35 m × 31 m × 31 m. The precinct wall was covered on the east and south exterior faces with carved reliefs that formed part of the sculptural program known as the "Long Wall." Within this space, the actual temple was placed in the northwest quadrant flush with the west wall and extending north, beyond the north wall of the precinct. In front of the temple was a courtyard of about the same dimensions as the temple with a cobbled floor. The porch area of the temple was paved in flat paving stones. At its southeast corner was a platform 4 m × 3 m placed against the inside of the south wall. To the east of this courtyard was a second court, the floor of which was 0.30 m lower. The cobbles selected for this courtyard floor were variegated pebbles from the Euphrates laid atop a gravel base. The east side of this court held a structure with three interior rooms. The entrance into the temple compound was through this court from the south.

Flanking the west side of the entrance and occupying a portion of the south side of the outer courtyard was a small room. The floor of this first court was higher by about 1 m from the level of the street outside. The precinct walls on the south and east side not only served to support the relief sculpture of the Long Wall but also operated as retaining walls for the courtyard, which was in effect a raised platform itself.

Woolley argued that this was the original distribution for the temple compound. At some point, the original courtyard space was extended beyond the initial perimeter wall, and a one-room structure was appended to the exterior east wall of the temple. Its north wall was shared with an even-more-northerly room, which was approached via a cobbled path that ran from the first courtyard northward. This path was flanked on its west by the new structure abutting the temple's wall and by a second structure added to the interior face of the east wall of the precinct. The new design created a much more congested albeit architecturally more ambitious complex (Woolley 1952: 167–71).

The small finds within the compound and the temple were limited, as was the case with all the excavations on the site (Winter 1983: 183). In the corner formed by the meeting of the original north precinct wall and the exterior east wall of the temple, an inscribed basalt stele with a hieroglyphic text that includes a reference to the "Great King" was unearthed (Woolley 1952: 167; Hawkins 1972). The inner courtyard yielded broken bones of small animals and birds as well as fragments of ivory inlay panels. Elsewhere in the small room on the south side of the outer court, part of a basalt relief of a winged griffin was found that resembles figures in the Long Wall program.

In the inner court, about 6.50 m from the temple entrance and beside a raised base of cut stone on which it may originally have stood was a fragmentary basalt group of 2 bulls (2.40 m long × 1.10 m high). Fragments of the hind quarter of the left side bull were recovered throughout much of the courtyard. Woolley argued that the bulls were part of a large installation that had stood on the base and had been destroyed deliberately. The bulls had been carved from a single block of basalt, and on the upper surface was a depression surrounded by a raised border. Woolley concluded that the smooth wear pattern on the raised edge of the depression was the result of friction and could have served to secure a metal basin. He noted that the bulls were unfinished in the back, a practice consistent with sculpture set against a wall but inappropriate for statues placed in the middle of a courtyard. He argued that the use of the grouping to support a base may have been a reuse. The original intent may have been for the unit to support a statue placed against a wall (Woolley 1952: 168–69). Bull imagery was found nearby in other sectors of the lower palace region.

Although the temple compound was probably a wing of the lower palace complex, neither the compound nor the temple proper had direct communication with the palace. The compound stood to the south and west of the palace and opened to the southwest, away from the entrance to the palace, onto a courtyard that was itself about the size of the temple. Walls on the west and south sides of the courtyard served to define and isolate it from the nearby area and created a temple precinct. The temple courtyard continued into another courtyard to the east, around the perimeter of which stood several more buildings. How these relate to the courtyard or to the temple is not at all clear, but they do serve to prevent any direct movement between the temple and the structure to the northeast, identified as the palace.

The basalt door jambs for the Temple of the Storm God carry hieroglyphic inscriptions authored by King Katuwas (Hawkins 1972). Woolley did not accept Katuwas as the individual responsible for the temple. He thought that the compound and temple had gone through at least two rebuildings and that in the earliest version it was a Late Bronze Age complex that Katuwas may have revamped, a conjecture that is reflected in the changes to the courtyards. However, since Woolley's publications, his dating, based on stylistic analyses of the reliefs, has been seriously challenged (Mallowan 1972: 63). Scholars do not accept the idea that the sculpture and the structures for the region of the lower palace belong in any form to the Late Bronze Age (P. J. James 1987b). The date for the temple and associated compound hinges on the date assigned to the Long Wall sculpture.[9] The compound is embedded within the sculptural program, bounded on one side by the processing figures, one of which is the Storm God himself, Tarhundas (Hawkins 1972: 95). Based on the epigraphic evidence of the inscriptions incorporated in the Long Wall, Hawkins argued that the Long Wall must have been erected by Suhis II, Katuwas's father. Suhis' wife, Watis, is represented as seated on the relief. Accepting Hawkins's reading, Mallowan proposed a date of ca. 890 B.C.E. for Suhis II (30 years later than the date proposed by Woolley). If Katuwas was responsible for the building of the Temple of the Storm God or even for its revamping, the construction must have happened in ca. 880 B.C.E.

Guzana (Tell Halaf)

Guzana dominated the Jezireh. Iron Age IIB Guzana was, like Carchemish, the seat of a local dynast. But unlike Carchemish, it had no Late Bronze Age settlement. It was a new foundation in the early Iron Age, probably beginning to assume importance in the tenth century B.C.E. The structure identified as a temple stood on a massive terrace that was placed on a lower terrace, and all of this stood in the citadel at Guzana (fig. 38). The temple consisted of two shallow but long rooms placed parallel to one another on their long sides. The front room was ca. 33 m × 5 m. The room behind was ca. 38 m × 7 m. The two main chambers were surrounded by long, narrow secondary rooms on the two short sides and the back side. These rooms could be entered from the main chambers. The entrance, on the north side, was fronted by an extended veranda ca. 38 m × 15 m. The entire unit identified as a temple has an L-shape, and at its maximum size is ca. 40 m × ca. 50 m.

The two main chambers were arranged so that they opened one on to the other from their long sides, and the connecting door aligned with the main door into the

---

9. The sculpture from Carchemish is on display in the Museum of Anatolian Civilizations in Ankara.

chambers. This entrance was in turn placed in line with the staircase that accessed the veranda and platform on which the temple was situated. Interestingly, this placement of the stairs, main entrance, and doorway between chambers was not an axial alignment. Neither the longitudinal nor the secondary axis of the complex was exploited in the design. The temple complex was structured so that each of the interior spaces had off-axis entrances. However, the largest of the chambers had secondary doors placed in each of the side walls on the longitudinal axis of the room. This axis was further emphasized by the row of columns that supported the roof. The stone bases for these columns survived. The design appeared to give primacy to the largest of the chambers, in which was found a portable hearth (Canby 1985: 336). However, the row of columns on the axis and the existence of the two secondary doors that provided access to much-smaller and seemingly less-significant spaces would have diminished the impressiveness of the interior and could well indicate that the main hall was not the focus of the design but functioned to bring people into the interior and then redistribute them into the surrounding rooms.

The temple was aligned so that it faced into the citadel, away from the lower city. The rear or south side was a wall 2 m thick that was punctuated with five buttresses or towers, the two corner towers of which were especially imposing. This construction must have appeared not unlike a secondary fortress within the citadel itself, raised above the level of the entrance. The temple opened to the north and faced the residential palace of the king across the terrace (Canby 1985: 334). The temple itself possessed a striking entrance, as can be seen in the reconstruction at the archaeological museum at Aleppo (fig. 39). Three caryatids, each 3 m high, standing on animals that were 1.5 m tall adorned the 9 m–wide entrance to the first chamber. The central figure was a man on a bull. To his left was a woman on the back of a lioness and to his right a man on a lion. The sides of the doorway were guarded by female sphinxes, and sculpted orthostats lined the lower portions of the exterior walls on either side of the entrance. The door between the first and second main chambers was also guarded by sculpted figures, this time griffins. These had large beaks similar to the beak of the sculpted bird of prey standing on a column in front of the temple on the terrace. The sculpted decoration was also carried around to the rear of the building. The 61 m–long rear wall of the temple platform was decorated with sculpted orthostats of alternating black volcanic basalt and limestone painted red. At the east side of the building was a gate that provided access to the temple and palace complex. This gate was also guarded by sculpted composite creatures with scorpion bodies and human heads. They stood 2 m in height (Canby 1985: 334–36).[10] The temple has also been

10. Much of the original sculpture was taken to Berlin by Max Freiherr von Oppenheim, the first excavator of the site. The sculpture was on display in a special museum in the city until the museum and much of the material from the site was destroyed during the allied bombings of Berlin in WWII (Elsen and Novak 1994: 115–26). Some of the reliefs can still be found in the archaeological museum at Aleppo,

identified as palace reception rooms because the construction identified as the king's residence across the terrace and to the north of the temple appears to have no formal reception area.

Some consider the most striking architectural feature of the Guzana temple to be the entryway, with its formal colonnaded space that provides entrance into an antechamber, which then opens into a deeper chamber. The design is a fully articulated example of the *bīt ḫilani* entrance, an architectural conceit found in first-millennium North Syrian palaces. It was probably a creation of the architects of the region that was taken east by Assyrians (Frankfort 1985: 151, 247, 276–88). The temple's dedication is not known, but the construction may have been the product of a building program by King Kapara (Dornemann 1997: 460–61), whose name is inscribed on several of the relief panels.

Tell Ta'yinat

The situation at Tell Ta'yinat, on the 'Amuq Plain at the northern bend of the Orontes River near ancient Alalakh (Tell Atchana), may have been analogous to that of the slightly older towns of Guzana and Carchemish: the site had seen settlement in the Early Bronze Age but had been abandoned for almost a millennium when it began to be redeveloped in Iron Age I. However, its proximity to the important Middle Bronze Age and Late Bronze Age city of Alalakh could well indicate that these were really "twin settlements" that shared a population moving between the two locations at various points in time (Yener et al. 2000: 189). The new excavations at the site have revealed that by the twelfth century B.C.E. there was settlement but either of foreign Aegean peoples, identified by their pottery, or by a population engaged in major trade of Aegean objects. This was followed by the first building period, which had a marked Hittite quality and a Luwian epigraphic tradition (T. Harrison 2009: 179–87). Hawkins has proposed that the site was the capital for King Taita, who ruled a territory that included the 'Amuq Plain, 'Ain Dara (even though others have argued that 'Ain Dara was an Aramean settlement), and Aleppo at some point in the eleventh–tenth centuries B.C.E. (Hawkins 2009: 170–71). Iron Age IIB Tell Ta'yinat of the ninth century B.C.E. was still the residence of a local ruler, probably the king of Patina (Unqi in Neo-Assyrian sources), which may actually still be Palistin. Whatever the actual name, the kingdom was destroyed by Tiglath-pileser III in 738 B.C.E.

The two temples on the site formed elements of a larger composition that included a palace. The first excavators, who knew of only one of the two temples (Building II), thought that it predated the palace and was joined to it in the larger composition at a later date. There was a difference in the levels of the exterior walls, and the area was refashioned into a terrace by the use of a retaining wall placed south of the

---

and associated materials are in the archaeological museum at Dayr az Zawr. The Metropolitan Museum of Art in New York City, the British Museum, and the Walters Art Museum in Baltimore each have small collections of reliefs from the site on display.

temple (McEwan 1937: 13). The temple (Building II) was a rectangular structure of 25 m × 13 m that was aligned west to east and opened on the east side (fig. 40). Though the south wall had totally disappeared, the excavators felt confident in their reconstruction (McEwan 1937: 13). The interior was divided into three distinct compartments arranged longitudinally along the axis, which is restated by each entryway. The porch area was 7 m wide and 5.60 m deep, and the sides of the porch were formed by the continuation of the main walls of the structure proper. The second chamber was the largest, at 10 m × 7 m, and the third chamber was the smallest. at 3 m × 7 m. The walls were just less than 2 m thick and were of mud brick veneered with stone in the lower levels that survived.

The temple was constructed on a high platform. The porch was approached via a flight of three stone steps on the east side. The entrance to the porch was through a pair of columns placed *in antis* that stood atop basalt bases sculpted as lions (fig. 41). The two doorways were ca. 4.5 m wide. The first door was rabbeted. The movement along the axis was interrupted in the third chamber by built installations. At right angles to the back wall projected two rows of flat stones. These had been placed above the floor level, and the space between the two rows was filled with mud brick. This construction rose to the same height as a mud-brick table placed in front of the installation on the back wall. These two elements were on the axis, though whether they were originally connected in some way could not be determined because the area had been disturbed (McEwan 1937: 13). Standing in front of these items was a still-smaller, arrow-shaped unit. This may have been the result of Assyrian influence, which entered the area in the eighth century B.C.E. (Busink 1970: 559–60).

Though originally the temple was thought to be older than the palace, subsequent work revealed that the palace (Building I) predated the temple (Building II), and both were placed in the second building phase at the site, which began at the end of the ninth century B.C.E. The temple was a later addition to the complex (fig. 42). The newly discovered temple (Field 2 temple) has the same design as Building II, a tripartite, longitudinal structure (T. Harrison 2009: 184–87). It was placed alongside but not parallel to the east wall the palace (Building I). Based on how it now appears, it dates to the last period of the site, when Tell Ta'yinat operated as a Neo-Assyrian provincial city. However, the structure appears to be a rebuilding of an earlier version, and so the original Field 2 temple probably dates back to the second building phase at Tell Ta'yinat. The extant remains show a structure ca. 18 m × 8.5 m, aligned on a north–south axis, with the entrance on the south side. The exterior walls are slightly under 2 m in thickness and were built in the "wood-crib" mud-brick construction, as were the walls of Buildings I and II. There is some evidence that the exterior walls of the Field 2 temple were plastered bright white. The three interior spaces—the porch, interior room, and the "holy of holies"—were separated from each other by mud-brick piers attached to the longitudinal walls. The south entrance was raised on a monumental stone staircase, which sat on a flagstone-paved plaza. The entrance to the porch was divided by a column placed in the middle, for which the base still exists. It was left in place when the temple was rebuilt, so only the top portion of the base is visible. This is part of the evidence for a rebuilding of the temple. The base itself closely resembles bases used for the columns on the porch of the palace (Building I).

Though the temple (Field 2 temple) was burned in a quite intense conflagration, enough of the final structure remains to provide some information about the interior treatment in the final phase of use. Wooden beams formed the roofing system. At least one of the thresholds was also of wood. The floor of the porch was of fired mud brick (Dessel 2008: 7). The main room was devoid of pottery or organic materials but did yield fragments of gold and silver foil and a fragment of a carved eye inlay, all of which could have come from a statue of a human figure. There were also bronze fragments and carved ivory inlays; both suggest the presence of rich furniture in the room. The "holy of holies" held an elevated, rectangular platform that filled most of the room. It could be ascended by means of steps in its two southern corners, and its top was covered in clay tiles. The excavators consider the platform to be a later intrusion into the space and not part of the original design. The room also suffered in the fire, but it did yield some cultic paraphernalia found on the platform and around the base: gold, bronze, and iron objects, libation vessels, and ritual objects of some type that were richly decorated. Found in the same area was a cache of Neo-Assyrian cuneiform tablets, probably part of an archive (Patel 2009: 11).

The palace was substantially larger than either of the temples—ca. 60 m × 25 m. The relation of the temples to the associated palace was different from the design at Carchemish or Guzana. The Tell Taʿyinat temples were to the south and east, behind the palace, the entrance for which was to the north. Nothing in the remains of the palace suggests any direct connection between the palace and the temples. There were no entrances to the palace in the south or east sides, and the line of rooms on the palace's south side indicated a series of small storerooms. On the other hand, the two temples formed a unit and were probably linked by a shared flagstone plaza, which has only partly survived. They were aligned at a right angle to one another, and clearly they were two versions of the same temple type but merely had different sizes.

The sanctuary remains from North Syria and southeast Turkey show that stone was normally used for prestigious structures, though the stone was integrated with "wood-crib"[11] and mud brick. Incorporation of sculpted bas-reliefs was found in both Aramean and Neo-Hittite contexts, and in both settings sculptors and designers had come to treat the reliefs, not as structural elements in the building, but as decorative accessories (Gurney 1954: 210). In this way, the Iron Age IIB builders separated their

---

11. See chap. 5.

new constructions from the older style of ʿAin Dara, where the sculpted stones were
structural features at several points in the temple. At Guzana and Carchemish, the
sculpted reliefs were used to line portions of processional routes, and this may also
have been the case at Samʾal (Zincirli), where sculpted orthostats line the southern
gate into the citadel (Frankfort 1985: fig. 335).

The larger Tell Taʿyinat temple (Building II) incorporated the sculpture as a decorative feature. The lion bases were used to support the columns of the porch, in a manner recalling the sculpted bases for the figures used as posts in the Guzana temple;
however, the Tell Taʿyinat lions have a rather Assyrian look and have been associated
with a later Assyrian refurbishing of the larger temple (Hawkins 2009: 168) that may
have happened when the Field 2 temple was also renovated. The temple-palace unit
was used by both Aramean and Neo-Hittite architects (see more fully below). In both
regions, the urban configuration included the citadel sector separated from the town
as a whole, though at Guzana—possibly following the pattern at the Aramean site of
ʿAin Dara—the separation between the lower town and the citadel was made bolder
by turning the temple structure so that it presented a blank face to the town proper.
Obviously, this may not be a specific feature of Aramean town planning so much as
the result of limited archaeological investigations of contemporary Neo-Hittite cities.
The Tell Taʿyinat temples show a clear debt to the older temple at nearby ʿAin Dara.
The tripartite division and deeply buried sanctuary was an old design conceit, but
the Iron Age IIB builders of the Tell Taʿyinat temple had the impressive old temple at
ʿAin Dara to consult. However, they did not aspire to the Iron Age IIA design with its
ambulatory and sculpted elements.

Phoenician Region

Unlike other areas of the Levant that seem to have suffered from the cultural
disruptions of about 1200 B.C.E., the Phoenician coast, with the exception of Ugarit
which was destroyed and depopulated, may have remained largely unmolested. The
coastal region of modern-day Israel, Lebanon, and Syria was an area of Canaanite
culture during the Middle Bronze and Late Bronze Ages. The city of Ugarit had dominated this coast during much of the Late Bronze Age, and to the south, Megiddo had
controlled movement from the coast inland via the Jezreel Valley. During the early
Iron Age, the region came to be considered the homeland of a culture known to the
Greeks as Phoenician. It is possible that this coastal strip does represent cultural continuity between the Late Bronze Age and early Iron Age (W. Anderson 1988: 365–67,
422–26; Bondi 1999c: 23–29; P. M. Bikai 1978a: 56). However, the archaeological record
for the area is not at all clear. In many cases, modern cities sit above ancient remains,
preventing systematic excavations (Moscati 1999: 1–19; Bondi 1999a: 316–17; Badre
1992: 37–44; P. Bikai 1992a: 25–36; P. M. Bikai 1992b; Jidejian 1992: 7–12). The absence
of good and lengthy textual material from the Phoenicians themselves and the lack of

substantial archaeological remains from any of the important Phoenician sites (Tyre, Sidon, Byblos) have led to the Phoenicians' being largely ignored as major players in the cultural developments of the Late Bronze Age and early Iron Age (P. M. Bikai 1990: 67–75).[12] No remains for monumental Late Bronze Age or early Iron Age Phoenician temples have yet been found in the major cities. Only the early Iron Age levels of Sarepta, Tell Sukas, Tell Arka, and Tell Abu Hawam have temples that date back to the early Iron Age. The biblical statements that King Hiram of Tyre played a substantial role in the construction of Solomon's temple in Jerusalem (1 Kings 5; 2 Chronicles 11) may indicate that Phoenician building skills were held in high esteem, at least in Iron Age II. Pierre Bikai, for many years director of the excavations at Tyre, is certain that one of the city's Iron Age temples can be found on the small island off the coast (probably the temple dedicated to Heracles and mentioned by Herodotus 2.44), but to date there have been no excavations (P. Bikai 1992b: 15). The small island in the harbor at Sidon that now holds a crusader castle is thought by some to have been the site of a temple at Sidon (fig. 43). While none of the important Phoenician temples survives on the mainland, the site of Kition (Larnaka) on Cyprus was the first Phoenician colony off the coast and an important Phoenician settlement. Remains of its significant temple dedicated to Astarte survived and offer some idea of the nature of monumental Phoenician religious architecture.

Tell Arka (Arqa)

Tell Arka is situated at the mouth of the Homs Depression. It has been identified as ancient Arqata. Though not on the coast, it prospered because of its access to the Orontes River plain and the cities of central Syria. The Late Bronze Age city was perhaps rich and strategically important enough to attract the attention of Tutmosis III since it seems to have been destroyed in the mid-fifteenth century, perhaps during one of his campaigns (Markoe 2000: 204). The site shows no signs of major recovery until Iron Age IIB, when a new settlement developed, moving out to the plain. At this time, a small sanctuary was built consisting of a building with a single rectangular room (Markoe 2000: 128, 204).

Kition (Larnaka)

There are remains of an important Phoenician temple dated to about 850 B.C.E. in the Kathari precinct at Kition (modern Larnaka) on the southeast coast of the island of Cyprus. Kition prospered in the Late Bronze Age, and remains of two sanctuaries (Temples 2 and 3) from this period have been identified in the excavations (Webb and Karageorghis n.d.: 3–4). Just as with Enkomi and Sinda, Kition shows signs of violent

---

12. In the 1990 reprint of the *CAH* vol. III.1 that treats the ancient Near East, there are no essays on Canaan or Phoenicia. The references are buried in other essays including those on the Neo-Hittite states and Israel. The 1988 exhibition at the Palazzo Grassi in Venice marked a change in the treatment accorded the Phoenicians; see Moscatti (1999). The entire *NEA* 73:2–3 (2010) is devoted to archaeology in Lebanon with a review of Phoenician excavations, but all from the later Phoenician period.

destructions associated with the arrival of the "Peoples of the Sea" (Drews 1993: 11–12). Temple 3 was completely eradicated and built over during the reconstruction, creating new Temple 1 (fig. 44), and Temple 2 was reused. At Kition, as elsewhere on Cyprus, evidence for the arrival of the "Peoples of the Sea" does not correlate with destruction followed by decline. At Kition, the town recovered (Webb and Karageorghis n.d: 6–7), and at other sites, the evidence points to a new occupation (Dothan and Dothan 1992: 197). Two additional temples (4 and 5) appear to have been constructed during this recovery phase at Kition. It is during this rebuilding after 1200 that ashlar masonry appears for prestigious construction.

The site suffered an earthquake in about 1075 B.C.E., and after a short period of abandonment, the town was reoccupied and the temples rebuilt along the lines that had existed prior to the destruction. One major change was the addition of an altar to the courtyard of Temple 4. The town remained viable until the end of the eleventh century B.C.E., when it was abandoned, perhaps the result of the harbor's silting up. In the ninth century B.C.E., it was reoccupied, now as a Phoenician colony, the first example of Phoenician expansion outside the city of Tyre (Webb and Karageorghis n.d.: 11).

The Phoenicians established temples atop the remains of the earlier Temples 1, 4, and 5. The new temple, dedicated to Astarte, stood above old Temple 1 and made use of the original ashlar masonry from the older temple, retaining the blocks in their original positions (fig. 45). The old and the new temples maintained the same east–west orientation. Temple 1 measured 35 m × 22 m and was designed around a central, open courtyard. This could be entered directly from the street on the south side through a monumental entrance. Another entrance was at the north end of the east wall. This provided access from another enclosed area, a courtyard (Temenos B) that served as the transitional space between a major street and the temple. The north wall of Temple 1 was penetrated by a door at the east end that provided access from still another courtyard region (Temenos A). The courtyard proper of Temple 1 was bounded on its south side by a wall that separated the courtyard from a walled corridor. The temple's north wall was constructed using drafted ashlar blocks for the interior façade and large, unhewn stones for the exterior face. The west, south, and east walls were built of rubble fill with ashlar facing on both the inner and outer façades. The west side of the courtyard and probably the end point and focus for the parallel corridor was a grouping of three chambers aligned in a row along the temple's west wall. The central chamber was the smallest, flanked by two larger, roughly equal rooms. This has been identified as a tripartite holy of holies (Webb and Karageorghis n.d.: 7).

The Phoenician builders retained the alignment of the temple. They made use of the basic outline of the building circumscribed by the fine ashlar masonry. The new temple could still be entered through the same doorways at the southeast and the northeast corners. These provided access to a large courtyard as in Temple 1, but the corridor along the south side of Temple 1 was removed and the courtyard made much larger. The courtyard now formed the entryway to a narrow chamber that ran the entire length of the west wall, where the three-chambered arrangement had been. Three doors now supplied access to this narrow chamber, and these doors were aligned with aisles described in the courtyard by parallel rows of columns, each with seven columns. These rows of columns must have supported roofing systems on the north and south sides that created flanking porticoes two columns deep. The roofed porticoes defined a central aisle that served as the main formal entrance into the central door to the narrow west room. This door was preceded by two large flanking pillars.

The new Temple of Astarte, destroyed by fire in ca. 800 b.c.e., was rebuilt soon thereafter but with some modifications. The four rows of wooden columns in the courtyard were replaced by four rows of stone piers, six piers to a row. The two lateral entrances to the holy of holies were walled up. In a final remodeling about 650 b.c.e. the spaces between the stone piers were walled in, creating three aisles where there had been a courtyard. Along the north and south walls, benches were built to hold offerings. At the southeast entrance, an altar was built, and Temenos B was subdivided (Webb and Karageorghis n.d.: 12).

The Phoenician Temple to Astarte had a door in its northeast corner that opened into the space that had been Temenos B in the first version of Temple 1. In the earlier form, Temenos B was defined on its south side by the north wall of Temple 2. Temenos B had a small opening in its southeast corner that provided indirect access to Temple 2. All of this disappeared in the Phoenician rebuilding. Temple 2 was not reconstructed, and Temenos B was enlarged to form a grand open space in front of the new temple. Across the street from the single entrance to Temenos B at its northeast corner, the Phoenician planners retained the placement of Temple 4. The Phoenician version of this temple was a long, rectangular courtyard divided in half by a central colonnade that formed the west portion of the temple. The east side consisted of the holy of holies. The plan was somewhat similar to that of the Temple of Astarte but on a much reduced scale. The altar table that had been added to the courtyard during the rebuilding after the earthquake of 1075 was retained, and a number of superimposed hearths next to it testify to its use during the Phoenician period (Webb and Karageorghis n.d.: 12).

Iron Age IIB is the time when Phoenician interests changed from merely exploiting maritime trade to establishing a type of overseas trade empire. The year 800 b.c.e. is the traditional date given for the foundation of Carthage and is also probably the date for the settling of Gadir on the Atlantic coast of Iberia. The expansion of Phoenician interests into the far west of the Mediterranean and the building of towns did not happen overnight, and the refounding of Kition as a Phoenician town was probably the first step. Kition is close enough to the Phoenician heartland to treat it as an annexation. There was a longstanding relationship between Cyprus and the Phoenician region, and it makes perfect sense that Tyre would have moved off its restrictive island to lay claim to Kition, the first stop on the voyage to the north and west. The temple at Kition was clearly a building of prestige, with its reused large-scale ashlar masonry and its unusual, partially roofed courtyard designed as a receptacle for a large number of people in front of the holy of holies. The unfortunate lack of contemporary architectural information from Tyre or Sidon makes it difficult for us to know how the new temple at Kition relates to monumental prestigious buildings in the two primary Phoenician cities. However, by looking at the modest remains of the temple at Tell Arqa, a town repopulated beginning in Iron Age IIA that possessed only a modest (possible) sanctuary, we may argue that the Kition temple was considered significant and therefore must be somehow reflective of what was happening in monumental temple construction in Tyre and Sidon.

Kingdom of Israel

Upper Galilee

Tel Dan

The archaeological record shows a sharp dividing line between the prosperous Late Bronze Age city and the early Iron Age village at the site of Tel Dan in the Golan region near Mount Hermon. In the Iron Age I village, the people were living in pit dwellings (Fritz 2002: 31). In the Iron Age I period, the site was probably within the Phoenician sphere, a situation that may have lasted into the beginning of Iron Age II (Raban and Stieglitz 1991: 41). By Iron Age II, the city had recovered (fig. 46), and a massive "high place" with subsidiary constructions dating to this period has been excavated on the northern flank at Tel Dan. The initial construction at complex 1 AII in stratum IVB (fig. 47) has been dated to the late tenth century B.C.E. (Biran 1994: 159–233) or early ninth century B.C.E. (Herr 1997c: 135). There is trace evidence of an earlier cult installation, from stratum V (Biran 1998: 40), though not in exactly the same area and perhaps associated with metalworking (Ilan 1997: 109).

The Iron Age IIB high place was constructed in Area T, near one source of the Jordan River. The earliest structure from stratum IVB had walls of large basalt and dolomite fieldstones and boulders. The complex included the open area, a stone-paved platform, storerooms, a podium of stone or *bāmâ*, and a plaster basin. The entire precinct was 60 m × 45 m arranged as a combination of closed rooms and open spaces and stone platforms. The *bāmâ* was constructed of large, dressed travertine blocks and was situated at the north part of the complex. It may have supported a temple that has now been robbed out completely. South of this major feature was a group of 3 storerooms.

Farther south was the heart of the complex, a 7.5 m × 5 m platform of basalt boulders partially covered by two layers of travertine blocks. A cobbled pavement surrounded the platform, creating a formal court that was open to the sky. A second platform was placed on the far south side, and on the west side of the compound was the actual spring, one of the sources of the Jordan River. The spring, or pool, was enclosed and incorporated into the cult complex. Steps led down into it, and the pool itself was reconfigured as a rectangular feature 1.5 m × 1 m. A terra-cotta tub, found broken into pieces, somehow functioned with the pool. Directly north of the pool was a second installation, a sunken basin with flanking basalt steps. This unit was constructed on a raised pebble and mud-brick terrace that stood along the west wall of the complex. The basin, 1.4 m × 0.88 m, occupied the center position on the terrace and was flanked by 2 large basalt slabs with associated sunken jars. A group of 12 heavy dolomite boulders of different sizes and weights stood to the east of the basin. The floor of the terrace sloped down to the south and east toward the rim of a large, sunken basalt receptacle in the southeast corner. This has been identified as an area for libations.

Finds from the complex do seem to confirm the cultic character of the space. From the storerooms came two upright pithoi painted in red and black stripes, red-slipped bowls, and an amphora stand. Some 40 vessels, mostly storage jars, were also located in the storerooms. One jug showed Phoenician influence. In the area of the courtyard and platform, there was a bar-handle bowl full of animal bones, with a trident incised on its base. Also from here came a terra-cotta incense stand and part of the head of a male figurine. The spring installation had the terra-cotta basin, already mentioned, and the possible "libation" installation contained a shallow bowl. Inside a jar at the southern end of the room was the faience head of a male figurine with Osiris crown. An Egyptian-style figurine of a man holding a staff or lotus stem was unearthed near the third pithos.

Biran argued that the first design of this high place with its associated cult installations should be attributed to Jeroboam I, who was king of Israel in the late tenth century B.C.E. and attempted to establish Dan and Bethel as rival cult centers to the temple in Jerusalem (Judg 18:30; 1 Kgs 12:29–30). He also set up images of the golden calf. Biran has suggested that Jeroboam's actions may also reflect a long and hallowed tradition at Dan that reached back to the time of the initial conquest of Canaanite Laish, possibly in the thirteenth century B.C.E. (Biran 1994: 165). The Jeroboam complex was burned within a generation or two. Layers of ash, broken pottery, and cult objects are scattered around the area.

The complex was rebuilt but with changes (see fig. 48; Biran 1994: 184–91). A new square *bāmâ* measuring 18.03 m × 18.63 m × 18.39 m × 18.82 m was constructed of travertine ashlars with drafted margins laid in the header-and-stretcher style. A row of cedar beams may have been inserted between rows of stones (Biran 1998: 40). The north wall, which was not visible, was built using boulders. Interior walls divided the large space into compartments of varying sizes. The exterior walls ranged from 1 to

2 m in thickness. This new travertine structure encompassed the older podium. Along the east face and portions of the south and west faces, there remain traces of a step that was 0.20 m wide × 0.12 m high that must have run along the lower course of the structure. This new construction could have supported a massive temple that is now missing completely (A. Mazar 1992a: 184–85).

A surface of crushed yellow travertine 0.10–0.20 m deep covered the east, south, and west sides of the structure as well as the remains of the earlier sanctuary with the exception of the central platform. This platform was retained from the earlier complex, and a new pavement of travertine blocks was added to its north side. On this new pavement were found two plaster circles 0.50 m in diameter and 1 m apart. These may mark the position of two columns. A column base was found reused in a later, Hellenistic construction. It could have been one of the pair. The two bases were aligned so that the mid-point between them was also the mid-point of the south face of the platform. A new building rose over the south-side installations of the previous complex. The pottery that was found beneath the crushed yellow travertine floor provides some dating evidence. It suggests a rebuilding in the first half of the ninth century B.C.E., the time of Ahab. Ahab is also credited with fortifying Dan with new walls and a gate complex. More recently, Athas has offered an alternative reading of this period. The find of an Aramaic inscription and the recognition that Bar-Hadad II, king of Aram and ruler of Damascus, had spread his influence if not direct control into the Galilee by the mid-ninth century B.C.E. and was followed by Hazael (who may have erected the Tel Dan Stele) have led Athas to posit an Aramean control of the city in the early ninth century B.C.E., when the second phase of the high place was constructed (Athas 2003: 256).

The sacred area was to undergo another redesign in the eighth century B.C.E. (see fig. 49; Biran 1994: 191–203; 1998: 40). The *bāmâ* and possible temple of the second phase were retained but now with a massive formal staircase, 8 m wide, on the south. This staircase replaced an earlier one that was built sometime between the completion of the second complex and the rebuilding that resulted in the third version (fig. 50). Ashlar masonry was used for the major structures. This staircase led south and down to the back wall of a large construction that replaced the paved platform of the previous two complexes. The new unit consisted of an outer enclosure wall of ashlar blocks 14 m × 12.5 m with entrances on the east and south. The entrances were 1.6 m wide with doorjambs protruding back into the courtyard. A large, shaped stone that was 0.50 m tall was found within the enclosure and may be the remnant of a larger platform or altar. The traces of stairs could be remnants of access to the top of the platform/altar. A small, 0.38 m × 0.40 m × 0.35, horned altar was found near the northwest corner of the enclosure and must have been used for small offerings. Traces of burning could be discerned on its surface.

The *bāmâ*-temple and paved platform area formed the major architectural features of this new sanctuary, but along the west side of the outer enclosure wall were two additional rooms that appear to have had cultic significance. The row of two rooms was about 15 m southwest of the platform. One room could be entered from the east side and from the west side. On the floor of the room, near the entrance, was a construction of 5 uneven limestone blocks that were arranged to form a square 1.03 m × 1.03 m and 0.27 m high, on top of which rested a round stone. Approximately 0.20 m south of this feature was half a jar that had been purposely sunk upside down into the floor. It contained ashes and burnt bone. The other room to the south could only be entered from the east. Here had been placed two basalt stones, 2.5 m apart. A 2 m–long burned wooden beam was found lying on the floor, one end on the southern stone. Charred wood fragments were also recovered on the north stone. These were probably the remains of columns that stood on the bases (Biran and Shanks 1987: 18–19).

Unlike the second phase, which yielded few finds, the third phase yielded rich material. In the small room to the southwest of the podium-temple that contains the feature of 5 limestone blocks, a bronze bowl was found with an omphalos base, as well as 3 ritual iron shovels, each shovel made of a single piece of iron. The discovery of ashes and animal bones in the vicinity suggests that the stone structure was used for animal sacrifices. Beneath the stone feature—the altar—was an object of silver and bronze that has been identified as a scepter head. It was decorated on the exterior with 5 figures around the top edge. These are quite corroded but may have been lion heads. Leaf patterns decorated the bulge portion. In the room to the south with the column remains, a single die of blue faience with dots inlaid in white was unearthed. In room no. 2049 on the west side of the sanctuary, a stamped amphora handle was found with the word *immasi-yo* or *immadi-yo* (belonging to Immasi-Yo or Immadi-Yo), which Biran has read as having a theophoric ending (Biran 1994: 206). Athas has observed that this is a Hebrew name of Israelite origin, the first clear evidence of a Israelite presence at the site (Athas 2003). Biran has further suggested that this area served as the residence for individuals who were affiliated with the sanctuary. A building to the southwest of the sanctuary proper, in which a great deal of domestic pottery was found, has been interpreted as the priests' house (Biran 1994: 206).

This third reconstruction of the Dan sanctuary is credited to Jeroboam II, whose rule ended a period of decline for the Northern Kingdom of Israel. Jeroboam took control in 785 B.C.E. The expanded and impressive third sanctuary at Dan may reflect the prosperity of his reign, and if Athas is correct, it also marked the Israelite domination of the site. The high place and associated cult buildings at Dan stand out distinctly from the other structures at the site. The constant rebuilding of the area but always along similar lines testifies to the continued hallowedness of the location.

The finds from the first and third sanctuaries testify to the special nature of this area within the urban fabric of Dan. The sanctuary and the possibly associated building to the southwest were destroyed by fire in the second half of the eighth century B.C.E.

In addition to the major "high place shrine," Tel Dan has also surrendered remains of shrines associated with the gate complexes. Within the first gate (fig. 51), in the paved plaza between the outer and inner gates, a raised platform of hewn limestone blocks was found. Four round-socketed bases of North Syrian style (fig. 52) may have supported poles for a canopy (Isserlin 1998: 245, fig. 55, pl. 18). These North Syrian elements offer support to Athas's view of an Aramean period of control at the site. Beside the installation stood a large monolith of basalt, possibly a *maṣṣēbâ* (Biran 1998: 40–44), and to the east of the installation 5 more *maṣṣēbôt* were located. Immediately preceding the upper gate on its southwest side were 5 basalt monoliths of various sizes. They stood abutting the city wall on the side of the paved square before the gate. Some type of bench or table was placed in front of them. They were arranged in their own niche-like space, an architecturally defined area. These have been identified as *maṣṣēbôt*. In the vicinity were recovered bones of sheep and goat, incense bowls, and votive vessels including an oil lamp designed to hold 7 wicks. There may also have been a structure similar to the structure just inside the outer gate—a canopied platform, here in the area of the upper gate (Biran 1998: 44–45). Opposite the installations on the west side of the gate was another grouping of 5 stones to the east of the gate. These were set on a stone platform. Outside the outer gate about 41 m alongside the city wall stood 5 stones on a solid foundation (Biran 1998: 44). These gate installations all date to no later than the mid-eighth century B.C.E. Athas has noted that proto-Aeolic capitals were found on the plaza of the gate (Barkay 1992: 319). The plaza is dated to the ninth century B.C.E., so the capitals must be later. Because these are regularly read as elements in formal, nonreligious Israelite architecture, they help support Athas's view that only in the third phase did the site become Israelite (Athas 2009: 256). Biran believed that the formal treatment of the gates reflected the "high place of the gate" mentioned in 2 Kgs 23:8 that formed a type of shrine that was suppressed in Judah during the seventh century by King Josiah. Isserlin accepts only the installation on the west side of the upper gate, with its offering table and associated votive vessels, as possibly relating to the "high place of the gate" (Isserlin 1998: 246).

Biran identifies all of the shrines except the shrine at the source of the Jordan as *maṣṣēbôt* shrines. No *maṣṣēbôt* has yet been found in association with the high place shrine, and it is possible that they may not have been a feature of this sanctuary. Biran has argued that these *maṣṣēbôt* shrines were intended to serve the needs of a popular cult as opposed to the cult of the high place shrine. One shrine located outside the first gate may have been installed for use by nonresident merchants who visited the city (Biran 1998: 45).

Kingdom of Judah

Negev

Tell Arad

The site of Tell Arad had been important and prosperous during the Early Bronze Age but had ceased to function in the Middle Bronze Age, Late Bronze Age, and Iron Age I (Amiran et al. 1978). B. Mazar (1965: 301) has argued that the location itself may have had special significance by the early Iron Age as a center point in the tribal territory of the Kenites.

The Iron Age II site is dominated by a great citadel (fig. 53) that originated in stratum XI. It was 55 m × 50 m, was well planned, and was surrounded by a casemate wall reinforced with towers. The citadel in stratum XI replaced an unwalled village, traces of which form stratum XII. The earlier publications of the site argued for a cultic installation in stratum XII that was later incorporated into the fortress (Herzog et al. 1984: 2–3). However, Herzog now reads the evidence differently and strongly doubts that there was any real line of continuity (Herzog 1997: 174).

The structure identified as a sanctuary first appeared in stratum X (late ninth century B.C.E.; see fig. 54), the period of the second fortress. There is no evidence to support placing it in the earlier, stratum XI fortress (Herzog et al. 1987: color plans 26–27; Herzog 1997: 174).[13] The citadel was a square oriented west to east with the entrance in the middle of the east side. The structure identified as the temple was in the northwest corner of the fortress up against the ninth-century B.C.E. outer wall. The temple consisted of a rectangular unit aligned west to east (fig. 55). At the west end was a broad room that ran north–south and was entered through a door on the long east side. Opposite the door was a niche, 1.2 m × 1.2 m. This was not placed exactly in the mid-point of the west wall. The north side extended a bit farther than the niche itself. The niche was approached by a low flight of stairs that was flanked by limestone blocks. The blocks belong technically to stratum IX but may have still been in use in stratum X. A courtyard 12 m × 7.50 m fronted the broad room and was flanked by an enclosed space on its north side. The entrance to the complex was on the east wall but not in line with the entrance to the broad room itself; instead, it was located in the southeast corner.

Within the broad room, plaster-covered benches lined the west and south walls. The courtyard was paved with small stones. Leading up to the niche were 4 shallow steps, and flanking them, on either side, were 2 pieces of worked limestone, identified as altars (fig. 56). Within the niche was found a low stone podium, on top of which may have stood an oblong stone with rounded edges and traces of red paint.

---

13. Herzog et al. 1984 (pp. 9–12) should be read with care because the earliest descriptions, which credited the major changes in the stratum-XI temple to stratum X, are no longer accepted by Herzog.

Within the courtyard was a large platform 2.40 m × 2.20 m and 1.50 m high, which Rainey translated into 5 × 5 cubits square × 3 cubits high (Rainey 1994: 338–39), constructed of unhewn fieldstones laid in mud mortar, perhaps reflecting the biblical injunction in Exod 20:24–25. At the foot of its south side was a stone step. On top of the platform had been placed a large flat fieldstone surrounded by a plaster channel. Rainey argued that it must have had a metal grill (Hebrew: *'ări'ēl*; or Moabite in line 12 of the Mesha Stele: *'r'l*; Rendsburg 2007: 9–14) on the top as well to allow for animal sacrifices (Rainey 1994: 338).[14] Adjacent to the platform and to its west was a small room that may have been used for storage (Herzog 1997: 175). Though modified over its period of use, the basic design for this sanctuary was to remain largely unchanged.

The finds of the first period included a red-slipped clay vessel of two parts that may have been an incense burner and that was found in the room west of the courtyard platform. It consisted of a high, hollow base topped by leaves and a deep, small bowl. A similar piece came from stratum V at Lachish, the time of the little Iron Age II shrine (Herzog et al. 1984: 12).

When rebuilt in stratum IX (eighth century B.C.E.), the sanctuary maintained the same format, but the floor of the courtyard was raised 1.20 m. The platform, therefore, only projected 0.40 m above the new floor. A new feature was added, a basin, 2 m south of the platform. A metal tub now may have sat on the platform (Herzog et al. 1984: 16). There were some additional changes that were also made to the sanctuary in the early eighth century B.C.E. Two chambers were made on the north side of the courtyard. The open space of the courtyard was reduced. From stratum IX came pots, storage jars, ceramic decanters, and dipper jugs as well as Cypro-Phoenician juglets and a small bronze lion in Syrian style that was found beside the platform in the courtyard.

Major changes took place in stratum VIII, in the late eighth century B.C.E., in both the fortress and the temple (fig. 57). These constructions replaced the stratum-IX complex, which was destroyed sometime in the latter half of the eighth century B.C.E. In the new design for the sanctuary (fig. 58), the courtyard was completely covered with a fill 1 m thick. The platform and the basin ceased to be used, and the courtyard became an open, level area fronting the broad room, which continued to function. The wall to the north of the niche was now doubled in thickness.

In the stratum VIII sanctuary, several ostraca were found. Each was inscribed with the single name of an individual or family. Two of the names have been associated with the priestly caste of Judah: Meremoth and Pashur (Ezra 8:33; 1 Chr 9:12); another bore the statement "sons of Kovah" and "sons of Bezal(el)." These may have been the Levitical guilds responsible for music in the temple and maintenance of the

---

14. A similar but slightly smaller altar has been discovered at nearby Beersheba, but there is no certainty regarding its original setting within a sanctuary (Rainey 1994: 333–49).

ritual artifacts (Herzog et al. 1984: 22). Still other names had Yahwistic elements: Eshi-yahu and Netanyahu.

The general design of the sanctuary space and the consistency of this design over several centuries must indicate the special nature of the space. The discovery in stratum X of two bowls on the step to the platform or altar in the courtyard incised with the Hebrew letters *qop* and *kap*—possibly the abbreviation for *qodeš kôhanîm* 'set apart for the priests' that was written on vessels intended to hold the portions of the sacrifices for the priests—seems to confirm the identification of this complex of rooms and spaces as being a sanctuary area from its inception (Herzog et al. 1987: 30–33).

The stratum VIII temple and fortress fell to the Assyrians or their Edomite allies. The rebuilt fortress of stratum VII, seventh century B.C.E., no longer shows any evidence of a shrine. All traces were wiped away.

Teman (Kuntillet ʿAjrud, Horvat Teiman)

The fortress at Teman is located on the Gaza road about 50 km south of the fortress at Kadesh-Barnea in the Sinai on the fringe of the Judean Negev. Originally there were two structures, of which the larger was a rectangular (15 m × 25 m), fortress-like building with a central court and corner bastions. Since it does not have the casemate rooms normally associated with Iron Age II fortresses, it has also been identified as a caravansaray or a defensible watering spot (see fig. 59; Isserlin 1998: 246–47; Nakhai 1994: 27; A. Mazar 1992a: 446–50). The entrance into the courtyard was through a bent-axis gate chamber. The outer unit, or forecourt, had benches along the walls. This space provided access to a narrow broad room that was also lined with benches. Both of these spaces were completely plastered in white: walls, benches, floors, a covering not used elsewhere in the structure. The plaster in the forecourt served as the background for wall paintings of floral and geometric patterns. Two broken pithoi were covered with drawings and Hebrew inscriptions in red ink. The inscriptions include references to Yahweh, Yahweh of Samaria, his Asherah, and El, in adddition to Baʿal. The site has been dated from the mid-ninth to mid-eighth century and classified as a religious center intended to serve the needs of travelers on this road leading to the Red Sea.

The breakup of the Kingdom of Israel resulted in two different processes of development in Iron Age IIB, since the north and south regions are environmentally quite distinct. The Northern Kingdom of Israel was richer. The land yielded more, and the kingdom was well situated to take advantage of the established trade linkages with the flourishing centers to the north in Syria and the west on the Phoenician coast. It was also involved with the emergence of the settled life in the Tranjordanian areas of Ammon and Moab. The wealth is reflected in the finds in the palace complex at Samaria (I–VI), which was itself a large compound built of ashlar masonry. It was a fortified sector of the city and must have resembled the contemporary developments of the North Syrian capitals at Guzana and Carchemish. The substantial collection of ivory fragments that must have decorated furniture in the palace testify to the luxury available to some in the Northern kingdom. No clear sanctuary has been found in association with the palace, but the sanctuary complex at Dan testifies to the investment made in religious architecture, which was probably patronized by the monarchy at one of the other royal cities of the north. To date, the excavations of the Dan sanctuary have not found it to be associated with a palace, but it was clearly a site that had controlled access. The space was built up with architectural elements, and it is doubtful that it could have held large numbers of people within the confines of the sanctuary proper, though its placement at the end of the major road through the town would have permitted it to function as part of a ceremonial procession. The physical space defined as cultic includes a number of features: a possible temple for which the platform exists, an outdoor altar area that becomes increasingly restricted as the sanctuary is rebuilt, and several secondary enclosed chambers to the side. Such a design allowed for a number of activities to occur simultaneously, some open to view, others hidden. The architecture of the sanctuary at Dan, particularly in its last stage, provided a space perfectly suited for complicated rituals. The space had a hierarchical structure. Some ceremonies were performed at ground level, while others occurred up on platforms. The development of sanctuaries at Dan and possibly Bethel, for which no actual archaeological evidence has been found, may have been the result of a desire on the part of the kings of the north to offer their people an alternative to the sanctuary of Jerusalem, which now stood in the capital of the rival Kingdom of Judah in the south.

Judah was a much poorer kingdom because of its more marginal agricultural environment and because it was much more isolated from the major trade networks. Iron Age IIB does witness the expansion of Jerusalem proper. Though the archaeological evidence is limited, it is possible that it was during this period that the tenth-century city began to expand off the limited area provided by the City of David and the Temple Mount by increasing the domestic area (fig. 129). Better understood is the contemporary development of Lachish (IV–III), which served as the winter capital for the kings of Judah. Here the walls enclosed a city with a certain amount of public architecture, in which was placed an impressive palace compound that was separated from the rest of the city. The arrangement recalls the layouts of Samaria, Guzana, and Carchemish. Again, as at Samaria, there is no sanctuary associated with the palace at Lachish, and the little cult room that appeared in Iron Age I over the ruins of the Late Bronze Age city was no longer operational.

However, there is evidence of other sanctuaries in the Kingdom of Judah at the fortress of Arad, which must have guarded the southern extent of the kingdom. How this little shrine operated cannot be ascertained from archaeology. It was a small space that could never have accommodated crowds of any type. In design, it is quite different from that of the temple of Solomon in Jerusalem as recorded in the Bible. It is a broad-room shrine preceded by a courtyard. The physical layout of the sanctuary was not suitable for any type of ceremonial processing, though its location deep within the fortress could have made it a suitable end point for a procession that somehow incorporated the entire fortress. The design, however, does allow for intimate interaction between the believer and the divine. There were not many changing spaces, as at Dan. In its most complicated form, the sanctuary included the holy of holies, the courtyard, and the outside altar. Ceremonies could not have become too complicated in such a limited special arrangement.

It is not at all clear what happened to the Arad sanctuary in the eighth century B.C.E., which is represented by the changes in stratum VIII. Aharoni argued that the sacrifices stopped at the end of the eighth century, reflecting the centralizing reforms of Hezekiah, and then the sanctuary ceased to exist completely in the late seventh century B.C.E. as a result of the Josiah's regulations against worship outside Jerusalem (Aharoni 1968a: 26). Herzog and his team thought that the entire sanctuary was terminated in the eighth-century stratum VIII (Herzog et al. 1984: 19–22). Naʾaman (1995: 185) has expressed strong doubts regarding the historical validity of the so-called reforms of Hezekiah and therefore sees no association with a royal decree and the changes in stratum VIII. Ussishkin (1988: 156) radically down-dated the earliest fortress to the eighth century B.C.E. and the sanctuary to the seventh century B.C.E. with an end in the sixth century B.C.E. completely separating the sanctuary from the reforms of Josiah or of Hezekiah.

The possible shrine at the fortress of Teman has no clear affiliation. It could have been Judahite. The inscriptions are Hebrew. Among the graffiti is a scene that has been interpreted as showing Yahweh and his consort, Asherah. The structure itself provides no clear evidence of ritual space. It is hard to know how the supposed shrine area might have operated, and it is just as possible that ritual was not the intended function. Most likely, this building was outside any real political control. It was a fortified caravansaray that offered protection to those who traveled the southern route between Gaza and the Wadi Arabah. Anyone who could pay could huddle behind its walls, and the shrine area was no more than a space that offered these temporary residents a place for some type of propitiation.

Philistia

By Iron Age IIB, the Philistine region had shrunk substantially from its greatest extent, which was reached during the latter part of Iron Age I. The rise of the Kingdom of Israel during the United Monarchy of Iron Age IIA had seen the Philistine region lose both territory and settlements to its powerful neighbor. The breakup of the United Monarchy allowed the Philistine communities some breathing room, but the archaeological record shows that there was little left that could be identified as distinctly Philistine. More and more, the Philistine communities were coming to resemble those of the other Northwest Semitic groups in the region, the Israelites and Phoenicians (Herr 1997c: 146–47).

Shephelah

Ashdod

A small sanctuary was built in Ashdod in the eighth century B.C.E. and operated into the period of Assyrian rule, in sector D (fig. 60). The Iron Age I sanctuary in Area H no longer functioned. The new sanctuary must have been constructed to serve the fortified, industrial, pottery-making quarter of the city (Dothan and Dothan 1992: 140), and the finds of female figurines indicate that the old cult of the "Ashdoda" was still flourishing (T. Dothan 1982: 234). The Area D temple consisted of several interconnected spaces distributed around courtyards and was quite different from the Iron Age I complex of buildings with the apsidal structure in Area H. A plastered mudbrick platform or installation was attached to a long wall in one of the rectangular spaces in the southern part of the Area D sanctuary.

Near the mud-brick platform and in associated spaces, the excavators recovered small ceramic figurines. Included are domestic animals, most attached to kernoi, male and female statuettes, miniature offering tables, figural plaques, most with female forms, and a single figure playing a lyre. Since the lyre player recalls the cult stand with musicians found in the twelfth-century grave of a warrior, the Dothans have used the two images to argue that music remained an important feature of cultic rituals at Ashdod (Dothan and Dothan 1992: 140, 174).

Though by Iron Age IIB, the Philistines were influenced by their neighbors, they were still an independent group. The "Ashdoda" figures suggest that the old beliefs were still viable. The Philistines' position along the coast allowed for much greater trade, and the finds of bones from Nile fish and Cypro-Phoenician pottery indicate that the people were still actively engaged with the two great cultural forces to the south and north. While the sanctuary in Area D of Ashdod is quite different from the great Iron Age I sanctuaries at Ekron and Tell Qasile, what does remain consistent is the focus on interior spaces and courtyard designs and the use of humble materials and building techniques.

Transjordan Region

The Transjordan region may have been partly under Israelite control during Iron Age IIA, but the division of the kingdom into Israel and Judah allowed the Transjordan area to develop on its own. Scholars assume that there were incipient states forming in the territories of Ammon and Moab, both of which were putting up major inscriptions if not monumental buildings. The sculptural finds from the Amman Citadel testify to a high level of sculptural competence and strong influence coming from the Phoenician region. The Amman Citadel inscription speaks of the god Milkom and of the temple dedicated to him that must have been built in the citadel.

Ammon

Rabbath-Ammon (Amman)

Excavations are beginning to reveal more about the Iron Age peoples of Trans-jordan. The 1993 excavations of the citadel in modern Amman, the ancient Rabbath-Ammon—the major city of the Ammonites—revealed fragmentary remains of an Iron Age IIB building under the standing remains of the Roman temple (Kanellopou-los 1994; Koutsoukou et al. 1997; Najjar 1993: 220–25; De Vries 1992: 529–30). There were ruins under and in front of the east end of the temple. Beneath the staircase, two walls were exposed, an east wall and a north wall. An additional stretch of wall was located within the confines of the Roman temple itself. The surviving portions of wall, 21.3 m running east to west and 6 m running north to south, indicate that this was a large structure. The lack of a partition wall suggests that this sizable building con-sisted of only a few large rooms or possibly a single large room. Traces of plaster on the floor could indicate that the structure was originally roofed. The walls themselves are of megalithic stonework, an unusual technique in the area. These features of the structure along with its position on the citadel overlooking the valley below and the later use of the site for a temple during the Roman period bolster the argument that the Iron Age building was also a sanctuary.

The Iron Age II ceramics were mostly coarse and plain wares with a small per-centage of cooking ware. The imported material included some Cypriot and Phoe-nician pieces. The Cypriot are mostly bowls. Twenty-seven figurines were recovered in the area around the excavations, and these too have been identified as Iron Age. These were handmade and included humans, horses-and-riders, horses, and birds. This possible temple stood on bedrock, and there is no evidence for an earlier build-ing on the site.

The picture that emerges of temple-building in Iron Age IIB is a picture of regional variation. There was no single political or cultural force that dominated the Levant, though by the end of the period, the Neo-Assyrian Empire had begun to conquer and control portions of the region. The other event that may have contributed to this variation was the Egyptian invasion of the southern Levant led by the Pharaoh Shi-shak. According to his victory inscription at Karnak, he laid waste to several centers in the south. While the invasion was not followed by the reestablishment of an Egyp-tian presence in the Levant, it must have been a shock, and the recovery showed how weak the local forces were. This must have encouraged a local response, and temple-building may have been just this sort of activity. Kings and temple-building seem to become a standard pairing during this era. The remains of temples in the Neo-Hittite and Aramean centers were all associated with royal projects, which was probably the case for the temple at the Amman Citadel. The situation was different at Dan, where the sanctuary may have been one of two (the other at Bethel) that were intended to compete with the better-established sanctuary at Jerusalem. The Northern Kingdom of Israel wanted to offer its people an alternative to the pilgrimage to Jerusalem in the rival Kingdom of Judah.

This period also marks the first phase of overseas expansion for the Phoenicians, who not only established outposts along the coasts of North Africa and Iberia but also introduced Levantine building forms and practices to these regions. The need for sanctuaries in these settings was quite different from the situation elsewhere in the Levant. The distant settlements needed the reassurance of a local sanctuary, so the temple-building was not limited to royal settings, which seems to have been the case with much temple-building in the Iron Age IIB Levant proper. The small sanctuaries at the Arad and Teman fortresses may well testify to the increased movement of soldiers as well as merchants through the region, both groups in need of some sacral reassurance in their dangerous undertakings.

The Ghor
Deir ʿAlla
The site of Deir ʿAlla had possessed an important Late Bronze Age sanctuary (fig. 61), but by Iron Age IIB, it was no longer functioning. However, the site was occupied and has yielded an important inscription. It fits with the developing writing culture in Ammon (Amman Citadel inscription) and Moab (Mesha Stele). The inscription from Deir ʿAlla was found painted on a wall with red pigment. It offers a prophecy by Balaam, son of Beor, and recalls the individual in Numbers 22–24. The inscription is poorly preserved, has no punctuation, and contains a number of rare words, making identifications of the language and script debatable (Herr 1997c: 148). It does, however, suggest that Deir ʿAlla played some type of prophetic role in Iron Age IIB, but there is nothing architectural to provide a framework for the inscription.

During Iron Age IIB, the kingdoms of Ammon and Moab became established. The Amman Citadel inscription and the Mesha Stele provide names of new state gods invoked in royal inscriptions. The Mesha Stele indicates that the solidification of the incipient state of Moab resulted from a revolt against the Northern Kingdom of Israel (2 Kings 3), which had controlled the region. Although the archaeological evidence is limited, there is good reason to see in both Ammon and Moab a process of change occurring as more settlements began to appear; among them were the capitals at Rabbath-Ammon for the Kingdom of Ammon and Dibon for Moab. The smaller towns are best understood with reference to the evidence available to us from the site of Jawa in Ammon. It was a walled town with a four-chambered gate enclosing several houses but not much of a clear urban plan. The gated entrance to the town of Jalul recalls the contemporary gate complex at Dan (Herr 1997c: 149). Similarly, the statues from the Amman Citadel have features that are best explained as deriving from Phoenician forms (Bienkowski 1991). As Ammon and Moab began to resemble the settled regions of the rest of the Levant, they were open to accepting influences from their neighbors.

Iron Age IIC Sites:
Late Eighth Century to the Mid-Sixth Century b.c.e.

Stratigraphic correspondences: Sarepta IIA/B = Tell Sukas H1/G3 = Khirbat al-Mudayna = Horvat Qitmit = ʿEn Hatzeva 5–4.

By the late eighth century b.c.e., the independence of much of the Levant had been brought to an end by the advance of Assyria. The North Syrian Neo-Hittite and Aramean kingdoms had all fallen before the Assyrian onslaught. The Kingdom of Israel was conquered, and in 701 b.c.e., the Assyrians invaded Judah. The Assyrians withdrew, and Judah was to remain independent until the end of Iron Age IIC. Philistia was not as lucky, but the Assyrians do seem to have made Philistia quite profitable, to judge from the extent of the olive-oil industry at Ekron.[15] In a similar way, the Phoenician cities, now also under Assyrian hegemony, established and maintained lucrative international trade throughout the Iron Age IIC period.

Phoenicia

Sarepta and Tell Sukas offer a glimpse of the development of sanctuaries within small towns in the Phoenician heartland during these centuries. Neither place was a major urban site or the residence of a ruler, so they must represent what might be found in any Phoenician town. Tell Sukas possibly illustrates the way that Greek elements, if not the Greeks themselves, were beginning to insinuate themselves into the fabric of life in the Levant, even at the village level.

Sarepta

The small site of Sarepta (Sarafand) has one of the few buildings to be recognized as an early Iron Age Phoenician sanctuary. As elsewhere in this coastal band, the site of Sarepta shows no signs of a break between Late Bronze Age and early Iron Age occupations, but instead evidences a continuous settlement stretching back to the Middle Bronze Age. The town was situated between Sidon and Tyre, and by the eighth century b.c.e., the town was considered a satellite of Sidon, based on evidence from the inscribed clay prism of the Assyrian king Sennacherib (704–681 b.c.e.; see *ANE Anth.*, 287–88). The structure identified as a shrine is from stratum IIA/B and stood on the edge of the tell, overlooking the modern harbor (Pritchard 1978: 131–48). It bordered what may have been an industrial quarter of the town. A narrow street separated the two areas. The building was rectangular, 6.40 m × 2.56 m, and was oriented east to west on the longitudinal axis (fig. 62). The east end was slightly wider than the west by about 0.32 m, because it based the foundations of the new building on the

---

15. During the Assyrian period, a temple was built (Temple Complex 650) in the Lower City, Field IV, but following a Neo-Assyrian design format. The remains of this temple yielded the inscription that identifies Ekron by name and lists five of its rulers, including Padi, who built the temple. Because it represents an imposed foreign import introduced at the very end of the period under consideration, the temple is not included as an object of investigation in this study (Dothan and Gitin 2005: 8).

older walls. The structure was embedded in the network of streets and was contained on the south and east sides. The building itself was near the principal north entrance to the city from the port. The construction reveals more care than is found in most of the other buildings on the site. The foundations are deep. The standing wall remains are of well-cut sandstone blocks arranged in a careful header-and-stretcher pattern. The floor is hard gray cement, ca. 0.10 m thick, laid over pebbles. This is not the norm for the site, where tramped earth was the most common flooring.

The structure went through at least two distinct periods of use. The variation between the width of the east and west ends is indicative of change and rebuilding. In the second phase, a door was cut into the north end of the east wall (G. R. H. Wright 1985: vol. 2, ill. 165a), and the earlier entrance was sealed up. This changed the entrance to the shrine from its first version, in which the door had been on the east end of the south wall. The shift in the placement of the entrance was probably occasioned by a structural problem. The street sloped downward toward the east. During heavy rains, it carried a massive volume of water, which deposited gravel and debris around the earlier entrance, raising the street to the height of the threshold and creating the possibility of water flooding into the temple through the door. However, G. R. H. Wright argues rightly that the change also resulted in a shift from an earlier bent-axis approach to something akin to but clearly not a long-room type (Wright 1985: 1.224), but in both versions, the cult focus remained the small west wall. During the second phase of use, the shrine was also enlarged by appending two rooms to the west side of the north end of the structure. These formed a unit 4 m × 4 m, with an internal wall dividing the space into two chambers. A door at the west end of the north wall of the main rectangular room permitted communication between the main room and the newly appended grouping.

During the first phase of the shrine, fieldstones set in mud mortar formed benches, 0.20 m high × ca. 0.35 m wide, that lined the inner four walls of the main rectangular room. The benches were covered in plaster, which created a smooth surface. A platform stood on the west wall in roughly the center position. Only an outline of the ashlar blocks survives because the stones have been robbed. The platform was placed flush against the west wall, and the three exposed sides were veneered with gypsum slabs, one of which was found in situ. To mount the platform, a step was provided in front. Twenty centimeters to the east of the platform was a rectangular socket, 0.50 m × 0.60 m that may have held a pillar. For the second phase of use, the pillar was removed, damaging the floor. A new floor was laid. The structure was expanded slightly on its north and west sides.

The benches and the platform from the first phase of the building are the features that helped excavators identify the structure as a cult building. The portable finds reinforced this conclusion: near the platform was found a rectangular stone worked on one side, with a square, stepped depression leading to a channel. The channel in turn opened into a cylindrical space that was originally hidden from view by a covering stone. From this chamber, two new channels emerged and ran to either side of the stone. This stone must have functioned as a libation table. The benches in the earlier version of the shrine contained no objects, but more than 200 items were found on and around the platform and pillar. Some of these were formal deposits, and others were scattered items. Most all of the offerings were of common materials and included several small figurines that are amulets of human and animal shapes. The figurines are of painted terra-cotta and can be categorized as women holding birds, seated women playing drums, and seated pregnant women. The last type was more common in the shrine's second phase. The only objects with intrinsic value found were 4 pieces of ivory and 1 alabaster vessel. Figures of Horus, Bes, Ptah, and Bastet; an eye of Horus; and a cat all testify to some Egyptian influence at the shrine; as does a small female figurine wearing a heavy Egyptian-style wig. The most significant find may be a terra-cotta throne flanked by 2 sphinxes. It had been broken before being buried in the shrine. The sphinx heads also have an Egyptian quality and wear false beards and high blue crowns. There were also finds with no obvious cultic associations: beads, game pieces, lamps, and cosmetic equipment. Notably absent were ceramic plates, cups, incense stands, and cooking pots.

A stylistic analysis of the finds has provided the dates for the operation of the shrine. The first version began in the eighth century B.C.E., and the shrine continued to function until the fourth century B.C.E. A dedicatory plaque, dated by letter forms to the late seventh or early sixth century B.C.E., described a statue of Tanit-Astarte made by one Shillem, son of Mapaʾal, son of ʿIzai. This suggests that the shrine was dedicated to this conflated goddess. Though Astarte is best known from eastern Mediterranean contexts, while Tanit is most commonly found in Phoenician settlements in the western Mediterranean (Ribichini 1999: 120–52), this dedication ties Tanit to the Phoenician homeland (Stern 2006: 177–80).

Tell Sukas (Suqas)

Tell Sukas,[16] possibly the Late Bronze Age city of Shukshu, has one of the longest archaeological records for the Phoenician region. It is situated on the Jebel Plain at the southern edge of the territory that Ugarit controlled in the Late Bronze Age. In both Late Bronze Age and early Iron Age strata, the finds reveal a wide variety of religious practices, suggesting a mixed population—more so than in other coastal sites. The discovery of a cremation cemetery with an associated open-air shrine in the harbor area that were used from the thirteenth century through the first half of the tenth

---

16. There are remains of two significant temples in the Phoenician region: one to Eshmun outside Sidon and the other dedicated to Melqart in the far south, near the border with Israel at Umm el-ʾAmed. Both of these are constructions belonging to the period of Persian control, later than the concerns of this book (Amiet 1964; Dunand and Duru 1962; Fisher-Genz 2008; Lipiński 1995; Stucky 2005).

century and contained votive deposits of small groups of vases has led some to argue that the site possessed a *tophet* (Ciasca 1999: 183).

There is also archaeological evidence for an Iron Age IIC sanctuary that consisted of a raised terrace and a trench to hold sacrifices. The remains of the structure are limited to a small building that enclosed a quadrangular room (Markoe 2000: 128; Bondi 1999a: 319). A later, seventh-century small temple with tiled roof, porch, and altar was built in the vicinity of the Phoenician sanctuary and over the remains of a hearth that could have been cultic in nature (Ciasca 1999: 183; Niemeier 2001: 15). Because the building had roof tiles of a type considered Greek, and Greek pottery remains have been found in some of the tombs at the site, this seventh-century temple has been posited to have served a small, resident Greek trading community (Riis 1970: 44–59), though this suggestion is not universally accepted.

Sarepta was situated along the coast between Tyre and Sidon, and as such it must have been influenced by developments in both of those cities. Its archaeological sequence shows that it was established at the end of the Late Bronze Age and was continuously occupied throughout the Iron Age. It provides the evidence for the relative speedy recovery of the coastal area from the ravages at the end of the Late Bronze Age. The town experienced major replanning during Iron Age IIB (Markoe 2000: 199). The little temple, although humble compared with the major royal buildings of Iron Age IIB, was nonetheless made special by the use of ashlar masonry.

Its position in the industrial quarter of the town with the evidence of nearby workshops for pottery, purple dyeing, jewelry manufacturing, and olive-oil processing recalls the location of the Iron Age IIB Ashdod shrine, which was also part of an industrial quarter. The placement may be nothing more than the accident of archaeological recovery. Other sites in the Levant may also have had shrines in industrial quarters, something that is known for the Late Bronze Age on Cyprus at Kition. However, for the moment, most of the other known Iron Age sanctuaries in the Levant come from nonindustrial sectors. It is worth mentioning that the high point of Sarepta, sector Y, was excavated down through these same levels and produced no evidence for a shrine. Whatever was at work here regarding the places chosen to be hallowed, height relationships may have played little or no role.

Interestingly, the shrine is small and thus could never have accommodated big groups within its walls, but it also had no courtyard and had no place to hold large numbers of people nearby. It was not designed for processional ceremonies. This is quite different from the sanctuaries at Tell Sukas. While small, these were set off from the surrounding areas by the use of platforms that established a cultic area, a temenos. The expansion of Phoenician economic interests overseas may partially explain the importance of the industrial quarter at Sarepta, which produced some of the goods taken in trade. It also probably helps clarify the possible presence of Greeks at the site of Tell Sukas, who were now establishing their own outposts throughout the Mediterranean, including the Levant.

Transjordan Region

Moab

Khirbat al-Mudayna

Only the fortified site of Khirbat al-Mudayna on the Wadi ath-Thamad has yielded structural remains identified as a shrine in Moab. The settlement probably sat on Moab's north frontier with Ammon. It was in the Moabite territory north of the Wadi Mujib. The site was situated on a small, oval hill, not far from the edge of the wadi (fig. 63). Excavation at the site has been limited, but to date, a major gate and a monumental building of ashlar masonry with hammer-dressed, rectangular stones have been unearthed (Daviau 1997: 224–25). South of the east end of the gate 2.50 m stood the building identified as a temple (Building 149; see fig. 64). It was a square structure 5.50 m × 5.50 m built up against the casemate wall and set within a courtyard. A door opened at the northwest corner, and two steps led down into the main room (R108). A second door was found at the southeast corner. Two square, composite stone pillars divided the space into two parts. The excavators assumed that pillars held up the roof, and between them was a platform or bench that defined the other smaller room, or annex (R110). The composite pillars may also have served to frame the two doors that led into R110. The walls were of limestone cobbles but were uneven in thickness. The casemate wall was the thickness of three rows of cobbles. The other walls were only the thickness of two rows of cobbles. The courses of cobbles were uneven, and the walls themselves were not straight (Daviau and Steiner 2000: 3–4). Benches of cobbles and packed earth partially lined the walls of the structure (Daviau and Dion 2002a: 42, 48), providing openings for the two doors, and were plastered on the tops and sides. They stood between 0.30 m and 0.40 m tall. The floor was of beaten earth but may have been plastered over, since there were traces of yellow plaster.

There was evidence of several replasterings of the interior, supporting the notion that the space was special and well maintained. Moreover, the building had at least two phases of operation, since the pillars were embedded in a layer below the excavated floor (Daviau and Steiner 2000: 4–5 n. 7). From R110 came a stone mortar found in situ, over which was a small, rectangular, limestone basin. A gaming board was found on the floor, probably having fallen from a nearby bench. R110 also yielded an Iron Age II lamp, a fragment of iron slag, and a ceramic leg fragment from a zoomorphic figurine. Finds from the larger space, R108, included several installations on or underneath the floor. In the center was a large pit 1.35 × 1.55 m, in which were found pottery sherds of 7 distinct vessels and a stone with a rectangular depression.

To the side of the door in the southeast corner was a smoothly polished, large, flat stone of a material different from the material used for the construction. It was part of a wall unit and was supported on top of 3 smaller stones. The wall unit supported 3 stone altars. The 3 limestone altars were discovered broken on top of a polished stone slab. One of the altars has been identified as a libation altar of an unusual type because it lacks the normal corner horns. Traces of red-painted horizontal lines framed a row of alternating red and black triangles on one side. The painted pattern has no clear parallel, though it is possible that textile motifs influenced the design. A second pattern on the right edge of the rim showed a red circle divided into four pie-shaped wedges. This element has been found on contemporary pottery from the site of Deir ʿAlla in the Ghor, not too far distant (Daviau and Steiner 2000: 9 n. 19).

A second, smaller altar, carved from a single block of limestone and hammer dressed, still had remains of soot from the burnt offerings it once held. The third altar was the tallest, at ca. 1 m. Cut from a single piece of limestone, it had a cylinder form with a conical foot and a cup-shaped depression on the top surface. The design was unusual. The altar was composed of a series of six distinct units, each separated from the other by a band of sculpted, petal-like forms that were originally painted alternately red and black. These individual units had facetted shapes not unlike beads. On one side of this altar had been painted red and black triangles, and below them a curving black line that ended in two prongs, possibly intended to represent a serpent. On the opposite side of the altar, some of the facets were decorated with a palm tree. There was also a Moabite inscription written perpendicular to the top rim of the altar, identifying the item as an incense altar made by Elishama for YSP, the daughter of ʿWT (Daviau and Steiner 2000: 10–11). Additional finds in the R108 included two limestone pegs that were possibly used as stoppers for jars, a fragment of a stone bowl, a spouted vessel with pedestal base, fragments of 5 ceramic oil lamps, a complete female figurine and a broken female figure, and some beads from jewelry. Four thousand animal bones along with two dozen ceramic figures of animals were recovered from the courtyard proper (150). The bones show clear cut marks (Daviau and Dion 2002b: 48–49).

A second shrine has also been discovered at Khirbat al-Mudayna but not within the settlement proper. About 4 km from the site, in the wadi system itself, the remains of a small shrine were found (Wadi ath-Thamad #13). A rectangular perimeter wall formed an enclosure in which stood a one-room structure (Daviau and Dion 2002b: 46, 49). Portions of stone benches that lined the walls survive. Only one small area of cobblestones and hard-packed soil was found intact and in situ.

While not much in the way of architecture remains, the finds from the site included several broken figurines, a model chair or throne, and fragments of pottery, all found beneath the undisturbed cobble floor. The figurines were of females, each of which held either a disc against her chest or a drum in her hands placed perpendicular to the body. Elsewhere in the disturbed remains, the excavators unearthed carnelian and shell beads, a scarab, seashells, fossils, coral, miniature ceramic vessels, limestone bowls, 3 limestone figures (one a modeled head), thousands of sherds from cooking vessels, jars, and pots, and 2 amulets—one with the god Horus and the other with Ptah. An important group of clay statues was also found at the site. One had a lamp placed on its head. A two-story model shrine with windows and perforated ceramic cups with tripod feet were also uncovered (Daviau and Dion 2002b: 48, 49, 63).

Edom

Horvat Qitmit

The site of Horvat Qitmit, in the northern Negev at the eastern margin of a broad valley, had one period of occupation during the seventh century B.C.E. with two phases of use (Beit-Arieh 1997: 390). It is the only site so far known from the Edomite region to yield a possible sanctuary complex, and moreover, the structures identified as forming the sanctuary are the only buildings at the site.

The total area covered was 1,300 square meters and consisted of two parts (fig. 65): complex A in the south and complex B in the north (Beit-Arieh 1991: 95–103). Complex A (fig. 66) had three rooms joined together as a single structure, a rectangular platform bounded on three sides by a stone wall to the southwest, and a second circular stone wall enclosing a basin, a pit, and an altar. Altogether, complex A comprised 300 square meters. The three-room structure was built of local flint stone and measured 10.5 m × 5 m. The walls were 0.6 m to 0.7 m thick and were preserved to a height of three courses or 0.60 m. The three rooms opened to the south, and each had a white floor of crushed and beaten lime on the ground layer.

The structure was modified at a slightly later date. The walls of two of the rooms were made thicker. A bench was added along the western wall of the west chamber. A threshold block and step were added to the east chamber. In all three of the rooms, podia-like wall segments with flat stones on top were built perpendicular to the entrances.

South and west of this grouping by about 11 m was the second feature of complex A. It consisted of a platform 1.25 m × 1 m that was constructed of medium-sized fieldstones laid on the bedrock. It survived to a height of 0.30 m. The platform was aligned with its corners at the cardinal points of the compass. Straight walls on the east, south, and west, which met and formed right angles, enclosed the platform on three sides. The north side was open, facing the grouping of rooms. The platform was situated at the southeast corner of the enclosure. All the surfaces were covered with white plaster.

To the south and east of the group of rooms and east of the feature just described, was the third element in the complex. This was another grouping of items: a small platform, a basin, and a pit all enclosed by a circular wall. The entire ensemble was bedded on a rock that sloped to the southeast. The platform was a large flat piece of flint stone (0.90 m × 0.70 m × 0.30 m) set on a base of smaller flint stone slabs. The round installation or basin (1 m in diameter) was 1.5 m from the platform and was constructed of fieldstones. The inner surface was plastered with the same coating used to cover the feature to the west. Near the basin was a pit hewn into the rock, 0.80 m deep. The wall that enclosed the grouping of elements was of medium-sized stones. A wall ran along the south from the circular space to the grouping of rooms and served to limit easy access from the south.

From the grouping of three rooms came a variety of wheel-made vessels, hand-made bowls and basins, some figurines, and bones of sheep and goats. These may all have come from the grouping in its second phase of use. The area to the southwest and enclosed on three sides also yielded finds, most coming from the area of the platform. These were clay figurines, ceramic stands, pottery vessels, bronze artifacts, seashells, and stone objects. One group of items consisted of 2 ostrich figurines, a hand from a statue, a clay dagger, and a fragment of an animal figurine. A second group had a life-sized hand grasping an object. A third group, found outside the enclosure to the south, included 20 figurines and fragments of pottery vessels. North of the platform were found 2 anthropomorphic stands, 1 cylindrical stand, a human figurine once attached to something else, 3 heads from human figurines, a fragment of an animal figurine, and a cooking pot of a type known as Judean. The general volume of finds from this area was high: 12 human figurines, 36 animal figurines, 14 statue parts, 20 anthropomorphic stands, and 5 bowls. There were also some bronze objects, including earrings and finger rings. The finds from the second, totally enclosed sector were fewer in number: fragments of statues, 10 figurines, and some pottery sherds. Noteworthy finds from the area were a sphinx figure, the clay head of a three-horned figure, and a stamp seal showing a human wearing a long cloak with left arm and hand raised.

Complex B (fig. 67) lay 15 m north of the three-room grouping of Complex A. It sat on lower ground and was a square construction 8.5 m × 8 m, built of stone, with walls ca. 1.20 m thick (Beit-Arieh and Beck 1995: 20–26; Beit-Arieh 1991: 103–9). The design seems to be that of a central unit, possibly an open court, surrounded by rooms. The structure went through two phases. In its first phase (fig. 68), the heavy walls were built, and the rooms were established on the north and west sides around a central courtyard. The rooms were constructed with heavy, pier-like supports. At the south end of the courtyard was a single standing stone (*maṣṣēbâ*). In the second phase, there was some rearranging of the rooms.

From this complex have come some figurine fragments, sherds, animal bones, and incised inscriptions. The pottery for the site falls into three categories: Edomite-type vessels with painting probably produced in the Arad-Beersheba Valley; generic Judah-Transjordan bowls that imitate Assyrian types; and domestic vessels mostly of local manufacture along with some Judean cooking pots. Among the pottery objects were perforated incense-burning cups of a kind known from other Transjordanian sites (Beit-Arieh 1988: 39). The ceramic cult stands show continuity with a long tradition throughout the ancient Near East. What is unusual is that the stands are not common at Iron Age II sites such as Horvat Qitmit. Their presence here testifies to either a revival of older forms or maintenance of a conservative tradition. Many of the pottery fragments came from anthropomorphic vessels. Some of these showed traces of painting. Included were bearded figures, nude female figures holding their breasts, and a figure grasping a sword. These were all wheel-made, hollow forms. The figural types developed from a long tradition in the Palestinian region stretching back to at least the seventeenth century B.C.E. The strong similarity between the sculpture and the pots at Horvat Qitmit has led P. Beck and others to conclude that the coroplast and potter were one and the same (Beit-Arieh and Beck 1995: 112). Among possible cult equipment were chalices decorated with attached pomegranates. Another group of fragments appeared to represent musicians playing lyres and tambourines (Beit-Arieh and Beck 1995: 161–68). Inscriptions have been found at Horvat Qitmit that record the name *qws*. This has been read as a reference to the primary male deity of the Edomite pantheon, Qos/Qaus, who was a martial god (Beit-Arieh and Beck 1995: 186–88).

In the early 1990s, a cache of 60 ceramic objects—which included anthropomorphic vessels, cylindrical stands, and chalices, all resembling the material from Horvat Qitmit—was unearthed at ʿEn Hatzeva. This site is also in the Negev and may have been a second sanctuary, though only minimal structural elements have been found to date (Cohen and Yisrael 1996b: 40–51 and cover).

The datable material from Horvat Qitmit shows that the sanctuary was in operation in the late seventh and early sixth centuries B.C.E. The evidence of the Edomite presence as revealed in the pottery and the inscriptions does pose a problem. It has been assumed that the Edomites were not established in this region of the Negev, only 10 km south of Arad. However, the major find of the sanctuary at Horvat Qitmit along with the discovery of the cache of objects at ʿEn Hatzeva and the unearthing of similar types of pottery at other Negev sites strongly suggests that in the late seventh and early sixth centuries this part of the Negev was Edomite territory (Beit-Arieh 1988: 41).

The developments at both Khirbat al-Mudayna and Horvat Qitmit share in common the catalyst of expanded trade from the south. Khirbat al-Mudayna was one of several sites that took shape in Moab during Iron Age IIB and IIC. In Iron Age IIB, local Moabite forces were responsible for the creation of fortified sites along the wadis of the Moab region, as the Kingdom of Moab established itself with the decline of the power of Israel. In Iron Age IIC, Moab was technically free, but its autonomy was curbed by its strong neighbor Assyria. However, the Assyrians did bring peace with them: Khirbat al-Mudayna and the other excavated site of Lehun show prosperous, albeit small towns. The finds from the sanctuary at Khirbat al-Mudayna testify to the far-flung trade connections of this little town on the eastern edge of the settled Levant. The incense must have come north on the King's Highway, which crossed the massive Wadi Mujib not far from the town. Daviau and Steiner (2000: 11–14) have noted that incense altars are rare in Transjordanian contexts, suggesting that their presence here at Khirbat al-Mudayna may reflect influences from western places, where incense altars have a longer history of use, and this seems to be supported by the fact that the closest parallels are found at Megiddo. Sites in Moab have also yielded 6 proto-Aeolic capitals such as were used for royal secular constructions in Israel and Judah (Herr 1997c: 173). Though it was removed from the main Levantine centers of cultural development to the north and west, Moab was connected via an extensive trade network to the larger Levantine world, and these connections were more than just sources of goods; ideas were also moving along the routes.

Horvat Qitmit was also stimulated by the trade that came out of the Wadi Arabah and passed through the Beersheba Valley to the Mediterranean. It must have been in part the needs of these caravans that motivated the establishment and maintenance of the sanctuary complex. No doubt the nomads of the previous periods now became the caravan leaders of Iron Age IIC, a pattern that is also well known in more-recent times with the Bedouin (Stephens 1991). Whether (like the little shrine at the fortified caravansaray at Teman from Iron Age IIB) the sanctuary at Horvat Qitmit was in some way pan-religious, or it was specifically dedicated to the gods of Edom cannot be determined. The tripartite arrangement of enclosed spaces does suggest a concern for tripartite divine relationships, which are well documented in Semitic religion. Herr has suggested that the national deity of Edom, Qaus (Qôs, *qws*), whose name appears inscribed at Horvat Qitmit, was probably the main deity worshiped at the site along with his consort, Asherah (or Astarte), in a pattern also known on the popular level for the cult of Yahweh (Herr 1997c: 176). The third deity is unknown, but all three may be represented in the ceramic sculptures found at Horvat Qitmit and ʿEn Hatzeva. Even specific dedications may not have deterred others from making use of the sanctuary, just as the little wayside shrine outside Khirbat al-Mudayna seems to have been used by anyone passing on the road. The Assyrian peace encouraged long-distance trade in part by providing some level of political stability to the Levantine region and by increasing the demand for tribute that could only be obtained by exploiting new markets. People who made their living by long-distance trade needed places to find solace. The political situation may have been more stable, but the realities of traveling through the Levantine world must still have posed many threats.

Architectural Patterns: A Post-colonial "Nationalist Revival"?

When analyzing the results of the excavations at Alalakh, Woolley noted that the Level III temple showed a change in the cult focus. During the Hittite period, the temple had been designed on a bent-axis format but later was changed to a direct-axis approach. Woolley argued that this was the result of a "nationalist revival" at the site that occurred as a result of the fall of Hittite hegemony. The direct-axis approach had characterized the temple prior to Hittite Imperial control of the region, and its dramatic reappearance after the Hittite collapse, Woolley thought, had political meaning (Woolley 1955: 78).

Kohlmeyer noted a similar change in the Aleppo Citadel temple. In the eleventh century B.C.E., the image of King Taita was introduced alongside that of the Storm God, which resulted in a change of cultic focus. The king's image altered the composition and meaning of the image from being a cult figure of the Storm God to being a dedicatory work. By removing the Storm God's cultic role, the workers reverted the focus of the room from its Hittite bent-axis format to its earlier, direct-axis design. Though Kolhmeyer does not actually argue that this is also evidence of a "nationalist revival," the fact that he introduces Woolley's argument for Alalakh makes it hard to believe that he is not suggesting something similar for Aleppo (Kohlmeyer 2009: 197).

At Beth-shean in the Palestinian area, both Mazar and James have noted the reappearance of a markedly Canaanite material culture in stratum V (Mazar Upper VI, James V), in which the two-temple format appears, showing a significant change from the earlier temple design. Though neither Mazar nor James proposes a "nationalist revival" in the political sense suggested for Alalakh and Aleppo, there is a suggestion that the stratum represents some type of intentional rejection of what had been present on the spot. For each of these instances, it is tempting to argue for a resurgence of preconquest, precolonial identity that perhaps emerged in the moment between the collapse of the two respective empires (the Hittite in the north and the Egyptian in the south) and the massive influx of new demographic forces (Arameans in the north and "Peoples of the Sea" and proto-Israelites in the south). But is this sort of reading valid?

Much work has been done in the field of postcolonial criticism in the last decade, and there is no reason to rehearse it all here (Chaturvedi 2000). At its heart lies the notion that colonized peoples retain a sense of their precolonized identities that both helps them to negotiate a new sense of self in the changed situation of being conquered and colonized and gives them a connection with the preconquest and precolonized past that can reemerge under the right circumstances to inform intellectual and artistic production. The study has mainly been concerned with conquest and colonization in the modern world, though there are a certain number of archaeologists, historians, and art historians who are beginning to examine these ideas as they related to the ancient world (Graves-Brown, Jones, and Gamble 1996; Lyons and Papadopoulos 2002). To date, however, no one has looked specifically at the Hittite and New Kingdom Egyptian empires from this postcolonial perspective. Do these three cases offer a glimpse of a preconquest sense that was reemerging in North Syria and Palestine in the eleventh century B.C.E.?

Even to address the question, we must answer two other questions: (1) Was there an actual sense of a specific identity attached to a place and manifested in cultural elements such as the direct-axis approach to a cult figure inside a temple or the building of paired temples? (2) Did the Hittite and Egyptian Late Bronze Age imperial aspirations include a colonization program that deracinated the local indigenous populations? Locating identity in ancient Levantine populations is usually limited to the pots-equal-peoples approach. Certain physical features in the archaeological record are argued to be representative of a specific culture's production, and their presence in the archaeological record in sufficient quantities or in a dramatic manner are considered evidence for the existence of the people who produced them on a particular site. Beyond this, it is difficult to ascertain what ancient Levantine peoples of the Bronze Age thought about in terms of identity beyond agricultural and ancestral ties to the land itself. So if the imperial forces did not separate the conquered peoples from their land physically, did a change in the overlords who exploited them also result in a change to their identity? For those in the upper echelon of the conquered society, the initial answer is certainly yes. This group had lost its position and, unless the conquering force wanted to use them to govern the conquered peasants, then they were effectively without an identity. But this would not seem to have been the case in either the Hittite or Egyptian imperial scenarios.

Day (2008) has isolated some nine stages by which conquering peoples take over, displace, and eventually eradicate the conquered peoples and their older claims to conquered land. In his structure, the Hittite and Egyptian empires had merely engaged in the first two stages. They had claimed a right to the land through the physical act of military conquest and had begun to name portions of the conquered territory. We can see this in the references to controlled territories in official inscriptions and documents. However, other than establishing a branch of the Hittite imperial family at Carchemish, there was no major demographic shifting. There is no evidence that residents of Hittite Anatolia or New Kingdom Egypt began to move into the North Syrian or Palestinian regions, requiring that the natives be displaced. What really seems to have existed in both areas were vassal kingdom structures, with some direct Hittite and Egyptian presence at Carchemish and Beth-shean. Under these circumstances, it is difficult to conceive that the imperial ambitions of either the Hittites or the Egyptians required a suppression of local identities, such as they might have been, because neither empire was really looking to annex the territories, to move their own peoples into them, or to push out the indigenous populations.

If this analysis is correct, then reading the events at Alalakh, Aleppo, and Beth-shean as evidencing a postcolonial response that can be labeled a "nationalist revival" seems unjustified. On the other hand, the changes made to the temples on the Aleppo Citadel and at Beth-shean do require some consideration of the historical setting in which they seem to have been created. As Kohlmeyer has pointed out, the image that King Taita erects of himself to accompany Teshub recalls the iconography of Hittite kingship. Even though the stylistic treatment of the body reflects features associated with the Neo-Hittite carvings, the attributes of costume and headdress belong to the older royal iconography (Kohlmeyer 2009: 197–98). King Taita may well have shifted the bent-axis format of the Hittite-period temple back to the pre-Hittite direct-axis format, but he chose to use in his own image attributes that had belonged to Hittite kingship. Visually he was aligning himself with what had just been and was not making any type of radical break.

In a similar manner, the new rulers at Beth-shean stratum V (Mazar VI) chose to treat all of the Egyptian New Kingdom royal material (the steles of Seti I and Ramesses II and the statue of Ramesses III) with great respect. They were erected outside the north temple in the large west side courtyard, and so they were clearly visible reminders of the older order that was no longer in operation. Rather than suggesting any type of "national revival," the eleventh-century b.c.e. finds at both Aleppo and Beth-shean suggest that the new local rulers were looking to align themselves with the older order and trying to place themselves back in the settings of now-vanished empires.

Something akin to this type of political anachronism in the choice of visual forms may also lie behind the strange arrangement of the two temples at Tell Taʿyinat that has so recently come to light. These two structures placed almost at a right angle to each other seem to be recalling the design of Temple V at Hattuša. In the earlier case, the design is of two cult chambers that share a common courtyard being placed at right angles within the larger temple. Given present dating to the eighth century b.c.e. for the Tell Taʿyinat temples, it seems unreasonable to posit a revived Hittite form. However, the excavations have shown that there is important building activity below the level of the remains of Buildings I and II, and so the present remains could replicate an older design at the site that goes back to at least the ninth century b.c.e. (T. Harrison 2009: 177).

Neo-Hittites and Arameans

The Neo-Hittite and Aramean cities probably began to build temples as soon as they were either secure or established. If ʿAin Dara is the rule and not the exception, then there must have been monumental religious buildings in the region by the end of Iron Age I, if not earlier, and the temple from the citadel at Aleppo supports this view. The fact that Ugarit and Alalakh did succumb to some type of outside force suggests that there were major disruptions of such a nature that one or more centuries were needed for strong urban centers to reemerge that were capable of monumental building. The archaeological record makes clear that the temples that survive from the Iron Age in this region were all prestigious buildings that used stone for part of the construction. They required major investments of labor to be constructed. Even the superstructures of mud-brick and wood-crib construction demanded skilled guidance. The temples were all separated from the general populace and, with the exception of ʿAin Dara, had become architectural features within palace complexes. Whether another group of temples existed in the lower cities to service the needs of the general population remains unknown from the present excavations.

Phoenician

Most standing remains of Phoenician sacred architecture are of Persian, Hellenistic, or Roman date. Even sanctuaries with an older core have these later accretions that make interpreting their original forms almost impossible. From the limited architectural evidence of remains of early Iron Age sanctuaries built along the Phoenician coast, some general architectural principles have been gleaned that seem still to have been used in building during later periods. Sanctuaries were most commonly modest, not monumental, affairs and fall into two categories: open-air precincts and enclosed buildings. Precincts open to the sky, such as at Tell Sukas, seem to have contained a paved, open, elevated courtyard with an installation such as a small shrine or altar. This form retained validity through the early Iron Age and into the Persian period. The post-sixth-century B.C.E. Sanctuary of Eshmun on the outskirts of Sidon (Bostan esh-Sheikh) is a monumentalized version of the early Iron Age type (fig. 69). Slightly less impressive was the sanctuary located at Amrit (fig. 70). A variation on the open-air sanctuary is found at Ain el-Hayat, near Amrit, where stood two opposing chapels decorated with Egyptianizing features; each rested on a cubic stone base, 3 m square. Certainly this type of precinct must have been more common in early Iron Age Phoenicia than the finds to date reveal.

None of the important Phoenician cities has yielded remains of monumental enclosed sacred architecture. Josephus, the first-century C.E. historian, records (*Ag. Ap.* 17.113) that King Hiram I (969–936 B.C.E.) engaged in a massive reconstruction program at Tyre that included the rebuilding and refurbishing of the city's sanctuaries, implying that they had existed for some time (eleventh-century buildings perhaps?). No specific building information is provided in the text, and Markoe has recently argued that the spatial constraints on the island of Tyre must have made real estate expensive and open space quite limited. Hiram may have needed to resort to building up rather than out in his reconstruction program.

A tower-like building rendered on the Assyrian relief from the palace of Sennacherib at Nineveh has been identified as a portrait of the Temple of Melqart at Tyre (fig. 71). If this is the case, then the placement of this tower near the water (and, one assumes, the city wall) does not match with the notion that the Temple of Melqart stood, along with the Temple of Astarte, on the acropolis in the southwest of the city (Markoe 2000: 196). However, the literary tradition and the Assyrian image, if properly interpreted, do suggest that the reemergent cities of Iron Age I probably did include some massive temples. The temples at Tell Abu Hawam and Kition suggest that, whenever possible, orientation with Late Bronze Age temples at the site and some continuity of cult were maintained.

Although the construction technique used for the Iron Age I temple at Abu Hawam indicates a coarsening in the level of technical ability, the quality of building for the Iron Age II temple at Sarepta reveals that once again, as in Late Bronze Age, a sacred building (even a modest building) could command greater resources and prestigious building technology than other structures in the town. At Kition, the ashlar masonry of the earlier building was reused. Interior spaces were kept modest, and the temples at Tell Arka, Sarepta, and Abu Hawam were fundamentally single, rectangular rooms. The reconstruction of the Phoenician temple at Kition indicates that only a small rectangular room at the west end of the complex was completely enclosed—again, a modest interior spatial design. The small temple at Sarepta evinced a built installation inside in its first version, and a similar interior installation may be what the excavators found in Iron Age I Abu Hawam's temple. Even though the interior space of the Sarepta temple was regularized by the removal of the installation in the second building phase, the next temple did retain the benches for the placement of votive offerings.

Nothing of temple architecture that survives in the Phoenician region proper attests to the high quality of stonework known from tenth-century city gates and walls at Tell Dor. Certainly the great temples at Tyre and Sidon and Byblos may have made use of prestigious techniques, which may explain why Solomon welcomed Phoenician technical assistance for the building of his new temple. On the other hand, the evidence for high-quality ashlar construction on Cyprus soon after 1200 B.C.E. may well indicate that this sort of construction entered Phoenician regions soon after as well and was probably carried by some of the groups of "Peoples of the Sea" settling in the coastal area. What does still exist seems to show that these high levels of building capability were not to be found in the secondary and tertiary levels of cities in the Phoenician region.

While it is generally agreed that the Phoenician coast did not suffer from massive destruction and depopulation in the disruptions of 1200 B.C.E., it seems that recovery in the region, as in North Syria, was not very rapid. The temple at Tell Abu Hawam is the only structure that testifies to a degree immediate response. All the other sanctuaries are from Iron Age II and, except for the sanctuary at Kition, do not demonstrate structural continuity with earlier remains below. They are from at least 400 years after the disruptions, and questions of continuity over such a long stretch, particularly in terms of architectural issues, are quite valid to raise. Even if residual Canaanite cultural forms still had some power to inform design decisions because of demographic continuity on the site, certainly 400 years of cultural development (which itself had come into being as a response to a dramatic shift in the surrounding economic and human environments) would have compromised any real direct linkages between the periods before and after 1200 B.C.E. On the other hand, Wen-Amon's one real description of an architectural setting, a second-story audience chamber, is found in the palace of the Phoenician prince of Byblos. It hints at architectural sophistication and sensitivity that could still be found in one of the Phoenician cities not long after the collapse of 1200 B.C.E. The prince sits before a large window that affords a view of the sea. He is framed by the landscape, and the sound of the pounding waves emphasizes his authority. Josephus's information about Hiram's rebuilding program in Tyre is interesting and may reflect a reality of the city in the tenth century. However, these two literary sources remain our only references to major architecture in the Phoenician region during the first two centuries of the early Iron Age. The possible portrait of the temple on the Assyrian relief from Nineveh seems to pose more questions than it answers. The temple is in the wrong place and, with its tower form, is not like anything else so far found in the region.

The Temple of Astarte at Kition is problematic because it is not clear whether it is a reflection of the building forms and techniques employed at the end of Iron Age I that might have been seen at Tyre or Sidon or whether it is strictly a response to the existing situation at Kition, where remains of a well-constructed monumental structure were obviously still visible and may have been reused. The temple does follow the form of large religious complexes as they developed on the opposite mainland in the sixth and fifth centuries B.C.E., with small holy of holies enclosed by a large, architecturally defined precinct. When it is possible to look at early colonial Phoenician sacral architecture, such as at Kommos on southern Crete (see fig. 72; Shaw 1989: 165–83), the structure is a small, rectangular, single-chambered building of modest proportions constructed on an older Minoan ashlar building. The chamber was equipped with benches along the two long walls, and in phase B (800–600 B.C.E.) with an elaborated, tripartite installation inside the chamber proper. Nothing of the Kommos shrine reflects the kind of architectural expression seen at Kition. The Kommos structure probably served the needs of a transient merchant community rather than an established town, and so perhaps the Kition temple was an example of major metropolitan sacred architecture as it was developing in Tyre and Sidon during the Iron Age I and Iron Age IIA.

Philistine

Two groups of Philistine sanctuaries seem to emerge from the archaeological evidence. There are the impressive, isolated structures that were built with some consideration for creating spatial hierarchies and interplays of interior and exterior spaces at Tell Qasile and Ekron. Quite different are the multiroomed, somewhat undefined, and perhaps less-formal sanctuaries of Ashdod. These all share in common the use of easily available mud brick. The spaces created are never large. There is no attempt to overwhelm or disorient individuals who were inside the spaces. The buildings, whether clearly separated from the fabric of the town as at Tell Qasile and Ekron or embedded into it as in all the shrines at Ashdod, are small. They show no signs of being associated with palaces but, rather, exist on their own.

Israelite and Judahite

Haran (1977: 12) noted that ancient Hebrew distinguished between enclosed temples and open spaces for worship where any Israelite could offer sacrifices—the latter called *bamôt*. Included in this category were "high places," though it needs to be noted that the concept of "high places" is itself the result of a mistranslation of *bāmâ* as *excelsus* in Jerome's Vulgate (Nakhai 1994: 19). It has come to be accepted that one type of sacred space that developed in the Israelite regions of Palestine during the early Iron Age was the high place. The high place has become a category of sacred space, and clearly there are shrines that were built as high places, though whether this was because the type was already recognized by the builders cannot be determined. The sanctuary at the source of the Jordan at Tel Dan and the possible sanctuaries at Mount Ebal, Shiloh, Hazor, and the Bull Site would all fit the description of high place shrines. The remains at Mount Ebal and the Bull Site are not accepted without reservations as being true hallowed spaces, nor do they conform comfortably to the criteria listed by Coogan (1987) for a sacred site. However, if they are sacred sites, then they represent the earliest examples of what might be called Israelite sacred architecture—basically enclosures with built platforms to serve as altars. The same is true for Tel Dan several centuries later and on a more elaborate scale. The extramural shrine at Makmish works in a similar way, but it is not set apart on a high piece of ground.

What does seem clear is that the high place form was only one option for early Iron Age architects in the region. Hazor's modest Iron Age I shrine seems to fit the high place definition, but it may also have been an actual room rather than just an enclosed area, and the same is true for the Iron Age II cult space at Lachish. It may be presumptuous to call them temples, but if they were roofed, then they were not solely focused on the exterior experience of the high place shrines. None of these early sanctuaries is architecturally impressive, despite the fact that the small cult structure at Lachish must be considered the best example of building at the site for the period.

The variety of shrine types, albeit all modest in terms of size, to be found in Iron Age I and II throughout the region that was to become ancient Israel is somewhat startling. Besides the "high places" already noted, there may have been domestic shrines—small chapels found within the confines of certain buildings, such as may have been the case at Megiddo and at nearby Taʿanach, the latter possibly associated with some type of industry. The shrine at the fortress of Arad may be argued to work in a similar way: a chapel intended to serve a specific group of people within a defined setting. Although the shrine is an impressive complex within the context of the fort, it in no way announces its presence from the outside. These religious spaces hidden within the confines of larger buildings seem the antithesis of complexes such as Tell el-Mazar and Makmish, which may have been designed to provide some sacred space for travelers. The function of the gate sanctuary at Kuntillet ʿAjrud may have been similar. It has a particularly unusual design, because one had to pass through the sacred space to enter the more fortified interior of the building, which does not seem to have had a religious function. This is quite different from the sanctuary of the fortress at Arad which was clearly set apart but was within the fortress itself. The *maṣṣēbôt* shrines at Tel Dan, the only such series found so far, may also have been intended for the needs of a transient community that passed through Tel Dan, though the shrines may just as well represent the more popular level of religion that existed in the ancient kingdoms of Israel and Judah in Iron Age II.

The structures associated with the first possible manifestations of religious building after 1200 B.C.E. are of modest construction. There is nothing noteworthy in the remains of Mount Ebal or Hazor or the Bull Site. This is certainly one reason for the lack of agreement about whether they were important structures. Much of what has been identified as sacred architecture is not noteworthy from the standpoint of building techniques. Lachish's little cult space is significant only in comparison with what surrounds it. Building 2072 at Megiddo could well represent the influence of the Philistines in the area; its more complicated design matches with the more precocious nature of sanctuary-building in the Philistine region as compared with building in the Israelite area during Iron Age I. The Building 2072 finds of Philistine loom weights and an example of figurative painted pottery suggest some degree of engagement with the Philistine region. By Iron Age II, on the other hand, portions of the Arad fortress shrine used cut-stone construction, and clearly, cut and fitted stones were the dominant technique of the construction of the Tel Dan sacred spaces. Of the surviving hallowed areas, those at Tel Dan stand out for the high quality of execution, even down to the North Syrian–style socket bases that held the poles for the canopy. This may be the result of residual Phoenician influence in the region, even in Iron Age IIB. It is also worth noting that the arrangement of Tel Dan with its paved road leading through a series of gates and climbing up to the hallowed place resembles (albeit it on a much more modest scale) the arrangement found at Carchemish and Guzana. These are all the products of royal patronage in Iron Age IIB.

Ammonite, Moabite, and Edomite

The evidence to date does indicate that, in all three of the Iron Age II kingdoms of Transjordan, there was some building of a sacral nature. There is no clear format that was shared by all three. Shrines without urban contexts may well have been the norm in all the area, though nothing has been found in early Iron Age Ammon to suggest that this was the case. However, the older, Late Bronze Age square temple found at the Amman airport indicates that isolated religious structures of this sort had been an architectural type in the previous period (Herr 1983b: 223–29). The Iron Age II examples in Edom and Moab may have served the expanded trade networks that seem to have emerged in the region. The possible Ammonite temple follows the pattern of citadel sanctuaries that were situated overlooking the town below that we know from the same period in North Syria. By contrast, the temple at Khirbat al-Mudayna is situated within the actual fabric of the town, and it resembles temples of the Phoenician and Philistine regions. Nothing in the actual construction of these buildings is notable other than the use of stone as opposed to mud, and even this was not uncommon in this area because stone is abundant. The blocks have not been specially treated. Much the same needs to be said about the sanctuary at Horvat Qitmit, which has nothing special to recommend it architecturally except for its novelty of place. It is the first and only sanctuary to be constructed in the region. Whoever commissioned it and whoever executed the commission had nothing to use as a model. Its plan does not resemble plans found anywhere else in the southern Levant. Herr may be correct in arguing that the three enclosed spaces indicate that the dedication was tripartite, but it is not common for this feature of Semitic religion to influence architectural forms in the Iron Age. Only the Phoenician temple at Kition can be argued also to have this feature. If the Edomite sanctuary did recall any other forms, they would be the Philistine Iron Age I sanctuaries at Tell Qasile and Ekron, with their interplays of courtyards and enclosed buildings. However, a gulf of 500 years separates the fully developed Iron Age I Philistine sanctuaries and this Edomite construction. The Philistine temples were not in operation and had probably been gone for centuries by the time the Edomite builder erected the sanctuary at Horvat Qitmit. Therefore, this complex was a new creation, the design of which was intended to serve a particular cultic need that was probably seeing its first physical manifestation.

Conclusion

The archaeological evidence is admittedly uneven, the result of the disparity in excavations in the region as a whole. Patterns, however, can be revealed. The first areas to begin to build sacred architecture after the turmoil of 1200 b.c.e. were the coastal and North Syrian regions. In this first period at the sites of Ashdod, Tell Abu Hawam, Tell Qasile, and Ekron, the structures may be the result of the recently settled "Peoples of the Sea." Remaining connections with the Aegean can be seen in the high percentage of Cypriot pottery found at Tell Abu Hawam and the "Ashdoda" figures at Ashdod that Dothan has argued are local versions of a Mycenean cult figurine. The sanctuary at Tell Qasile suggests that, at some of these new settlements, there was a kind of steady development and growing prosperity that is reflected in the increased opulence with each rebuilding of the sanctuary over a 200-year period. A similar pattern has emerged at Ekron, where the earliest temple buildings in Field I on the acropolis and at Field IV in the lower city testify already to rather impressive initial constructions—complexes of connected rooms rather than single spaces that, in the case of the Field IV sanctuary, were embellished and elaborated in the second version. The lack of excavation in the appropriate levels at the major Phoenician sites deprives us of the ability to determine whether there was any major cultural force emerging from this region during this first period of recovery. The finds of local versions of Aegean-style pottery in the region of the ʿAmuq Plain seems to suggest that this area was also feeling some of the impact of Aegean penetration—perhaps by some group of "Peoples of the Sea." In North Syria, the finds from the Aleppo Citadel excavations suggest a rapid recovery and perhaps the emergence of a new kingdom, Palistin, the king of which, Taita, chose to associate himself with older Imperial Hittite forms, even if his kingdom was some type of amalgamation of native people and a newly arrived group from the "Peoples of the Sea" with strong Aegean associations. ʿAin Daraʾs initial rise may have been stimulated by the same catalyst.

The Beth-shean evidence indicates that the Egyptian cultural influence in southern Canaan was still a powerful force in the half century after 1200 B.C.E. It may have been an outpost, because there is no evidence for any other major foreign or native site anywhere in the interior during Iron Age I. However, by the eleventh century B.C.E., the Egyptian presence was gone, and an indigenous force was again in control but was still using Egyptian visual associations to bolster its claims. The evidence at Hazor, which may have been destroyed as early as the first quarter of the thirteenth century B.C.E., suggests that the recovery in other sites in the interior was at best a modest level of cultural achievement. Where once there had stood impressive Late Bronze Age towns, there now may have existed villages with resources capable of only small-scale building. Where new building is found during this early phase, such as at Mount Ebal and the Bull Site, the structures are modest affairs without clear diagnostic features to allow for easy identification as being cultic. But the slightly later, extramural sanctuary at Tell el-Mazar in the Jordan Valley does suggest that, within a century of the collapse of the Late Bronze Age, even small communities were able to design more-architecturally-complex spaces for cultic purposes.

The lack of accepted dates for the Megiddo material poses a problem, since it is not at all clear whether the possible shrines at the site should be dated to a time of recovery after 1200 B.C.E., to an intermediate period in the history of the site, or to the tenth century. Kempinski's desire for the evidence to point to the architectural development of the domestic shrine that can possibly be related to literary evidence in Judges results in the argument that the material must belong to the next phase of development and not to the period of initial recovery. Stern's arguments against a domestic shrine and in favor of the remains' just being elements in a larger building, perhaps a Solomonic-period palace, raise the issue of Solomon's role in the development of Megiddo in Iron Age II—an issue that is hotly contested by the present excavators. For the moment, the Megiddo material is difficult to fit into a clear chronological schema. If Kempinski is correct, then this is the only existing architectural evidence for the supposed domestic cult, because nothing of an architectural form survives to distinguish the cultic corner at Taʿanach. On the other hand, Ussishkin has read the evidence as coming from a real temple at the site, which was an important if not massive building that was set apart by a courtyard and use of the prestigious building technique of ashlar masonry for some portions. He has argued that this was an Israelite structure and therefore must belong to the period after the initial recovery at other sites but perhaps before the Solomonic period.

Perhaps Building 2072 points to some type of interface between the emerging communities of the early Iron Age during the period between the initial recovery and the Iron Age II building phases. The design looks to be an import from the Philistine area. Philistine loom weights and a painted pot were also found in the building, so perhaps it is not too farfetched to argue that the structure was intended to serve the needs of a small resident Philistine population at Megiddo, a population that may have become established at the site following the turmoil of 1200 B.C.E. It is true that the Philistine region is a distance from Megiddo, but certainly not so far as to rule out the presence of a small resident community at Megiddo in the eleventh century. Certainly the building design by itself could represent an architect's independent discovery or an exotic design imported for some reason, but the loom weights and the painted jug found in association with the structure argue for some type of Philistine presence at the site.[17] The markedly important courtyard is a feature that does appear in most Philistine sanctuaries and becomes a significant feature in the Iron Age II Israelite sanctuaries at Tell Arad and Tel Dan. Whether this was the result of borrowing the concept from the Philistines during Iron Age I or was an independent creative discovery cannot be determined from the evidence.

The majority of the archaeological evidence comes from the Iron Age IIA and B periods, dating from the tenth to the eighth centuries B.C.E. By this point in time, an Aramean dynast in North Syria had begun to construct an impressive temple and palace complex at Guzana. The neighboring Neo-Hittite communities were also building, and the mixing of iconography that has been noted for the third group of reliefs from the Aleppo Citadel temple may well indicate that the sharp divisions between Arameans and Neo-Hittites had broken down, at least in the realm of rulers. However, the evidence from the Temple of the Storm God at Carchemish suggests that a sanctuary could operate with a degree of autonomy from the palace, at least in one Neo-Hittite center. Clearly the palace was close to the temple, but the temple had its

17. The roles that resident communities of alien peoples within ethnically defined urban settlements has not been widely explored as a feature of Near Eastern Late Bronze and Iron Age societal development; however, it is most definitely a field of archaeological investigation in ancient Mexico and China, where important urban centers with a defined ethnic population supported recognized alien neighborhoods (R. Millon, "The Place Where Time Began: An Archaeologist's Interpretation of What Happened in Teotihuacan History," in *Teotihuacan Art from the City of the Gods* [ed. K. Berrin and E. Pasztory; New York: Thames and Hudson 1993] 16–43; L. Feng, "Sogdians in Northwest China," in *Monks and Merchants: Silk Road Treasures from Northwest China* [ed. A. Juliano and J. Lerner; New York: Abrams, 2001] 220–29).

own precinct and was entered not directly from the palace compound but from the main street. Granted, the street was designed as a processional way with relief sculpture distinguishing the entire area as special and, in this sense, the palace was part of the larger design complex. However, the temple still seems to have had a degree of architectural autonomy that is not apparent at Guzana.

The situation at Tell Ta'yinat is difficult to decipher. It is not obvious how the area behind the palace actually functioned within the larger urban fabric itself. The temples form their own little precinct, but this area is not separate and seems to have been accessible quite easily, though this may not be true. It is obvious that the palace faces away from the temple and has no direct, clear architectural connection with the temple established by entrances; on the other hand, the two are related in terms of building techniques and formal entrance designs. Phoenicians, particularly Tyreans, were beginning to settle elsewhere, and the rebuilt temple at Kition on Cyprus testifies to Phoenician expansion and to the development of skills needed for massive stone architecture.

At the same time, the sanctuary at Sarepta indicates that smaller Phoenician settlements had also formulated a sacred type of architecture that fit comfortably into the fabric of the community. In the case of the sanctuary at Tell Qasile, there is evidence that, even after the city had become an Israelite outpost on the Mediterranean, the old Philistine temple in its final form was being used by the new Israelite community. Other Israelite sanctuaries are difficult to detect until the late tenth century. The initial manifestation of a sanctuary at Tel Dan is dated to the first period of the divided kingdom. Its later incarnations as well as the additional shrines at the site are all understood as architecture of the Kingdom of Israel. The same is the case for the little temple in the fortification at Arad. It is a sanctuary of the Kingdom of Judah.

It is in Iron Age IIB that temples appear again in Transjordan. The Late Bronze Age had seen temples at Deir 'Alla (fig. 61) and Pella (fig. 24) in the Jordan Valley and in the high country in the region of the modern-day Amman airport (fig. 73). Two of these structures have been recognized as isolated sanctuaries that must have served the needs of a nomadic society that lived in the region during the Late Bronze Age. In Iron Age II, the formation of political states similar to those developing north in Syria and west in Israel and Phoenicia must have played some role in the concurrent development of a sacred architecture. In Ammon and Moab, these shrines seem to belong within an urban context and therefore are even closer in their parallels to developments outside the region. The single extramural shrine at Khirbat al-Mudayna (Wadi ath-Thamad #13) may well reveal the needs of the traders who now plied the various routes. The same certainly may be the case for the gate shrine at Teman and the little extramural shrine on the Sharon Plain at Makmish. For each of these shrines, there were urban settings not very far away. They may have been frequented by small-scale traders. The Edomite shrines at Horvat Qitmit and 'En Hatzeva were truly isolated manifestations of religious devotion. They may have served the need of caravan traders (who were often at great distances from settlements and security) to find a place for ritual acts of piety in otherwise potentially inhospitable settings.

All of the Iron Age architectural remains identified as religious are modest in terms of interior size. With the exception of the paired structures at Beth-shean and two of the Philistine temples, none of the remains exhibits evidence for interior posts to support a complex roofing structure. The tradition throughout the Levantine region was for flat roofs, as is still largely the case today. The width of an interior space was dictated by the length of a single timber beam that could be used to form the lintel placed on opposing walls. A large interior space had to be formed either with long single beams, usually only available from the famed cedars of Lebanon, which can grow to a height of 40 meters, or by the use of interior supports, columns, on which the ends of two beams could rest. Interior supports may have been operative in the Philistine temples: Building 350 at Ekron and Temple 131 at Tell Qasile. However, the posts in Building 350 seem more likely to have supported a sun shade for one part of the courtyard than a complete roofing system. The supports for Temple 131 seem unnecessary because the room is not very wide, but they certainly could have supported a roofing structure.

On the other hand, what appear to be architectural supports in the remains may have been freestanding posts that had a cultic significance rather than a structural function. During the Late Bronze Age, there were temples in the Canaanite south at Hazor, Lachish, and at Beth-shean that show evidence for interior columns that could well have provided the needed structural support necessary for creating large interior spaces.[18] Both Beth-shean and Lachish were within the orbit of Egyptian influence (G. R. H. Wright 1985: 1.236). Beth-shean was the site of an Egyptian garrison, so the creation of such large interiors may have been the result of an Egyptian temple-building tradition, albeit on a much smaller scale. The tradition may have persisted through the building of the paired temples at Beth-shean since there is also evidence for the retention of the Egyptian steles and statue. Hazor sits between the Canaanite and Syrian regions. The Orthostat Temple could well point to a Canaanite Late Bronze Age practice of creating large interiors that has just not been found elsewhere to date, but the possible support columns are really only clear in the Middle Bronze Age version. The situation for the Late Bronze Age temple is not as obvious. In the Syrian region during the Late Bronze Age, the interiors show no signs of additional supports and are usually less than 10 m wide, a width that could easily have been spanned with single beams made from the cedars of Lebanon. The tradition for single-spanned interior spaces continued with the Iron Age constructions, which also do not exceed 10 m in width.

18. For a complete listing with drawings of all the supposed temples with structural columns from the Chalcolithic to Iron Age IIB, see G. R. H. Wright 1985: vol. 2, ill. 181.

Chapter 4

Continuity

Hallowed Ground

Continuity between Late Bronze Age and early Iron Age sanctuaries can be considered in a number of ways. Some of the early Iron Age shrines stood directly atop Late Bronze Age sacred structures. This was true for ʿAin Dara, Aleppo's Citadel temple, Abu Hawam, Kition, and Beth-shean. Of these, there may have been some cultic continuity at ʿAin Dara, Aleppo, Abu Hawam, and Beth-shean, because none of these sites exhibits any type of demographic shift at about 1200 B.C.E., though Beth-shean did witness a major change about half a century later, when the Egyptian garrison was removed. At Kition, there was a marked break in occupation between the Late Bronze Age and the Iron Age II sanctuary; this break is also evidenced elsewhere at the site—a break followed in the early Iron Age by a population shift. Therefore, though the spot may have retained a hallowed association, the Late Bronze Age cult probably did not survive into the early Iron Age. Something similar may have happened at Beth-shean between strata VII/VI (Mazar's Lower VI) and stratum V (Mazar's Upper VI), which marks the aftermath of the Egyptian withdrawal.

Carchemish, Lachish, Megiddo, and Hazor were all important Late Bronze Age cities that remained significant into the early Iron Age. However, in none of them is there evidence that the Late Bronze Age sacred topography continued to hold sway into the early Iron Age. The modest structures identified as shrines in Lachish, Megiddo, and Hazor have nothing to do with the much more impressive Late Bronze Age temples. The Middle Bronze Age *migdāl* temples at Shechem and Megiddo, which appear to have functioned in the Late Bronze Age, may still have been in use in the early Iron Age. The Middle Bronze Age *migdāl* at Pella had ceased operations in the Late Bronze Age when it was replaced by a smaller, far less robust structure. This in turn changed substantially in Iron Age II, when the final version of the temple was built, but the hallowed nature of the spot at Pella was never lost. Something similar may have happened at Aleppo, where the Iron Age I temple was erected over a Middle Bronze Age temple that must have functioned into the Late Bronze Age. At Carchemish, the evidence of the Late Bronze Age Hittite city is still unclear, but the

Neo-Hittite Temple of the Storm God shows no signs of being constructed over an earlier sanctuary.

Construction Techniques

Many of the structures identified as sanctuaries were constructed using traditional building materials and methods for the Levantine region. Most commonly walls are of mud brick, sometimes laid on top of a type of stone socle or foundation.[1] The tradition of using stone, not ashlar, but worked and fitted stone blocks as well as unworked, unhewn fieldstones for walls remains a constant for important structures. The caveats that G. R. H. Wright introduced (1985: 1.118–20) regarding the isolation of a standardized measuring system in the archaeological remains that can be argued to have been employed in Levantine building are still valid, as are his general observations. Levantine builders in the Bronze and Iron Ages probably used a measuring system borrowed either from Mesopotamia or Egypt, depending on where they were working. The cubit (Hebrew *ʾammoh*; Akkadian *ʾammatu*; Ugaritic *ʾmt*) was derived from the human body, the distance from the elbow to the tip of the middle finger. This unit was then subdivided into palms (Hebrew *topah/tepah*) and fingers (Hebrew *ʾeṣbaʾ*). Ezek 40:5 mentions a reed (Hebrew *qaneh*, Akkadian *qanu*) that equals 6 cubits in length, a more suitable measuring device for laying out large areas. G. R. H. Wright specifies a cubit of ca. 44.4 cm and a longer sacred cubit as used by Eziekial as just under 52 cm.[2] More recently, Barkay and Usssishkin have measured the public buildings in Level IV (ninth to eighth centuries B.C.E.) at Lachish with an eye to identifying the measurement system in use. They isolate a standard Egyptian cubit of 52.5 cm, which they argue was widely employed and that contrasts with a short cubit of 45 cm, which was used in Level III (eighth-century B.C.E.) structures. In discussing the city wall of level IV, they note that the walls of the tower are 6.20 m thick, and the goal may have been to achieve a thickness of 6.3 m when the plaster coating was still adhering. This would have resulted in the equivalent of 12 cubits or 2 royal Egyptian

---

1. It should be stressed that mud-brick building is neither easy nor necessarily cheap in terms of labor expended. The reconstruction of a 65 m–long stretch of the mud-brick city wall for Hattuša that is on average 12–13 m high required 2,700 tons of loam, 100 tons of straw, 1,500 tons of water for the mud-brick mixture alone. See J. Seeher, *A Mud brick City Wall at Hattusa: Diary of a Reconstruction* (Istanbul: Ege Yayınları, 2007). It is also worth noting that Western-trained archaeologists often lack sensitivity to mud-building traditions. The term *mud brick* is rather ubiquitous in its use and may not reveal so much the reality of what was built as the limitations of the archaeologist who reads all mud structures as mud brick or as a generic way of referring to what must have been the most likely superstructure if nothing has survived. Certainly, I must confess that I often used the term in this latter way in this book. In point of fact, mud can be employed for walls in a number different applications—that is, layered mud, rammed earth, and mud balls—none of which can be discerned from the stone socles if the mud superstructure is gone (Van Beek and Van Beek 2008: 3).

2. *The New Oxford Annotated Bible* (Oxford: Oxford Bible, 1962: 1052 n. 40.5) suggests 17.5 in. for the ordinary cubit, 20.68 in. for the long cubit, and 10 ft. 4 in. for the reed.

kanim. The use of the Egyptian cubit has been attested in other state constructions in the Kingdom of Judah and may well be indicative of the level of formal control of state-sponsored construction projects (Barkay and Ussishkin 2004: 417, 423). Unfortunately, the individual temple remains have not been systematically measured in the field with these units in mind, so it is impossible actually to take the published remains and work them into the proposed system in order to determine whether there was a standard. Moreover, since the temples range from the southwestern through the northeastern Levant, Wright's caveat still applies: the measurement system in use would probably have depended on whether Egypt or Mesopotamia was the dominant cultural force in the region.

Plans and Orientation

The plans of the Levantine temples have formed the basis for almost all analyses of sanctuaries. Temple plans have been categorized and studied in terms of deviation from an accepted norm. A consideration of the plans is an appropriate place to begin any new investigation. In 1971, G. R. H Wright published what remains the most comprehensive morphological study of temple plans of the Levant (Wright 1971a: 17–32)[3]. His six groupings of temple types recognized the individual design trends that had been noted by other scholars, who were examining more discrete units of material, and the categories have continued to be used by other investigators over the last 30 years (A. Mazar 1992b: 161–87; Fritz 1987b: 38–49; Ben-Tor 1973: 92–98).

Wright distinguished six types of temple plans in existence before the Iron Age: a long room, a broad room, a bent axis, a centralized square, a courtyard format, and a general high place. He maintained that these types were already identifiable in the archaeological record for the late Neolithic and by the Middle Bronze Age were in full flower throughout ancient Palestine. Many of the Iron Age temples presented in chap. 2 can be slotted into one or, occasionally, more than one of these divisions. The temples at Carchemish, Tell Ta'yinat, 'Ain Dara, Abu Hawam, and possibly the strata VII/VI (Mazar's Lower VI) temple at Beth-shean can all be classified as versions of long-room types. The shrine at Tell Arad is a broad-room type. The stratum X version of the sanctuary at Tell Qasile is a bent-axis design. The strata XII/XI temples at Tell Qasile could be taken as centralized square plans, considering that the buildings are generally square, and the focus of cult activity may have been the platform roughly in the center of the unified space. The lack of a clear focus for the shrine formed from Complexes A and B at Horvat Qitmit suggests that it should be treated as a courtyard type. Building 350 at Ekron may also be treated as a courtyard complex, as can Building 2072 at Megiddo. The constructions at Mount Ebal, the "Bull Shrine," and the

---

3. This remains the basic structure that Wright used in his more involved discussion of temples in his large architectural survey (G. R. H. Wright 1985: 1.215).

small shrine at Hazor can be classified as "high-place" types, while the sacred compound at Tel Dan may be categorized as a combination of a courtyard and a high place.

This quick review shows that there is some level of architectural continuity in the use of temple plans, which had a heritage stretching back in some instances to the Early Bronze Age in the Levant. It is also obvious that the categorization does not reveal a great deal. Several of the temples do not fit comfortably: the parallel long halls at Guzana, the apsidal structure at Ashdod, Building 351 at Tel Miqne/Ekron, and the temples of stratum V (Mazar, Upper VI) at Beth-shean. The temples of strata XII and XI at Tell Qasile seem to stretch the pigeonhole that Wright called a centralized square type to a rather large extent. Even where a case can be made for the appropriateness of a label, the label itself says little about the temple.

The plan, however, is valuable. Iron Age architects left behind traces of the ways in which they responded to the architectural traditions of the past in the plans for the buildings that they erected during the Iron Age. The plans show how these architects manipulated space and how they conceived spatial relationships. In several of the plans, it seems reasonable to argue for a line of architectural continuity. The early Iron Age architects were responding to known spatial arrangements and design concepts, and so it is appropriate to consider how older forms were reworked in the early Iron Age. Just as no single type of temple served the needs of all the Iron Age communities of the Levantine region, there was no particular orientation that distinguished temples from other buildings in the area. It is certainly possible and even likely that particular cults may have required a specific orientation for a temple, but in most instances the cult associated with a particular sanctuary ruin cannot be ascertained. The excavated temple remains have not revealed a pattern that shows that the issues of terrain, astronomy, sun position, or even wind direction dictated orientation on a regular basis (Wright 1985: 1.258; Ottosson 1980: 115; Busink 1970: 252). What does seem clear is that there are no direct links between specific types of temples and particular orientations. On the other hand, significant changes to the orientation of a temple structure that was one of a series of temples in operation for a long time at a site cannot be ignored. The changes in the orientations of the Iron Age Aleppo and Pella temples from their predecessors' temples on the same spots must indicate a significant shift of some type, but exactly what the shift indicates is not at all clear.

Long-Room Temples

Orientation of Axis

Long-room temples form the largest single group.[4] The category itself is problematic, with a number of variations, the result of which is a complicated architectural history. A long-room temple is an elemental form, a rectangular space in which the

---

4. Not all students of temples agree with the inclusion of these particular temples under the classification of long-room type; see A. Mazar (1992b: 161–87), whose classification system is quite different.

longitudinal axis is emphasized, usually at the terminal points, by means of entrances and built items. The long-room format stresses a steady progression through space in a fixed direction. Within this definition, there is wide latitude for forms. The Carchemish (fig. 36) and Abu Hawam (fig. 11B) temples are unified single-room interior spaces. The Tell Ta'yinat (fig. 96) and 'Ain Dara (fig. 5) temples are versions of a tripartite format. The Beth-shean strata VII/VI (Mazar's Lower VI; see figs. 26–27) temples are a modified tripartite form. What these structures share in common is a rectangular shape, alignment on the longitudinal axis, and a design emphasis placed on this axis, usually through the use of the doorways and niches.

A glance at the plans for the temples at Carchemish (fig. 36) and Abu Hawam (fig. 11B) shows that they are not conceived in the same way. The Carchemish temple is quite formal in its arrangement, the longitudinal axis is an important feature in the design, and the significance of the space enclosed by the walls of the temple is made evident by the use of a shallow porch that already serves as a transitional region between the outside and the inside. Moreover, the walls of the temple at Carchemish are thick—thicker than any other nearby structural walls; this must have given the exterior of the building a degree of ponderousness not matched by any other construction in the vicinity. None of these features is at play in the Abu Hawam temple. It cannot even be determined from the remains that the longitudinal axis prevailed in the design since the entrance to the building is not known. The Late Bronze Age Building 50 that Building 30 replaced does seem more like a long-room design (fig. 11A). The buttresses on each of the long sides reinforce the notion of longitudinal movement, the possible niche at the midpoint of the small east wall heightens the sense of longitudinal priority, and the circular feature laid in the middle of the building on the axis seems to clinch the argument that Building 50 did operate as a long-room structure—probably a temple. Only the shared placement and orientation of Buildings 30 and 50 really allow the latter structure to share the identification of the former. The possible internal arrangement of the west side of Building 30 seems to argue against the structure's actually being understood as a long-room type, however. There is no emphasis being placed on the longitudinal axis.

Building 30 (fig. 11B) does resemble a Late Bronze Age structure at Tel Mevorakh that has been identified as a sanctuary (fig. 74). Tel Mevorakh is located north of Hadera on the south bank of the Nahal Tanannim (Crocodile River) at the point where the Carmel coast separates from the Plain of Sharon. It is not very distant from Abu Hawam, though the Carmel Range does intervene. During the Late Bronze Age (strata XI–IX), the site appears to have been an isolated roadway shrine (Stern 1984: 4–6, 28).[5] The temple structure went through three rebuildings, each time with modifications. However the general format of the first shrine survived the modifications.

---

5. The Tel Mevorakh shrine was an isolated structure, and it has been proposed that it served the needs of Late Bronze Age coastal nomadic peoples (Bunimovitz 1994: 199 n. 105).

The sanctuary was a single room of rectangular shape, 10 m × 5 m, aligned west to east, with emphasis probably on the longitudinal axis, though this is difficult to determine since the entrance has not been found. Along the north and west walls were the remains of benches made of earth plastered with lime. The west side was occupied by an elaborate system of platforms (fig. 75). A platform 20 cm above the floor level covered much of the west side of the room. In the northwest corner, 4 earthen steps ascended 60 cm to a higher platform. Near the southwest corner of the room stood 2 raised installations attached to the lower platform. Near the steps leading up to the higher platform was a depression coated with lime that could have served as the base for a wooden post. While this first configuration was modified in the two successive versions of the shrine, the treatment of the west side as special survived at least through the second iteration (Stern 1977: 89–91). The first two phases of the shrine were from the sixteenth to the thirteenth centuries B.C.E. Obviously, there was no direct association between the Tel Mevorakh shrine and Building 30 at Abu Hawam. The two intermediaries, the third shrine at Tel Mevorakh and Building 50 at Abu Hawam, bear no resemblance to one another and are not, in terms of format, like the other temples that succeeded or preceded them.

For the moment, it must be assumed that the Tel Mevorakh shrine and the sanctuary represented by Building 30 are both points on an architectural continuum of shrine-building that spans from the Late Bronze Age to the early Iron Age and was used for smaller and probably less important shrines that, in formal terms, can be labeled long rooms but that exhibit interior arrangements that technically disqualify them as true long-room structures. That such a tradition could have influenced both buildings is not at all unlikely in light of the fact that the two sites are not far distant from one another, and variants on this type of shrine may have existed in many small Canaanite coastal communities of the Late Bronze Age and early Iron Age. However, if the plan for Building 30 at Abu Hawam is related to the Canaanite form at Tel Mevorakh, then it seems that the possible non-Canaanite population at Abu Hawam was not uncomfortable with building its prestigious structure using a native form. Building 30 both continued the placement and alignment of the older sanctuary and was isolated from the dense urban matrix, giving it increased status. It was a significant building in the town.

While the Beth-shean temple that survives through strata VII (fig. 27) and VI (Mazar's Lower VI; see fig. 26) on the acropolis is perhaps best classified as a long-room temple, it seems to fit into this category somewhat uncomfortably, particularly since the entrance is not on the longitudinal axis in either version of the temple but is instead slightly off center. The temple itself is a rectangular structure, and the longitudinal force is maintained on the interior. The axial sensibility is reinforced by the single column on either side of the axis. The axis in the earlier stratum VII temple is less pronounced because none of the features in the main hall and at the temple's north end is aligned symmetrically with the axis. In the stratum VI (Mazar's

Lower VI) temple, axial symmetry becomes the dominant force. The two versions of the Beth-shean temple are at best only distantly related to the temples at Carchemish, Tell Taʿyinat, and ʿAin Dara.

The temples at Beth-shean must have served a mixed community. The town was garrisoned by Egyptian soldiers. This Egyptian presence dates back to at least the Eighteenth Dynasty. If the dates of the twelfth and eleventh centuries are accepted for strata VII and VI (Mazar's Lower VI), with the end of VII being at the close of the Nineteenth Dynasty, then division between these two strata marks the transition from Late Bronze Age to early Iron Age. The architectural continuity between the two strata suggests that the break was not of major cultural significance, though it may well have had important political ramifications. The early Iron Age temple of stratum VI (Mazar's Lower VI) was still heavily dependent on the Late Bronze Age design from stratum VII. The interesting features of this design, which remain constant through both versions, are the entrance set slightly off axis and defined by a vestibule area, a kind of antechamber to the main apartment of the temple, the large main hall, and the raised area at the north end that is privileged by being physically lifted above the rest of the room. The closest Late Bronze Age parallel for this design is the Fosse Temple at Lachish, phase III (fig. 76).

Lachish (Tell ed-Duweir) was situated in the Judean foothills of the Shephelah, near a major road leading from the coastal plain to the Hebron hills (Ussishkin 1997: 317). It was one of the Canaanite settlements of the Middle Bronze Age. The Fosse Temple was built during the city's Late Bronze Age period and evidences three distinct phases (Tufnell et al. 1940: 19–45; Ussishkin 1985: 219–20).[6] The phase III temple (fig. 76) seems to reflect some of the same design elements as the stratum VII temple at Beth-shean. The entrance to Fosse Temple II is designated by a vestibule space, in this case almost a secondary item to the large main hall, which is more a square. In the main cult room, columns frame the longitudinal axis, which terminates at the raised platform. There are secondary rooms behind the built installations on the wall opposite the entrance. Whether these small, seemingly hidden spaces should be understood as even more sacred and more restricted regions of the temple like the third chamber in the Tell Taʿyinat temple (fig. 96) or whether these are just indications of storerooms cannot be determined from the remains or the plans. While a case can be made to include both the Beth-shean and Lachish structures in the category of long-room temples, they can also be treated as "temples of irregular plan," a category

6. Ottosson (1980: 81–92) does not accept the identification of the Fosse Temple as a temple. He identifies it as pottery workshops. A. Mazar (1992b: 179) has no problem with the temple identification but has questioned some of the structural features reported by the excavators, especially the south-wall exit. Finkelstein (1988: 343–44) has argued that, because the temple was built outside the wall of the city, it must have served the needs of a pastoral population in the area.

defined by Stern that contains several Late Bronze Age Canaanite examples (Stern 1984: 33–34, figs. 4a–b).

Interestingly, the formal elements increase when the stratum VI (Mazar's Lower VI) temple at Beth-shean (fig. 26) is compared with the phase III version of the Fosse Temple. In both, the axial symmetry is a strong feature, because the installations on the back wall are emphatically an element in the axial alignment. In both, the rooms behind the back wall that are somehow associated with the platform installations are clearly of secondary importance, at least from the design perspective. The destruction of the phase III temple at Lachish has been dated to the twelfth century, and it is possible that both the phase III Fosse Temple and the strata VII/VI (Mazar's Lower VI) Beth-shean temples could have existed contemporaneously.

If the entrance is removed as a diagnostic feature for the stratum VI (Mazar's Lower VI) temple at Beth-shean, then the design appears a great deal like a long-room temple, symmetrically aligned along the longitudinal axis and possessing well-defined high space at the end of the axis, opposite the entrance. The high platform is approached by a quite formal set of stairs placed on axis and preceded by the pair of columns framing the axial line. The raised platform itself is deep enough to be treated as a chamber. This treatment of the interior space can be more closely paralleled by the other temple at Lachish—the Acropolis or Summit Temple. The Lachish temple (fig. 77) was a rectangle consisting of two rooms: an antechamber and a main chamber (Ussishkin 1978: 10–25; 1983: 109). On the east wall of the main chamber, opposite the entrance, was a formal stone staircase of 7 risers well hewn from nari and chalk that led to a doorway, which in turn opened into a third chamber. The three entrances and the staircase were in a line just slightly off the axis of the room. The axis itself seems to have been framed by 2 wood columns, the bases of which have been found in the main chamber (Clamer and Ussishkin 1977: 73–76).[7] This treatment of the main hall and the setting off of the sacred space by use of a formal staircase seem quite close to the design of the stratum VI (Mazar's Lower VI) temple at Beth-shean. Considering that the Lachish temple dates to the last period of the Late Bronze Age at the site, it certainly could have overlapped with the stratum VII temple at Beth-shean.

During the late thirteenth and twelfth centuries, the Egyptian presence in Canaanite Palestine was particularly strong. The Nineteenth-Dynasty pharaohs marched through Palestine in the battles to wrest territory from Hittite control on the northern frontier and to punish the Canaanite cities for inappropriate behavior (A. Mazar 1992a: 232–94; Redford 1992: 125–40). Beth-shean was an Egyptian garrison town, and Lachish certainly felt the Egyptian presence, considering its location in the southern region of Palestine. Rowe, who first excavated the Beth-shean acropolis, argued that

---

7. Note that the Acropolis temple also had an entrance on the north side. This was a formal entrance with steps leading up to the door of an anteroom. This entrance was on line with the columns and provided an accent to the main chamber's secondary axis (Clamer and Ussishkin 1977: 73).

the stratum VII temple at Beth-shean was destroyed by a great conflagration at the end of the Eighteenth Dynasty, making the stratum VI temple a product of the Nineteenth-Dynasty date (Rowe 1930: 23–31). These dates allowed Rowe to compare the format of the stratum VII temple with the Eighteenth-Dynasty, fourteenth-century B.C.E. chapels at Tell el-Amarna (A. Mazar 1992a: 253).

There are certainly some superficial similarities between the Egyptian and Canaanite temples. Since the Middle Kingdom, Egyptian architects had been designing temples that followed a rigid bilateral symmetry and that progressed in a linear fashion through space toward a "holy of holies" situated at the end of the axial line. The movement along the axis was accompanied by a closing down of space. This is clear in the plan for the funerary complex of Mentuhotep (Arnold 1997: 76, fig. 32), and this continued as a feature in New Kingdom temples as well. This is not the level of comparison that Rowe favored, however. Rowe was looking at the small chapels known from the estates of the nobles and the workmen's village at Tell el-Amarna. These retain the marked axial symmetry and linear movement but are reduced to a single chamber, an unroofed or half-roofed space defined by the walls and the door and lifted above the ground on a platform, and Wright offered reconstructions of the strata VII temple (identified as the Amenophis Temple) and VI temple based on the Egyptian estate temple prototype (G. R. H. Wright 1985: vol. 2, ills. 151, 152, 154). There is a fair amount of variability in the chapels associated with the workmen's village, and the estates that actually had chapels were quite few in number (Lacovara 1999: 68–70).

While these could in some way relate to the design at Beth-shean, which might in turn have influenced Lachish's two temples, there are several elements that argue against such a relationship. The most recent dating for the Beth-shean stratum VII temple makes it a century later, after the Amarna changes had largely been forgotten. The Beth-shean temple was larger than these private chapels, was not an estate temple but part of the urban fabric (as was also the case for the two Lachish temples) and was probably fully roofed (see G. R. H. Wright 1985: vol. 2, ills. 152 and 155 for alternative restorations). Considering the special nature of the Amarna temples and their role in the cult of the city, it is hard to see how their designs could have traveled to Canaanite Palestine, especially since Akhenaten took such an inactive role in affairs in the western and northern regions of the Empire. The stratum VII temple looks much more like the Late Bronze Age temples from elsewhere in the Canaanite region. Considering that the Egyptian presence was never very large at the site (perhaps at a maximum only one-quarter of the population and that Canaanite material cultural forms survived the Egyptian occupation), it is not unreasonable to assume that the temple was retained in local form, especially if the cult was Canaanite not Egyptian (McGovern, Fleming, Swann 1993: 3, 24).

The North Syrian Background for the Long-Room Type

The long-room temple at Carchemish (fig. 36) can be related to a couple of lines of architectural development. It was built in a Neo-Hittite city—a city that had been

Hittite since at least thirteenth century B.C.E. (Güterbock 1954: 114), when it served as the capital for the district called Aštata and was the residence for the Hittite king's representative (Gurney 1954: 74). It seems reasonable to assume that, as a Neo-Hittite city, it might have retained a lingering aspect of the Imperial Hittite style, though it is important to note that some three centuries separate the city's role as a major Hittite center and its position as the capital of a Neo-Hittite kingdom. With regard to its long-room format, the temple itself looks like nothing from the Hittite homeland of Anatolia. The long-room type was not used for Hittite imperial temple architecture. It is true that the long-room format at Carchemish (which is really a porch that leads into a large single unified space) might ultimately be derived from the megaron type—a type normally considered to have its origins in Early Bronze Age Anatolia (Fritz 1987b: 38–49). However, the spread of the megaron form took place millennia before the building of the Carchemish temple. There are possible megara in Early Bronze Age Megiddo.[8] What does seem special about the Carchemish temple that might link it to Hittite forms is the employment of thick walls that were sturdy enough to have held up a tower-like superstructure. Woolley argued for a two-story building, which is how Busink (1970: fig. 151) reconstructed the temple. The reconstruction resembles Naumann's restoration of the gatehouse for the Late Bronze Age Imperial Hittite sanctuary at Yazılıkaya (Naumann 1955: 387). That a gatehouse, even within a sacred setting, could have affected the design of a temple in a provincial center several centuries later and after the demolition of the gatehouse seems doubtful.

On the other hand, Carchemish was a North Syrian city with a long pre-Hittite history. The Middle Bronze Age in North Syria had seen the proliferation of long-room temples. They are the standard temple type at Middle Bronze Age Ebla. Like the early Iron Age temple at Carchemish, Temple B1 (fig. 78) at Ebla has the same thick walls, though it is clearly conceived differently, for the longitudinal movement is more noticeable because of the pronounced rectangular shape of the building and the single interior chamber (Matthiae 1981: 126–28). This type of massive long-room temple, often with a set-off porch, retained its currency throughout the Late Bronze Age in North Syria, where it can be found in the Hittite period temples at Emar (figs. 79–80; see also Margueron 1983: 180–83).

This long-room type, also called a Syrian-style temple, spread into Canaanite Palestine during the MBA II, where it has been argued (A. Mazar 1992a: 211–13) that it served as the basis for the Middle Bronze Age *migdāl* temples at Shechem (fig. 81) and Megiddo (fig. 82). As with the North Syrian versions, these Palestinian temples have the thick walls that could have resulted in temples of more than one story. They also have clearly defined porch areas. And like the North Syrian Middle Bronze and Late Bronze Age examples, they are focused on the longitudinal movement.

---

8. The stratum XVI temple and the twin temples of stratum XV. These are not long-room forms. They are broad-room types; see Kempinski 1992: 54–56.

The Migdāl-Temple Type

The term *migdāl* ('tower') was initially coined to describe the two structures at Shechem and Megiddo (2048), which were argued to have served as temples but that also possessed fortress aspects. The buildings shared in common thick exterior walls and similar plans. The porch spaces seem to have been set off by paired towers (Matthiae 1990: 111–13; Jaroš 1998: fig. 21; G. E. Wright 1965: fig. 48). At Megiddo, the flanking towers seem to have been added at a later date, were built over two small rooms (Epstein 1965: 214), and at this same time two columns may have been added to the entrance porch. The Shechem temple also shows some evidence for the use of columns in the porch. Kohlmeyer has argued that the Middle Bronze Age temple on the citadel at Aleppo was also a *migdāl* type (Kohlmeyer 2009: 194).

The formation of a classification of *migdāl*-temple type is not without problems. G. E. Wright first employed the term for the Middle Bronze Age Shechem temple. He then redated the Megiddo temple (2048). The excavators of Megiddo had identified the temple as coming from stratum VIII (Loud 1948: 102), which made the structure Late Bronze Age in date. Wright (1957: 20; 1965: 94) wanted to place it in strata X or XI (MBA II) so that it would be contemporaneous with the Shechem temple. The association of the two buildings based on the morphological element of the towers is also troublesome. Epstein has shown that the Megiddo temple towers were made of ashlar masonry, did not fit with the fabric of the rest of the building, and were a later addition. However, in her analysis, she also pushed for an earlier dating of the basic structure. She argued that there was a stratum XII temple that was replaced by the first *migdāl* in stratum XI or X, to which the towers were added in stratum VIIB (Late Bronze Age; Epstein 1965: 210). Epstein's dating for the initial version of the *migdāl* temple fits more comfortably with the Shechem temple, although her Middle Bronze Age version lacks the diagnostic feature of the towers (Dunayevsky and Kempinski 1973: 180–85).

Shechem is located in the hill country north of modern Jerusalem. Jaroš has argued that the city began to develop rapidly in the MBA IIB period, when the city was enclosed by a massive wall of cyclopean masonry. It was in this same period that the *migdāl* temple was constructed (see fig. 83; see also Jaroš 1998: 51–53, figs. 20–21). It was built on a podium, which elevated it and allowed it to dominate the area. Its walls were thick. It had the long-room format with a single unified cult chamber preceded by a clearly defined porch area (fig. 84A). It is slightly larger than the Megiddo temple (G. E. Wright 1965: 87–95; Bull 1960: 113–14). Wright and Bull argued that, although the area inside the temple remained in operation into the early Iron Age, the actual structure changed significantly. Their second temple, Temple 2, built over the older *migdāl* temple, was a far less-substantial building. Stager has refuted this whole notion of a second temple at Shechem and has argued that the Middle Bronze Age *migdāl* continued in use, substantially unchanged, into Iron Age I (fig. 84B/C; see Stager 2003: 31).

Megiddo (Silberman et al. 1999: 32–39) had been established in the Early Bronze Age on the major road that connected Egypt with the northeast, occupying the end of a narrow pass that cuts through the Carmel Range at the Wadi ʿArah and looks out onto the beginning of the Esdraelon Valley. It was strategically placed to profit from the north–south commerce along the coast and the east–west trade between the coast and the Jordan Valley. It also was well watered and possessed an agriculturally rich hinterland. Middle Bronze Age Megiddo replaced the earlier Early Bronze Age city. Whether there was real continuity with the earlier Early Bronze Age city is doubtful (Fritz 1995: 18). However, the Early Bronze Age cultic area on the northeast side of the tell remained hallowed in the Middle Bronze Age city. The earliest temples date to EB III. They are three roughly square structures that were divided into two spaces by internal walls. The front space appears to be a porch that then leads into a separate chamber. In each building, the remains of pairs of stone bases seem to indicate that columns were used to support the roof. The three structures line up more or less on a southwest to northeast incline, and they all open to the southeast. The plans have been identified as megaron forms (Jaroš 1998: 39–40, fig. 14). However, G. R. H. Wright thought that the Megiddo structures were broad-room temples (Wright 1971a: 18–19). So both types of temple architecture may have been known in Megiddo in the Middle Bronze Age, when building 2048 was constructed.

Building 2048 (figs. 30 and 82) dominated the cultic sector of the city throughout the Middle Bronze Age (strata X–VI). The structure was rebuilt five times during the course of the Middle Bronze Age and remained in operation into the Late Bronze Age (Kempinski 1972: 10–15; 1989: 170–85; Ben-Tor 1973: 92–98; Epstein 1973: 54–57; Dunayevsky and Kempinski 1973b: 161–87). The temple always retained the same north–south alignment and stood on a podium that raised it above the surrounding ground level and probably raise it higher than any nearby structures. The walls were always thick compared with the walls of other structures in the vicinity. The alignment on the longitudinal axis was further emphasized by a niche built into the rear wall of the main chamber. The main chamber itself was a single unified space, but the design eventually included an obvious porch area that served as the transitional space between the profane and sacred realms.[9]

More recently, S. Bourke, the excavator of the large Middle Bronze Age temple at Pella (fig. 24B), has argued that this temple was also a *migdāl*, and it is the largest example so far known—at 32 m × 24 m. The temple was a mud-brick structure resting on stone foundations and socles. One of the probable 2 flanking entrance towers has been excavated. It appears to have been a tripartite design: with a porch flanked by the towers, a central room, and a deep holy of holies. The Late Bronze Age temple of 1350 B.C.E. did not follow the same design as the Middle Bronze Age temple, though

---

9. In its original form, the porch could not be established with certainty (A. Mazar 1992b: 165).

the orientation remained the same. Almost all of the Middle Bronze Age superstructure was removed, making it difficult for archaeologists to do a clear analysis of the Middle Bronze Age temple. In the one restored view so far published, the central chamber is shown as unroofed, though it is not certain that it was unroofed (Bourke 2007; Churcher 2003).

Should these Middle Bronze Age temples be classified by a term that is used in the Bible to describe Late Bronze Age or early Iron Age structures? The association of a temple with a fortress rests on a passage in Judges (9:46), in which men of Shechem are said to have taken refuge in the "House of God" (the god Berith or El-Berith) at the moment when Abimelech attacked and captured the city.[10] Whether this was a fortified element that was part of a temple proper as G. E. Wright and, earlier, May contended (May 1939), or it was a separate, distinct construction is not at all obvious from the text. All that the text really indicates is that early Iron Age Shechem possessed a defensive structure associated with the city god. In reality, the people took refuge in the ṣěriaḥ of the Temple of El-berith, and ṣěriaḥ is usually translated 'stronghold' (Stager 2003: 32). If it was still operating in the early Iron Age, then it must have been the only structure in the town large enough to have held a large number of people, as is suggested by the passage. On the other hand, the archaeological work at the site has indicated that Shechem suffered a massive destruction around 1100 B.C.E. and was probably depopulated for a century (van der Toorn 1996: 242–44). In such a scenario, it seems unlikely that the ruined form of the Middle Bronze/Late Bronze Age temple would have been pressed into service by the population that reestablished Shechem about 1000 B.C.E. A second passage in Judges (8:17), often brought into the discussion, refers to the so-called castle of Penuel that was destroyed by Gideon. Here there are no clear temple associations.

The textual references to possible *migdāl* structures describe early Iron Age settings. Van der Toorn has argued that the two stories record events from the period when the Israelites were first entering the hill country. This was a period of mixed population in the area, a time of demographic and cultural transition, when structures that had functioned in the last part of the Late Bronze Age were still being used in some cases (van der Toorn 1996: 242–53). The actual buildings identified as *migdāl* temples (and in the case of Shechem, associated with the textual reference) are all Middle Bronze Age in origin. If G. E. Wright's (1965: 94–95) date for the first She-

---

10. The problem is with the translation and meaning of the text; the NJPS translation of the *Tanakh* (Pelikan 1985: 396) reads, "they went into the tunnel of the temple," and the *New Oxford Annotated Bible with Apocrypha* (RSV; Oxford, 1962: 307) reads, "they entered the stronghold of the house of El-berith." The issue seems minor to the translator but is a serious issue for anyone trying to recover the actual architectural feature. What does seem clear from both texts is that the structure was chosen for strength rather than simply because, as a hallowed place, it was thought possibly to offer safety and sanctuary during an attack.

chem temple is accepted, then they are constructions of the nineteenth or eighteenth century B.C.E. The gap between archaeological remains and textual references is at least 600 years and probably more. There has been a tendency to make the fit more comfortable by suggesting that the temples continued to operate throughout the Late Bronze Age. This is somewhat difficult to prove from the archaeological evidence. There was still a temple in operation in area H of Shechem, where the *migdāl* had stood, but Wright argued that it was a different temple form, although it did retain the thick walls and rectangular shape. Wright himself noted a century of abandonment between the end of the Middle Bronze Age phase and the first phase of Late Bronze Age use, which he dated to the thirteenth century B.C.E. (G. E. Wright 1965: 95–100; Bull 1960: 114–15). The final temple at Megiddo (strata VIIB–VIIA) had thinner walls. The tower appendages had been moved away from the building's core, and the west tower was built over an earlier structure in the temple precinct (Epstein 1965: 214).

G. E. Wright wanted a specific temple type that could be linked to the biblical references and that would meet the specific design requirements implied by the textual descriptions: fortified, defensive, and having towers.[11] Since one reference was specifically to Shechem, and he had found a possible candidate (albeit from a much earlier period), he pressed for continuity between the Middle Bronze Age temple and its Late Bronze Age successor. He tried to make the Megiddo parallel stronger by pushing for a redating of the initial building of the temple so that it would correspond with his date for Shechem. The building chronology for the Megiddo temple is not very clear (Kempinski 1989: 181–86). It has been postulated that, in its first form, the Megiddo *migdāl* did not have flanking towers. If this is correct, then should it be considered to parallel the design at Shechem? The entire discussion becomes more confused if another possible *migdāl* temple is added to the list. Rowe identified a building in stratum VII of the acropolis at Beth-shean as a *migdāl* but not as a temple (Rowe 1930: 20–21). It is a rectangular structure with thick walls and two flanking towers. Instead of having a unified, rectangular interior as the main chamber, the walls enclose five rooms and a staircase that leads to an outer room. Since Rowe could isolate nothing in the design of the building or in the finds that indicated a religious function, he labeled it a military construction. He argued that the staircase led from the core of the building to an outer room where troops could be assembled on the fortress walls.

Josh 19:38 mentions a town in the Galilee known as Migdāl-el. Wright noted that *mig* appears in several place-names and seems to refer to the defensive properties of the sites (G. E. Wright 1965: 95). He took the line of reasoning further and argued that defensive and fortress temples were a common feature of Canaanite towns. For

---

11. Wright's view of the *migdāl* form was of a totally roofed, defensive structure (see fig. 81), but more recently Churcher has presented a partially roofed version of the *migdāl* for the Middle Bronze Age Pella temple (see fig. 24B).

Wright, this was just more evidence for the validity of a category of *migdāl* temples. The term itself might indeed be an apt description that would have been recognized as such in the early Iron Age, when *mig* appears in the biblical passages and when some of the towns with *mig* in their names must have existed.

Burke (2007) has shown that the variations on *mig* have a wide distribution throughout the Levant and probably began to be used in the Middle Bronze Age. However, he has argued that the term was associated with watchtowers and small defensive structures, not temples. He sees Wright's interpretation of *migdāl*-Shechem in Judg 9:46 as a reference to "the Temple of El-Berith" (which Wright thought that he had found in the ruins of Shechem) as misguided in two ways. First, Burke argues that the reference is to a place, Migdāl-Shechem, not a building in Shechem. The *mig* suggests that this town had a watchtower. Second, Wright's insistence on the text's being tied to a specific structure has led to the creation of a category that never existed: fortified temples.

However, B. Mazar (1968: 93) and Kempinski (1989: 184) proposed that the *migdāl* form was a real Middle Bronze Age type that developed in the Syrian region and was connected to the religious and political shifts that took place in Syria beginning around 1700 B.C.E. While the archaeological evidence for the break between the Early Bronze Age and Middle Bronze Age is quite stark in the south, in the north there is nowhere near as much reason to see the end of the Early Bronze Age and the beginning of Middle Bronze Age in such dramatic terms (Matthiae 1981: 65–111; 1990: 111–21). This suggests that two quite different cultural histories developed in the two regions. The northern area saw continuity. The south witnessed a major break. Sites such as Megiddo were abandoned or reduced to village status. The urban culture of the south had to be reinvented in the Middle Bronze Age, whereas it continued without as much interruption in the north. As the Middle Bronze Age developed in the south, more-sophisticated influences from the north entered the region, including the *migdāl* temple form. Mazar argued for demographic forces' carrying the notions into the region; Kempinski favored some type of cultural filtering. The movement of the Hurrians into southern Canaan with the development of MBA IIB Canaanite civilization that took shape in the wake of the Hyksos invasion of Egypt and the subsequent florescence of Levantine culture may have involved both possibilities. The development of the *migdāl*-temple type in the south resulted, then, from earlier architectural experiments in the north that had been brought south.

The renaissance of urbanization in southern Canaan during the Middle Bronze Age was paralleled by the continued prosperity and development in the north, especially in the cities of Alalakh and Ebla. These two Syrian cities may not have been Canaanite, but they clearly engaged the cities of Canaan and played a role by providing design options for builders elsewhere. The Alalakh temple in level VII (fig. 90) was one of several superimposed buildings that may have been dedicated to the city's patroness, the goddess Ishtar (Woolley 1955: 33–90). The temple produced some of the city's archives (Wiseman 1953). Woolley maintained that the level VII temple was built by Yarim-Lim, whose statue probably stood inside the temple's cult chamber (Woolley 1955: 64, 235–37). The level VII temple had thick walls; at 4 m, they were thicker than the walls that enclosed the temples at Megiddo or Shechem. It is possible that the Alalakh temple was more than a single story high, and the Middle Bronze Age Aleppo Citadel temple was perhaps of the same format. The Alalakh level VII temple could well have been a fortress as well as a temple (Woolley 1953: 39). One of the inscribed texts from Alalakh (AT 243:9, 13) mentions the distribution of rations to a fortress (*bit duri*) of Ishtar.

It also seems apparent that the temple was attached to a palace, both physically and economically, because there are several documents that refer to debts owed by the palace to the temple (Na'aman 1980: 212–13). The fortress quality certainly does seem to connect the Alalakh level VII temple to the two temples farther south, in Canaan, but the more square room format of the main chamber seems to present a different idea of interior spatial configuration. Instead of the steady accent on the longitudinal movement provided by the long-room format, the square room creates a kind of spatial tension by introducing a contrasting axis.

Though the Alalakh level VII temple has been proposed as the prototype for the *migdāl* temples in the south, Middle Bronze Age developments at Ebla cannot be ignored. At Ebla, the Middle Bronze Age saw the building of Temples B$_1$, N, D (Mardikh IIIA–B), and P$_2$ (from area P). These are rectangular spaces aligned on the longitudinal axis and are best described as long-room temples. They are not exactly the same. Temples B1 and N (figs. 78 and 85) are simple single-rectangular enclosed spaces defined by thick walls, over 2 m. There are no porches or entrance areas; rather, the flagstone steps enter directly into the main and only chamber (Matthiae 1981: 126–27). The plan for Temple D (fig. 86) appears to be quite different in the details. Instead of a single, unified interior space, the larger rectangular space is preceded by two smaller antechambers, one totally enclosed and the second forming a porch for the building. Temple P$_2$ (fig. 87) is somewhat similar to Temple D in possessing a defined entrance space that is separate from the main chamber, but the interior space is a single, unified area. Temples D and P$_2$ have the same thick walls as found on Temples B$_1$ and N, but they seem less substantial in comparison with the overall size of the buildings. While the four buildings share the same rectangular format and longitudinal alignment, they are neither the same with regard to the treatment of the interior spaces nor with regard to the role of structurally defined entrances. Matthiae has identified both Temples D and P$_2$ as palace chapels (Matthiae 1981: 201–3; 1990: 111–21). He has also argued that Temple D marked a spot as sacred that was already hallowed in the earlier history of the site and probably dominated the side of the acropolis that overlooked the west side of the lower town.

The temples at Megiddo and Shechem are not the only evidence for temple architecture in southern Canaan during the Middle Bronze Age. Some scholars have iden-
tified the remains of a temple in Area H at Hazor (fig. 88) as another Middle Bronze
Age *migdāl* temple (Tubb 1998: 68; A. Mazar 1992b: 211; B. Mazar 1968: 93). Hazor, like
Megiddo and Shechem, was a major city in the Middle Bronze Age. It is mentioned in
the records of the palace at Mari (Ziffer 1990: 14). It sits in the northeastern region of
Canaan (modern Galilee) and was probably the most significant Middle Bronze and
Late Bronze Age city in the region (Kempinski 1989: 195). It was one of the largest cities in the Levant, probably the equal of many important Mesopotamian cities (Yadin
1972a: 106–7). Area H is in the lower city, just inside the ramparts. Unlike at Megiddo,
the earliest evidence for sacred architecture in this region is MBA II. However, the
region retained its hallowed nature up until the destruction of the city in the Late
Bronze Age.

Orthostat blocks were recovered from the excavation site, and the Late Bronze
Age temple has come to be known as the Orthostat Temple (Yadin 1959: 3–8; 1972a:
75–96; 1975: 101–11). The Late Bronze Age temple (fig. 89) was a rectangular structure
aligned on the longitudinal axis with thick exterior walls, 2.3 m. The walls enclosed
two interior spaces: a main chamber and antechamber and entrance porch. A narrow wall constructed opposite the entrance and in front of the rear wall of the main
chamber further emphasized the axis and created a small secondary space within the
chamber (Bonfil 1997: 87). Yadin (1972a: 75–76, fig. 18) suggested that the porch was
strong enough to have supported towers. There has been a tendency to classify this
temple as a Late Bronze Age version of a *migdāl*—an architectural cousin of the temples at Shechem and Megiddo. It shares the thick defensive walls, the main chamber-
porch layout, the alignment along the longitudinal axis, and the possible towers. But
it is also different from the temples at Shechem and Megiddo, for the main chamber
is not rectangular. It has a broad-room rather than a long-room format. Two basalt
bases found in the main chamber probably supported columns to hold up the roofing
system. Basalt stairs provided entrance from the court area in front of the temple to
the porch area. The temple, like those at Shechem and Megiddo, was raised on a platform above the ground level and the neighboring buildings. The design of the Area
H, stratum II temple at Hazor, with its main chamber as a broad-room rather than
long-room type seems more like the level VII temple at Alalakh (fig. 90).

The Megiddo and Shechem temples are single unified cult spaces arranged on
the longitudinal axis, which is accented by the placement of the single entrance. The
common features of the rectangular format and the thick walls join these temples
with those of contemporary vintage from Ebla. A closer look at the temples, however, reveals some important differences in the plans. Temples B_1, N, and P_2 from Ebla
all share the same rectangular, unified-interior spatial configuration, and in this they
compare quite easily with the Megiddo and Shechem temples. Temple D falls outside

this line of classification. The interior space is subdivided into two distinct chambers, and then the ensemble is preceded by a formal entrance space; thus, Temple D is different. Similarly, Temples B$_1$ and N have no specially defined entrances. The stairs lead up and into the main room. This type of design can be found in the coastal Canaanite region of Byblos in Early Bronze Age temple XIV, where the temple is a composition of three single room units, each having the long-room type, that are arranged side by side (Saghieh 1983: 93, 119–20, 122–25). This may ultimately be a variant of the megaron temple form that was already known in Early Bronze Age Megiddo (Bonfil 1997: 98).

Only Temple P$_2$ at Ebla (fig. 87) has both the unified main chamber and the entrance porch analogous to the designs at Megiddo and Shechem. Matthiae thought that the three temples were related. The basic similarities outweighed the differences. The Ebla temple was merely larger than the Palestinian versions (Matthiae 1990: 113–14). Ultimately, the form can be traced back to the region of the middle Euphrates in northeastern Syria, where Matthiae has suggested that prototypes might be found in EB IV temples at Tell Biʾa (ancient Tuttal) and Area L at Tell Halawa. In Matthiae's reasoning, the unified long-room temple with formal entrance was an invention of the North Syria region during EB IV that then moved south in the Middle Bronze Age, perhaps through the intermediary of Ebla, into Canaan, where it was adopted by builders at Megiddo and Shechem during the great period of urban revitalization, the Middle Bronze Age, in southern Canaan. Bietak has argued that the temples in stratum E/3–2 at Tell el-Dabʾa, the site of the Middle Bronze Age Hyksos capital in the eastern Nile Delta, followed this same format, indicating just how far south this design traveled (Bietak 1979: 247–60). These were massive constructions and must have stood as proud monuments in the cities that possessed them; they were statements of the wealth of the individual cities and rulers that were capable of building them.

Fowler (1983: 49–53) has pointed out that the whole discussion of *migdāl* temples has become circular. It rests, in part, on Albright's appropriation of Wright's description of a *migdāl*-temple type, into which category Albright placed the Shechem and Megiddo temples and added the Late Bronze Age acropolis temples at Ugarit. He posited a wide distribution for the type through Canaan with a staying power well into the Late Bronze Age. For the moment, the archaeological evidence does not sustain the hypothesis. While rectangular, long-room temples are constructed throughout the Late Bronze Age and into early Iron Age; in most instances, these do not have any clear fortress associations, and nothing really ties the later biblical accounts to any existing remains (Campbell and Ross 1968: 2–27).

The entire issue is significant for the early Iron Age because there may have been a Middle Bronze Age fortified-temple type that survived in some form, no doubt heavily modified, into the first centuries of the Iron Age and could have influenced other architectural forms. The small but sturdy Temple of the Storm God at Carchemish seems as though it may have used the fortress format. Whether this was a recognized category and whether the term *mig* actually referred to temples of this sort or to structures of a quite different nature cannot be determined. It is certainly possible that these North Syrian and Palestinian temples in some manner influenced the creation of the Iron Age II temple in the Neo-Hittite city of Carchemish, but if they did so, it must not have been a direct influence. Only the *migdāl* temples at Shechem and Megiddo may have still been operating in the early Iron Age and, then, in a much less impressive form.[12] What is more likely is that the tradition of building fortress-like temples using the long-room format was well established in North Syria and parts of the Canaanite region.[13] The architect for the temple at Carchemish was neither designing a new form nor making a particularly novel statement architecturally for a Levantine city, even with a Hittite overlay.

The Long-Room Type with Tripartite Design

The two temples at Tell Taʿyinat (fig. 42) are quintessential long-room temples. They have a tripartite design consisting of a porch, a long main chamber, and a final room. The design is symmetrically aligned along the longitudinal axis, and the buildings are raised on platforms that can only be approached via the front stairs that lead to the porches. The porch of the recently excavated temple has a single column on the axis while the porch of the first-discovered temple is defined by two columns *in antis*. When McEwan first introduced the building in 1937, he described it as a megaron (McEwan 1937: 13), an identification that was maintained by Haines in his 1971 publication (Haines 1971: 53), though it was not used by Harrison in his description of the newly unearthed temple. Haines thought that the basic megaron format had been somewhat modified by the addition of the pronounced porch or *prodromus* to the basic structure, and while he acknowledged that the inspiration for the type could be western, the presumed origin of the megaron in the third millennium B.C.E., he also noted that the temple resembled some north Mesopotamian temple remains. Frankfort supported the megaron comparison but noted that, unlike a true megaron, in which the second apartment should be the primary space, the Tell Taʿyinat temple has a deeper, third chamber assumed to be the focus of the cult, and this is also the case with the newly discovered temple. Frankfort actually favored Assyrian influence on the design, in which the Assyrian entrance lobby opened up to form a more formal porch space (Frankfort 1985: 290). Hawkins wonders if the temple (Building II) might not actually postdate the Assyrian conquest of the region (Hawkins 2009: 168). The construction of the temple has been dated to the second building phase at the site, in the beginning of the eighth century B.C.E. (Haines 1971: 64–66). Technically, however, this was a period when the North Syrian cities were largely independent of Assyrian

---

12. This view has recently been disputed by Stager (2003: 26–35), who believes that the Shechem temple was still the fully developed Middle Bronze Age *migdāl* operating in the early Iron Age.

13. Stager (2003: n. 5) has identified the remains of a temple at Pella on the east side of the Jordan River as a *migdāl* temple as well.

rule and may well have been pursuing anti-Assyrian policies (Gurney 1954: 44–45); thus, it does not seem to have been a time when they were most likely to have been emulating Assyrian architectural models.

The temple at Tell Taʿyinat has a couple of special features. It was clearly conceived as a tripartite structure with emphasis on the longitudinal axis, and this seems even more the case with the newly discovered temple and its column placed on the longitudinal axis. There are no comparable early Iron Age building remains in the Levant. The ʿAin Dara temple has been used as a parallel to the original Tell Taʿyinat temple (Monson 2000: 31), but the two temples and the newly discovered temple are quite different in their treatment of space, though they may ultimately derive from the same source. There are two distinct features that mark the Tell Taʿyinat temples. The first is the tripartite format, which emphasizes the steady penetration of layers of space. Privileging a space by burying it within layers of surrounding spaces is well known in Mesopotamian sacred architecture going back to the early second millennium and in New Kingdom Egyptian temple architecture (L. Bell 1997: 148). The practice was in use during the Late Bronze Age in the Levant as well. This layering of spaces can be seen in the Fosse Temple at Lachish (fig. 76), the Area H Orthostat Temple at Hazor (fig. 89), and the level IV temple at Alalakh (fig. 91). It carries through as a feature of some early Iron Age temples: the temple at ʿAin Dara (fig. 5) and the strata VII/VI (Mazar's Lower VI; see figs. 26–27) temples on the acropolis at Beth-shean.

What makes the Tell Taʿyinat design special is the emphasis on three clearly designated chambers rather than just defined areas. A Late Bronze Age prototype for this is harder to find; only the stratum IV temple at Alalakh (fig. 91) might be seen as a progenitor. The Alalakh temple also possesses the second feature that sets off the Tell Taʿyinat form—the symmetrical arrangement along the longitudinal axis. This element gives to the movement through space a strong feeling of direction. It is true that this can be found in the Early Bronze Age megara from western Anatolia, but the movement along the axis is disrupted in those buildings by the placement of the hearth in the main apartment. At Tell Taʿyinat, nothing disturbs the steady pace from porch to platform in the third room, and this is also true of the Alalakh temple. There is no way in which the level IV temple at Alalakh could have directly played a role in the plan for the Tell Taʿyinat temples. Though the two sites are near neighbors, the stratum IV temple was buried under four later iterations, and the city itself had ceased to function in the twelfth century B.C.E. What the level IV temple shows is that in the Late Bronze Age there was a North Syrian architectural penchant for tripartite designs aligned along the longitudinal axis, creating very formal spaces that were perfectly suited to be enhanced by the addition of the formal *bīt ḫilani* entrance format, which is what Frankfort noted about the Tell Taʿyinat temple (1985: 290).

The stratum IV temple at Alalakh was not a new creation of Late Bronze Age architects. The excavations at Ebla have shown that, as early as the Middle Bronze

Age, the tripartite format with longitudinal axial symmetry was an established type. Temple D at Ebla (fig. 86) must be seen as the general prototype (Matthiae 1981: 134). Ebla had ceded power to other cities to the west in North Syria by the time of the Middle Bronze Age and did not exist as a Late Bronze Age city. Therefore, there is no manner in which its Middle Bronze Age temple D could have directly influenced any early Iron Age temple design. What it does demonstrate is that the type had developed by the Middle Bronze Age in North Syria. Temple D was an important temple in Ebla and was associated with a palace. The temple at Alalakh shows that the form was alive and well in the Late Bronze Age, where once again the temple was probably associated with a palace complex. It was still being used as a type and maintaining its palatial connection in eighth-century B.C.E. Tell Taʿyinat.

The temple at ʿAin Dara also belongs in this discussion. The site is not very distant from Tell Taʿyinat, and the temple's core is a version of the long-room type (fig. 3). It seems clear that the present remains for the temple at ʿAin Dara result from a major change in the conception of the temple (fig. 5). The ambulatory is a later addition that changed the form of the original temple in a dramatic and significant way. The earlier temple, which did survive as the heart of the final version, was a rectangular structure with two chambers arranged along the longitudinal axis. While it did resemble the temple at Tell Taʿyinat and probably partook of the same lineage, even in its first manifestation it was different in several important ways.

It is not a tripartite design. It consists of only two chambers. The second, larger chamber is divided into two parts by the raised platform that covers the final third of the space. While the platform may be analogous to the third chamber in terms of function, it is not analogous in architectural conception. The platform serves to elevate and set apart something within the larger space. Though a wood screen could have been used to hide the platform from view, the platform was still in a shared space. In the design with three rooms, the third chamber isolates something. It may hide its existence. These are two quite different operations, though they may have the same function. Another point of difference is the porch. It is appended to the main structure and not integrated into the architectural unit. Rather than providing the first space in a succession of interior spaces, it provides a final area on the building's exterior before the transition into the interior proper. Finally, the chambers themselves are separated by short but architecturally significant corridors. This means that the progression into the temple is of the sort in which space is being compressed and then expanded rather dramatically. The porch opens, not into the antechamber but, rather, into a narrow and constricted hall, the real transition space between the exterior and interior realms.

This hall then expands into the first chamber. There is a relationship between the hall and the chamber. The chamber's width is roughly three times the hallway's depth. The length of the hall and the depth of the chamber from the edge of the hallway to the set of stairs that leads to the next hallway is more or less the same. Again there is a constriction of space. The notion of change in relationships is heightened by the fact that stairs must now be mounted to reach the level of the next chamber. The second hallway is about the same depth and width as the first. The width of the second chamber is five times the width of the hall, and twice the depth of the hall, which is, more or less the depth of the free space before the platform of the second chamber.

All of this suggests careful and thoughtful manipulations. The closing and opening of spaces is controlled, and it must have been done quite consciously. The hallways are paved with large single slabs that contrast with the smaller, more loosely arranged paving stones for the chamber floors. It is into the paving stones of the hallways that the enormous feet (fig. 9), thought to represent the feet of the resident deity, were carved. The linear movement through the spaces was an intended part of the temple design. The arrangement of the core of the temple at ʿAin Dara is much more sophisticated than the arrangement of the temple at Tell Taʿyinat and, while they may both ultimately trace their origins back to the Middle Bronze Age tripartite plans (such as the plan of Temple D at Ebla), they represent two quite different reconceptions of that prototype in the early Iron Age. The temples at Tell Taʿyinat and ʿAin Dara are two variations on the Middle Bronze Age tripartite plan as seen in Temple D at Ebla, and both variations have Late Bronze Age predecessors.

The Long-Room Temple as Part of a Palace Complex

The Temple of the Storm God at Carchemish seems to have been loosely part of a larger grouping of buildings that seems to have included a palace, though the temple was defined as architecturally autonomous from the palace. If the Iron Age II temple was at all responding to a specific prototype, then the prototype was probably the palace temple of stratum VII at Alalakh (Tell Atchana; see fig. 90). It should be noted that the supposed temple at Alalakh is just that: conjectural. Nothing was found in any of its levels to prove that it functioned as a religious building rather than as a residential or administrative structure (Frankfort 1985: 276). By the Late Bronze Age, Alalakh had usurped Ebla's position as the major city of North Syria. Alalakh was also vassal to the Hittite Empire during the Late Bronze Age (Woolley 1955: 133–55), though it did not recover as an early Iron Age city after its twelfth-century destruction (Woolley 1955: 164). The building identified as a temple (the only temple so far excavated) was continually used—built, destroyed, and rebuilt—through 16 incarnations over two millennia. In its final forms, strata IB and IA (figs. 92–93), it bore little resemblance to the Carchemish temple, but Woolley argued that the Late Bronze Age level III temple, which had existed during part of the period of Hittite dominance, was a tower structure of at least two stories (Woolley 1955: 135–37)—not unlike the proposed reconstruction for the Temple of the Storm God at Carchemish. In plan, however, the even earlier Middle Bronze Age level VII temple (fig. 90) looks quite similar to the Carchemish temple. Its similarity to the Carchemish design is limited to neither the form of the temple's plan nor the possible tower-like superstructure. The distribution of buildings and courtyards for the palace-temple complexes at Middle Bronze Age Alalakh and Iron Age IIB Carchemish (fig. 36) is strikingly similar, and the pattern continued to be used at Alalakh through the Late Bronze Age. The temple precincts were positioned away from the palace entrances. Though part of a bigger architectural ensemble, the temples were accorded a separate status, a type of autonomy, within the larger composition.

The temples at Tell Taʿyinat (fig. 42) probably formed some type of loosely defined architectural unit with the palace (Building I)—a complex similar to that of Middle Bronze and Late Bronze Age Alalakh or Hazor (Bonfil and Zarzecki-Peleg 2007) or Iron Age IIB Carchemish. This complex was located at the south side of a larger grouping of buildings arranged around an open plaza that dominated the northwestern quadrant of the acropolis, and it probably formed the major feature of the entire acropolis (fig. 94).[14] The later, Assyrian palace was built south of this complex and on the other high point of the acropolis (Haines 1971: 61). The acropolis itself may have formed a citadel that was approached via a gate, the remains of which have been found on the east side of the mound (Haines 1971: 60).

Building I has been identified as a developed version of the North Syrian *bīt ḥilani*. It was erected in the first building period and shows four building phases (Haines 1971: 44–53, 64–66). Throughout its history, Building I opened to the north with a formal entrance that faced onto the large plaza, and while the entrance was modified—sometimes columns, sometimes no columns—its placement and direction of movement never changed, and its relationship to the structure opposite, Building IV (which seems to have operated from the first through the fourth building phases at the site), remained constant.

Building IV was also a *bīt ḥilani* (Haines 1971: 41–43), and thus these two major constructions (Buildings I and IV) were arranged as an architectural dialogue across the plaza (fig. 95). Their relationship remained constant even as the structures around them were removed and new designs introduced. The temples—Building II and Field 2 temple—were added in the second period (figs. 42, 96) and were in operation during only two of the complex's four phases: phases two and three (Haines 1971: pls. 106–7). Building II's north wall was constructed parallel to the palace's south wall. It opened to the west onto a plaza shared with the Field 2 temple and a street, and had nothing to do with the palace plaza composition. Building II was even set back from the west side of the palace, so that the presence of the temple was not evident from the northwest exterior corner of the palace. There was no means of direct communication between the palace, with its northern orientation, and the temples behind it. The

14. For the drawings based on those of Haines 1971, I have not tried to incorporate the recently discovered Field 2 temple.

south and east walls of the palace shows no evidence of doors. The plans suggest that the Field 2 temple, Building II, and Building I really should not be considered a unit. The planners at Tell Ta'yinat knew how to create architectural dialogues, for they did this with Buildings I and IV, the formal porches of which established a line of visual communication that could not have been missed by anyone standing in the plaza.

However, Buildings I and II do share an important feature that joins them together: their building technique. Both structures were built of unbaked mud brick, using alternating courses of square and rectangular faces to achieve a bonding. At every fourth course, a layer of reeds was laid across the walls in the mud-plaster joints. This sort of technique is not very unusual, but wood was also integrated into the building process for both structures, making the technique novel. In the palace around the porch area and the exterior of the south wall, horizontal wood beams were placed flush with certain sections of the wall, and in the porch these horizontal members alternated with wood beams that actually penetrated the wall up to 1 m—a wood-crib construction (Haines 1971: 45, 53–54, figs. 91A–E). It is difficult to know if any of this technique was visible, but the presence of plaster remains on some fragments of the wall argues that it was not visible. Most likely, the technique was not used as a device for visually uniting the buildings; however, its employment on both the palace and the temple, Building II, may well indicate that they were considered a unit. The temple may have been constructed at the same time that the palace was being restored, and the same work crews may have been responsible for both structures.

The design of a palace complex with a temple annex—a palace chapel of sorts— seems to have been an invention of North Syrian architects in the Middle Bronze Age that continued in use through the Late Bronze Age. Besides the complex at Alalakh, another example is known from Tell Brak and possibly Qatna. The discovery of a similar grouping from Late Bronze Age Hazor indicates that the design concept also spread south (Bonfil and Zarzecki-Peleg 2007). In all of these complexes, the temple is a substantially smaller building than the palace that it serves. Its connection to the palace is established by proximity and the shared courtyard region that would have permitted ceremonial movements between palace and temple. Therefore, while it is reasonable to posit a linkage between the Late Bronze Age pattern and the Iron Age IIB manifestations of palace complexes with long-room temples at Carchemish and Tell Ta'yinat, it is also important to realize how differently these latter examples functioned. The formats rendered the temples independent from the palaces that they somehow served.

The most famous tripartite long-room temple was also intended to operate as a palace chapel. Solomon's temple was clearly but one element in a larger grouping of buildings. No physical traces of this temple or of any of the associated palace constructions remain. What exists are the long descriptions provided first in 1 Kgs 5:15–9:25 and, later, in 2 Chronicles 2–8. The value of these accounts can certainly be debated, and the details about the temple building itself are highly suspect (Hurowitz 1992: 25–27, 106, 243–44; see also chap. 1). However, there is no doubt that what the authors of the two narratives recount is the building of a long-room temple consisting of three parts labeled ʾûlām, hêkāl, and děbîr (fig. 97) set within a palace compound. How these spaces in the temple relate to one another is not really clear from the literary record (Aharoni 1973: 1–3). Since nothing of the temple stands, it is not profitable to devote too much time to making the textual material accord with archaeological remains from elsewhere. What is worth noting is that the type of building—a rectangle, aligned on its longitudinal axis, entered via one of the short sides, and possessing a distinct entrance area, a main chamber, and a "holy of holies"—was not a new architectural type. Moreover, its inclusion in a palace complex responded to an older, Middle Bronze Age design notion that had already entered the southern region by the Late Bronze Age at Hazor. Solomon's palace-temple grouping must have been among the first in the Iron Age. How the structures related to one another is difficult to determine. Busink (1970: 46–57) proposed that the complex consisted of a series of independent buildings spread over an enclosed space—an arrangement that was quite different from the layout known from the Late Bronze Age examples.

To build his temple, Solomon called on Hiram, king of Tyre, to send him cedar lumber and men skilled at working the timbers (1 Kgs 5:6; 2 Chr 2:8–10). The author of Kings also suggests that the Tyrians assisted with the stonework (1 Kgs 5:18). Whether the architect was also from Tyre is not at all clear, though in the Chronicles account Solomon requests a more-skilled craftsman who was capable of working with metal and dyed fabrics (2 Chr 2:7). The design of the temple as described by both authors could easily have been the work of architects from Tyre. However, nothing of Late Bronze Age or early Iron Age Tyre's architecture has been unearthed, and the same is true for the great Phoenician city of Sidon (Markoe 2000: 195–201; Ciasca 1988: 168–84). Byblos's monumental remains are from the Early and Middle Bronze Ages (Jidejian 1968: 25–74). No physical remains exist to provide us an idea of Phoenician monumental architecture or a model for the plan for Solomon's temple or for the palace complex. However, the Phoenician coastal region had been part of the region controlled by the city of Ugarit during the Late Bronze Age. The acropolis at Ugarit (Ras Shamra near Latakia) on the north cost of Syria (fig. 98) has the remains of two Late Bronze Age temples. The city consisted of a major urban core with servicing sectors at Minet el-Beida and Ras Ibn Hani. The city's two major Late Bronze Age sanctuaries were identified within the first decade of work at the site (Schaeffer 1931: 8–11; 1933: 119–26; 1935: 141–76; 1937: 127–28). Both temples stood on a high point, a low acropolis rising about 20 m above the coastal plain (fig. 99). They were not features in a larger palace arrangement but instead overlooked the royal palace in the lower city (fig. 100). They did not exist in isolation but were part of an architectural matrix that included noncultic structures. The stratigraphy of the temple area has been difficult to read, making it impossible to sketch a complete record of the development and use of the temples over their three centuries of operation (Dornemann 1981: 62).

The two structures may have been visible from the sea, thereby making them the emblem of the city itself (Yon 1992a: 116). Temple 1 (fig. 101) sits on the northwest side of the acropolis and consists of two chambers arranged as a T-shape along a north–south axis. The temple stood on a high podium and was approached by a massive staircase leading up to a large doorway. A small, almost square monument (2.20 m × 2 m) stood in front of the staircase and showed the same alignment. The antechamber, a long-room type, formed the stem of the T.[15] The main chamber was a broad-room type formed by the cross bar of the T. The surviving walls are of cut and fitted blocks of stone and are almost 2 m thick (1.70 m). A secondary stairway, also of cut stone construction, provided access to the podium via the exterior of the west wall (Hult 1983: 26).

Temple 2 is southeast of Temple 1. It shares with its neighbor the same plan and similar dimensions and orientation. The socle of Temple 2 is constructed of a rubble fill core with cut and fitted stone-masonry facing and coarser blocks used for the interior facing. The walls of the temple itself are thicker than those for Temple 1—between 4 and 5 m. The thickness of the walls for both temples, their placement on a high point of land near the coast, and their being raised on high podia has led Yon to argue that both temples were really tower structures that served as beacons for the city (Yon 1992a: 116).

Both temples seem to have been erected overlooking courtyards defined by secondary buildings forming the perimeter (Yon 1992b: 27–29; Courtois 1979). The cut and fitted stone-masonry technique is also found in the lower city on the great complexes identified as palaces (fig. 102). The shared technique links the buildings as high-prestige structures, since most other buildings are of rubble stone construction (Hult 1983: 22–26, 62). The temples, however, were raised above the other structures on podia, while the palaces were entered directly from the street.

The T-shape for the two structures makes them different from any other buildings on the site. It is a form without a parallel in the Levantine region in either the Middle Bronze Age or Late Bronze Age. Schaeffer thought that the use of the same unusual design for both temples must have resulted from a shared cultic role. Two steles found on the south face of Temple 2 carry Ugartic dedications to Dagon, thereby possibly identifying the cult of the temple.[16] A relief carving on a stele found in association

---

15. G. R. H. Wright (1985: 1.232) reads these remains as broad-room temples approached through a vestibule or courtyard.

16. The two inscribed steles (KTU 6.13, 6.14) indicate that Dagan is to receive offerings. The god is also listed on other offering-lists and similar texts found at Ugarit. In the pantheon lists, he is placed after El but before Ba'al. He is twice referred to as *dgn ttl* (KTU 1.24:14; 1.100:15), or 'Dagan of Tuttul', which ties him to Mari. Since he plays no role in the Ugaritic story of Ba'al, he may actually be a late arrival on the coast coming from the east (van der Toorn, Becking, and van der Horst 1999: 216–17).

with Temple 1 portrays a figure wearing a tall headdress with spiral curls who strides to the right, which Schaeffer read as Baʿal,[17] an identification reinforced by a second stele[18] of imported Egyptian sandstone found nearby with an inscription in Egyptian hieroglyphs, a dedication to Baʿal of Ṣaphon from Mami, a royal scribe (Yon 2007: nos. 17, 18). Therefore, the two cults would have had a familial linkage.

The two temples at Ugarit present some interesting points of convergence and divergence with Middle Bronze Age forms. The thickness of the walls, especially in Temple 2, certainly suggests that both these temples are related to the fortress-like temples of the Middle Bronze Age. They are not *migdāl* temples as defined in Palestine, with towers but, rather, are closer to the original Syrian model as developed at Ebla and probably elsewhere. They may well have stood quite tall, perhaps a development out of the fortress type suitable for an elevated site, on which they could serve as an announcement of the city to anyone approaching by sea. The temples are really larger complexes with courtyards, and in this they also recall the forms of the Middle Bronze Age. Where they do not conform is in the actual design. The interplay of broad-room and long-room elements within the same structure and the use of the long-room longitudinal axis as the organizing force can be seen in Middle Bronze Age temples but not the combination of the two elements that form the T-shape. This is a new feature for Levantine architecture and may be a local invention. This may also be the case with the other feature of interest—the pairing of the temples. These two structures respond to one another, as evidenced by the repetition of the unusual plan; they are in an architectural association. It may be, as Schaeffer argued, the result of the familial association of the cults, but it could also be an architectural tradition. The pairing of the temples creates an architectural ensemble and increases the visual stature of the structures.

The pairing of long-room temples at Ugarit is not at all unique.[19] At Late Bronze Age Emar, also in the North Syrian region, stood another pair of temples. Emar (Meskene) was an old settlement in northern Syria at the confluence of the Euphrates and Balikh rivers. The third-millennium tablets from Ebla indicate that diplomatic, strategic, and commercial concerns joined the two cities (Pettinato 1981: 45, 87, 101, 161). An Old Babylonian text details a trade itinerary from Larsa in the south through northern Mesopotamia and the Khabur Plains that ends with Emar as the final destination. However, the Early Bronze Age city has not been found, and only a few tablets provide evidence of the Middle Bronze Age city. What has been excavated is the Late Bronze Age city (Kohlmeyer 1985: 260).

---

17. RS 4.427 (Louvre Museum AO 15775).
18. RS 1[089]+ RS 2[033] + RS 5183 (Louvre Museum AO 1.3176).
19. G. R. H. Wright (1985: 1.230) identified the twin temple scheme as a feature of Early Bronze architecture in the Levant and Anatolia.

Emar was a newly constructed city in the Late Bronze Age, probably resulting from the need to relocate the city to a higher level because of changes in the flow of the rivers. The ruins are positioned on a limestone plateau at the valley's edge. Three sides are protected by the naturally steep slopes. The west side has a moat. Because the site slopes significantly from east to west, the builders used terraces to create large flat areas (Pitard 1996: 15–16). It is most likely that the new city of Emar was founded by one of the great Hittite kings, Šuppiluliuma I or Muršili II (Beckman 1996: 4). The local kings of Emar were vassals of the Great King's viceroy at Carchemish (Beckman 1996: 4; Kohlmeyer 1985: 248) and protected the eastern fringe of the empire.

In the southwest corner of the site, on the highest point of land (Area E), there are two structures identified as temples (fig. 79). The two buildings appear to have been constructed as a pair. They stood side by side in a north–south line, and the entrances opened to the east. They were not parallel. The front ends fanned slightly apart from each other. The south temple was slightly larger than the other, and its floor level was 1 m higher. The temples consist of a single long-room design with a porch defined by the extension of the wall of the main chamber. The entrances are through the east walls and are aligned on the longitudinal axes. Both temples have raised benches along the rear walls and podia built in front of the benches (Margueron 1983: 180–81, figs. 3–4). The temples have yielded tablets: 21 tablets from the south temple, 5 from the north temple.

A second grouping of temples is found at Area M in the center of the urban fabric. Temple M_1 (fig. 80) is also a long-room type but lacks the porch defined by the side walls. Instead the porch is much smaller, defined by massive buttresses on the *antae* of the temple walls. It is aligned southwest to northeast, opening to the northeast. The door is placed on the longitudinal axis. A bench runs the length of the rear wall, and a podium stands two-thirds of the way into the main chamber. Temple M_1 (Temple du devin) yielded 650 tablets and has been associated with a specific family of archive priests, "the diviners of the gods of Emar," who may have lived in a nearby house (Pitard 1996: 18). A second temple in the region, M_2, shares the same west-to-east orientation as the paired temples in area E. It also is a long room but with a small porch. The interior has a podium, and the exterior may have been decorated with ceramic cones. Both temples M_1 and M_2 and the temples in sector E are on the edge of large artificial terraces that define architectural units (Margueron 1982: 236–37). They face away from the terraces, which open behind them. They are not architecturally joined to the courtyards but, rather, are juxtaposed with them. They are similar in their long-room plans, which place emphasis on the longitudinal axis and emphasize it further by the entrance (Fleming 1992a: 288–89).

Ugarit, Emar, and Alalakh provide North Syrian Late Bronze Age prototypes for long-room temple variations, paired temples, and palace-temple complexes that could have been known to Phoenician architects. The temple forms were not themselves an invention of the Late Bronze Age. There was the earlier, tripartite long-room temple (Temple D) from Middle Bronze Age Ebla, and Canaanite Palestine had the *migdāl* temples at Megiddo and Shechem. The Megiddo and Shechem temples may have functioned into the early Iron Age. These variations on a long-room type developed in the Canaanite cities of Palestine in MBA IIB. Prior to this, Middle Bronze Age sanctuaries had been limited to open-air shrines. How much of the Late Bronze Age palace complexes would have been visible to Iron Age I architects is difficult to determine. Nothing suggests that these were in use after the fall of the Late Bronze Age cities. Moreover, the lack of any clear design association between the Iron Age IIB examples that do survive at Carchemish and Tell Taʿyinat and the Late Bronze Age predecessors probably indicates that nothing more than the idea of the connections was actually still known in the early Iron Age. What the archaeological evidence makes clear is that the long-room temple type had a long history in the Levantine region. Its development and use during the course of the Early Bronze Age, Middle Bronze Age, and Late Bronze Age were informed by several different design influences coming from Anatolia and northern Mesopotamia. Local needs were instrumental in the ways in which the long-room type was shaped and used at the various sites. The creation and spread of a possibly fortified version in the Middle Bronze Age from Syria into southern Canaan suggests that as a type the long room was a versatile structure easily adapted to different needs. Its reappearance in the early Iron Age can only be seen as a continued validation of its recognized utility as a religious building form.

Broad-Room Temples

The Iron Age IIB temple within the citadel at Arad represents the continuation of the other major temple type, the broad room, from the Bronze Age into the Iron Age. In a long-room temple, the longitudinal axis dominates the design, and the entrance is somehow associated with this axis. In a broad-room design, the power of the longitudinal movement within a rectangular space is balanced by emphasis placed on the secondary axis of the space. The entrance is placed on one of the long sides, and the focal point of the interior space is opposite the entrance at a position on the other long wall. The main chambers of the Early Bronze Age megara at Megiddo are technically broad-room forms. This is also the case for the main chamber of the Area H temple at Hazor, which throughout its Middle Bronze Age and Late Bronze Age versions (strata III, II, IB, and IA) was always a broad-room form encased in a long-room temple type (Yadin 1972b: 80–119). G. E. Wright, the excavator of Shechem, argued that the Middle Bronze Age *migdāl* temple there was a broad-room type (Wright 1965: 97). Simple broad-room temples with no associated long-room elements do exist but are not at all common in the Late Bronze Age, where only the temple in Area C at Hazor (fig. 103) can really be cited as a Late Bronze Age example (Yadin 1972a: 68–69). While G. E. Wright thought that the broad room was a type with a history that could be traced back in Palestine to the Early Bronze Age—a view that was seconded by Kempinski (1992: 54)—G. R. H. Wright questioned the essential existence of the type in the Palestinian corpus, arguing that it was really a Sumerian invention with no true Bronze Age Palestinian examples (Wright 1971a: 25; see his slightly different discussion in 1985: 1.232–34). This view has been echoed by Yeivin in his study of Early Bronze Age temples (Yeivin 1973: 163–75).

The temple at Arad is a true broad-room type (fig. 55). It stands alone and is not part of a long-room structure. Through the history of the site and its several rebuildings, the broad-room format was never abandoned. The striking feature about the Arad temple is that it clearly was a complex in which the broad room formed one element. The courtyard in front of the chamber with its own cult installation at some periods and the side room paralleling the courtyard and placed at a right angle to the broad room were also integral elements in the design. This is a much more formal and hierarchical space than is the case with the broad room in Area C at Hazor. Moreover, the broad room itself is clearly the end goal of the complex rather than a transitional space, as it is in the Area H temple at Hazor. The Arad shrine is a new concept built of old parts. Many have seen the resemblance between the Arad temple, which exists as the only Iron Age example at the moment,[20] and the four-room and three-room house types that developed in the Late Bronze Age and early Iron Age in the hill country of Palestine (Fritz 1995: 148).[21] These are usually oblong overall plans, with the broad room at the back end of a courtyard and forming the main enclosed space of the house and the subsidiary three or two rooms laid out in a row on one side of the courtyard and at a right angle to the broad room (Netzer 1992: 193). However, Bunimovitz and Faust (2002: 33–41) have seen in the design and longevity of the four-room house a kind of conscious marker of identity created and sustained by the emergent Israelite population. This view could point to a connection between house form and temple type. On the other hand, these four-room houses show a great variation and tend to demonstrate ad hoc adaptations (A. Mazar 1992a: fig. 8.22). The Arad temple is much more rigid and fixed in its treatment of the relationships of the parts. It is certainly possible that the architects for the citadel shrine borrowed a house type and then regularized it, but it is also possible that the resemblance between domestic design and temple is more fortuitous than intentional.

The tripartite holy of holies at the end of the colonnaded courtyard of the Phoenician Temple of Astarte at Kition (fig. 45) does resemble the broad-room type. It is certainly possible that this form was pushed into service to create this portion of the

---

20. Two large houses of the four-room type from Tell en-Naṣbeh were unearthed in the 1930s and identified as temples and could indicate that the Arad temple was not really so unique, but Shiloh has argued strongly against the temple identification (Shiloh 1979a: 147).

21. Shiloh (1970: 180–90) has argued against this view for many of the four- and three-room structures found. For an alternative view of the Arad temple as a version of a high place, see Welten 1972: 19–37.

larger sanctuary. Unlike the Arad shrine, however, in which the hierarchical design indicates that the holy of holies is more significant than the courtyard that fronts it, the unusual treatment of the courtyard of the Kition temple renders it a more-significant architectural element in the design, which suggests that the courtyard and holy of holies should be taken together as a single unit.

Bent-Axis Temples

A bent-axis design is a more complicated arrangement of the interior forces of a space. The directionality introduced by the entrance is abruptly broken, usually at a 90-degree angle, by the main axis of the space established by the primary cultic focus. Temple 131 from stratum X in Area C of Tell Qasile (fig. 21) and the Iron Age II version of the temple at Pella can be identified as bent-axis type temples from the Iron Age. In the previous versions of the Tell Qasile temple, entrance to the single chamber of the sanctuary had been accessed by a door in the east wall opposite what appears to have been the side with the cult focus. In the changes introduced in stratum X, a new vestibule was added to the sanctuary chamber, creating a two room shrine, and entrance into this vestibule was from the north. Entering the main cult chamber required a right angle turn, thus breaking the movement along the initial axis.

The change in format for the Pella temple is much more striking. What had been a long-room temple, in its Middle Bronze Age form probably a *migdāl* temple, was quite suddenly and dramatically changed to a bent-axis format. The interior probably still retained a longitudinal focus, but it was now entered from a corner door. Since the temple was now a secondary feature of a larger complex, perhaps a palace, the change probably reflected a new pattern of use, though in most palace-temple complexes from the Late Bronze Age and Iron Age II, the long-room temple is by far the most common.

The north temple in stratum V (Mazar's Upper VI) at Beth-shean (fig. 28) may be a version of a bent-axis type. It does appear to be designed with a vestibule on the west side that established one direction of movement through the space, which then was abruptly shifted by a right-angle turn to enter the main chamber proper.

The bent-axis type of temple has only a limited history in the Levant. G. R. H. Wright thought that the first version of the Fosse temple at Lachish was a bent-axis form, his only example from the Late Bronze Age. He identified the MBA IIC structure at Nahariyah as a version of the bent axis, again the only example that he could find from the Middle Bronze Age. He had one Early Bronze Age example, the EBA III acropolis temple at Ai. Wright thought that the bent axis may have been a major form in Early Bronze Age Palestinian architecture but that it was displaced by the long room at the time the cultural disruptions in Palestine, about 2000 B.C.E., after which it never again assumed importance (G. R. H. Wright 1971a: 17–32). The bent axis is a well-known Mesopotamian type, and the earliest versions can be traced back to temple VII at Eridu (Abu Shahrein) from the Al ʿUbaid period (Frankfort 1985: 19, fig. 3). The redesign of the Tell Qasile temple could partake of an old but rarely used architectural form in the Levant, though this hardly seems likely. Considering the drama of the break with the previous versions of the temple, the change to the plan should probably be seen not as the revival of some quite ancient building form but as the result of a shift in the functioning of the cult that resulted in the need for a new type of temple format. Something similar must lie behind the change in temple forms in stratum V (Mazar's Upper VI) at Beth-shean.

Centralized Square Temples

The Temple of the Storm God at Carchemish and the first two versions of the temple at Tell Qasile seem the most likely heirs of the centralized square plan, which does seem to have had a wide distribution in the Late Bronze Age. The Carchemish temple has already been discussed as a variant of the long-room type. It does, however, have a square-like form and a single chamber that make it closer to a square than the rectangle that would be expected in a true long room. On the other hand, the marked axial movement along the longitudinal axis and the reinforcing of this sense by means of the porch suggest that any association with the Late Bronze Age square temple design is probably more accidental than intentional. The two early versions of the Tell Qasile temple (strata XII and XI) are more serious contenders (fig. 20A/B). Neither of them is a real square with right-angle corners, and the walls are somewhat uneven in their thickness, but it is obvious that they were conceived as squared structures enclosing a square chamber. The earliest form of the shrine (stratum XII) was designed to highlight the two axes of the chamber. The entrance was placed more or less in the middle of the east wall and established the east–west axis. This line intersected with the edge of a platform attached to the east side of the partition wall that protrudes from the shrine's north wall. The platform was roughly in the middle of the room and therefore defined the north–south axis as well as occupying the crossing of the two axes. The measurements are not hard and fast, and it is possible that the associations just described were not intentional. They certainly disappear in the next iteration of the temple (stratum XI). Nothing in this version restates either of the two main axes. However, if the absence of any notice of axial forces was the intention of the architect, then it might be safe to assume that these forces were understood and exploited by the builder of the stratum XII version.

Neither of the two temples resembles the square centralized temple plans of the Late Bronze Age. G. R. H. Wright knew of the Amman airport temple (fig. 73). He also included the MBA IIC temple at Tananir on Mount Gerizim near Shechem in the list (G. R. H. Wright 1971a: 19–22). Excavations have revealed another possible square building dating to the Bronze Age at Hazor. These all evidence an internal format of two concentric squares, with secondary dividing walls that create a series of chambers surrounding a central square space. None of these structures has any architectural reason to be labeled a temple, and Burke (2007: 43–47) has argued that they were watchtowers. The structure at Hazor functioned within an urban setting. The structures at Amman and Tananir stood alone. Only the Amman building has yielded prestigious finds that support the identification of the remains as belonging to a building with a special function (Herr 1983a). It has been pointed out that the interior square spaces in both the Amman and Tananir buildings were too large to have been roofed (Campbell and Wright 1969: 111–12). Both of these buildings had a round, column-like installation in the central square space, and Campbell and Wright suggested that these were bases to hold up sacred pillars, which they argued commemorated covenants taken among tribes who used these two isolated sanctuaries as tribal league shrines. Yadin thought that the smaller square building at Hazor had served a similar tradition in an earlier phase at the site (Yadin 1972a: 100).

Herr, who excavated at the Amman airport site, disagreed with the tribal league association for these buildings, and for the remains at the Amman airport he suggested a mortuary function (Herr 1983b: 224–29). Herr's reading of the remains required the practice of cremation burial, which was not the norm for the region of Transjordan, and so he posited a Hittite presence in the area, for which no evidence exists independent of the Amman airport structure. Herr's interpretation has not been universally accepted (A. Mazar 1992a: 256–57 n. 21).

While there was a tradition for square buildings with central focus in the Levant, particularly in the area of Canaan in the Middle Bronze Age and Transjordan in the Late Bronze Age, these earlier forms have little in common with the two square versions of the temple at Tell Qasile. The Tell Qasile structures were not designed as paired concentric squares encasing a series of rectangular chambers that in turn defined an inner square. There is no reason to believe that the Tell Qasile structures were unroofed, and while the first version of the temple may have intentionally laid stress on the central feature at the axial crossing, nothing like this is present in the second version.

Courtyard Temples

In Wright's typology, the courtyard sanctuaries are those that combine enclosed spaces and courtyards, treating both elements with equal importance. This is different from the use of a courtyard to set off a temple building by separating it from any nearby buildings, which is a standard feature of most of the Late Bronze Age and early Iron Age temple complexes. The category is somewhat amorphous, since it is difficult, based solely on the remains, to identify when a courtyard and an enclosed space are accorded equal weight in the design. Moreover, it is not clear in many instances whether a space was roofed, unroofed, or partially roofed. Wright thought that he had one example, the MBA IIC complex at Nahariyah (G. R. H. Wright 1971a: 19; A. Mazar 1992b: 162), but no examples from the Late Bronze Age have been found. Three Iron Age structures, however, seem to belong to the category: the final complex in stratum

X at Tell Qasile, the Phoenician Temple of Astarte at Kition, and the complex of rooms and spaces that form Building 350 at Ekron.

The final design of both the stratum X sanctuary 131 at Tell Qasile (fig. 22) and the Phoenician Temple of Astarte at Kition (fig. 45) consists of the main temple and secondary shrines' all being embedded within a series of courtyards. At Tell Qasile, the sacred part of the temple was buried at the far west end of the building. Spaces open up to the east. The main chamber leads out into the vestibule to the east. The vestibule exits to the north into a walled courtyard to the east. This plan served to render the holiest portion of the temple as largely inaccessible to all but a few, while at the same time creating a series of layered hallowed spaces that provided shells around the most sacred area and isolated it from the profane region outside. The courtyard was designed to interact with the temple, since it funnels any visitor toward the temple and directs worshipers' movements. It also functions in crowd control, since it makes at least one if not two turns that would limit the number of the people crowding at the door. The small secondary exit from the courtyard leads directly onto the street and may have allowed people to escape if the pressure of the crowd grew too great. The presence of a built installation within the courtyard suggests that it also could have been used for services.

The small second shrine (Shrine 300) attached to the exterior of the west wall of temple 131 at Tell Qasile was also fronted by an L-shaped courtyard. This courtyard could have functioned in a manner analogous to that of the other courtyard, directing and controlling crowds. Unlike the courtyard associated with the main temple, which in its present remains is not much larger than the temple proper, the courtyard leading into the shrine is about two times the size of the shrine. Interestingly, in neither case did the courtyard provide an architectural accent for the structure. The main entrance into the big courtyard must have been to the east. The view from this entrance would have been a blank wall, the east wall of the vestibule. Only a bench along the south half of the wall gives any type of articulation to the expanse of masonry. Reaching the entrance required movement through the courtyard space. Even at the entrance, the temple was not raised above the level of the courtyard. Moreover, the west wall of the courtyard intersected the north wall of the temple just to the west of the entrance. There was no visual suggestion of the size of the enclosed space of the temple proper. Similarly, the entrance to the shrine's courtyard faced the blank wall that is the western extension of the temple's north wall. When the turn was made to the south into the corridor that leads to the shrine's entrance, the major feature in the space was the north wall of the shrine.

At Kition, the smaller courtyard or temenos leads into the colonnaded courtyard in front of the holy of holies, creating a similar system of layering. As I mentioned above, the holy of holies does seem to use the broad-room format, but it cannot be separated from the colonnaded courtyard. The courtyard clearly organizes the movement of people through the space and directs the approach to the holy of holies. The architectural devices that frame the holy of holies are part of the architecture of the courtyard. Moreover, the courtyard retained the prestige ashlar masonry treatment of the earlier version of the temple.

Building 350 (fig. 18) at Ekron is slightly different. The main entrance into the complex is known, and it clearly defines a special space by the use of the wide opening, the *antae*, and the two columns placed *in antis*. The two chambers along the west side of the complex, which are the same width, could have been an open courtyard, though the three bases, probably for columns, along the longitudinal axis of the second chamber, do suggest that this space was roofed, at least partly. As in the design for the stratum X temple at Tell Qasile, the courtyards again seem to have functioned as a means of restricting and directing crowds. They establish a specific line of motion through the space, a north-to-south movement that is then broken because the actual cult chambers are located to the east, introducing a bent-axis aspect to the design. The courtyards provide the same construct of spatial penetration as do the two courts at Tell Qasile, but they do this in a different manner. The layering is more formally arranged, one space leading into the next, and the overriding sense of geometry is much more apparent than at Tell Qasile, where there are no real right angles. The evidence for possible installations in the second court of Building 350 may indicate that this deeper court was also used for ritual. Another design similar to this is the possible Philistine Building 2072 at Megiddo (fig. 31). Whether these Philistine experiments with courtyard sanctuary designs affected the later developments of Israelite sanctuaries in Iron Age II at Tell Arad and Tel Dan cannot be determined. What is clear is that Philistine architects of Iron Age I played with rather sophisticated courtyard designs in southern Palestine.

The Carchemish temple compound (fig. 36) is somewhat similar to Building 350 at Ekron. There is the same type of layering in the courtyard spaces, so that access to the temple is through a series of liminal regions. The changing nature of the flooring in each space—the outer, and inner courtyards, and the interior of the temple—seem to reinforce the idea that the spaces have different meanings and probably different functions. There is also the same type of break in directional focus that is noted at Ekron. The courtyards are aligned on an east–west axis, while the temple is on a north–south line, as is the entrance to the compound. However, at Carchemish, the the courtyards help to set off the actual temple building, which seems to have priority.

The Late Bronze Age sanctuary at Kamid el-Loz (ancient Kumidi; see fig. 104) at the southeastern end of the Baqʿah Valley in Lebanon is the best-preserved example of a courtyard design and may have provided a prototype.[22] This was a minor Late

---

22. G. R. H. Wright (1985: 1.232) classified Kamid el-Loz as a broad-room temple type rather than a courtyard type. I think that the courtyard is actually the defining feature of the structure, and thus I treat it in this category.

Bronze Age center with a palace and a temple (Badre 1997: 265; Hachmann 1989: 59–68) and was within the orbit of the Canaanite cultural sphere. The final complex on the site, T2 (M. Metzger 1991: 144–90), showed clear structural and design affiliations with the previous complex, T3. It comprised two separate groups of spaces arranged on both sides of a common wall. The east grouping consisted of spaces A, B, and C, which have been interpreted as two enclosed rooms (A and B) flanking the east and south sides of an open, brick-paved courtyard (C), in which stood a series of built installations (Hachmann 1983: 72–73). The courtyard was actually buried deep within the complex. The entrance was via a small patio at the southeast corner of the grouping, with a door that opened into the south wall of room B. Another door in the west wall of B gave access to the courtyard.

How space A related to the other spaces is not as clear. The western grouping was similar, in that courtyard G was deeply embedded within the core of the complex. It was the only feature in the northeast quadrant of the grouping of rooms, which consisted of H, J, K, and L. Spaces F, H, J, and K formed a block of three parallel rectangular chambers aligned on their longitudinal axis, which lined up to the west of courtyard G. Somehow attached to them to the south was room L, which was aligned in opposition, with its longitudinal axis running north–south. Parallel to L was room F, a large rectangular space, entered on the far west of its long south side.

The plan of the complex arranged around courtyard G was strikingly similar to the plan employed for Building 350 at Ekron and, more distantly, to the plan at Carchemish. The plans all included the same distribution of spaces, the same orientation of axes, and the same relationship between antechamber and courtyard. Inside room H, situated along its west wall, was an E-shaped fixture of mud brick, and with it were found animal bones and ceramic fragments. In the south room, L, there was a bronze knife with lion-headed handle and the fragment of a figurine of a woman with a Hathor-style hair treatment (Hachmann 1983: 68). This suggests that these side chambers, like those in Building 350, were centers for cult activities. Kamid el-Loz was not an important site and probably served the needs of the agricultural communities of the northern Baqʿah Valley (Ward 1994: 66–85). However, the location of the site in the valley that served as a major conduit for north–south trading and that was crossed by an important east–west road does not rule out the possibility that design ideas introduced at Kamid el-Loz could have moved outside its immediate area. The role of the temple as part of a palace complex may have rendered it more viable as a source for architectural inspiration. Because the Baqʿah Valley was probably one of the migration routes used by the land-moving groups of the "Peoples of the Sea" as they headed south, many people must have passed by the ruins of the temple as they headed south.

Although the other half of the complex at Kamid el-Loz does not match the later early Iron Age examples at Tell Qasile, Ekron, or Building 2072 as closely, it does suggest that the courtyards may have had real cultic functions. The installation in courtyard C (fig. 105) was massive, consisting of a mud-brick podium mounted by stairs and flanked on one side by an I-shaped feature holding two stone bases that in turn probably supported columns. Slightly to the south of this massive unit was a clay basin set into the floor of the courtyard. It has been suggested that this was a separate shrine within the larger sacred complex. Several house models were found in courtyard C (Hachmann 1983: no. 101). Nothing this dramatic has been discovered in the courtyards of the Tell Qasile or Ekron complexes, though both have yielded some evidence of courtyard installations. The findings at Kamid el-Loz indicate that there was an established tradition of using courtyards for cult purposes.

The Edomite sanctuary at Horvat Qitmit (fig. 65) is best treated as a courtyard-type sanctuary, though with a far less-formalized concept of spatial relationships. Complex B (fig. 67) seems to be nothing more than a series of rooms surrounding a small patio. Complex A (fig. 66) appears more planned—a true architectural composition. Three enclosed, long, parallel rooms open onto three distinct spatially defined areas: an unpaved and unarticulated plaza, a region designated by an enclosing wall on three sides, and a fully enclosed circular area. The entire composition is balanced, with the built structures forming half the sanctuary; and the plaza, which is partially enclosed, and circular spaces forming the other half. The two halves are linked by means of stone: a single row of stones runs from the circle to the three rooms, and fieldstones were used for construction. The similarity of building materials also relates Complex B to Complex A. All this suggests an architectural sensibility, albeit modest, in the creation of the Horvat Qitmit complexes.

The modest nature of the Horvat Qitmit complex also makes it difficult to be certain that the sanctuary identification is appropriate. It was clearly not conceived as a courtyard sanctuary in the same way as the stratum X temple at Tell Qasile or Building 350 at Ekron or even Building 2072 at Megiddo. In these instances, the courtyards form important elements in an architectural ensemble—open space played against enclosed space in a rather carefully contrived manner. The open and enclosed relationship at Horvat Qitmit seems much more accidental. Moreover, the poor quality of building materials and the humble nature of the actual structures resembles much more the types of constructions that have been associated with Iron Age I high place building. If there is some type of association between the seventh-century B.C.E. sanctuary at Horvat Qitmit and the twelfth-century B.C.E. "high places," it can be no more than the suggestion that this type of modest sanctuary construction continued to have currency over a 500-year period. Since the twelfth-century B.C.E. sites are assumed to be early manifestations of the Israelite culture, there is no way that they link culturally to the Edomite shrine at Horvat Qitmit.

High Places

Wright defined the high place, or *bāmâ*, as an open-air sanctuary placed on a protruding crest of ridge back and usually associated with a pillar—menhir, *maṣṣēbâ*—which he thought to be a surrogate for the tree of life, representing the male principal or a pole or wooden image (*xóanon*); or an *Asherah*, standing in for the female principal (Wright 1971a: 17).[23] He distinguished the type as distinct from the courtyard-temple complex, though clearly the two were related. Wright's definition warrants some reconsideration. Nakhai (1994: 18–29) has explained that the whole concept of a high place as a distinct sacred, architectural type comes from Jerome's mistranslation of *bāmâ* as *excelsus*, which in turn led to the English gloss as 'high place'. The word appears over 100 times in the biblical text, but it does not necessarily carry associations with a physically lifted place. In fact, the word in its cognates in several other Semitic languages does not even carry sacred connotations.

The two sites that are considered possibly to be the first of the Iron Age I high places—the Bull Site of Manasseh (fig. 33B) in the Samarian hills (A. Mazar 1982) and the cult place on Mount Ebal (fig. 33A) north of Shechem (Zertal 1985: 26–43; 1986: 49–53; 1987 105–65; 1988: 137–53)—are not universally accepted as sacred spaces (Nakhai 1994: 23; Kempinski 1986: 44–49). Both of these sites consist of installations built with local stone, possibly altars, set in the open and defined as specific areas set apart by encircling stone walls. The finds of ritually cleaned bones of young male animals in the first level at Mount Ebal; and offerings including a small, bronze statuette of a bull placed on a paved area in front of a single standing stone (a *maṣṣēbâ*) at the site of Manasseh (A. Mazar 1992a: 348–52) evidence a sanctuary identification more than the architecture. This is much the same at Horvat Qitmit, where the finds of ceramic sculpture and ritual objects provide the rationale for the identification rather than the structures and their arrangements.

There are several biblical references to early Iron Age *bāmôt* in the periods of Judges, the United Monarchy, and the Divided Monarchy, but the only fully developed high-place complex from the early Iron Age is at Tel Dan, which was in use from the tenth through the early eighth centuries B.C.E.[24] The complex is separated from the rest of the settlement at Dan and is approached by ascending the street (fig. 106), but its location is not on a particularly high spot. In all three of its iterations, it consisted of a flat paved area and a raised high platform. These two features were somehow enclosed or set off by walls that defined a precinct, and on the west side it contained secondary rooms. The three versions of the complex show a growing level of architectural complexity as the platforms became more dramatic architectural forms, with staircases and levels to the platforms and walls that were used to manipulate movement around

23. For general study of the tree cults in the ancient world, see Butterworth 1970.

24. Tell Sukas, the Phoenician site (see above, chap. 3), may have had a high place by the fourth century B.C.E. (Bondi 1999a: 319).

and through the individual units. The remains have not yielded clear evidence of the *maṣṣēbâ* and *Asherah* elements that Wright included in his definition, though two nonstructural columns may have stood on the lower, smaller platform during the second phase of operation (fig. 48). Groupings of nonstructural columns stood at three locations on the paved road that led from the city gate up to the sanctuary, including a grouping outside the city gate proper (fig. 51).

The sites identified as high place sanctuaries were among the first type to appear in the Middle Bronze Age. This is how the first sanctuary at Nahariya is categorized (A. Mazar 1992b: 161); it consisted of a platform attached to a small square building enclosing a single room. High places combined with courtyard sanctuaries may be found in the Levant back to the Early Bronze Age. The temple at Byblos ("Temple en L") may well have been an early form of this type of complex. In the Middle Bronze Age, it evolved into the Temple of the Obelisks (fig. 107), in which form it appears to have operated as a high place set off by courtyard elements (Jidejian 1968: 20–21, 35–37). It contained a single structure, probably defining the high place, and was surrounded by obelisks—all enclosed in a kerb wall.

A high place complex may have existed in MBA IIC at Gezer (Dever 1997c: 396–400; Macalister 1912: 377–411). In this instance, the high place was defined by a row of 11 large stone monoliths aligned north–south, in the center of an open area. These are quite different from the situation at Tel Dan. The Tel Dan spaces are arranged in a hierarchical fashion, with a paved platform serving as the front drop for the *bāmâ*, with a temple behind. The final phase is a bit more confused because the two major elements in the sanctuary are each given their own integrity using stairs and enclosure walls (fig. 50). However, there is no doubt that the two main features in the center of the open space defined by the enclosing precinct walls take priority over the secondary chamber on the west side. Over the course of the three rebuildings, the relationship between the *bāmâ* and the podium-temple was made more rigid by aligning the two structures on the main longitudinal axis of the precinct. The other feature that separates the Tel Dan high place from any of the predecessors is the quality of the construction technique. From the first versions, ashlar stone masonry was used for the primary structures. In the second phase, these were laid in a careful header-and-stretcher pattern. None of the other high places exhibit this care in both layout and construction.

Although it does seem that the concept of selecting an isolated high point as a religious locale and giving it some architectural embellishment, as well as preventing it from sharing space with secular structures can be traced back at least to the Middle Bronze Age in the Palestinian region, the concept still had currency in the early Iron Age. If Biran is correct, the high place at Tel Dan was established in a location devoid of any pre-Israelite cultic associations. The Canaanite sanctuaries for the Middle Bronze Age and Late Bronze Age city were located elsewhere, more toward the center of the site (Biran and Shanks 1987: 18). This may indicate that the high place design was really a new form in the Israelite early Iron Age. Yadin noted something similar at Hazor, where he argued that the new Israelite population that settled on the ruins of the Canaanite city (stratum XI), sometime before the reign of Solomon—as early as the eleventh century B.C.E.—created a new sanctified area, a high place. It was a small rectangular enclosure, a building (?), containing a bench-like structure in its southern half. The area to the west of the enclosure was paved and held four stone pillars, *maṣṣēbôt* (?); the areas to the south and east were also paved. On the southern paved area, 2 broken incense burners were found. The area was then built over in the next stratum. There is nothing to indicate that the spot had previously been hallowed, which would be appropriate in the case of newcomers, as at Tel Dan. However, the finds from the site included a small bronze figure of a seated male, read by Yadin as a possible Warrior-God image (Yadin 1975: 254–57). While Yadin favored a new population at the site residing on the ruins of the Canaanite city, the bronze image could also be explained as the product of a returning Canaanite population. What is clear is that the area's sacred nature was respected in the next period. This high place is earlier than that at Tel Dan and nowhere near as architecturally developed.

Conclusion

The issue of architectural continuity is, of course, another way of addressing the question of cultural continuity between the Late Bronze Age and the early Iron Age in the Levant. The historical evidence for the demographic disruption at the end of the Late Bronze Age followed by the arrival of new peoples throughout the early Iron Age and the development of new political and societal structures by Iron Age IIA does demand that we inquire what from the Late Bronze Age culture survived to influence the evolving culture of the early Iron Age. A number of the early Iron Age sanctuaries do not possess a plan definitive enough for reasonable categorization. To this group belong the Iron Age sanctuaries of Sarepta, Lachish, Teman, Khirbat al-Mudayna, Amman, Tell Sukas, Tell Arka, and Ekron Field I. Several other structures reveal plans that were clearly conceived but do not belong in the categories that have been proposed for Levantine temples and must be treated as something new.

Certain lines of investigation about architectural continuity seem to yield little of value for answering the deeper question of cultural continuity. Building materials were largely determined by local geology, and the traditions of efficient building methods using these materials were the result of centuries of practice. There is little reason to expect that successful adaptations to local resources will necessarily be abandoned with the arrival of newcomers. One need only remember that the Spanish who colonized the southwestern United States adapted their structures to employ building practices perfected by the local Pueblo peoples.[25] Moreover, in the case of

---

25. This was also true for the development of Spanish colonial architecture along the coastal region of Peru, where local, indigenous forms of construction had to be adopted (even though they were not

the early Iron Age Levant, the newcomers had few if any traditions of monumental building.

The presence of early Iron Age sanctuaries raised above the remains of earlier Late Bronze Age sanctuaries does seem more revealing. At the Aleppo Citadel, ʿAin Dara, Abu Hawam, and Beth-shean, they should be an indication that, even if there were changes brought about as a result of Late Bronze Age–early Iron Age population shifts, these topographic spots retained a numinous quality that could be fit into the new societal structures taking shape. In a similar way, the total break with earlier hallowed grounds in many sites argues for a major shift in the concept of the sanctity of older topographical features between the Late Bronze Age and early Iron Age. As G. R. H. Wright (1985: 1.245–47) has concluded, the continuity of plans is not necessarily indicative. The individual plans do not provide any particular indication of the ethnicity of the builders. These were plans that could be adapted and changed to suit new ritual needs, whatever the initial ritual practices were that had influenced their design. Since all of these plan types had long pedigrees in the Levantine region, their continued use into the early Iron Age suggests merely that, whatever the rituals, the spaces were still viable and could be altered to function. The variety of changes made to the plans may actually indicate that there were several ways in which ritual space was conceived and used in the early Iron Age. Forms such as the centralized square and the courtyard are of limited help in understanding continuity because they do not have specific diagnostic features, and it is difficult to determine how closely the early Iron Age versions carried on with forms employed in the Late Bronze Age. At the most basic level, courtyards serve to create greater sanctity for the enclosed temple area by offering an entrance that is only accessible through an already privileged and semi-hallowed space.

The long-room type is a bit easier to consider. It is probably not surprising that it is at the older, established settlements—which have Middle Bronze, Late Bronze, and early Iron Age strata, for example, Megiddo, Shechem, and Hazor—that evidence for the possible continued use of the *migdāl* version of the long room into the early Iron Age is seen. These are sites regarded as having formed their Canaanite identities in the Middle Bronze Age, maintained them through the Late Bronze Age, and retained them into the early Iron Age more fully than other sites. However, this does not mean that the *migdāl* long-room temple was a marker of Canaanite identity. Its origins are Syrian. More likely, the survival of the long-room type in the old Canaanite region is evidence of continued ritual practices that were best performed in these spaces. On the other hand, the revival and development of the form in North Syria in the Neo-Hittite and Aramean centers seem to suggest some degree of affiliation between the

---

appropriate to the Spanish notion of the proper building of public structures) because of limitations of materials and the danger of earthquakes; V. Fraser, *The Architecture of Conquest: Building in the Viceroyalty of Peru, 1535–1635* (Cambridge: Cambridge University Press, 1990) 110–11.

new Iron Age settlements and their Late Bronze Age ancestors. Considering that the long-room type has no history as a temple form in the Hittite heartland, its presence and popularity in the Iron Age centers may point to a sense of local identity, though it should not be read as a sign of a "nationalist revival," because Hittite elements were still being promoted by local Iron Age kings.

The use of the broad-room type for the Arad temple, however, must be seen as something new. While the type is well known in earlier contexts elsewhere in the Levant, its use at Arad is quite definite and has no earlier tradition in the region. It must be seen as either a new discovery for the area or as the revival of an older form but in a totally new context. Its possible association with the four-room house type cannot be ignored (G. R. H. Wright 1985: 1.237). The use of the format in the setting of a frontier fortress by the kings of the newly independent Kingdom of Judah may be an indication that architectural form had been invested with some sort of meaning tied to the early history of the Israelite people.

Based on the archaeological record, it is difficult to determine how the Iron Age temples compared in scale to the Late Bronze Age structures that they replaced. By the Late Bronze Age, there were structures with an area of 1,000 m², and the *migdāl* temple at Shechem had a total area of 550 m² (G. R. H. Wright 1985: 1.120–21). Certainly in Iron Age I, nothing being built would have equaled the major temples of the Late Bronze Age. The renovated Aleppo Citadel temple may have retained the grandeur of its predecessor; perhaps the ʿAin Dara Iron Age version still presented an impressive form; and if they were still in use, then the surviving *migdāl* temples must have commanded some respect. Otherwise, the Iron Age I structures were poor relations at best. In Iron Age II, Wright thinks that once again large buildings developed (some with areas of 1,000 m²–2,000 m²) at several places in the region, and a culminating point was reached in the long-room temple type with the temple of Solomon which, based on the biblical descriptions, must have been a noticeably long and somewhat narrow structure.

Chapter 5

New Forms

It should be clear that, while it is possible to link features of many of the early Iron Age temples to Middle Bronze and Late Bronze forms, the similarities also serve to highlight significant differences that may actually suggest that some of the early Iron Age temples were quite new conceptions and that some lines of continuity with the earlier forms may be only superficial. This can be seen in the temple in the citadel at Arad. Although the main chamber is an old form, a broad-room temple the origins of which can be traced back to the Early Bronze Age, its combination with a front courtyard and with secondary chambers makes the complete complex something quite new, as does its specific context, a frontier fortress. The Tel Dan high place design has a long pedigree, but not its particular hierarchy of parts or its high-quality technical execution of the individual elements.

Of course, the problem is one of the need to classify. Obviously, no early Iron Age architect thought in terms of Wright's (1971a) sexpartite morphology. There were real points of continuity between some Bronze Age temples and their Iron Age successors. The most important was the notion of the types of spaces that were appropriate for conducting ritual. These remained constant. Both enclosed spaces and open spaces could be made suitable, and this was true for both Bronze Age and Iron Age sites of worship. Whether enclosed or open, spaces were arranged to focus attention on select features; size, placement, and height were all employed to privilege certain areas over others. Space itself could be manipulated into hierarchical structures, and this was done by controlling access to space and movement through space. Certain very specific, recognizable forms did seem to survive the end of the Bronze Age and enter the first part of the Iron Age. The long-room, tripartite, rectangular temple is certainly the prime example of this survival. It is not impossible that the formula of courtyard and secondary chambers found at the Late Bronze Age site of Kamid el-Loz was specifically recalled in the design of Building 350 at Ekron, though the distance in time and space suggests that there were intermediaries that simply have not been found. However, the point remains that the specific architectural feature seems too closely replicated and complicated to be the result of simple independent discovery.

It is valuable to debate the degree of continuity and discontinuity among the particular temples already discussed, and it is valid to argue for some level of linkage between these Iron Age temples and their possible architectural kin from the Bronze Age. It is also true that the Iron Age architects produced new forms that are best understood as novel developments. These are not without Bronze Age antecedents, but they excited greater interest in early Iron Age builders and were developed more fully.

Building Techniques

Ashlar Masonry

The primary construction technique to be used fairly widely in the early Iron Age was ashlar masonry. The use of carefully cut and fitted stones either to build entire structures or to provide a sheathing for certain faces had a long history in Egypt (Boardman 2000: 20). It spread to or developed independently in the Levant, where, as early as the third millennium, monumental stone walls could be found in the sacred region of Byblos, though these were not truly ashlar masonry (fig. 107; Jidejian 1968: figs. 25–28). A finer quality of masonry was to be seen in the Middle Bronze Age Temple of the Obelisks erected over the Early Bronze Age temples at Byblos (Jidejian 1968: 66). Ashlar masonry was employed by builders on Crete during the neo-palatial period (Rehak and Younger 1998: 108).

Ashlar masonry developed during the second millennium in Late Bronze Age contexts on the island of Cyprus at Alassa, Enkomi, Kition, Maa-Palaeokastro, and Salamis. During the same period, it appeared at Ugarit (fig. 102) and Ras Ibn Hani, south of Ugarit (Raban and Stieglitz 1991: 37 with illustration). Karageorghis notes that ashlar masonry construction appeared on Cyprus in the context of sites with new populations that arrived in the LC IIIA period. These he has identified as the first wave of "Peoples of the Sea" to take up residence on the island, but the technique of ashlar construction was not used in the Aegean region from which these newcomers emerged. He has argued that the population must have included refugees from Ugarit, one of the major cities destroyed by the "Peoples of the Sea," who then introduced the technique on the island, where it was used for major LC III temple constructions at both Kition (fig. 108) and Palaeopaphos (Kouklia) (fig. 109; see Karageorghis 1982: 91–99). Raban and Stieglitz (1991: 37–39) have read the archaeological evidence a bit differently, arguing that the thirteenth-century appearance of ashlar construction in both Cypriot and Levantine contexts was the result of the migration of the various groups that formed the "Peoples of the Sea." Since Tel Dor had ashlar construction as early as the thirteenth century and was perhaps settled by the Sikels, they could well have been the specific group responsible for introducing the technique throughout the area in the last period of the Late Bronze Age.

Ashlar masonry construction spread during the early Iron Age, particularly after the tenth century B.C.E. The corners of the tenth-century north gate tower at Ashdod were constructed using ashlars (M. Dothan 1993: 99). The temple at Sarepta made use of finely cut stone blocks, and there were remains of other ashlar structures in City D at Sarepta (Pritchard 1978: 82–84). The ʿAin Dara temple was also built of ashlar blocks (fig. 110), and the masonry style was employed for the ninth-century buildings at Samaria (Boardman 2000: 27–29). It is regularly argued that ashlar masonry is a distinct, diagnostic feature of Solomonic state buildings (Isserlin 1998: 250; A. Mazar 1992a: 382; Reich 1992: 211–12). The walls associated with the possible Temple of Astarte/Juno at Tas-Silġ on Malta are ashlar masonry, though probably of third-century B.C.E. date and therefore Punic rather than Phoenician (Bonanno et al. 2000; Sagona 2002: 274).

Framework Technique

Another stone construction technique that is sometimes called "Phoenician-Israelite construction," or *framework technique* consists of piers constructed of stone blocks arranged in a regular, rhythmic pattern, with an infill of rubble stone or mud brick. The technique reappeared in Roman times as *opus africanum* (Mierse 1999: 274) but developed in the Levantine region during the early Iron Age. It does not figure in any of the temple remains so far discovered, but it does appear at sites during these centuries, and its absence from the temple remains may be nothing more than the lack of substantial superstructures for most of these buildings. It is best documented in the Levant on coastal sites and was in use from the tenth through the fourth centuries B.C.E. (Stern 1993: 22 and 24 with illustration). It was also taken west to the Phoenician colonies (Bondi 1999a: 330 and illustrations 323, 332).

Wood-Crib Construction

All of the sanctuary structures from the early Iron Age were built with mud brick to some degree. This had been the standard building material for the Late Bronze Age. In some instances, the mud-brick walls were built on stone socles; in other instances, they rest on the bedrock. At Guzana, the builders adapted an old Mesopotamian technique (Frankfort 1985: 42) of building with mud-brick arches (Albright 1956a: 79). There is nothing noteworthy in the mud-brick material or in the form of the bricks to distinguish the early Iron Age buildings from their predecessors. There are, however, some technical innovations that warrant discussion.

In the North Syrian region, mud-brick wall construction was combined with wood structural elements. The temple-palace at Guzana and the palace and temple at Tell Taʿyinat display a distinctive technique that integrates wood with the mud brick in a system that is termed *wood-crib construction* (fig. 111). This is found in the porch areas of the palaces and in portions of the porch of the temple at Tell Taʿyinat.[1] The contractors for each site employed wood slightly differently. At Tell Taʿyinat (Haines 1971: 45–46, 53–54), horizontal beams were placed flush with the wall and alternated

---

1. Haines (1971: 53) states that evidence for the wood-crib construction survived at the northwest corner of the temple and at the east end of the north wall. It is assumed that it was employed in the other two corners, which have been lost over the centuries.

with rows of regularly inserted beams that penetrated the wall from 75 to 100 cm. The mud brick formed the fill between the wood elements. At Guzana (Langenegger et al. 1950: 60, 80–86, 382), two systems of wood integrated with mud brick were employed, both used to secure the orthostats to the mud-brick walls of the temple-palace. Along the north façade, the sculpted face of the structure, a complex wood grill was used in which wood beams transversely cut across the thickness of the walls at regular intervals to be joined with the horizontal members on the exteriors of the walls. The builders anchored the orthostats to this wood armature. Something similar was used at the North Syrian site of Zincirli (Samʾal) for Bīt Ḥilani III. The south wall of the temple-palace at Guzana was much more massive, being both higher and thicker than the north façade. Here, the orthostats were employed along the lower edge of the walls to visually form a socle. They were each secured by a wood beam placed above that penetrated the wall for about 50 cm. Resting atop the row of beams was a horizontal wood member.

Wood was, of course, available in the North Syrian region, though more wood was used at Zincirli than at Guzana, suggesting that local resources probably did vary, and the construction technique had to be adapted. Frankfort recognized this mixing of building media, which can include stone along with the wood and mud brick—a characteristic combination of North Syrian early Iron Age architecture (Frankfort 1985: 285; Ussishkin 1966a: 109). In fact ,it was a continuation of a construction style that can be found as early as the Middle Bronze Age in Yarim-Lim's palace in level VII at Alalakh (Woolley 1939: 25, pl. 90.1; 1953: 68; Frankfort 1985: 253). Use of wood in building was probably spread more widely by Hittite constructions in the Late Bronze Age, since it was a well-developed Anatolian style of building. The Middle Bronze Age palace at Beycesultan was partly of timber construction (Lloyd and Mellaart 1965). Woolley argued that its use in Late Bronze Age contexts in the North Syrian region was restricted to prestigious buildings. Timber construction was never a widespread technique (Woolley 1961: 130), though it did penetrate as far south as Hazor, where the Late Bronze Age palace included a section with wood structuring in the mud-brick walls (Ben-Tor and Rubiato 1999: 31). Interestingly, while the use of the wood-crib construction technique can be found at several Iron Age IIB sites—Tell Taʿyinat, Guzana, Tell Hamath, and Zincirli—it does not seem to function in the same manner at all the sites. At Guzana, the builders employed it only in the areas in which orthostats needed to be affixed to mud-brick walls. At Tell Taʿyinat, there is no evidence that orthostats were ever an element in the decorative program for the palace or temple. Most likely, the visual traces of construction techniques would have been hidden under a coating of plaster, and this was probably also the case with building IV at Tell Hamath, which Ussishkin has read as a temple but which the excavators believe was part of the city's gate structure (Ussishkin 1966a: 104–10). Why the technique was used at Tell Taʿyinat and Hamath is not clear since its most valuable function was not employed, though it is worth remembering that Tell Taʿyinat was the sister site to Alalakh (Tell Atchana). At both sites, timber was rather extravagantly employed. The builders of Tell Taʿyinat may have been continuing the tradition begun at Alalakh. The remains of the *bāmâ* at Tel Dan showed a variation on the technique: wooden beams inserted between rows of ashlar blocks (Biran 1998: 40).

The evidence from Tell Taʿyinat and Hamath points to continuity with nearby Late Bronze Age Alalakh in the use of timber construction for prestigious buildings. However, they changed in that the buildings now included temples. The development of the technique at Guzana suggests a change as the architect for the temple-palace exploited the technique in quite a new way, to assist with the placement of the sculpted orthostats. This allowed the architect to integrate sculpture into architecture in a manner not seen in Late Bronze Age buildings. This application was obviously understood and appreciated by other builders since it also appears at Zincirli. The Tel Dan evidence suggests that builders were comfortable experimenting with the technique and were still developing it well into Iron Age II.

Timber construction and ashlar masonry were widely used and perhaps most developed in the North Syrian region in the early Iron Age, where it seems they answered specific needs of the early Iron Age builders. Earthquakes are, of course, a fear in the area, and perhaps this was an attempt to create walls that were capable of adjusting to movements, as has been suggested for similar wood and rubble constructions in Late Bronze Age Minoan buildings.

Though there is some limited evidence for this type of technique in the Levant during the Middle Bronze Age and early Late Bronze Age (the time of the Minoan experiments with similar building methods), the 400-year gap between the latest Late Bronze Age and the earliest early Iron Age examples suggests that its appearance in the early Iron Age should be treated as a new architectural form. The Late Bronze Age examples all came from the west, where Hittite influence was strongest, and Iron Age II Zincirli, Tell Taʿyinat, and Hamath all belonged to this geographical area and were part of the Neo-Hittite cultural sphere.

However, Guzana was at the opposite end of the region, in an area much closer to Mesopotamia, and was a city with no Hittite or Neo-Hittite affiliations. The technique could have revived or even survived in the west and then been brought east, where it was readapted for a new and quite specific architectural function. Other features do appear to have moved from west to east in Iron Age II. The lion sculptural form first used at Carchemish, Malatya, and Zincirli was picked up and developed as a motif for Aššur-nasirpal II's palace at Nimrud (Winter 1980: 357). Moreover, even before the political and military power of Assyria assured that whatever the Assyrian kings might want from the west they could get, there is some evidence to suggest that artisans, at least sculptors, were moving about from one commission to another. A number of the North Syrian sites share sculptural forms that are quite close to the treatment of specific features, suggesting some exchange of artists (Mallowan 1972: 72; Ussishkin 1967: 190–92).

Whether something similar was occurring with builders is not so clear. However, within royal settings during the Asssyrian period, builders did have value. They were treated as a distinct group among captives (Winter 1976: 19). Winter has also proposed that, during Iron Age II, Levantine centers were once again producing high quality luxury goods for courtly exchanges—in some degree recreating the Late Bronze Age exchange network system (Winter 1981: 130). In such a setting, it is not inconceivable that architectural styles and building techniques were moved around from court to court.

The features of ashlar masonry and timber construction were limited to prestigious structures for the most part. Artisans were not free agents, and their movements must have been controlled by the central authorities. A later, fifth-century B.C.E. letter written in Babylon or Susa (Arshain letter VII 7) indicates that an artisan could be attached to an estate and marked with a tattoo in the manner of a slave (Driver 1957: 29 and 66). While the source is late, the terminology employed is derived from Aramaic, perhaps reflecting the older order of the Iron Age II period, when the language began to spread. Shared groups of contractors among North Syrian cities could account for the similarities, though the suggestion creates even more confusion about why a building technique developed for a specific function would be employed when the reason for its use is not in evidence. Perhaps the builders of the palace and temple at Tell Taʿyinat knew the technique but not the reason for its use. They employed it because it seemed appropriate somehow—a special technique for prestigious constructions perhaps. For a builder, acquiring this type of technology required training and experience to reach a high level of skill. It is only normal human nature that those who possessed the skill would not be prone to abandon it or modify it greatly if the patron was willing to accept it. This would certainly seem to explain the spread of ashlar construction after the tenth century B.C.E. If indeed it became the tell-tale sign of early Israelite state architectural commissions, then it was used both to announce the prestige of selected items and to lend additional prestige to specific edifices. Ashlar masonry is a more difficult and more costly way in which to build.

Building Forms

Bīt Ḥilani

Much has been written about the *bīt ḥilani* as a distinct architectural form. The term *bīt ḥilani* was Amorite or Akkadian but was used in Assyrian texts to refer to a specific type of porticoed building found with palaces (Luckenbill 1927: 11, para. 84) and associated with Hittite lands, probably understood to be North Syria. Puchstein (1892) and, slightly later, Koldewey (Humann and Koldewey 1898) offered the basic definition that is still operative: a large, formal opening flanked by rooms and serving as an entrance into a more significant space. Weidhaas (1939) refined the description slightly by insisting that the opening also held columns. Frankfort identified the *bīt ḫilani* in its fully developed form as part of palace architecture of the Iron Age II North Syrian cities (Frankfort 1952). In the palaces at Tell Taʿyinat, Guzana, and Zincirli, the *bīt ḫilani* unit provided the organizing element around which all other architectural features of the palace were arranged. Frankfort, following Woolley (1961: 136–37), thought that the architectural form could first be seen, albeit in an inchoate form, in the Middle Bronze Age palace of Yarim-Lim at Alalakh and then in a slightly more defined version in the Late Bronze Age palace of Niqmepa, also at Alalakh (though Woolley also maintained that the fundamental form might have derived from an Early Bronze Age temple type). More recently, Late Bronze Age prototypes of the *bīt ḫilani* palace entrance have been noted for palaces at Emar in Syria.[2] It was not, however, until the early Iron Age that the architectural construct became a formalized and easily recognizable element that could be defined by a specific term, *bīt ḫilani*, and that was borrowed wholesale by Assyrian builders for palace F at Khorsabad, perhaps at Sargon's request (Frankfort 1985: 151–52, 247, 253–54, 276–77, 283–89). Akurgal favored this view but also thought that Naumann's recognition that certain aspects of the *bīt ḫilani* form were already present in Minoan architecture (Naumann 1955: 356) should not be dismissed. Akurgal saw the *bīt ḫilani* as a development of the Neo-Hittite cities that first manifested itself in the citadel palace (Building J) at Zincirli but reached it fullest flowering in the design of the palace temple at Guzana, a building that he dated to the late eighth century B.C.E. based on stylistic elements (Akurgal 1966: 69–77).

More recently, *bīt ḫilani* palaces have been identified in Iron Age II contexts farther south, in Israel.[3] Megiddo's Palace 6000 and Building 1723 (fig. 34) have been treated as *bīt ḫilani* forms,[4] though Shiloh has argued against the interpretation for Building 1723 (Shiloh 1979b: 83–87). The site of Bethsaida also yielded a possible *bīt ḫilani* palace form (Bernett 2000). Disagreement on the dating of the stratigraphy at Megiddo makes it difficult to determine whether the form should be understood to have moved south from North Syria or to have been developed earlier, in the early

---

2. The reference is in the Web newsletter for the Tübingen excavations: *EMAR 2001 Excavation Report*, http://www.uni-tuebingen.de/emar/en/excavation.html.

3. In his article for the *Dictionary of Art* ([ed. J. Turner; New York: Grove, 1996], s.v. "Syria–Palestine IV: Bronze Age"), R. C. Chapman identifies the earliest *bīt ḫilani* as appearing in the Alalakh (Tell Atchana) palace of Yarim-Lim (level VII). The style then spread in the Late Bronze Age and can be found in the royal palaces at Ugarit and the Alalakh (level IV) palace.

4. *Revelations from Megiddo: The Newsletter of the Megiddo Expedition*, November 1998, http://www.tau.ac.il/humanities/archaeology/Megiddo/revelations3.html; and *Rostock Universität Newsletter*, http://www.uni-rostock.ed/fakult/theofak/Niemann/Artik. However, Lehmann and Killebrew (2010: 13–33) offer an alternative view, arguing that the southern Levantine structures are not southern versions of the North Syrian *bīt ḫilani* but are, rather, a local architectural form, "a central hall tetra-partite" plan developed out of the four-room house type.

Iron Age contexts of southern Canaan. The two structures are in stratum VA/IVB. Yadin dated this as Solomonic, in part because of the ashlar masonry used for Palace 6000. This would provide a date of about 1000 B.C.E., predating the North Syrian examples. Finkelstein's revised dating of stratum VA/IVB to the ninth century and Omride Dynasty makes Palace 6000 and Building 1723 contemporaneous with the North Syrian examples. On the other hand, if one accepts Lehmann and Killebrew's (2010:27–30) assertion that Palace 6000 is a "central hall tetra-partite" plan derived from the four-room house type found in the southern area and not a variation on a *bīt ḫilani*, then the structure no longer needs to be fit into the developmental sequence for the *bīt ḫilani*.

Winter (1980: 357–64) has noted that the information on the existence of the architectural form rests on Assyrian texts from the second half of the eighth century, which identify the term *bīt ḫilani* as being foreign and as referring to a western architectural idea. The texts were not particularly clear about what the architectural form might be but, looked at in the fuller context, the *bīt ḫilani* appears to have been some part of a palace.[5] However, Winter is not convinced that it needs to include columns or operate as a façade type of space. She has suggested that the term refers to a series of interconnected rooms associated with public reception, particularly throne rooms. She has also suggested that the real problem is that the term, which she argues is ultimately derived from a Hittite word, in Assyrian usage might have been a somewhat vague reference to a suite of one or more transverse rooms with a major façade accent and with multiple accesses.

The *bīt ḫilani* would not enter into a discussion of early Iron Age Levantine temple-building were it not for two places where the palace and the temple collide. The first is at Guzana, where the *bīt ḫilani* was elaborated by the use of sculpted elements for the vertical supports and the flanks of both the exterior and interior doors of the temple-palace structure (fig. 39). This sculpted ensemble was then integrated into the larger program of the orthostat reliefs of the north façade and the freestanding sculpture on the terrace. The program for all the sculpture has been read to be religious, and the building has come to be treated as a temple-palace rather than just a palace.

This might have been an isolated case, but at the site of Tell Taʿyinat, the entryway of the temple building (Building II) located behind the palace received special treatment. The *bīt ḫilani* in the palace at Tell Taʿyinat is quite conservative when compared with that in Guzana. In its most elaborate treatment, it contained 3 columns that stood on top of decorated bases. The decoration was restrained, limited to applied patterns.

---

5. In his article on Neo-Assyrian architecture for the *Dictionary of Art* ([ed. J. Turner; New York: Grove, 1996], s.v. "Mesopotamia II: Architecture (1) Neo-Assyrian (b) Royal Building Project"), J. Russell cites the *bīt ḫilani* of the palace at Tarbigh built by Esarhaddon for the crown prince as the only example of a true *bīt ḫilani* structure in Assyrian architecture.

However, the little temple behind (which was a tripartite design of a porch forming an antechamber, long main chamber, and small adyton or altar room—all arranged on the longitudinal axis) was given an impressive façade by the use of two sculpted column bases, each one of dual lions placed side by side and standing over one meter in height (fig. 41).[6] The columns and their bases served to set off the porch in exactly the same way that the columns do on the porch of the palace at Tell Ta'yinat or the statues do on the porch of the temple-palace at Guzana. This treatment of the porch or antechamber of the temple at Tell Ta'yinat seems to be a modified version of the *bīt ḥilani* developed in the more secular realm of palace architecture at the same time. It is grafted onto a much older architectural form—the tripartite, longitudinal temple— and therefore, it functions in a slightly different manner.

The temple at 'Ain Dara may represent the earlier movement of the *bīt ḥilani* from the palace to the temple front (though there may well have been a palace associated with the temple that has not yet been found). The façade was clearly designed so that 2 columns flanked the entrance and were set *in-antis* between the side units of the ensemble (fig. 5). The design resembles that of the Tell Ta'yinat temple, which was not far away.

The description of the temple of Solomon has led several investigators to argue that it must have followed the format of the Tell Ta'yinat temple, with a prominent porch (A. Mazar 1992a: 376–77). As with the long-room reconstruction for the temple, the *bīt ḥilani* form depends on how the literary sources are interpreted. If the *'ûlām* (1 Kgs 6:3) is understood to be a separate porch fronting the main chamber, then there is potential for the design to have borrowed the *bīt ḥilani* format, especially since the temple seems to have been an element in a larger complex that included the palace of Solomon. To many, this has seemed even more likely when the named columns, Boaz and Jachin, are brought into the discussion (1 Kgs 7:15–22). The biblical account devotes some attention to describing these two large bronze columns, which were placed on the façade in some manner. The columns have received added emphasis from a nonbiblical source, Herodotus (2.45), who reports that the Temple of Heracles (Melqart) in Tyre, a temple associated with Hiram I, who assisted with Solomon's temple, also had two special columns: one golden and the other of emerald appearance. The word choice, *stela*, does not help to clarify whether these were structural elements or freestanding items within the sanctuary, and Herodotus does not indicate where they were placed in relationship to the main temple building.

The discovery of the Tell Ta'yinat and (more recently) the 'Ain Dara temples with the columns placed *in-antis* in the porch has led several scholars to argue that a similar treatment must have existed for the temple of Solomon (figs. 112 and 113; see also Monson 2000: 30–32; Fritz 1987b: 41). This is even more the case because the entrance

---

6. Hawkins (2009: 168, illustration caption) identifies the lion bases as "purely Assyrian" and thinks that they provide evidence of an Assyrian refurbishing of the temple (Building II).

to the ʿAin Dara temple is a separate unit, perhaps not unlike the *ʾûlām*. The alternative view, that the columns stood free from the structure and framed the door's two sides, still has adherents (Meyers 1981: 38). Busink's reconstruction (fig. 114) shows his use of the descriptions in both Kings and Chronicles. 2 Chr 3:15–17 is a little more vague and may suggest that there were two sets of columns: the named columns placed free-standing in front of the temple, and a second, smaller pair serving the load-bearing function of holding up the architrave of the porch. Busink's reconstruction has two columns *in-antis* in the porch and the named columns larger and in front.

Columns

The Tell Taʿyinat find of sculpted column bases that lent stature to the column shafts, the impressive use of statues with massive sculpted animal bases for the façade of the Guzana structure, the biblical description of the two columns of the temple of Solomon, and Herodotus's discussion of two significant columns associated with the Temple of Heracles (Melqart) in Tyre (Bonnet 1988: 101, 219; Katzenstein 1973: 87)—all raise the question of the role of columns in early Iron Age sanctuaries. Columns were not a new architectural item in the early Iron Age, and their use in façade designs can be traced back to Late Bronze and possibly Middle Bronze Age monumental palace entrances. However, within the context of the *bīt ḥilani* form modified for use as a temple front, they were a new development in Iron Age II.

Freestanding nonstructural columns as reported for the temples of Solomon and Heracles (Melqart) were certainly a new form in Iron Age II. There is a long tradition of erecting stones, *maṣṣēbôt*, in the Levantine region. The Middle Bronze Age Temple of the Obelisks at Byblos (fig. 107) is an example, and the practice continued well into Iron Age II with Tel Dan's *maṣṣēbôt* shrines at several places in the town, but the stones had no architectural pretense. This was not the case with the columns associated with the Iron Age II temples. Whether they were actually load bearing or served as framing devices, these columns took part in the architectural form. Moreover, based on the literary sources, they required a high degree of specialized technical skill to manu-facture. They were much more than just stone columns. The columns associated with the temple of Solomon were cast bronze with a great deal of applied decoration. The columns in the sanctuary at Tyre were gold and emerald in color, possessing a radiant quality. Herodotus was not reporting on these by quoting another source; he had seen the columns and was impressed by them. Columns with an independent quality that drew attention, even if they functioned in a structural manner, seem to have been a development of the Iron Age II builders.

The Louvre has a small terra-cotta *naiskos* model collected from Idalion on Cy-prus and dated to the Cypro-archaic period (mid-seventh to sixth century B.C.E.).[7] It was one of two shrine models from the site, and it shows a long-room building with

7. In the section of Near Eastern Antiquities. Colonna-Ceccaldi 1869 N3294.

the entrance door flanked by two columns (Karageorghis 1982: 151–52; García y Bellido 1963: 118, fig. 28). They stand on defined bases and are capped by lotus flower capitals that hold up a lintel. They are not like the Tell Ta'yinat columns placed *in-antis* within the porch but stand separate; however, they are structural because they support the roof over the door—a kind of baldachino. Another ceramic model from Tell el-Far'ah (North) in northern Israel shows a door flanked by two columns (fig. 116a).[8] The capitals reach above the height of the door opening, and between them is a decorative infill, perhaps indicating that they represented nonfunctional columns (A. Mazar 1992a: 377, fig. 9.6).

Interior columns were a well-known feature of several Late Bronze Age temples. The stratum XIII temple from Area H at Hazor evidenced 2 sets of paired columns, one pair flanking the holy of holies and the other pair framing the door from the first chamber into the second chamber. The strata VII/VI (Mazar's Lower VI) temple at Beth-shean (figs. 27–28) and the Acropolis Temple (Stratum VI) at Lachish (fig. 77) had paired columns within the main hall aligned along the main axis. The Fosse Temple at Lachish (fig. 76) had 4 columns arranged in pairs and flanking the main axis of the principal chamber. With the exception of the columns placed on platforms in the Fosse Temple, all these Late Bronze Age columns could have been load-bearing, structural elements. In the early Iron Age sanctuaries, interior structural columns largely disappeared. The columns that have been found followed more the pattern of the platform columns in the Fosse Temple. The first phase of the little temple at Sarepta (fig. 62) had an ashlar platform topped with a standing column. The main temple at Tell Qasile in its final form had 2 columns (fig. 21), one possibly structural, and the other placed on a platform. Room 49 at Lachish may have had paired standing stones, *maṣṣēbôt* inside, and Room 340 of Building 338 stratum IV at Megiddo had remnants of possible *maṣṣēbôt* as well. The inclusion of these elements in an interior setting is not new to the early Iron Age. The Fosse Temple at Lachish was a Late Bronze Age prototype, but the use spreads more widely in the early Iron Age.

Windows

The window appears as a prominent motif in the story of Ba'al's palace. Ba'al does not want the window, but Kothar-wa-Khasis insists. Finally Ba'al realizes the need, and Kothar opens the palace with a window (Pritchard 1969: 92–118: Ginsberg 1973: 106). The story as we possess it comes from Late Bronze Age Ugarit. None of the surviving Late Bronze Age temple remains supplies evidence of windows, though almost all reconstructions of temples show windows. In the early Iron Age, the window mo-

---

8. It was found in the courtyard of a residential structure, stratum VIIb, tenth century B.C.E. Dever (2008b) describes and discusses a similar unprovenanced terra-cotta shrine. For a more complete consideration of ancient architectural models in Levantine contexts, see Daviau 2008 and Muller 2000.

tif was picked up by ivory carvers and turned into the "woman at the window" type (fig. 117) known in the collections from Arslan Tash, Samaria, and Khorsabad (Winter 1981: 116). The little *naiskos* from Idalion has figures peering out the windows of the cult chamber, and the other temple model from the site shows windows as part of the structure. Musicians placed in windows appear on a clay stand from Ashdod (fig. 14), and on another stand from Tell Qasile dancing figures are shown in windows (Braun 2002: 165–79). These may not specifically be representations of temples. The stand from Tell Qasile did come from the temple complex. The Ashdod musician stand was found in the twelfth-century grave of a warrior (Dothan and Dothan 1992: 175) and thus may not be tied to any notion of a cult building. The eighth-century B.C.E. figure of a lyre player, also from Ashdod, came from the context of a shrine structure in the industrial sector of Area D (Dothan and Dothan 1992: 140), suggesting that it is not unreasonable to see the stand with musicians as cultic in nature and perhaps representing a temple or shrine setting. The 2 sculpted clay stands found in a chamber at Taʿanach have supplied the rationale for labeling the chamber a shrine (Rast 1994: 355). The 2 have apertures that have been classified as windows (P. Beck 1994: 353–55). This admittedly circumstantial evidence may suggest that, from quite early in the early Iron Age, windows had become a feature of cultic architecture, possibly developing out of Late Bronze Age settings but also possibly representing something new.

The archaeological evidence for windows in a temple setting is also questionable. At ʿAin Dara, a series of carved stone panels from the walls of the first chamber represented a lattice-like pattern in horizontal bands set into a unit with rabbet-draft edges. Monson proposed that these were intended to operate as false windows. Kohlmeyer argued that a similar series of panels from the Hittite Late Bronze Age temple on the Aleppo Citadel were likewise stand-ins for windows (Kohlmeyer 1999: 195; Gonnella, Khayyata, and Kohlmeyer 2005). On either side of the extant cult statue base in Temple 1 at Hattuša (fig. 120, "holy of holies"), there are well-preserved, dressed, flat stone blocks that may be indicative of windows.[9] McMahon has noted at least one reference to participants in a festival in the temple taking their places behind the windows (McMahon 1991: 263–64 [KUB 55.43 iv 31]). Windows do seem to have been a feature in Hittite domestic architecture as well, which probably carried over into temple designs. When Telepinus flies into a rage, we are told that "mist seized the windows" (Pritchard 1969: 87–91, Goetze translation, 5). On the other hand, the rabbet-draft frames of the ʿAin Dara panels are not unlike the treatment of the frames of the later Iron Age II ivory carvings from the Northwest Assyrian palace at Nimrud featuring the "woman at the window" (fig. 117). Monson has argued that a problematic section of the description of Solomon's Temple (1 Kgs 6:4), the Hebrew *šĕqupîm*

---

9. Personal communication with Gregory McMahon.

ʾaṭumîm, which has been glossed as some type of blocked opening, may refer to false windows, as at ʿAin Dara (Monson 2000: 32, 34).

Ambulatories

In its last building phase—eighth century B.C.E. (Abu ʿAssāf 1993: 161)—the temple at ʿAin Dara was changed in a fundamental way. What had stood as the temple (fig. 3)—the rectangular block with porch, antechamber, and main chamber—was now encased by a massive ambulatory (fig. 5), perhaps standing two stories high. The regularly placed thick piers along the inner and outer walls of the ambulatory could have supported the weight of the second story. The ambulatory was designed as an independent unit with access via doors on either side of the porch that provided entrance to the main body of the temple. There is no evidence of any type of direct connection between the interior of the old temple block and the new ambulatory other than the two entrances flanking the porch. As was the case with the main temple, the interior of the ambulatory held sculpted reliefs; some 80 panels lined the walls of the corridor, and 30 carved steles with figural scenes also stood inside the halls (Monson 2000: 28). Lions guarded the two entrances. The degree of decoration indicates that the ambulatory space was not for storage, and the nature of the reliefs (images of divinities and of offerings) points to a ceremonial function. The lack of direct connection between the corridors and the main temple suggests independence of ceremonial function. Like the ambulatories of the great pilgrimage churches of the Romanesque and Gothic periods in Western Europe, this ambulatory was designed to be used while the main temple was functioning as well.

The ambulatory of the ʿAin Dara temple is the only structure of this sort unearthed so far in the Levant for the early Iron Age. There are no easily recognizable prototypes. The great Hittite rock shrine at Yazılıkaya (fig. 118) incorporates sculpture into natural rock corridor between the cliffs, but this would be, at best, a very distant relation to the much more-formal and totally built environment at ʿAin Dara, in which the natural landscape plays no role at all. The great Temple of the Weather God at Hattuša incorporates a kind of ambulatory space into the design (fig. 119). The main block of rooms that includes the dual cult chambers is set off and separated from the surrounding storerooms by a corridor that extends along all four sides (fig. 120). As with the rock shrine at Yazılıkaya, the similarities seem too superficial to infer a direct association. Moreover, the Hittite sanctuaries had ceased to function with the collapse of the Hittite Empire in the early twelfth century B.C.E. At least four centuries separate the monuments.

The south temple at Beth-shean (fig. 28), stratum V (Mazar's Upper VI) may incorporate a version of the ambulatory. Its northern brother is a simple rectangular chamber with 4 interior columns and entrance at the southwest corner. It is probably a version of the unified rectangular interior space that has a long history in the Levant. However, the southern building, which is not unanimously considered a temple, is different. The core is a large rectangular hall that was divided into 3 naves by 2 colonnades, the members of which are joined each to the next by a mud-brick wall. Surrounding the hall were storerooms. These partitions may have served to create a type of ambulatory surrounding the interior core of the building. This design poses problems of interpretation. The use of columns to support a roof system can be found in several Late Bronze Age temples in the Levant, but these are limited to paired columns. This grouping of 6 columns in 2 parallel rows is not an outgrowth of the earlier version, and joining the columns in this fashion at least at some point causes a strange arrangement in the interior. It is possible that this building is not a temple but a storage depot, in which case the design may relate to the contemporary tripartite pillared buildings that have been interpreted as stables as well as storehouses (Kochavi 1999: 44–50; Herr 1988) and have been found throughout Palestine during the early Iron Age. There is nothing in the treatment of the interior that rules out its use as a magazine rather than as a cult space.

Monson has argued that the ambulatory at ʿAin Dara can be understood to be the same as the problematic architectural featured called the *ṣĕlāʿôt* in the description of Solomon's temple (1 Kgs 6:5–6). Monson is certain that the *ṣĕlāʿôt*, which is normally translated 'side chambers', actually describes a formal ambulatory space that encompassed the cult chamber of the temple (Monson 2000: 33–34). From the architectural perspective, there is little to work with one way or the other. The biblical text is problematic. There is disagreement about whether the structure intended by the term *ṣĕlāʿôt* was even part of the original design (Fritz 1987b: 39). The word itself and the associated term, *yāṣîaʿ*, caused the Greek translators trouble (Ouellette 1972: 187–88, 190). There is general agreement among those who have attempted to reconstruct the temple based on the literary materials that the core of the temple, its cult building, was surrounded in some manner by chambers on three of its sides. These may have held cultic paraphernalia or the state treasuries (fig. 97; see A. Mazar 1992a: 377; Waterman 1943: 293–94). Although treasuries have not been identified for other early Iron Age temples, storage rooms are a common enough feature, usually holding objects somehow associated with cultic activities. The ʿAin Dara ambulatory could have served this sort of function, but considering the role that sculpture plays inside the ambulatory structure, such a role seems less likely. The space has more a cultic quality—perhaps more in line with the *bīt* gate of the *bīt ḫilani* referred to in an Assyrian text and thought to indicate a side wing in which the statues of the gods were kept (Ouellette 1972: 190). However, this role is not appropriate to our present conceptions of the functioning of the temple of Solomon.

Monson's hypothesis can be treated only as a hypothesis because there are no archaeological remains from Solomon's temple. For the present, ʿAin Dara is the only temple with a fully articulated ambulatory. As an architectural feature, it was not borrowed by other builders of temples in the region, unless the south building at Beth-shean does indeed incorporate storerooms flanking the main hall as a sort of ambulatory (Isserlin 1998: 250). On the other hand, Stager has argued that the *seriah*, or stronghold, at Shechem—to which the townspeople fled to escape Abimelech—was in reality an ambulatory space surrounding the fortified or *migdāl* temple. In other words, it was the feature that made the temple fortified. If Stager is correct, then the feature may have originated in the Middle Bronze Age (Stager 2003: 32), but no archaeological evidence supports the interpretation.

Architectural Sculpture

One of the outstanding features of monumental architecture of the early Iron Age North Syrian cities is the importance accorded to architectural sculpture, including both reliefs and three-dimensional forms. Architectural sculpture is attested at Hazor in the Late Bronze Age temple at Area H (Yadin 1972a: 89–91). The Middle Bronze Age temple D at Ebla had guardian lion figures placed before the entrance into the main cult chamber (Kohlmeyer in Weiss 1985: 214–15), and a similar guarding lion probably stood at the entrance to the Middle Bronze Age temple on the Citadel at Aleppo (Gonnella, Khayyata, and Kohlmeyer 2005: 112). Some of the sculptural material from ʿAin Dara has been identified as being Late Bronze Age—that is, the first stage of the temple's construction (Kohlmeyer 2008: 123).[10] The Late Bronze Age Hittite temple on the Citadel at Aleppo was richly decorated with interior sculpture (Kohlmeyer 2009: 194–96). These examples make the absence of sculptural elements in most Middle Bronze and Late Bronze Age temple architecture all the more noticeable. This situation changed dramatically during Iron Age I in North Syria. There was a sudden outburst and prodigious production of sculptural decoration integrated with major architecture (Kohlmeyer 2008: 124; 2009: 197–99). Evidence for massive displays of relief sculpture is found in both the Neo-Hittite regions and the Aramean areas. Albright has argued that the sculpture demonstrates a continuation of the older Hittite cultural force in the region, which never really saw a major break between the Late Bronze and early Iron Age cultures (Albright 1956b: 146, 154–55), a view earlier expressed by Woolley specifically for the site of Carchemish (Woolley 1921: 49). Frankfort thought that the ultimate source for this type of decoration was Assyria (Frankfort 1985: 290), while Akurgal (1966: 60–62) and Bittel (1976: 238) saw a continuation of Hittite forms. Albright's contention that there was no real break between Hittite and Neo-Hittite culture and art was opposed by Frankfort (1985: 279–80). Winter has suggested that North Syria was its own center of artistic experimentation

---

10. The Ishtar relief from ʿAin Dara has been dated as early as Iron Age IA (Orthmann 1993: 245–51) and as late as Iron Age IIB (Abu ʿAssāf 1983: 8).

which in turn influenced the developments in Mesopotamia (Winter 1983: 177–97), a view also espoused by Collon in regard to seals (Collon 1987: 83).

It is worth noting that the earliest great Assyrian relief compositions that decorate palace walls date to the ninth century. If Albright's date for the Kapara inscription at Guzana is accepted, then the sculpture at the site would date to the second half of the tenth century B.C.E.—predating any possible Assyrian model (Albright 1956a: 75–85; 1956b: 152)—and this certainly seems to be the case for the first reliefs in the Aleppo Citadel temple. The highly developed format of the Assyrian relief sculptures, given their involved programs and large-scale narrative presentations, is quite at odds with the small-scale, metope-like reliefs of the North Syrian form (fig. 121). The Assyrian reliefs were used to decorate interior spaces of palaces, but the North Syrian sculptures were most commonly placed outside (although the finds from the Aleppo Citadel temple, which are all interior decoration, and the sculpture that decorated the ambulatory and interior of the ʿAin Dara temple indicate that interior relief sculpture was also used). The exterior sculpture gave a special meaning to public areas. Ultimately, sources and prototypes are not terribly important in the context of early Iron Age architectural forces in the Levant. What is essential is to recognize that sculptors and architects must have worked together on these massive compositions, which were clearly designed as programs.

The compositions do not fit a single format. At Carchemish, the reliefs lined the processional way leading from the King's Gate to the entrance of the lower palace, where the Temple of the Storm God was located (figs. 36, 122, and 123; see Woolley 1921: 110–16; 1952: 158–60, 164–67). The reliefs stood along the processional way, in a pattern also known from the nearby site at Zincirli (Frankfort 1985: fig. 335). However, at Carchemish the program incorporated the exterior wall of the temple precinct. The reliefs followed the same color pattern as seen elsewhere in North Syria, which was alternating dark basalt and white limestone slabs. The reliefs stood above a base of plain limestone masonry (Woolley 1952: 164–65). The Carchemish design placed the sculptural decoration and the temple in the transitional area between the palace complex on the acropolis and the lower town. The sculptural display at Guzana is largely confined to the acropolis region (Moortgat 1955). From the lower town, it was possible to see the sculpted sphinxes that announced the gate to the acropolis region and the reliefs on the blank façade of the temple-palace that faced the lower town. However, the most impressive sculpture was reserved for the temple-palace front, which faced inward, away from the lower town. It was the presence of what have come to be recognized as divine portraits that line the lower portion of the north side of the temple-palace complex that convinced Langenegger to define the building as a temple-palace and not merely a royal residence (Langenegger et al. 1950: 27). These carved orthostats covered the actual building fabric of mud brick. At ʿAin Dara, where the building fabric is itself ashlar blocks, the sculpted reliefs formed an integral part of the structure (fig. 6) and are found throughout the building, including the ambu-latory. The relief orthostats in the Aleppo Citadel temple provided the visual base on which the superstructure of mud-brick walls rested. Like the later compositions at Carchemish and Zincirli, the figures were presented as though in a procession, though without a clear connection between the figures, as found at Carchemish. The images at Aleppo are more similar to the metope structure at Guzana: most of the figures are self-contained, with the exception of the earlier relief of the Weather God and king and the later relief of two bulls flanking a tree.

The sculptural decoration was not limited to relief-carved orthostats. The two doorways of the *bīt ḫilani* on the temple-palace at Guzana were both guarded by pairs of animals: lions at the front door and winged griffins at the inner door between the two chambers (fig. 124; Frankfort 1985: 293). The porch itself had 3 standing figures, each about 3 m tall, that held up the architrave. These were 2 males and a female, not divinities according to Frankfort (1985: 291), and each one stood on the back of a carved animal (1 m to 1½ m in height): a bull in the middle, with 2 flanking lions. While only Guzana has yielded structural freestanding statues, several of the North Syrian sites have provided sculpted stone bases that must have supported columns. The temple at Tell Taʿyinat had 2 sculpted lion bases in the temple porch (fig. 41). Each base was itself composed of 2 snarling lions placed side by side. These were set in bitumen on a large stone slab 1.38 × 1.64 m. The bases themselves stood 0.72 m high and were 1.12 m wide and 1.58 m long (Haines 1971: 54). The porch of the palace in its second phase (Floor 3) also had 3 supports across the front, columns rather than stat-ues, but they stood on sculpted bases. They were of basalt and stood on foundations of rough stone. The bases (fig. 125) consisted of 2 parts, a minimally decorated lower register and a more heavily ornamented upper register—the 2 separated by a central torus with running guilloche pattern (Haines 1971: 46).

Several of the North Syrian sites with sculpted decoration must have shared mo-tifs if not actual workmen. There were repeated stylistic features at more than one site. The treatment of the column bases for the palace at Tell Taʿyinat was similar to that for the column bases of building K at Zincirli (Haines 1971: 46 n. 13). The lions from ʿAin Dara resembled some lions found at Carchemish and dated to the period before the tenth century B.C.E. (Özyar 1991: 23–25, 30). The front-facing figure from the sec-ond group of the Aleppo Citadel Temple resembled the front-facing figures from ʿAin Dara (Kohlmeyer 2000: 34). Even when stylistic similarities cannot be found, motifs joined the sites. There were bull-men at ʿAin Dara, Guzana, and Carchemish and, although they were not stylistically related, they must, as an iconographic motif, be traced to the same origin, probably older Mitannian forms (Özyar 1991: 21). In addi-tion to shared motifs and stylistic forms, another shared element was the alternation and interplay of the two types of stone used in all of the sculpture: white limestone and gray basalt. This was a notable feature in the arrangement of the paving of the

great courtyard in front of the temple at ʿAin Dara. It can also be seen in the orthostats of the temple-palace at Guzana. It may have been present in the Aleppo Citadel
temple. The earlier reliefs on the east wall were in limestone, while the later reliefs on
the north wall were of basalt. However, it is not clear that the two groups functioned
together in the second version of the early Iron Age temple.

The description of the temple of Solomon includes two references to sculpture:
on the doors leading into the temple and into the shrine (1 Kgs 6:31–36); and, within
the main chamber, the 2 cherubim that guarded the ark (1 Kgs 6:27). The images on
the doors are clearly nonnarrative—cherubim, palms, calyxes. These are presented as
having iconographic meaning, but in their arrangement as single isolated units, they
recall the display of the metope forms at Guzana. The 2 great statues of cherubim
that were part of the decoration of the ark area were quite different. These recalled
the guardian sphinx figures found at both Guzana and at Carchemish, though in the
latter two cases, they are relief carvings and not freestanding sculptures. Waterman
(1943: 290–94) argued that these cherubim inside the temple itself are not described
as they had originally been placed. He noted that the description of them makes them
much too large for the ark itself, and they even towered over the screen that shielded
the ark from the eyes of those in the main chamber. They were about half the size of
the shrine itself. He thought that they originally had served to guard the entrances
into the treasury of Solomon located in the ambulatory space. Only later were they
repositioned to protect the ark. It is worth noting that the craftsman who worked for
Solomon to create most of the interior fittings, though not necessarily the sculpture,
was Phoenician, sent by Hiram of Tyre (1 Kgs 7:13) and thus could have been aware
of developments from the North Syrian region. If there were indeed massive pieces of
freestanding sculpture inside the building itself, then they represent something new.
In North Syria, interior sculpture seems to have been limited to relief work, while fully
independent sculptures were used for entrances and exterior decoration.

Aegean Elements

It has long been recognized that among the groups that made up the "Peoples of
the Sea" were peoples of Aegean origin.[11] As they settled along the Levantine coast,
either before attacking Egypt or as the result of that attack,[12] they introduced Aegean
forms into the old Canaanite culture of the region, most notably seen in the development of LM IIIC:1b style pottery.[13] Aegean influence may have been penetrating
into the North Syrian region at the same time (Lehmann 2002a: 82; 2002b: 85). A

11. The possibility of kinship was first observed during research on Philistine pottery (Heurtley
1936: 90–110).
12. This is a debated point; see the discussion in chap. 2.
13. A challenge was been put forward by S. Sherratt (1998: 292–313), who argued that the appearance
of the new material assemblage is better explained as the result of trade rather than settlement of new

number of architectural anomalies that cannot be explained as developing from the Late Bronze Age Canaanite building traditions and that do seem to have Aegean *comparanda*, such as the spread of ashlar masonry, may be evidence for the introduction of Late Bronze Age Aegean building traditions into early Iron Age Levantine contexts.

The apsidal structure in area H of Ashdod (fig. 13) survived through two strata, XIII–XII. It was introduced in stratum XIII, built above the ruins of the destroyed Late Bronze Age city, and had no apparent Late Bronze Age predecessors in the region (Dothan and Dothan 1992: 160–61). The apsidal form has been found in Early Bronze Age strata as a domestic unit. At one time thought to be the dominant house of the Early Bronze Age, it is now recognized as having been employed only occasionally (Ben-Tor 1992a: 60–61). During the centuries of the Iron Age I in the Levant, the apsidal form continued as a building type in Dark Age Greece. It had a long history of use in the Aegean. In Aetolia, there is a continuous tradition for using the apsidal form that stretches back to the prehistoric period (Ainian 1997: 111–13 n. 682). Monumental apsidal constructions are known from Late Helladic contexts, such as House P from Rakhmani (de Pierpont 1990: fig. 1), and they continued to be built as substantial structures during the Dark Age, as evidenced by a number of apsidal structures throughout the Aegean region (Fusaro 1982: 7). If the evidence of the Sanctuary of Hera at Perachora is valid beyond the one site, then the apsidal form had also assumed a cultic role by the eighth century B.C.E. (Payne 1940: 34, fig. 8). It may well have been a building form that migrants took with them.

The Ashdod apsidal structure in Area H was not really like the structures known from Aegean contexts, because it was an apsidal element that surrounded and encased a rectangular depression. Because of the presence of a courtyard in the vicinity and discovery of the Ashdoda figurine in a nearby context, the Dothans identified the apsidal structure as a temple (Dothan and Dothan 1992: 153–55). The apses on Aegean buildings did not function in this manner. If the apsidal plan is ultimately the result of the presence of Aegean people at Ashdod, they clearly modified the prototype.

The other interesting feature at Ashdod is from Area G, stratum XIIIb. This was a pottery workshop area, and the finds of LM IIIC:1b–style pottery allow for a date at the very beginning of Iron Age I, the time when the "Peoples of the Sea" first settled at the site. The feature consisted of a square platform made from plastered bricks and a separate round base that had supported a pillar that was reused from a Late Bronze Age context. We know that this base served as an altar because it was blackened by fire. Sherds and animal bones were found scattered around the two structural elements. This has been interpreted to have been an outdoor shrine. Nanno Marinatos

---

peoples, a thesis developed by A. Bauer (1998: 149–67). For the opposing view, see Barako and Yasur-Landau 2003: 32.

argued for a Bronze Age Aegean cult that was practiced in the open air, during which devotees bent over a stone or pithos, and she has isolated a number of images in Minoan and Mycenean seal impressions that she argues show figures involved with the ritual (Marinatos 1990: 87–90). The open-air shrine at Ashdod could be a localized version of this cult, which required minimal architecture.

Interior hearths have been found in Building 351 at Ekron (fig. 17) and the first sanctuary building at Tell Qasile. The Dothans observed that the prominence accorded the hearth in Building 351 cannot be explained by earlier Canaanite traditions. The first version of the hearth was large and took up much of the interior space of the chamber in which it was located. It was a plastered hearth with modeled edge, forming a broad flat rim that encircled the great plate of the hearth. The plaster floor lapped the edge of the hearth. The later hearths maintained the position but were of a smaller size. The hearth remained a feature throughout the twelfth century B.C.E. and the first half of the eleventh century B.C.E. (T. Dothan 1995: 42–45). The first version of the temple at Tell Qasile may also have contained an interior hearth, though it was not of the same shape or grandeur as the hearth at Ekron. Dothan sees these interior hearths as architectural linkages with the Aegean world. The large interior hearth around which the rest of the space was designed was a well-known feature of Late Bronze Age Aegean architecture, particularly in the Mycenean regions. Dothan has argued that the prominence accorded the hearths during early Iron Age I indicates the residual force of Aegean cult and architectural practices. By the mid-eleventh century, these had dissipated, and the function of the hearths had been forgotten, and hence they disappear as architectural elements.

The Dothans associated the hearths with the Mycenean palace culture of mainland Greece. It is from the sites of Mycene, Tiryns, and—best of all—Pylos that the evidence for the significant role of hearths came. These great hearths were situated in the main room of the royal megaron. They were surrounded by 4 columns, which, though clearly structurally important to hold up the opening in the roof for the smoke to escape, also gave to the hearths a special emphasis within the space. They emerged in LH III as a formal ritual place in the palace and were probably tied to a political-religious cult (de Pierpont 1990: 255–62). Of the recovered hearths in the Philistine region, only the hearth from Ekron resembles these Mycenean palace hearths. It also is larger than is needed for cooking purposes, but it was situated in the first room of the sanctuary. As reconstructed, it would have obstructed easy entrance into the complex and was clearly not designed to be an interior hearth. Building 351 was not a megaron, nor was it even close. It was a square enclosure with a series of smaller spaces or chambers, but these were not arranged in a linear fashion. This was not a longroom design in the megaron tradition. While hearths were a common enough feature in Aegean Bronze Age domestic architecture, there was no evidence to suggest that they were used for ritual purposes. Only those within the megara, the great hearths, have been defined as having some sort of cultic function beyond standard use (Rutkowski 1986: 18–19). If the hearth came from an Aegean background, then only the physical hearth was retained; the rest of the architectural framing had been abandoned. Yasur-Landau (Barako and Yasur-Landau 2003: 36) pointed out that the Aegean migrants that formed the "Peoples of the Sea" did not come from the elite world of the LH III palace culture. They emerged from the post-palace period. The evidence of the material culture of these people as found in the lowest stratum of their occupation in the Levantine region shows that they carried nothing of LH III elite culture with them. Certainly nothing found at Ekron or Tell Qasile other than the hearths echoed mainland Greek Mycenean architecture. There was no use of cyclopean masonry, no evidence for fresco painting, and neither of the structures identified as sanctuaries was a megaron. This view of the Aegean refugees is not universally accepted. Although Stager is certain that eventually evidence of remnants of the LH III Mycenean palace culture will turn up, most likely in the form of Linear B inscriptions (Stager 1991: 36), this evidence has not yet come to light, and the points of comparison between the hearths seem weak at best.

It is worth noting that the hearth did not retain its importance in the post-palace period in the Mycenean homeland. While the megaron continued as a form and was modified and used well into the early Geometric period (Ainian 1997: 386–87), the interior hearth disappeared as a formal architectural element. There was no clear linkage between LH III megara with their possible cultic associations and the megara of the Early Geometric period, which may represent nothing more than the continuation of a formal design rather than a function. By the eighth century B.C.E., the Greek sanctuary had emerged as focused on an outdoor altar and only secondarily on a temple proper (Sourvinou-Inwood 1993: 5). Of course, the hearth may be argued to have continued as the formal altar that became so important in the archaic period (Hoffmann 1953: 189–95), but this would represent a substantial change in architectural form and cultic practice. Clearly, by the Geometric period, the concept of the common hearth for the polis, the *koine hestia*, had developed. The Late Bronze Age demonstrates little separation of sacred and nonsacred space in the context of Mycenean culture. The fact that the great hearths, if indeed they functioned for cultic fires, were located within the confines of structures that were used by rulers either as houses or as political areas demonstrates this mingling of more than one function for the spaces. This seems also to be the case with the large room XV in the Sacred Area of Mycene, where a possible cultic space was embedded within the dense fabric of a residential area of the city (fig. 126; Rutkowski 1986: 180). It has been argued that one major break between the Late Bronze Age and the early Iron Age in the Greek region was in the development of a specifically religious space. I. Morris has suggested that spatial indeterminacy continued through the Greek Dark Age but that, by 700 B.C.E., a change had emerged: sacred spaces were differentiated from living spaces (Morris

1989: 317). If Morris is correct, and certainly not all agree (Sourvinou-Inwood 1993: 5–6), then something similar may have happened in the Levant with the invasion of the "Peoples of the Sea" but at an earlier point.

If the massive hearth at Building 351 is difficult to relate compellingly to known Mycenean prototypes, then the hearths at Tell Qasile are even harder to associate. Small-scale hearths in Aegean contexts have sometimes been argued to have served for cult fires, but this is not accepted unanimously, and the evidence is not strong (Rutkowski 1986: 13, 54,146). There is one possible prototype: a hearth in shrine room XV (in Wace's Building) of the Sacred Area at Mycene (Rutkowski 1986: 180). Room XV (fig. 127) was part of a complex of rooms, most of which were probably cultic in nature, and all were embedded in a denser urban fabric and shared common walls. This concentration was located along the southwest side of the lower acropolis and was packed against the inner face of the cyclopean wall. From this complex have come a number of cultic objects and fresco fragments. It may somewhat resemble the arrangement that the Dothans argued was characteristic of the early shrines at Ashdod, which do not seem to be separated physically from the rest of the urban matrix. Room XV was dominated by a large oval hearth more or less in the center of the room. Two large stones, one north and the other west of the hearth may have served to support columns, and there may have been a third column. These columns may have been used to support some type of opening in the roof to allow for the smoke to dissipate, but how they would have functioned is not clear since they do not frame the hearth in the same way as the four columns in the megaron pattern. A stone bench stood along the south wall, and the east wall held a platform placed at right angles to the wall. On the ledge of the platform, 3 discs were discovered that show evidence of ash and may also have functioned as hearths. The east wall itself was plastered and painted with a fresco containing registers of figures. The hearth at Tell Qasile (fig. 21) was more similar to the raised-disc hearths in Room XV than to the massive floor hearth. It may be possible to argue that the oval-floor hearth in Room XV was really the prototype for the hearth at Ekron (fig. 17), since both dominated their spaces and obstructed movement. Room XV may have been unroofed, resembling the Dothans' proposed reconstruction of the hearth chamber in Building 351, or they may only have been partially roofed; it depends on how the columns were actually functioning. On the other hand, the oval hearth was not constructed as an architectural feature: built up with plaster to form a structural element in the space in the same way as the hearths in the megara or at Ekron.

If Yasur-Landau is right that the refugees brought with them a debased form of the Mycenean palace culture, then they might have been familiar with rituals associated with fire and requiring a hearth, such as rituals practiced outside the confines of the palace megaron area and in spaces such as are represented by Room XV. If the scenario is accepted that sometime around 1200 B.C.E. the palace-based rule and economy collapsed but the citadels were still occupied for another generation, then perhaps the nonpalatial cult areas also continued to function, and therefore some aspects may have been brought with the colonists. On the other hand, if the view of the Dothans and Stager is accepted that the migrants were actually coming from the context of the Mycenean palace culture and were attempting to transplant aspects of that culture in the Levant, then it seems that the transplanted items were significantly modified almost immediately. Perhaps more importantly, the entire political topography was shifted at the Philistine sites.

At Mycene, the cult complex was located physically below the level of the megaron, and the complex itself may have had an internal hierarchy of parts subordinated to the megaron (Negbi 1988: 341). The megaron itself was tied to rulership, with the throne room most likely being located inside (Rehak 1995: 95–118). Probably the megaron was the locus for the official state cult (Hägg 1995: 387–91). The complex on the west slope of the citadel had to have played a secondary role, though it may well have been tied to the megaron cult site with some type of processional path. It was also operating as a workshop center (Hägg 1992: 30). Something similar is seen at Phylakopi IV, the Late Bronze Age fortified settlement on the island of Melos. The sanctuary complex (fig. 128) (which consisted of the east and west shrines) stood opposite the megaron and some distance away on the south side of the site and was part of the fortification wall (Renfrew et al. 1985: 370–91; Renfrew and Wagstaff 1982: 43).

The setting for the temples at Tell Qasile does not resemble the setting at Mycene or Phylakopi in any manner. The Tell Qasile temple buildings occupied a high point that was somewhat aloof from the other structures and was not embedded within the complex. In its last phase, with two separate sanctuaries sharing a common wall and separate courtyard areas, it may have come to look and operate somewhat like the Mycenean complex with Room XV, but the final phase of Tell Qasile (fig. 21) was at the very end of the Philistine period, long after the influences of the Mycenean homeland could be expected to have informed design practices.

It is worth noting that Building 2072 at Megiddo (fig. 31) may have retained the Late Bronze Age Aegean pattern in the period immediately after the chaos of 1200 B.C.E. This phase of the site seems to be represented by stratum VIA. Building 2072 was located on the northwest of the site near what must have remained of the earlier fortifications (fig. 31) and distant from the *migdāl* temple. If it was a cult structure intended to serve a newly arrived population (one of the groups forming the "Peoples of the Sea"), then it is not unreasonable that it would have been positioned in a manner that recalled the non-elite forms of the Aegean homeland. The sanctuaries at Mycene and Phylakopi show that this arrangement of cult areas separate from the megaron itself was somewhat widespread.

Negbi (1988: 350–57) has argued for shared formal features that can relate the west-slope complex at Mycene with the final temple at Tell Qasile. Both have storeroom spaces located behind the temple space; both have internal columns as support elements (Negbi reads both columns at Tell Qasile as structural); and both have internal platform units. These seem rather minor items in reality. The columns did not occupy the same role in both settings and may not have been fully functional in the Tell Qasile structure. Similarly, the platform placements did not reproduce one another, suggesting that the rituals used in each setting were quite different. Storerooms have been found in several of the Levantine complexes, though the particular arrangement behind the temple may be a distinct feature. The differences seem more significant than the similarities. There was no evidence that the Tell Qasile shrine also functioned as a workshop space. It was not placed in a secondary position to any other structure. It dominated the hill and the town that it served. The excavator has denied any connections with Aegean forces and has argued that all the features in the Tell Qasile temple can be shown to have Levantine pedigree dating back to the Bronze Age (A. Mazar 1980: 62–68).

While the sanctuary complex at Phylakopi followed the Mycenean pattern of placement, and in this respect was quite different from what developed in the Philistine region, it did share the prominence accorded to the courtyard in common with the stratum X complex at Tell Qasile, Building 350 at Ekron, and even Building 2072 at Megiddo. At Phylakopi, the two shrines shared a common courtyard off which each shrine had an entrance and that must also have played a role in rituals, because it contained a baetyl and a bench that no doubt was supposed to hold offerings. The courtyard was a restricted space, with access carefully directed. It does seem likely that both Building 350 and Building 2072 owe something of their design format to an earlier Late Bronze Age pattern of courtyard use as seen in the Kamid el-Loz sanctuary. Perhaps the newcomers found a happy resonance with an already existing architectural conceit. The format at Tell Qasile, on the other hand, shows no such strong connection with Late Bronze Age Levantine forms and in fact seems closer to the arrangement found at Phylakopi IV, suggesting that, while the Aegean elements may indeed have been limited at such a late date in the Philistine region, some design ideas may have survived.

The little Late Bronze Age roadside temple at Tel Mevorakh (fig. 75), which is not very far from Tell Qasile, did share some features with the later Iron Age I structure (Shrine 300), particularly the rectangular space and the internal platforms. Negbi (1988: 352) noted that the Tel Mevorakh temple actually seemed rather close to the East Shrine at Phylakopi IV. The East Shrine was appended to a larger sanctuary, which included the West Shrine in about 1270 B.C.E. (Renfrew and Wagstaff 1982: 43). The East Shrine and the Tel Mevorakh temple shared the single-room format with a dominant corner platform. This was also the design for the secondary shrine (Shrine 300) at Tell Qasile. The Tell Qasile shrine and the Phylakopi shrine likewise shared a bent-axis alignment; the alignment for the Tel Mevorakh temple cannot be determined because the temple lacks its entrance. Negbi saw these as significant points to share in common but does not argue that they were the result of Aegean influences penetrating the Levantine coastal regions. Instead, Negbi suggests the reverse, that Levantine architectural influences were carried into the Aegean during the Late Bronze Age to influence the developing forms of non-megaron shrines. In this scenario, the shared features of the Tell Qasile shrines and the Late Bronze Age sanctuaries at Mycene and Phylakopi could be the result of these ideas' being reintroduced to the region by the arrival of groups from the "Peoples of the Sea," especially since they do not represent the architectural forms associated with the palace cult but the forms associated with the more popular cults. On the other hand, they could equally well point to survivals of forms from the Canaanite period that the new arrivals saw fit to borrow, perhaps because they looked familiar or because the Canaanite cultural force was still strong enough to influence the early development of cultic forms in Iron Age I settlements in the region.

Whether the hearths and the specific interior furnishings and the alignments of the parts in these Iron Age I Levantine sanctuaries are best understood as the result of new peoples' bringing with them their cult architecture or as the continuing vitality of the older Late Bronze Age Canaanite architectural forms—the fact remains that the Iron Age I temples were operating in quite new settings. Their features, at best, resembled but did not reproduce the proposed prototypes. The hearth in Building 350 was unlike any Mycenean hearth in terms of its location, and the hearth at Tell Qasile does not compare much more comfortably with its possible Mycenean prototype. The same is clearly true for the placement of the Tell Qasile temple, which was the dominant building at the site. On the other hand, it was not an isolated roadside shrine like the Tel Mevorakh temple. It was integrated into the town fabric, and this was true for the entire history of its operation. Building 350 at Ekron stood as a major structure in the site, not as a grouping of rooms buried in a denser urban fabric, as was the case with the Late Bronze Age sanctuaries at Mycene and Phylakopi. Building 2072 and the sanctuaries at Ashdod, which may date to the first phase of settlement by the "Peoples of the Sea," showed the Late Bronze Age arrangement of sacred spaces integrated into the urban fabric that is attested in the Aegean—but now in a Levantine context.

It is worth noting as a final point that the hearth also played a role in the eighth-century B.C.E. temple-palace at Guzana. The back room of the *bīt ḫilani* contained the remains of a bronze cart that had been designed to move a portable hearth around the space (Langenegger et al. 1950: 44–49, figs. 14, 15). This may have been nothing more than a heating device, but it could have also played some type of cult role, especially since it was designed to be moved and was a well-made construction. Considering the physical and chronological distances, it is likely that the Philistine hearths of the twelfth century and the North Syrian portable hearth of the eighth century have no direct association, but their presence testifies to the importance of the hearth in early Iron Age architecture in select settings.

There is one last Aegean issue that needs to be considered. Building 30 at Abu Hawam has already been discussed as a possible temple for a mixed community in the town. It does seem to bear some similarities with the Tel Mevorakh shrine, as does Tell Qasile. However, its designation as a sanctuary seems to fit rather uncomfortably; the change in construction, the lack of special interior arrangements, and the loss of the building's separation from the surrounding structures seem to indicate a major change in conception if nothing else. There is an alternative interpretation for the structure. It could have been a feasting hall. Similar specialized architectural forms have been found in early Iron Age contexts in the Aegean. These are rectangular megaron-style halls with a porch-like area preceding the main room. Granted, the halls that are known are all eighth century B.C.E. and, thus, quite distant in time from the hall at Abu Hawam. Nevertheless, this was an Aegean type of structure, used to house the *daites* (*dais*, sing.), which had developed as an important feature of aristocratic life in the Greek settlements of the Dark Ages, at least in the Homeric epics. Buildings of this sort have been identified at Emporio on Chios and at Zagora on Andros, where the buildings appear to be integrated into the fabric of the town (Boardman 1967: 32; Cambitoglou et al. 1988). Whether this aristocratic feasting tradition is something that formed only in the changing economic world of the eighth century B.C.E. (Tandy 1997: 142–49) and therefore has nothing to do with the Iron Age I reconfiguration of Abu Hawam or first took shape during the disruptions and resettlements following the collapse of 1200 B.C.E. and could have been introduced into a setting such as Abu Hawam, with its heterogeneous population that included "Peoples of the Sea," cannot be determined with certainty from the archaeological record.

Plans

Of the plans that developed during the early Iron Age, the most unusual was the plan of the Temple of Astarte in Phoenician Kition (fig. 45). What appeared was a small sacred space, a holy of holies, that was embedded in one end of a large colonnaded court. It was the most lavish use of colonnades for any structure in the early Iron Age and recalled, if anything, the New Kingdom hypostyle halls of Karnak and Luxor and the hypostyle hall of the Hittite palace complex at Büyükkale at Hattuša. The suggestion that the columns held up only a partial roofing structure so that the center aisle leading to the entrance to the holy of holes was open makes the design all the more unusual. For the moment, there is nothing else like it in Levantine architecture. It stands as an isolated example of a new type of monumental space. However, the basic concept of a pavilion that (1) was set apart to serve as the cultic focus, (2) had a surrounding space to set it off, and (3) was demarcated by an exterior wall—this plan had a future life in Levantine sanctuary design. The sixth-century B.C.E. Phoenician Sanctuary of Melqart at Amrit on the south Syrian coast (fig. 70) developed along these lines, though with the colonnades now placed within encircling stoas (Jourdain-Annequin 1992: 11–23).

Complexes

Although it is possible that the south building in Stratum V (Mazar's Upper VI) at Beth-shean was a storehouse rather than a temple, the fact remains that it was the second element in a larger building complex (fig. 28). Its north wall was designed to relate to the south wall of the north building. The two structures were set in a plaza area, and the space to the west was contrived to direct movement in a particular manner. This contrasted with the densely packed construction that surrounded the ensemble to the north, south, and east. It was certainly possible that the storehouse was important enough—more a treasury perhaps—to receive a privileged position within the larger architectural composition. At Beth-shean, the buildings were not conceived as being isolated and self-contained. This was made especially obvious in the treatment of the corridor that ran between the north and south structures. The architect worked to establish a conversation with several speakers. How this actually played out in three dimensions cannot be determined because none of the superstructure survives. The shared building material, which was mud brick, automatically joined all the constructions together—massive and humble. Whether the architect was able to incorporate elements into the superstructure that allowed the two monumental structures to respond to one another cannot be known.

The sculptural displays in the North Syrian cities worked in a similar way to link together several separate, autonomous units. At Carchemish and Zincirli, the reliefs were placed so that they provided backdrops for processions along the formal avenues. At ʿAin Dara and Guzana, they were incorporated into the fabric of the buildings proper. They may still have been used within some type of staged performance, but it could not have been a processional movement in the same way. Rather, the sculpture here focused attention on a specific building.

Beth-shean is not the only site that possessed this type of complex planning and design. It was clearly at play in the forms given to the palace compounds of the North Syrian cities. At Guzana, the temple-palace was so placed that it formed a single unit with the main gate into the citadel region, the Scorpion Gate. The sculpted decoration began at that point. The long ramped corridor leading from the gate entrance up to the main plaza limited the view of anyone entering the space and then deposited the visitor on the plaza in front of the temple-palace terrace. The exterior face of the temple-palace, its enormous south wall, loomed over the lower city outside the citadel and provided no hint of what appeared to the visitor who confronted the north façade and the *bīt ḫilani*. The reliefs on the south side were arranged in alternating panels of basalt and limestone. These were reused panels. The iconography on the south façade, therefore, was meaningless (Özyar 1991: 172). The north face was different. Here the reliefs were arranged to form an iconographic program, a display of divine figures that held aloft the terrace on which was placed the great porch, the *bīt ḫilani,* a niche in which the king and his retinue would appear (Langenegger et al. 1950: 27). Opposite the temple-palace to the north was another major structure, smaller than the temple-palace but still clearly important. This may have been the formal residence for the king. Together, the Scorpion Gate, the north building, and the temple-palace formed an architectural ensemble.

The pattern for the complex at Guzana was repeated and made even grander at Tell Taʿyinat (fig. 94). What Tell Taʿyinat lacked in sculptural decoration it made up in thoughtful architectural manipulation. The *bīt ḫilani* of the palace opened to the north onto a patio space that served to connect it to a slightly smaller, square building to the north. This building, in turn, opened to the south, facing the palace. It too had a *bīt ḫilani* treatment, and an architectural dialogue ensued between the two structures. This dialogue was maintained over the four phases during which the two buildings existed, even though the space between them was modified quite dramatically (fig. 95). The temples existed for two of these periods (fig. 42). They were architecturally never part of this ensemble. When they were constructed during the second building period, the main palace had a major wing that extended to the north off of the east side of the palace block. This wing prevented any type of easy movement between the palace and the temples located behind the palace. In the third building period, the north wing was replaced by a raised terrace that covered a large area extending from the new north façade of the palace all the way up to the north building and incorporated the east face of that structure. This effectively blocked any direct movement between palace and temples. The designs at both Tell Taʿyinat and Guzana placed all emphasis on the space in front of the façade of the main palace (or temple-palace) structure.

With the exception of Beth-shean, none of the early Iron Age Palestinian temples came from contexts where the larger setting was well enough known to determine whether or not they formed elements in larger architectural ensembles, even in a peripheral way as at Tell Taʿyinat. The description of the Temple of Solomon places it within a royal architectural ensemble that included several other buildings, among them the palace itself (Busink 1970: 161, fig. 46). Like at Tell Taʿyinat, the palace appeared to have been a more significant piece of architecture than the temple, and it has been argued that the temple was initially no more than a palace chapel (Wright 1944: 77; Waterman 1943: 284–94) which only later assumed its larger national identity. The confusion over building 338 at Megiddo makes it somewhat difficult to bring it comfortably into the discussion. If Ussishkin, following Schumacher's interpretation, is correct, then the structure was a temple placed on a courtyard, perhaps within a gated precinct. However, there is not enough surviving to argue for any type of large architectural grouping. Herzog has noted that during the early Iron Age two types of urban plans come to dominate: peripheral plans and orthogonal plans. The latter type was less common, but it did have a significantly higher number of structures built using monumental construction techniques like ashlar masonry (Herzog 1992: 247). Ashlar masonry may have been used for Building 338 according to Schumacher.

It might be possible to argue that the building techniques were used to lend prestige to constructions in Palestine in the way that formal architectural compositions and orthostat revetments were used in North Syria. The complex at Tel Dan may be the lone survivor of this Palestinian approach. Though the complex went through three iterations, the basic hierarchy of parts never varied (figs. 47–48): a main podium probably holding up a temple, a paved platform to the south, and a series of auxiliary chambers built into the side walls of the precinct. In these various versions of the complex, a dialogue was maintained between the temple podium (and one assumes the temple) and the platform that balanced it to the south by the repeated use of fine stone construction. In the first two phases, the conversation may well have been one of opposing forces: the temple rising atop its podium, the platform being a restatement at the ground level; the temple enclosing space, the platform being an open space. The oppositions were harmonized in the final version (fig. 49), when both temple and platform rose in height, and both used walls as enclosures.

The Edomite sanctuary at Horvat Qitmit (fig. 65) also seems to be understood best as an architectural complex, though of a far less formalized type. Complex B seems to have been no more than a series of rooms surrounding a small patio, but complex A (fig. 66) was apparently a planned space, an architectural composition. There were 3 enclosed, long, parallel rooms. They faced out to 3 distinct units: a negative space that was a rather unarticulated and unpaved plaza, an area defined by a low wall enclosing 3 of its sides, and a fully enclosed circular area. The circular and the three-sided areas formed one-half of the sanctuary and opposed the enclosed space of the 3 rooms. The 2 halves were joined by a single row of stones running from the circle to the enclosed rooms and by the use of local fieldstones for all the building. Similarity of building material also allowed complex B to be related to complex A. The design of complex A was not formal enough to indicate architectural intent clearly. The arrangement of the parts may have been quite accidental. However, the fact that the 3 enclosed rooms opened out and into the space bordered by the 3-sided unit and the circular enclosure seems to indicate that the 2 parts were intended to operate together. The small wall that swung out of the circular enclosure toward the 3 rooms reinforces this reading.

The establishment of large complexes using architectural devices and building positions as devices for making the parts form a whole was not new to the early Iron Age. However, the particular methods that have been discussed do reveal patterns that were not known in Late Bronze Age Levantine contexts. Moreover, the North Syrian settings were especially sophisticated, combining as they did building placements, architectural dialogues, and sculptural elements. The Palestinian experiments, by comparison, were less well defined, though the treatment of a corridor between the

2 major building walls at Beth-shean reveals thoughtful manipulation. It is also interesting to consider that the ashlar building technique may have been accorded a kind of pseudo-iconographic value in the setting of the early Iron Age Palestinian cities.

Conclusion

The early Iron Age temples reveal that a number of new forces were influencing architectural choices. Some elements already existed in the region during the Late Bronze Age but had been exploited only rarely, and some were perhaps the result of new peoples' entering the region and introducing foreign building forms, though there is nothing to suggest that the Arameans came with a long tradition of building. The "Peoples of the Sea" are equally problematic, because it is not at all clear that migrant groups would have been the most likely to retain ideas about prestigious building types. It also seems that many of the new building concepts reflected architectural adaptations that Levantine peoples were making to changing circumstances. Where old forms still had currency they were used, and this is seen in the lines of continuity that do exist between temples of the early Iron Age and their Late Bronze Age predecessors. However, the early Iron Age represented a severe sociological and cultural break with the Late Bronze Age. Not all Late Bronze Age forms still had value, and the new societies taking shape needed to create meaningful architectural types for themselves. Both the aspects that were retained and the aspects that were developed fresh are best explained as serving the needs of the new societal forms of the early Iron Age.

Chapter 6

Societal Forces and
Early Iron Age Temple-Building

A temple was a significant structure. In certain settings such as Sarepta or Tell Qasile, the temple was the only prestigious building in the community. In other situations, such as Guzana and Tell Taʿyinat, it could be one element in the royal building program. Temples were physical manifestations of the coming together of the creative and intellectual lives of the communities that built and used them, and as such, the Iron Age temples drew to their service the best artists of the day. The best builders worked on them; the best artisans created for them. To suit their rituals, the best musicians created new sounds.

The Creative and Intellectual Aspects of Temple-Building

Craftsmen and Builders

The concept of skilled craftsmanship in the ancient Near East was tied to the capability of manipulating materials. Levels of skill had to depend on the availability of materials. Craftsmen earned their status by the value of the raw materials that they shaped (Gates 1990: 30). Our knowledge of craftsmen is limited to a few written sources, of which the Middle Bronze Age Mari documents have been the most useful, and they concern craftsmen who produced small-scale works; our concept of the craftsmen is probably also suitable to the skilled builder. Categories of technical expertise that would nowadays be treated as artisan, such as carpet maker, carpenter, and gardener, were listed in the Mari sources along with other technical jobs such as doorkeeper and palace guard (J. Sasson 1990: 23). The hierarchy stressing first the materials and second the ability to re-form them suggests that craftsmen must have been very dependent on the resources that were available for demonstrating their skills and earning their keep. While certain artisans might have made their name working with limited imported materials—precious metals and semiprecious stones—a builder would always be confined to working with the available building materials. Resources defined the builder even more than was true of other craftsmen. Builders learned their craft from an early age, and since the materials were most commonly those at hand, certain individuals basically perfected skills that many people in the area must have possessed, albeit on a more rudimentary level. At Tell Qasile and again in Jerusalem for Solomon's temple, the use of unusual building materials for the region raises the question: From where did the skilled workmen come? To build using cut and fitted stone blocks required trained craftsmen. At Tell Qasile, perhaps the knowledge was one that the ancestors of the Philistines brought with them and kept alive. However, the first version of the temple, the mud-brick form, stood for 50 years, and no other structure at the site used cut stone during the half century, so how the technique was passed down without any practical use is difficult to say. On the other hand, the second temple at Tell Qasile could attest to the arrival of skilled workmen from elsewhere. Jerusalem is rich in stone, but David and his followers represented a new group on the site. The biblical account credits Hiram, the king of Tyre, with sending men to do stonework on the temple at Jerusalem. Solomon's men labored side by side with these foreigners, perhaps learning the techniques; however, the Late Bronze Age or Iron Age I great box-terrace-retaining-wall construction on the eastern slope of the "City of David" (A. Mazar 1992a: 374, fig. 9.3) and the possible remains of a Late Bronze Age Egyptian-style temple (Barkay 2000) indicate that impressive stone construction may already have been known as an architectural feature in pre-Solomonic Jerusalem.

Both these examples suggest that skilled craftsmen were themselves part of the economic matrix. Elsewhere in the accounts in Kings and Chronicles, Solomon requests of Hiram a worker skilled in treating materials that will be used to embellish the temple. Artisans of the early Iron Age, and probably included among these would be builders, were still part of the "reciprocal" economy that had developed during the early Middle Bronze Age. They could be sent by rulers to work for other rulers (Gunter 1990a: 12). In many instances, there was no need for outside builders because the temples were constructed using the traditional techniques of the region—techniques that had long been practiced to exploit the local resources fully. However, if the desire was to erect something novel, then outside technical expertise needed to be obtained.

Of course, the situation described in the Mari archives may not be completely valid for an early Iron Age Levantine setting. The Late Bronze Age Ugaritic texts introduced the Builder-God Kothar-wa-Khasis, who was responsible for creating palaces for both Yamm and, later, Ba'al (M. S. Smith 1997: 95; Coogan 1978: 80; Ginsberg 1973: 93). There are a couple of significant points about Kothar that warrant attention. First, he served other gods, thus following the pattern of craftsmen as recorded in the Mari documents. El ordered the construction of Yamm's palace, and Kothar was sent to build it. He was at the disposal of his ruler; not only was he required to go erect the palaces of Yamm and Ba'al, he had to leave his home and appear before El to receive his commission. All this seems to reflect the Middle Bronze Age pattern that appears in the Mari documents. He was also multitalented, or at least was expected to be able to do more than one kind of craft. He made the magical clubs with which Baʿal defeated Yamm (M. S. Smith 1997: 103; Ginsberg 1971: 96). He also worked in precious materials, casting furniture ornaments in gold and silver (Smith 1997: 121), and though he used cedar for the palace, he also worked gold and silver into the construction (Smith 1997: 131–32). Obviously, this last element resulted from poetic license to befit the supernatural setting in which Baʿal's palace operated, but it suggests that materials provided value to the monument's design—to the object created. Here it is worth remembering the description of the interior of Solomon's temple with its cedar paneling (1 Kgs 6:9), its gold leaf (1 Kgs 6:30), and the gold furnishings (1 Kgs 7:48–50). It may be possible to recognize an architect-builder as well as a craftsman in metal in the figure of Hiram,[1] the craftsman sent by King Hiram to serve Solomon. He is never actually described as the builder; he is always presented as the bronzeworker (1 Kgs 7:13–47), but so is Kothar.

There is a final point in the Kothar–Baʿal narrative that is worth considering: the debate over the window (M. S. Smith 1997: 133–36; Ginsberg 1971: 104–6). Kothar wanted to incorporate a window into the design, a large window (probably not unlike the window believed to have been present in the palaces at Amarna—a window for the purpose of royal appearances), but Baʿal did not want it. The issue here is the debate. Kothar's engagement with Baʿal may indicate that, while a craftsman was at the disposal of the ruler, there was room for the individual artisan to assert some individuality in making design decisions. Kothar could not override Baʿal's desires (he was a craftsman serving a patron), but he assured Baʿal that he was making a mistake and later laughed when Baʿal reversed himself and asked for the window. For the exchange to have meaning, there must have been an element of reality. Craftsmen had to have had some say in how they created to meet the demands of a given commission.

The Late Bronze Age story of Kothar and Baʿal survives in a version found in the library of the so-called House of the High Priest at Ugarit along with a number of other religious texts. The library may have functioned in a scribal school situated on the acropolis between the two temples (M. S. Smith 1997: 81; Saadé 1979: 171–81). The world that it reflects is that of a prosperous fourteenth-century B.C.E. Levantine city enmeshed in the great international eastern-Mediterranean trade network of the Late Bronze Age. How much of this is applicable to the early Iron Age is certainly questionable, especially in light of the changed demographic and economic landscape that emerged after 1200 B.C.E. However, the Aegean element in the composite population that formed the "Peoples of the Sea" may have carried with them these same notions about craftsmen. S. Morris has argued that already in the Late Bronze Age the Levantine Craftsman God had found a home in the Mycenean palace world (Morris 1992: 73–100). If she is correct, then among some of the Aegean peoples who immigrated

---

1. Huram-abi in 2 Chr 2:13–14.

to the Levantine region as part of the "Peoples of the Sea" population, the concept of the Craftsman God possibly tied to palace/temple-building may also have been present. Blakely (1998) has postulated that, not only did finished metalwork travel around the eastern Aegean, so did metalworkers, not unlike Kothar himself (who lived in either Egyptian Memphis or on the island of Crete but traveled to his commissions). This old Late Bronze Age association between a Craftsman God and hands-on production—including architecture (palace/temple-building)—may have survived the upheavals of 1200 B.C.E. and come back into the Levant with some of the "Peoples of the Sea." Interestingly, the early Iron Age novel *The Tale of Ahiqar* has the king of Egypt requesting that an architect be sent by the king of Nineveh. This suggests that the practice may have been common enough to become a literary trope in the early Iron Age, because it appears in both the Ahiqar story and the account of Solomon's building program (Burkert 1992: 24).

The mixing of manufacturing, particularly bronzeworking, with a sanctuary setting is not well attested in the Late Bronze Age Levant. There may be some evidence at Hazor, Ugarit, and Enkomi (S. Morris 1992: 108, 112), but for the most part, Late Bronze Age Levantine temples stood apart from industrial settings. However, in the Aegean area, particularly on Cyprus, which had a mixed population of indigenous people and Mycenean Greeks in the last phase of the Late Bronze Age, the industrial and the sacred coexisted in the same space. This is true of the area of the later Temple of Astarte at Kition, which in the twelfth century B.C.E. contained several temples (fig. 44), and there is evidence for copperworking (Webb and Karageorghis n.d.: 4–5). The connection of metallurgy and sanctuary has also been noted for the contemporary sanctuaries at Palaeopaphos and Myrtou-Pigadhes. Karageorghis argued that, while the creation of monumental, ashlar-masonry sanctuary buildings on Cyprus coincided with the arrival of "Achaean settlers" on the island, he was not comfortable assigning responsibilities for the introduction and spread of the masonry technique or for religious developments to these new people. The longstanding importance of Cyprus to the copper trade of the Middle Bronze Age and Late Bronze Age explains why in the Late Bronze Age some sanctuaries become tied to industrial operations (Karageorghis 1982: 104). On the other hand, during the early Iron Age, the mixed setting of sanctuary and industry shows up at a few Levantine sites, mostly those associated with the new arrivals. At Ashdod, the apsidal building found in the earliest level of the early Iron Age town—the level settled by the "People of the Sea" according to the Dothans—was situated in an industrial quarter. Though it seems likely that the shrine at Timna had ceased to operate at the end of the Late Bronze Age, the early Iron Age stratum revealed some industrial work at the site, and the ruins of the old shrine may have retained a hallowed quality.

However, two of the references in the discussion of Solomon's temple warrant some investigation. Clearly, the craftsman that Hiram sent Solomon fit the pattern of

Kothar. He came as a man skilled at working many things, including metals, textiles, and precious stones. Though he was not specifically an architect, his curriculum vitae leaves little reason to doubt that he could build as well, and he most assuredly did create architectural features, including 2 columns with decorated capitals. Since he came from Hiram's kingdom, from the region with old Canaanite survival, he was a residual figural type, a Late Bronze Age craftsman sent by his king to undertake work for another king. Neither the old system nor the old concepts were totally dead. But this craftsman did not do his own casting. The objects that he designed were massive, and Solomon had them cast in the Jordan Valley between Succoth and Zarethan (1 Kgs 7:46). This had been a marginal region in the Late Bronze Age, with some settlement at Pella and Tell el-Mazar. The Deir ʿAlla sanctuary (fig. 61) operated in the area and probably served the needs of a largely nomadic population. There is no evidence for a Late Bronze Age center for bronzeworking. However, this was a region that did develop during the early Iron Age. It benefited from its position near the north of the Wadi Arabah and thus participated in the copper trade that moved out of the Arabah and then north and west. First Pritchard and later Tubb argued that the metalworking developments in the region were probably the result of settlement in the Jordan Valley by one of the groups of the "Peoples of the Sea." Evidence for early Iron Age Aegean-style metallurgy was found at Tell es-Saʾidiyeh, now identified as Zarethan (Pritchard 1968: 79–112; Negbi 1991: 205–43; Tubb 1998: 96–100). These newcomers to the region, possibly Sherden, established themselves during a time when the Jordan Valley, along with the site at Timna, was still under Egyptian control. It was easy enough for some of the raw material to end up servicing the craft needs of the new population.

The evidence suggests that, in the early Iron Age, the Late Bronze Age concepts of the craftsman and his position in society were still operative. Not only did they survive with some of the residual Canaanite population, they may have returned in the form of Aegean reconfigurations. Two elements are of most significance: (1) the idea that craftsmen traveled; and (2) the notion that, while a craftsman served the needs of his patron, he may also have offered his own advice and solutions to artistic and design problems when asked. In the Late Bronze Age, craftsmen traveled at the request or command of local rulers. The situation probably continued in the early Iron Age, but new forces must also have intervened, allowing for skilled men to move on their own (Burkert 1992: 24). It may be possible to see the hand of individual craftsmen in some of the unusual features that began to appear on early Iron Age structures but were not picked up and repeated. It is against a background of moving craftsmen-builders, sometimes arriving as the result of the contacts of a local ruler but in some instances of their own volition, that we should see the change in building techniques at Tell Qasile. The first arrivals, who established the new settlement on the Yarkon, relied on the traditional method of building for the area, but some 50 years later, a craftsman trained in the working of cut stone built a temple for the residents that was more in the style of what they may have known elsewhere, perhaps on Cyprus.

Rituals and Musicians

The temples that were in the settings of royal compounds were, no doubt, intended to provide backdrops for the presentation of kingship. How this took place and what role the physical structure of the temple played cannot be determined from the extant epigraphic and literary sources. The Late Bronze Age texts from Ugarit indicate that, by the end of the Late Bronze Age, blood sacrifices of cattle and sheep were taking place at the temples (Pardee 1995b). It is not clear how large the participating group was, though the temples known from Ugarit were within the city itself and not placed in the palace complex. This suggests that a wider public was involved. The Iron Age II Amman Citadel inscription, on the other hand, provides some notion of limited access to a temple because it forbids certain individuals to enter, which may indicate that, by Iron Age II, participation in rituals was a more limited affair (Shea 1991: 62–66). The references to rituals associated with the temple of Solomon are problematic because they seem to reflect a retrojection of practices from the Second Temple back onto Solomon's temple (Kraeling and Mowry 1957; Haran 1978; Weitzman 1997: 101).

All the early Iron Age temples, even those outside the royal areas, may have had restricted access to the cult chamber itself, but a certain amount of ritual activity must have taken place outside the temple proper, in the courtyard regions, which could accommodate more viewers and participants. There is evidence for processions at Ugarit (Clifford 1979: 137–46), something that also may have been a common feature of the Late Bronze Age Canaanite cities and that could have survived or been revived in early Iron Age contexts. Certainly the arrangement of the relief sculptures at Carchemish (fig. 122) suggests that processions were a feature of the ritual-political life of the city, and what was true for Iron Age II Carchemish must have been true of other North Syrian centers. How much Canaanite ritual practice would have survived the collapse of Canaanite culture is hard to say, but Garner has argued for connections between the Ugaritic and Hebrew terminology for classes of sacrifice such as burnt offerings and peace offerings (Garner 1985: 51–60). If the Ugaritic terminology informed early Hebrew terminology, then certain ritual practices may also have continued. Franklin thinks that biblical descriptions of the role of music in the Davidic and Solomonic periods reveal continuity with Late Bronze Age and even Middle Bronze Age Canaanite practices. He notes especially the organization of musicians by families, which can be traced back to the Mari texts.[2] From Tell Arad have come two ostraca with the statements "sons of Kovah" and "sons of Bezal(el)," which Herzog has argued attest the presence of Levitical guides responsible for temple music

---

2. I want to thank my colleague John Franklin, Department of Classics, University of Vermont, for allowing me to read portions of his unpublished book manuscript, *Kinyras: The Divine Lyre.*

(Herzog et al. 1984: 22) who must have attended to the musical needs of the small fortress shrine. On the other hand, the finds of small ceramic figures playing drums at Sarepta, Horvat Qitmit, and Khirbat al-Mudayna may well indicate that, within the confines of smaller, less-prestigious, and perhaps non-state-regulated religious settings, music-making was a less-formal affair.

The biblical descriptions suggest some public dancing for rituals associated with military victories (Exod 15:20), worship of the Golden Calf (Exod 32:19), celebrations at Shiloh (Judg 21:21), and the movement of the ark into Jerusalem (2 Sam 6:14–16). The particular dance performance associated with the movement of the ark may represent the introduction of a type of musical performance that had developed in the Late Bronze Age Levantine royal settings that David was introducing into the old tribal structure of premonarchic Israel (Franklin 2011). His wife, Michal, the surviving daughter of Saul, was appalled by the display, and David was forced to reprove her (2 Sam 6:21).[3] Certainly the prominent role that courtyards play in the designs of several of the early Iron Age temples indicates where the dances and processions may have taken place. The incense stand with dancers from Tel Dan testifies to the significance of dance as the subject for a cult object, but it does not indicate that the dancers are inside the temple or even physically near it. Music-making is evidenced also at Ashdod with the lyre-playing figure.

During the Late Bronze Age, music seems to have reached a somewhat sophisticated level in the Levant, and much of the development took place in association with temples as well as with royal courts (J. Franklin 2007: 27–37). An ensemble of a *kinnôr* (lyre), *nēbel* (strings), a *tof* (frame drum), and a *halil* (pipe) formed the "Canaanite or Levantine temple orchestra" that accompanied professional singers and could also include *metsiltayīm* (cymbals) and a *shofar* (trumpet; see J. Franklin in press). Finds of several different sorts of instruments attest to a variety of types of audio production, and the presence of Hittites and Egyptians, both with distinct musical traditions, can only have served to stimulate some degree of experimentation at the local level (Braun 2002: 69–71). These discoveries may have survived into the early Iron Age. Within the Philistine and Phoenician realms, there is good evidence for the development of ensemble playing—pairs of pipers and drummers (Braun 2002: 155). The terra-cotta stands from Tell Qasile (stratum X) with dancers and from Ashdod with instrumentalists (fig. 14) and the so-called "Orpheus Jug" (fig. 32) from Building 2072 at Megiddo with its standing musician could indicate that dance and accompanying music were performed within the confines of sacred spaces to delight the god. The "Orpheus Jug" was identified as a Philistine painted vase found within the remains of a structure that could have been Philistine inspired, so the image very likely references

---

3. Halpern (2001: 333) thinks that the issue is the moving of the ark itself to Jerusalem and not the procession that disturbs Michal.

Philistine rituals rather than surviving Canaanite practices at Megiddo.[4] The dancing figures from Tel Dan (Biran 2003: 128; 1986: 169–87) and from Horvat Qitmit should also represent individuals engaged in activity that pleased the gods to watch (Biran 2003: 128) and took place within the precinct, if not the cult room of the temple.

What special role, if any, women may have played in the ritual aspect of the temples is difficult to determine. Ackerman has suggested that a major shift downward in the social status of women in the emerging Kingdom of Israel may have occurred between Iron Age I and Iron Age II (Ackerman 2003). Women, who had been active participants in the village-level life in Iron Age I and who are cited as dancing in ritual settings (Exod 15:20; Judg 21:21), were restricted in the emerging urban life of Iron Age II Israel. Whether the higher social status of women in Iron Age I translated into a more engaged role in religious ritual is a different matter. It is impossible to ascertain whether the situation in Israel had meaning for other regions of the Levant. Though Renfrew does not actually identify the gender of the priests serving the cult space on Phylakopi, the reconstruction of the interior shows a woman making a sacrifice (Renfrew et al. 1985: 9.6). This follows a long-standing pattern in Aegean studies, in which the notion of a female priesthood is regularly posited, at least for the Late Bronze Age. As with all other supposed connections between the Philistine region and the Aegean, teasing out the ties is difficult. There is no Philistine evidence for cult practices involving priestesses, but nothing in the finds makes it clear that the sanctuaries were serviced by a male priesthood either.

Several of the sanctuaries have yielded ceramic finds most commonly associated with food preparation, serving, and eating. As Renfrew warns, finds may not necessarily be part of the original fixtures of the temple but could have migrated in through any number of means (Renfrew et al. 1985: 387–88), but if we can trust the finds of ceramic materials, then it seems reasonable to assume that food preparation and consumption occurred within the temple precincts in several cases. Food preparation is most commonly assigned a female gender classification in the Levant of the early Iron Age, and here there may be the indication of a role that women played within the ritual life of at least some of the sanctuaries. Though none of the excavated temples has produced evidence for weaving, Meyers (2003b: 425–44) has argued that this may also have been a role assigned to women in a temple setting. There is a reference in 2 Kgs 23:7 to women working within the confines of the temple in Jerusalem, probably in a secondary space in the precinct rather than in the temple itself, weaving garments to garb the Asherah. This may provide a window onto a much later development with no connections to the ritual practices of the Iron Age I and II, or it could be the continuation of an older, well-established practice for which archaeological evidence

---

4. Again the issue of the date is problematic. The jug was found in stratum VIA, which has been dated to 1050–1000 B.C.E. by A. Mazar (1992a) or 900–850 B.C.E. by Finkelstein and Silberman (2001); see Lawergren 2003. King and Stager (2001: ill. 163) give the work an eleventh-century B.C.E. date.

is just not available. Where women most commonly exercised a powerful role in religious life would have been in the context of household practice (Meyers 2003a: 189), but how this connected with temples is not at all obvious.

The finds from some sanctuaries do suggest that one aspect of ritual life where women could have had a prominent role was music making. The small figures from the Moabite wayside shrine at Wadi ath-Thamad #13 depict women or girls, several of whom hold drums. A similar model of a woman or girl with an upright drum, a tambour, was found in the conjectured palace structure at Pella (trench XXXIIAA) that was probably associated with the Iron Age temple (Bourke 2007) and thus perhaps reflects a continuing Canaanite aspect that survived into the Iron Age. Mitchell thinks that there are an adequate number of similar ceramic figurines throughout the region to treat them as a classification (Mitchell 1992: 128 fig. 4). A ceramic model of a one-room naiskos, possibly from Karak in Jordan, shows two nude female figures, each on the porch and playing a tambour held against her left shoulder (Daviau 2008: 297)[5]. The image seems clearly to connect female musicians with cultic settings. The biblical description of women accompanying themselves with drums in the performance of victory songs provides a context for these terra-cotta figurines (Braun 2002: 120) while the findspots of the Pella and Wadi ath-Thamad figures clearly place female musicians within a sacred space. The Karak naiskos takes the association even further by combining together ritual building, female musicians, and public nudity.

The Economics and Politics of Temple-Building

Patronage

The destruction at the end of the Late Bronze Age wiped out the political structures that had obtained for most of the second millennium throughout the Levant. The individual rulers of the city-states of the Canaanite Levant who had dominated the political life of the region were gone. Nascent nation-states emerged throughout the region. Where independent cities still operated, as in the Philistine area, they were grouped into confederations. By the tenth century B.C.E., the Phoenician coastal cities had come to recognize the authority of Tyre. No single outside power replaced Egyptian and Hittite presences until the aggressive reemergence of Assyria in the ninth century B.C.E.

Late Bronze Age temples had functioned in the city-state environment. They were agents of Late Bronze Age religions as they had developed throughout the region. Though there are examples of temples at Alalakh (Frankfort 1985: 276–77) and Kamid el-Loz that may have been placed in close association with a palace, the majority of Late Bronze Age temples stood physically apart from (now-recognizable) palace structures. Independent temples in an urban setting continued to function, albeit on

---

5. In the Amman Citadel Museum–National Museum of Jordan, J5751.

a more modest scale in the early Iron Age, but a whole category of palace-temple constructions came into being. These were not the only sanctuaries in operation during the early Iron Age. Small shrines independent of an urban context appeared as well. There were Late Bronze Age predecessors such as the Amman airport temple, the sanctuary at Deir ʿAlla, and the Tel Mevorakh shrine, but the placement of the early Iron Age shrines attests to changes in religious practice and the emergence of new routes of movement in the region.

The early Iron Age Levantine temples fall into three categories: they owed their existence to an individual's patronage, a community's efforts, or a royal project. Obviously, the resources available in each instance were different, and they informed the nature of the design and the physical aspects of the final structure.

Individual Patronage

The actual temple remains, with the exception of the royal constructions, do not present themselves as examples of individual patronage. None of the remains comes with epigraphic evidence to supply the identity of the builder. Although it is possible to make some claims for royal patronage based on factors other than epigraphic, the same is not the case for nonroyal patrons. The most likely candidates to be the result of private patronage would have been those which stand independent of an urban fabric—sanctuaries that had their own separate identity for a limited period of operation, which would have been the lifetime of the patron and the immediate heirs.

Private ancestral cults have been identified as a feature of the religious life of the Late Bronze Age Levant that can be traced back to the Middle Bronze Age and may well have continued to play an important and formative role in the early stages of early Iron Age religion in Israel (van der Toorn 1996: 206–35) as well as elsewhere in the Levant. The little Late Bronze Age shrine known as the Stela Temple in area C at Hazor (fig. 103; see Yadin et al. 1958: Loci 6135 and 6136), which contained a seated stone figure and several small shaped-stone items, has been identified as dedicated to a funerary cult. The crudely worked steles may have been images of the ancestors (P. Beck 1990: 91–95). If the identification is correct, then there is nothing particularly diagnostic about the architecture. The shrine was modest, a single chamber entered through a door on one of the long sides, technically a broad-room type of building.

A cult of dead rulers is postulated for Late Bronze Age Ugarit on the basis of the textual material, though no archaeological remains have been associated with the cult, so nothing can be suggested about the nature of the architecture. At Guzana, tombs were found on the temple-palace terrace, suggesting that there was a connection between royal burials and the ritual structure. Ussishkin suggested that a carved piece of soft white limestone found in the early Iron Age context of Building 338 at Megiddo placed atop the southernmost column was an idol (Ussishkin 1989: 155), and Beck has included it as a possible late example of the continuance of the ancestor cult into the early Iron Age (P. Beck 1990: 94). If this is correct and if Building

338 was indeed a prestigious building in early Iron Age Megiddo, then it might have been the private shrine within the context of a palace at the site, as Kempinski has suggested—a royal version of the private shrine of Micah (Kempinski 1989: 186–89), a royal mortuary cult perhaps following the Late Bronze Age precedent. Again, there is nothing significant about the architecture. The space is modest and isolated. The proto-Aeolic capitals that have been associated with the room were not found in it, and thus have no clear affiliations, and the capital type is most commonly adjudged to belong to secular constructions (Reich 1992: 212–13). Ussishkin prefers to follow the views of Schumacher, the original excavator, and identify the structure as an independent temple that did possess some specific architectural features: a paved courtyard from which a monumental staircase provided access to the temple proper (Ussishkin 1989: 149–72).

The little wayside shrine at Wadi ath-Thamad (WT #13; see fig. 64) located outside the confines of the town at Khirbat al-Mudayna could have been a private installation. This was a small shrine, unsuitable for a large-scale congregation. What survived suggested that the interior of the structure had stone benches that lined the walls. The floor was cobbled. The finds seemed to indicate votive offerings: broken figurines, carnelian and shell bead jewelry, faience amulets, and many sherds from household, cooking pottery (Daviau and Dion 2002: 49). All of this was appropriate to a modest shrine that may have been used at certain times by people other than just the builder.

A subsidiary category may be shrines belonging to a clan. Van der Toorn has argued that the tomb of Samuel at Ramah-of-the-Zuphites (1 Sam 25:1; 28:3) is best understood in these terms; it was a shrine that served the needs of a select group of individuals within a larger community (van der Toorn 1996: 253–55). The story was set in the hill country of ancient Israel, so it may represent a particular feature of early Israelite religious architecture that is not applicable to anywhere else in the Levant. The possible altar on Mount Ebal north of Shechem (fig. 33A) may have served the needs of a clan. The remains, if read as sacred, consisted of a rectangular feature of local fieldstones that has been interpreted as an altar by some, but by no means by all (Zertal 1985; 1986; 1987; 1988; Finkelstein 1988b: 82–85; Soggin 1988; Kempinski 1986). Zertal identified this structure with Joshua's altar on Mount Ebal (Deut 27:4; Josh 8:30–35). Considering that the alternative identification for the remains is a watch-tower with no religious affiliations (Kempinski 1986), it is difficult to argue for any diagnostic features in the remains. It may be reasonable to include the shrines in the Negev at ʿEn Hatzeva and Horvat Qitmit (figs. 65–68) in this subcategory of clan shrines. There is no evidence of communities in association with the shrines during their period of operation. They could have provided a religious focus for a nomadic clan group that operated in the region and came together infrequently for organized rituals.

There is nothing architecturally distinct about these sanctuaries and shrines to point to either individual or clan patronage. At best, it is possible to argue for the inclusion of the category as a means of explaining shrine buildings that otherwise are too distant from settlements to have been easily recognized as the result of a community's concerns. These are modest affairs. The literary evidence for this sort of category is strictly biblical, and at present, the only possible examples of this type of sanctuary are confined to the areas of modern-day Israel and Jordan.

The story of Micah (Judg 17:1–18:21) provides evidence of the tradition of private shrines, though, as with all biblical accounts of the early Iron Age, its value for reconstructing religious and social settings in the period immediately after the collapse of 1200 B.C.E. is questionable. The story clearly records the establishment of a private shrine, complete with a priest (van der Toorn 1996: 246–51). This is not presented as an unusual practice, and it may be reasonable to assume that such private shrines were a feature for a select number of individuals in the early Iron Age society of Israel. On the other hand, Judges 18 has been recognized as an intentional mockery of the movement of the tribe of Dan to the north and the establishment of its sanctuary. The Danites are portrayed as brigands who abuse Micah's hospitality by stealing his cult image and inducing his priest to follow them (Naʾaman 1994: 270). How much stock to place in the validity of the details in this story is highly questionable. However, the shine that Micah builds is intended to house a silver cult statue, suggesting that the rite is not especially associated with Yahweh (Jacobsen 1987: 15–29), though the ban on graven images was not yet in effect. If it was not the Yahwist cult, then it could have been a surviving Canaanite cult, thus suggesting that private, domestic shrines were not an unknown feature of Iron Age I and II Levantine architecture.

Community Sanctuaries

Several of the sanctuaries were functioning features in an urban landscape. Their existence had some influence on the way the urban matrix took shape. All the Philistine temples known to date came from urban settings. The temple at Tell Qasile occupied the highest position at the site. From its inception, the sanctuary was incorporated into a larger complex of structures. Its entrance had to be defined by the use of a courtyard. The Area H sanctuary at Ashdod formed part of the constructions on the acropolis and contained an apsidal space, a design feature not seen in other buildings on site. The later Area D sanctuary was an extensive complex: 12 distinct spaces arranged around courtyards. This complex was integrated into an industrial quarter of the city. The sanctuaries at Ekron, like those at Ashdod, stood out because of their design features. The Field I sanctuary in the upper city was located within the confines of a residential sector, and the sanctuary from Field IV in the lower city seems to have been a feature in an elite district of the city. None of these buildings was isolated and separated from the urban complex; rather, each was tightly woven into the fabric of the city. Their interior spaces and the use of courtyards provided some distinction to these buildings and made them different from their neighbors, but they were not architecturally separated and must somehow have been serving the needs of the community residing around them.

Building 30 at Abu Hawam maintained the general form of the older temple, Building 50, as well as continuing to treat the particular spot as distinct, hallowed. Thus, it is better understood as a sanctuary designed for the needs of a community. On the other hand, there were some significant changes to the building. The older Building 50 had stood isolated from nearby structures, surrounded by an open, neutral space. Moreover, its walls had been different from those of other constructions, because they were thicker and had external buttresses. Building 30 was nowhere near as isolated. Its west side remained open with a large courtyard area, but buildings came right up to its north wall. It was no longer allowed to stand aloof. Similarly, its style of construction was changed so that it fit more comfortably into the pattern used for other structures. The walls were thinned, and there were no external buttresses. Perhaps Building 30 gained status by being placed over the remains of a ruined temple, but it also may have functioned in a different manner, especially since the town's Iron Age I population clearly included a significant element of Aegean people.

The modest shrine from Sarepta appears to have been intended to serve the needs of an industrial quarter of the town. Like the Philistine shrines, it was completely integrated into the urban fabric of Sarepta. It was even less architecturally distinguished than were the Philistine temples. It was a single room without courtyards and was entered directly from the street. Nothing about the design separated it from surrounding buildings. Only the arrangement of the interior space with benches provided an architectural element that announced its special use. On the other hand, the actual techniques of construction did announce that the building was special. It has deep foundations, and the walls were of well-cut sandstone blocks laid in a header-and-stretcher pattern. These features along with the gray cement pavement in the interior set off the space as special. The little sanctuary at Sarepta was Phoenician. The lack of Late Bronze Age sanctuaries from the Phoenician region makes it impossible to know whether the Sarepta sanctuary represents continuity or discontinuity. What did exist as Late Bronze Age temples, the temples at Ugarit and Kamid el-Loz, were temples that in some way served the needs of a city or a palace and therefore are not comparable with the sanctuary at Sarepta, which has no such associations.

These were all sanctuaries best understood as being the products of a specific community's needs. Whether they satisfied a group within a larger community or were the result of larger community effort cannot be ascertained. None of these buildings was allowed to dominate the setting in which it operated. The architecture may show that the buildings were special—manifest by the number of rooms, their unusual configuration, the use of prestigious building techniques, or the structure's physical location within a city—but they were nonetheless structures that operated in the daily ebb and flow of the communities in which they were situated and which must have been responsible for their building and their maintenance.

Royal Temples

Certainly the building of some temples was the prerogative of kings in the Late Bronze Age. If one uses the Ugaritic text of Baʿal's story, it becomes immediately obvious that a temple was the same as a god's house. Just as kings commissioned the creation of the cult statues for sanctuaries, they were responsible for the building of the temples themselves. The Ugaritic texts demonstrate that the kings were regularly involved with some of the cults, participating in processions and rituals. The destruction of the social structure of parts of the Levant during the turmoil of the period around 1200 B.C.E. cut the connection between kings and temples, at least in some areas. Where the old arrangements remained intact, the old systems were probably maintained; but in much of the area, the new social structures that resulted from the devastation or from the change in the demographic makeup of a region meant that the old order was no longer operative.

During Iron Age I, there is little evidence for any type of strong kingship. Possibly the new settlements at Ashdod and Tell Qasile had kings, but nothing in the finds from the sites supports this sort of view. Even though there is some agreement that the Phoenician cities of the Lebanese coast probably did not sustain serious damage during the troubles that witnessed the end of Ugarit and the Hittite cities farther east, there is nothing archaeological to indicate that the cities were ruled by kings. The Egyptian story of Wen-Amon's journey to Byblos is usually argued to present a picture of the Phoenician coast in about 1100 B.C.E. In the narrative, Wen-Amon does deal with local rulers, the princes at Dor and Byblos. It is not obvious from the text how extensive their powers were. However, the description of Wen-Amon's audience with Zakar-Baʿal, the ruler of Byblos, shows that the prince still possessed a sense of theatrical staging for his presentation. One of his formal activities was tending the cult in the city, for it was during the process of his offering actions that one of his young attendants was seized by some type of frenzy. Therefore, the one narrative text from the period does indicate a continuity of rulership pattern for the coast after the destruction of 1200 B.C.E. In fact, Wen-Amon begins his journey with a stop at the court of Ne-su-Ba-neb-Deb and his wife Ta-net-Amon at Tanis in the south. As one would expect, there are no stops along the southern coast of Palestine, since the area is not conducive to harbors. It is only at Dor that Wen-Amon puts in to shore. However, with local princes at Tanis and at Dor, it seems likely that the communities established by the "Peoples of the Sea" in between would follow a similar social structure, especially since Dor at this point in time was ruled by the Tjeker. The find of the Iron Age I relief of the Storm God as approaching the king from the citadel temple at Aleppo clarifies that kingship had survived in the region, but since the Aramean and Neo-Hittite cities do not emerge as major entities until Iron Age II, it is safe to assume that kings in this region were operating on a most limited basis. Rulership, though not kingship, may have continued to be involved with the temple-building program at Beth-shean, which remained a Egyptian garrison for at least another half-century after the rebuilding on the acropolis around 1200 B.C.E., and in the Canaanite cities that survived the changes of the period, local kings could have continued to maintain the older practices. An ivory plaque from Megiddo, on the left side portraying a ruler seated in a winged-sphinx throne and approached by a woman in Syrian headdress accompanied by musicians and on the right side showing the same prince presenting naked captives, may have been created either just before or just after the devastations of 1200 B.C.E. and thus may show some continuity between Late Bronze Age and Iron Age I, though it also reflects the continued Egyptian influence in the region through the first half of the twelfth century B.C.E. The subject is, however, a Canaanite war and victory cycle (Frankfort 1985: 270, fig. 316). The motif of the ruler seated in a sphinx throne is repeated on Ahiram's sarcophagus from Byblos. Frankfort dated the Megiddo ivory, which was found in a cache beneath the destruction level of Megiddo VII, to the thirteenth and even fourteenth centuries B.C.E., and he dated the sarcophagus to the thirteenth century. Albright took exception to this Late Bronze Age dating and argued that the greater part of the ivories dated to the first half of the twelfth century. In a similar vein, he insisted that Ahiram's sarcophagus dated to the tenth century B.C.E. (Albright 1956b: 158–59). Certainly Albright's reasoning is stronger for the sarcophagus. Frankfort was willing to concede that the inscription of the sarcophagus was tenth century, but he insisted that it had been added later. Albright argued against such a deliberate falsehood since the inscription clearly states that the coffin was made for the individual buried within it. The point is that, whether the Megiddo ivory dates to Late Bronze Age or early Iron Age, its motifs are Late Bronze Age. The similarities with the treatment of the enthroned ruler on Ahiram's sarcophagus show continuity in motif between the Late Bronze Age and the early Iron Age, which may also reflect continuity in concepts of rulership in the Phoenician coastal region, but nothing in the archaeological record indicates major new building programs at these sites during these first centuries of the early Iron Age.

New Kings and New Gods

It was with the advent of Iron Age IIA that the political institution of kingship once more emerged as a force throughout the Levantine region. But there was a change. Where in the Late Bronze Age, kings had their power confined to a city and its hinterland, many of the Iron Age IIA and B kings were now rulers of petty states. The Phoenician kings followed the older pattern, though, by about 1000 B.C.E., the city of Tyre was emerging as the dominant power and the real political force among the cities, and its kings had come to play the major role in Phoenician expansion and foreign policy (Markoe 2000: 32–39; Katzenstein 1973: 130–35). Iron Age II witnessed the establishment of strong states in northern Syria, and for several of these the names of the kings have survived. Unlike the situation in Phoenicia, where the names of kings were recorded but no standing temple remains can be associated with royal patrons, at the Neo-Hittite city of Carchemish and at the Aramean city of Guzana royal names and sacred structures can be joined together. Certainly the most famous of royal sanctuary commissions—that of Solomon—was erected during this period. While these projects follow the old tradition that kings should build temples, they differ in that these temples were often elements in political programs of territorial expansion, and they were items in a larger restructuring of religion in the Levant that saw the creation of new cults to new gods.

By far the longest-lasting of the new cults was that of Yahweh, which took shape in the region of Palestine throughout Iron Age I and possibly earlier in the Late Bronze Age. It became closely aligned with the monarchy of the newly emergent state of Israel under its first kings Saul and David. In a similar vein, the cults of Milkom among the Ammonites, Chemosh among the Moabites, and Qaus among the Edomites were all developments of the early Iron Age, which first appeared in the epigraphic record in Iron Age II. Melqart from Tyre,[6] the newly promoted god, was to play an important role in Tyre's colonial expansion to the West.

The first kings known by name to emerge in the early Iron Age were those of the new kingdoms that appeared in these centuries of Iron Age IIA: Saul, David, and Solomon in Israel, Abi-baꜤal and Hiram I in Tyre. The biblical sources and Josephus record their names.[7] Mesha of Moab and Sanib and his grandson Yerah꜐azar from Ammon put up inscriptions. Kapara from Guzana was associated specifically with a building. His inscriptions came from the temple-palace complex that he rebuilt. These were the kings under whose rule new religious forces were set in motion by the creation of new gods. They were also the builders of the major temples of the early Iron Age. The temples of Iron Age I may have served the needs of communities that were emerging from the disruptions of the twelfth century B.C.E. or were just trying to survive, or

---

6. Melqart's identity is still a debated point. No one doubts that the name makes him "King of the City." Bonnet (1988) assumes that the city is Tyre, a conjecture with no obvious support since the earliest inscription that identifies Melqart as the BaꜤal of Tyre is from Malta and dates to the second century B.C.E. (*KAI* 47:1; van der Toorn, Becking, and van Horst 1999: 563). The notion that he was the patron of Tyre seems further complicated by the fact that the gods BaꜤal Shamên and Bethel both appear in position before Melqart on the treaty of Esarhaddon (M. S. Smith 1990b: 590). Dussaud (1946–48) argued that Melqart was a Weather God of the Haddad type and associated with fertility, a view strongly rejected by Albright (1969) and more recently by Baumgarten (1981) who instead propose that he was a chthonic deity somehow connected with the Resheph and Nergal types, a king of the underworld city whose fertility associations were prosperity through his underworld role. This view is shared by Ribichini and Xella (1979), who have seen in Melqart a version of Milkashtart, an older Canaanite chthonic god connected with Ugaritic Rephaim. Lipiński (1995: 226) sees Melqart as deriving from the earlier Milku, a god from Ugarit who appears in the royal theophoric name of King Abimilku.

7. The name Hiram appears in 1 Kgs 5:1, but it is Huram in 2 Chr 2:3.

they may been responding to the needs of new communities that took shape in foreign lands; however, the royal patronage of certain Iron Age IIA and B temples caused some temples to become elements in the political propaganda of Iron Age II statecraft.

Hiram I (969–936 B.C.E.)

Hiram I, king of Tyre, was the first ruler-builder to emerge in the early Iron Age. Two sources record his actions: the Hebrew Bible and Josephus. Hiram was recorded in Samuel, Kings, and Chronicles as a friend of David and Solomon, a supplier of materials and labor for building projects. Hiram was an important player in two of Josephus's works: *Against Apion* (*Ag. Ap.*) and *Jewish Antiquities* (*Ant.*). In both works, Josephus was trying to marshal evidence of the great age of Israel, so neither work was neutral. However, Josephus was at pains to assure the reader that the information about Phoenician matters came from primary documentation, from the Phoenician archives themselves (*Ag. Ap.* 17.106–8). The redactors of the biblical material were interested in Hiram only with regard to his associations with the Israelite kings and the newly emergent state. Josephus was actually concerned with establishing Hiram as a significant player with historical pedigree because it then allowed him to link David and Solomon to an accepted historical figure. With this in mind, Josephus provided information about Hiram and Tyre that was quite independent of involvement with Israel.

Hiram assumed the throne of Tyre after his father, Abi-ba'al, and thus was part of a dynasty rather than being a usurper. According to Katzenstein, he already was involved in diplomatic ventures as crown prince. However, Josephus stated that one of his major actions as king was the destruction of the old temples in the city and their rebuilding. This information came not from Josephus's knowledge of archival matters but from the work of two other historians. One historian, Dius (*Ag. Ap.* 17.113–16), is known to us only from Josephus. The other, Menander of Ephesus (*Ag. Ap.* 17.18.116–17; *Ant.* 8.144–47), may also appear in the later work of Clement of Alexandria, where he is referred to as Menander of Pergamon (*Strom.* 1.114).[8] The age of Tyre was problematic. Josephus recorded that it was an old city, but the archaeological evidence is not as compelling, compared with other cities on the Phoenician coast. Whatever the reality, if Josephus can be trusted on this point, and there is probably no reason not to trust this information, Hiram was credited with a massive building campaign in the city, one element of which was the rebuilding of temples. This made him a royal patron on a grand scale. Of the temples that he rebuilt, two received attention from Josephus: the Temple of Olympian Zeus and that of Heracles. Dius claimed that Hiram erected embankments on the eastern end of the town (one must assume the island), in order to shore up this section and to enlarge the building surface of the city. He also built a causeway to join the island containing the city proper to a smaller island holding the

---

8. See Boyes 2012: 34 and n. 1 for reservations about Josephus's reliability.

Temple of Zeus. Menander's discussion confirmed the general information. Hiram was responsible for building an embankment, the purpose of which may have been to join the new island city of Tyre with the older mainland site. Besides the Temple of Zeus, he also built temples to Heracles and Astarte. However, all this information really served a specific purpose for Josephus, which was to set up the discussion of Solomon's temple in Jerusalem. This was made quite clear in *Jewish Antiquities*, in which the king of Tyre was decidedly secondary to Solomon.

The Josephus account does provide some useful information. Hiram was a temple builder. He may well have destroyed older shrines for the express purpose of rebuilding them. Moreover, the reconstructing of sanctuaries was part of a larger urban renewal project. Both accounts consulted by Josephus noted Hiram's use of timber from Mount Lebanon, obviously the cedars. This was not a new feature, but the emphasis given to this point by both authors may indicate that Tyre's claims to the cedars represented something new. Byblos clearly had been trading in cedar from the time of the Old Kingdom, but Byblos is in the north, close to some of the cedar groves. Hiram must have been exploiting the cedars in the south of the Lebanon range—the cedars of the Chouf. This emphasis on Hiram's expeditions to obtain the cedar reflected the new geopolitical reality of Iron Age IIA. Tyre had become the dominant city on the Phoenician coast, controlling not just the major portion of sea-borne trade but also access to the major natural resource in the Lebanon itself. Dius merely reported that the cedar was used for the rebuilding of the temples, but Menander stated clearly that the cedar was for the roofing of structures. This is to be expected because wood was the only option for roofing. There is one other potentially important bit of information, though the two sources report it slightly differently. Dius claimed that Hiram adorned the Temple of Zeus with gold offerings, and Menander said that Hiram dedicated a gold pillar (*kiona*) in the Temple of Zeus. These were probably reporting the same thing but in different ways.

Herodotus also knew something of the temples in Tyre. He visited the city specifically to see the Sanctuary of Heracles (2.44–45). This was part of a larger discussion about the spread of the cult of Heracles around the eastern Mediterranean. He reported on two temples dedicated to Heracles: one to Heracles and the other to Thasian Heracles. Of these, he said only that the Temple to Heracles was richly adorned with two remarkable columns (*stelai*): one of gold, the other of emerald—both of which gleamed in the dark with a strange radiance.

There is potentially one last piece of information about Tyrian sanctuaries of Iron Age II. From the palace of Sennacherib in Nineveh came a relief showing the king of Tyre, Luli, fleeing before the arriving Assyrians (fig. 71). The image of the city was of a wall on which seems to be the façade of a building with two columns flanking the entrance. This has been read as a portrait of the Temple of Heracles (Markoe 2000: fig. 9).

The information from Josephus can be translated into an early Iron Age context. The Sanctuary of Olympian Zeus must be that of Baʿal-Shamên ('Lord of Heavens'), the chief deity of the city according to the seventh-century B.C.E. treaty between Esarhaddon and Baʿal, king of Tyre (van der Toorn et al. 1999: 149). This was the local manifestation of the Late Bronze Age Baʿal, the powerful Levantine god of the Ugaritic texts. On the other hand, the Sanctuary of Heracles was that of Melqart. Melqart had become conflated with Heracles by the sixth century B.C.E., perhaps on Cyprus or even Thasos (Karageorghis 1982: 144). When these later Greek writers discussed Heracles in the context of Phoenician Tyre, they were really describing Melqart in his Hellenic guise. Herodotus did not know the author of the shrines to Melqart-Heracles at Tyre. He knew only that the main temple was old. The claim was made that it was as old as the city itself, which the priests claimed was 2,300 years of age. This does not agree with what is known of the archaeological history of Tyre, which is nowhere near this old. However, it may well indicate that the temple had stood prior to Hiram's destruction and rebuilding campaigns. On the other hand, there is no evidence that the cult of Melqart dates earlier than Iron Age IIA (Röllig 1983: 88). However, an earlier form of the god may have already appeared in the Ugaritic texts.[9]

Hiram was credited by Menander with initiating the celebration of the *egersis* 'the Awakening' of Melqart, a major festival in Tyre (*Ag. Ap.* 1.118–19; *Ant.* 8.146–47; Bonnet 1988: 33–40). Katzenstein associated this with the rebuilding of the temple rather than the establishment of a festival (Katzenstein 1973: 92–93). The information in Josephus is not enough to claim that Hiram actually was responsible for the creation of the cult of Melqart, but it does seem that he was a strong supporter and gave some degree of royal patronage to the cult. It was clearly not the only cult to be given royal support. In fact, if taken at face value, the statements in both Dius and Menander about Hiram's actions suggest that he successfully placed all the cults in the city under some type of royal authority. About the temples themselves, not too much can be gleaned from the written sources. Clearly the Temple of Baʿal-Shamên received the most precious objects.

The Temple of Melqart may have been a double cult. It depends on whether the Temple to Astarte was a separate sanctuary or part of the Sanctuary of Melqart. Menander placed the two deities in close association (Bonnet 1988: 35). The columns or pillars pose a bit of a problem. Menander knew of only one, which was a gold pillar; the choice of *kiona* seems significant. It is a pillar, an architectural element, even if not used in an architectural manner. This is different from Herodotus's account. He discusses two *stelai* in the Sanctuary of Melqart (Heracles). The term was often used to indicate freestanding, nonarchitectural units, sometimes inscribed. Herodotus did not describe these as forming architectural elements in the temple; rather, they were

---

9. See n. 6 above.

discussed in terms of their intrinsic value—one stele of gold and the other of emerald, and the latter possessing an unusual radiant property. Certainly it is possible that these were both references to the same element, the differences in description having to do with any number of transmission problems. Supposedly, Menander was reporting on the state of the Sanctuary of Baʿal-Shamên when Hiram patronized it, based on the evidence of the Phoenician archives, while Herodotus was reporting firsthand observations of Tyre made half a millennium later. Much could have transpired.

Herodotus did not mention the Temple of Baʿal-Shamên (Olympian Zeus). Perhaps it no longer stood; the gold pillar was moved to the Sanctuary of Melqart (Heracles), and another pillar was added. Menander could have misunderstood the source and placed the column in the wrong sanctuary. At some point, both sanctuaries were equipped with the feature of freestanding pillars, not an unusual element in early Iron Age Levantine temple settings. *Maṣṣēbôt*, freestanding stone pillars, were a common enough feature in early Iron Age archaeological contexts in Israel and can be found in the Phoenician region in the Temple of Obelisks at Byblos (fig. 107), a complex that dates back to the Early Bronze Age (Dunand 1973: 48–54). Bonnet has argued that the *stelai* were actually natural features associated with the sanctuary—rocks that had formed part of the initial foundation of the city on the island. Nonnios (*Dion.* 40.465–500) knew these as the Ambrosienne Rocks. For Bonnet, it was these natural features that were somehow given a treatment in the sanctuary and that later Herodotus discussed, though he did not really understand them (Bonnet 1988: 31–33).

The relief from the Southwestern Palace of Sennacherib at Nineveh (fig. 71) may show an image of the Temple of Melqart at Tyre. The association with this temple is largely based on the emphasis given to the two columns that flank the entrance of the façade. This seems to correspond with the columns mentioned by Herodotus, assuming that these were indeed elements within the architectural setting. The image of the temple appearing above the city wall does seem unusual. It breaks with the representation of buildings in Phoenician towns seen elsewhere in the reliefs. For example, in a scene of the looting of a Phoenician town from the same palace, Room XLVIII, slabs 11–13, there are buildings shown above the city wall, and these do not have the two flanking columns indicated.

However, the specific relief in question no longer exists. It was still visible as late as 1903–5, because a photograph shows a little of it in situ next to the east jamb of Door d (Russell 1991: fig. 129). What does exist is a drawing by Layard made when he first discovered it (Russell 1991: 37–39). The photograph shows how shallow the relief was and how difficult it must have been to interpret. The question is whether the prominence accorded the nonfunctioning flanking columns was the intent of the artist or the result of the way Layard interpreted the damaged panels (Harden 1962: 308, no. 50). The reliefs, nos. 14–15, come from what Layard designated as Room B of the Southwest Palace of Sennacherib.

The room was later renamed Room I of what has come to be recognized as a throne-room suite of 6 interconnected rooms (I–VI) that open off courtyard H. The scene of the city by the sea in which the people are fleeing by boat (because, one assumes, the city is being assaulted by the Assyrian army) is just one of several scenes of cities attacked and captured that line the walls of the large room. Nothing survives to identify the city or the campaign. However, there are a number of topographical and landscape elements included in the relief program for the room to indicate that the represented cities are those in the west that were the subject of Sennacherib's third campaign, the details of which are preserved on the inscribed Rassam Cylinder (British Museum, WAA 80-7-19,1; Russell 1991: 160–64). As part of this campaign, the Assyrian army marched down the Phoenician coast. Barnett first suggested that the image captured on slabs 14–15 is the escape of King Luli of Tyre from Sennacherib (Barnett 1956: 91),[10] and therefore the building peeking above the city wall must have been one of the structures best known from the city, one that would serve to visually identify the city image for the viewer. It is the columns that have allowed for the connection with the Temple of Melqart.

On the other hand, the Temple of Melqart was not the only temple in Tyre that Hiram rebuilt. Significant as the cult was to Hiram, it was not the cult of the chief deity of the city. The importance that the Temple of Heracles-Melqart receives from Herodotus is simply because he is interested in the spread of the cults involving Heracles. His concern with the sanctuary is not a concern for prestige of architecture. For an Assyrian artist charged with representing the fall of an important foreign city before the onslaught of his king, the best-known temple from the conquered city, the temple of its chief deity would be a better emblem to use in his composition. It would stand a better chance of being recognized by a knowledgeable viewer.

Nothing of monumental Iron Age II sacred architecture survives from the Phoenician region. There is no way to connect Hiram the builder with any extant remains. The small shrine building from Kommos (fig. 72) on the south coast of Crete has been identified as a Phoenician shrine and probably represents the type of modest architecture that Phoenician sailors carried with them and introduced throughout the regions of the Mediterranean where they established a presence—and in some instances, colonies, at a later date. This modest structure, a single room, cannot be a reflection of the architecture being built in Tyre proper.

While there is no evidence for Phoenician settlements outside the Levantine region before the ninth century b.c.e., the temple remains at Kition and Paphos from Iron Age IIB may reflect some aspect of the reality of sacred buildings in the Phoenician region. Kition came under the control of Tyre in the ninth century b.c.e.

---

10. However, in Luckenbill's (1924: 27–31) translation of col. 2 of the Rassam Cylinder, Luli is identified as king of Sidon.

By the middle of the century, a new temple was built on the ruins of the Late Bronze Age Temple I in Area II (fig. 45; see also Karageorghis 1982: 123–24; Karageorghis and Webb n.d.: 11–12). This has been identified as a Temple to Astarte, but considering that the cult of Melqart-Heracles was an important feature of the religious life of later Kition and that Astarte may well have already shared Melqart's temple in Tyre, it is likely that from the start it was a temple that had associations with both deities. The Phoenician builders made use of the ashlar masonry surviving from the earlier temple that had been a feature of the last phase of Late Bronze and Iron Age I Cypriot architecture (Hadjisavvas 2003: 31–34). The ashlars were incorporated into the new fabric, and the plan of the new temple retained much of the plan of the older structure. However, what had been an open courtyard in the earlier design was now reconceived with double colonnades on either side of an open central corridor. The corridor and flanking porticoes followed the longitudinal axis of the building. The plan is aligned on more or less an east–west axis. The entrance was in the northeast corner. The holy of holies occupied the entire west side. Therefore, the movement through the porticoes and corridor was from east to west. Three doors penetrated the wall separating the colonnaded space and the holy of holies. The central door was at the west end of the corridor, and the side porticoes had secondary entrances into the most sacred space. Two large pillars seem to have stood flanking the main entrance from the corridor into the holy of holies, offering support to the notion for the pair of columns for the Temple of Melqart at Tyre, and between the pillars stood some type of offering table.

The temple at Kition offers a possible plan type that became associated with the cult of Melqart as it was first established at Tyre and then sent out as part of the colonial apparatus (Mierse 2004); no other temple type can be associated with any specific cult. Melqart was probably a cult promoted by Hiram and his successors, but according to the Esarhaddon and Baʿal treaty, he was not the main god of Tyre. Baʿal-Shamên occupied this position. It is more likely that his temple is shown on the Assyrian relief.

Solomon

Hiram I was a rebuilder of temples and crafty user of religious cults. His contemporary, Solomon, king of the newly formed state of Israel, was equally engaged in building, though only one religious structure was to concern him—the great temple in Jerusalem. Like Hiram, Solomon exists in the biblical record and in the references to his reign and building projects made by later historians, particularly Josephus. Nothing contemporary exists for certain. Solomon's building did not come out of nowhere. His actions completed a project first envisaged by his predecessor and father, David. His building of the temple was not very different from Hiram's destruction of the standing temples and then rebuilding them. In fact, Hiram was actively involved in the building programs of both David and Solomon.

The setting for Solomon's building program in Jerusalem has not been established archaeologically. The biblical account of David's taking of the city indicates that something existed on the site of what was to become the capital of the new kingdom of Israel. It was a Jebusite city, therefore a Late Bronze Age or transitional early Iron Age Canaanite city[11] of some type that had survived the upheavals of the demographic shifts of the two centuries since the arrival of the "Peoples of the Sea" and the Israelites themselves (Zwickel 1999: 14–17). However, little from the excavations in the city has revealed any of this early city. Kenyon and, later, Shiloh found evidence of pre–Iron Age occupation in the region east and south of today's "Old City" on a spur of land overlooking the Kidron Valley. Chalcolithic sherds from stratum 21 were the earliest sign of human presence, and there were possible traces of Early Bronze Age habitations and a Middle Bronze Age wall (Bahat and Hurvitz 1996: 286–306). Shiloh exposed a series of massive stepped walls in the lower strata of his Area G, and earlier, Kenyon unearthed fragments of retaining walls in her Area A. These are at the north end of the eastern slope of the City of David. More recently, Bahat and Hurvitz have combined the evidence from these two excavations and reconstructed a series of massive retaining walls using the evidence from Shiloh's and Kenyon's digs. In their reconstruction, the complex of walls was a massive box terrace designed to hold aloft a major structure. Both Kenyon and Shiloh argued that the ceramic evidence from these lower walls provided a Late Bronze Age date for the construction.

Tarler and Cahill have argued that Kenyon and, later, Shiloh misinterpreted the evidence, and in reality the constructions at this level were from the transitional thirteenth–twelfth centuries B.C.E. (Tarler and Cahill 1992: 55). Kenyon's and Shiloh's readings of the remains would allow for a Late Bronze Age structure of some size and impressiveness to have existed on the site now assumed to have later become the early Iron Age city of David and Solomon. This would mean that the site had a significant Canaanite architectural presence. Cahill and Tarler's dating would imply that the site did not take form until just before David's conquest. Either interpretation would allow for the massive retaining wall to be the support for the Jebusite stronghold where David lived after taking the city (2 Sam 5:9; Mazar and Mazar 1989: 40).

The only other archaeological material with possible Late Bronze Age associations came not from Jerusalem proper but from a nearby site. At Giloh, a village site to the southwest of Jerusalem, were the remains of a tower-like structure somewhat similar in construction to the stepped walls from Shiloh's and Kenyon's excavations (A. Mazar 1994a: 86–87). In Jerusalem proper, Barkay recovered items that he argued were the remains of a small Nineteenth-Dynasty Egyptian temple. None of these came from an archaeological context. They were loose finds—a fragment of a stele with hieroglyphic inscription, 2 Egyptian alabaster vessels, an Egyptian serpentine statuette,

11. Na'aman (1994: 239–43) identifies the Jebusites as one of the non-Canaanite peoples who migrated into the region of Canaan in the wake of the destructions of the twelfth century B.C.E.

an offering table, and lotus-shaped column capitals (Barkay 2000: 55). Of these, only the capitals and the offering table were architectural in nature; the rest were offerings, appropriate to a temple but not necessarily indicative of a temple. Barkay associated the items based on findspots and the Egyptian stylistic affiliations and proposed that a small Egyptian temple stood somewhere in Late Bronze Age Jerusalem, possibly servicing the needs of an Egyptian administrator and staff resident in the Canaanite city (Barkay 2000: 48–51). Amarna letter 287 mentions a Jerusalem garrison, but Barkay assigned a Nineteenth-Dynasty rather than an Eighteenth-Dynasty date to the temple because of its possible dedication to Seth, a deity popular in Nineteenth-Dynasty contexts and absent in the Eighteenth Dynasty (Barkay 2000: 57). Barkay's temple combined with Kenyon's and Shiloh's evidence for a massive substructure to support a Late Bronze Age structure may indicate that a Canaanite city of some prestige did stand at the site of the later early Iron Age city of Jerusalem.

There are five other letters in the corpus of the Amarna letters that are argued by some to refer to Jerusalem. The six letters were authored by a Canaanite prince, Abdi-Hepa (Abdi-Khepa), possibly the ruler of Late Bronze Age Jerusalem during the Eighteenth Dynasty.[12] Redford suggested that Abdi-Hepa was the child of a local Canaanite chief who had spent his youth in Egypt and was placed on the throne by Egyptian interests, possibly in violation of another son's prerogative. His letters placed emphasis on his allegiance to Egypt and the importance of the maintenance of the Egyptian garrison and administration in his city (Redford 1992: 270). The six Amarna letters and Barkay's Egyptian temple could be the evidence for a Late Bronze Age city somewhere in the vicinity of the later early Iron Age city, very possibly at the site of the City of David, where Kenyon and Shiloh have argued for evidence of Late Bronze Age monumental construction.

If Redford and Barkay were correct, then the Late Bronze Age city had a strong Egyptian presence. Throughout the Late Bronze Age, Egyptian pharaohs exercised varying degrees of control throughout the Canaanite region. Beth-shean played an important role in the Egyptian control of the Canaanite region and yielded temple remains that offer some idea of how sacred architecture in an Egyptian-controlled sphere developed in the Late Bronze Age. If Late Bronze Age Jerusalem was strongly Egyptianized, then it may have possessed similar features.

Steiner read the same evidence differently, arguing that the site of Late Bronze Age Jerusalem was not a town but an Egyptian estate, a baronial estate protecting the route from Beth-shean and providing the pharaoh with slaves (Steiner 1998: 28–32). An actual city did not appear until the late tenth or early ninth century B.C.E.—a view

---

12. The recent find in the fill from the area of the Iron Age II gate complex of a fragment of an Akkadian cuneiform document dated to the fourteenth century B.C.E. and written in court scribal style has been identified by some as coming from court archives, possibly supporting the existence of a Late Bronze Age city at Jerusalem (Shanks 2011: 42–43).

that is in opposition to the standard view that Jerusalem developed under David and Solomon in the early and mid-tenth century (Steiner 1998: 32). The lack of good archaeological evidence from Jerusalem dating to the Late Bronze Age and Iron Age I has been blamed partly on the topography of the site itself. The tendency of later builders was to scrape away all remains of earlier structures in order to reach bedrock on which to place the new buildings (Na'aman 1998: 44). Furthermore, the archaeological practice of keeping only select sherds from a dig site rather than the full collection has made it difficult, if not impossible, for later researchers to reconstruct respective quantities of pottery types (Cahill 1998: 35; Shanks 2000).

However, Shiloh's excavations showed (Shiloh 1985: 129–34) that an Iron Age II city did develop. By the eighth century, the city wall incorporated the possible earlier Jebusite region as well as the City of David, the Temple Mount, and a large western addition (Shanks 2000: 39–41). E. Mazar offered a tentative reconstruction of the chronology of the spread based on her work as well as the work of B. Mazar and Shiloh (see fig. 129; also see Mazar and Mazar 1989: 38–41). The Jebusite city of Iron Age I was limited to an area of about 9 acres, restricted by its placement on a spur of land surrounded by valleys. The city then spread north to the region known as the Ophel, a location already reinforced at its southern end by Kenyon and Shiloh's massive construction. Based on biblical accounts, for which no independent archaeological evidence exists, she posited that David, with the help of Hiram, built himself a palace, which Mazar argued was located at the southern end of the Ophel, perhaps incorporating the old Jebusite stronghold. The excavation works of Benjamin and later Eilot Mazar on the Ophel revealed a possible gatehouse (B. Mazar's building C). It has been recognized as a four-chamber structure with a main tower and secondary tower that overlooked the Kidron Valley, a design somewhat similar to that at Megiddo. It seems to date to the ninth century and probably provided access from the south to the palace-temple complex (Shanks 2011: 39–41: Mazar and Mazar 1989: 48–51). Bahat and Hurvitz offered a bit of refinement to Mazar's reading of the evidence. They agreed that the Ophel was the saddle that separated the Jebusite city from the later city to the north. They argued that it was filled in and leveled during the tenth century to allow for the old city and the new developments to the north to form a continuous whole. The older, Jebusite region yielded some ashlar blocks and a proto-Aeolic capital, possible evidence to support the notion that David's palace was in this area (Bahat and Hurvitz 1996: 293).

David may have intended to build a temple to house the ark. He did acquire the threshing floor from Araunah, the Jebusite (2 Sam 24:24; or the Jebusite named Ornan, 2 Chr 3:1; see Zwickel 1999: 31–33). The biblical descriptions provide no clarity about the location of this threshing floor. Because Araunah was identified as a Jebusite, perhaps the spot was within the confines of the old Jebusite city and not north, where the Temple Mount (Haram al-Sharif) later stood. The texts do not indicate that the purchase was for land on which to build a temple but, rather, to erect an altar. It is certainly not impossible that David intended to build a temple; later texts suggest that he did (1 Kgs 8:16–21; 2 Chr 6:41–42; Ps 132:8–10), but these texts are suspect and may be evidence of later manipulations of the David story (Meyers 1987: 358; Rupprecht 1977: 5–17).

The biblical tradition credits Solomon with building the temple, but nothing in the texts locates the temple in the city. 2 Chr 3:1 states that Solomon erected it on Mount Moriah over the threshing floor of Ornan, but this does not clarify the actual space in the urban setting. Later biblical references suggest that it was situated on a rise. Josiah's scribe needed to go up to the House of the Lord (2 Kgs 22:3–4), and in Jeremiah (26:10) court officials went up from the king's palace to the House of the Lord. It has long been assumed that the later position of Herod's temple must have been more or less consistent with the earlier temple of Solomon (Josephus, *J.W.* 15.184; Ritmeyer 1996: 48). One stretch of masonry forming the retaining wall of the present-day Temple Mount was identified by Laperrousaz as being a survival from the Solomonic constructions (Laperrousaz 1987: 34–45). At the base of the southwest corner, 35 m from the corner was a straight joint marking the spot where two different ashlar walls met but did not bond. The spot was usually considered evidence of Herod's extension to the platform of the Temple Mount. Laperrousaz argued that 10 courses of rough and irregular ashlar belonged to the older, Solomonic period of building. Ritmeyer (1992: 38), considering the same stretch of wall, read the rough bossed ashlar blocks as remnants of the Hasmonean work on the platform, a view earlier put forward by Mazar (B. Mazar 1985: 466). Of the actual temple and its dependencies, nothing survived on the Temple Mount, and therefore, the physical placement of the ancient structure cannot be determined with any type of certainty. Three popular accounts have tried to locate the temple by using the present-day topography of the Temple Mount. They all focused on the Dome of the Rock and argued that the Solomonic structure stood somewhere in the neighborhood (A. Kaufman 1983; Ritmeyer 1992: 24–45; 1996: 46–55; Jacobson 1999a; Zwickel 1999: 36–42).

Like the temples at Tell Ta'yinat, Carchemish, and Guzana, the temple built by Solomon was placed in some type of close association with his new palace (Busink 1970: 154–59). The biblical text makes clear that Solomon constructed a new palace along with the temple. The accounts of both building projects are interwoven. Based on the biblical descriptions, Solomon commissioned it as a temple-palace complex, with both buildings using prestigious materials and building techniques.

Nothing in the texts provides any information about the location of the palace in relationship to the temple, though it has long been recognized that the temple was initially serving more as a royal chapel than an independent entity (G. E. Wright 1944: 77). Waterman has gone further and argued that the side chambers of the temple served as the royal treasury (Waterman 1947: 161–63), which further stressed the connection between palace and temple and suggested physical proximity. A common placement has been on the southern edge of the Temple Mount, between the northern edge of the City of David and the temple proper. If the palace was located here, it fits the description of ascending to the temple from the palace suggested by 2 Kgs 22:3–4 and Jer 26:10 because there is a rise of about 70 m (Shanks 2011: 44–45). However, Ussishkin has proposed that the palace was actually to the north of the temple, where a more spacious area could accommodate the palace complex and remove it from the steady traffic headed from the City of David to the temple (Shanks 2011: 45). Ussishkin further maintains that the palace was the largest building that Solomon commissioned ,and its limited coverage in the biblical account reflects not its importance but the attitude of the later editor of the book of Kings (Ussishkin 1966b: 174–86).

1 Kings provides the names of several structures of the palace: "the house of the forest of Lebanon," "porch of pillars," "porch for the throne," and "the house for the pharaoh's daughter." There is also a reference to courtyards. The structure seems to have been a series of independent units or wings, probably arranged around courtyards. Ussishkin, using the then-recently-excavated Building 1723 at Megiddo that Yadin had dated to the Solomonic period as a guide, proposed a reconstruction of the palace of Solomon in Jerusalem. He argued that both buildings were based on the Syrian *bīt ḥilani* prototype (Ussishkin 1966b: 186). These associations have been more recently thrown into doubt by the revised dating of stratum VA–IVB at Megiddo, in which Building 1723 sits. While Yadin proposed a tenth-century date for the stratum, Ussishkin and Finkelstein have argued for a ninth-century occupation (Finkelstein 1996: 177–85). This change in date has prompted debate and outrage (Shanks 1998b: 57–61; A. Mazar 1997c). As with all debates about Late Bronze and early Iron Age Jerusalem, the lack of clearly recognizable and undisputed archaeological evidence from the problematic centuries makes it difficult to determine the merits of the arguments. Based on the evidence of Kenyon and Shiloh's massive structure, Mazar's ninth-century gatehouse, the long-standing tradition both biblical and nonbiblical for the existence of Solomon's temple, and the presence of good archaeological evidence for an expanded city by the mid-ninth century, it seems perverse not to accept that something was happening at the site of the City of David and the Temple Mount during the tenth and early ninth centuries. It is quite a different matter to go so far as to posit a major capital city, as some have done (Naʾaman 1997: 43–47).

Kingship and Temples in Neo-Hittite and Aramean Cities

One of the reasons that the first Tell Taʿyinat temple (Building II)[13] was easy to associate with Solomon's temple in Jerusalem was that it was built in a region in which

---

13. The second long-room temple at Tell Taʿyinat was only discovered in 2008. All earlier discussions of the temple of Solomon and its relationship to Tell Taʿyinat refer only to Building II.

temple-building and the politics of kingship had developed in a distinct pattern. The patron for the temples at Tell Taʿyinat cannot be determined, but the temples are clearly elements in a larger architectural program that includes the *bīt ḫilani* palace type complex. While the specifics of the Tell Taʿyinat temple commissions has eluded investigators, this is not the case for the Temple of the Storm God at Carchemish or the temple-palace complex at Guzana. In both of these instances, the nature of the political commission can be somewhat reconstructed.

Katuwas and Carchemish

The Temple of the Storm God was an architectural element set into a large sculptural ensemble in the lower palace area. This formed the region at the southeastern foot of the acropolis (fig. 122). The temple compound, a walled-off area, was directly to the southwest of the grand staircase that led into the lower palace proper, which rose on a series of terraces up the side of the acropolis to the upper palace, which was largely destroyed by Hellenistic- and Roman-period settlements on the site (Woolley 1952: 157–58). The actual entrance to the temple compound was on the south wall, opposite the King's Gate and the Herald's Wall. The temple with its precinct was located immediately west of the grand staircase. The compound's east wall formed part of the architecture of the staircase. Joining the exterior south and east compound walls to the staircase was a continuous sculpted frieze of figures, which shows that the temple compound was conceived as an element in the palace design. The find of a basalt stele in the small triangular area behind the shrine proper and the north wall of the compound, which carried an inscription referring to the "Great King" and a winged disk carved in relief (Woolley 1952: 167), furthers the association between palace and temple.

The identity of the king who was actually responsible for the commission has been much debated. The basalt jambs of the doorway into the shrine itself bore inscriptions by King Katuwas. Woolley argued that this was the monarch responsible for the erection of the first version of the King's Gate (Woolley 1952: 169). An architectural dialogue among the palace, including the temple compound, and the opposite wall (the Herald's Wall) and the King's Gate did seem reasonable, considering that there appeared to be carefully controlled movement. The formal corridor that entered from the Water Gate to the east was narrow, probably defined by the lower terrace of the palace and the continuation of the Herald's Wall. Any traffic entering this region of the town would have been funneled into the large triangular plaza defined by the northwest bend of the palace, the southwest turn of the east wall of the temple compound, and the southwest movement of the Herald's Wall. This was the plaza from which the grand staircase moved up to the upper acropolis. At its widest, the plaza was ca. 63 m. This same pattern of constriction and opening was continued to the west so that the southeast corner of the temple complex came closer to the Herald's Wall, and then on the opposite side, the space opened up again so that the entrance to the temple compound and the King's Gate formed a second, parallel triangular plaza region that complemented the plaza in front of the grand staircase. Woolley described this as the ceremonial center of town (Woolley 1952: 158).

However, Woolley believed that the temple for which Katuwas was responsible was a redesign of an earlier compound, a structure dating to the Late Bronze Age Hittite period. It was the Hittite king that was being referred to on the basalt stele (Woolley 1952: 170). However, Woolley's dates, especially those based on stylistic considerations, were dismissed by most scholars who considered the material (Mallowan 1972: 63).

Hawkins (1972: 96) argued that Suhis II, Katuwas's father, was responsible for the building and decorating of the Long Wall, though he did not debate the evidence of the Katuwas inscriptions for the date of the temple proper. Hawkins worked with the epigraphic evidence, and Mallowan supported his view by use of the stylistic evidence from the reliefs themselves (Mallowan 1972: 65). Therefore, Hawkins and Mallowan dated the Long Wall to about 890 B.C.E. and the temple to around 880 B.C.E. These dates were substantially earlier than those proffered by Akurgal, who argued that certain stylistic features in the treatment of the chariots and horses on the Long Wall could only be explained as the influence of Assyrian reliefs and therefore indicated a date in the middle eighth century B.C.E. (Akurgal 1966: 109) for the Long Wall. However, he separated Katuwas from the Long Wall project. Akurgal dated the king to as early as 850 or as late as 700, based on stylistic elements in the treatment of his image on a different relief (Akurgal 1961: pl. 118). Frankfort was undecided on the actual date for Katuwas (Frankfort 1985: 403 n. 84).

Ussishkin offered a compromise by suggesting that the composition of the Long Wall was not the work of a single ruler but, rather, was two separate compositions, which he based on the archaeological evidence of the wall itself. He pointed out that the Long Wall did not fit the pattern for normal structures with orthostats. Instead of a structure that was supported by the walls—so that the orthostats became an element in the structure itself—the Long Wall was a self-supporting wall, not part of a building. As such, it was not difficult to add or change the orthostat composition. He thought that the Long Wall actually divided into northern and southern portions discernible from differences in the actual construction of the wall and in the treatment of the composition of the relief program itself. The southern section was what formed the exterior east wall of the temple compound, and Ussishkin argued that this section could have been erected by Katuwas at the time that he either built or refurbished the temple, though there are also reasons to favor Sangara, who succeeded Katuwas (Ussishkin 1976: 105–11).

Although Ussishkin was certain that the composition of the Long Wall was not unified, in reality, it seems quite unified. The reliefs of the northern portion, those flanking the grand staircase, were of the gods, and the Storm God took pride of place. This was followed by the nude goddess and the seated figure of a queen, identified in the accompanying inscription as Watis, possibly the wife of Suhis II (Hawkins 1972: 94–97) or Sangara's queen (Ussishkin 1976:107). This was not Katuwas's queen, who was identified in an inscription as Ana in A11a at the north end of the Long Wall Procession. The war chariots trampling the enemy came next, and finally the foot soldiers arrived (Mallowan 1972: 69). The presence of the Storm God at the inception of the procession—at its northern end, and flanking the grand staircase headed up to the palace—locked together the temple compound and the tutelary deity. Inscription A1a clearly associated the Storm God of Carchemish, Tarhundas, with military victory and the ruler as the active agent for the victory; and lines 3–4 seem actually to describe part of the procession program (Hawkins 1972: 88–94). Therefore, the iconography that incorporated the god within the procession of chariots and foot soldiers, all headed in the direction of the acropolis palace seems perfectly unified.

Whether Katuwas is considered to be the prime designer of the entire complex of temple compound and sculptural program or the second member in the dynasty responsible for the completion of the project, and whether the temple is treated as his conception or his redesign of an older compound (Woolley 1952: 167), it seems obvious that Katuwas was a ruler who used architecture and sculpture as part of his public presentation. Twice in inscriptions, he associated himself with the Temple to the Storm God—once on the inscription on the jambs of the temple door (A2a, A3a), in which he claimed to have founded the temple, and then in A11a, in which he claimed to have built the Temple of the Storm God of the Lions. Barnett assumed that the Temple of the Storm God of the Lions was what existed in the temple compound (Woolley 1952: 260). Elsewhere, in inscriptions A23 and A20a—both of which came from the door jambs on the Grand Staircase that Hawkins read as forming a single text—Katuwas identified himself as he who reestablished the Goddess Kupapa as great queen of Carchemish. Somewhere else in the city, there must be another temple that Katuwas rebuilt or refurbished (Hawkins 1972: 102–3).

Hawkins has no candidate for this other temple, though there was a *ḥilani* structure that Woolley discovered on the south side of the main road to the Water Gate (fig. 130). This was a square structure, 18 m per side, with a thick lower wall on the east side and evidence of an internal staircase. It was a two-story affair. It had a single inner chamber approached through a porch flanked by 2 columns *in antis*—hence, its appellation, the *ḥilani*. Woolley reported that the stratigraphy of the *ḥilani* region was confusing, with evidence of older structural material below the *ḥilani* and much later building activity above it. He could not date the specific time span for the operation of the *ḥilani* other than to assume that it was in operation contemporaneously with the Water Gate Road, onto which it opened, and which was destroyed in the final destruction of Carchemish by the Assyrians, 604 B.C.E. It was also unclear to Woolley how the Water Gate and the Water Gate Road connected with the Herald's Wall and the lower palace region. Again, this was due to disruptions to the stratigraphy resulting from the later Roman building in the region.

However, the structure must have been impressive. The *ḫilani* was set back about 1 m from the edge of the underlying platform. The walls had been sheathed in ortho-stats. Woolley reconstructed the building as possessing a façade of 2 thick piers fram-ing 2 large columns set within a deep porch. The door to the interior chamber was large, with a width of 4 m, and was placed in the center of the design. The entryway was paved with large, hard, white limestone slabs. The interior corridor was paved in basalt slabs that are polished by use. The exceptional width of the doorway suggested to Woolley that there had been some type of internal supports to hold up the lintel. He reconstructed these as piers set on sculpted bases. The actual chamber was 14 m × 6.50 m, and within it, buried up to its rim, was a krater containing animal bones and pottery fragments. Outside the building was found a fragment of a relief with an ithyphallic, bull-legged figure in horned headdress and broad belt, grasping a tree. Nearby was a second sculpture, a headless basalt statue of an enthroned figure, wear-ing a cloak and ankle-length undergarment, seated with hands resting on its knees. A fragmentary statue of a basalt lion was found in the vicinity. There was also a basalt offering table (Woolley 1952: 176–81).

Woolley thought that the building must have served some type of ritual function for the king (Woolley 1952: 184). It occupied its own small precinct and was not easy to see. The precinct could never have held many people, yet it was near the ceremo-nial region of the lower palace defined by the Grand Staircase and Herald's Wall. It could have served as a scene for private royal rituals. Nothing in the material found or in the building itself identified it as a temple, much less the temple of Kupapa, but the long history of rebuilding on the site, the unusual design, and the private nature of the temple and precinct—all these factors would indicate that it was suitable as a sanctuary for the goddess associated with royal rule at Carchemish and not as a mili-tary display. If it did function with the Grand Staircase, Long Wall, Herald's Wall, and Storm God's Temple compound, then the whole region that opened up at the foot of the staircase could have been used for large-scale processional rituals linking the lower city with the acropolis palace.

While there is no agreement about the date of Katuwas's reign, which is pos-ited within the range of a century, there is no debate that the temple was his work. Whether the temple compound directly relates to the erection of the Long Wall relief sculpture or whether it is something that needs to be treated separately is also not generally agreed on by scholars. On the other hand, there is no doubt that Katuwas did more than merely build the temple. There is a relief with his image (Mallowan 1972: 67–68; Akurgal 1961: 130, pl. 118). He may or may not have commissioned some of the Long Wall sculpture, though for Hawkins, his temple project must be seen as an element associated with his father's patronage of the Long Wall, which means that the two items are elements in a dynastic art program (Hawkins 1972: 96). If one accepts the maximum view of Katuwas, he was a major builder, a user of art within some type of dynastic program. The works would include the relief image of him, a portion of the Long Wall sculpture, and the temple compound. This is a fairly massive program.

Kapara and Guzana

The city of Guzana was the capital of the Aramean Kingdom of Bit Bahiani. The region it controlled, the Khabur Plain, was a fertile zone with a long history of occupation. The Chalcolithic settlement gave its name to a cultural phase. The Early Bronze Age site of Tell Brak is not too distant from Guzana, and during the Late Bronze Age, the region was under Hurrian control (Elsen and Novak 1994: 117). However, by the last period of the Late Bronze Age and certainly through Iron Age I and II, the pressure from the westward expansion of the Neo-Assyrian Empire was first felt here. The Khabur region formed the frontier zone between the Neo-Hittite and Aramean city-states of Iron Age II and the Assyrians. At some point during Iron Age II, King Hadiami engaged in some major building at his capital of Guzana. No structure that survives has been attributed to him, but a number of reliefs that had originally been intended for a temple to the Storm God were reused by Hadiami's son, Kapara, who had them inscribed "Kapara, son of Hadiami." The reliefs were reused as elements in the exterior decoration of the massive building identified as a temple-palace that occupies the south side of the upper citadel, and it is the standard view that this structure was commissioned by Kapara (Langenegger et al. 1950: 25).

As is the case with all the Iron Age II monarchs, there is no agreement regarding the date of Kapara's reign. The Assyrian annals make clear that the Khabur region passed into Assyrian control under Adad-Nirari III in 808 B.C.E., and Šalmanassar III claimed that this region collapsed during his Syrian campaigns of 853 B.C.E. (Dion 2002: 56). Assuming that the palace predated the Assyrian annexation of the area, dates for Kapara and for the temple-palace have ranged from Albright's contention that Kapara ruled in the tenth century; to Frankfort's placement of him in the second half of the ninth century (therefore, not long before the Assyrian arrival); to Lipiński (2000: 132), who has dated him to around 830 B.C.E.; to Akurgal, who has argued for a date in the last third of the eighth century, after the Assyrian advance into the region.[14] Both Albright and Akurgal are in agreement that the sculpture associated with the great temple-palace at Guzana shows no strong evidence of Assyrian stylistic influence (Albright 1956a: 76; Akurgal 1966: 111–15). However, Akurgal does note that the kings at Guzana used Assyrian script and perhaps spoke the language. Moreover, he sees Assyrian elements in the specifics of costume and coiffure as revealed on some

---

14. E. Herzfeld, who was the first systematically to study the sculpture from the site, argued for a tripartite chronological division of the material, with the earliest pieces dating to the third millennium B.C.E. (Early Bronze Age). This view is not accepted by any other students of the material (Herzfeld 1934).

of the reliefs, which could well argue for a strong Assyrianizing element in the court life at Guzana.

Albright reads the evidence quite differently. The Assyrian textual evidence shows that the Khabur region was already under strong Assyrian control by the early ninth century. Adad-nirari II accepted the submission of Guzana sometime between 911 and 891 B.C.E. This westward expansion continued under Tukulti-Ninurta II and Assur-nasirpal II in the first half of the ninth century. Against this backdrop of unrelenting Assyrian aggressiveness, it seems highly unlikely that a local vassal prince would have erected a major temple-palace complex, especially a structure that was so lacking in Assyrian design features. Albright has therefore argued that Kapara's temple-palace must date to the second half of the tenth century, just before the major expansion but at a point when Assyrian prominence was beginning to be felt in the region (Albright 1956a: 84–85)—the view opposite Akurgal's. Below the level of the terrace of the temple-palace, a tomb was discovered. This was a carefully constructed underground chamber that may predate the terrace proper. The small finds inside—a small, semioval gold plaque, perhaps part of a headdress, and 2 Phrygian-style bronze vessels—have all been dated to the last third of the eighth century B.C.E. Using this as a datum point, Akurgal argued that the temple-palace that incorporated the tomb must therefore date to the same period. Kapara and his construction are late eighth century B.C.E. However, the find from the tomb need not date the building of the structure, which may have been constructed earlier and reused. Since a portion of the sculpted reliefs for the exterior decoration of the terrace are identified by inscriptions as belonging to another structure, these, Akurgal maintained, were from an earlier building dating to the middle of the eighth century (Akurgal 1966: 117–19).

Frankfort has argued for a date for Kapara and the temple-palace complex in between Albright's and Akurgal's dates. As is the case with Akurgal's dating, Frankfort's date is based on stylistic assessments of the reliefs and freestanding sculptures associated with the temple-palace. While Frankfort sees strong Mesopotamian influences in the sculptures, he considers them to have entered mainly by means of portable arts. The sculptures represent reinterpretations of elements explored in the minor arts in Mesopotamia and Assyria but not in sculpted forms. This leads him to conclude that the sculptures for the temple-palace could not have been created after Assyria took direct control of the region, with the establishment of an Assyrian residence for the governor in 808 B.C.E. It was only after this political pattern was repeated throughout the North Syrian region that the local princes begin to commission sculptural programs that reflected what was happening in sculpture in Assyria proper. The reliance on imagery that resulted from looking at ivories and similar items indicates that the temple-palace at Guzana predated this shift (Frankfort 1985 297).

The actual design of the temple-palace has features that reveal it to be related to other North Syrian structures. Its moveable bronze hearth placed in the main room behind the portico is not unlike the hearth found in the Upper Palace at Zincirli. The format of the portico that leads into a large rectangular room that parallels the throne room behind, both aligned to the façade, is a distinct feature of North Syrian palace architecture found at Zincirli and the Tell Taʿyinat palace next to the temples as well as the Guzana temple-palace. The lost upper palace at Carchemish may well have followed the same design. This plan may have an Assyrian version, though in the posited Assyrian plan, there is no architecturally distinct portico, and the first room entered is the throne room—hence, the most important space (Frankfort 1985: 282–89).

Like the program at Carchemish, the structure at Guzana seems to have been a royal project, intended to serve the needs of the palace itself, although the space created and decorated was the public sector. The sculpture and architecture were mixed. This combination was also found at the North Syrian site of Zincirli. However, at both Zincirli and Carchemish, there is no real integration of the sculpture and architecture. The relief-carved orthostats decorated freestanding walls that served to direct traffic and probably designated important spaces in the urban plan.

At Guzana, the sculptural program is much more an element in the full architectural display. The gate that designates the entrance to the upper citadel is flanked by relief sculptures of scorpion-men that verge on three-dimensional works. The front of the lower terrace on which the temple-palace stands is decorated with large reliefs that were probably cut for the structure, while the back side of the temple-palace that looks out over the lower city is decorated with the reused relief slabs arranged in an alternating pattern of black basalt and reddish limestone. The use of the reliefs is not unique at all, and the lack of coherence in the arrangement of slabs suggests that the design had no great significance; this is quite different from the more-thoughtful structuring of the slabs at Carchemish. However, it is the employment of freestanding, three-dimensional sculpture in the program that really sets Guzana and Kapara's temple-palace apart.

The portico architrave is held up by 3 statues, each over 3 m in height (fig. 39). Each stands on an animal that is 1-1/2 m high. This is a monumental composition not equaled by surviving designs anywhere else in the North Syrian region. The figures are clearly human; none carries or wears attributes of divinities. The inscriptions that each statue carries also make no reference to gods. All this has led to the suggestion that they could be representatives of the ruling family (Frankfort 1985: 290–91). Larger-than-life-size statues of rulers are known from Zincirli and Malatya, and there is a large relief of Katuwas at Carchemish. Portraits of rulers were not unheard of in the North Syrian cities, but if this is a correct identification for the figures at Guzana, then they have assumed a much more monumental aspect. The arrangement of 2 men standing atop lions flanking a woman standing on a bull in the middle, if portraits, may be of Kapara, his father Hadiami (Hadiânu), and the latter's wife. Among the inscriptions that Kapara left are those in which he claims to have surpassed his father and grandfather in achievements (Albright 1956a: 81–82). Since these identify the palace as belonging to Kapara, then the association must be with building projects. This competitive quality seems to be found in many of these Iron Age II building projects. Hiram destroys so that he can rebuild. Solomon undertakes what David could not. Katuwas probably finishes what his father started, and Kapara baldly states that he is more capable than his father or grandfather.

The design of Guzana was different from the design at Carchemish in that the program did not reveal itself until one had already entered a restricted region. But the two programs shared in common their use of sculpture and architecture to define a public space that must have served the royal needs for display. The Guzana project was more involved than what survived of the Carchemish, since it incorporated both relief and three-dimensional sculptures and arranged them in three distinct areas: (1) fully exposed decorative relief slabs and one standing statue of a bird on a column; (2) transitional, fully articulated statues and reliefs that occupy the portico space; and (3) sculpture fully inside the temple-palace. This was the most sophisticated of any sculpture-architecture combination known from the Iron Age II Levantine contexts.

Kingdoms of Transjordan

The Transjordan region has not provided connections between structures and named rulers. Only at Amman on the citadel have traces of a massive structure been found, but these cannot be connected with the reigns of Sanib or Yeraḥʾazar or with the cult of Milkom. However, the Ammon citadel has also yielded 4 carved-stone, double-faced female caryatid heads with mortise holes drilled in the tops and bottoms (Prag 1989: 69–70).[15] They were found reused in a Hellenistic drain but have been dated to the eighth–seventh century B.C.E. The size of these elements ranges from 26 cm to 30 cm, and probably the heads formed architectural features somewhat analogous to the famous "Woman at the window" ivories (fig. 117). Whether the heads were placed individually above a row of palm-tree volute capitals of the type found at Ramat Rahel, outside Jerusalem—which probably decorated the balustrade of the upper story of the royal palace (fig. 116 B)[16] to form a repeated pattern of narrow openings—or the heads themselves were used in place of capitals cannot be determined (Prag 1987: 122–27). However, they do suggest that by the eighth century B.C.E. there was some type of major structure on the Amman Citadel that had decorative stonework. The palm-tree volute capitals from Ramat Rahel were found in a Stratum Vb building of the late eighth or early seventh century B.C.E. (Lipschits et al. 2011: 19–21) that has been identified as a palace, and they have been restored as the balustrade for a

---

15. Archaeological Museum, Amman, Inv. J11689.
16. Israel Museum, IAA 1964–87; See also the home page for the Ramat Rahel Archaeological Project–Archaeology of the Site, http://www.tau.ac.il/~rmtrachl/archaeology of site.htm.

window following the pattern of the ivories. In addition, a carved relief with the same pattern of capitals forming a balustrade was found in a cave at Ramat Rahel and is not dissimilar from reliefs from funerary complexes on Cyprus (Shiloh 1985: 135–39). The stone capitals from Ramat Rahel and the stone caryatid heads from the Amman Citadel did not come from tombs; they were from built structures that stood on the surface. The Amman heads were most likely from a palace structure like the Ramat Rahel capitals, perhaps a palace associated with the temple.

Rulers, Temples, and Politics

The temples that remain from Guzana and Carchemish were clearly parts of larger architectural ensembles. The temples were in some way associated with palaces. This was even more true with the temples at Tell Taʿyinat. The palace predated the temple (Building II) and probably the newly excavated temple, but the temples were appended to the larger palace grouping. They were clearly not the most important buildings, since they could not be accessed directly from the palace and actually sat behind the palace court and second structure grouping. However, the shared construction techniques and the close physical proximity made it obvious that this was a temple-palace complex. A similar arrangement may have existed on the acropolis at Hamath, where the royal enclosure for a Neo-Hittite king was excavated in level E (Ussishkin 1966a: 104–10). The same was made quite clear in the narrative of the building of Solomon's temple. The description of the temple was interrupted by the description of the palace complex, of which it was one element.

There were Late Bronze Age precedents for this physical association of temple to palace. This was not, however, the Late Bronze Age norm. Temples at most Late Bronze Age sites throughout the Levantine region were independent entities. Kings may well have been expected to play roles within the ritual life of temples, but the structures were not features in palace compounds. Many of the great Late Bronze Age temples—those at the Hittite capital at Hattuša, at Emar, Ugarit, Megiddo, Hazor, and and Lachish—all stood as autonomous architectural features in the urban landscape. The massive royal temples of Iron Age II were often integrated into larger ensembles.

The question of Jerusalem in the tenth century now enters into the picture. The literary description of Jerusalem during the reigns of David and Solomon provides some of the most complete information about Iron Age II urban development, but the description cannot be sustained by the archaeological evidence at Jerusalem proper. On the other hand, a number of sites throughout Israel have been argued to evidence major building projects that can be dated to ca. 1000 B.C.E. and that show a tendency toward a standardization of forms, suggesting that a centralized power was directing development (Dever 1982: 286). The buildings included in this list are possible palaces at Megiddo; gateways at Megiddo, Hazor, and Gezer; and casemate walls at Megiddo, Hazor, Gezer, Tell Beit-Mirsim, Beth-Shemesh, and Tell Qasile (Dever 1982: 289–95).

Recently these associations have been questioned by the redating of the Megiddo material to the ninth century B.C.E. (Finkelstein 1996: 177–87). The issue is of some importance in determining possible cultural forces. The traditional biblical view treats Jerusalem and its development during the United Monarchy as the major cultural force in the Levant during the tenth century B.C.E., Iron Age IIA. If in reality Jerusalem was but a minor place during the century, then it could hardly have influenced the developments elsewhere in the Levantine region.

The issue then becomes how to understand the role of Solomon's temple. Bright (1981: 217–18) has argued that the temple must be understood as just one of several projects undertaken by Solomon throughout the kingdom. The view is based on accepting that the various buildings dated to the tenth century B.C.E. are indeed products of the Solomonic period. In Bright's view, the temple was not a special feature. Meyers has proposed an opposing view (C. Meyers 1987: 357–76). For her, the temple was a major element in Solomon's political propaganda. It may well have been planned initially by David, to be finished by his son, which was a statement of dynastic succession; a similar situation obtained at both Guzana and Carchemish. As the earthly home of a god, the temple was a key building that a king might well be expected to erect. Moreover, in Iron Age II settings, these new temples were jealously guarded because kings incorporated them into the palace grounds. To the known list can probably be added the Amman Citadel and the temple and palace at Hamath, which may well have been the capital of a Syrian kingdom of the same name (Ikeda 1979: 82). In this regard, temple-building with royal connections took on a form quite different from what can be seen in the Late Bronze Age. In Egyptian and Hittite contexts, the main temples operated physically independent from the palace. The same was true for the two principal temples in Ugarit and the temples at Emar. This common Late Bronze Age pattern can be seen earlier in Middle Bronze Age settings at Ebla, Shechem, and Megiddo. The tradition was broken in Iron Age II with the emergence of the palace-temple compound as a common urban feature. At the same time, there were nonroyal sanctuaries also being built.

The only information on how these temples may have been constructed comes once again from the biblical accounts of the building of Solomon's temple. Forced labor of some type was used, though whether Israelite or non-Israelite is left ambiguous.[17] Soggin notes that the use of the forced labor of conquered people was enjoined on rulers in Deut 20:11 (Soggin 1982: 266). Forced labor pools drawn from peoples in conquered territories may have been a device used by all the Levantine rulers, though only for Israel is there any suggestion that these sorts of project extended beyond the immediate confines of the capital city.

---

17. 1 Kgs 5:13–14 mentions generic forced labor. 2 Chr 2:17–19 describes forced labor required of resident foreigners in Israel. 1 Kgs 9:15–22 and 2 Chr 8:8–10 make clear that forced labor was imposed on conquered peoples.

How does not answer why. The royal temples break with the Late Bronze Age tradition and point to something new that was developing in the region in Iron Age II. The Late Bronze Age political reality was quite different from what emerged in Iron Age II. Where there had been a number of independent, rival city-states sandwiched between the powerful empires of the Hittites to the north and the Egyptians to the south, the Iron Age II *realpolitik* was one of independent territorially based states vying with one another for the control of land, trade routes, and cities. Pockets of conquered peoples formed a new feature of the landscape. The city-state template continued to operate along the Phoenician coast and in the Philistine area. However, the Phoenician city of Tyre was coming to control the other cities by engaging in some type of expansion on the mainland as well as out into the Mediterranean (Boyes 2012: 41). The Philistine cities had come together in Iron Age I as a federation: the Pentapolis. It is against the backdrop of these emerging territorial kingdoms that Meyers explains the role of Solomon's temple, a structure erected to benefit both the Israelite and the subjected populations. It was a royal vehicle to communicate to the widest possible audience the authoritative presence of the ruler who had built it (Meyers 1987: 364). A similar situation may have existed for the temples at Amman and the royal cities of Syria. Where there is epigraphic material to flesh out the picture, the dynastic connections with the temples are patently clear. These were royal temple-palace complexes with dynastic associations, very likely constructed with forced labor supplied by conquered peoples, and this may have been the pattern for all of the royal architectural ensembles in Iron Age II contexts of the Levant. It may be possible to see David as the initiator of the process when he first purchased the threshing floor from Araunah and erected an altar in his newly conquered capital city (Ahlström 1961: 115). The whole story may have much deeper significance, for it has been suggested that Araunah was actually the old, defeated Jebusite king, in which case, David's action is even more provocative (Ahlström 1961: 117). If the text of 2 Chronicles is followed instead of 1 Kings, then the nature of the dynastic expropriation becomes even more dramatic. Solomon builds his temple on the threshing floor that had been the property of the old Jebusite king (Ornan in Chronicles). The act of building the temple becomes the final act of erasing all traces of the prior monarch.

If one accepts the traditional biblical chronology augmented with the epigraphic material from Syria and Josephus's texts, then a picture can be constructed of the royal temple-building process in the Levant at the beginning of Iron Age II. Hiram I became king of Tyre by succeeding his father, and he undertook major building projects in Tyre. Solomon, in a similar pattern, took the throne from his father and pursued a program of building that included both the capital and significant cities in the newly formed kingdom of Israel. Late in the tenth century B.C.E., the southern Levant was assaulted by a newly revived Egypt led by Shishak (ca. 925 B.C.E.). While it appears that Judah and Israel suffered most in this attack, the Pharaoh's passage up the Jordan

Valley would have caused some degree of chaos to the emerging states of Ammon and
Moab (B. Mazar 1957: 57–66). During this same period, the aggressive movement of
Assyria into northern Syria was halted and pushed back as the Aramean migration
into the region became much more pronounced (B. Mazar 1962: 98–120). By the late
tenth century B.C.E., the North Syrian capital cities of Carchemish and Guzana witnessed a developmental pattern similar to what had taken place a generation earlier
in Phoenicia and Israel. Katuwas assumed power at Carchemish and completed and
perhaps expanded construction projects begun by his father. Kapara did much the
same at Guzana.

In each of these cases, dynastic succession and building were tied together, and
the commissioning of temples clearly played a significant role. The temple of Solomon
has generated the most abundant literature, discussing the political role of the temple
in the setting of an emerging dynastically structured monarchic Iron Age II kingdom.
It is certainly true that rulers building temples and participating in state rituals associated with the temples were nothing new. This practice was a feature of imperial ritual
in Late Bronze Age New Kingdom Egypt and the Hittite Empire, and even the local
Late Bronze Age Canaanite rulers at Ugarit and Emar followed similar protocol to
judge from the surviving textual evidence. But what does seem new in Iron Age IIA is
the strong dynastic affiliations between some sanctuaries and ruling houses. Equally
significant is the appearance of either new gods or gods of lesser importance who were
now pushed into prime positions. Melqart becomes the god who directs Tyre's expansion. At Damascus, Hadad, whose temple is probably under the Roman Temple to Ju-
piter Damascinus, which is covered partly by the Ummayad mosque, is the principal
deity of the Kingdom of Aram and is tied to the royal family (B. Mazar 1962: 106–11).
A similar situation is apparent with Milkom at Ammon. The best known is Yahweh in
Jerusalem and his association with the ruling House of David.

While the biblical text is suspect, it is not impossible that it supplies some guidance in understanding how rulers were using these new gods and their sanctuaries.
Interestingly, in all these cases, it is not the first generation of rulers who are responsible for what survives. It is not until at least the second generation, if not beyond, that
the new cult, the security of rule, and the building of the sanctuary come together.
The biblical treatment of David describes his connections with Jerusalem. He captures
the city, which was outside of the area of Canaan that had already been distributed to
the Israelite tribes, and he makes this neutral city his capital. In doing this, he aban-
dons his birthplace, Hebron. Then he has the ark moved from Shiloh to Jerusalem,
effectively relocating the cultic center for the tribal federation (Eissfeldt 1957: 138–47).
Bringing the ark to Jerusalem only has great meaning if the ark had a supratribal cult
status—a view that is not universally accepted (van der Toorn and Houtman 1994:
209–31). David's act of building an altar to Yahweh on the threshing floor of Araunah
has been interpreted by several scholars as an act intended to neutralize and lay claim

to the older Jebusite royal cultic area (Rupprecht 1977: 5–17; Ahlström 1961: 113–16). David does build a palace but is never able to construct a temple, though this may have been his intention (Meyers 1987: 365). The construction of the sanctuary falls to Solomon, who erects the temple as an element in the larger compound that includes his palace, and the original plan may have been for the temple to serve as a palace chapel rather than as a public sanctuary.

This pattern does seem to be repeated. Katuwas at Carchemish was responsible for the Temple to the Storm God and probably a portion of the great frieze on the Long Wall and the Grand Staircase. The reigns of Katuwas and Kapara are probably only one generation after the reigns of Hiram I and Solomon. The building programs with their sculptural programs can be considered alongside that of Solomon. Kapara is the third generation of his family to rule at Guzana; he cites his grandfather and father, and he too is forging a kingdom out of a tribal federation. The architectural ensemble at his capital is the physical manifestation of the new order. Like the description of Solomon's temple and like the actual temple remains at ʿAin Dara, elements of the structure are large—overwhelming in fact—especially the freestanding sculpture of the 3 figures and the bird of prey that stand separate on the terrace in front of the entrance to the *bīt ḫilani*. In the remains of Guzana and ʿAin Dara, and in the description of the temple of Solomon, there is an emphasis on grandeur of scale suggesting a setting appropriate for a divinity (Bloch-Smith 1994: 18–31). The great barefoot prints on the stone treads leading into the holy of holies (fig. 9)at ʿAin Dara, about 1 m in length, would posit a God who stood perhaps 20+ m tall (Stager 2000: 44), exhibiting what Ezekiel calls the *kāvôd* (radiant glory) of Yahweh (Ezek 9:3, 10:18). So in this respect, the ʿAin Dara and the Israelite temples share the notion of a god residing whose presence is overwhelming (Hurowitz 2011: 54). Maybe something similar was operating at Guzana with its grand statues. The setting at Carchemish is slightly different. The scale of the buildings and the sculpture is not as overwhelming, though the quantity of relief sculpture is impressive. However, the gods are included among the figures that march in the great procession, so divinity interacts with the king in the same space, recalling the pattern at the Late Bronze Age Hittite sanctuary at Yazılıkaya and the surviving relief from the Iron Age I temple on the Aleppo Citadel.

The focus on new divinities associated with new dynasties was a distinguishing feature of several of the Iron Age IIA political entities that came into being. In the cases of the Israelites, the peoples of the Transjordan, and the Arameans, these political changes marked a significant social shift from nomadic to sedentary, territorial lifestyle. In the areas where these peoples settled, older populations had to be absorbed or removed. The situation was different in the Phoenician and Neo-Hittite areas, where the new political structures derived from the same populations. There may have been some demographic disruption, some new migrants who had to be incorporated into the surviving Late Bronze Age populations, but the political reality of

Iron Age II does not indicate a demographic change to the region. It is therefore not surprising that the older gods still thrived, even as new gods did appear. This is not to say that the old Late Bronze Age model was operating unchanged and unmodified. Tyre under Hiram I became a territorial force with claims to lands stretching inland and along the coast. The new god, Melqart, was closely aligned with the royal house. In fact, it is reasonable to classify all the Iron Age II states in the Levant as secondary states. None had the history of long internal development to be found in Egypt or even Mesopotamia (Master 2001: 124–25 and n. 33). Several of the Iron Age II monarchies represented relatively recent shifts from nomadic chiefdoms to lineage-based dynastic monarchies, and the shift happened quite quickly, over the century between the lull in Assyrian aggressiveness and the beginning of the resurgence of Egypt followed by Assyria.

Tadmor has argued that over the first two centuries of Iron Age II, when the monarchy was established and passed first through the dynastic line of the United Monarchy and then the lines of the Divided Monarchy, structures were developed and put in place that prevented any return to nonmonarchic, tribal self-governance (H. Tadmor 1982: 239–57). While Tadmor's concern is with Israel, much the same process must have been ongoing throughout the Levantine region. One of the concepts that may have been merging with the new monarchies was the notion of the king's righteousness as the mirror image of the god's righteousness. In this manner, the new kings could be subsumed within the cosmic order that battles chaos (Brueggemann 1971: 317–32). This notion of the king as one of tools being used by divine forces in the fight against chaos supports Stager's suggestion that the temple of Solomon and the city of Jerusalem are a manifestation of Eden. The temple of Solomon and the new city become part of a mythic topography (Stager 2000: 36–47). If such is the case for Solomon's temple and capital, then something quite similar may well gird the other royal temples being built in Levantine cities. The association between the king and the god can be given a stronger bond if something physical within the temple references the god's involvement with his people through the vehicle of the king. At Jerusalem, this item was the ark that David had moved to Jerusalem and that Solomon had built the temple to house.

The recent find of a later Assyrian vassal treaty of Esarhaddon in the new or second temple at Tell Taʿyinat that may have been deposited in the holy of holies of the temple may point to a similar concept at work (Hurowitz 2011: 57). The treaty is a list of curses, similar to those in Deut 28:25–32, in which the god is asked to punish the violator of the treaty—the local king of Tell Taʿyinat, one assumes. In this instance, the presence of the vassal treaty in the temple of a god of the subordinate city suggests that the temple and the god have been co-opted by the Assyrians but only because it is assumed that the god will operate to provide punishment for any ruler who defies the sacred nature of the covenant enacted between two rulers before a god. Certainly the notion that the deity resides in the temple is well attested for the Jerusalem temple and may be considered characteristic of the other temples. This is, of course, the Late Bronze Age literary trope behind the story of Baʿal's palace-temple. The temple, then, is the microcosmic house of the god, the earthly version of the heavenly abode (Friedman 1981: 21–30)—a Late Bronze Age concept that is revived and given new meaning in the setting of Iron Age II monarchies.

There may be a difference in the way the gods were thought actually to occupy the spaces. Yahweh was understood to be resident in a garden, seen in the imagery of palm trees and cherubs, at Solomon's temple: a static presence. Quite different is god's presence at ʿAin Dara, if one reads the relief sculpture on the walls as providing a hint about the nature of the divine presence. Hurowitz (2011: 51–55) thinks that the various figures (bull-man, lion-man, eagle-man, and human) with arms uplifted carved along the base of the raised platform of the innermost room are the equivalent of the 4 *ḥayyôt* who support Yahweh's chariot that carries his throne (Ezekiel 1). These figures have the 4 faces of a man, a lion, a bull, and an eagle and, while there are indeed differences between the literary description and the sculptural interpretation, the reliefs can be made to work with the text. Hurowitz then suggests that the ʿAin Dara temple must have functioned akin to a vehicle. Instead of providing a firm and fixed spot in which the god could reside in a static mode, the god here was in effect in flight, moving as though seated on a chariot-borne throne. This same movement motif, though in a more obvious presentation, is seen in the Iron Age I rebuilt temple on the Aleppo Citadel (Hurowitz 2011: 55). At Carchemish, the gods form part of a sculpted procession, so movement is a fundamental aspect of the presentation. At both Aleppo and Carchemish, the temples are dedicated to the Storm God, which would explain the shared theme. The Guzana statues seem to be stressing a more static presence, though here there is no floral or arboreal imagery to suggest a garden or paradisiacal setting. So perhaps there were two different, possibly opposing or contrasting notions of how gods resided within the confines of their sanctuaries.

What is not so clear is how these temples, which served as physical manifestations of a new political order blessed by new gods, actually operated in the emerging urban fabric of the Iron Age II cities. Where they do survive, the temples are not really integrated into the larger city. At both ʿAin Dara and Guzana, the temples are located on an acropolis, physically separated from the main habitation regions of the city—a situation that also seems to describe Solomon's temple. True enough, there is a large courtyard in front of the temple-palace terrace at Guzana that could have accommodated a crowd; a similar situation may have been in operation at ʿAin Dara. At Carchemish, the precinct of the Storm God's Temple is an element in the processional way that leads to the Grand Staircase and the palace, so it is possible that more individuals than the king and courtiers had some sort of access. This must have been the situation in Jerusalem; however, it is worth remembering that the temples at Tell

Taʿyinat are quite different in this respect. They are located behind the palace, but they neither share access to the great courtyard, nor do they have any precinct of their own.

Meyers (1983: 167–78) has argued that the named columns of the temple of Solomon actually provide a clue about the way the structure was integrated into the city. Jachin and Boaz were elements of the *ʾûlām*, the relationship of which to the rest of the temple is not at all clear from the texts. According to the description, it was not enclosed by the side chambers that framed the main portion of the temple, the *hêkāl* and the *děbîr*. These two sections are treated as a single unit in terms of measurements given, while the *ʾûlām*'s measurements are reported separately. Moreover, while doors of olivewood close off the *děbîr*, and doors of cypress wood do the same for the *hêkāl*, no doors are mentioned for the *ʾûlām*. Its construction of large hewn stones surmounted by cedar beams agrees more with the construction of the palace and palace court than with the temple. Meyers has concluded that the *ʾûlām* is not an enclosed, internal space—a porch or formal entrance—the most common identification provided for the architectural feature; rather, it is a large courtyard fronting the temple. It is not an integral architectural element in the structure of the temple building itself, which is why the *ʾûlām* is absent in the description of the tabernacle, which otherwise parallels the description of the temple (Cross 1981: 161–80). The columns, Jachin and Boaz, were gateposts marking the entrance into the courtyard. They were the public face of the sanctuary complex, the aspect seen by the larger community, which probably had little or no access to the temple building itself. Thus, the columns must have been part of Solomon's iconographic program. They were a constant reminder to the general populace of the great moment when Yahweh came to the city. The ark had been carried from Shiloh to Jerusalem by David, and Solomon had it carried to the new house. The columns announce the space where Yahweh dwells among his people.

Meyers's stress on the role of the courtyard and the formal entrance to this space should not be dismissed. Certainly, one of the features that marked the early Iron Age temples was the role played by courtyards. Already in the Iron Age I temple at Tell Qasile, the courtyard had assumed an architectural importance in the design. This was also true for the temple at Ekron. Courtyards had not been a major feature in the Late Bronze Age temple designs. At Beth-shean, it was the temple complex erected after the Egyptian period that showed the courtyard being used as a means of establishing an architectural relationship between the two parts of the compound.

The courtyards used in the Iron Age II royal temple designs assumed an even greater significance. At Guzana, there were in reality two courts: one court on the upper terrace forming a raised entrance into the temple-palace, and a lower court that also served to connect the residential palace with the temple-palace. This was a courtyard that could have held the general population from the lower city but was also appropriate for displays of pomp in the form of ceremonial processions moving from residential palace to temple-palace.

The Temple of the Storm God at Carchemish was placed in a precinct with two distinct courtyards. One fronted the entrance to the temple. The other formed the first space within the precinct. The two courtyards met but were distinct in paving and height. While no special features survived to mark the entrance to the precinct of the Storm God, it was clear that there was a door that led into a walled-off precinct, and the temple was placed deep within the precinct; this is a model that may have been applicable to the temple in Jerusalem. The entrance that marked the transition from the lower town to the citadel at Guzana was embellished with relief sculpture. These were not columns; they were guardian figures, mythical beasts, but they must have served the purpose of designating that the region behind was different from the space in front. On the other hand, where actual paired columns in association with architecture have survived—the temples at Tell Taʿyinat (Building II) and ʿAin Dara—they were elements in the physical structure of the temple buildings and were formal features of the porches; they were columns *in antis* in the truest sense of the term. While Meyers's interpretation is worth considering, it does require that the physical survival of columns defining an entrance porch in a temple setting be dismissed as the closest parallel to the biblical description.

The temples at ʿAin Dara and Tell Taʿyinat are most commonly compared with the description of the temple of Solomon. They are all thought to share in common the long-room format. The Tell Taʿyinat temple (Building II) has been promoted as the closest parallel to the lost temple since its discovery in the 1930s.[18] But its eighth-century B.C.E. date renders it impossible as a prototype, assuming the normally accepted tenth-century B.C.E. date for Solomon's temple. However, the ʿAin Dara temple—which appears to have had a fully developed long-room format by its tenth century B.C.E. incarnation, even if the surrounding ambulatory element was added later—could be considered, if not the prototype, a contemporaneous construction with the temple of Solomon. Because the long-room temple type is seen to have been a Syrian invention, though in use in Palestine as early as the Middle Bronze Age, its reappearance in the Iron Age II temple of Solomon may have been the result of foreign influence, most likely coming from the Phoenician court of Hiram I, who supplied material and labor to Solomon to build the temple.

Hiram I does seem to have initiated the use of a major building as a royal tool of propaganda in the Iron Age II Levant. He was responsible for rebuilding a number of temples in Tyre and was responsible for the promotion (though probably not the invention) of the cult of Melqart, a god with fertility and resurrection connotations, who lacks any real Late Bronze Age pedigree (Dussaud 1946–48: 205–30). In time, Melqart came to be conflated with Heracles, at least in Greek minds. The dual god appears on Cypriot coinage of the fifth century B.C.E. It is assumed that Hiram I

---

18. And as recently as Hurowitz 2011: 48.

constructed a Sanctuary to Melqart as part of his massive rebuilding program in Tyre and that this was the sanctuary that Herodotus visited and described as the Sanctuary of Heracles. According to the logic of this approach, Hiram I was the protagonist who introduced the long-room temple back into Israel, and the Temples of Melqart and of Yahweh must have been quite similar.

Considering Hiram I to be the force behind the revival and spread of the long-room temple type in Iron Age II and the Temple of Melqart in Tyre the prototype for the other long-room temples seems reasonable at first blush. All the sources point to Hiram I as a monarch who especially saw the potential for massive building, and the biblical accounts and, later, Josephus are clear that David and Solomon looked to him for help with building. His architects must have known how to work with stone as well as how to use cedar support timbers and beams to best effect.[19] However, this revival of the long-room form seems to exhibit some marked differences from the earlier appearance of the type. The Iron Age II long rooms that survive are all used for temples associated with palaces. This was not the situation in the Late Bronze Age, when the long room was used in a number of different settings. Only the level VII temple at Alalakh can be said to be specifically a royal temple. Hiram I or his architect may well have seen a value in making use of the old form within the new, specific context of royal architecture. The long-room format that was revived was specifically the tripartite form, which stresses the penetration of space through layers and which invited formal linear processional movements. Was the Temple of Melqart at Tyre the vehicle by which the long-room temple made its reappearance?

Melqart, although not a new god, was newly promoted to importance. Though he was tied to the royal family, he was not the chief deity of Tyre. This role was probably still held by Baʿal-Shamên, who is invoked in the treaty between Esarhaddon and Baʿal, king of Tyre (Clifford 1990: 55–64: Katzenstein 1973: 90). The Late Bronze Age god Baʿal, in various guises was still a strong force throughout the Phoenician region. He was present at Mount Carmel, where he battled with Yahweh (1 Kgs 18:17–40), and he was the god taken to Israel by Jezebel (1 Kgs 16:31–33). The Sanctuary to Baʿal-Shamên may have been on an island next to Tyre that Hiram had joined to the city by means of a causeway (Josephus, *Ag. Ap.* 1.113; Markoe 2000: 196; Katzenstein 1973: 87). Melqart was actually a secondary deity, promoted by Hiram I, whose importance expanded after 800 B.C.E., as Tyre undertook colonial expansion. This role in colonialization may be manifested at Kition, where the rebuilt temple is dedicated to Astarte, the consort of Melqart, and the temple is not a long-room type.

The long-room temple within the setting of Tyre, if it was used, was more likely employed for the Temple of Baʿal-Shamên, a temple that Hiram I may have restored

---

19. Boardman (2000: 27–31) argues strongly against the notion that Phoenicians were particularly able stoneworkers.

at the same time that he had the island sanctuary joined to the city proper. If Solomon borrowed, or better, accepted the notion of the long-room temple as appropriate for Yahweh, it makes most sense that the choice would have seemed suitable only if the temple type had come to be associated with the prime deity at Tyre. Yahweh may have been like Melqart in his connection with the royal family and his newness as a major deity in the landscape but, unlike Melqart, he was the prime god, and his parallels were with El and Baʿal, not Melqart. He was already laying claim to older topographical features of the landscape that had been El's in the Late Bronze Age (Cross 1983; Clifford 1972). Architectural iconography developed for Melqart was inappropriate for Yahweh.

Hiram's connections with the developing Kingdom of Israel are but one example of the Phoenician king's commercial and diplomatic interests. If Hiram was somehow responsible for the introduction of the long-room temple into the setting of palace architecture in Jerusalem, it was probably not from Tyre that the direct importation was done. Tyre had an older sacred topography that Hiram and his architects needed to respect, and the implication in the texts is that he rebuilt but not *ex nihilo*. The population at Tyre was not a conquering force: it was directly related to the older, Late Bronze Age population and had no reason to disregard what already stood.

The situation was the opposite in Jerusalem. The Israelites were a new people, and the conquest of the city was an element in David's campaign to unify the country and subject the older populations. The biblical texts provide no real sense of the Jebusite city, and so David and Solomon were for all intents and purposes creating *ex novo*.

It is possible that the long-room temple with palace connections that had been in use in Late Bronze Age Alalakh could have somehow been known in Tyre, perhaps because it survived in one of the older centers along the Phoenician coast. While Wen-Amon's descriptive information is limited, since architecture is not his interest, he does indicate that the prince of Byblos was sacrificing when one of the attendants was possessed by a fit, which could indicate that the ritual was happening within the palace precinct, perhaps in the vicinity of a palace-temple, but this is total guesswork and is in no way supported by the text. Phoenician contacts with other North Syrian centers where the design conceit had been present in the Late Bronze Age and survived, such as ʿAin Dara, could have prompted the architect from Tyre to carry the form to Jerusalem. However, there was limited Phoenician cultural exchange with North Syrian centers before the late eighth and seventh centuries—when Phoenician artifacts begin to appear in these contexts (Winter 1976: 15–17)—and when Carchemish begins to produce small ivory sculpture (Winter 1983: 182). There is certainly no reason to believe that the long-room temple type was reintroduced to North Syria by Tyre, since Carchemish and the other North Syrian cities were in the process of creating their own cultural identity quite independent of influences from the Phoenician coast.

If one accepts the notion of a greater Israel under David and Solomon, then the kingdom's control stretched north to the Syrian region around Damascus (2 Sam 8:6; Katzenstein 1973: 94), making it the largest political entity in the Levant during the tenth century B.C.E. With this sort of status accrues cultural prestige. Solomon's new royal compound with its long-room temple could easily have provided the inspiration for the spread of the long-room temple type back into Syria, although whether it was the ʿAin Dara temple or the temple of Solomon that informed the later temples at Tell Taʿyinat is impossible to determine. By the eighth century B.C.E., when the Tell Taʿyinat temples were built, greater Israel no longer existed, and Jerusalem was capital of a much reduced Kingdom of Judah. It seems unlikely that it would have served as any type of model for a state in Syria. The design of the Tell Taʿyinat complex exhibits what appears to have been a significant change. The temples have been pushed off the main plaza and away from the focus of the palaces.

Even if Solomon's political control was not as far reaching as advocates of the greater-Israel scenario suggest, he may still have been involved with developments in the Syrian region. Ikeda has pointed out that Solomon's agents were probably reselling horses and chariots obtained from elsewhere to the new dynasts of the Syrian Neo-Hittite and Aramean states. The late tenth century B.C.E. witnessed a series of disruptions in the region. The earlier Assyrian presence established by Tiglath-pileser I (at Pitru and Mutlinu near Carchemish) had been displaced by Aramean aggression. Within Carchemish itself, there was a dynastic overthrow, and the older Ura-Tarhunda Dynasty was replaced by the Suhi Dynasty, from which emerged Katuwas (Ikeda 1982: 231–34). The whole great building program at Carchemish, of which the Temple of the Storm God was one element, must be seen as a political statement by a new dynasty that took power during a period of foreign penetration into the region. This may also be the setting into which the second phase of the ʿAin Dara temple should be placed. This older, long-room tripartite temple, which may date back to the last decades of the Late Bronze Age, received an elaborate face-lift with the new treatment of the porch and the embedded paired columns, and in about 900 B.C.E., it was enlarged by means of the ambulatory that surrounds three sides.

So, while it is possible that the temple of Solomon had an impact on the design of the ʿAin Dara temple, it is also quite clear that the political situation in the Syrian region was serving as a catalyst for new architectural designs every bit as strong as that of David's establishment of the Kingdom of Israel and Solomon's program of solidifying the kingdom. If the Suhi Dynasty at Carchemish is at all indicative of what these rulers were doing, then there is no surprise that temple architecture was being employed. Of course, with building activities in Tyre, Jerusalem, and several North Syrian cities, it may be better to think in terms of design ideas' being moved about because of the density of building projects within the Levantine region.

The problem for our understanding of how forms might have passed from region to region is the result of our placing emphasis on the wrong aspects of the story. Tandy has argued that a major economic disruption occurred in the eighth century B.C.E. in the Greek area, as the old warrior-based aristocracy that had developed in the period after the fall of the Late Bronze Age Mycenean culture gave way to a new aristocracy controlled by a market economic structure. One of the catalysts that effected the change was the contact that the Greeks began to have with the North Syrian kingdoms through the port at Al Mina, which connected with the ʿAmuq Plain and was not far from Tell Taʿyinat. A second Levantine agent that promoted the development of a market-based economic structure was Tyre. The description of Tyre that appears in Ezekiel (27:3–9) testifies to the city's wealth acquired through long-distance trade. This was a market dependent on luxury and prestigious goods, quite separate from the local market that operated on basic needs for the local population. For Tandy, Al Mina and Tyre represent controlled markets through which passed a specialized type of commodity destined for a prestigious setting (Tandy 1997: 119); and in the Levant, one end point for these goods was temples, as can be seen from the finds associated with the temples. Even in the troubled period after 1200 B.C.E., the finds in temple settings are often prestigious goods—imported pottery, much from Cyprus, or imitations of the imported ware, as well as items in precious metals. In the early Iron Age setting, the Levantine kings had become active agents in this commerce, as can be seen in the figures of Hiram I and Solomon. Solomon attempted to become directly engaged with the seaborne trade by providing ships to sail alongside Hiram's (1 Kgs 10:21). Hiram and Solomon had established between themselves a reciprocal relationship. As independent rulers, they exchanged as equals, always trying to maintain the opposite king's indebtedness. This is seen in the temple-building project in which Hiram provides labor and expertise and Solomon pays with wheat, but always the economic implications are hidden in terms of gift-giving (Tandy 1997: 97). Surviving records from elsewhere in the Levant do not provide for parallels in the region, but they must have existed. Just as Hiram sent help for a royal building project in Jerusalem, a similar situation probably existed in other royal building commissions. Since so many of these royal projects included temples as an element, it seems likely that the skilled labor trained on one project would have been considered valuable to another ruler.

Whether the long-room temple type as it appears in the Iron Age II royal settings is best understood as a survival from the Late Bronze Age (which can actually be traced back to the Middle Bronze Age at Shechem and Megiddo) or whether it was a new discovery of Iron Age II architects searching for a form that suited the needs of rulers who were seeking novel forms for their new palace-temple complexes cannot be decided. Its existence as a form at ʿAin Dara during Iron Age I suggests that the form continued to retain some degree of currency even as the Late Bronze Age world disappeared. Hiram's architects could have spread it south. The architects working for the North Syrian dynasts may have reintroduced it in the north. Solomon's builders may have been responsible for its revival. Whether or not Jerusalem played a leading role in the architectural experimentation of Iron Age II, the fact remains that temples during the period were to form an important aspect in the political iconography of the monarchies that was taking shape throughout the Levant.

Certainly the political role played by temples in Iron Age IIA continued during and to the end of Iron Age II. The great sanctuary compound at Tel Dan can best be understood as the attempt of the kings of the Northern Kingdom of Israel to create a rival sacred site to the temple in Jerusalem that was now under the control of the kings of the Southern Kingdom of Judah. Dan was probably positioned to provide a pilgrimage destination for the people of Israel that substituted for the temple in Jerusalem.

Though Solomon may have built his temple as a royal chapel, it emerged as the national shrine for Yahweh during the period of the divided monarchy. The archaeological evidence supports the notion that centralizing forces were brought to bear, and alternative shrines were eliminated so that all focus was directed on the Jerusalem temple. This is clearly witnessed in the closing down of the small shrine in the fortress at Arad. The suppression of the fortress sanctuary at Arad is probably just one of several pieces of evidence for the increasing power of centralized religious control by the royal figures and a focus of devotion on select shrines that could be watched. In the setting of Judah, this has been read as a distinct feature of the development of the cult of Yahweh, but the archaeological findings from the North Syrian region and the Kingdom of Israel do not suggest that anything much different was happening here. The evidence may be skewed by the nature of archaeological investigations in early Iron Age settings, which have concentrated on urban environments and monumental building projects (Faust 2003: 147; Meyers 2003a: 186–89). Future closer examinations of the rural settings may reveal more evidence of small-scale religious architecture throughout the Levantine region in Iron Age II that can now only be glimpsed at Sarepta and the Edomite Negev and wayside shrines at Wadi ath-Thamad #13 outside Khirbat al-Mudayna and Kuntillet ʿAjrud. Some notion of the development of Levantine sacred architecture free from the royal aspect can be examined in the colonial setting that emerged in the eighth century B.C.E., to which we now turn.

Chapter 7

Levantine Architecture Goes West

The scholarly consensus is that the first real Levantine settlements in the far West were not established until the end of the ninth century or beginning of the eighth century B.C.E. (Aubet 1993). While there is good reason for believing that some type of commerce existed between the Levant and the coastal band of the western Mediterranean in the Late Bronze Age, this communication did not lead to any significant cultural interactions and certainly not settlements. The Phoenicians are credited with the colonization. However, it is worth remembering that 'Phoenician' is a Greek term: *Phoinikeïa, Phoinikes*, used and perhaps coined by Homer, who alternates it with 'Sidonian' (*Sidones*; Winter 1995: 247). Interestingly, Tyrians are absent in Homer's account, at least as a specific group. He may have known that the audience would read *Tyrians* for *Phoenicians* as well as *Sidonians*, or his information about Phoenicians may reflect the older order of Iron Age I and Iron Age IIA, when Sidon was in a position of greater power than Tyre. Interchangeability of Phoenicians and Sidonians suggests that, for Homer, and perhaps his audience, there was a specific geographic locality in which to place these people: the Lebanese coast. Certainly, during the Iron Age I period, this must have been the most likely region from which long-distance travel would have emanated, since the best ports were here and, by the late ninth century, the estuary of the Orontes River was once again a viable port facility.

The Greek establishment at Al Mina opened up the region and permitted direct communication from the ʿAmuq Plain and the North Syrian cities. Al Mina, probably established by Euboeans as the eastern end of their iron-trading commercial network (Tandy 1997: 69), was visited by other Greeks, as evidenced by the finds of Corinthian pots, and very likely Levantine peoples from the north used it as well, sometimes sailing on Greek ships and perhaps at other times supplying their own. The important issue is to recognize that, while Homer had a specific place and people in mind when he referred to Phoenicians and Sidonians, in reality the Levantine people who became part of the Iron Age II exchange network were not solely from the Lebanese coast. As S. Morris has pointed out, the easterners referred to with the collective noun

Phoenicians by their Greek competitors were probably an amalgam of eastern peoples (Morris 1992: 130). It is equally important to see that the north Levantine coast actually had two distinct affiliations. By the eighth century B.C.E., Al Mina offered a way for North Syrian and southeastern Anatolian materials and peoples to engage with the expanding Mediterranean economy. On the other hand, during the first centuries of Iron Age II, the southern coast of Lebanon was integrated into a cultural and political network with the emerging centers of Jerusalem, the towns and cities of the Jezreel and Beth-shean valleys, and the northeast site of Tel Dan in the Golan Heights. Tyre had associations with the newly emerging United Monarchy of Israel under David and Solomon. In the mid-eighth century B.C.E., Sidon provided Ahab of the Omride Dynasty of the Northern Kingdom of Israel with his bride. The cultural ties of the southern Lebanese coast with the interior must have extended during this eighth century B.C.E. all the way to the Kingdom of Ammon, based on the evidence of sculptural finds (Zayadine 1991).

While Homer knows the Phoenicians or Sidonians as seafarers, he does not seem to know that they are also settlers, colonizers. For Homer, they are not like his fellow eighth-century B.C.E. Greeks, who are beginning to settle in southern Italy and Sicily. Rather, they are pirates who carry pretty trinkets but are not to be trusted. The economic structure that the Levantine traders were involved in establishing in the course of Iron Age IIA represented a change from the structure that had dominated international economic exchange during the Late Bronze Age. The palace network of the Late Bronze Age incorporated the palace structures of New Kingdom Egypt, the Canaanite Levant, Hittite Anatolia, and the Mycenean Aegean through the movement of high-status materials and finished products, many from the palace workshops. The Amarna letters reveal that the economic process was characterized by reciprocity among the ruling elites.

The discoveries of the fourteenth-century B.C.E. shipwreck at Ulu Burun and the twelfth-century B.C.E. shipwreck off Cape Gelidonya (Bass 1967; 1986; 1987) indicate that there was a separate, parallel international economic network operating in the Late Bronze Age in which high-status goods were reconfigured and moved around as part of the more significant trade in copper and tin. In this second network, the merchantmen collected materials from throughout the eastern coastal region, and the crews were probably equally mixed ethnically. There is good reason to believe that no single group monopolized the trade that, on both the palace level and the lower level, engaged Egyptians, Canaanites, Hittites, and Aegean peoples (S. Morris 1992: 104). The palace economic structure did not survive the collapse of 1200 B.C.E., but the more adaptable maritime trade of the parallel economy probably did continue. It may well have become more mercenary, and the piratical aspects could well have come to dominate, especially if the influx of new peoples with maritime backgrounds represented by some of the "Peoples of the Sea" entered into the network as a result of

settling along the Levantine coast just before and after 1200 B.C.E. This seems to be reflected in the story of Wen-Amon, who is chased by pirates. The catalyst that served to
change this modest coastal trawling during Iron Age I into the trans-Mediterranean
exchange of Iron Age IIA was probably the need to seek out new sources of metals
that led the emerging royal economies of Iron Age II to encourage merchantmen to
sail toward locales that were potentially rich in metal ores: the northern Aegean, the
Bay of Naples, and the Atlantic coast of southern Iberia.

Actual colonization in the West did not begin until after the greatest period of
prosperity for the coastal Levantine cities. Although Tyre may have moved to take
control of portions of eastern Cyprus, in particular Kition, under Hiram I in the tenth
century B.C.E., the establishment of settlements in the far West cannot be traced before about 800 B.C.E. At this point, the situation in the Levant was changing. The
Neo-Assyrian aggression had become much stronger and, during the course of the
eighth century B.C.E., the Assyrian forces began indirectly to dominate much of the
economic and political life in the Levantine region. One of the major new pressures
that led to the push west was the need to find new sources of silver to pay the Assyrian
tributes.[1]

Although Homer does not seem to know of the Tyrians, by the ninth century
B.C.E., they had become the dominant group involved in Levantine colonization. Tyre
established the network of significant settlements that brought the Western Mediterranean into the cultural sphere of the East, with emporia at Gadir on the Iberian coast,
Lixus on the Atlantic coast of North Africa, and Carthage opposite Sicily on the North
African littoral. These were nodes in a new type of economic system, a market-based
network quite different from the reciprocal model of the Late Bronze Age palace network. In this new structure, the exchange was between two parties lacking strong
social bonds. The relationship was of short duration and clearly delineated (Tandy
1997: 113). It often involved peoples unable to communicate with one another verbally.
The goal was not to establish debt-obligation relationships that mark the reciprocal
structure but, rather, to allow for obtaining specific commodities at the best market
price. The arrangement was to have profound effects on the social structures of some
of the native peoples of the West with whom the Phoenician merchants did business
(Cunliffe 1988: 12–58).

While Tyrians and perhaps even Sidonians led the way in the formal process of
establishing colonial settlements outside the Levant, there is no reason to assume that
all who sailed from the region were from Tyre and Sidon. Not only was there an alternative port farther north that could provide access to the Mediterranean, but the ties

---

1. Certainly the social forces played a role in this movement to the West, especially as the nature
of sailing and shipbuilding among the Levantine peoples changed as a result of new sailing technology
introduced and developed by the maritime folk among the "Peoples of the Sea" (Wachsman 1998).

of both Sidon and Tyre with the emerging kingdoms of Israel and Ammon must have meant that people from these areas also headed West, either as members of crews or as passengers—or even in their own ships. Even if Tyrians dominated the actual shipping process, they probably did not provide all of the settlers of these small outposts. It is perhaps worth recalling that, while it was indeed the English who technically established the colonial outposts in India and Canada by means of the East India Company and the Hudson's Bay Company, any research on the people who staffed these settlements quickly shows the strong presence of Scots in the mix. One finds a similar type of diverse background for those who formed the settlement of Dutch Manhattan (Dalrymple 2002; Shorto 2005). Since these were establishments with economic foundations and not the result of demographic shifts, only certain sorts of individuals would have seen fit to move so far away from the world that they knew.

Phoenicians and Greeks

Phoenicians engaged in long-distance trade before the Greeks began to set up a colonial structure in the mid-eighth century B.C.E. As early as the tenth century B.C.E., Levantine goods show up in Greek settings, probably the result of Phoenician traders, perhaps the heirs of the coastal trawlers of the Late Bronze Age (S. Morris 1992: 133–40), and the argument has been put forward that some Levantine emigrants sought refuge in Greek settings during Iron Age II. This may have been quite possible for craftsmen who by nature were a mobile force in the Levantine and early Greek world (Burkert 1992: 21–25). It is in the environment of Phoenician-Greek exchange that the first Greek temples appear. There has long been recognition that Levantine forces informed the initial experiments with temple-building using the Ionic order (Dinsmoor 1975: 58–61). The discovery of the little Phoenician shrine on the south coast of Crete at Kommos must have marked a meeting place for already-existing Levantine forms and developing Greek forms (Burkert 1992: 20–21). No one has gone so far as to argue that the Levantine developments in architecture informed the basic elements of Greek temples, which are still treated as a type of internal response to specifically Greek needs (Dinsmoor 1975: 41–48). However, the fact remains that Greek merchants residing in the newly established port of Al Mina were clearly in a position to observe the impressive architectural developments taking place at nearby Tell Ta'yinat if not at North Syrian centers farther inland. There may have been a Greek community at Tell Sukas that commissioned a Greek-style temple (Riis 1970).

The question of how much influence the architectural forms of the Levant had on early Greek architectural experiments is not worth asking, because Greek architecture followed its own path quite quickly. What is worth considering is what the Levantine merchants built for sanctuaries outside their homelands: what architectural forms did they carry West with them, and what shape did these take in the setting of isolated outposts in foreign territories? Their history provides some sense of how architecture traveled and, although the possible influence of Levantine forms on early Greek architecture may be largely dismissed from this study, the same is not necessarily true for other places where Levantine settlements and architecture interfaced with native populations.

The First Settlements

Cyprus

Kition: Temple of Astarte

Cyprus was the first place that Phoenicians established themselves once they began to leave the mainland. The Temple to Astarte at Kition, which incorporated remains from older temples on the site dating back to the Late Bronze Age, was probably the first substantial Phoenician construction outside the major coastal cities. The ninth-century B.C.E. ruins at Kition preserve the largest surviving Phoenician temple still to be seen (fig. 45), since none of the mainland sites have yielded their Iron Age II temples. Hiram I established Tyrian control over Kition and thereby established a larger economic and political entity. He controlled two points on a trade route and the sea between them. It is reasonable to regard Kition in the tenth and ninth centuries B.C.E. as a Tyrian outpost because the town seems to have been refounded by Tyrian settlers after a period of abandonment. However, the fact remains that Cyprus and Kition cannot really be considered colonies in the same way as the others in this discussion. Cyprus had a long association with the coastal communities that stretched back to at least the Middle Bronze Age. It was tied economically and also culturally. Some of the groups associated with the "Peoples of the Sea" had settled for a time on Cyprus before making their final move to the Levantine coast. This tied the island not just to the Lebanese section but also to the newly emerging states in the south: the Philistines, Tejeker, and Shardana. On the other hand, the island seems to have hosted Canaanites fleeing from the destruction caused by the newly arrived "Peoples of the Sea," and so Canaanite culture also survived on the island, perhaps to be replanted back on the mainland after the calm returned in Iron Age I (Negbi 1992: 604–5; Dothan and Dothan 1992: 191–98). Therefore, while direct control of Kition by a mainland city may have been a new experience, to see Kition as a colonial outpost is not entirely correct. There was too much cultural overlap between the Cypriots of the east coast and the mainland folk.

The Temple of Astarte at Kition is best understood as an example of high-quality, cosmopolitan Phoenician architecture, and it probably resembled the sanctuaries in Tyre and Sidon. Consequently, it does provide a few key pieces of information. The scale of the actual shrine portion, the holy of holies, is modest. The impressive portion of the structure is taken up by a colonnaded space that may be a partially open courtyard. This type of arrangement was to remain a common feature of the later temples in the Phoenician region, as can be seen in the later, sixth-century B.C.E. Sanctuary of Marathus (Amrit) dedicated to Melqart near modern Tartous (fig. 70), which also consisted of a small holy of holies set within a courtyard defined by a portico on three sides (Jourdain-Annequin 1992: 11–18).

The Phoenician temple at Kition stood above the ruins of a temple that had been erected following the 1200 B.C.E. destruction of the site by the "Peoples of the Sea." This temple had in turn replaced a still-earlier sanctuary built not too long before the destruction, perhaps by an arriving group of Myceneans (Ionas 1984: 99). It was very possible that it was this first temple that introduced the structural elements of a small holy of holies and a large courtyard all enclosed by a surrounding wall. This does not appear to have been a Mycenean form that was brought to the island. Rather, it seems to have developed here and was then rebuilt in several iterations, until its final form as the Phoenician temple. On the other hand, considering the role that Cyprus played as host to both invading "Peoples of the Sea" and fleeing mainland Canaanites, it seems likely that the forms developed at Kition were taken to the mainland to influence the later developments.

Kition: Bamboula

Cyprus should be seen as a location where Levantine architecture developed parallel to what was happening on the mainland. It may also have had a role to play in the formation of colonial forms, since the site at Kition was probably a standard port-of-call for ships leaving Tyre and heading west. The little Sanctuary of Melqart-Heracles on the Bamboula in Kition began to operate in the mid-seventh century. This is the first known Sanctuary dedicated to the Tyrian god Melqart conflated with the Greek hero Heracles. The sanctuary went through two phases of operation between 650 and 500 B.C.E. (Caubet 1984: 107–13). In the first phase, the actual structural elements were modest (fig. 131a). The building identified as a temple shared one wall with the exterior wall that also defined the temenos space. The altar was the dominant feature but was not located on any type of axis with the temple itself. In the second phase, the original temple retained its position, but the altar disappeared, and a second structure, possibly a chapel, was erected at a 90° angle with the older temple, which was on a north–south axis and occupied most of the west side of the precinct. The new chapel stood to the south and was the dominant feature on the south side of the complex, which was also where the entrance to the precinct was to be found. The east side of the precinct was defined by a colonnaded structure, a type of stoa.

For Caubet, the design of the sanctuary is one of interplay between positive (Buildings) and negative (Courts) spaces (Caubet 1984: 113, fig. 4). The interplay is significant since the courtyards have become much more complicated in their placement and interrelationships than was the case with the earlier courtyard of the Temple of Astarte, even as the size of the courtyards has become much smaller. The Sanctuary of Melqart-Heracles shows a kind of spatial hierarchy. Clearly different courtyards function in different ways and for different purposes. There are liminal spaces, places that were neither fully enclosed nor fully exposed, spaces such as the entrance into the main temple and the stoa. How these functioned in ritual or regular use cannot be determined from the remains themselves.

Ionas has argued that the open-air elements of the design were a fundamental feature of the religious architecture that developed on Cyprus from the Middle Bronze Age through Iron Age II (Ionas 1984: 97). In this respect, however, Cypriot architecture was not unique. The interplay of closed and open was a common enough feature of Late Bronze and Iron Age architecture on the mainland as well, but the design of the Kition sanctuary does suggest how this interplay had become a sophisticated feature, even in a small space and in a modest complex. The particular design of the phase 2 sanctuary resembled the complex of the Storm God at Carchemish (fig. 36): the placement of the temple to the side and the use of hierarchy in the arrangement of the courtyards. This could indicate that this particular interplay resulted from some other influences entering Kition—a result of the Tyrian trade network. The North Syrian ideas about the arrangement of structural elements would have found a receptive audience already used to playing with combinations of closed and open spatial arrangements. However, the sanctuary also had a strange similarity to Building 351 at Ekron. There was the same type of penetration of the space, which is similarly layered. Not all the spaces were equal. In this case, the connection was to an earlier Philistine sanctuary. If the design for the sanctuary in Bamboula was reflective of others on Cyprus, then the feature at Ekron could have been the result of Cypriot influence carried to the Philistine region as the "Peoples of the Sea" dispersed from Cyprus to take over the south coast of the Levant in Iron Age I. Whether the Cypriot sanctuary represents the receipt of a foreign idea that found a congenial host or whether it suggests that Cyprus was the initiator of the design and sent it forth to the mainland with the "Peoples of the Sea" cannot be determined from the archaeological evidence.

Crete: Kommos

While developments on Cyprus rightly need to be treated as an aspect in the complete picture of architectural forms within the Levantine region itself, the manifestations of Levantine architecture on the south coast of Crete present a quite different situation. Crete had been a trading partner with Cyprus and the Levant since the days of the Minoans, and certainly the integration of the island within the economic network of the Cypriot and Levantine coastal cities had only increased during the period of Mycenaean hegemony. However, the cultural life of Crete was quite distinct from that of Cyprus and the Levantine coastal communities, and the appearance of a Levantine shrine on the island needs to be considered alien, with no previous cultural connections of this type.

The shrine was built at the small south coast anchorage of Kommos, not far from the ancient palace of Phaestos, and on the remains of an earlier Minoan structure

(Waltrous et al. 2004: 310). The earliest evidence indicates a shrine in operation in the late tenth century B.C.E., and it must have been established to service the needs of Levantine merchants sailing along the coast. Probably these were merchant ships sailing out of Sidon or Tyre, and so it is probably best to assume that the shrine is an example of Phoenician overseas architecture. The ruins provide the first glimpse of what Phoenician merchantmen were carrying west in their architectural kit bag.

The first structure was dated to about 925 B.C.E. (Shaw 1989: 165–72). The interior furnishings, however, belong to the second phase (800–600 B.C.E.). The structure was a small rectangle that contained a single room entered from one of the short sides. A pillar stood in the doorway and divided the entrance in half. In the structure's second phase (fig. 72), benches were built along the two long walls, and the axial line was highlighted by the placement of the doorway pillar. Behind it, in the chamber itself stood a sandstone block designed to hold three upright pillars. In front of this was a hearth, and behind it was a shield followed by an offering bowl. Outside the small structure, there was nothing more to the sanctuary. There were no courtyards, and secondary structures were minimal. The shrine must have been designed to serve as a container for offerings made by seamen en route to or from one of the Phoenician cities. There were no finds of objects to suggest any type of elaborate ritual.

The dedication cannot be determined any more than the identity of the builders. If the temple was a Tyrian foundation, then Melqart is a likely guess. Nothing points specifically to Melqart. The raised stones on the sandstone block recall the stones placed outside the gates of Tel Dan. Tel Dan was not a Phoenician settlement but was within the orbit of Phoenician contact as it developed in late Iron Age I and Iron Age IIA.

Greece: νΤhasos

The modest temple at Kommos suggests the nature of sacred building that the merchants who formed the vanguard of the Phoenician colonization movement of the late ninth century B.C.E. brought with them. It was an easy structure to erect and provided nothing more than a place for some contact with the gods of home for individuals who were headed away for extended periods of time. Something similar may have stood in the northern Aegean on the island of Thasos. Both Herodotus (2.44) and later Strabo (5.25.12) suggest that the Phoenicians did establish themselves on the island. Unlike the situation on Crete, which was probably nothing more than a way station for sailors, the Thasos settlement was intended to exploit the mineral wealth of the island (Servadio 2000: 28). Herodotus identifies the god associated with this settlement as Heracles. Since Heracles was already joined to Tyre's Melqart by Herodotus's day, it seems safe to assume that the original god serving as patron for the community was Melqart. This was clearly the role that he assumed most commonly as the Tyrians set forth to establish settlements. Herodotus actually states that he has seen the Temple

to Heracles on Thasos. The discovery during the 1913 excavations of a fifth-century
B.C.E. inscription referring to the cult regulations for individuals who were making
sacrifices to *Herakles Thasias* supports the notion that the cult existed on the island
(van Berchem 1967: 89–90; Pouilloux 1954: 85). Several other epigraphic finds have led
to the suggestion that the island knew two distinct cults to Heracles: one cult to the
god and the other to the hero (van Berchem 1967: 90–91). However, whether either
one of these should be seen as a later development of the older Phoenician cult of Melqart has been widely questioned, and the Phoenician association with the island was
rejected by the excavators, especially since nothing of certain Phoenician provenance
was found in the excavations (Launey 1944).

Recent work on the island has brought back the question of Phoenician involvement in the settlement during the early Iron Age (de Courtils and Pariente 1988: 123),
so the temple that was unearthed should not be completely dismissed from any consideration of Phoenician colonial architecture, though it needs to be stressed that the
island and its shrines quickly assumed a Greek quality. Van Berchem (1967: 104–5) has
noted that the epigraphic evidence for the cult practices makes clear that the shrine
was served by a yearly appointed priesthood following Greek practice and not by a
professional priesthood, as would be expected for a Levantine sanctuary. Even some
of the features of ritual practice—the banning of women from participating in rituals and the refusal to allow pork offerings—can also be found in Greek practices and
need not represent Semitic survivals.

The early excavations did uncover a temple, probably the one that Herodotus
knew, since it dates to the late sixth century B.C.E. (Launey 1944: 84). It was almost a
square, 23 m × 25 m, and of Ionic order with 8 columns on the long sides and probably
6 on the short sides. This was a Greek building. It still could have served a Phoenician cult since eventually Greek forms were incorporated within Phoenician cultural
settings, but as architecture, it provides no information about Phoenician notions. It
did replace an earlier structure, more modest in scale, but more impressive than the
sanctuary at Kommos. It was constructed using polygonal masonry, often an indication of importance, and consisted of a pronaos, naos, and adyton, a long-room type
of temple. When the new Ionic temple was erected, the older temple was incorporated
into a secondary portico that was used for the ritual meals associated with the cult.
Such meals were a common enough feature of Greek practice and may in no way represent a survival of an older ritual pattern, just as van Bercham has argued for other
features sometimes regarded as Semitic survivals. However, the banning of women,
the rejection of pork, and the incorporation of the older temple into the section of the
new complex associated with the ritual meals could all point to older cultic survivals
of Semitic origin, which may further strengthen the idea that the first sanctuary was
Phoenician. The more complex design for the second sanctuary also may point to a
more-involved and sophisticated play with space, such as has been noted for the Mel-

qart Sanctuary at the Bamboula at Kition, with its closed and open and liminal spaces. A pronaos and naos may suggest this sort of spatial hierarchy.

Malta: Tas-Silǧ

Tas-Silǧ is located in the southeast of Malta on the Delimara-Zejtun highway and near Marsaxlokk Bay and is probably the coastal town that Ptolemy discusses (*Geographia* 4.3.13). It was first inhabited during the prehistoric period and was continuously occupied through antiquity. Sagona, based on an analysis of the pottery finds, suggests that the beginning of the Phoenician use of the site dates to Archaic phase I, which she argues is prior to the eighth century B.C.E. (Sagona 2002: 29, 274) and lasted until the Romans took control of the island at the end of the second Punic War. Many of the ceramics that span the Phoenician period carry inscribed dedications to Astarte, which has led to the conclusion that the site was sacred to the goddess and must have had a temple—perhaps the same one that is described by Cicero as dedicated to Juno and rich in offerings that were stripped by Verres (*In Verrem* 2.4.46.104).

Excavations at the site were undertaken between 1963 and 1970 by the Missione Archeologica Italiana (Cagiano et al. 1973). Italian excavations resumed in 1997 and were augmented by excavations of the University of Malta. Of the architectural features associated with the temple, there are only fragmentary remains that have so far been published (Bonanno et al. 2000). There are some ashlar foundation walls, which certainly fit with a Phoenician construction. These date to the third–second century B.C.E. and would represent Punic rather than Phoenician construction. Nothing of the earlier, Phoencian-period temple has yet been published. Thus, though there may have been a significant temple of early Phoenician date on the southeast of Malta, it is not possible to use it in this analysis.

The Iberian Peninsula

The arrival of Phoenicians in the far West and particularly on the Iberian Peninsula can be dated no earlier than the late ninth century B.C.E. Ancient sources speak of Phoenician settlements along the Mediterranean and Atlantic coasts, and archaeological investigations have discovered a number of settlements. The sudden appearance of evidence for incipient urban planning and rectilinear structures reveal a change from the Late Bronze Age building tradition of the native peoples of the region (Neville 2007: 11–46). These new forms of architecture are associated with Levantine materials and testify to a new presence along the coast.

Gadir: Temple of Melqart

The foundation of Gadir (Cádiz) on the Atlantic coast of Spain just beyond the end of the Mediterranean was one of the most important settlements established by the Tyrians. Attempts to place the Phoenicians on the coast as early as Iron Age I have largely failed. The city of Gadir probably dates to about 800 B.C.E., perhaps at the same time as the foundation of Carthage (Escacena 1986: 39–58; Negbi 1992: 599). All the evidence points to the placement of the major temple at Gadir, the Temple dedicated to Melqart, not in the city proper but several kilometers distant from the city at the opposite end of the long narrow island (Strabo 3.5.5). García y Bellido (1963: 80–82) located this spot as the present-day little island of Sancti Petri. Possibly the site reflects the initial purpose for the sanctuary, which was to service sailors engaged in coastal trade, not settlers (Mierse 2004: 564–65). Its location on the end of the island nearest to Gibraltar would mean that ships sailing out of the Mediterranean and north would spot this comforting sight not too long after entering the Atlantic. It may have been a place of refuge for shipwrecked foreign travelers (Herodotus 2.115). It has been suggested that a hallowed spot was created in part to offer a special, "protected" area in which a sense of trust might be fostered for the Phoenician merchants and their new customers, with whom they had no other kind of historical association (Neville 2007: 87). Niemeyer has proposed that the western movement followed a three-stage scenario. The first stage was coastal exploration, which perhaps began as early as 1000 B.C.E. The second stage was when the settlements along the coast, often on islands, were established: ninth and eighth centuries B.C.E. The final stage witnessed the direct influence of the newcomers on the native populations: the eighth and seventh centuries B.C.E. (Niemeyer 1984: 3–94).

The lack of any standing remains makes all discussions of the temple entirely speculative. If the initial temple dates to Niemeyer's first phase, then it was part of the exploration but not the settlement, which is probably why the actual town was established at the opposite end of the island, putting it in a better position to exploit the estuary of the Guadalquivir River (ancient Betis) to the north and the native city at Huelva, which was probably the center for the native kingdom of Tartessos. At this point, the Tyrians could access the mineral wealth of the Rio Tinto by dealing with the native community at Huelva as well as finding trade partners up the Guadalquivir in the rich agricultural land along the river. Recent studies of the geology of the Guadalquivir estuary have revealed that there was quite a different coastline in antiquity. What is today the Cota Doñana wildlife refuge, at the time of the Phoenician arrival was a large inlet of the Atlantic Ocean that penetrated quite far inland to the region of modern-day Seville (Neville 2007: 123, fig. 4.6; Ruiz Mata 2002: 167–70). Gadir itself was at the mouth of the Guadalete, a smaller and less significant river, but a river that must have offered some degree of access to the native communities of the nearby interior. While it is not at all clear what the native cultural level was at the time of the Phoenician exploration and first settlement in the region, it is certain that within about a century a native culture of some significance had developed, possibly the result of the catalyst of Phoenician involvement with the area (Cunliffe 1988: 1–11; R. Harrison 1988).

Gadir is known to have held several temples within the city proper, though no actual ruins have yet been identified (Escacena 1986: 43–45). In this regard, Gadir is different from the towns that have yielded archaeological evidence for sanctuaries in the

West. Motya and Kerkouane, both later settlements, have yielded evidence for single major sanctuaries, with perhaps a couple of small secondary shrines. At Lixus on the Atlantic coast of Morocco, there was an important Sanctuary to Melqart, which may have been found in its later Roman state but is the only sanctuary so far discovered (Rebuffat 1985; Ponsich 1982). Gadir's greater number of sanctuaries may point to its significance in the colonial enterprise. These sanctuaries within the confines of the city proper were all no doubt products of the urbanization process and therefore may well have been different from the Sanctuary of Melqart, which began life in quite a different setting. The Melqart Sanctuary never lost its importance. Long after the end of Phoenician and even Punic control, when the city was completely incorporated into the Roman world, the Melqart Sanctuary continued to function and attract the attention of Roman-period writers, though in its newer guise as the Sanctuary of Hercules Gaditanus (Mierse 2004: 547–55).

The sanctuary played several roles in the Roman-period literary works. For Silius Italicus, it served as an exotic backdrop for a scene in his epic poem the *Punicia* (3.14–60). Though he provided some information about the buildings and about the rituals conducted in the sanctuary, none of it can really be taken at face value since Silius Italicus had no firsthand knowledge of the sanctuary, nor was his interest in it greater than for its exotic appeal. Strabo (3.5.5–9) seems to have used Polybius and Poseidonius, good sources of information, for the section on Gadir and the sanctuary, but his concerns were not particularly with the architecture. The information was hit or miss, and his main source, Poseidonius, was a philosopher focused on grounding his philosophical and theoretical investigations on personal experience; whatever information he supplied Strabo about architecture was accidental and merely part of the larger issue that concerned him. Consequently, Strabo's discussion of the sanctuary is disjointed at best.

This is also true of Philostratus's biography of Apollonios of Tyana. Apollonius did spend time at the sanctuary in the late first century c.e. but not for the purpose of considering the architecture or even the rituals (*VA* 5.5). Apollonios was an eastern Greek philosopher, a neo-Pythagorean who was exploring the variety of religious life during the first century c.e. He traveled to a number of sanctuaries throughout the Roman world and beyond but never demonstrated any interest in architecture. He came to Gadir because of the fame of the peoples of Gadir for their religious wisdom, though what this meant was never made clear.

All of the Greek and Latin sources[2] share in common the fact that the sanctuary to which they refer was a late manifestation—one that no doubt had gone through several changes over all the centuries of its operation. The archaeological investigations at Kition, Kommos, and Thasos reveal that none of these shrines remained as it

---

2. For a complete discussion of all the sources, see García y Bellido 1963: 97–134.

was founded. It is reasonable to assume that as time went on more and more Greek architectural elements appeared at the Gadir temple. This is certainly true for Punic sites in North Africa, where Greek architectural vocabulary is found to creep in during the Hellenistic period. How much of the older, Phoenician structure could be seen by any visitor to the Sanctuary of Melqart or Hercules Gaditanus in the first century B.C.E. or first century C.E. cannot be determined from literary sources, nor can it be documented with any archaeological evidence. It is probably safe to assume that not much of it remained.

A second group of sources, from the medieval period, may provide some indication that the ruins of the sanctuary still stood at least until the thirteenth century C.E. The information is not of much greater value than the information in the Classical sources for reconstructing the architecture itself. These were all written by Arab geographers and historians—some with direct knowledge of the site and others working from lost sources. None of them knew what they were seeing; none of them had any sense of the earlier history of the region (Mierse 2000: 1–9).

There is one other item that has been employed to reconstruct the temple. The city of Gadir struck coins in the first century B.C.E. with the image of a temple façade used on the reverse. This is a highly questionable source, since the coin image reproduces an image that was first developed by the mint of Rome, and thus the image probably did no more than reference the temple in Gadir (Mierse 1993: 38–41).

The lack of any physical evidence for the temple did not stop García y Bellido from trying to reconstruct it. He used the few references to architectural features, the evidence from excavations of Levantine temples (mostly from the Late Bronze Age) that had been published by 1963, and the biblical descriptions of the temple of Solomon. His reconstruction closely resembled the reconstruction that had been offered of the temple of Solomon and remains to this day the accepted version for the otherwise lost temple (Aubet 1993: 232–34; R. Harrison 1988: 123–26). The problem with García y Bellido's reconstruction is the model. He did not realize that the temple that Hiram helped Solomon construct was an archaistic structure and an element in the newly developing palace-temple complexes of Iron Age II. That was how it was intended to be used in Solomon's design. García y Bellido assumed, as have others, that Hiram's builders would have constructed for Solomon what they had built in Tyre for the Sanctuary of Melqart, but there is no reason to accept this sort of conclusion. García y Bellido thought that there must be a connection because of the role that the independent columns seem to play in both the temple of Solomon (Joachim and Boaz) and Temple of Melqart at Tyre, at least according to Herodotus. Moreover, columns do seem to appear as an important motif in the Latin and Greek literary references to the Sanctuary of Hercules Gaditanius. However, in Herodotus's discussion of the columns of the Sanctuary of Melqart in Tyre, it is not at all clear that these features form any part of the architecture. He could well be referring to something akin to the freestanding stones that are found at the gate shrines in Tel Dan. He is far more interested in their materials than in their architectural role. To some extent. the same may be true for the columns in the temple of Solomon since they also are not really architectural. It is the materials and the decorations that concern the author of the description in Kings. The columns that are described by Strabo (3.5.5) and by Philostratus (*VA* 5.5) as connected with the Temple of Hercules Gaditanus are inscribed, and it is the writing that really interests the two authors, not the placement or architectural role of the columns. At best, what these sources supply is information that within these sanctuaries there were freestanding stones (columns, steles, baetyls, *maṣṣēbôt*), a not unusual feature within the setting of Semitic sanctuaries. If one drops the ties established via the columns, then nothing really joins the Sanctuary of Melqart in Tyre to the temple of Solomon in Jerusalem, and certainly nothing allows for the Temple of Hercules Gaditanus to be related to the temple of Solomon.

If the first Temple to Melqart outside Gadir belonged to the period before real settlements were established in the West, then the temple must have been much more in line with the little shrine erected at Kommos, something easy to build and to maintain where sailors trading along the coast could stop and give thank offerings (Mierse 2004).

EL Cerro de San Juan de Coria del Río

The recent find of a small temple of the late eighth century B.C.E. to the north of Gadir on the ancient estuary coastline of the Guadalquivir at El Cerro de San Juan de Coria del Río may offer an idea of what the initial temple at Gadir might have looked like (Neville 2007: fig. 4.6). The settlement has been identified as that referred to as Mons Cassius by Avienus in the *Ora Maritima* 255. The poem, though composed in the fourth century C.E., relied on a much older work for its information about the sights along the south coast of Spain. The lost source is usually identified as a periplus of the sixth century B.C.E. (Cunliffe 2001: 38–45). The sanctuary was part of the fabric of the settlement and therefore must have been erected during the second phase of Phoenician penetration, when permanent communities were being established. It was a small, single-chambered building with an associated courtyard. While it went through five rebuildings over three centuries, its basic form remained constant (fig. 132). The interior floor was of tamped earth covered with red clay at some stages, and the courtyard was of cobbles; thus, the two spaces were distinguished by flooring. The walls of the structure were adobe bricks placed on socles of irregular stones (Escacena Carrasco and Izquierdo de Monte 1998: 971–74; Escacena et al. 1993: 144–46).

In the third iteration, the seventh century B.C.E., a bench ran along the side of one wall, and in the center of the room stood a platform 15 cm high and 80 cm × 55 cm in size, shaped like an oxhide, and oriented toward the rising sun of the summer solstice (Neville 2007: 128). This structure has been interpreted to have been an altar around which was found a glass scarab with Egyptian hieroglyphs and another with an image of Isis. Also found were fragments of an ostrich egg with red pigment (Belén Deamos

2001: 7). The discovery of anchors in association with the shrine has led to an identifiaction of the deity as Ba῾al Ṣaphon, who was worshiped at Tyre—a god associated with storms and a protector of navigation.

Seville: El Carambolo

Another possible temple has been suggested for ruins at El Carambolo, near Seville. These may well have been near the coast of the ancient estuary of the Guadalquivir, as it is now being reconstructed. Today, they are quite far inland. If the reconstructed coast is correct, then the estuary and associated bay for the delta of the Guadalquivir was quite large and would have allowed Phoenicians to establish settlements deeper into the native region than is suggested by the present coastline. The ruins were excavated in the mid-twentieth century (Carriazo 1973: 256–77). The ceramic finds date the first building to about 750 B.C.E.—thus, within the second stage as defined by Niemeyer. A small bronze figure of Astarte may provide the dedication (Belén Deamos 2001: 3–7). The structure went through four different reconstructions but retained a basic form of rectangular and square units but without any clearly defined transit spaces (fig. 133). Walls were of adobe, set on socles of large stones. The earliest version, level IV, showed the finest masonry work (Carriazo 1973: 278). In this stratum was unearthed one room in the complex with a bench and a pillar (Carriazo 1973: 262). Surrounding this room were secondary spaces, although no real plan could be articulated. That the complex should be identified as a temple cannot be argued from any of the architectural features, though the benches obviously could have been for offerings, and the pillar might actually be the remains of an altar. Belén Deamos thinks that in the next level, III, there is evidence for a baetyl cult. This was not an unusual feature to be associated with Astarte, if indeed the bronze figurine of Astarte identified the main dedication (Belén Deamos 2001: 6–7). The level has also yielded bronze spits, terra-cotta bird figurines, a fibula, and alabaster vases. These are all common sorts of offerings in Levantine shrines, and the bronze spits may indicate that the complex also hosted cultic meals.

Carriazo thought that El Carambolo was a native town, part of the region controlled by Tartessos but with strong Phoenician influences. More recently, Belén Deamos has argued that in its foundation phase, level IV, the site was a Phoenician settlement.[3] She points out that the later Latin name for the nearby town of Seville was Hispalis, which could well have its root in the Semitic *Spal*. If the original dedication was to Astarte, then there was a connection with Melqart, since Astarte was Melqart's consort. The connection then would have been due to the Phoenician colonial movement.

---

3. Salvage excavations at the site in 2002–4 revealed a second sanctuary that operated for two centuries (8th–6th centuries B.C.E.) and went through 5 phases of development. The excvators identified it as an indigenous sanctuary but with Near Eastern influences in its initial form (Fernández Flores and Rodríguez Azogue 2005).

The finds of possible temples at El Cerro de San Juan and at El Carambolo represent the earliest remains of religious architecture in the far West. The complex at El Carambolo poses problems simply because there is nothing else like it, but the actual temple portion may consist of no more than a single room provided with the furnishings of benches and an altar. As such, it is not unlike the temple at El Cerro de San Juan, a single-room shrine. Both of these resemble the temple at Kommos in their modest forms. Possibly some of the spaces that Carriazo uncovered at El Carambolo were actually courtyards, placing the small temple in a setting not very different from that at El Cerro de San Juan. If the early temple at Thasos is indeed of Phoenician origin, then it represents a slightly more sophisticated design, given its three distinct parts.

None of the finds of early Phoenician constructions outside the Levant itself supports the notion that the Temple of Melqart at Gadir looked at all like the temple of Solomon as described in the Bible, at least not in its initial form. It is certainly reasonable to assume that the temple did not remain a small, modest shrine on the model of the temple at Kommos as the city of Gadir developed on the opposite end of the island. Obviously, if the sanctuary did already exist as a stopping point for sailors during the initial stage of the Phoenician movement west, then as the second stage progressed and Gadir emerged as the dominant Phoenician center in the far West, the Sanctuary of Melqart, the patron god of these overseas enterprises must have received some embellishment. The Temple of Astarte at Kition offers the best notion of how the temple might have been elaborated. The holy of holies was no doubt made more monumental, perhaps even assuming the tripartite format known at Kition and referenced in items such as the installation inside the temple at Kommos. Standing upright stones, baetyls, may well have become a feature in the sanctuary since these are probably what both Poseidonius and Apollonios saw at the sanctuary (Mierse 2004: 572). Because the earliest remains of temples in this region show evidence of courtyards and variations in paving, it may be that the initial Temple of Melqart at Gadir also had this feature. This would, no doubt, have been developed in a more sophisticated manner in later iterations of the sanctuary, paralleling the sorts of development in the Phoenician region, including Cyprus, during Iron Age IIC. The finds of an ostrich egg and a glass scarab at Cerro de San Juan and the alabaster vases at El Carambolo suggest that these sanctuaries were operating to draw prestigious items toward them, as was the case at Levantine sanctuaries. The bronze spits at El Carambolo hint at ritual meals taken within the sanctuary precinct. The courtyards would have provided the needed space. The interior furnishings of benches and platforms suggest that the main cult rooms held offerings, as did their Levantine models.

A Second Phoenician Colonization

The general tendency has been to treat the period of Phoenician colonization as a single, static enterprise that was initiated, led, and overseen by the two centers of the Phoenician coast, Tyre and Sidon. The notion that Phoenicians were engaged almost exclusively in obtaining the metal riches of the Iberian Peninsula to ship back to the Levant seems to explain poorly many of the choices for settlement along the coasts. Not only were these settlements often exchanging goods for items other than metals, several of the sites seem to have been producing goods for the trade (Dietler 2009: 7). The Phoenician sites on the Peninsula can be separated into two distinct groups: (1) sites that were centered around the Straits of Gibraltar on both the European and African sides and that must have been dominated by Gadir (Sanmartí 2009: 54–55). This group would have included the settlements along the Guadalquivir (river) and Guadalete estuaries. (2) A separate settlement pattern emerged during the same period along the south coast of the Peninsula, the sites of the Costa del Sol (Neville 2007: 105–8). Our knowledge of temple-building activity is limited to a few of the sites in the Straits of Gibraltar group.

While the actual dates for foundations stretch over more than a century, little consideration has been given to whether the nature of the colonization changed. In 1989, C. González Wagner and J. Avar published an article in which they proposed that Phoenician colonization had shifted radically in the late eighth and early seventh centuries B.C.E. What had begun as a mercantile concern that was in part driven in the eighth century B.C.E. by the need to obtain silver to pay growing Assyrian tribute demands and that largely concerned the two great commercial cities of Tyre and Sidon was altered as Assyrian aggression became much more destructive. The Assyrian drive into the Levant was accompanied by devastation of the old agricultural base particularly in retribution for any type of rebellion by conquered peoples. The damage to the hinterland by Assyrian armies brought to an end a precarious balance that has been maintained by farmers. The amount of arable land was limited, there was a change in rain patterns in part due to deforestation of the coastal mountains, which left less land available for farming, and the population pressures along the coast placed greater stress on the agricultural region. The increased destructive aggressiveness and territorial annexation on part of Assyrian kings, beginning with Tiglath-pileser III (754–725 B.C.E.) and climaxing with the destruction of Sidon and the scorched-earth policy of Esarhaddon (681–668 B.C.E.) throughout North Syria, the Levant, and elsewhere resulted in an exodus of rural folk and individuals from outside the Phoenician littoral.

In the West, there is a new pattern seen to be emerging with the development of Phoenician colonies that had an agricultural basis and that were not located in the traditional manner on easily defended islands, as Thucydides describes (6.2). Instead, these new sites are often found inland rather than on the coast (González Wagner and Alvar 1989). Aubet Semmler disagrees and points out that the González Wagner and Alvar theory ignores all the evidence, both ancient and modern, that the Iron Age Phoenicians had developed as a merchant–commercially driven society rather than a primarily agriculturally based society (Aubet Semmler 2002: 99). However, while he did not offer such a radical theory of migration to explain it, Culican did note that the products used to identify Phoenician sites break into two chronologically distinct periods: a first group dating to 1200–850 B.C.E., and a second group dating from 850 to 650 B.C.E. (Culican 1982: 45–82). The second group contains the ceramic objects most commonly associated with Phoenicians in the West: trefoil-mouth jugs and mushroom jugs (Bisi 1986: 348 n. 54). The dates do not correlate specifically with the González Wagner and Alvar theory, though they do overlap, but the division in objects may support the contention of two distinct waves of arrivals with different agendas. Whether or not one accepts the particular interpretation offered by González Wagner and Alvar, the fact remains that that a second wave of settlement seems to have to happened in the West.

Motya and Kerkouane

González Wagner and Alvar have argued that the settlement of Motya on the west coast of Sicily felt some of this second wave of emigration from the Levant, since it possesses substantial agricultural hinterlands (González Wagner and Alvar 1989: 82–83). The sanctuaries identified among the ruins at Motya date to this second period, whether or not they were indeed the product of a different group of migrants. The area of the site known as the *cappidazzu* is in the northeastern sector, which seems to have been the sacred quarter of the town. The impressive rectangular building (27.40 m × 35.40 m) that has been excavated dates to the fourth century B.C.E. (fig. 134), after the destruction of the Phoenician settlement by Dionysus I of Syracuse in 397 B.C.E. One feature of this complex was a second, smaller structure in front, probably designed to hold 3 baetyls, which would have stood on a rectangular slab of stone pierced through by a large hole in the center with two partial holes at either end. This fourth-century complex replaced an earlier complex dating to the seventh century. It consisted of a smaller building made of rough, undressed stones and somehow related to a lustral well. The two elements were enclosed by a wall built in the sixth century. The few architectural details found in connection with the earlier shrine included an Egyptian cyme decoration (Tusa 1999: 234–36; Tusa and de Miro 1983: 91). Another shrine, probably of sixth-century B.C.E. date, seems to have stood just outside the north gate. In its first phase, it incorporated Doric columns, suggesting early Greek influence at the site (Bondi 1999a: 329–30).

González Wagner and Alvar do not discuss Kerkouane on Cape Bon in the region near Carthage, though they do suggest that, even in this area, the settlement pattern changed in the later periods (González Wagner and Alvar 1989: 84–85). The ruins at Kerkouane date to the sixth century B.C.E. The sanctuary is the largest remaining Phoenician temple found in the western Mediterranean.[4] Kerkouane is on the coast of modern Tunisia not far from Carthage. The temple was integrated into the gridded fabric of the town. It consisted of a vestibule entered directly from the street. This in turn led to an oblong room (7 m × 10 m) with two benches. The hall was located in

---

4. It is also known as the "House of Columns."

a courtyard and divided it into two parts. The front part had a platform, probably an altar, making the front courtyard the center for ritual sacrifices. The rear courtyard was arranged for ritual dining. The outbuildings associated with the temple housed a workshop that produced terra-cotta figurines. Found in the workshop were storage areas for clay, tubs, and a kiln (Fantar 1999: 211–12; Bondi 1999a: 326).

Iberian Sites of the Second Emigration

Carmona

While none of the Iberian sites that González Wagner and Alvar discuss as possibly having been settled by Levantine peoples looking to establish an agricultural rather than a mercantile basis for the support of the community have yielded evidence for temple structures (González Wagner and Alvar 1989: 88–102), Belén Deamos has identified two possible examples of sanctuaries that would have been intended to service just these sorts of Levantine settlements in the rich agricultural heartland of the Guadalquivir Valley.[5] The latest structure at Carmona, from the fifth century B.C.E., consists of three contiguous rooms running NE to SW, two showing evidence of red pavement, and all arranged on one side of a courtyard. The stones of the foundations and socles were carefully selected for size so that the medium and large stones formed the exterior facing, and the smaller stones formed the interior. The standing wall fragments are 0.55–0.56 m wide and probably held up tapis or adobe walls. This fifth-century B.C.E. complex stands above two earlier versions, the oldest dating to the seventh century B.C.E.[6] The earliest is a rectangular structure enclosing a single room and is longitudinally oriented NE to SW (fig. 137). It was built with adobe or tapis walls placed on stone socles of the same width as the later three-room complex, but the stones for the foundations and socles are not as carefully chosen. The interior floor shows signs of being red. While nothing about the design of either structure indicates a temple, the finds in all three levels of constructions do suggest ritual uses. The red pigment on the floors is distinct and is found in the native sanctuary at Cancho Roano (see below) as well as the shrine at El Cerro de San Juan. The orientation was maintained in all three versions. Built benches are part of the architectural furnishings of the final structure, and these are often found as part of temple structures. The architecture of the middle temple (sixth century B.C.E.) cannot be discerned, but there are finds: 4 marble ladles in the form of the paws of an ungulate, 3 large pithoi with Levantine-style painted decoration, a red ceramic plate, 2 gray ceramic cups, and 2 roughly made vases (Belén et al. 1997: 145–80). Among the painted designs on the 3 pithoi are figures of griffins marching in a line, and vegetal filler, including rosettes and lotus forms. Belén argues that these are funerary motifs usually connected with Astarte (Belén Deamos 2001: 9–10) and may indicate the nature of the temple's dedication.

---

5. The excavators tended to view these sites as being of native origin with Phoenician influence.
6. During the Roman-period occupation, a cistern was dug down through the Iron Age remains. It appears as the circular element in the drawings.

Montemolín

A second possible temple has been found at El Cerro de Montemolín (Marchena) (Chaves 1993; Chaves and de la Bandera 1992). The site is not far from the important later, native, Roman period town of Urso (Osuna) and has yielded a series of super-imposed structures that could have been a temple. These stand on a hill, maybe an acropolis, so perhaps a high place in the old Semitic sense. The oldest level dates to the late eighth–early seventh centuries B.C.E. (fig. 135). This first structure, Building A, is of mud brick or tapis set on stone socles about 0.80 m thick and in an oval form oriented SW to NE on the longitudinal axis, and the oval building survives through another iteration. Building D, the next structure, continues the orientation but not the shape. The new building is a rectangle with interior subdivisions that create a se-ries of spaces (fig. 136). There is a small entrance vestibule that leads into a courtyard surrounded on two sides by long rooms that can be entered from the courtyard. It is this last version of the temple, sixth century B.C.E., that yields the evidence for cultic function (Belén Deamos 2001: 12). In the vestibule are ceramic finds along with bones of domestic sheep, pigs, and cattle—probably remains of animals slaughtered in sacri-fices at the entrance to the temple and then consumed in ritual meals. In the courtyard are traces of hearths and fragments of cooking pots along with plates, which had all been broken after being used to prepare and cook the meat. In a small pit, there is a possible votive deposit that is a mixture of animal bone fragments, ash, sherds of painted pots, and a belt buckle.

Cancho Roano

The oval shape of the first two buildings at El Cerro de Montemolín is unknown in any other building on the Iberian Peninsula for this period. It is not found in Levan-tine sacred architecture. Only the unusual apsidal building at Ashdod from the period of the settlement by the "Peoples of the Sea" relates at all, and this is only because it is unusual. However, at the site of Cancho Roano in southeastern Extremadura, the recent excavations have unearthed remains of an oval-shaped feature in the lowest level of the building. This oval element is not defined by the foundation walls of the structure but is, rather, a roughly oval platform made of stones. This feature does not remain an architectural element in the later three phases of the complex at Cancho Roano, which have been identified as a possible native temple. The excavator has ar-gued, however, that the earlier feature may have marked the tomb of a local warrior who was buried with great ceremony on the site. This hero's tomb was then incorpo-rated into the later versions of the massive structure. Indeed the decision to build the temple on the site could have been motivated by its already hallowed nature (Celes-tino Pérez 2001: 22). Although the Cancho Roano building is a native construction influenced by Levantine developments, the earlier tomb probably predates the arrival of any Semitic influences in the region.

It is certainly possible that a similar situation existed at el Cerro de Montemolín. The oval structure may mark an earlier, Late Bronze Age native heroic tomb that was honored through one rebuilding before the hallowed nature of the spot was converted to a temple rather than strictly a funerary monument. In the first version of the Cancho Roano temple (CR level C), the oval feature was hidden by the new building, which was partially built on top of it. The complex centered on unit H-7, which was to remain the focal point of the design through phases B and A, during which time the building was greatly enlarged with additional rooms and courtyards, and the oval feature was lost (Celestino Pérez 2001: 26–37).

Conclusion

Of these possible sanctuaries in the colonies that were part of the second wave of emigration, only the remains from Kerkouane provide enough architecture to suggest anything about the building itself. The locking of the sanctuary complex into the urban grid recalls the treatment of the little shrine at Sarepta. The format of vestibule preceding the main cult chamber can be found as early as the third version of the temple at Tell Qasile and seems to have remained as a feature of even modest sanctuary designs. The placement of the shrine within a large grouping of courtyards clearly follows the pattern seen in several of the Iron Age II Levantine and Cypriot sanctuaries, such as Bamboula, and could be a precursor to the developments that took place in the Phoenician region during the Persian period. The evidence for ritual meals is known from several Levantine shrines. Interestingly, the Kerkouane sanctuary has associations with a terra-cotta workshop. The mixing of sanctuary and workshop is not a common feature of Levantine sacral design for Iron Age I or II but has been noted for sacral Iron Age IA sites on Cyprus (Webb and Karageorghis n.d.: 4–5; Karageorghis 1982: 104) and in the Levant at Ashdod and Sarepta (see chap. 3).

Far less survives of the sanctuaries on the Iberian Peninsula for this second period. What can be concluded is that the sanctuaries are still quite modest structures, though there is some evidence for the more careful selection of building materials. The possible incorporation of older, native graves into the first sanctuaries at Cerro de Montemolín and Cancho Roano poses an interesting question. Was this undertaken as a means of usurping the older native hallowedness of the ground? At Cancho Roano, the builders were most likely native but very strongly influenced by new foreign, Levantine forces in the area. At Cerro de Montemolín, there is a good chance that the site had become a Levantine outpost, and here the final version of the temple, Building D, with its rectangular shape and rooms connected to an internal courtyard, recalls the design of Building 350 at Ekron, or perhaps in some way it mimics the form of the small shrine in the Tell Arad fortress. While the spaces in the fortress shrine are hierarchical in a manner that is quite different from the shrine at Montemolín, the basic formats for the Tell Arad fortress shrine and Montemolín Building D do resemble one another.

What is noteworthy about the González Wagner and Alvar theory is that it allows for the influences entering the West to come from a much wider distribution of Semitic sources. The traditional view of Phoenician colonization lays stress on the cities of Tyre and Sidon and can be expanded legitimately to include eastern Cyprus. However, if González Wagner and Alvar are correct, then the second wave of emigrants came from a much wider region of the Levant, from all the areas being damaged by Assyrian aggression. They also were not coming from urban centers only but from the rural regions as well. Moreover, while the settlers from Tyre and Sidon may well have brought with them older Canaanite concepts that had survived the disruptions of 1200 B.C.E., the newer emigrants were moving out of the regions that had developed in the wake of the 1200 B.C.E. destructions. They were moving away from Iron Age IIB settings. The temples at Motya and Kerkouane are integrated into the urban fabric of their towns, not unlike the little sanctuary at Sarepta. The positions of the sanctuaries at Motya, one in the northeast near the north gate and the other just outside it, recall the situation of the Moabite sanctuary at Wadi ath-Thamad #13. The greater diversity of peoples making up the later migrations might help explain the appearance of a temple type at Cerro de Montemolín which, at least in Iron Age contexts, developed in the Philistine region rather than in the Phoenician area and may have been further developed later in the setting of a Judean fortress outpost.

Whether or not one accepts the González Wagner and Alvar explanation, the fact remains that the seventh-century B.C.E. Phoenician settlements on the Iberian Peninsula were quite different from the settlements that first appeared in the eighth century B.C.E. In her analyses of the changing urban fabrics and burial patterns at Phoenician sites, Neville has noted that, by the seventh century, clearly the settlements were permanent; individuals who were living in them were part of the far Western setting. These were people who lived and died in the West, by choice, one assumes. Houses at several sites become more impressive, being carefully constructed with stone. Some of the cemeteries attached to the towns include impressive chamber tombs with rich grave gifts, including imported Egyptian and Greek objects. The cemeteries seem to attest a greater degree of social stratification in these communities, and some of the wealth may have been acquired from the production of the towns themselves, since there is now evidence of local craft workshops. It seems safe to assume that some of the commercial interaction between Phoenicians and the indigenous populations involved the local production (Neville 2007: 75).

It is striking in such settings of prosperity to find so little evidence of rich temple-building, yet the answer may lie in the nature of the emigration itself. In her excavations of the cemetery at Al-Bass that served some of the population of Iron Age Tyre,

Aubet Semmler has noted the strong egalitarian nature of the burials themselves. She has posited that, if any elements of social stratification were encoded in the burials, they may have appeared in the level of the "secondary rites," which would have occurred at the grave but would not necessarily be indicated in the burial contents or the tomb itself. At the same time, she has pointed out that there is evidence for more-elaborate cut-rock tombs elsewhere around Tyre, and these could have served the needs of the more affluent and prestigious members of Tyrian society, which seems to have been the situation at Sidon. So the Al-Bass burials reflect the reality for a large portion of the population but not for all members (Aubet 2010: 154–55).

Something similar may have been happening on the Iberian Peninsula, with a few high-ranking burials set off by the mass of more common burials. Neville (2007: 76) has suggested that this arrangement could reflect the reality of the structure within which the Phoenician overseas adventure was undertaken. Members of the great mercantile families of Tyre led the movement west and established the first outposts. They were the ancestors of unilineal corporate descent groups, who came to control much of the commercially obtained wealth and, by the seventh century, probably also the local craft workshops. The prominent members of these groups formed the network of ties back to the Levantine coast and continued to oversee the movement of peoples west, particularly if the González Wagner and Alvar thesis is correct.

This picture somewhat agrees with C. Bell's analysis of the change in trade patterns in the Levant following the collapse of 1200 B.C.E. (Bell 2006: 112–13). She has argued that, as the palace control of long-distance trade ceased, the merchant communities, probably comprising merchant families, of Cyprus and the Phoenician coast were able to step into the void because they were largely free of the Late Bronze Age imperial trade agendas. Since the Iberian Peninsula may have already been a loose part of the extended Late Bronze Age trade network by Iron Age IA—to judge from the Villena treasure of eastern Mediterranean luxury materials dated to between the thirteenth and tenth centuries B.C.E. and probably a gift to a local chief from a Cypriot or Sardenian middleman merchant (Neville 2007: 31)—Phoenician trading families were poised to head back to the West. In this scenario, the kings of Tyre did not play much of a role. Because most of the major temple construction at Tyre probably had some type of royal affiliation (at least in the tenth century, with Hiram's projects), this royal construction would have had no currency in the context of overseas outposts, either in their initial phases or later, in their permanent forms. If, as is suggested above, the demographic makeup of the Western settlers became more varied in the seventh century, then specifically Tyrian forms would had had even less reason to be favored in the new communities. Instead, what appears are modest sanctuaries of a type built by Levantine communities but not by kings.

Chapter 8

Conclusion

Formal Patterns

No major architectural shifts occurred between the Late Bronze Age and the early Iron Age that strike me as indicating a fundamental change in the concept of a structure. A Late Bronze Age architect would have recognized all the forms that were employed in temples in the early Iron Age. The Levant would have to wait until the advent of Greek rule before truly new forms entered the region. However, early Iron Age temples are not completely interchangeable with their Late Bronze Age forerunners.

Vernacular versus Prestigious Temple Types

Many of the surviving remains of Late Bronze Age temples fall in the category of prestigious buildings. The temples that were constructed in urban settings were usually large compared with other structures and were solidly built. Some had the pedigree of age because their usage reached back to the Middle Bronze Age. They represented major investments by their communities, and this was true of even the sanctuaries that may have serviced nomadic populations at Deir ʿAlla and the Amman airport. The exception is the wayside shrine of Tel Mevorakh.

The early Iron Age temples divide into those that were built to be prestigious structures and those erected as elements of the vernacular built environment. In the former category are the temples from the Late Bronze Age that continued to function into the early Iron Age and the new temples constructed as part of larger palace-temple complexes. The vernacular temples are small, modest affairs. Their special significance is usually only clear due to the internal arrangements of the furnishings. These items may manifest clues in terms of placement or the use of limited prestigious building materials that help to reveal their separation from other structures in the community, but there is nothing unusual about their size, orientation, or most of the materials used for their construction that makes their special role immediately apparent. The shrine at Sarepta and the temples at Abu Hawam, Tell Qasile, and Ekron are all integrated into the urban fabric. Their slightly larger size and nondomestic plans indicate their particular role. Tell Qasile's temple was placed on the highest point in the town, a location that does distinguish it, and courtyards were used to create a kind of buffer between the temple itself and the encroaching neighborhood, but this is quite different from the clear separation for prestigious temples. Interestingly, the Late Bronze Age and first early Iron Age temples at Beth-shean maintain the characteristics that give the temples a clear prestigious status within the urban setting. This changes when the site loses any associations with Egyptian control of the region. The later temples become much more deeply enmeshed in the dense urban development on the acropolis.

The placement of a little shrine in the fortress at Arad was new. There is nothing parallel from Late Bronze Age settings. It was clearly a product of the new Iron Age II political reality of territorial kingdoms rather than city-states, which needed to protect frontier interests with permanent garrisons. The shrine, though small and not distinguished by building materials, was still accorded prestige by the use of an encircling wall that served to create a separate precinct. The courtyard in the front space also provided some protection for the most sacred space, the holy of holies. The importance accorded the area is evidenced by the way in which it was respected in the rebuildings of the fort itself.

At Tel Dan, enough of the urban fabric survives to permit comparisons of the prestigious and vernacular aspects of cultic spaces. The main sanctuary is a high place defined by both its physical position and its separation from the rest of the town at the end of the cobbled road that leads up to it directly from the main gate. It is a space that could be easily restricted. The road provided a perfect formal processional route, thereby emphasizing the importance of the events that occurred in the space at the end of the road. The structures within the precinct include those that were built of good stone masonry. Stone is not rare in the region, but it is not the material of most domestic architecture. The precinct is also large with several distinct areas. This may have permitted a number of simultaneous activities. The other shrines along the road are modest affairs—spaces set aside for the placement of *maṣṣēbôt*. These are shrines that could be approached by anyone on the road and were not physically restricted. They are not significant in terms of their housings, which are no more than cutbacks in the wall that frames the main road.

The pattern that emerges for the early Iron Age temples appears more complex than the pattern for the Late Bronze Age. While many temples of the earlier period were clearly given prestige by scale, in the early Iron Age prestige is more likely to come from the inclusion of the temple in a complex with a palace. In the designs at Tell Taʿyinat and Guzana, the dialogue between palace and temple is seen in the architectural interplay of materials and design features. The lack of surviving evidence for the palace at Carchemish makes it impossible to assess how the two units related, but it is obvious that the temple was intentionally incorporated into the design of the processional way. The notion of kingship as it developed in Iron Age II was associated with the physical manifestation of the presence of the divine in the same sphere as the king himself. The king had direct access to the divine, who resided in the same space.

The movement of Levantine peoples to the far West, first as merchantmen and later as settlers, brought the architectural concept of buildings devoted to cultic function into new regions. In the Aegean, there already existed a tradition of shrine-building, albeit on a modest scale, that had taken shape in the Late Bronze Age. Farther west, this sort of architectural notion does not seem to have formed already among the native peoples of the Mediterranean coast. The Levantine travelers took with them the vernacular form of their religious architecture. The surviving temples in the West exhibit the same traits as noted for the vernacular forms in the Levant. They are modest structures built of easily available, worked materials. The plans, where they survive, show no outward manifestation of the cultic functions intended for the building. This is in perfect accord with the function of these distant outposts of Levantine cults. Initially, they were intended to serve the needs of sailors and merchants—adventurers, granted—but not kings or rulers. In their earliest forms, these temples were not even built for resident communities, since most likely the traffic moved through them and out again fairly quickly. This is probably why more attention was paid to the storage facilities of these factories than to the religious buildings. Though a later wave of migration brought settlers who expanded the Levantine presence deeper into the West, these were village settlers whose traditions of sanctuary buildings were of the vernacular type. Their temples reflect what they knew in their Iron Age IIC villages, not the prestigious temples associated most often with the royal projects of Iron Age IIA and B.

Temples and Their Settings

Whether a temple was of the vernacular type or was a feature in a royal enclosure, it was conceived in cosmic terms. The early Iron Age communities, despite all the demographic changes that had taken place, still treated their temples as the physical residence of the god, a belief that extended back to the third millennium B.C.E. (Pitkänen 2003: 27–28). Carrying a cult to the West required that a house be built for the god, even on a modest scale. The physical presence of the god provided the populace with the assurance of divine beneficence and prosperity, and the temple offered the best evidence of the god's existence within the community. The ancient descriptions of Tyre suggest that several temples could be found within the confines of the city. Even if one temple was sequestered inside the royal region, there were others available to the general population. The excavations at Guzana, Carchemish, and Tell Taʿyinat have not expanded to the cities themselves, so it is not clear whether more than the royal temples are to be found. The placement of the Tell Taʿyinat temple behind the palace rather than in the courtyard that actually defined the royal enclosure may have rendered it more available to the residents of the city.

While no single type can be identified as either vernacular or prestigious, there are clear features that seem to distinguish the two types. The prestigious temples all contain spaces arranged in such a manner that they can accommodate processions, a formal movement through the space. In some instances, this type is in the form of a tripartite design, but not always. This sort of arrangement does not occur with the vernacular temples. In them, the internal spaces are small and often subdivided. They could never accommodate stately, formal movements through them. Many of the vernacular temples are designed so that they require a directional shift after an individual has entered the building. The benches that are often found as architectural features of these temples must have been intended to hold votive offerings. The intimacy of the space and the denial of any formal movement would have encouraged a more intimate involvement with ritual, though by whom, we cannot determine from the architecture.

The two wayside shrines were the least well defined in terms of architecture. This may be the result of their role. They were places that offered solace in a region that had become ethnically and religiously more diverse in the early Iron Age. They were perhaps intended to be neutral spaces. By limiting their architectural definition and internal furnishings, the shrines could function for a wider range of cultic needs. This may also have been the case for the shrines that were built in the West. The mixed groups of people who probably sailed out of Levantine ports were perhaps best served by sanctuaries that were as undefined as possible. While something similar could also have influenced the design of the Negev sanctuary at Horvat Qitmit, the find of a rich assortment of ceramic items including probable cultic statues at ʿEn Hatzeva suggests that a very specific cult was involved at these two sites—that is, a cult that served the needs of the nomadic Edomite population of the region. The individual units that constituted the Horvat Qitmit grouping may well have been created to serve quite specific rites, some of which took place in designated spaces outdoors, and others in enclosed areas.

Certainly the interplay between the enclosed areas and the open areas that were related to those enclosures was a feature of most of the early Iron Age sanctuary designs, though the treatment of the open space as equivalent to another room seems to have been more fully developed in the nonroyal settings for temples. Courtyards within sanctuary complexes—such as at Ekron, Tell Qasile, the Temple of Astarte and the later Temple of Melqart at Kition, and the fortress shrine at Tell Arad—may have permitted select members of the community to have a greater connection with the divine without actually allowing them to enter the holiest spaces. These design features were not new in the early Iron Age, but their appearance in small, modest, vernacular shrines could reflect some type of change in the way in which some early Iron Age communities understood how the divine could be approached and by whom.

Collapse and Regeneration

It is interesting to note that, in the studies of collapses and regenerations of society that have appeared over the last decade (Schwartz and Nichols 2006; Yoffee and Cowgill 1988), none has elected to look closely at the end of the Late Bronze Age and the birth of the early Iron Age in the Levantine context. Certainly the question of what forces led to the collapse of the Late Bronze Age has generated numerous studies (Joukowsky and Ward 1992), as has the question of the birth of the ancient Israelite state, but investigations from the point of view of models that are applicable to the wider Levantine region have largely been ignored.

The revival of the Levant occurred quite quickly in certain areas, and the process warrants a large-scale reassessment. That sort of consideration is beyond the scope of this book, but it seems obvious that temples were a very basic item in the architectural repertoire of the reemerging societies of the early Iron Age and thus provide fundamental testimonia to revived social and economic structures within the region. The political situation in the Late Bronze Age Levant favored the formation of centralized, small city-states under some type of control from either the Egyptian Empire in the south or the Hittite Empire in the north, or the struggle to remain somewhat independent. Within this setting, the temples formed the physical manifestations of the local religious hierarchy (Yoffee 1988 12). No doubt the use of localized rituals tied to specific manifestations of a cult—even a cult with wide distribution—helped to assure residents of a city who had limited economic and political independence some notion of their own uniqueness. Temples were the locus for activities that assured this sort of identity. The temples themselves differed very little from one place to another, but they probably did not need to be varied; they were the backdrop for rituals that the general public only partially observed, because access to the interior was denied.

The problem posed by the collapse at the end of the Late Bronze Age is a problem of definition. Did the Late Bronze Age civilization cease to be, and did the civilization that rose to replace it in the early Iron Age represent a significant break (Yoffee 1988: 15)? The answers seem to depend on what areas one is investigating. The Phoenician region shows good evidence for demographic and cultural continuity. Freeing the coast from the control of outside powers allowed the early Iron Age Phoenician cities to flourish and to emerge as powerful local city-states in the Late Bronze Age model, though, by early Iron Age II, Tyre was dominating and controlling the overseas territorial expansion. Elsewhere, demographic shifts suggest quite new cultural forces at work: the Arameans in the north and the Philistines in the south. Any Late Bronze Age forces that remained vital were now viewed through new cultural lenses. The situation for early Israelites and the peoples of Transjordan remains less clear, since there is no agreement about whether these were new peoples in the area or old human stock with a new identity. Under these circumstances, the local societies that begin to emerge in early Iron Age I and then flourish in early Iron Age II must largely be seen as new. They were the products of the regeneration of the region that began not long after the destructions of 1200 B.C.E. and the following societal collapse. The temples that began to appear in early Iron Age I represented one of the most potent statements of this regeneration. They were emblematic of a return to a degree of social complexity because they required some redistribution of society's resources to build and to maintain, even in their early, modest forms. The first to appear were basically of the vernacular sort, serving the needs of these first reviving communities. The early Iron Age I temples may well testify to the security of places such as Tell Qasile. The steady embellishment and enlargement of the temples suggest a degree of increased prosperity, and thus funds were available that could be funneled into building projects. The great palace-temple complexes of early Iron Age II speak of renewed political and economic power that was concentrated in the hands of the individuals who commissioned them. Widespread use of the design form of these temple-palace units, from Jerusalem in the south to Tell Taʿyinat in the north, from Guzana in the east to possibly Tyre in the west may be an indication of the interconnected nature of the political and economic spheres in the Levant of the ninth century B.C.E.

Nothing in the archaeological finds or the designs of the temples helps to clarify whether the temples in the early Iron Age settings functioned differently from those in the Late Bronze Age in any way. The wider distribution of the vernacular type may support the argument for wider community involvement in some aspects of religion than there had been in the Late Bronze Age. There is reason to posit an enriched role for music in early Iron Age society that must have been reflected also in the ritual setting. At a minimum, there may have been greater demand for temple musicians, who would then have increased the accessibility of the divine to the larger community (Schwartz 2006: 9).

The dynasties that we know came to power in the early Iron Age II were new, and with the possible exception of the Tyrian, were born of new peoples, who either arrived in the region or had shifted positions as a result of the collapse of Late Bronze Age society. These dynasties may have consciously looked to older forms of architecture to help legitimize their claims to power. This would explain the archaizing tendency of some of the temples associated with palaces (Schwartz 2006: 12) and would certainly fit with the situation at Tell Taʿyinat, which is physically close to the site of the great temple-palace complex of Late Bronze Age Alalakh. At Tell Taʿyinat, the Alalakh precedent may have been too strong to ignore, although 400 years had intervened. Something similar could lie behind the temple-palace arrangement at Carchemish, but with no knowledge of the Late Bronze Age city, we cannot know. In a similar manner, the form of early Iron Age Tyre may have intentionally evoked Late Bronze Age Tyre, but with remains of neither Late Bronze Age nor early Iron Age city to work with, we cannot say.

On the other hand, the design of the temple in the Guzana complex can be related to no other existing remains, which suggests that here on the eastern fringe of the Levant in a territory that had only recently come under Aramean control and that had a long history of direct Mesopotamian connections, there was an environment conducive to architectural experimentation. The Guzana temple is, however, an exception. More common is the revival of the long-room temple type for these temple-palace compounds, and its use may well have resulted from a need to dress new dynasties in old clothes in politically uncertain settings.

Solomon and His Temple

Nothing in this book helps one side or the other in the debate about the date for Solomon and his temple. As described, the temple could have been built in the tenth or the ninth century B.C.E. It is clearly dependent on older models. From the Middle Bronze Age onward, architectural influences in the region tended to move from Syria down into Palestine. Making the Jerusalem temple-palace complex the precursor to those at Tell Taʿyinat, Carchemish, and Guzana would clearly break this pattern, but the early Iron Age was a new world with far less continuity than was true of the Middle Bronze and Late Bronze Ages. On the other hand, the rise of the Davidic Dynasty was not without problems. Jerusalem was only incorporated into the emerging state of Israel during David's years, and thus it was free from any previous traditions that needed to be considered, since it was conquered territory. Moreover, David's claim to the right to rule was not uncontested (Finkelstein and Silberman 2006). If the events recorded in the book of Kings are dated to the ninth century B.C.E. rather than the tenth, then the building project that engaged Solomon's attention fits into a pattern that was seen in several political centers at the same time. The use of the long-room temple format combined with the palace construction would then mean that the Solomonic program was part of the larger pattern of royal complexes being constructed by new dynastic heads. It would have been the expected architectural statement of kingship—something that might be found in the political center of any ruler.

Ethnicitvy and Architecture

There is good evidence to support the notion of a demographic shift in the Levantine region, probably beginning in the Late Bronze Age and culminating in the two centuries of Iron Age I. But whether this change of people was accompanied by a changed sense of identity or a sense of possessing a specific ethnicity is not at all certain. Throughout this book, terminology laden with ethnic resonances has been employed as a means of keeping the various groups and areas clear. Phoenician, Philistine, Israelite, Neo-Hittite, and Aramean have all been established as categories into which temples have been slotted, but the use of the device for the purposes of presentation and arrangement of information should not blind us to the fact that the terminology was very likely meaningless during the centuries under investigation. There is no compelling reason to believe that the peoples living in Iron Age I North Syria knew themselves to be Arameans or (Neo-)Hittites. Clearly the peoples on the Phoenician coast did not refer to themselves as Phoenicians, because the label is of Greek derivation. Whether the highland people of Palestine considered themselves to be Israelites is certainly one of the most contested points of scholarship on this period (R. Miller 2005), as is the question of whether or not the Philistines would have known themselves by this term.

Specific terminology apart, the larger question is did these different human groups identify themselves as units? Did they possess what Killebrew has called a sense of "group identity" (Killebrew 2005: 8) that would allow us to recognize each one as a distinct ethnos that somehow manifested its distinctness in material culture? Setting aside the use of pottery, which has caused many problems when employed as a marker of specific ethnicity, can any other manifestation of material culture help to mark a specific group in the Levant during these centuries? Architecture would seem to be a reasonable choice, and certainly the literature on the four-room house as a possible indicator of Israelite presence testifies to this sort of use. However, the arguments have not proved persuasive, and the evidence is anything but clear. This is similarly true of sanctuaries and temples.

Although it makes it easier for us to discuss and compare temples when they are presented in identifying categories, these categories do the disservice of suggesting that there really was a specific (Neo-)Hittite, Aramean, Phoenician, Israelite, or Philistine type of temple. Nothing seems to be further from the truth. The buildings considered in this book do not appear to have any particular affiliation with a specific people. A possible argument can be made that the Iron Age I Philistine structures maintained some features of Aegean origin that were perhaps identity markers that still carried meaning for the people of Philistine settlement on the coast, but these features are limited, quite different in their use from the use of their supposed prototypes, and do not persist. If they ever had a specific role of serving to remind the Philistines of their origins, clearly that role ceased early.

The Arameans were a nomadic people with no tradition of monumental building, who learned to build as they settled. This lack of tradition combined with a similar lack of concern for the remnants of what still existed in the areas where they settled may have freed them to explore quite novel forms, such as the Guzana structures, which do not seem to fit exactly with contemporary developments elsewhere.

The other newcomers in the region, the Israelites, on the other hand, built temples and sanctuaries in Israel and Judah in Iron Age II that follow patterns known from elsewhere: a long-room temple to accompany the palace of Solomon, a high place with altars and possible temple at Tel Dan, and a broad-room temple at Arad. None of the generally held views about the origins of the Israelites gives them a tradition of architecture that could have influenced these structures.

However, even when there is a degree of demographic continuity with which to argue, as with the Phoenicians and Neo-Hittites, the structures that appear do not exhibit enough specific elements to support their being considered a particular type of temple associated with a group—a Neo-Hittite or Phoenician temple type.

What did seem to exist during Iron Age I and II was a variety of sanctuary and temple forms—some with older pedigrees, some new—that had wide distribution. What perhaps dictated which form to use was the temple's function in social, economic, and political terms, rather than any notion of an appropriate style for a specific people. Village-level temples, whether from Sarepta on the Phoenician coast or Khirbat Mudayna in Moab, were small, modest affairs that were probably intended to serve as receptacles for offerings made by the residents of the villages and as the focal point for community rituals. Function and resources determined the forms. Similar forces girded the designs of the great royal temple-palace complexes, which were much more about the appropriate setting for the presentation of divinely sanctioned rule than about any announcement of ethnic identity.

It may well have been during the Iron Age that the fundamental breakdown in the religious unity of the Levant began that continued for at least a thousand years and that in time would come to have ethnic associations, but Iron Age I andII temples do not evidence this collapse. The temples within the same social, economic, or political setting seem to have been interchangeable. The little chapel outside Khirbat Mudayna could have changed places with the little shrine at Teman. Solomon's temple could have stood at Tell Taʿyinat. The rich sculptural decorations at Guzana, Aleppo, and Carchemish may not have been suitable in Solomon's Jerusalem, but the biblical description does offer a temple with interior sculpture and sculpture on the doors, and the Late Bronze Age orthostat temple at Hazor had sculpture; so even on this point, there may not have been a problem.

The situation of the sanctuaries of the Iron Age I and II Levant may find its closest parallel in the Romanesque church architecture of Western Europe. The churches built in England, France, and Spain in the eleventh and early twelfth centuries c.e. were largely interchangeable. They did not represent national styles. In this regard, Romanesque architecture was quite different from the Gothic forms that next appeared, which were very much about regional styles associated with the identity of the people in whose locales they were built; they were anything but interchangeable.

The Spread of the Levantine Forms

The most far-reaching architectural development in the early Iron Age Levant was the spread of Levantine forms outside the homeland. This diffusion must have occurred in two distinct ways—both tied to commerce. The Greek presence at the port of Al Mina on the Syrian coast from the eighth century B.C.E. on corresponded with the birth of monumental Greek temple architecture. While there is more than adequate evidence of the lines of continuity that joined eighth-century B.C.E. Greek temple experimentation (particularly the form of naos and pronaos) with the designs of earlier early Iron Age rulers' houses and even Late Bronze Age Mycenean shrines, the fact remains that Greeks at Al Mina must have had the opportunity to see some of the monumental temples going up at nearby locations such as Tell Taʿyinat and ʿAin Dara. Both of these temples were on their respective acropolis citadels but were not completely hidden in palace enclosures and thus may have been visible even if not fully accessible to interested Greeks. They would have provided a chance to see contemporary monumental stone temple buildings. Greek artists displayed openness toward other aspects of Levantine art that began to enter Greece during these years of the Orientalizing period, which suggests that there was an environment in which architects who wanted to construct important temple buildings may have been free to imitate Levantine structures, which had religious pedigree as well as foreign allure. Certainly the earliest evidence that we have for temples in the Greek world reveals forms that are too similar to contemporary Levantine long-room temples to be entirely accidental.

The other vehicle promoting the spread of Levantine temple forms to the West was the movement of Eastern Mediterranean peoples out of their homelands. The first phase took merchants west, and these merchants needed some type of cultic site to serve them during their long journeys. This need was satisfied by modest, vernacular-type shrines at sites such as Kommos, perhaps Thasos, and maybe the first iteration of the sanctuary at Gadir. Later, Levantine settlers established real outposts in the West, and these communities also needed to have sanctuaries. In both of these movements, the populations headed west were probably mixed populations. Even though the ships sailed out of the Phoenician ports and were elements in the Phoenician mercantile expansion, the sailors and settlers probably came from all over the region, as was certainly the case when Levantine settlers moved west in the wake of Assyrian aggression throughout the region. This must have been even more true if, as C. Bell has stressed, much of this was largely private enterprise rather than state controlled (Bell 2006: 113–14). Merchant families looking to establish profitable trading outposts in the far West would have been seeking settlers capable of being deracinated without losing their ability to perform vital duties at such an outpost. They would have been less in need of people who merely originated from the mother city.

In the Aegean, Levantine architectural forms encountered local architectural forces with long traditions. However, in the far West, no architectural traditions for sacred building existed. Here the new forms introduced to serve Levantine needs were the first to be built, and any potential study of the development of indigenous sacred architecture in the regions open to Levantine settlement cannot be considered without a serious examination of the role played by the Levantine forms. The Levantine builders introduced temples of the Levantine vernacular types, and it was in response to these that the indigenous architects created the first native temples during the sixth and fifth centuries B.C.E. These indigenous temples were not copies of Levantine forms, but they only appear in the context of the newly emerging native societies in the far West that took shape as a direct result of the catalyst of a foreign presence (Cunliffe 1988).

Bibliography

Abdul Salam, A.
  1996   Physical Geographical Environment in the Tadmorian Desert and the Silk Road. *AAAS* 47: 27–28.
Abu ʿAssāf, A.
  n.d.   *Le temple de ʿAin Dara.* n.p. [site guide]
  1982   ʿAin Dara: Eine neu entdeckte Residenzstadt. Pp. 349–52 in *Land des Baʿals: Syrien- Forum der Völker und Kulturen.* Mainz am Rhein: von Zabern.
  1983   Ein Relief der kriegerischen Göttin Ischtar. *Damaszener Mitteilungen* 1: 7–8.
  1985   Ain Dara. Pp. 347–50 in Weiss 1985.
  1990   *Der temple von ʿAin Dara.* Damaszener Forschungen 3. Mainz: von Zabern.
  1993   Der Tempel von ʿAin Dara in Nordsyrien. *Antike Welt* 24: 155–71.
  1997   ʿAin Dara. Pp. 33–35 in vol. 1 of *OEANE.*
  2000   Die Stadt im alten Orient. Pp. 76–82 in *Damaskus-Aleppo: 5000 Jahre Stadtentwick- lung in Syrien.* Mainz am Rhein: von Zabern.
Ackerman, S.
  2003   Digging Up Deborah. *NEA* 66/4: 172–84.
Aerts, E., and H. Klengel, eds.
  1990   *The Town as Regional Economic Centre in the Ancient Near East,* Session B-16: *Pro- ceedings of the Tenth International Economic History Conference. Leuven, August 1990.* Leuven: Leuven University Press.
Aharoni, Y.
  1968a Arad: Its Inscriptions and Temple. *BA* 31/1: 1–32.
  1968b Trial Excavation in the "Solar Shrine" at Lachish: Preliminary Report. *IEJ* 18: 157–69.
  1973   The Solomonic Temple, the Tabernacle and the Arad Sanctuary. Pp. 1–8 in Hoffner 1973.
  1974   The Building Activities of David and Solomon. *IEJ* 24: 13–16.
  1975   *Investigations at Lachish: The Sanctuary and the Residency (Lachish V).* Publications of the Institute of Archaeology 4. Tel Aviv: Tel Aviv University Press.
  1979   *The Land of the Bible: A Historical Geography.* Philadelphia: Westminster.
  1982   *The Archaeology of the Land of Israel.* Philadelphia: Westminster.
Ahlström, G. W.
  1961   Der Prophet Nathan und der Tempelbau. *VT* 11: 113–27.
  1982   *Royal Administration and National Religion in Ancient Palestine.* Leiden: Brill.
  1984   Giloh: A Judahite or Canaanite Settlement? *IEJ* 34: 170–72.
Ainian, A. M.
  1997   *From Rulers' Dwellings to Temples: Architecture, Religion and Society in Early Iron Age Greece (100–700 B.C.).* Studies in Mediterranean Archaeology 121. Jonsered: Åströms.

Akkermans, P. M. M. G., and G. M. Schwartz
  2003   *The Archaeology of Syria, from Complex Hunter-Gatherers to Early Urban Societies (ca. 16,000–300 BCE).* Cambridge World Archaeology. Cambridge: Cambridge University Press.
Akurgal, E.
  1961   *Die Kunst der Hethither.* Munich: Hirmer.
  1966   *The Art of Greece: Its Origins in the Mediterranean and Near East.* New York: Crown.
  1985   *Ancient Civilizations and Ruins of Turkey: From Prehistoric Times until the End of the Roman Empire.* Istanbul: Haşet.
Albright, W. F.
  1920   The Babylonian Temple-Tower and the Altar of Burnt-Offerings. *JBL* 39: 137–42.
  1954   *The Archaeology of Palestine.* London: Penguin.
  1956a The Date of the Kapara Period at Gozon (Tell Halaf). *AnSt* 6: 75–85.
  1956b Northeast-Mediterranean Dark Ages and the Early Iron Age Art of Syria. Pp. 144–64 in *The Aegean and the Near East: Studies Presented to Hetty Goldman on the Occasion of Her Seventy-Fifth Birthday,* ed. S. Weinberg. Locust Valley, NY: Augustin.
  1957   The High Place in Ancient Palestine. Pp. 242–58 in *Volume du Congrès Strasbourg, 1956.* VTSup 4. Leiden: Brill.
  1968   *Yahweh and the Gods of Canaan: A Historical Analysis of Two Contrasting Faiths.* Garden City, NY: Doubleday.
  1969   *Archaeology and Religion of Israel.* 5th ed. Baltimore: Johns Hopkins University Press.
Almagro-Gorea, M., and T. Moneo
  2000   *Santuarios urbanos en el Mundo ibérico.* Madrid: Real Academia de la Historia.
Alt, A.
  1953   Ägyptische Tempel in Palastina und die Landnahme der Philister. Pp. 216–30 in *Kleine Schriften zur Geschichte des Volkes Israel,* vol. 1. Munich: Beck.
Amiran, R.
  1969   *Ancient Pottery of the Holy Land from Its Beginnings in the Neolithic to the End of the Iron Age.* Jerusalem: Massada.
  1972   A Cult Stele from Arad. *IEJ* 22: 86–88.
Amiran, R., U. Paran, Y. Shiloh, and R. Brown
  1978   *Early Arad I: The Chaleolithic Settlement and Early Bronze Age City. First–Fifth Seasons of Excavations, 1962–1966.* Jerusalem: Israel Exploration Society.
Amiet, P.
  1964   Review of *Omm el-ʿAmed: Une ville de l'époque hellénistique aux Échelles de Tyr,* by M. Dunand and R. Duru. *Syria* 41: 157–61.
  1987   Der Königsweg. Pp. 15–25 in Mittmann et al. 1987.
Amiet, P., J. Balensi, and A.Lemaire
  1987   Späte Bronzezeit. Pp. 106–16 in Mittmann et al. 1987.
Anati, E.
  1962   *Palestine before the Hebrews: A History from the Earliest Arrival of Man to the Conquest of Canaan.* New York: Knopf.
Anderson, G.
  1981   The Praise of God as a Cultic Event. Pp. 15–33 in *Priesthood and Cult in Ancient Israel.* JSOTSup 125. Sheffield: JSOT Press.
Anderson, P.
  1976–77 The Antinomies of Antonio Gramsci. *New Left Review* 100: 5–78.

Anderson, W.
1988   *Sarepta I: The Late Bronze and Iron Age Strata of Area II, Y.* Beirut: University of Lebanon Press.

Andrae, W.
1930   *Das Gotteshaus und die urformen des Bauens im alten Orient.* Berlin: Schoetz.

Antonelli, C.
1995   I santuari micenei ed il mondo dell'economia. Pp. 415–21 in Laffineur and Niemeier 1995.

Archi, A.
1992   The City of Ebla and the Organization of Its Rural Territory. *AoF* 19: 24–28.

Archi, A., ed.
1984   *Circulation of Goods in Non-palatial Context in the Ancient Near East.* Rome: Ateneo.

Arnold, D.
1997   Royal Cult Complexes of the Old and Middle Kingdoms. Pp. 31–85 in Shafer 1997.

Artzy, M.
1990   Pomegranate Scepters and Incense Stand with Pomegranates Found in Priest's Grave. *BAR* 16/1: 48–51.
1994   Incense, Camels and Collarded Rim Jars: Desert Trade Routes and Maritime Outlets in the Second Millennium. *OJA* 13: 121–47.

Astour, M. C.
1965   *Hellenosemitica: An Ethnic and Cultural Study in West Semitic Impact on Mycenaean Greece.* Leiden: Brill.
1973   Ugarit and the Aegean: A Brief Summary of the Archaeological and Epigraphic Evidence. Pp. 17–27 in Hoffner 1973.

Åström, P.
2000   Cyprus. Pp. 150–53 in Bietak 2000b.

Athas, G.
2003   *Tell Dan Inscription: A Reappraisal and New Interpretation.* London: T. & T. Clark.

Aubet (Semmler), M. E.
1986   Los fenicios en España, estado de la cuestión y perspectivas. Pp. 9–30 in Olmo Lete and Aubet 1986.
1990   Die Phönizier, Tartessos und das frühe Iberien. Pp 65–74 in Gehrig and Niemeyer 1990.
1993   *The Phoenicians and the West: Politics, Colonies, and Trade* Cambridge: Cambridge University Press.
2002   Phoenician Trade in the West: Balance and Perspectives. Pp. 97–112 in Bierling 2002.
2010   The Phoenician Cemetery of Tyre. *NEA* 73/2–3: 144–55.

Auld, A. G.
1975   Judges I and History: A Reconstruction. *VT* 25: 261–85.

Badawy, A.
1965   *Ancient Egyptian Architectural Design: A Study of the Harmonic System.* University of California Publications: Near East Studies 4. Berkeley: University of California Press.

Badre, L.
1992   Canaanite Tyre. Pp. 37–44 in Joukowsky 1992.
1997   Kamid el-Loz. Pp 265–66 in *OEANE*, 3.

Baffi Guardata, F.
1991   Il culto practicato ad Ebla. *La Parola del Passato: Rivista di studi antichi* 46: 394–416.

Bahat, D., and G. Hurvitz
  1996   Jerusalem, First Temple Period: Archaeological Exploration. Pp. 268–306 in Westenholz 1996.
Balensi, J., P. Amiet, C. Clamer, and B. Couroyer
  1987   Das 2. Jahrtausend v. Chr. Pp. 88–103 in Mittmann et al. 1987.
Balensi, J., M. D. Herrera, and M. Artzy
  1993   Abu Hawam Tell. Pp. 7–14 in vol. 1 of *NEAEHL*.
Bandera, M. L. de la
  1993   Montemolín: Evolución del asentamiento durante el bronce final y el periodo orientalizante (campañas de 1980 y 1981). *Anales de Arqueología Cordobesa* 4: 17–47.
Barako, T.
  2000   The Philistine Settlement as Mercantile Phenomenon? *AJA* 104: 513–30.
Barako, T., and A. Yasur-Landau
  2003   One if by Sea . . . Two if by Land: How Did the Philistines Get to Canaan? *BAR* 29/2: 24–39.
Barkay, G.
  1992   The Iron Age II–III. Pp. 302–73 in *The Archaeology of Ancient Israel*, ed. A. Ben-Tor. New Haven, CT: Yale University Press.
  2000   What's an Egyptian Temple Doing in Jerusalem? *BAR* 26/3: 48–57.
Barnett, R. D.
  1956   Phoenician and the Ivory Trade. *Archaeology* 9: 87–97.
  1975   The Sea Peoples. Pp. 359–78 in *CAH* 2/2: *History of the Middle East and the Aegean Region c. 1380–1000 b.c.*, ed. I. E. S. Edwards et al. Cambridge: Cambridge University Press.
Bartlett, J. R.
  1997   Edom. Pp. 189–90 in vol. 2 of *OEANE*.
Barth, F., ed.
  1969   *Ethnic Groups and Boundaries: The Social Organization of Culture Difference*. Boston: Little, Brown.
Bass, G. F.
  1967   *Cape Gelidonya: A Bronze Age Shipwreck*. TAPS 57. Philadelphia: American Philosophical Society.
  1986   A Bronze Age Shipwreck at Ulu Burun(kaş): 1984 Campaign. *AJA* 90: 269–96.
  1987   Oldest Known Shipwreck Reveals Splendors of the Bronze Age. *National Geographic* 172/6: 693–733.
Bauer, A.
  1998   Cities of the Sea: Maritime Trade and the Origin of Philistine Settlement in the Early Iron Age Southern Levant. *OJA* 17: 149–67.
Baumgarten, A.
  1981   *The Phoenician History of Philo of Byblos: A Commentary*. Leiden: Brill.
Beck, A., J. A. Sanders, and D. N. Freedman, eds.
  1998   *Leningrad Codex: A Facsimile Edition*. Grand Rapids, MI: Eerdmans / Leiden: Brill.
Beck, P.
  1990   A Note on the "Schematic Statues" from the Stelae Temple at Hazor. *TA* 17: 91–95.
Beckman, G.
  1989   The Religion of the Hittites. *BA* 52/2–3: 98–108.

1992   Hittite Administration in Syria in Light of the Texts from Hattusa and Emar. Pp. 41–49 in *New Horizons in the Study of Ancient Syria*. Biblioteca Mesopotamia 25. Malibu, CA: Undena.

1994   The Cult-Stands from Tannach: Aspects of the Iconographic Tradition of Early Iron Age Cult Objects in Palestine. Pp. 352–81 in Finkelstein and Naʾaman 1994.

1996   Emar and Its Archives. Pp. 1–9 in Chavalas 1996.

Beer, C.

1992   Ethnic Diversity and Financial Differentiation in Cypriote Sanctuaries. Pp. 73–84 in *Economics of Cult in the Ancient Greek World: Proceedings of the Uppsala Symposium 1990*, ed. T. Linders and B. Alroth. Acta Universitatis Upsaliensis: Boreas 21. Uppsala: Academiae Ubsaliensis.

Beit-Arieh, I.

1987   *Edomite Shrine: Discoveries from Qitmit in the Negev*. Jerusalem: Israel Museum.

1988   New Light on the Edomites. *BAR* 14/2: 28–41

1991   The Edomite Shrine at Horvat Qitmit in the Judean Negev: Preliminary Excavation Report. *TA* 18: 93–116.

1997   Qitmit Horvat. Pp. 390–91 in vol. 4 of *OEANE*.

Beit-Arieh, I., and P. Beck

1995   *Horvat Qitmit: An Edomite Shrine in the Biblical Negev*. Tel Aviv: Institute of Archaeology Tel Aviv University.

Belén Deamos, M.

2001   Arquitectura religiosa orientalizante en el Bajo Guadalquivir. Pp. 1–16 in Ruiz Mata and Celetino Pérez 2001.

Belén, M., R. Anglada, J. L. Escacena, A. Jiménez, R. Linceros, and I. Rodríguez

1997   *Arqueología en Carmona (Sevilla): Excavaciones en la Casa-Palacio del Marqués de Saltillo*. Carmona: Junta de Andalucia.

Bell, C.

2006   *The Evolution of Long Distance Trading Relationships across the LBA/Iron Age Transition on the Northern Levantine Coast: Crisis, Continuity and Change*. British Archaeological Reports International Series 1574. Oxford: Archaeopress.

Bell, G.

1987   *The Desert and the Sown*. Boston: Beacon.

Bell, L.

1997   The New Kingdom 'Divine' Temple: The Example of Luxor. Pp. 127–84 in Shafer 1997.

Ben Avraham, Z., and S. Hough

2003   Promised Land. *Natural History* 112/9: 44–49.

Ben-Dor, I.

1950   A Middle Bronze Age Temple at Nahariya. *QDAP* 14: 1–41.

Ben-Shlomo, D., I. Shai, and A. Maeir

2004   Late Philisitne Decorated Ware ("Ashdod Ware"): Typology, Chronology, and Production Centers. *BASOR* 335: 1–35.

Ben-Tor, A.

1973   Plans of Dwellings and Temples in Early Bronze Age Palestine. *ErIsr* 11 (Dunayevsky memorial vol.): 92–98. [Hebrew]

1989   *Hazor III–IV: An Account of the Third and Fourth Seasons of Excavation, 1957–1958*. Jerusalem: Israel Exploration Society and Hebrew University.

1992a Early Bronze Age Dwellings and Installations. Pp. 60–67 in Kempinski and Reich 1992.

1992b Introduction: The Early Bronze Age. Pp. 52–53 in Kempinski and Reich 1992.

1992c New Light on Cylinder Seal Impressions Showing Cult Scenes from Early Bronze Age Palestine. *IEQ* 42/3–4: 153–64.

1997a Hazor. Pp. 1–5 in vol. 3 of *OEANE.*

1997b The Yigael Yadin Memorial Excavations at Hazor, 1990–93: Aims and Preliminary Results. Pp. 1–7-127 in *The Archaeology of Israel: Constructing the Past, Interpreting the Present.* JSOTSup 237. Sheffield: Sheffield Academic Press.

2000   Hazor and the Chronology of Northern Israel: A Reply to Israel Finkelstein. *BASOR* 317: 9–16.

Ben-Tor, A., and R. Bonfil, eds.

1997   *Hazor V: An Account of the Fifth Season, 1968.* Jerusalem: Israel Exploration Society and Hebrew University.

Ben-Tor, A., and M. T. Rubiato

1999   Excavating Hazor, Part Two: Did the Israelites Destroy the Cananite City? *BAR* 25/3: 22–39.

Bentzen, A.

1952   *Introduction to the Old Testament II.* Copenhagen: Gad.

Berchem, D. van

1967   Sanctuaires d'Hercule-Melqart: Contribution à l'étude de l'expansion phénicienne en Méditerranée. *Syria* 44: 73–109.

Bergquist, B.

1973   *Heracles on Thasos.* Acta Universitatis Upsaliensis: Boreas 5. Uppsala: Academia Ubsaliensis.

1993   Bronze Age Sacrificial *Koine* in the Eastern Mediterranean? A Study of Animal Sacrifice in the Ancient Near East. Pp. 11–43 in Quaegebeur 1993.

Bernett, M.

2000   The bit hilani at Bethsaida: Its Place in Aramean/Neo-Hittite and Israelite Palace Architecture in the Iron Age II. *IEJ* 50: 47–81.

Best, J.

1991   Linguistic Evidence for a Phoenician Pillar Cult in Crete. *JANES* 20: 7–14.

Bienkowski, P.

1990   The Chronology of Tawilan and the 'Dark Age' of Edom. Pp. 35–44 in *Proceedings of the First International Conference of ARAM*, vol. 2/1–2. Oxford: Oxford University Press.

1991   *The Art of Jordan: Treasures from an Ancient Land.* Gloucestershire: Stroud.

1992   The Beginning of the Iron Age in Southern Jordan: A Framework. Pp. 1–2 in *Early Edom and Moab: The Beginning of the Iron Age in Southern Jordan*, ed. P. Bienkowski. Sheffield: Sheffield Academic Press.

Bienkowski, P., and E. van der Steen

2001   Tribes, Trade, and Towns: A New Framework for the Late Iron Age in Southern Jordan and the Negev. *BASOR* 323: 21–47.

Bierling, M.

2002   *The Phoenicians in Spain: An Archaeological Review of the Eighth–Sixth Centuries B.C.E.—A Collection of Articles Translated from Spanish.* Winona Lake, IN: Eisenbrauns.

Bietak, M.
1979   *Avaris and Piramesse: Archaeological Exploration in the Eastern Nile Delta.* Oxford: Oxford University Press.
1985   The Philistines Reconsidered. Pp. 216–19 in *Biblical Archaeology Today: Proceedings of the International Congress on Biblical Archaeology,* ed. J. Amitai. Jerusalem: Israel Exploration Society.
1995   Connections between Egypt and the Minoan World: New Results from Tell El-Dabᶜa/ Avaris. Pp. 19–28 in Davies and Schofield 1995.
1996   *Avaris, the Capital of the Hyksos: Recent Excavations at Tell el-Dabᶜa.* London: British Museum.
2000a   Egypt. Pp. 83–95 in Bietak 2000b.
2000b   *The Synchronisation of Civilisations in the Eastern Mediterranean in the Second Millennium B.C.: Proceedings of an International Symposium at Schloss Haindorf, 15th–17th of November 1996 and the Austrian Academy, Vienna, 11th–12th of May 1998.* Vienna: Österreichischen Akademie der Wissenschaften.
Bietak, M., and K. Kopetzky
2000   Israel/Palestine. Pp. 96–129 in Bietak 2000b.
Bikai, P.
1992a   The History of the Excavations. Pp. 25–36 in Joukowsky 1992.
1992b   The Land of Tyre. Pp. 13–24 in Joukowsky 1992.
Bikai, P. M.
1978a   The Late Phoenician Pottery Complex and Chronology. *BASOR* 229: 48–56.
1978b   *The Pottery of Tyre.* Warminster: Aris and Phillips.
1989   Cyprus and the Phoenicians. *BA* 52: 203–9.
1990   Black Athena and the Phoenicians. *JMA* 3/1: 67–75.
1992a   The Phoenicians. Pp. 132–41 in Joukowsky and Ward 1992.
1992b   Phoenician Tyre. Pp. 45–54 in Joukowsky 1992.
Bikai, P., and Bikai, P. M.
1987   Tyre at the End of the Twentieth Century. *Berytus* 35: 67–96.
Bimson, J.
1990–91 The Philistines. Their Origins and Chronology Reassessed. *JACF* 4: 58–76.
1992–93 Shoshenk and Shishak: A Case of Mistaken Identity? *JACF* 6: 19–32.
Bimson, J., and D. Livingston
1985   Redating Exodus. *BAR* 13/5: 40–53.
Binst, O., et al.
1999   *The Levant: History and Archaeology in the Eastern Mediterranean.* Cologne: Könemann.
Biran, A.
1981   *Temples and High Places in Biblical Times.* Jerusalem: Hebrew Union College.
1986   The Dancer from Dan, the Empty Tomb and the Altar Room. *IEJ* 36:168–87.
1993   *Biblical Archaeology Today: Proceedings of the Second International Congress on Biblical Archaeology, Jerusalem—June–July 1990.* Jerusalem: Israel Exploration Society.
1994   *Biblical Dan.* Jerusalem: Israel Exploration Society.
1998   Sacred Spaces of Standing Stones: High Places and Cult Objects at Tel Dan. *BAR* 24/5: 38–45.
2003   The Dancer from Dan. *NEA* 66/3: 128–32.

Biran, A., and H. Shanks
 1987 Avraham Biran: Twenty Years of Digging at Tel Dan. *BAR* 13/4: 12–25.
Bisi, A. M.
 1986 Le Rôle de Chypre dans la Civilisation Phénicienne d'Occident: Etat de la Questions et Éssai de Synthèse. Pp. 341–50 in *Acts of the International Archaeological Symposium "Cyprus between the Orient and the Occident"—Nicosia, 8–14 September 1985,* ed. V. Karageorghis. Nicosia: Department of Antiquities, Cyprus.
Bittel, K.
 1976 *Die Hethiter.* Munich: Beck.
Blakely, J., and J. W. Harden
 2002 Southwestern Judah in the Late Eighth Century B.C.E. *BASOR* 326: 11–64.
Blakely, S.
 1998 Trade, Cult, and the Mythic Imagination: The Aegean and the Levant in the Late Bronze Age and Iron Ages, 1400–700 B.C. *Albright News* 4/December: 8–10.
Bloch-Smith, E.
 1992 *Judahite Burial Practices and Beliefs about the Dead.* JSOT Sup. 123: ASOR Monograph Series 7. Sheffield: Sheffield Academic Press.
 1994 Who Is 'The King of Glory'? Solomon's Temple and Its Symbolism. Pp. 18–31 in Coogan et al. 1994.
Bloch-Smith, E., and B. A. Nakhai
 1999 A Landscape Comes to Life: The Iron Age 1. *NEA* 62/2: 62–127.
Boardman, J.
 1967 *Excavations in Chios, 1952–1955: Greek Emporio.* London: British School of Archaeology at Athens.
 2000 *Persia and the West: An Archaeological Investigation of the Genesis of Achaemenid Art.* London: Thames and Hudson.
 2001 Aspects of Colonization. *BASOR* 322: 33–42.
 2002 Al Mina: The Study of the Site. Pp. 315–31 in *Ancient West and East,* vol. 1/2, ed. G. Tsetskhlandze. Leiden: Brill.
Boling, R. G.
 1969 Bronze Age Buildings at the Shechem High Place: ASOR Excavations at Tananir. *BA* 32/4: 81–105.
 1975 Excavations at Tananir. Pp. 25–85 in *Report on Archaeological Work at Suww'net eth-Than'ya, Tananir, and Khirbet Minha (Munhata),* ed. G. M. Landes. BASORSup 21. Missoula, MT: Scholars Press.
Bondì, S. F.
 1999a City Planning and Architecture. Pp. 311–48 in Moscatti 1999.
 1999b The Course of History. Pp. 30–46 in Moscatti 1999.
 1999c The Origins in the East. Pp. 23–29 in Moscatti 1999.
Bonfil, R.
 1997 Middle Bronze Age to Persian Period. Pp. 25–101 in Ben-Tor and Bonfil 1997.
Bonfil, R., and A. Zarzecki-Peleg
 2007 The Palace in the Upper City of Hazor as an Expression of a Syrian Architectural Paradigm. *BASOR* 348: 25–47.
Bonanno, A., A. J. Frendo, and N. C. Vella, eds.
 2000 Excavations at Tas-Silġ, Malta: A Preliminary Report on the 1996–1998 Campaigns Conducted by the Department of Classics and Archaeology of the University of Malta. *Mediterranean Archaeology* 13: 67–114.

Bonnet, C.
1988   *Melqart: Cultes et mythes de l'Héraclès tyrien en Méditerranée.* Studia Phoenicia 8. Leuven: Peeters.

Bordreuil, P.
1991   Recherches Ougaritiques I: Où Baʿal a-t-il remporté la victoire contre Yam? *Semitica* 40: 17–38.
2000a   An Efficiently Administered Kingdom. *NEA* 63/4: 190–91.
2000b   The South-Arabian Abecedary. *NEA* 63/4: 197.

Borowski, O.
1995   Hezekiah's Reforms and the Revolt against Assyria. *BA* 58/3: 148–55.

Bossert, H. T.
1951   *Altsyrien: Kunst und Handwerk in Cypern, Syrien, Palästine, Tranjordanien und Arabien von de Anfängen bis zum völligen Aufgehen in grechisch-römischen Kultur.* Tübingen: Wasmuth.

Bourke, S.
2005   Excavating Pella's Bronze Age Temple Precinct: The 1999 and 2001 Season. *Mediterranean Archaeology* 18: 109–18.
2007   Pella in Jordan 2007: Early Settlements, Mudbrick Temples and Iron Age Palatial Residence. *Bulletin of the Near Eastern Archaeology Foundation* 51: 1–3.

Bourke, S., and P. Descoeudres, eds.
1995   *Trade, Contact, and the Movement of Peoples in the Eastern Mediterranean: Studies in Honor of J. Basil Hennessey.* Mediterranean Archaeology Supplement 3. Sydney: Meditarch.

Boyes, P.
2012   "The King of the Sidonians": Phoenician Ideologies and the Myth of the Kingdom of Tyre–Sidon. *BASOR* 365: 33–44.

Brandl, B.
1984   A Proto-Aeolic Capital from Gezer. *IEJ* 34: 173–76.

Braun, J.
2002   *Music in Ancient Israel/Palestine: Archaeological, Written and Comparative Sources.* Grand Rapids, MI: Eerdmans.

Briend, J., and J.-B. Humbert, eds.
1980   *Tell Keisan (1971–1976): Une cité phénicienne en Galilée.* Fribourg: Editions universitaries.

Bright, J.
1981   A *History of Israel.* Philadelphia: Westminster.

Brody, A.
2002   From the Hills of Adonis through the Pillars of Hercules: Recent Advances in the Archaeology of Canaan and Phoenicia. *NEA* 65/1: 69–80.

Bronson, B.
1988   The Role of Barbarians in the Fall of States. Pp. 196–218 in Yoffee and Cowgill 1988.

Broshi, M., and I. Finkelstein
1992   The Population of Palestine in Iron Age II. *BASOR* 287: 47–60.

Brouquier-Reddé, V.
1992   *Temples et cultes de Tripolitaine.* Paris: Centre national de recherche scientifique.

Brueggemann, W.
1971   Kingship and Chaos: A Study in Tenth Century Theology. *CBQ* 33: 317–32.

Bruyère, B.
1930 Rapport sur les fouilles de Deir el-Medineh. Pp. 9–10, 17–50, 61–72 in *Fouilles de l'FAOC*. Cairo: Institut Français d'Archéologie Orientale de Caire.
1952 *Rapport sur le fouilles de Deir el-Medineh (1935–40)*. Cairo: Institut Français d'Archéologie Orientale de Caire.

Bruyère, B., and G. Nagel
1924 *Rapport sur les fouilles de Deir el-Médinet (1922–23)*. Cairo: Institut Français d'Archéologie Orientale de Caire.

Bryce, T.
1997 Luwians. Pp. 385–86 in vol. 3 of *OEANE*.

Buccellati, G.
1988 The Kingdom and Period of Khana. *BASOR* 270: 43–62.

Buccellati, G., and F. Deblaume
1992 A Study of Accessibility and Circulation Patterns in the Sin Temple of Hafagi from the Third Millennium B.C. *Mesopotamia* 27: 89–118.

Bull, R.
1960 A Re-examination of the Shechem Temple. *BA* 23/4: 110–19.

Bulliet, R.
1990 *The Camel and the Wheel*. New York: Columbia University Press.

Bunimovitz, S.
1990 Problems in the "Ethnic" Identification of the Philistine Culture. *TA* 17: 210–22.
1994 Socio-Political Transformations in the Central Hill Country in the Late Bronze–Iron I Transition. Pp. 179–202 in Finkelstein and Na'aman 1994.
1995 On the Edge of Empires: Late Bronze Age (1500–1200 B.C.E.). Pp. 320–32 in Levy 1995.

Bunimovitz, S., and A. Faust
2001 Chronological Separation, Geographical Segregation, or Ethnic Demarcation? Ethnography and the Iron Age Low Chronology. *BASOR* 322: 1–10.
2002 Ideology in Stone: Understanding the Four-Room House. *BAR* 28/4: 33–41.
2003 Building Identity: The Four Room House and the Israelite Mind. Pp. 411–23 in Dever and Gitin 2003.

Burke, A.
2007 Magadalūma, Migdālîm, Magdoloi, and Majādīl: The Historical Geography and Archaeology of the Magdalu (Migdāl). *BASOR* 346: 29–57.

Burkert, W.
1992 *The Orientalizing Revolution: Near Eastern Influence on Greek Culture in the Early Archaic Age*. Cambridge: Harvard University Press.

Burney, C., and D. M. Lang
2001 *The Peoples of the Hills: Ancient Ararat and Caucasus*. London: Wiedenfield and Nicholson.

Burns, R.
1994 *Monuments of Syria: An Historical Guide*. London: Tauris.

Busink, T.
1963 Les origines du Temple de Salomon. *Jaarbericht Ex Oriente Lux* 17: 165–92.

1970   *Der Tempel von Jerusalem von Salomo bis Herodes: Eine archäologisch-hisorische Studie enter Berücksichtigung des westsemitischen Tempelbaus*, vol. 1: *Der Tempel Salomos*. Leiden: Brill.

1980   *Der Tempel von Jerusalem von Salomo bis Herodes: Eine archäologisch-hisorische Studie enter Berücksichtigung des westsemitischen Tempelbaus*, vol. 2: *Von Ezechiel bis Middot*. Leiden: Brill.

Busto Saiz, J.

1987   On the Lucianic Manuscripts in 1–2 Kings. Pp. 305–10 in *IV Congress of the International Organization for Septuagiant and Cognate Studies: Jerusalem 1986*, ed. C. Cox. Atlanta: Scholars Press.

Butterworth, E. A. S.

1970   *The Tree at the Navel of the Earth*. Berlin: de Gruyter.

Butzer, K.

1984   Long-Term Nile Variation and Political Discontinuities in Pharaonic Egypt. Pp. 102–12 in *From Hunters to Farmers*, ed. J. D. Clark and S. Brandt. Berekeley: University of California Press.

Byrne, R.

2003   Early Assyrian Contacts with Arabs and the Impact on Levantine Vassal Tribute. *BASOR* 331: 11–25.

2007   The Refuge of Scribalism in Iron I Palestine. *BASOR* 345: 1–31.

Cagiano de Azevedo, M., A. Caprino, F. Ciasca, A. D'Andria, M. Guzzo Amadasi, and M. Rossignani

1973   *Missione archeologica italiana a Malta: rapporto preliminare della campagna 1970*. Rome: Consiglio Nazionale delle Ricerche, Centro per la Civiltà Fenicia e Punica.

Cahill, J.

1998   David's Jerusalem: Fact or Fiction? It Is There: The Archaeological Evidence Proves It. *BAR* 24/4: 34–41, 63.

Camacho, H.

1986   The Altar of Incense in Hebrews 9:3–4. *AUSS* 24: 5–12.

Cambitoglou, A., A. Birchall, J. Coulton, and J. R. Greene

1988   *Zagora*, vol. 2: *Excavation of a Geometric Town on the Island of Andros*. Athens: Athenais Archaiologike Hetaireia.

Campbell, E. F., and G. E. Wright

1969   Tribal League Shrines in Amman and Shechem. *BA* 32/4: 104–16.

Campbell, E. F., and J. F. Ross

1968   The Excavation of Shechem and the Biblical Tradition. *BA* 26: 2–27.

Canby, J. V.

1976   The Stelereihen at Assur, Tell Halaf, and Maṣṣebôt. *Iraq* 38: 114–21.

1985   Guzanna (Tell Halaf). Pp. 332–38 in Weiss 1985.

Caquot, A.

2000   At the Origins of the Bible. *NEA* 63/4: 225–27.

Caquot, A., and A. Lemaire

1977   Les textes araméens de Deir ʿAlla. *Syria* 54: 189–208.

Caquot, A., and M. Sznycer

1980   *Ugaritic Religion*. Leiden: Brill.

Carriazo Arroquia, J. de Mata

1973   *Tartessos y El Carambolo*. Madrid: Patronato Nacional de Museos.

Casevitz, M.
1984   Temples et sanctuaires: Ce qu'apprend l'étude lexicologique. Pp. 81–95 in Roux 1984.

Catling, H. W.
1980   *Cyprus and the West, 1600–1050 B.C.* Sheffield: Sheffield Academic Press.

Caubet, A.
1984   Le sanctuaire chypro-archaique de Kition-Bamboula. Pp. 107–18 in Roux 1984.
1992   Reoccupation of the Syrian Coast after the Destruction of the 'Crisis Years.' Pp. 123–31 in Joukowsky and Ward 1992.

Celestino Pérez, S.
1995   El periodo orientalizante en Extremadura. *Extremadura Arqueológica* 4: 67–89.
1997   Santuarios, centros comerciales y paisajes sacros. *Quaderns de Prehistòria i arqueologia de Castelló* 18: 359–89.
2001   Los santuarios de Cancho Roano: Del indigenismo al orientalismo arquitectónico. Pp. 17–56 in Ruiz Mata and Celestino Pérez 2001.

Cenival, J.-L. de
1964   *Living Architecture: Egyptian.* New York: Grosset and Dunlap.

Charpin, D.
1992   Mari entre l'est et l'ouest: Politique, culture, religion. *Akkadica* 78: 1–10.

Chaturvedi, V., ed.
2000   *Mapping Subaltern Studies and the Postcolonial.* London: Verso.

Chavalas, M. W.
1992   Ancient Syria: A New Historical Sketch. Pp. 1–21 in *New Horizons in the Study of Ancient Syria.* Bibliotheca Mesopotamica 25. Malibu, CA: Undena.

Chavalas, M. W., ed.
1996   *Emar: The History, Religion, and Culture of a Syrian Town in the Late Bronze Age.* Bethesda, MD: CDL.

Chaves, F.
1993   Investigación arqueológica en Montemolín. Pp. 501–13 in *Investigaciones arqueológicas en Andalucía, 1985–1992: Proyectos. Communicaciones que se presentan a las VI Jornadas de Arqueología Andaluza a celebrar en Huelva, 25–29 de enero de 1993.* Seville: Dirección General de Bienes Culturales.

Chaves, F., and M. L. de la Bandera
1991   Aspectos de la urbanística en Andalucía occidental en los siglos VII–VI a.C. a la luz del yacimiento de Montemolín (Marchena, Sevilla). Pp. 691–714 in *Atti del II Congresso Internationale di Studi Fenici e Punici,* vol. 2, ed. E. Acquaro. Rome: Consiglio nazionale della ricerche.
1992   Problemática de las cerámicas 'orientalizantes' y su contexto. Pp. 49–89 in *Lengua y cultura en la Hispania prerromana: Actas del V Congreso sobre lenguas y culturas prerromanas de la Península Ibérica,* ed. J. Untermann and F. Villar. Salamanca: University of Salamanca.

Churcher, B.
2003   Pella's Canaanite Temple. http://*www.astarte.com.au/html/pella_s_canaanite_temple .html.*

Ciasca, A.
1999   Phoenicia. Pp. 168–84 in Moscati 1999.

Clamer, C., and D. Ussishkin
1977   A Canaanite Temple at Tell Lachish. *BA* 40/2: 71–81.

Clarke, D. L., ed.
1977   *Spatial Archaeology*. London: Academic Press.
Clifford, R.
1971   The Tent of El and the Israelite Tent of Meeting. *CBQ* 33: 221–27.
1972   *The Cosmic Mountain in Canaan and the Old Testament*. Cambridge: Harvard University Press.
1979   The Temple in the Ugaritic Myth of Baʿal. Pp. 137–46 in *Symposia Celebrating the Seventy-Fifth Anniversary of the Founding of the American Schools of Oriental Research (1900–1975)*, vol. 2, ed. F. Cross. Cambridge: Harvard University Press.
1990   Phoenician Religion. *BASOR* 279: 55–64.
Cline, Eric H.
2000   *The Battles of Armageddon*. Ann Arbor: University of Michigan Press.
Cohen, R.
1991   En Hazeva, 1988/1989. *ESI* 10: 46–47.
Cohen, R., and Y. Yisrael
1995a   The Iron Age Fortress at ʿEn Haseva. *BA* 58: 223–35.
1995b   *On the Road to Edom: Discoveries from ʿEn Hazeva*. Jerusalem: Israel Museum.
1996a   En Hazeva, 1990–1994. *ESI* 15: 110–16.
1996b   Smashing the Idols: Piecing Together an Edomite Shrine in Judah. *BAR* 22/4: 40–51.
Collon, D.
1987   *First Impressions: Cylinder Seals in the Ancient Near East*. Chicago: University of Chicago Press.
Coogan, M. D.
1978   *Stories from Ancient Canaan*. Louisville: Westminster John Knox.
1987   Of Cults and Cultures: Reflections on the Interpretation of Archaeological Evidence. *PEQ* 119: 1–8.
Coogan, M. D., J. C. Exum, and L. E. Stager, eds.
1994   *Scripture and Other Artifacts: Essays on the Bible and Archaeology in Honor of Philip J. King*. Louisville: Westminster John Knox.
Cooper, L.
2006   The Demise and Regeneration of Bronze Age Urban Centers in the Euphrates Valley of Syria. Pp. 18–37 in Schwartz and Nichols 2006.
Coote, R., and K. Whitelam
1987   *The Emergence of Early Israel in Historical Perspective*. Sheffield: Sheffield Academic Press.
Correia, V. H.
2001   Arquitectura oriental e orientalizante em terrirório português: Uma revisao. Pp. 57–68 in Ruiz Mata and Celestino Pérez 2001.
Courtils, J. de, and A. Pariente
1988   Excavations in the Herakles Sanctuary at Thasos. Pp. 121–23 in Hägg, Marinatos, and Nordquist 1988.
1991   Problèmes topographiques et religieux à l'Hérakleion de Thasos. Pp. 67–73 in *L'espace sacrificial dans las civilizations méditerranéennes de l'antiquité*, ed. R. Étienne and M. T. Couilloud. Lyon: Maison de l'Orient.
Courtois, J.-C.
1979   L'architecture domestique à Ugarit au bronze récent. Pp. 105–34 in *Ugarit-Forschungen Internationales Jahrbuch für die Altertumskunde Syrien-Palästinas*, vol. 11: *Festschrift für Claude F. A. Schaeffer*. Münster: Ugarit-Verlag.

1984   *Alasia III: Les objets des niveaux stratifiés d'Enkomi.* Paris: Editions Recherche sur les civilisations.

Cowgill, G. L.
   1988   Onward and Upward with Collapse. Pp. 244–76 in Yoffee and Cowgill 1988.

Crocker, P.
   1987   Recent Finds from Tell Dan. *Buried History* 23/3: 37–43.

Curtis, A.
   1985   *Cities of the Biblical World: Ugarit.* Cambridge: Lutterworth.

Cross, F. M.
   1973   *Canaanite Myths and Hebrew Epic.* Cambridge: Harvard University Press.
   1979   *Symposia Celebrating the Seventy-Fifth Anniversary of the Founding of the American Schools of Oriental Research (1900–1975).* Cambridge, MA: American Schools of Oriental Research.
   1980   Newly Found Inscriptions in Old Canaanite and Early Phoenician Scripts. *BASOR* 238: 1–20.
   1981   The Priestly Tabernacle in the Light of Recent Research. Pp. 169–80 in Biran 1981.
   1998   *From Epic to Canon: History and Literature in Ancient Israel.* Baltimore: Johns Hopkins University Press.

Culican, W.
   1970   Almuñecar: Assur and Phoenician Penetration of the Western Mediterranean. *Levant* 2: 28–36.
   1982   The Repertoire of Phoenician Pottery. Pp. 45–82 in Niemeyer 1982.

Cunchillos, J. L., and J. P. Vita
   1993   Crónica de la destrucción de una ciudad del reino de Ugarit (TUOO-2.61). *Sefarad* 53: 243–47.

Cunliffe, B.
   1988   *Greeks, Romans, and Barbarians: Spheres of Interaction.* New York: Methuen.
   2001   *The Extraordinary Voyage of Pytheas the Greek.* London: Allen Lane.

Dalley, S., A. T. Reyes, D. Pingue, A. Salvesen, and A. McCall
   1998   *The Legacy of Mesopotamia.* Oxford: Oxford University Press.

Dalrymple, W.
   2002   *White Mughals: Love and Betrayal in Eightennth-Century India.* London: HarperCollins.

Daviau, P. M. M.
   1997   Moab's Northern Border: Khirbat al-Mudayna on the Wadi ath-Thamad. *BA* 60: 222–28.
   2008   Ceramic Architectural Models from Transjordan and the Syrian Tradition. Pp. 294–308 in *Proceedings of the 4th International Congress of the Archaeology of the Ancient Near East (March 29–April 3, 2004),* vol. 1: *The Reconstruction of Environment: Natural Resources and Human Interrelations through Time; Art History: Visual Communication,* ed. H. Kühne, R. Czichon, and F. J. Kreppner. Wiesbaden: Harrassowitz. .

Daviau, P. M. M., and P.-E. Dion
   2002a   Economy-Related Finds from Khirbat al-Mudayna (Wadi ath-Thamad, Jordan). *BASOR* 328: 31–48.
   2002b   Moab Comes to Life. *BAR* 28:1: 38–49.

Daviau, P. M. M., and M. Steiner
   2000   A Moabite Sanctuary at Khirbat al-Mudayna. *BASOR* 320: 23–48.

Davies, W. Vivian, and L. Schofield, eds.
1995   *Egypt, the Aegean and the Levant: Interconnections in the Second Millennium* BC. London: British Museum.

Day, D.
2008   *Conquest: How Societies Overwhelm Others.* Oxford: Oxford University Press.

Dearman, J. A.
1992   *Religion and Culture in Ancient Israel.* Peabody, MA: Hendrickson Publishers.
1997   Roads and Settlements in Moab. *BA* 60: 205–13.

Dearman, J. A., and J. M. Miller
1983   The Melqart Stele and the Ben Hadads of Damascus: Two Studies. *PEQ* 115: 95–101.

Deger-Jalkotzy, S.
2000   The Aegean. Pp. 162–68 in Bietak 2000b.

Delaume, F.
1994   Spacings and Statistics, or a Different Method to Analyze Buildings: A Test with Mesopotamian Houses from the Late Bronze and Iron Ages. *Akkadica* 89–90: 1–8.

Demsky, A.
1998   Discovering a Goddess. *BAR* 24/5: 53–58.

Dessel, J. P
2008   Activities. *University of Tennesse: The Newsletter of the Fern and Manfred Steinfeld Program in Judaic Studies* 15: 7.

Dever, W.
1967   Excavations at Gezer. *BA* 30/2: 47–62.
1982   Monumental Architecture in Ancient Israel in the Period of the United Monarchy. Pp. 269–306 in Ishida 1982.
1987a The Contribution of Archaeology to the Study of Canaanite and Early Israelite Religion. Pp. 209–47 in Miller, Hanson, and McBride 1987.
1987b The Middle Bronze Age: The Zenith of the Urban Canaanite Era. *BA* 50/3: 148–177.
1992   The Late Bronze–Early Iron Horizon in Syria–Palestine: Egyptians, Canaanites, 'Sea Peoples', and Proto-Israelites. Pp. 99–110 in Joukowsky and Ward 1992.
1997a Abu Hawam, Tell. P. 9 in vol. 1 of *OEANE.*
1997b Ashdod. Pp. 219–20 in vol. 1 of *OEANE.*
1997c Gezer. Pp. 396–400 in vol. 2 of *OEANE.*
1997d Timna. Pp. 217–18 in vol. 5 of *OEANE.*
2008a Review of *Israel's Ethnogenesis: Settlement, Interaction, Expansion and Resistance,* by A. Faust. *BAR* 34/6. http://members.bib-arch.org/search.asp?PubID=BSBA&Volume=34&Issue=6&ArticleID=15&UserID=0&.
2008b A Temple Built for Two: Did Yahweh Share a Throne with His Consort Asherah? *BAR* 34/2: 55–62.

Dever, W., and S. Gitin, eds.
2003   *Symbiosis, Symbolism and the Power of the Past: Canaan, Ancient Israel, and Their Neighbors from the Late Bronze Age through Roman Palaestina.* Winona Lake, IN: Eisenbrauns.

De Vries, B.
1992   Archaeology in Jordan. *AJA* 96: 457–520.

De Vries, L. F.
1987   Cult Stands: a Bewitching Variety of Shapes and Sizes. *BAR* 13/4: 26–37.

Diakonoff, I. M.
  1992   The Naval Power and Trade of Tyre. *IEJ* 42: 168–93.
Diés Cusí, E.
  2001   La influencia de la arquitectura fenicia en las arquitecturas indígenas de la Península Ibérica (s. VIII–VII). Pp. 69–122 in Ruiz Mata and Celestino Pérez 2001.
Dietler, M.
  2009   Colonial Encounters in Iberia and the Western Mediterranean: An Exploratory Framework. Pp. 3–48 in Dietler and López-Ruiz 2009.
Dietler, M., and C. López-Ruiz, eds.
  2009   Colonial Encounters in Ancient Iberia: Phoenician, Greek, and Indigenous Relations. Chicago: University of Chicago Press.
Dinsmoor, W. B.
  1975   *The Architecture of Ancient Greece.* 3rd ed. New York: Norton.
Dion, P.
  2002   Review of Edward Lipiński, *The Aramaeans: Their History, Culture, Religion*, by E. Lipiński. *BASOR* 327: 55–61.
Donner, H.
  1982   The Interdependence of Internal Affairs and Foreign Policy during the Davidic-Solomonic Period (with Special Regard to the Phoenician Coast). Pp. 205–14 in Ishida 1982.
Dornemann, R. H.
  1981   The Excavations at Ras Shamra and Their Place in the Current Archaeological Picture of Ancient Syria. Pp. 59–69 in *Ugarit in Retrospect: Fifty Years of Ugarit and Ugaritic*, ed. G. D. Young. Winona Lake, IN: Eisenbrauns.
  1997   Halaf, Tell. Pp. 460–62 in vol. 2 of *OEANE*.
Dothan, M.
  1973   The Foundation of Tel Mor and of Ashdod. *IEJ* 23: 1–17.
  1977   The Musicians of Ashdod. *BA* 40/1: 38–39.
  1979   Ashdod at the End of the Late Bronze Age and the Beginning of the Iron Age. Pp. 125–34 in Cross 1979.
  1981   Sanctuaries along the Coast of Canaan in the MB Period. Pp. 74–81 in Biran 1981.
  1993   Ashdod. Pp. 93–102 in vol. 1 of *NEAEHL*.
Dothan, T.
  1982   *The Philistines and Their Material Culture.* New Haven, CT: Yale University Press.
  1992   Social Dislocation and Cultural Change in the 12th Century B.C. Pp. 93–98 in Joukowsky and Ward 1992.
  1995   Tel Miqne–Ekron: The Aegean Affinities of the Sea Peoples' (Philistines') Settlement in Canaan in the Iron Age 1. Pp. 41–60 in *Recent Excavations in Israel: A View to the West. Reports on Kabri, Nami, Miqne-Ekron, Dor, and Ashkelon*, ed. S. Gitin. Archaelogical Institute of American Colloquia and Conference Paper 1. Dubuque, IA: Kendall/Hunt.
Dothan, T., and M. Dothan
  1992   *People of the Sea: The Search for the Philistines.* New York: Macmillan.
Dothan, T., and S. Gitin
  1990   Ekron of the Philistines. *BAR* 16/1: 20–36.
  1993   Miqne, Tel (Ekron). Pp. 1051–59 in vol. 3 of *NEAEHL*.
  1997   Philistines. Pp. 310–13 in vol. 4 of *OEANE*.

2005   *Tel Miqne–Ekron: Summary of Fourteen Seasons of Excavations, 1981–1996 and Bibliography 1982–2005*. Jerusalem: W. F. Albright Institute of Archaeological Research and the Institute of Archaeology, Hebrew University of Jerusalem.

Dothan, T., and A. Zukerman

2004   A Preliminary Study of the Mycenaean IIIC:1 Pottery Assemblages from Tel Miqne–Ekron and Ashdod. *BASOR* 333: 1–54.

Doumet-Serhal, C.

2010   Sidon during the Bronze Age: Burials, Rituals and Feasting Grounds at the College Site. *NEA* 73/2–3: 114–29.

Drews, R.

1993   *The End of the Bronze Age: Changes in Warfare and the Catastrophe ca. 1200 B.C.* Princeton: Princeton University Press.

Driver, G. R.

1957   *Aramaic Documents from the Fifth Century*. Oxford: Clarendon.

Dunand, M.

1973   *Fouilles de Byblos*, vol. 5. Paris: Geuthner.

Dunand, M., and R. Duru

1962   *Oumm el-ʿAmed: Une ville de l'époque hellénistique aux échelles de Tyr*. Paris: Maisonneuve.

Dunayevsky, I., and A. Kempinski

1973a   The Megiddo Temples. *ErIsr* 11(Dunayevsky memorial vol.): 8–29. [Hebrew]
1973b   The Megiddo Temples. *ZDPV* 89: 161–87.

Dunham, S.

1988   Review of *Die Tempel und Heiligtümer im alten Mesopotamien* (Denkmäler antiker Architektur 15) Berlin 1984, by E. Heinrich. *JNES* 47: 210–14.

Dunn, R. S.

1989   *The Adventures of Ibn Battuta: A Muslim Traveler of the 14th Century* Berkeley: University of California Press.

Dussaud, R.

1941   *Les découvertes de Ras Shamra et l'Ancien Testament*. 2nd ed. Paris: Geuthner.
1945   *Les religions des Hittites et des Hourrites, des Phéniciens et de Syriens*. Paris: Presses Universitaires de France.
1946–48   Melqart. *Syria* 25: 205–30.

Edelman, D. V., ed.

1995   *You Shall Not Abhor an Edomite for He Is Your Brother*. Atlanta: Scholars Press.

Edgerton, W. F., and J. A. Wilson

1936   *Historical Records of Ramesses III: The Texts of Medinet Habu*, vols. 1–2. Chicago: University of Chicago Press.

Effendi, Habeeb Risk Allah

2001   *The Thistle and the Cedar of Lebanon*. London: Garnet.

Eisenberg, E.

1977   The Temples at Tell Kittan. *BA* 40/2: 78–81.

Eisman, M.

1978   A Tale of Three Cities. *BA* 41/2: 47–60.

Eissfeldt, O.

1957   Silo und Jerusalem. Pp. 138–47 in *Volume du Congrès: Strasbourg 1956*. VTSup 4. Leiden: Brill.

1965   *The Old Testament: An Introduction Including the Apocrypha and Pseudepigrapha, and Also Works of Similar Type from Qumran*, trans. P. R. Ackroyd. New York: Harper & Row.

Eisenstadt, S. N.
1986   *The Origins and Diversity of Axial Age Civilizations.* Albany: State University of New York Press.
1988   Beyond Collapse. Pp. 236–43 in Yoffee and Cowgill 1988.

Elayi, J.
1981   The Relations between Tyre and Carthage during the Persian Period. *JANES(CU)* 13: 15–30.
2010   An Unexpected Archaeological Treasure: The Phoenician Quarters in Beruit City Center. *NEA* 73/2–3: 156–69.

Ellenbogen, M.
1962   *Foreign Words in the Old Testament: Their Origin and Etymology.* London: Luzac.

Ellis, P.
1968   *The Yahwist: The Bible's First Theologian.* Collegeville, MN: Fides.

Elsen, G., and M. Novak
1994   Der Tall Halaf und das Tall-Halaf-Museum. *Das Altertum* 40: 115–26.

Epstein, C.
1965   An Interpretation of the Megiddo Sacred Area during Middle Bronze II. *IEJ* 15: 204–21.
1973   The Sacred Area at Megiddo in Stratum XIX. *ErIsr* 11 (Dunayevsky Memorial Volume): 54–57. [Hebrew]

Escacena, J. L.
1986   Gadir. Pp. 39–58 in Olmo Lete and Aubet Semmler 1986, vol. 1.

Escacena Carrasco, J., and R. Izquierdo de Montes
1998   Intervención arqueológica de urgencia en el Colegio Público "Cerro de San Juan" de Coria del Río (Sevilla). Pp. 971–78 in *Anuario Arqueológico de Andalucía 3.* Seville: Junta de Andalucia.

Escacena, J., M. Belén, J. Beltrán, M. del Rosario Pardo, and J. Ventura
1997   Proyecto estuario: Actuaciones de 1993. Pp. 142–48 in *Anuario arqueológico de Andalucía 1993.* Seville: Junta de Andalucia.

Falconer, S. E.
1986   The Development of Middle Bronze Age Villages in the Jordan Valley: New Perspectives from Tell el-Hayyat. P. 227 in *Abstracts of Biblical Literature, Annual Meeting 1986.*
1987   *Heartland of Villages: Reconsidering Early Urbanism in the Southern Levant.* Ph.D. dissertation, University of Arizona.
1994   The Development and Decline of Bronze Age Civilization in the Southern Levant: A Reassessment of Urbanism and Ruralism. Pp. 305–34 in *Development and Decline in the Mediterranean Bronze Age.* Sheffield Archaeological Monograph 8. Sheffield: Collis.

Falconer, S. E., and B. Magness-Gardiner
1989   Hayyat. *AJ* 1: 254–61.

Fantar, M.
1993   Formules propitiatoires sur des stèles puniques et néopuniques. Pp. 125–33 in Quaegebeur 1993.

1999 North Africa. Pp. 199–230 in Moscatti 1999.

Faust, A.

1999 Socioeconomic Stratification in an Israelite City: Hazor VI as a Test Case. *Levant* 31: 179–90.

2000 The Rural Community in Ancient Israel during Iron Age II. *BASOR* 317: 17–40.

2003 Abandonment, Urbanization, Resettlement and the Formation of the Israelite State. *NEA* 66/4: 147–61.

2006 *Israel's Ethnogenesis: Settlement, Interaction, Expansion and Resistance.* London: Equinox.

Faust, A., and E. Weiss

2005 Judah, Philistia, and the Mediterranean World: Reconstructing the Economic System of the Seventh Century B.C.E. *BASOR* 338: 71–92.

Ferjaoui, A.

1990 Dèdicase d'un sanctuaire à ʿAštart découverte à Mididi (Tunisie). *Semitica* 38 (Hommages à Maurice Sznycer): 113–19.

Fernández Flores, A., and A. Rodrígez Azogue

2005 El complejo monumental del Carambolo Alto, Camas (Sevilla): Un santuario orientalizante en la paleodesembocadura del Guadalquivir. *Trabajos de Prehistoria* 62: 111–38.

Fernández Marcos, N.

1991 The Antiochian Text in I–II Chronicles. Pp. 301–11 in *VII Congress of the International Organization for Septuagint and Cognate Studies: Leuven 1989*, ed. C. Cox. Atlanta: Scholars Press.

1995 The *Vetus Latina* of 1–2 Kings and the Hebrew. Pp. 153–63 in *VIII Congress of the International Organization for Septuagint and Cognate Studies: Paris 1992*, ed. L. Greenspoon and O. Munnich. Atlanta: Scholars Press.

Finegan, J.

1979 *Archaeological History of the Ancient Middle East.* New York: Dorset.

Finkel, I. L., and M. J. Seymour, eds.

2008 *Babylon.* Oxford: Oxford University Press.

Finkelstein, I.

1984 The Iron Age "Fortresses" of the Negev Highlands: Sedentarization of Nomads. *TA* 11: 189–209.

1986a Iron Age Sites in the Negev Highlands: Military Fortresses or Nomads Settling Down? *BAR* 12/4: 46–53.

1986b Shiloh Yields Some but Not All of Its Secrets. *BAR* 12/1: 22–41.

1988a Arabian Trade and Socio-Political Conditions in the Negev in the Twelfth–Eleventh Centuries B.C.E. *JNES* 47: 241–52.

1988b *The Archaeology of Israelite Settlement.* Jerusalem: Israel Exploration Society.

1988c Search for Israelite Origins. *BAR* 14/5: 34–45.

1994 The Emergence of Israel: A Phase in the Cyclic History of Canaan in the Third and Second Millennia BCE. Pp. 9–17 in Finkelstein and Naʾaman 1994.

1996 The Archaeology of the United Monarchy: An Alternative View. *Levant* 28: 177–87.

1999 State Formation in Israel and Judah: A Contrast in Context, a Contrast in Trajectory. *NEA* 62/1: 35–52.

Finkelstein, I., and N. Naʾaman, eds.
  1994   *From Nomadism to Monarchy: Archaeological and Historical Aspects of Early Israel.* Jerusalem: Israel Exploration Society.

Finkelstein, I., and N. A. Silberman
  2001   *The Bible Unearthed: Archaeology's New Vision of Ancient Israel and the Origins of Its Sacred Texts.* New York: Simon & Schuster.
  2006   *David and Solomon. In Search of the Bible's Sacred Kings and the Roots of the Western Tradition.* New York: Free Press.

Finkelstein, I., and D. Ussishkin
  1995   Back to Megiddo. *BAR* 21/1: 26–43.

Fisher, C. S.
  1923   Beth-Shean Excavations of the University Museum Expedition 1921–1923 (University of Pennsylvania). *Museum Journal* 14: 229–31.
  1929   *The Excavation of Armageddon.* Chicago: University of Chicago Press.

Fisher, P.
  1999   Chocolate-on-White Ware: Typology, Chronology, and Provenance—The Evidence from Tell Abu al-Kharaz, Jordan Valley. *BASOR* 313: 1–30.
  2000   Jordan. Pp. 130–35 in Bietak 2000b.

Fisher-Genz, B.
  2008   Review of *Das Eschmun-Heiligtum von Sidon: Architektur und Inscriften*, by R. A. Stucky. *Gnomon* 80: 620–24.

Fisk, R.
  2002   *Pity the Nation: The Abduction of Lebanon.* New York: Thunder's Mouth / Nation Books.

Fitch, J. M., and D. P. Branch
  1960   Primitive Architecture and Climate. *Scientific American* 203: 134–44.

Fitzgerald, G. M.
  1930   *The Four Canaanite Temples of Beth-Shan*, part 2: *The Pottery.* Philadelphia: University of Pennsylvania Museum.
  1932   Excavations at Beth-Shan in 1931. *PEFQS* 64: 141–45.

Fleming, D.
  1992a *The Installation of Baʿal's High Priestess at Emar.* Atlanta: Scholars Press.
  1992b The Rituals from Emar: Evolution of an Indigenous Tradition in Second-Millennium Syria. Pp. 47–61 in *New Horizons in the Study of Ancient Syria.* Bibliotheca Mesopotamica 25. Malibu, CA: Undena.
  1996   The Emar Festivals: City Unity and Syrian Identity under Hittite Hegemony. Pp. 81–121 in Chavalas 1996.

Forsén, B.
  1996   *Griechische Glieder-weihungen.* Helsinki: Finnish Institute at Athens.

Fortin, M.
  1984   The Enkomi Tower. *Levant* 16: 173–76.
  1999   *Syria: Land of Civilizations*, trans. J. Macaulay. Quebec: Musée de la civilisation.

Fowler, M. D.
  1983   A Closer Look at the 'Temple of El-Berith' at Shechem. *PEQ* 115: 49–53.

Fox, M.
  1988   *Temple in Society.* Winona Lake, IN: Eisenbrauns.

Frankel, R.
1994   Upper Galilee in the Late Bronze–Iron I Transition. Pp. 18–34 in Finkelstein and Naʾaman 1994.

Franken, H. J.
1967   Texts from the Persian Period from Tell Deir ʿAlla. *VT* 17: 480–81.
1989   Deir ʿAlla (Tell). *AJ* 2: 201–5.
1992   *Excavations at Tell Deir ʿAlla: The Late Bronze Age Sanctuary.* Louvain: Peeters.
1997   Deir ʿAlla, Tell. Pp. 137–38 in vol. 2 of *OEANE*.

Frankenstein, S.
1979   The Phoenicians in the Far West: A Function of the Neo-Assyrian Imperalism. *Mesopotamia* 7: 263–94.

Frankfort, H.
1952   The Origin of the Bit-Hilani. *Iraq* 14: 120–31.
1985   *The Art and Architecture of the Ancient Orient.* 4th ed. Harmondsworth: Penguin.

Franklin, J.
2007   The Global Economy of Music in the Ancient Near East. Pp. 27–37 in *Sounds of Ancient Music*, ed. J. G. Westenholz. Jerusalem: Bible Lands Museum.
2011   "Sweet Psalmist of Israel": The *Kinnôr* and Royal Ideology in the United Monarchy. Pp. 99–113 in *Strings and Threads: A Celebration of the Work of Anne Draffkorn Kilmer*, ed. W. Heimpel and G. Frantz-Szabo. Winona Lake, IN: Eisenbrauns.

Franklin, N.
2007   A Response to David Ussishkin. *BASOR* 348: 71–73.

Freunde eines Schweizerischen Orient-Museums
1985   *Vom Euphrat zum Nil: Kunst aus dem alten Ägypten und Vorderasien.* Zurich: Freunde eines Schweizerischen Orient-Museums.

Frick, F. S.
2000   Ritual and Social Regulation in Ancient Israel: The Importance of the Social Context for Ritual Studies and a Case Study: The Ritual of the Red Heifer. Pp. 219–32 in *Away from the Father's House: The Social Location of* naʿar *and* naʿarah *in Ancient Israel.* JSOTSup 301. Sheffield: Sheffield Academic Press.

Friedman, R. E.
1987   *Who Wrote the Bible?* Englewood Cliffs, NJ: Summit Books

Friedman, R. E., ed.
1981   *The Creation of Sacred Literature.* Near Eastern Studies 22. Berkeley: University of California Press.

Friedrich, J. G., R. Meyer, A. Ungnad, and E. F. Weidner
1940   *Die Inschriften vom Tell Halaf.* AfOBeiheft 6. Berlin: Self-published.

Fritz, V.
1977   *Tempel und Zelt: Studien zum Tempelbau in Israel und zu dem Zeltheiligtum der Priesterschrift.* Neukirchen-Vluyn: Neukirchener Verlag.
1983   Tel Masos: A Biblical Site in the Negev. *Archaeology* 36/5: 30–37.
1987a   Conquest or Settlement? The Early Iron Age in Palestine. *BA* 50/2: 84–100.
1987b   What Can Archaeology Tell Us about Solomon's Temple? *BAR* 13/4: 38–49.
1995   *The City in Ancient Israel.* Sheffield: Sheffield Academic Press.
2002   Israelites and Canaanites: You Can Tell Them Apart. *BAR* 28/4: 28–31.

Fritz, V., and P. R. Davies, eds.
1996   *The Origins of the Ancient Israelite State.* JSOTSup 228. Sheffield: Sheffield Academic.

Furumark, A.
  1941   *The Mycenaean Pottery: Analysis and Classification*. Stockholm: Kungl.
Fusaro, D.
  1982   Note di architettura domestica greca nel periodo tardo-geometrico e arcaico. *Dialoghi di Archeologia* n.s. 1/4: 5–30.
Gal, Z.
  1994   Iron I in Lower Galilee and the Margins of the Jezreel Valley. Pp. 35–46 in Finkelstein and Na'aman 1994.
Galling, K.
  1956   Review of *Tell Halaf III: Die Bildwerks* by D. Opitz and A. Moortgat. *BO* 13: 36–37.
García y Bellido, A.
  1963   Hercules Gaditanus. *Archivo Español de Arqueología* 36: 70–153.
Garner, G.
  1974   City of the Golden Calf: ` Discoveries at Tell Dan. *Buried History* 10/4: 122–26.
  1985a God or Baʿal? Discoveries at Ras Shamra, Syria. *Buried History* 21/3: 51–60.
  1985b The Temple and Fortress at Tell Arad. *Buried History* 21/1 : 3–17.
Garrido, J. P.
  1978   La colonización fenicia en el área atlántica de la península ibérica. Pp. 381–86 in *The Proceedings of the Xth International Congress of Classical Archaeology*, ed. E. Akurgal. Ankara: Türk Tarih Kurumu.
Gates, M.-H.
  1990   Artisans and Art in Old Babylonian Mari. Pp. 29–38 in Gunter 1990b.
  1996   Archaeology in Tukey. *AJA* 100: 277–335.
Gaube, H.
  1999   Foreword and The Levant. Pp. 7–11 in Binst et al. 1999.
Gehrig, U., and H. G. Niemeyer, eds.
  1990   *Die Phönizier im Zeitalter Homers*. Mainz am Rhein: von Zabern.
George, A.
  2008a Ancient Descriptions: Babylonian Topographical Texts. Pp. 54–59 in Finkel and Seymour 2008.
  2008b A Tour of Nebuchadnezzar's Babylon. Pp. 60–65 in Finkel and Seymour 2008.
Geva, S.
  1989   *Hazor, Israel: An Urban Community of the 8th Century B.C.E.* British Archaeological Reports, International Series 543. Oxford: Archaeopress.
Gilboa, A.
  2005   Sea Peoples and Phoenicians along the Southern Phoenician Coast—A Reconciliation: An Interpretation of Sikila (*SKL*) Material Culture. *BASOR* 337: 47–78.
Gilboa, A., and I. Sham
  2003   An Archaeological Contribution to the Early Iron Age Chronological Debate: Alternative Chronology for Phoenicians and Their Effects on the Levant, Cyprus and Greece. *BASOR* 332: 7–80.
Ginsberg, H. L.
  1958   Poems of Baal and Anath in *ANE Anth*.
Gitin, S.
  1989   Tel Miqne–Ekron: A Type-Site for the Inner Coastal Plain in the Iron Age II Period. Pp. 23–58 in Gitin and Dever 1989.
  1992   Last Days of the Philistines. *BAR* 45/3: 26–31.

2002   The House That Albright Built. *NEA* 65/1: 5–10.

Gitin, S., and W. Dever, eds.
1989   *Recent Excavations in Israel: Studies in Iron Age Archaeology.* AASOR 49. Winona Lake, IN: Eisenbrauns.

Gitin, S., and T. Dothan
1987   The Rise and Fall of Ekron of the Philistines. *BA* 50: 197–222.

Gitin, S., A. Mazar, and E. Stern, eds.
1998   *Mediterranean Peoples in Transition: Thirteenth to Early Tenth Centuries b.c.e. (In Honor of Trude Dothan).* Jerusalem: Israel Exploration Society.

Giveon, R.
1978   *The Impact of Egypt on Canaan: Iconographical and Related Studies.* Fribourg: Universitätsverlag / Göttingen: Vandenhoeck & Ruprecht.

Gjerstad, E.
1944   The Colonization of Cyprus in Greek Legend. *Acta Instituti Romani Regni Sueciae: Opscula Atheniensia* 3: 107–23.
1946   Decorated Metal Bowls from Cyprus. *Opuscula Archaeologica* 4: 1–18, pls. 1–11.

Goldwasser, O.
2010   How the Alphabet Was Born from Hieroglyphs. *BAR* 36/2: 36–50.

Gonnella, J., W. Khayyata, and K. Kohlmeyer
2005   *Die Zitadelle von Aleppo und der Tempel des Wettergottes: Neue Forschungen und Entdeckungen.* Münster: Rhema.

González Prats, A., and E. Ruiz Segura
1990–91   Nuevos datos sobre urbanística y cultura material en el Hierro Antiguo del sudeste (Peña Negra, 1986). *Lucentum* 9–10: 51–75.

González Wagner, C. G., and J. Alvar
1989   Fenicios en occidente: La colonización agrícola. *Rivista di Studi Fenici* 17: 61–102.

Gooding, D. W.
1965   An Impossible Shrine. *VT* 15: 405–20.
1967   Temple Specifications: A Dispute in Logical Arrangement between the MT and the LXX. *VT* 17: 143–72.

Gordon, C.
1949   *Ugaritic Literature: A Comprehensive Translation of the Poetic and Prose Texts.* Rome: Pontifical Biblical Institute.
1955   *Ugaritic Manual*, vol. 3. Rome: Pontifical Biblical Institute.
1989   Ebla, Ugarit and the Old Testament. *Orient* 25: 134–68.
1992   The Mediterranean Synthesis. Pp. 188–96 in Joukowsky and Ward 1992.

Gorman, F. H.
1990   *The Ideology of Ritual: Space, Time, and Status in Priestly Theology.* Sheffield: Sheffield Academic Press.

Goshen-Gottstein, M. H.
1979   The Aleppo Codex and the Rise of the Massoretic Bible Text. *BA* 42/3: 145–63.

Gottwald, N.
1989   *The Hebrew Bible: A Socio-Literary Introduction.* Philadelphia: Fortress.

Graves-Brown, P., S. Jones, and C. Gamble, eds.
1996   *Cultural Identity and Archaeology: The Construction of European Communities.* London: Routledge.

Gray, J.
1957   *The Legacy of Canaan.* Leiden: Brill.

1966   Social Aspects of Canaanite Religion. Pp. 370–92 in *Volume du Congrès: Geneva 1965.* VTSup 15. Leiden: Brill.

Grayson, A. K.
1990   Assyria: Ashur-dan II to Ashur-Nirari V (934–745 B.C.). Pp. 238–81 in *CAH* 3/1: *The Prehistory of the Balkans: The Middle East and the Aegean World, 10th to 8th Centuries B.C.* Cambridge: Cambridge University Press.

Greaves, A. M., and B. Helwing
2003   Archaeology in Turkey: The Stone, Bronze, and Iron Ages. *AJA* 107: 71–103.

Guardata, F. B.
1991   Il culto praticato ad Ebla paleosiriana. *La Parola del Passato* 46: 394–416.

Gunter, A. C.
1990a   Artists and Ancient Near Eastern Art. Pp. 9–20 in Gunter 1990b.
1990b   *Investigating Artistic Environments in the Ancient Near East.* Washington, DC: Arthur M. Sackler Gallery, Smithsonian Institution.

Gurney, O. R.
1954   *The Hittites.* Harmondsworth: Penguin.

Güterbock, H. G.
1954   Carchemish. *JNES* 13: 102–14.
1975   The Hittite Temple according to the Written Sources. Pp. 125–32 in *Nederlands Historisch-Archeologisch Instituut te Istanbul 1975.*
1992   Survival of the Hittite Dynasty. Pp. 53–55 in Joukowsky and Ward 1992.

Guy, P. L. O.
1931   *New Light from Armageddon: Second Provisional Report (1927–1929) on the Excavations at Megiddo in Palestine.* Chicago: University of Chicago Press.

Haas, V., and L. Jakob-Rost
1984   Das Festritual des Gottes Telipinu in Hanhana und in Kašha: Ein Beitrag zum hethitischen Festkalender. *AF* 11: 10–91.

Hachmann, R., ed.
1983   *Frühe Phöniker im Libanon: 20 Jahre deutsche Ausgrabungen in Kamid el-Loz.* Mainz am Rhein: von Zabern.
1989   *Kamid el-Loz, 1963–1981: German Excavations in Lebanon* (Part 1). *Berytus* 37: 5–187.

Hadidi, A., ed.
1987   *Studies in the History and Archaeology of Jordan.* London: Routledge and Kegan Paul.

Hadjisavvas, S.
2003   Ashlar Buildings. Pp. 31–35 in *From Ishtar to Aphrodite: 3200 Years of Cypriot Hellenism—Treasures from the Museums of Cyprus*, ed. S. Hadjisavvas. New York: Alexander S. Onassis Public Benefit Foundation, Onassis Cultural Center.

Haeny, G.
1997   New Kingdon 'Mortuary Temples' and 'Mansions of Million Years.' Pp. 86–126 in Shafer 1997.

Hagens, G.
2002   The Chronology of Tenth-Century Assyria and Babylon. *JACF* 9: 61–70.

Hägg, R.
1992   Sanctuaries and Workshops in the Bronze Age Aegean. Pp. 29–32 in Linders and Alroth 1992.
1995   State and Religion in Mycenaean Greece. Pp. 387–91 in Laffineur and Niemeier 1995.

Hägg, R., and N. Marinatos, eds.
1981   *Sanctuaries and Cults in the Aegean Bronze Age: Proceedings of the First International Symposium at the Swedish Institute in Athens, 12–13 May 1980.* Stockholm: Svenska Institutet i Athen.

Hägg, R., N. Marinatos, and C. Gullög Nordquist, eds.
1988   *Early Greek Cult Practice: Proceedings of the Fifth International Symposium at the Swedish Institute at Athens, 26–29 June 1986.* Stockhom: Svenska Institutet i Athen.

Haines, R. C.
1971   *Excavations on the Plains of Antioch, II: Structural Remains of the Later Phases— Chatal Hüyük, Tell al-Jadaidah, and Tell Taʿyinat.* OIP 92. Chicago: University of Chicago Press.

Hallo, W.
1992   From Bronze Age to Iron Age in Western Asia: Defining the Problem. Pp. 1–9 in Joukowsky and Ward 1992.
1993   Albright and the Gods of Mesopotamia. *BA* 56: 18–24.

Halpern, B.
1981   Sacred History and Ideology: Chronicles' Thematic Structure—Indications of an Earlier Source. Pp. 35–54 in Friedman 1981.
1987   Radical Exodus Redating Fatally Flawed. *BAR* 13/6: 56.
1996   The Construction of the Davidic State: An Exercise in Historiography. Pp. 44–75 in Fritz and Davies 1996.
1998   Research Design in Archaeology: The Interdisciplinary Perspective. *NEA* 61/1: 53–65.
2001   *David's Secret Demons: Messiah, Murderer, Traitor, King.* Grand Rapids, MI: Eerdmans.

Hamblin, W., and D. Seely
2007   *Solomon's Temple, Myth and History.* London: Thames and Hudson.

Hamilton, R.
1934   Excavations at Tell Abu Hawam. *QDAP* 4: 1–69.

Handy, L. K.
1993   Review of Seow 1989 in *JNES* 52: 159–60.

Hankey, V.
1974a   A Late Bronze Age Temple at Amman, I: The Aegean Pottery. *Levant* 6: 131–59.
1974b   A Late Bronze Age Temple at Amman, II: Vases and Objects Made of Stone. *Levant* 6: 160–78.
1995   A Late Bronze Age Temple at Amman Airport: Small Finds and Pottery. Pp. 169–85 in S. Bourke and J.-P. Descoeudres 1995.

Hankey, V., and H. Hankey
1985   A Mycenaean Pictorial Krater from Lachish, Level VI. Pp. 88–99 in *Palestine in the Bronze and Iron Ages: Papers in Honour of Olga Tufnell*, ed. J. N. Tubb. London: Institute of Archaeology.

Har-El, M.
1978   The Pride of the Jordan: The Jungle of the Jordan. *BA* 41/2: 64–75.

Haran, M.
1977   A Temple at Dor? *IEJ* 27: 12–15

1978   *Temples and Temple-Service in Ancient Israel: An Inquiry into Biblical Cult Phenomena and the Historical Setting of the Priestly School.* Oxford: Clarendon. [Repr. Winona Lake, IN: Eisenbrauns, 1985]

Harden, D.
1962   *The Phoenicians.* New York: Thames & Hudson.

Hardin, J. W.
2004   Understanding Domestic Space: An Example from Iron Age Tell Halif. *NEA* 67/2: 71–83.

Harding, G. L.
1956   Excavations in Jordan. *ADAJ* 3: 80.

Harif, A.
1974   A Mycenaean Building at Tell Abu-Hawam in Palestine. *PEQ* 106: 83–90.
1978   Coastal Buildings of Foreign Origin in Second Millennium B.C. Palestine. *PEQ* 110: 101–6.

Harrison, R.
1988   *Spain at the Dawn of History: Iberians, Phoenicians and Greeks.* London: Thames & Hudson.

Harrison, T.
2003   The Battleground: Who Destroyed Megiddo? *BAR* 20/6: 28–35.
2007   The Late Bronze/Early Iron Age Transition in the North Orontes Valley. Pp. 83–102 in *Societies in Transition: Evolutionary Processes in the Northern Levant between the Late Bronze Age II and the Early Iron Age. Papers Presented on the Occasion of the 20th Anniversary of the New Excavations in Tell Afis, Bologna, 15th November 2007.* Studi e testi orientali 9, Serie Archeologica 2. Bologna: Clueb.
2009   Neo-Hittites in the ʻLand of Palistineʼ: Renewed Investigations at Tell Taʻyinat on the Plain of Antioch. *NEA* 72/4: 174–89.

Hauer, C.
1980   The Economics of National Security in Solomonic Israel. *JSOT* 18: 63–73.

Hawkins, J. D.
1972   Building Inscriptions of Carchemish: The Long Wall of Sculpture and the Great Staircase. *AnSt* 22: 87–108.
1977   *Trade in the Ancient Near East.* London: British School of Archaeology in Iraq.
1982   The Neo-Hittite States in Syria and Anatolia. Pp. 372–441 in *CAH* 3/1: *The Prehistory of the Balkans: The Middle East and the Aegean World, 10th to 8th Centuries B.C.* Cambridge: Cambridge University Press.
1988   Kuzi-Tesub and the ʻGreat Kingsʼ of Karkamis. *AnSt* 38: 99–108.
1996–97   A New Luwian Inscription of Hamiyatas, King of Masuwari. *Abr-Nahrain*: 108–17.
2009   Cilicia, the Amuq, and Aleppo: New Light in a Dark Age. *NEA* 72/4: 164–73.

Heinrich, E.
1984   *Die Tempel und Heiligtümer im alten Mesopotamien* Denkmäler antiker Architektur 15. Berlin: Deutsches Archäologisches Institut.

Hennessy, J. B.
1966   Excavations of a Late Bronze Age Temple at Amman. *PEQ* 98: 155–62.
1985   A Thirteenth Century B.C. Temple of Human Sacrifice at Amman. *Studia Phoenicia*: 85–104.

Hermann, A.
1938   *Die ägyptische Königsnovelle.* Leipziger ägyptologische Studien 10. Gluckstadt, NY: Augustin.

Hermann, S.
1953–54   Die Königsnovelle in Ägypten und Israel: Ein Beitrag zur Gattungs-Geschichte des Alten Testaments. *Wissenschaftliche Zeitschrift der Karl Marx Universität, Leipzig* 3: 33–44.
1985   2 Samuel VII in the Light of the Egyptian Königsnovelle–Reconsidered. Pp. 119–28 in *Pharaonic Egypt, the Bible and Christianity*, ed. S. Israelit-Groll. Jerusalem: Magnes.

Herr, L.
1983a   *The Amman Airport Excavations, 1976.* AASOR 48. Ann Arbor, MI: American Schools of Oriental Research.
1983b   The Amman Airport Structure and the Geopolitics of Ancient Transjordan. *BA* 46: 223–29.
1985   The Servant of Baʿal’s. *BA* 48: 169–72.
1988   Tripartite Pillared Buildings and the Market Place in Iron Age Palestine. *BASOR* 272: 4–67.
1993   What Ever Happened to the Ammonites? *BAR* 19/6: 26–35.
1997a   Amman Airport Temple. Pp. 102–3 in vol. 1 of *OEANE*.
1997b   Ammon. Pp. 103–5 in vol. 1 of *OEANE*.
1997c   The Iron Age II Period: Emerging Nations. *BA* 60: 114–83.

Herzfeld, E.
1934   Der Tell Halaf und das Problem der hettischen Kunst. *Archäologische Mitteilungen aus Iran* 6/3–4: 111–223.

Herzog, Z.
1980   A Functional Interpretation of the Broadroom and Longroom House Types. *TA* 7: 82–89.
1992a   Administrative Structures in the Iron Age. Pp. 223–30 in Kempinski and Reich 1992.
1992b   Settlement and Fortification Planning in the Iron Age. Pp. 231–74 in Kempinski and Reich 1992.
1997   Arad. Pp. 174–76 in vol. 1 of *OEANE*.

Herzog, Z., M. Aharoni, and A. Rainey
1987   Arad: An Ancient Israelite Fortress with a Temple to Yahweh. *BAR* 13/2: 16–35.

Herzog, Z., M. Aharoni, A. F. Rainey, and S. Moshkovitz
1984   The Israelite Fortress at Arad. *BASOR* 254: 1–34.

Hess, R.
1993   Early Israel in Canaan: A Survey of Recent Evidence and Interpretations. *PEQ* 125: 125–42.

Hestrin, R.
1991   Understanding Asherah: Exploring Semitic Iconography. *BAR* 17/5: 50–59.

Heurtley, W. A.
1936   The Relations between ‘Philistine’ and Mycenaean Pottery. *QDAP* 5: 90–110.

Hiebert, T.
1996   *The Yahwist’s Landscape: Nature and Religion in Early Israel.* Oxford: Oxford University Press.

Higginbotham, C. R.
1998   The Egyptianizing of Canaan. *BAR* 24/3: 36–43.

2000   *Egyptianization and Elite Emulation in Ramesside Palestine.* Leiden: Brill.

Hijazi, H.
1991   *The Late Bronze Age Temples in the Vicinity of Amman, Jordan.* M.A. thesis, Yarmouk University, Jordan.

Hodder, B. W.
1965   Some Comments on the Origins of Traditional Markets in Africa South of the Sahara. *Transactions of the Institute of British Geographers* 36: 97–105.

Hölscher, G.
1923   Das Buch des Könige, seine Quelle und Seine Redaktion. Pp. 158–213 in *Eucharisterion: Studien zur Religion und Literatur des Alten und Neuen Testaments, H. Gunkel Festschrift,* ed. H. Schmidt. Göttingen: Vandenhoeck & Ruprecht.

Hoffman, J.
2004   *In the Beginning: A Short History of the Hebrew Language.* New York: New York University Press.

Hoffmann, H.
1953   Foreign Influence and Native Invention in Archaic Greek Altars. *AJA* 57: 189–95.

Hoffner, H. ed.
1973   *Orient and Occident: Essays Presented to Cyrus H. Gordon on the Occasion of His Sixty-Fifth Birthday.* Neukirchen-Vluyn: Neukirchener Verlag.

Hoftijzer, J.
1976   The Prophet Balaam in a 6th Century Aramaic Inscription. *BA* 39: 11–17.

Hoftijzer, J., and G. van der Kooij
1976   *Aramaic Texts from Deir ʿAlla.* Documenta et Monumenta Orientis Antiqui 19. Leiden: Brill.

Hollinshead, M.
1999   'Adyton,' 'Opisthodomos,' and the Inner Room of the Greek Temple. *Hesperia* 68: 181–218.

Holladay, J. S.
1987   Religion in Israel and Judah under the Monarchy: An Explicitly Archaeological Approach. Pp. 249–99 in Miller, Hanson, and McBride 1987.

Homès-Fredericq, D.
1989   Lehun. *AJ* 2: 339–59.

Hooke, S. H.
1958   *Myth, Ritual, and Kingship: Essays on the Theory and Practice of Kingship in the Ancient Near East and Israel.* Oxford: Clarendon.

Hopkins, D. C.
1993   Pastoralists in Late Bronze Age Palestine: Which Way Did They Go? *BA* 56: 200–211.

Horden, P., and N. Purcell
2000   *The Corrupting Sea: A Study of Mediterranean History.* Oxford: Blackwell.

Horn, S.
1969   The Amman Citadel Inscription. *BASOR* 193: 2–19.
1973   The Crown of the King of the Ammonites. *AUSS* 11: 170–80.

Howie, C. G.
1950   *The Date and Composition of Ezekiel.* Journal of Biblical Literature Monograph 4. Philadelphia: Society of Biblical Literature.

Hübner, U.
1992   *Die Ammoniter: Untersuchungen zur Geschichte, Kultur und Religion eines transjordanischen Volkes in 1. Jahrtausend v. Chr.* Wiesbaden: Harrassowita.

Hult, G.
1983   *Bronze Age Ashlar Masonry in the Eastern Mediterranean: Cyprus, Ugarit, and Neighboring Regions.* Studies in Mediterranean Archaeology 66. Gothenburg: Åström.

Humann, C., and R. Koldewey
1898   *Ausgrabungen in Sendschirli,* vol. 2. Mitteilungen aus den Orientalischen Sammlungen 12. Berlin: Spemann.

Hunger, H.
2000   The Current State of Research on Mesopotamian Chronology (Absolute Chronology III). Pp. 60–61 in Bietak 2000.

Hurowitz, V.
1992   *I Have Built You an Exalted House: Temple Building in the Bible in Light of the Mesopotamian and Northwest Semitic Writings.* JSOTSup 15. Sheffield: Sheffield Academic Press.
2011   Solomon's Temple in Context. *BAR* 37/2: 46–57, 77–78.

Ibrahim, M.
1987   Geographische und ökologische Rahmenbedingungen vom Paläolithikum. Pp. 38–52 in Mittmann et al. 1987.

Ibrahim, M., and Z. Kafafi
1987   Mittlere und Späte Bronzezeit. Pp. 86–87 in Mittmann et al. 1987.

Ikeda, Y.
1979   Royal Cities and Fortified Cities. *Iraq* 41: 75–87.
1982   Solomon's Trade in Horses and Chariots in Its International Setting. Pp. 213–38 in Isheda 1982b.

Ilan, D.
1997   Dan. Pp. 107–12 in vol. 2 of *OEANE.*

Ionas, J.
1984   L'architecture religieuse au chypriote récent (Kition et Enkomi). Pp. 97–105 in Roux 1984.

Irwin, W. A.
1943   *The Problem of Ezekiel: An Inductive Study.* Chicago: University of Chicago Press.

Ishida, T.
1982a Solomon's Succession to the Throne of David: A Political Analysis. Pp. 175–87 in Ishida 1982b.
1982b *Studies in the Period of David and Solomon and Other Essays: Papers Read at the International Symposium for Biblical Studies, Tokyo, 5–7 December 1979.* Winona Lake, IN: Eisenbrauns.

Isserlin, B. S. J.
1982   Motya: Urban Features. Pp. 113–31 in Niemeyer 1982.
1998   *The Israelites.* London: Thames & Hudson.

Jacobsen, T.
1987   The Graven Image. Pp. 15–32 in Miller, Hanson, and McBride 1987.

Jacobson, D.
1999a Sacred Geometry: Unlocking the Secret of the Temple Mount, Part 1. *BAR* 25/4: 42–53.

1999b Sacred Geometry: Unlocking the Secret of the Temple Mount, Part 2. *BAR* 25/5: 54–63.

James, F.
  1966 *The Iron Age at Beth Shan: A Study of Levels VI–IV.* Philadelphia: University Musuem, University of Pennsylvania.

James, F., and P. McGovern
  1993 *The Late Bronze Egyptian Garrison at Beth Shan: A Study of Levels VII and VIII.* Philadelphia: University Museum, University of Pennsylvania.

James, P. J.
  1987a Southeastern Anatolia and Northern Syria: Dating Neo-Hittite Art and Architecture. *JACF* 1: 36–40.
  1987b Syro-Palestine: Conflicting Chronologies. *JACF* 1: 44–49.
  1991 *Centuries of Darkness: A Challenge to the Conventional Chronology of Old World Archaeology.* London: Cape.

Jaroš, K.
  1998 *Kanaan, Israel, Palästina: Ein Gang durch die Geschichte des Heiligen Landes.* Mainz am Rhein: von Zabern.

Jidejian, N.
  1968 *Byblos through the Ages.* Beruit: Dar el-Machreq.
  1992 An Introduction to Tyre. Pp. 7–12 in Joukowsky 1992.

Joukowsky, M. S., ed.
  1992 *The Heritage of Tyre.* Dubuque: Kendall/Hunt.

Joukowsky, M. S., and W. Ward, eds.
  1992 *The Crisis Years: The 12th Century* B.C. *from beyond the Danube to the Tigris.* Dubuque, IA: Kendall/Hunt.

Jourdain-Annequin, C.
  1992 *Héraclès-Melqart à Amrith, Recherches iconographiques: Contribution à l'étude d'un syncrétisme.* Paris: Geuthner.

Kanellopoulos, C., ed.
  1994 *The Great Temple of Amman: The Architecture.* Amman: American Center for Oriental Research.

Kaniewski, D. E. Paulissen, E. Van Campo, M. Al-Maqdissi, J. Bretschneider, and K. Van Lerberghe
  2008 Middle East Coastal Ecosystem Response to Middle-to-Late Holocene Abrupt Climate Changes. *Proceedings of the National Academy of Science of the United States of America* 105: 13941–46.

Kaniewski, D., E. Paulissen, E. Van Campo, H. Weis, T. Otto, J. Bretschneider, and K. Van Lerberghe
  2010 Late Second – early First Millennium BC Abrupt Climate Changes in Coastal Syria and Their Possible Significance for the History of the Eastern Mediterranean. *Quaternary Research* 74: 207–15.

Kapelrud, A. S.
  1963 Temple Building: A Task for Gods or Kings. *Or* 32: 56–62.

Karageorghis, V.
  1982 *Cyprus from the Stone Age to the Romans.* London: Thames & Hudson.
  1990 À propos de Kitiens portant la tiare. *Semitica* 39 (Hommages à Maurice Sznycer): 1–5.

1992   The Crisis Years: Cyprus. Pp. 79–86 in Joukowsky and Ward 1992.

Katzenstein, H. J.

1973   *The History of Tyre, from the Beginning of the Second Millennium* B.C.E. *until the Fall of the Neo-Babylonian Empire in 538* B.C.E. Jerusalem: Schocken Institute for Jewish Research–Jewish Theological Seminary of America.

1979   Tyre in the Early Persian Period (539–486 B.C.E.). *BA* 42/1: 23–34.

Kaufman, A.

1983   Where the Ancient Temple of Jerusalem Stood. *BAR* 9/2: 40–59.

1984   A Note on Artistic Representations of the Second Temple of Jerusalem. *BA* 47: 253–54.

1988   Fixing the Site of the Tabernacle at Shiloh. *BAR* 14/6: 46–53.

Kaufmann, H.

1988   The Collapse of Ancient States and Civilizations as an Organizational Problem. Pp. 219–36 in Yoffee and Cowgill 1988.

Kempinski, A.

1972   The Sin Temple at Khafaje and the En-Gedi Temple. *IEJ* 22: 10–15.

1986   Joshua's Altar: An Iron Age 1 Watch-Tower? *BAR* 12/1: 44–49.

1989   *A City, State and Royal Centre in North Israel.* Munich: Beck.

1992   Chalcolithic and Early Bronze Age Temples. Pp. 53–59 in Kempinski and Reich 1992.

Kempinski, A., and R. Reich, eds.

1992   *The Architecture of Ancient Israel from the Prehistoric to the Persian Periods: In Memory of Immanuel (Munya) Dunayevsky.* Jerusalem: Israel Exploration Society.

Kenyon, K. M.

1966   *Amorites and Canaanites.* London: British Academy.

Khalifeh, I. S.

1988   *Sarepta II: The Bronze Age and Iron Age Periods of Area II.* Beirut: Université Libanaise.

Khazanov, A. M.

1984   *Nomads and the Outside World.* Cambridge: Cambridge University Press.

Killebrew, A.

1998   *Ceramic Craft and Technology during the Late Bronze and Early Iron Ages: The Relationship between Pottery Technology, Style, and Cultural Diversity.* Ph.D. dissertation, Hebrew University.

2005   *Biblical Peoples and Ethnicity: An Archaeological Study of Egyptians, Canaanites, Philistines, and Early Israel, 1300–1100* B.C.E. Atlanta: Society of Biblical Literature.

Kinet, D.

1981   *Ugarit: Geschichte und Kultur einer Stadt in der Umwelt des Alten Testaments.* Stuttgart: Katholisches Bibelwerk.

King, P. J., and L. E. Stager, eds.

2001   *Life in Biblical Israel.* Louisville: Westminster John Knox.

Kinglake, A. W.

1982   *Eothen.* London: Century / Gentry.

Kitchen, K. A.

1989   Shishak's Military Campaign in Israel Confirmed. *BAR* 15/3: 32–33.

1999   Notes on a Stela of Ramesses II from near Damascus. *Göttinger Miszellen* 173: 133–38.

2000   Regnal and Genealogical Data of Ancient Egypt (Absolute Chronology I). Pp. 39–52 in Bietak 2000b.

2001   How We Know When Solomon Ruled. *BAR* 27/5: 32–37.

Klengel, H.
1996 Palmyra and International Trade in the Bronze Age: The Historical Background. *AAAS* 47: 159–64.

Knapp, A. B.
1989 Complexity and Collapse in the North Jordan Valley: Archaeometry and Society in the Middle–Late Bronze Ages. *IEJ* 39: 129–48.

Knapp, G.
1988 Linguistic and Cultural Geography of Contemporary Peru. Pp. 223–33 in *Texas Papers on Latin America: Pre-Publication Working Papers of the Institute of Latin American Studies*. Austin: University of Texas Press.

Knoppers, G.
1992 The God in His Temple: The Phoenician Text from Pyrgi as a Funerary Inscription. *JNES* 51: 105–20.
1995 Prayer and Propaganda: Solomon's Dedication of the Temple and the Deuteronomist's Program. *CBQ* 57: 229–54.

Kochavi, M.
1999 Divided Structures, Divided Scholars. *BAR* 25/3: 44–55.

Koenig, J.
1983 La déclaration des dieux dans l'inscription de Deir Alla. *Semitica* 33: 77–88.

Kohlmeyer, K.
1985a Egyptian and Hittite Influences in Syria. Pp. 246–49 in Weiss 1985.
1985b Emar (Meskene). Pp. 260–61 in Weiss 1985.
1985c Ugarit (Ras Shamra). Pp. 249–52 in Weiss 1985.
2000 *Der Tempel des Wettergottes von Aleppo*. Münster: Rhema.
2008 Zur Datierrung der Skupturen von ʿAin Dārā. Pp. 119–30 in *Fundstellen: Gesammelte Schriften zur Archäologie und Geschichte Altvorderasiens ad honorem Hartmut Kühne*, ed. D. Bonatz, R. M. Czichon, and F. J. Kreppner. Wiesbaden: Harrassowitz.
2009 The Temple of the Storm God in Aleppo during the Late Bronze and Early Iron Ages. *NEA* 72/4: 190–202.

Kondoleon, C.
2001 The City of Antioch: Introduction. Pp. 3–11 in *Antioch: The Lost City*, ed. C. Kondoleon. Princeton: Princeton University Press.

Kooij, G. van der, and M. M. Ibrahim, eds.
1989 *Picking Up the Threads: A Continuing Review of Excavations at Deir Alla, Jordan*. Leiden: University of Leiden, Archaeological Center.

Kouchoukos, N.
2001 Satellite Images and the Representation of Near Eastern Landscapes. *NEA* 64/1–2: 80–93.

Koutsoukou, A., K. Russell, M. Najjar, and A. Momani
1997 *The Great Temple of Amman: The Excavations*. Amman: American Center for Oriental Research.

Kraeling, C. H., and L. Mowry
1957 Music in the Bible. Pp. 282–312 in *New Oxford History of Music*, vol. 1: *Ancient and Oriental Music*, ed. E. Wellesz. London: Oxford University Press.

Krahmalkov, C. R.
1981 The Foundation of Carthage, 814 B.C.: The Douïmès Pendant Inscription. *JSS* 26: 177–91.

Kreiger, B.
1997   *The Dead Sea: Myth, History, and Politics*. 2nd ed. Hanover, NH: University Press of New England.

Kuschke, A.
1967   Der Tempel Salomos und der 'syrische' Tempeltypus. Pp. 124–32 in *Das Ferne und Nahe Wort: Festschrift Leonhardt Rost*, ed. F. Maass. Berlin: A. Töpelmann.

Lacovara, P.
1999   The City of Amarna. Pp. 61–71 in *Pharaohs of the Sun*, ed. R. Freed, Y. Markowitz, and S. D'Aura. Boston: Museum of Fine Arts.

Laffineur, R., and W.-D. Niemeier, eds.
1995   *Politeia: Society and State in the Aegean Bronze Age. Proceedings of the Fifth International Aegean Conference, University of Heidelberg, Archäologisches Institut, 10–13 April 1994*. Aegaeum 12/2. Brussels: Université de Liège.

Lagarce, E., and J. Lagarce
2000   Coastal Syria and Lebanon. Pp. 140–46 in Bietak 2000b.

Lambert, W. G.
1985   Trees, Snakes and Gods in Ancient Syria and Anatolia. *BSOAS* 48: 435–51.

Langenegger, F., K. Müller, and R. Naumann
1950   *Tell Halaf*, vol. 2: *Die Bauwerke*. Berlin: de Gruyter.

Laperrousaz, E.-M.
1987   King Solomon's Wall Still Supports the Temple Mount. *BAR* 13/3: 34–45.

Lapp, P. W.
1967   The 1966 Excavations at Tell Ta'annek. *BASOR* 185: 2–39.

Launey, M.
1944   *Études thasiennes*, vol. 1: *Le sanctuaire et le culte d'Hérakles á Thasos*. Paris: Boccard.

Lawergren, B.
2003   Review of *Music of Ancient Israel/Palestine* by J. Braun. *BASOR* 332: 100–102.

Lawler, A.
2009   Temple of the Storm God. *Archaeology* 62/6: 20–25.

Lebrun, R.
1987   L'Anatolie et le monde phénicien du Xᵉ au IVᵉ siècle au J.C. *OLA* 5: 23–33.
1993   Aspects particuliers de sacrifice dans le monde Hittite. Pp. 225–33 in Quaegebeur 1993.

Lefebvre, P.
1991   Salomon et Bacchus. Pp. 313–23 in *VII Congress of the International Organization for Septuagint and Cognate Studies, Leuven, 1989*, ed. C. Cox. Atlanta: Scholars Press.

Lehmann, G.
2002a   Review of *Iron Age Pottery in Northern Mesopotamia, Northern Syrian and South-Eastern Anatolia: Papers Presented at the Meetings of the International "Table Ronde" at Heidelberg (1995)*, ed. A. Hausleiter and A. Reiche. *BASOR* 325: 81–83.
2002b   Review of *The Iron Age Settlement of ʿAin Dara, Syria: Survey and Soundings*, by E. C. Stone and P. Zimansky. *BASOR* 325: 83–85.

Lehmann, G, and A. Killebrew
2010   Palace 6000 at Megiddo in Context: Iron Age Central Hall Tetra-Partite Residencies and the Bīt-Hilāni Building Tradition in the Levant. *BASOR* 359: 13–33.

Lemaire, A.
  1978 Les Benê Jacob. *RB* 85: 321–37.
  1984 La Haute Mésopotamie et l'origine de Benê Jacob. *VT* 34: 95–101.
Lemche, N. P.
  1998 Greater Canaan: The Implications of a Correct Reading of EA 151:49–67. *BASOR* 310: 19–24.
Leonard, A., Jr.
  1989 The Late Bronze Age. *BA* 52/1: 4–39.
Lesko, L.
  1992 Egypt in the 12th Century B.C. Pp. 151–56 in Joukowsky and Ward 1992.
Lévy, E., ed.
  1985 *Le système palatial en Orient, en Grèce et à Rome.* Travaux du Centre de Recherche sur le Proche-Orient et la Grèce Antiques 9. Leiden: Brill.
Levy, T., ed.
  1995 *The Archaeology of Society in the Holy Land.* New York: Facts on File.
Lewis, T.
  1996 The Disappearance of the Goddess Anat: The 1995 West Semitic Research Project in Ugaritic Epigraphy. *BA* 59: 115–21.
Linders, T., and B. Alroth, eds.
  1992 *Economics of Cult in the Ancient Greek World: Proceedings of the Uppsala Symposium, 1990.* Acta Universitatis Upsaliensis: Boreas 21. Uppsala: Academia Ubsaliensis.
Linders, T., and G. Nordquist, eds.
  1987 *Gifts to the Gods: Proceedings of the Uppsala Symposium 1985.* Uppsala: Academia Ubsaliensis.
Lipiński, E.
  1993 Rites et sacrifices dans la tradition phéncio-punique. Pp. 257–81 in Quaegebeur 1993.
  1995 *Dieux et déesses de l'univers phénicien et punique.* OLA 64. Leuven: Peeters.
Lipschits, O.
  2005 *The Fall and Rise of Jerusalem: Judah under Babylonian Rule.* Winona Lake, IN: Eisenbrauns.
Liverani, M.
  1966 Il Setore B. Pp. 31–58 in *Missione archeologica italiana in Siria 1965: Rapporto preliminare della Campagna 1965 (Tell Mardikh).* Rome: Università di Roma.
  1979 *State and Temple Economy in the Ancient Near East.* Leuven: Departement Oriëntalistiek.
  1987 The Collapse of the Near Eastern Regional System at the End of the Bronze Age: The Case of Syria. Pp. 66–73 in *Centre and Periphery in the Ancient World,* ed. M. Rowlands, M. Larsen, and K. Kristians. Cambridge: Cambridge University Press.
  1988a *Antico Oriente: Storia, società, economia.* Rome: Laterza.
  1988b The Growth of the Assyrian Empire in the Habur/Middle Euphrates Area: A New Paradigm. *State Archives of Assyria Bulletin* 2: 81–98.
  2000 *The Aramaeans: Their History, Culture, Religion.* Leuven: Peeters.
Lloyd, S., and J. Mellaart
  1965 *Beycesultan,* vol. 2: *Middle Bronze Age Architecture and Pottery.* Occasional Papers of the British Institute of Archaeology at Ankara 8. London: British Institute of Archaeology at Ankara.

Lockhart, J.

1992   *The Nahuas after Conquest: A Social and Cultural History of the Indians of Central Mexico, Sixteenth through Eighteenth Centuries.* Stanford: Stanford University Press.

Long, B.

1984   *1 Kings: With an Introduction to Historical Literature.* Grand Rapids, MI: Eerdmans.

Lonsdale, S.

1993   *Dance and Ritual Play in Greek Religion.* Baltimore: Johns Hopkins University Press.

Loud, G.

1948   *Megiddo II: Seasons 1935–39.* 2 volumes. Chicago: University of Chicago Press.

Lowery, R. H.

1991   *The Reforming Kings: Cult and Society in First Temple Judah.* JSOTSup 120. Sheffield: Sheffield Academic Press.

Luckenbill, D.

1924   *The Annals of Sennacherib.* OIP 2. Chicago: University of Chicago Press.

1927   *Ancient Records of Assyria and Babylonia.* Chicago: University of Chicago Press.

Lyons, C., and J. K. Papadopoulos

2002   *The Archaeology of Colonialism.* Los Angeles: Getty Research Institute.

Macalister, R. A. S.

1912   *The Excavation of Gezer: 1902–1905 and 1907–1909.* 3 volumes. London: Committee of the Palestine Exploration Fund.

MacDonald, B.

1994   *Ammon, Moab and Edom.* Amman: Al Kutba.

Machinist, P.

1986   On Self-Consciousness in Mesopotamia. Pp. 183–202 in Eisenstadt 1986b.

Macqueen, J. G.

1986   *The Hittites and Their Contemporaries in Asia Minor.* London: Thames & Hudson.

Maeir, A., and C. Ehrlich

2001   Excavating Philistine Gath. *BAR* 27/6: 32–41.

Malamat, A.

1954   Cushan Rishathaim and the Decline of the Near East around 1200 B.C. *JNES* 13: 231–42.

1982   A Political Look at the Kingdom of David and Solomon and Its Relations with Egypt. Pp. 189–204 in Ishida 1982b.

1989   *Mari and the Early Israelite Experience.* Oxford: British Academy.

Malbran-Labat, F.

2000   Commerce at Ugarit. *NEA* 63/4: 195.

Mallet, J.

1987   Le temple aux rhytons. Pp. 213–48 in Yon et al. 1987.

Mallinson, M.

1999   The Sacred Landscape. Pp. 72–79 in *Pharaohs of the Sun*, ed. R. E. Freed, Y. J. Markowitz, and S. H. D'Auria. Boston: Museum of Fine Arts.

Mallowan, M. E. I.

1972   Carchemish: Reflections on the Chronology of the Sculpture. *AnSt* 22: 63–86.

Margueron, J.-C.

1976   Maquettes architecturales de Meskéné–Emar. *Syria* 53: 193–232.

1980   *Le moyen-Euphrate: Zone de contacts et d'échanges. Actes du Colloque du Strasbourg, 10–12 mars 1977.* Leiden: Brill.

1981   Ras-Shamra: Nouvelles Perspectives des fouilles. Pp. 71–78 in *Ugarit in Retrospect: Fifty Years of Urgarit and Ugaritic*, ed. G. D. Young. Winona Lake, IN: Eisenbrauns.

1982   Rapport préliminaire sur les 3e, 4e, 5e et 6e campagnes de fouilles à Meskéné–Emar. *AAAS* 32: 233–49.

1983   Emar. *AAAS* 33: 175–85.

1984   Prolégomènes à une étude portant sur l'organisation de l'espace sacré en orient. Pp. 23–36 in Roux 1984.

1985   Les palais syriens à l'Age du Bronze. Pp. 127–58 in Lévy 1985.

1995   Emar: Capital of Aštata in the Fourteenth Century B.C.E. *BA* 58: 126–38.

2000   A Stroll through the Palace. *NEA* 63/4: 205–7.

Marʾi, ʿA.
1996   Palmyra as an Important Station on the Caravan's Road during the Second Millennium B.C. *AAAS* 47: 137–38.

Marinatos, N.
1990   The Tree, the Stone and the Pithos: Glimpses into a Minoan Ritual. *Aegaeum* 6: 79–91.

Markoe, G.
1990   The Emergence of Phoenician Art. *BASOR* 279: 13–26.

2000   *Phoenicians*. Berkeley: University of California Press.

Master, D.
2001   State Formation Theory and the Kingdom of Ancient Israel. *JNES* 60: 117–31.

Matthews, V., and D. C. Benjamin
1993   *Social World of Ancient Israel*. Peabody, MA: Hendrickson.

Matthiae, P.
1967   I frammenti di sculture in pietra. Pp. 111–38 in *Missione archeologica italiana in Siria: Rapporto preliminare della Campagna 1966 (Tel Mardikh)*. Rome: Università di Roma.

1975   Unité et développement du temple dans la Syrie du bronze moyen. Pp. 43–72 in Nederlands Historisch-Archeologisch Instituut te Istanbul 1975.

1981   *Ebla: An Empire Rediscovered*. Garden City, NY: Doubleday.

1984   New Discoveries at Ebla: The Excavations of the Western Palace and the Royal Necropolis of the Amorite Period. *BA* 47/1: 18–32.

1990   A New Monumental Temple of MBII at Ebla and the Unity of Architectural Tradition in Syria–Palestine. *AAAS* 40: 111–21.

2000   Studies in the Relative and Absolute Chronology of Syria in the IInd Millennium B.C.: An Integrated Parallel Project. Pp. 136–39 in Bietak 2000b.

Mattingly, G. L.
1997   A New Agenda for Research on Ancient Moab. *BA* 60: 214–21.

May, H. G.
1939   *Material Remains of the Megiddo Cult*. Chicago: University of Chicago Press.

Mazar, A.
1975   Excavations at Tell Qâsile, 1973–1974. *IEJ* 25/2–3: 77–88.

1977   Additional Philistine Temples at Tell Qasile. *BA* 40/2: 87.

1980   *Excavations at Tell Qasile*, part 1: *The Philistine Sanctuary: Architecture and Cult Objects*. Qedem 12. Jerusalem: Institute of Archaeology, Hebrew University of Jerusalem.

1982   The 'Bull-Site': An Iron Age 1 Open Cult Place. *BASOR* 247: 27–41.

1983   Bronze Bull Found in Israelite 'High Place' from the Time of Judges. *BAR* 9/5: 34–40.

1985a The Emergence of the Philistine Material Culture. *IEJ* 35: 95–107.

1985b   *Excavations at Tell Qasile*, part 2: *The Philistine Sanctuary: Various Finds, the Pottery, Conclusions, Appendixes.* Qedem 20. Jerusalem: Institute of Archaeology, Hebrew University of Jerusalem.

1986   Excavations at Tell Qasile, 1982–1984: Preliminary Report. *IEJ* 36: 1–15.

1988   On Cult Places and Early Israelites: A Response to Michael Coogan. *BAR* 4/4: 45.

1992a   *Archaeology of the Land of the Bible 10,000–586 B.C.E.* New York: Doubleday.

1992b   Temples of the Middle and Late Bronze Age and Iron Age. Pp. 161–87 in Kempinski and Reich 1992.

1993a   Beth Shean in the Iron Age: Preliminary Report and Conclusions of the 1990–1991 Excavations. *IEJ* 43: 201–29.

1993b   The Excavations at Tel Beth-Shean in 1989–1990. Pp. 606–19 in Biran 1993.

1994a   Jerusalem and Its Vicinity in Iron Age 1. Pp. 70–91 in Finkelstein and Naʾaman 1994.

1994b   The Northern Shephelah in the Iron Age: Some Issues in Biblical History and Archaeology. Pp. 247–67 in Coogan et al. 1994.

1997a   Beth-Shean. Pp. 305–9 in vol. 1 of *OEANE*.

1997b   Four Thousand Years of History at Tel Beth-Shean: An Account of the Renewed Excavations. *BA* 60: 62–76.

1997c   Iron Age Chronology: A Reply to I. Finkelstein. *Levant* 29: 160–63.

2006   *Excavations at Tel Beth Shean, 1989–1996*, vol. 1: *From the Late Bronze Age IIB to the Medieval Period.* Jerusalem: Israel Exploration Society

Mazar (Maisler), B.

1951   The Stratification of Tell Abu Huwam on the Bay at Acre. *BASOR* 124: 21–25.

1957   The Campaign of Pharaoh Shishak to Palestine. Pp. 57–66 in *Volume du Congrès: Strasbourg 1952.* VTSup 4. Leiden: Brill.

1965   The Sanctuary of Arad and the Family of Hobab the Kenite. *JNES* 24: 297–303.

1967   The Philistines and the Rise of Israel and Tyre. Pp. 1–22 in *Proceedings of the Israel Academy of Sciences and Humanities*, vol. 1/7. Jerusalem: Israel Academy of Sciences and Humanities.

1968   The Middle Bronze Age in Palestine. *IEQ* 18/2: 65–97.

1975   Jerusalem in the Biblical Period. Pp. 1–8 in *Jerusalem Revealed: Archaeology in the Holy City, 1968–1974*, ed. Y. Yadin. Jerusalem: Israel Exploration Society.

1986   *The Early Biblical Period: Historical Studies.* Jerusalem: Israel Exploration Society.

Mazar, E.

1989   Royal Gateway to Ancient Jerusalem Uncovered. *BAR* 15/3: 38–51.

1997a   Excavate King David's Palace! *BAR* 23/1: 50–57.

1997b   What Did King David's Palace Look Like? *BAR* 23/1: 57.

Mazar, E., and B. Mazar

1989   *Excavations in the South of the Temple Mount: The Ophal of Biblical Jerusalem.* Qedem 29. Jerusalem: Institute of Archaeology, The Hebrew University of Jerusalem.

Mazzoni, S.

1990   Tell Afis and the Chronology of the Iron Age in Syria. *AAAS* 40: 76–92.

McCarthy, D. J.

1982   Compact and Kingship: Stimuli for Hebrew Covenant Thinking. Pp. 75–92 in Ishida 1982b.

McClellan, T.
  1992 Twelfth Century B.C. Syria: Comments on H. Sadler's Paper. Pp. 164–73 in Joukowsky and Ward 1992.
McEwan, C. W.
  1937 The Syrian Expedition of the Oriental Institute of the University of Chicago. *AJA* 41: 8–16.
McGovern, P.
  1980 Explorations in the Umm ad-Danʾnir Region of the Baqʿah Valley, 1977–1978. *ADAJ* 24 (Gerald Lankester Harding Memorial Volume): 55–67.
  1981a Baqʿah Valley Project, 1980. *BA* 45: 122–24.
  1981b Baqʿah Valley Project, 1981. *Liber Annus* 31: 329–32.
  1985 *Late Bronze Palestinian Pendants: Innovation in a Cosmopolitan Age.* Sheffield: JSOT Press.
  1986 *The Late Bronze and Early Iron Ages of Central Transjordan: The Baqʿah Valley Project, 1977–1981.* Philadelphia: University Museum, University of Pennsylvania.
  1987 Central Transjordan in the Late Bronze and Early Iron Age: An Alternative Hypothesis of Socio-economic Transformation or Collapse. Pp. 267–73 in Hadidi 1987.
  1989 Baqʿah Valley Survey. *AJ* 1: 25–44.
McGovern, P., S. Fleming, and C. Swann
  1993 The Late Bronze Egyptian Garrison at Beth Shan: Glass and Faience Production and Importation in the Late New Kingdom. *BASOR* 290–91: 1–27.
McGuire, R., and M. Schiffer
  1983 A Theory of Architectural Design. *Journal of Anthropological Archaeology* 2: 277–303.
McMahon, G.
  1989 The History of the Hittites. *BA* 52/2/3: 62–77.
  1991 *The Hittite State Cult of the Tutelary Divinities.* Assyriological Studies 25. Chicago: Oriental Institute of the University of Chicago.
McNicoll, A. M.
  1992 *Pella in Jordan*, vol. 2. Mediterranean Archaeology Supplement 2. Sydney: Meditarch.
Meissner, B.
  1933 Die Keilschrifttexte auf den steinernen Orthostaten und Statuen aus dem Tell Halaf. Pp. 71–79 in *Aus fünf Jahrtausend morgenländischer Kultur: Festschrift Max Freiherrn von Oppenheim.* Archiv für Orientforschung, Beiband 1. Berlin: Biblio-Verlag.
Mellaart, J.
  1968 Anatolian Trade with Europe and Anatolian Geography and Culture Provinces in the Late Bronze Age. *AnSt* 18: 187–202.
Mellink, M.
  1977 Archaeology in Asia Minor. *AJA* 81: 289–321.
Mettinger, T.
  1982 YHWH Sabaoth: The Heavenly King on the Cherubim Throne. Pp. 112–18 in Ishida 1982b.
Metzger, B. M., and M. D. Coogan
  1993 *The Oxford Companion to the Bible.* Oxford: Oxford University Press.
Metzger, M.
  1991 *Kamid el-Loz 7: Die spätbronzezeitlichen Tempelanlagen. Stratigraphie, Architektur und Installationen.* Bonn: Habelt.

Metzger, M., and U.-R. Barthel
 1993 *Kamid el-Loz 8: Die spätbronzezeitlichen Tempelanlagen. Die Kleinfunde.* Bonn: Habelt.

Meyers, C.
 1981 The Elusive Temple. *BA* 45: 33–42.
 1983 Jachin and Boaz in Religion and Political Perspective. *CBQ* 45: 167–79.
 1987 David as Temple Builder. Pp. 357–76 in Miller, Hanson, and McBride 1987.
 1991 Of Drums and Damsels: Women's Performance in Ancient Israel. *BA* 54: 16–27.
 2003a Engendering Syro-Palestinian Archaeology: Reasons and Resources. *NEA* 66/4: 185–97.
 2003b Material Remains and Social Relations: Women's Culture in Agrarian Households of the Iron Age. Pp. 425–44 in *Symbiosis, Symbolism, and the Power of the Past: Canaan, Ancient Israel, and Their Neighbors from the Late Bronze Age through Roman Palaestina*, ed. W. G. Dever and S. Gitin. Winona Lake, IN: Eisenbrauns.

Mierse, W. E.
 1993 Temple Images on the Coinage of Southern Iberia. *Revue belge du Numismatique* 139: 38–45.
 1994 Review of V. Brouquier-Reddé 1992. *AJA* 98: 178–79.
 1999 *Temples and Towns in Roman Iberia: The Social and Architectural Dynamics of Sanctuary Designs from the Third Century* B.C. *to the Third Century* A.D. Berkeley: University of California Press.
 2000 The Sanctuary of Hercules-Melkart at Gades and the Arabic Sources. *Miscellanea Mediterranea: Archaeologia Transatlantica* 18: 1–10.
 2004 The Architecture of the Lost Temple of Hercules Gaditanus and Its Levantine Associations. *AJA* 108: 545–76.

Millar, F.
 1993 *The Roman Near East.* Cambridge: Harvard University Press.

Millard, A.
 1989 The Doorways of Solomon's Temple. *ErIsr* 20 (Yadin volume): 135–39.
 1991 Writing in Jordan: From Cuneiform to Arabic. Pp. 133–49 in Bienkowski 1991.

Miller, J. M.
 1977 The Israelite Occupation of Canaan. Pp. 255–77 in *Israelite and Judean History*, ed. J. H. Hayes and J. M. Miller. Philadelphia: Westminster.
 1981 Solomon: International Potentate or Local King? *PEQ* 123: 28–31.
 1997 Moab. Pp. 38–39 in vol. 4 of *OEANE*.

Miller, M.
 1997 Ancient Moab: Still Largely Unknown. *BA* 60: 194–204.

Miller, P. D., P. D. Hanson, and S. D. McBride, eds.
 1987 *Ancient Israelite Religion: Essays in Honor of Frank Moore Cross.* Philadelphia: Fortress.

Miller, R.
 2004 Identifying Earliest Israel. *BASOR* 333: 55–68.
 2005 *Chieftains of the Highland Clans: A History of Israel in the Twelfth and Eleventh Centuries* B.C. Grand Rapids, MI: Eerdmans.

Milson, D.
 1987 The Design of the Temples and Gates at Shechem. *PEQ* 119: 97–105.

1988   The Design of the Early Bronze Age Temples at Megiddo. *BASOR* 272: 75–78.

1989   Megiddo, Alalakh, and Troy: A Design Analogy between the Bronze Age Temples. *PEQ* 121: 64–68.

1992   The Bronze Age Temples at Troy (VIC) and Hazor (Area H): A Design Analogy. *PEQ* 124: 31–41.

Miron, R.

1990   *Kamid el-Loz 10: Das 'Schatzhaus' in Palastbevich. Die Funde.* Bonn: Habelt.

Miroschedji, P. de

1999   Yarmouth: The Dawn of City-States in Southern Canaan. *NEA* 62/1: 2–21.

Mission Archéologique de Ras Shamra

1979   *Ras Shamra, 1929–1979.* Lyon: Maison de l'Orient méditerranée.

Mitchell, T. C.

1992   The Music of the Old Testament Reconsidered. *PEQ* 124: 124–43.

Mittmann, S., W. Röllig, T. Podella, D. von Boeselager, B. Jacobs, and U. Bechmann

1987   *Der Königsweg: 9000 Jahre Kunst und Kultur in Jordanien.* Mainz am Rhein: von Zabern.

Monson, J.

2000   The New ʿAin Dara Temple: Closest Solomonic Parallel. *BAR* 26/3: 20–35.

Montgomery, J. A.

1934   Archival Data in the Book of Kings. *JBL* 53: 46–52.

Montgomery, J. A., and H. S. Gehman

1951   *A Critical and Exegetical Commentary on the Book of Kings.* Edinburgh: T. & T. Clark.

Moortgat, A., and D. Opitz

1955   *Tell Halaf III: Die Bildwerke.* Berlin: de Gruyter.

Moorey, P. R. S., and S. Fleming

1984   Problems in the Study of the Anthropomorphic Metal Statuary from Syro-Palestine before 330 B.C. *Levant* 16: 67–90.

Morgan, L.

1995   Minoan Painting and Egypt: The Case of Tell el-Dabʿa. Pp. 29–53 in Davies and Schofield 1995.

Morris, I.

1989   Attitudes towards Death in Archaic Greece. *Classical Antiquity* 8: 296–320.

Morris, S.

1992   *Daidalos and the Origins of Greek Art.* Princeton: Princeton University Press.

Moscati, S., ed.

1999   *The Phoenicians.* New York: Tauris.

Mostyn, T., and A. Hourani, eds.

1988   *The Cambridge Encyclopedia of the Middle East and North Africa.* Cambridge: Cambridge University Press.

Mountfort, G.

1965   *Portrait of a Desert: The Story of an Expedition to Jordan.* London: Collins.

Muhly, J. D.

1984   The Role of the Sea Peoples in Cyprus during the LCIII Period. Pp. 39–56 in *Cyprus at the Close of the Late Bronze Age*, ed. V. Karageoghis and J. D. Muhly. Nicosia: A. G. Leventis Foundation.

1985   End of the Bronze Age. Pp. 261–70 in Weiss 1985.

1992   The Crisis Years in the Mediterranean World: Transition or Cultural Disintegration? Pp. 10–26 in Joukowsky and Ward 1992.

Muhly, J. D., R. Maddin, and V. Karageoghis, eds.
1982   *Early Metallurgy in Cyprus, 4000–500 B.C.* Nicosia: The Foundation.

Mullen, E. T.
1980   *The Assembly of the Gods: The Divine Council in Canaanite and Early Hebrew Literature.* HSM 24. Chico, CA: Scholars Press.

Muller, B.
2000   Images d'architecture de deux et an trois dimensions au Proche-Orient ancient: Mésopotamie, Syrie, Palestine. Pp. 1137–70 in *Proceedings of the First International Congress on the Archaeology of the Ancient Near East: Rome, May 18th–23rd, 1998*, ed. P. Matthiae et al. Rome: Università degli studi di Roma, "La Sapienza."

Mylonas, G.
1981   *Mycenae: A Guide to Its Ruins and Its History.* Athens: Ekdotike Athenon.

Naʾaman, N.
1980   The Ishtar Temple at Alalakh. *JNES* 39: 209–14.
1986   Migdal-Shechem and the Home of El-Berith. *Zion* 51: 270–75.
1992   Israel, Edom and Egypt in the 10th Century B.C.E. *TA* 19: 71–93.
1994   The 'Conquest of Canaan' in the Book of Joshua and in History. Pp. 218–81 in Finkelstein and Naʾaman 1994.
1995   The Debated Historicity of Hezekiah's Reform in Light of Historical and Archaeological Research. *ZAW* 107: 179–95.
1997   Cow Town of Royal Capital? Evidence for Iron Age Jerusalem. *BAR* 23/4: 43–47.
1998   It Is There: Ancient Texts Prove It. *BAR* 24/4: 42–45.
1999   Four Notes on the Size of Late Bronze Age Canaan. *BASOR* 313: 31–38.
2000   The Contribution of the Trojan Grey Ware from Lachish and Tel Miqne–Ekron to the Chronology of the Philistine Monochrome Pottery. *BASOR* 317: 1–8.

Najjar, M.
1993   Amman Citadel Temple of Hercules Excavations: Preliminary Report. *Syria* 70: 220–25.

Nakhai, B. Alpert
1994   What's a Bamah? How Sacred Space Functioned in Ancient Israel. *BAR* 20/3: 18–29.
1997a   Kitan, Tel. P. 300 in vol. 3 of *OEANE*.
1997b   Syro-Palestinian Temples, *s.v.* Temples. Pp. 169–74 vol. 5 of *OEANE*.

Naumann, R.
1955   *Architektur Kleinasiens von ihren Anfängen bis zum Ende der hethitischen Zeit.* Tübingen: Wasmuth.

Nederlands Historisch-Archeologisch Instituut te Istanbul
1975   *Le temple et le culte compte rendu de la vingième rencontre assyriologique internationale organisée à Leiden du 3 au 7 juillet 1972 sous les auspices der Nederlands Instituut voor het Nabije Oosten.* Uitgaven van het Nederlands Historisch-Archaeologisch Instituut te Istanbul 37. Istanbul: Nederlands Historisch-Archeologisch Instituut te Istanbul.

Negbi, O.
1986   The Climax of Urban Development in Bronze Age Cyprus. *Annual Report of the Department of Antiquities, Cyprus, 1986*: 97–121.

1988   Levantine Elements in the Sacred Architecture of the Aegean at the Close of the Bronze Age. *Annual of the British School at Athens* 83: 339–57.

1991   Were There Sea Peoples in the Central Jordan Valley at the Transition from the Bronze Age to the Iron Age? *TA* 18: 205–43.

1992   Early Phoenician Presence in the Mediterranean Islands: A Reappraisal. *AJA* 96: 599–615.

Negev, A., ed.

1986   *The Archaeological Encyclopedia of the Holy Land.* Revised ed. Nashville: Thomas Nelson.

Netzer, E.

1992   Domestic Architecture in the Iron Age. Pp. 193–201 in Kempinski and Reich 1992.

Neumann, J., and S. Parpola

1987   Climatic Change and the Eleventh–Tenth Century Eclipse of Assyria and Babylonia. *JNES* 46: 161–82.

Neumann, J., and R. M. Sigrist

1978   Harvest Dates in Ancient Mesopotamia as Possible Indicators of Climatic Variations. *Climatic Change* 1: 239–56.

Neville, A.

2007   *Mountains of Silver and Rivers of Gold: The Phoenicians in Iberia.* Oxford: Oxbow.

Newgrosh, B., D. Rohl, and P. van der Veen

1992/93   The el-Amarna Letters and Israelite History. *JACF* 6: 33–64.

Nichols, J. J., and J. Weber

2006   Amorites, Onagers, and Social Reorganization in Middle Bronze Age Syria. Pp. 38–57 in Schwartz and Nichols 2006.

Niemeier, W.-D.

2001   Archaic Greeks in the Orient: Textual and Archaeological Evidence. *BASOR* 322: 11–32.

Niemeyer, H. G.

1982   *Phönizier im Westen.* Madrider Beiträge 8. Mainz am Rhein: von Zabern.

1984   Die Phönizier und die Mittelmeerwelt im Zeitalter Homeros. *Jahrbuch des Römisch-Germanischen Zentralmuseums, Mainz* 31: 3–94.

1990   Die phönizischen Niederlassungen im Mittelmeerraum. Pp. 45–64 in Gehrig and Niemeyer 1990.

2004   Phoenician or Greek: Is There a Reasonable Way out of the Al Mina Debate? Pp. 38–48 in *Ancient West and East*, vol. 3/1, ed. G. Tsetskhlandze. Leiden: Brill.

North, R.

1973   Ugarit: Grid, Strata, and Find-Localizations. *ZDPV* 89: 113–60.

Northedge, A.

1980   Survey of the Terrace area at Amman Citadel. *Levant* 12: 135–54.

Noth, M.

1968   *Könige.* Neukirchen-Vluyn: Neukirchener Verlag.

Noureddine, I.

2010   New Light on the Phoencian Harbor at Tyre. *NEA* 73/2–3: 176–81.

Ofer, A.

1994   'All the Hill Country of Judah': From a Settlement Fringe to a Prosperous Monarchy. Pp. 92–121 in Finkelstein and Na'aman 1994.

Olmo Lete, G. del
1986   Ritual procesional de Ugarit (KTU 1.43). *Sefarad* 46/1–2: 363–71.
1991   Pervivencias cananeas (Ugariticas) en el culto fenicio—III. *Sefarad* 51/1: 99–114.
1993   Royal Aspects of the Ugaritic Cult. Pp. 51–66 in Quaegebeur 1993.
Olmo Lete, G. del, and M. E. Aubet, eds.
1986   *Los fenicios en la Península Ibérica.* 2 vols. Sabadell/Barcelona: Ausa.
Orrieux, C.
1984   Le Temple de Salomon. Pp. 51–59 in Roux 1984.
Orthmann, W.
1971   *Untersuchungen zur späthethitischen Kunst.* Bonn: Habelt.
1975   *Der alte Oriente* Berlin: Propyläen.
1990   L'architecture religiuese de Tell Chuera. *Akkadica* 69: 1–18.
1993   Zur Datierung des Istar-Reliefs aus Tell ʿAin Dārā. *Istanbuler Mitteilungen* 43: 245–51.
Ottosson, M.
1980   *Temples and High Places in Palestine.* Uppsala Studies in the Ancient Mediterranean and Near Eastern Civilisations 12. Uppsala: Academia Ubsaliensis.
1987   Sacrifice and Sacred Meals in Ancient Israel. Pp. 133–36 in Linders and Nordquist 1987.
Ouellette, J.
1969   Le vestibule du Temple de Solomon était-il bit hilâni. *RB* 76: 365–78.
1972   The *Yasin* and the *Ṣelaʿot:* Two Mysterious Structures in Solomon's Temple. *JNES* 31: 187–91.
Ousterhout, R.
2010   Archaeologists and Travelers in Ottoman Lands: Three Interesting Lives. *Expedition* 52/2: 9–20.
Oxford Bible
1962   *The New Oxford Annotated Bible with Apocrypha.* Revised Standard Version. Expanded edition. Oxford: Oxford University Press.
Özyar, A.
1991   *Architectural Relief Sculpture at Karkamish, Malatya and Tell Halaf: A Technical and Iconographic Stud*y. Ph.D. dissertation, Bryn Mawr College.
Pardee, D.
1979   Literary Sources from the History of Palestine and Syria II: Hebrew, Moabite, Ammonite, and Edomite Inscriptions. *AUSS* 17: 47–69.
1995a   Review of *The Ideology of Ritual: Space, Time, and Status in Priestly Theology* by F. H. Gorman. *JNES* 54: 62–64.
1995b   RS 1:009 (CTA 36, KTU 1.46): Reconstructing an Ugaritic Ritual. *BSOAS* 53: 229–42.
1997   Moabite Stone. Pp. 39–41 in vol. 4 of *OEANE.*
2000   Divinatory and Sacrificial Rites. *NEA* 63/4: 232–34.
Parker, S.
1997   *Ugaritic Narrative Poetry.* Atlanta: Scholars Press.
2000   Ugaritic Literature and the Bible. *NEA* 63/4: 228–31.
Parrot, A.
1938   Les Fouilles de Mari: Quatrième campagne (hiver 1936–1937). *Syria* 19: 1–29.
Parunak, H. Van Dyke
1978   Was Solomon's Temple Aligned to the Sun? *PEQ* 110: 29–33.

Patel, S.
  2009 World Roundup. *Archaeology* 62/6: 10–11.
Patrich, J.
  1986 The *Mesibah* of the Temple according to the Tractate *Middot*. *IEJ* 36: 215–33.
Payne, H.
  1940 *Perachora I: The Sanctuaries of Hera Akraia and Limenia*. Oxford: Clarendon.
Peet, T. E., and C. L. Woolley
  1923 *The City of Akhenaten I*. London: Egyptian Exploration Society.
Pelikan, J., ed.
  1985 *Sacred Writings 1. Judaism: The Tanakh* (the New JPS Translation). New York: Book
        of the Month Club.
Pelon, O.
  1984 Le palais minoen en tant que lieu de culte. Pp. 61–79 in Roux 1984.
Pendlebury, J. D. S.
  1935 *Tell el-Amarna*. London: Dickson & Thompson.
Pettinato, G.
  1979 *Culto ufficiale ad Ebla durante il regno di Ibbi-Sipiš*. Rome: Istituto per l'Oriente, Cen-
        tro per le antichità e la storiea dell'arte del Vicino Oriente.
  1981 *The Archives of Ebla: An Empire Inscribed in Clay*. Garden City, NY: Doubleday.
  1991 *Ebla: A New Look at History*. Baltimore: Johns Hopkins University Press.
Picard, C.
  1990 Les sacrifices Molk chez les puniques certitudes et hypothèses. *Semitica* 39 (Hom-
        mages à Maurice Sznycer): 77–88.
Pierpont, G. de
  1990 Le rôle du foyer monumental dans la grande salle du palais mycénien. Pp. 255–62 in
        *L'habitat égéen préhistorique: Actes de la Table Ronde internationale organisée par le
        Centre National de la Recherche Scientifique, l'Université de Paris I et l'École française
        d'Athènes (Athènes, 23–25 juin 1987)*, ed. P. Durcque and R. Treuil. Paris: Boccard.
Pitard, W. T.
  1988 The Identity of the Bir-Hadad of the Melqart Stela. *BASOR* 272: 3–21.
  1996 The Archaeology of Emar. Pp. 13–24 in Chavalas 1996.
Pitkänen, P.
  2003 *Central Sanctuary and Centralization of Worship in Ancient Israel: From the Settle-
        ment to the Building of Solomon's Temple*. Piscataway, NJ: Gorgias.
Polak, F.
  2001 The Septuagint Account of Solomon's Reign: Revision and Ancient Recension.
        Pp. 139–64 in *X Congress of the International Organization for Septuagint and Cog-
        nate Studies: Oslo 1998*, ed. B. Taylor. Atlanta: Society of Biblical Literature.
Polany, K.
  1975 Traders and Trade. Pp. 133–54 in *Ancient Civilization and Trade*, ed. C. C. Lamberg-
        Karlovsky and J. Sabloff. Albuquerque: University of New Mexico Press.
Ponsich, M.
  1982 Lixus: Informations archéologiques. Pp. 817–49 in *Aufstieg und Niedergang der rö-
        mischen Welt* 2, ed. H. Temporini. Berlin: de Gruyter.
Pope, M.
  1955 *El in the Ugaritic Texts*. VTSup 2. Leiden: Brill.

Popko, M.

1986 Ein neues Fragment des hethitischen nuntarrijašhaš-Festrituals. *AF* 13: 219–23.

1987 Hethitische Rituale für das Große Meer und das tarmana-Meer. *AF* 14: 252–62.

Porada, E.

1956 A Lyre Player from Tarsus and His Relations. Pp. 185–211 in *The Aegean and the Near East: Studies Presented to Hetty Goldman on the Occasion of Her Seventy-Fifth Birthday*, ed. S. Weinberg. Locust Valley, NY: Augustin.

1992 Sidelights on Life in the 13th and 12th Centuries B.C. in Assyria. Pp. 182–87 in Joukowsky and Ward 1992.

Porter, B. N.

1993 Sacred Trees, Date Palms, and Royal Persona of Ashurnasirpal II. *JNES* 52: 129–39.

Porter, R.

1994–95a Dating the Beth-Shean Temple Sequence. *JACF* 7: 52–69.

1994–95b Dating the Stela from Tel Dan. *JACF* 7: 92–96.

Potter, E.

2001 Jordan's Jericho: Report on the General Monthly Meeting. http://*nsw.royalsoc.org.au/talks_2001/talk_Oct2001.html*.

Pouilloux, J.

1954 *Recherches sur l'histoire et les cultes de Thasos*, vol. 1. Paris: Boccard.

Prag, K.

1987 Decorative Architecture in Ammon, Moab and Judah. *Levant* 19: 121–27.

1989 A Comment on the Amman Citadel Female Heads. *PEQ* 121: 69–70.

Pritchard, J. B.

1968 New Evidence on the Role of the Sea Peoples in Canaan at the Beginning of the Iron Age. Pp. 79–112 in *The Role of the Phoenicians in the Interaction of the Mediterranean Civilization*, ed. W. A. Ward. Beirut: American University of Beirut Press.

1971 The Phoenicians in Their Homeland. *Expedition* 14: 14–21.

1978 *Recovering Sarepta, a Phoenician City: Excavations at Sarafand, Lebanon, 1969–1974, by the University Museum of the University of Pennsylvania*. Princeton: Princeton University Press.

Puchstein, O.

1892 Die Säule in der Assyrischen Architektu. *Jahrbuch des Archäologischen Instituts* 7: 1–24.

Puchstein, O., and C. Humann

1890 *Reisen in Kleinasien und Nordsyrien*. Berlin: Reimer.

Quaegebeur, J., ed.

1993 *Ritual and Sacrifice in the Ancient Near East: Proceedings of the International Conference Organized by the Katholieke Universiteit Leuven from the 17th to the 20th of April 1991*. Leuven: Peeters.

Raban, A., and R. R. Stieglitz

1991 The Sea Peoples and Their Contributions to Civilization. *BAR* 17/6: 24–43.

Rabinovich, A., and N. Silberman

1998 The Burning of Hazor. *Archaeology* 51/3: 50–55.

Rahmani, L. Y.

1982 A Votive Stele with Proto-Aeolic Capital. *IEJ* 32: 199–202.

Rainey, A.
1994   Hezekiah's Reform and the Altars at Beer-sheba and Arad. Pp. 333–54 in Coogan et al. 1994.
2001   Stones for Bread: Archaeology versus History. *NEA* 64/3: 140–49.

Rast, W. E.
1978   *Taanach I: Studies in the Iron Age Pottery.* Cambridge, MA: American Schools of Oriental Research.
1994   Priestly Familes and the Cultic Structure at Taanach. Pp. 355–65 in Coogan et al. 1994.

Rebuffat, R.
1985   A propos du quartier des temples de Lixus. *RAr* n.s. 1: 123–28.

Redford, D.
1992   *Egypt, Canaan, and Israel in Ancient Times.* Princeton: Princeton University Press.

Rehak, P., ed.
1995   *The Role of the Ruler in the Prehistoric Aegean: Proceedings of a Panel Discussion Presented at the Annual Meeting of the Archaeological Institute of America, New Orleans.* Aegaeum 11. Austin, TX: University of Texas at Austin, Program in Aegean Scripts and Prehistory.

Rehak, P., and J. G. Younger
1998   Review of the Aegean. Prehistory VII: Neopalatial, Final Palatial, and Postpalatial Crete. *AJA* 102: 91–173.

Reich, R.
1992   Palaces and Residences in the Iron Age. Pp. 202–22 in Kempinski and Reich 1992.

Renfrew, C. P.
1981   Questions of Minoan and Mycenaean Cult. Pp. 27–33 in Hägg and Marinatos 1981.
1994   The Archaeology of Religion. Pp. 47–53 in *The Ancient Mind: Elements of Cognitive Archaeology*, ed. C. Renfrew and E. Zubrow. Cambridge: Cambridge University Press.

Renfrew, C. P., et al.
1985   *The Archaeology of Cult: The Sanctuary at Phylakopi.* British School of Archaeology at Athens Supplement 18. London: British School of Archaeology at Athens.

Renfrew, C. P., and M. Wagstaff
1982   *An Island Polity: The Archaeology of Exploitation in Melos.* Cambridge: Cambridge University Press.

Ribichini, S.
1999   Beliefs and Religious Life. Pp. 120–52 in Moscatti 1999.

Ribichini, S., and S. Xella
1979   Milkʾštart, *mlk (m)* e la tradizione siropalestinese sui Refaim. *Revsita di Studi Fenici* 7: 145–58.

Richard, S.
1987   The Early Bronze Age: The Rise and Collapse of Urbanism. *BA* 50: 22–44.

Richter, D.
2001   *Facing East from Indian Country: A Native History of Early America.* Cambridge: Harvard University Press.

Riis, P. J.
1970   *Sūkās I: The North-East Sanctuary and the First Settling of Greeks in Syria and Palestine.* Publications of the Carlsberg Expedition to Phoenicia 1. Copenhagen: Munksgaard.

Risberg, C.
1992a   Location of the Original Temple Mount. *BAR* 18/2: 24–37.

1992b Metal-Working in Greek Sanctuaries. Pp. 33–40 in Linders and Alroth 1992.
Ritmeyer, L.
1996 The Ark of the Covenant: Where It Stood in Solomon's Temple. *BAR* 22/1: 46–55.
Roberts, J. J. M.
1982 Zion in the Theology of the Davidic-Solomonic Empire. Pp. 93–108 in Ishida 1982b.
Robinson, S.
1991–92 The Chronology of Israel Re-examined: The First Millennium BC. *JACF* 5: 89–98.
Rodríguez, A. M.
1986 Sanctuary Theology in the Book of Exodus. *AUSS* 24: 127–45.
Rollefson, G. O.
1996 The Neolithic Devolution: Ecological Impact and Cultural Compensation at ʿAin Ghazal, Jordan. Pp. 219–29 in *Retrieving the Past: Essays on Archaeological Research and Methodology in Honor of Gus W. Van Beek*, ed. J. D. Seger. Winona Lake, IN: Eisenbrauns.
Röllig, W.
1983 On the Origin of the Phoenicians. *Berytus* 31: 79–93.
Rothenberg, B.
1972 *Timna: Valley of the Biblical Copper Mines.* London: Thames & Hudson.
1988 *The Egyptian Mining Temple at Timna.* London: Institute for Archaeo-Metallurgical Studies and Institute of Archaeology, University College Press.
Rose, M.
1977 Yahweh in Israel—Qaus in Edom. *JSOT* 4: 28–34.
Routledge, B.
2004 *Moab in the Iron Age: Hegemony, Polity, Archaeology.* Philadelphia: University of Pennsylvania Press.
Routledge, C.
1995 Pillared Buildings in Iron Age Moab. *BA* 58: 236.
Roux, G., ed.
1984 *Temples et sanctuaires: Séminare de recherche 1981–1983 sous la direction de G. Roux.* Maison de l'Orient 7. Lyon: Maison de l'Orient méditerranéen.
Rowe, A.
n.d. New Light on the Old Testament: The Six Canaanite Temples of Beth-Shan, Discovered in the Years 1925–1927. *Palestine Annual and Near East: Syria, Transjordan, Cyprus, Rhodes, ʿIraq, Persia* 1/2: 41–48.
1927 The Discoveries at Beth-Shan during the 1926 Season. *The Museum of the University of Pennsylvania Museum Journal* 19: 9–45.
1930 *The Topography and History of Beth-Shan*, vol. 1. Philadelphia: University of Pennsylavania Press.
1940 *The Four Canaanite Temples of Beth-Shan*, part 1. Philadelphia: University of Pennsylvania Press.
Rubiato Díaz, M. T.
1991 Volver a Hatsor: I campaña de excavaciones arqueológicas in memorian Y. Yadin. *Sefarad* 51/1: 183–98.
1993 Tell Hatsor. II y III campañas de excavaciones arqueológicas. *Sefarad* 53/1: 193–208.
1994 Tell Hatsor. IV campaña de excavaciones arqueológicas. *Sefarad* 54/1: 151–54.

1995 Hatsor Solomónica y Hatsor Cananea: V campaña de excavaciones arqueológicas en Tell Hatsor. *Sefarad* 55/1: 195–206.

Ruiz Mata, D.
2002 The Ancient Phoenicians of the 8th and 7th Centuries B.C. in the Bay of Cádiz: State of the Research. Pp. 155–98 in Bierling 2002.

Ruiz Mata, D., and S. Celestino Pérez, eds.
2001 *Arquitectura oriental y orientalizante en la Península Ibérica.* Madrid: Consejo Superior de Investigaciones Científicas.

Rupprecht, K.
1977 *Der Tempel von Jerusalem: Gründung Salomos oder jebusitisches Erbe?* Berlin: de Gruyter.

Russell, J. M.
1991 *Sennacherib's Palace without Rival at Nineveh.* Chicago: University of Chicago Press.

Rutkowski, B.
1986 *The Cult Places of the Aegean.* New Haven, CT: Yale University Press.

Rutter, J.
1992 Cultural Novelties in the Post-Palatial Aegean World: Indices of Vitality or Decline. Pp. 61–78 in Joukowsky and Ward 1992.

Saadé, G.
1979 *Ougarit, métropole canaanite.* Beirut: Imprimerie Catholique.

Sader, H.
1992 The 12th Century B.C. in Syria: The Problem of the Rise of the Aramaeans. Pp. 157–63 in Joukowsky and Ward 1992.

Saghieh, M.
1983 *Byblos in the Third Millennium.* Warminster: Aris & Phillips.

Sagona, C.
2002 *The Archaeology of Punic Malta.* Ancient Near Eastern Studies: Supplement 90. Louvain: Peeters.

Saidel, B. A.
2001 Abandoned Tent Camps in Southern Jordan. *NEA* 64/1: 150–57.

Sams, G. K.
1992 Western Anatolia. Pp. 56–60 in Joukowsky and Ward 1992.

Sandars, N. K.
1987 *The Sea Peoples: Warriors of the Ancient Mediterranean.* London: Thames & Hudson.

Sanmartí, J.
2009 Colonial Relations and Social Change in Iberia (Seventh to Third Centuries BC). Pp. 49–88 in Dietler and López-Ruiz 2009.

Sasson, J.
1990 Artisans . . . Artists: Documentary Perspectives from Mari. Pp. 21–28 in Gunter 1990b.

Sasson, V.
1979 The Amman Citadel Inscription as an Oracle Promising Divine Protection: Philological and Literary Comments. *PEQ* 111: 117–25.

Savage, S. H., and S. Falconer
2003 Spatial and Statistical Inference of Late Bronze Age Polities in the Southern Levant. *BASOR* 330: 31–45.

Schaeffer, C. F. A.
1931 Les fouilles de Minet-el-Beida et de Ras Shamra: Deuxième campagne (printemps 1930) rapport sommaire. *Syria* 12: 1–14.
1933 Les fouilles de Minet-el-Beida et de Ras-Shamra: Quatrième campagne (printemps 1932) rapport sommaire. *Syria* 14: 93–127.
1935 Les fouilles de Ras Shamra–Ugarit: Sixième campagne (printemps 1934), rapport sommaire. *Syria* 16: 141–76.
1937 Les fouilles de Ras Shamra–Ugarit: Huitième campagne (printemps 1936) rapport sommaire. *Syria* 18: 125–54.
1966 Nouveaux témoignages du culte de El et de Baʿal à Ras Shamra–Ugarit et ailleurs en Syrie–Palestine. *Syria* 43: 1–19.
Schäfer, J.
1983 Bemerkungen zum Verhältnis mykenischer Kultbauten zun Tempelbauten in Kanaan. *AA* 4: 551–58.
Schloen, J. D.
2001 *The House of the Father as Fact and Symbol: Patrimonialism in Ugarit and the Ancient Near East.* Studies in the Archaeology and History of the Levant 2. Winona Lake, IN: Eisenbrauns.
2002 W. F. Albright and the Origins of Israel. *NEA* 65/1: 56–62.
Schloen, J. D., and A. S. Fink
2009 Searching for Ancient Samʾal: New Excavations at Zincirli in Turkey. *NEA* 72/4: 203–19.
Schmidt, W.
1982 A Theologian of the Solomonic Era? A Plea for the Yahwist. Pp. 55–73 in Ishida 1982b.
Schumacher, G.
1908 *Tell el-Mutesellin I: Fundbericht.* Leipzig: Rudolf Haupt.
Schwartz, G. M.
2006 From Collapse to Regeneration. Pp. 3–17 in Schwartz and Nichols 2006.
Schwartz, G. M., and J. J. Nichols
2006 *After Collapse: The Reorganization of Complex Societies.* Tucson: University of Arizona Press.
Seger, J.
1997 Shechem. Pp. 19–23 in vol. 5 of *OEANE*.
Sekine, M.
1982 Lyric Literature in the Davidic-Solomonic Period in the Light of the History of Israelite Literature. Pp. 1–11 in Ishida 1982b.
Sellin, E.
1932 Der gegenwärtige Stand der Ausgrabung von Sichem und ihre Zukunft. *ZAW* 50: 303–8.
Seow, Choon Leong
1989 *Myth, Drama, and the Politics of David's Dance.* Atlanta: Scholar's Press.
Servadio, G.
2000 *Motya: Unearthing a Lost Civilization.* London: Gollancz.
Shafer, B. E., ed.
1997 *Temples of Ancient Egypt.* Ithaca, NY: Cornell University Press.

Shanks, H.
1985   *Recent Archaeology in the Land of Israel.* 2nd ed. Washington, DC: Biblical Archaeology Society.
1988   Two Early Israelite Cult Sites Now Questioned. *BAR* 14/1: 48–52.
1998a   David's Jerusalem: Fiction or Reality? *BAR* 24/4: 25.
1998b   Where Is the Tenth Century? *BAR* 24/2: 56–67.
2000   2700-Year-Old Tower Found? *BAR* 26/5: 39–41.
2010   Prize Find: Oldest Hebrew Inscription Discovered in Isralite Fort on the Philistine Border. *BAR* 36/2: 51–54.

Shaw, J.
1989   Phoenicians in Southern Crete. *AJA* 93: 165–83.

Shea, W.
1979   Milkon as the Architect of the Rabbath-Ammon's Natural Defenses in the Amman Citadel Inscription. *PEQ* 111: 17–25.
1988   Sennacherib's Description of Lachish and Its Conquest. *AUSS* 26: 171–80.
1991   The Architectural Layout of the Amman Citadel Inscription. *PEQ* 123: 62–66.

Shefton, B. B.
1988   The Paradise Flower, a 'Court Style' Phoenician Ornament: Its History in Cyprus and the Central and Western Mediterranean. Pp. 97–117 in Tatton-Brown 1988.

Sherratt, A., and S. Sherratt
1991   From Luxuries to Commodities: The Nature of Mediterranean Bronze Age Trading Systems. Pp. 351–84 in *Bronze Age Trade in the Mediterranean: Papers Presented at the Conference Held at Rewley House, Oxford, in December 1989*, ed. N. H. Gale. Jonsered: Åströms.

Sherratt, S.
1992   Immigration and Archaeology: Some Indirect Reflections. Pp. 316–47 in *Acta Cypria: Acts of an International Congress on Cypriote Archaeology Held in Göteborg on 22–24 August 1991*, part 2. Jonsered: Åströms.
1994   Commerce, Iron and Ideology: Metalurgical Innovation in the 12th–11th Century Cyprus. Pp. 59–106 in *Cyprus in the 11th Century B.C.: Proceedings of the International Symposium Organized by the Archaeological Research Unit of the University of Cyprus and the Anastasios G. Leventis Foundation, Nicosia, 30–31 October 1993*, ed. V. Karageoghis. Nicosia: A. G. Leventis Foundation.
1998   Sea Peoples and the Economic Structure of the Late Second Millennium in the Eastern Mediterranean. Pp. 292–313 in Gitin, Mazar, and Stern 1998.

Shiloh, Y.
1970   The Four-Room House: Its Situation and Function in the Israelite City. *IEJ* 20: 180–90.
1977   The Proto-aeolic Capital: The Israelite 'Timorah' (Palmette) Capital. *PEQ* 109: 39–52.
1979a   Iron Age Sanctuaries and Cult Elements in Palestine. Pp. 147–58 in Cross 1979.
1979b   *The Proto-Aeolic Capital and Israelite Ashlar Masonry.* Qedem 11. Jerusalem: Institute of Archaeology, Hebrew University of Jerusalem.
1984   *Excavations at the City of David I: 1978–1982, Interim report of First Five Seasons.* Qedem 19. Jerusalem: Institute of Archaeology, Hebrew University of Jerusalem.
1985   The Material Culture of Judah and Jerusalem in Iron Age II: Origins and Influences. Pp. 113–46 in *The Land of Israel: Cross-Roads of Civilizations*, ed. E. Lipiński. Leuven: Peeters.

Shorto, R.
2005 *The Island at the Center of the World: The Epic Story of Dutch Manhattan and the Forgotten Colony That Shaped America.* New York: Vintage.
Sigrist, M.
1993 Gestes symboliques et rituels à Emar. Pp. 381–410 in Quaegebeur 1993.
Silberman, N. A.
1991 Desolation and Restoration: The Impact of the Biblical Concept on Near Eastern Archaeology. *BA* 54: 76–87.
Silberman, N. A., I. Finkelstein, D. Ussishkin, and B. Halpern
1999 Digging at Armageddon. *Archaeology* 52/6: 32–39.
Singer, I.
1983 Western Anatolia in the Thirteenth Century B.C. according to the Hittite Sources. *AnSt* 33: 205–17.
1985 The Beginning of Philistine Settlement in Canaan and the Northern Boundary of Philistia. *TA* 12: 109–22.
1988 Merneptah's Campaign to Canaan and the Egyptian Occupation of the Southern Coastal Plain of Palestine in the Ramesside Period. *BASOR* 269: 1–10.
1992 How Did the Philistines Enter Canaan? A Rejoinder. *BAR* 18/6: 44–46.
1995 A Hittite Seal from Megiddo. *BA* 58: 91–93.
Smith, M. S.
1990a *The Early History of God: Yahweh and the Other Deities in Ancient Israel* San Francisco: Harper and Row.
1990b Review of Bonnet 1988. *Journal of the American Oriental Society* 110: 3: 590–92.
1997 The Baʿal Cycle. Pp. 80–180 in Parker 1997.
2002 Ugaritic Studies and Israelite Religion: A Retrospective View. *NEA* 65/1: 17–29.
Smith, W. S.
1965 *Interconnections in the Ancient Near East: A Study of the Relationships between the Arts of Egypt, the Aegean, and Western Asia.* New Haven, CT: Yale University Press.
Smith, W. S., and W. K. Simpson
1986 *The Art and Architecture of Ancient Egypt.* Harmondsworth: Penguin.
Snell, D.
1985 The Aramaeans. Pp. 326–29 in Weiss 1985.
Soggin, J. A.
1982 Compulsory Labor under David and Solomon. Pp. 259–67 in Ishida 1982b.
1988 The Migdal Temple, *Migdal Sekem*: Judges 9 and the Artifact on Mount Ebal. Pp. 115–19 in '*Wünschet Jerusalem Frieden*': *The Collected Communcications of the XIIth Congress of the International Organization for the Study of the Old Testament, Jerusalem, 1986,* ed. M. Augustin and K.-D. Schunk. Frankfurt am Main: Peter Lang.
Soldt, W. H. van
1985–86 The Queens of Ugarit. *Jaarbericht Ex Orient Lux* 29: 68–73.
Sourvinou-Inwood, C.
1993 Early Sanctuaries, the Eighth Century and Ritual Space: Fragments of a Discourse. Pp. 1–17 in *Greek Sanctuaries: New Approaches,* ed. N. Marinatos and R. Hägg. London: Routledge.
Soyez, B.
1972 Le bétyle dans le culte de l'Astarté phénicienne. *Mélanges de l'Université Saint-Joseph* 47: 149–69.

Spottorno, M. V.
  1995   Josephus' Text for 1–2 Kings (3–4 Kingdoms). Pp. 145–63 in *VIII Congress of the International Organization for Septuagint and Cognate Studies, Paris 1992*, ed. L. Greenspoon and O. Munnich. Atlanta: Scholars Press.

Stager, L.
  1985   The Archaeology of the Family in Ancient Israel. *BASOR* 260: 1–35.
  1991   When Canaanites and Philistines Ruled Ashkelon. *BAR* 17/2: 24–43.
  2000   Jerusalem as Eden. *BAR* 26/3: 36–47.
  2003   The Shechem Temple Where Abimelech Massacred a Thousand. *BAR* 29/4: 26–35.

Stager, L., and P. King
  2001   *Life in Biblical Israel*. Louisville: Westminster John Knox.

Stein, G. J., ed.
  2005   *The Archaeology of Colonial Encounters: Comparative Perspectives*. Santa Fe: School of American Research Press.

Steiner, M.
  1998   It's Not There: Archaeology Proves a Negative. *BAR* 24/4: 26–33.

Stephens, J. L.
  1991   *Incidents of Travel in Egypt, Arabia Petraea, and the Holy Land*. San Francisco: Chronicle Books.

Stern, E.
  1977   A Late Bronze Temple at Tell Mevorakh. *BA* 40/2: 89–91.
  1984   *Excavations at Tel Mevorakh (1973–1976), part 2: The Bronze Age*. Qedem 18. Jerusalem: Institute of Archaeology, Hebrew University of Jerusalem.
  1990a   Hazor, Dor and Megiddo in the Time of Ahab and under Assyrian Rule. *IEJ* 40: 12–30.
  1990b   New Evidence from Dor for the First Appearance of Phoenicians along the North Coast of Israel. *BASOR* 279: 27–34.
  1990c   Schumacher's Shrine in Building 338 at Megiddo: A Rejoinder. *IEJ* 40: 102–7.
  1993   The Many Masters of Dor, Part 2: How Bad Was Ahab? *BAR* 19/2: 18–29.
  1994   *Dor, Ruler of the Seas: Twelve Years of Excavations at the Israelite-Phoenician Harbor Town on the Carmel Coast*. Jerusalem: Israel Exploration Society.
  2006   Goddesses and Cults at Tel Dor. Pp. 177–80 in *Confronting the Past: Archaeological and Historical Essays on Ancient Israel in Honor of William G. Dever*, ed. S. Gitin, J. E. Wright, and J. P. Dessel. Winona Lake, IN: Eisenbrauns.

Stieglitz, R.
  1990   The Geopolitics of the Phoenician Littoral in the Early Iron Age. *BASOR* 279: 9–12.

Stone, B. J.
  1995   The Philistines and Acculturation: Cultural Change and Ethnic Continuity in Iron Ages. *BASOR* 298: 7–32.

Stone, E. C., and P. Zimansky
  1999   *The Iron Age Settlement at ʿAin Dara, Syria: Survey and Soundings*. British Archaeological Reports, International Series. Oxford: Archaeopress.

Strommenger, E.
  1985   Assyrian Domination, Aramaean Persistence. Pp. 322–25 in Weiss 1985.
  1986   Ausgrabungen in Tell Biʾa, 1984. *Mitteilungen der Deutschen Orient-Gesellschaft zu Berlin* 118: 7–44.

Stucky, R. A.
2006   *Das Eschmun-Heiligtum von Sidon Architektur und Inscriften.* Basel: Vereinigung der Freunde antiker Kunst.

Tadmor, H.
1982   Traditional Institutions and Monarchy: Social and Political Tensions in the Time of David and Solomon. Pp. 239–57 in Ishida 1982b.

Tadmor, M.
1982   Female Cult Figures in Late Canaan and Early Israel: Archaeological Evidence. Pp. 139–73 in Ishida 1982b.

Talmon, S., and M. Fishbane
1976   The Structuring of Biblical Books: Studies in the Book of Ezekiel. *ASTI* 10: 129–53.

Tandy, D. W.
1997   *Warriors into Traders: The Power of the Market in Early Greece.* Berkeley: University of California Press.

Taracha, P.
1985   Zu den hethitischen taknáz da: Ritualen. *AF* 12: 278–82.

Tarler, D., and J. Cahill
1992   David, City of. Pp. 52–67 in vol. 2 of *ABD*.
1994   Excavations Directed by Yigal Shiloh at the City of David, 1978–1985. Pp. 31–45 in *Ancient Jerusalem Revealed*, ed. H. Geva. Jerusalem: Israel Exploration Society.

Tatton-Brown, V.
1988   *Cyprus and the East Mediterranean in the Iron Age.* London: British Musuem.

Taylor, B. A.
1997   The Lucianic Text and the MT in 1 Reigns. Pp. 1–9 in *IX Congress of the International Organization for Septuagint and Cognate Studies, Cambridge, 1995*, ed. B. Taylor. Atlanta: Scholars Press.

Thalmann, J.-P.
2010   Tell Arqa: A Prosperous City during the Bronze Age. *NEA* 73/2–3: 86–101.

Thomason, A. K.
2001   Representations of the North Syrian Landscape in Neo-Assyrian Art. *BASOR* 323: 63–96.

Thompson, J. A.
1985   Foreign Religious Influences on Israel. *Buried History* 21/4: 89–97.

Thorpe, I. J., and P. J. James
1987   Bronze to Iron Age Chronology in the Old World: Time for a Reassessment? Section One: Introduction. *JACF* 1: 6–8.

Toombs, L.
1979   Shechem: Problems of the Early Israelite Era. Pp. 69–83 in Cross 1979.

Toombs, L., and G. E. Wright
1963   The Fourth Campaign at Tell Balatah (Shechem). *BASOR* 169: 1–61.

Toorn, K. van der
1996   *Family Religion in Babylonia, Syria and Israel: Continuity and Change in the Forms of Religious Life.* Leiden: Brill.
2007   *Scribal Culture and the Making of the Hebrew Bible.* Cambridge: Harvard University Press.

Toorn, K. van der, B. Becking, and P. W. van der Horst
1999   *Dictionary of Deities and Demons in the Bible.* 2nd ed. Leiden: Brill.

Toorn, K. van der, and C. Houtman
 1994   David and the Ark. *JBL* 113: 209–31.
Tubb, J. T.
 1985   Tell Es-Sa'idiyeh: Preliminary Report on the First Three Seasons of Renewed Excavations. *Levant* 20: 23–88.
 1988   The Role of Sea Peoples in the Bronze Industry of Palestine/Transjordan in the Late Bronze–Early Iron Age Transition. Pp. 251–70 in *Bronzeworking Centers of Western Asia c. 1000–538 B.C.*, ed. J. E. Curtis. London: Kegan Paul and the British Museum.
 1998   *Canaanites.* Norman: University of Oklahoma Press.
Tufnell, O., C. Inge, and H. Lankester
 1940   *Lachish II: The Fosse Temple.* London: Published for the Trustees of the late Sir Henry Wellcome by Oxford University Press.
Tusa, V.
 1999   Sicily. Pp. 231–49 in Moscatti 1999.
Tusa, V., and E. De Miro
 1983   *Sicilia occidentale.* Itinerari archeologici 10. Rome: Newton Compton.
Ussishkin, D.
 1966a   Building IV in Hamath and the Temples of Solomon and Tell Tayanat. *IEJ* 16: 104–10.
 1966b   King Solomon's Palace and Building 1723 in Megiddo. *IEJ* 16: 174–86.
 1967   On the Dating of Some Groups of Reliefs from Carchemish and Til Barsip. *AnSt* 17: 181–92.
 1970   On the Original Position of Two Ionic Capitals at Megiddo. *IEJ* 20: 213–15.
 1976   The Monuments of the Lower Palace Area in Carchemish: A Rejoinder. *AnSt* 26: 105–11.
 1978   Excavations at Tel Lachish, 1973–1977: Preliminary Report. *TA* 5: 1–97.
 1980   Was the 'Solomonic' Gate at Megiddo Built by King Solomon? *BASOR* 239: 1–18.
 1983   Excavations at Tel Lachish 1978–1983: Second Preliminary Report. *TA* 10: 97–175.
 1985   Levels VII and VI at Tel Lachish and the End of the Late Bronze Age in Canaan. Pp. 213–30 in *Palestine in the Bronze and Iron Ages: Papers in Honour of Olga Tufnell*, ed. J. Tubb. London: Institute of Archaeology.
 1987   Lachish: Key to the Israelite Conquest of Canaan? *BAR* 13/1: 18–41.
 1988   The Date of the Judaean Shrine at Arad. *IEJ* 38: 142–57.
 1989   Schumacher's Shrine in Building 338 at Megiddo. *IEJ* 39: 149–72.
 1990   Notes on Megiddo, Gezer, Ashdod, and Tell Batasa in the Tenth to Ninth Centuries B.C. *BASOR* 277/278: 71–91.
 1997   Lachish. Pp. 317–23 in vol. 3 of *OEANE.*
 2007   Megiddo and Samaria: A Rejoinder to Norma Franklin. *BASOR* 348: 49–70.
Van Beek, G., and O. Van Beek
 2008   *Glorious Mud! Ancient and Contemporary Earthen Design and Construction in North Africa, Western Europe, the Near East, and South Asia.* Washington, DC: Smithsonian Scholarly Press / Lanham, MD: Rowman & Littlefield.
Van Seters, J.
 1983   *In Search of History, Historiography in the Ancient World and the Origins of Biblical History.* New Haven, CT: Yale University Press.
Vaux, R. de
 1965   *Ancient Israel: Social Institutions.* New York: McGraw Hill.
 1978   *The Early History of Israel.* London: Darton, Longman & Todd.

Veen, P. van der

1989–90 The El-Amarna *Habiru* and the Early Monarchy in Israel. *JACF* 3: 72–78.

2006 A Revised Chronology and Iron Age Archaeology: An Update. *JACF* 10: 49–56.

Vermeule, E.

1974 *Toumba tou Skourou: The Mound of Darknesss—A Bronze Age Town on Morphou Bay in Cyprus.* Boston: Musuem of Fine Arts.

Vincent, L. H.

1956 *Jérusalem de l'Ancien Testament II: Recherches d'Archéologie et Histoire.* Paris: Gabalda.

Vogelstein, M.

1950–51 Nebuchadnezzar's Reconquest of Phoenicia and Palestine and the Oracle of Ezekiel. *HUCA* 23: 197–229.

Voos, J.

1985 Zu einigen späthethitischen Reliefs aus den Beständen des Vorderasiatischen Museum Berlin. *AF* 12: 65–86.

Wachsmann, S.

1998 *Seagoing Ships and Seamanship in the Bronze Age Levant.* College Station, TX: Texas A. & M. University Press.

Waldbaum, J.

1994 Early Greek Contact with the Southern Levant, ca. 1000–600 B.C.: The Eastern Perspective. *BASOR* 293: 53–66.

Waltrous, L. V., D. Hadzi-Villianou, H. Blitzer

2004 *The Plain of Phaestos: Cycles of Social Complexity in the Mesara Region of Crete.* Los Angeles: Cotsen Institute of Archaeology, University of California–Los Angeles.

Warburton, D.

2003 Lore and War in the Later Bronze Age: Egypt and Hatti. Pp. 75–100 in *Ancient Perspectives on Egypt,* ed. R. Metthews and C. Roemer. London: University College of London.

Ward, W.

1994 Archaeology in Lebanon in the Twentieth Century. *BA* 57: 66–85.

Ward, W., ed.

1968 *The Role of the Phoenicians in the Interaction of Mediterranean Civilizations: Papers Presented to the Archaeological Symposium at the American University of Beirut, March 1967.* Beirut: American University of Beirut Press.

Ward-Perkins, J. B.

1981 *Roman Imperial Architecture.* Harmondsworth: Penguin.

Warren, P., and V. Hankey

1989 *Aegean Bronze Age Chronology.* Bristol: Bristol Classical Press.

Wasilewska, E.

1993 Organization and Meaning of Sacred Space in Prehistoric Anatolia. Pp. 471–500 in Quaegebeur 1993.

Waterman, L.

1943 The Damaged 'Blueprints' of the Temple of Solomon. *JNES* 2: 284–94.

1947 The Treasuries of Solomon's Private Chapel. *JNES* 6: 161–63.

Watzinger, C.

1929 *Tell el-Mutessellim II: Die Funde.* Leipzig: Haupt.

1933 *Denkmäler Palästinas: Eine Einfürung in die Archäologie des Heiligen Landes I—Von den Anfängen bis zum ende der israelitischen Königszeit.* Leipzig: Hinrichs.

Webb, J. M.
  1977   Late Cypriot Altars and Offering Structures. *Annual Report of the Department of Antiquities, Cyprus, 1977*: 113–32.
  1986   The Incised Scapulae. Pp. 317–28 in *Excavations at Kition V*, part 2: *The Pre-Phoenician Levels*, ed. V. Karageorghis and M. Demas. Nicosia: Department of Antiquities.

Webb, J. M., and V. Karageorghis
  n.d.   *A Short Guide to the Excavations at Kition.* Cyprus.

Weidhaas, H.
  1939   Der bit hilani. *Zeitschrift für Assyriologie und vorderasiatische Archäologie* 45: 108–68.

Weinfield, M.
  1964   Cult Centralization in Israel in the Light of a Neo-Babylonian Analogy. *JNES* 26: 202–12.

Weinstein, J.
  1992   The Collapse of the Egyptian Empire in the Southern Levant. Pp. 142–50 in Joukowsky and Ward 1992.

Weiss, B.
  1982   The Decline of the Late Bronze Age Civilization as a Possible Response to Climate Change. *Climate Change* 4: 173–98.

Weiss, H.
  1985   *Ebla to Damascus: Art and Archaeology of Ancient Syria.* Washington, DC: Smithsonian Institution.

Weiss, H., and K. Kohlmeyer
  1985   Ebla. Pp. 213–16 in Weiss 1985.

Weitzman, S.
  1997   *Song and Story in Biblical Narrative: The History of a Literary Convention in Ancient Israel.* Bloomington: Indiana University Press.

Welten, P.
  1972   Kulthöhe und Jahwetempel. *ZDPV* 88: 19–37.

Welter, G.
  1932   Stand der Ausgrabungen in Sichem. *AA* 3–4: cols. 313–14.

Werner, K.
  1993   *The Megaron during the Aegean and Anatolian Bronze Age: A Study of Occurrence, Shape, Architectural Adaptation, and Function.* Jonsered: Åströms.

Westenholz, J. G.
  1996   *Royal Cities of the Biblical World.* Jerusalem: Bible Lands Museum.

Whybray, R. N.
  1968   *The Succession Narrative: A Study of II Samuel 9–20; I Kings 1 and 2.* Naperville, IL: Allenson.

Will, E.
  1996   Palmyre et les routes de la soie. *AAAS* 47: 125–28.

Winter, I.
  1976   Phoenician and North Syrian Ivory Carving in Historical Contexts: Questions of Style and Distribution. *Iraq* 38: 1–22.
  1979   On the Problems of Karatepe: The Reliefs and Their Context. *AnSt* 29: 115–51.
  1980   Art as Evidence for Interaction: Relations between the Assyrian Empire and North Syria. Pp. 355–82 in *Mesopotamien und seine Nachbarn, Politische und kulturelle*

Wechselbeziehungen im alten Vorderasien vom 4. bis 1. Jahrtausend v. Chr., vol. 1, ed. H.-J. Nissen and J. Renger. Berlin: Reimer.

1981   Is There a South Syrian Style of Ivory Carving in the Early First Millennium B.C.? *Iraq* 43: 101–30.

1983   Carchemish *ša Kišad Puratti. AnSt* 33: 177–97.

1995   Homer's Phoenicians: History, Ethnography, or Literary Trope? A Perspective on Early Orientalism. Pp. 247–71 in *The Ages of Homer: A Tribute to Emily Townsend Vermeule*, ed. J. B. Carter and S. P. Morris. Austin: University of Texas Press.

Wiseman, D. J.

1953   *The Alalakh Tablets.* London: British Institute of Arcaheology in Ankara.

Wood, B. G.

1991   The Philistines Enter Canaan: Were They Egyptian Lackeys or Invading Conquerors. *BAR* 17/6: 44–53.

1994   Review of *Excavations of Tell Deir ʿAlla: The Late Bronze Age Sanctuary*, by H. J. Franken. *BASOR* 295: 94–96.

Woolley, C. L.

1921   *Carchemish: Report on the Excavations at Djerabis on Behalf of the British Museum*, vol. 2: *The Town Defences*. Oxford: Oxford University Press.

1939   Excavations at Atchana–Alalakh, 1938. *Antiquaries Journal* 19: 1–37.

1948   Excavations at Atchana–Alalakh, 1939. *Antiquaries Journal* 28: 1–19.

1952   *Carchemesh: Report of the Excavations at Djerabis on Behalf of the British Museum*, vol. 3: *The Excavations in the Inner Town*. Oxford: Oxford University Press.

1953   *A Forgotten Kingdom.* Baltimore: Penguin.

1955   *Alalakh: An Account of the Excavations at Tell Atchana in Hatay, 1937–1949.* London: Society of Antiquaries.

1961   *The Art of the Middle East Including Persia, Mesopotamia, and Palestine.* New York: Crown.

Worschech, U.

1997   Egypt and Moab. *BA* 60: 229–37.

Wright, G. E.

1944   Significance of the Temple in the Ancient Near East, part 3: The Temple in Palestine–Syria. *BA* 7/4: 65–77.

1955   The Stevens' Reconstruction of the Solomonic Temple. *BA* 18: 41–44.

1957   The Second Campaign at Tell Balâtah (Shechem). *BASOR* 148: 11–28.

1965   *Shechem: The Biography of a Biblical City.* New York: McGraw-Hill.

1967   Shechem. Pp. 355–70 in *Archaeology and Old Testament Study*, ed. D. Winton Thomas. Oxford: Clarendon.

1968   Temples at Shechem. *ZAW* 80: 2–9.

1970   The Significance of Ai in the Third Millennium B.C. Pp. 299–320 in *Archäologie und Altes Testament: Festschrift für Kurt Galling*, ed. A. Kuschke and E. Kutsch. Tübingen: Mohr/Siebeck.

Wright, G. R. H.

1966   The Bronze Age Temple at Amman. *ZAW* 78: 351–57.

1968   Temples at Shechem. *ZAW* 80: 1–9.

1971a   Pre-Israelite Temples in the Land of Canaan. *PEQ* 103: 17–32.

1971b   Shechem and the League Shrines. *VT* 21: 572–603.

1972   Square Temples East and West. Pp. 380–87 in *The Memorial Volume of the Vth International Congress of Iranian Art and Archaeology*, ed. A. Tajvidi and M. Y. Kiani. Tehran: Ministry of Culture and Arts.

1973   Co-ordinating the Survey of Shechem over Sixty Years, 1913–1973. *ZDPV* 89: 188–96.

1985   *Ancient Building in South Syria and Palestine.* 2 vols. Leiden: Brill.

Wright, J. C.
1995   The Archaeological Correlates of Religion: Case Studies in the Aegean. Pp. 341–48 in Laffineur and Niemeier 1995.

Wright, J. E.
2002   W. F. Albright's Vision of Israelite Religion. *NEA* 65/1: 63–68.

Wright, M.
1985   Contacts between Egypt and Syro-Palestine during the Protodynastic Period. *BA* 48: 240–53.

Wyatt, N.
1983   The Stela of the Seated God from Ugarit. *UF* 15: 271–77.

1988   The Source of the Ugaritic Myth of the Conflict of Baʿal and Yam. *UF* 20: 375–85.

Xella, P.
1980   L'Influence babylonienne à Ougarit: D'après les textes alphabétiques rituels et divinatoires. Pp. 321–38 in *Mesopotamien und seine Nachbarn: Politische und kulturelle Wechselbeziehungen im alten Vorderasien vom 4. bis 1. Jahrtausend v. Chr.*, vol. 1, ed. H.-J. Nissen and J. Renger. Berlin: Reimer.

Yadin, Y.
1952   The Blind and the Lame and the Conquest of Jerusalem by David. Pp. 222–25 in *Proceedings of the First World Congress on Jewish Studies.* Jeruslaem: World Union of Jewish Studies.

1959   The Fourth Season of Excavations at Hazor. *BA* 22/1: 2–19.

1967   The Temple Scroll. *BA* 30/4: 135–39.

1972   *Hazor: The Head of All Those Kingdoms.* The Schweich Lectures of the British Academy 1970. London: Oxford University Press for the British Academy.

1975   *Hazor: The Rediscovery of a Great Citadel of the Bible.* New York: Random.

1979   Transition from a Semi-Nomadic to a Sedentary Society in the Twelfth Century B.C.E. Pp. 57–68 in Cross 1979.

Yadin, Y., Y. Aharoni, R. Amiran, T. Dothan, I. Dunayevsky, and J. Perrot
1958   *Hazor I: An Account of the First Season of Excavations, 1955.* Jerusalem: Magnes.

1960   *Hazor II: An Account of the Second Season of Excavations, 1956.* Jerusalem: Magnes.

Yadin, Y., and S. Geva
1986   *Investigations at Beth Shean: The Early Iron Age Strata.* Qedem 23. Jerusalem: Institute of Archaeology, Hebrew University of Jerusalem.

Yassine, K.
1983   El Mabrak: An Architectural Analogue of the Amman Airport Building? *ADAJ* 27: 491–93.

1984   *Tell El Mazar I: Cemetery A.* Amman: University of Jordan.

Yasur-Landau, A.
2001   The Mother(s) of the Philistines: Aegean Enthroned Deities of 12th–11th C. Philistia. Pp. 329–43 in *Potnia: Deities and Religion in the Aegean Bronze Age.* Aegaeum 22. Liège: Université de Liège.

Yeivin, S.

1968   Mycenaean Temples and Their Possible Influence on the Countries of the Eastern Littoral of the Mediterranean. Pp. 1130–48 in *Atti e memorie del 1° Congresso internazionale di micenologia, 1967*. Rome: Ateneo.

1973   Temples That Were Not. *ErIsr* 11 (Dunayevsky Memorial Volume): 63–173. [Hebrew]

Yener, K. A.

2005   *The Amuq Valley Regional Projects: Surveys in the Plain of Antioch and the Orontes Delta, Turkey 1995–2002*, vol. 1. Chicago: Oriental Institute of the University of Chicago Press.

Yener, K. A., C. Edens, T. Harrison, J. Verstraete, and T. Wilkinson

2000   The Amuq Valley Regional Project, 1995–1998. *AJA* 104: 163–220.

Yoffee, N.

1988   Orienting Collapse. Pp. 1–19 in Yoffee and Cowgill 1988.

2006   Notes on Regeneration. Pp. 222–28 in Schwartz and Nichols 2006.

Yoffee, N., and G. L. Cowgill, eds.

1988   *The Collapse of Ancient States and Civilizations*. Tucson: University of Arizona Press.

Yon, M.

1984   Sanctuaires d'Ougarit. Pp. 37–50 in Roux 1984.

1985a   Baʿal et le roi. Pp. 177–90 in *De l'Indus aux Balkans: Recueil à la mémoire de Jean Deshayes*, ed. J.-L. Huot, M. Yon, and Y. Calvet. Paris: Recherche sur les civilisations.

1985b   La ville d'Ougarit au XIIIe s. av. J.C. Pp. 705–23 in *Comptes rendus des séances de l'Académie des inscriptions et belles-lettres*. Paris: Boccard.

1987   Les rhytons du sanctuaire. Pp. 343–50 in Yon et al. 1987.

1992a   The End of the Kingdom of Ugarit. Pp. 111–22 in Joukowsky and Ward 1992.

1992b   Ugarit: The Urban Habitat. The Present State of the Archaeological Picture. *BASOR* 286: 19–34.

2000a   Daily Life. *NEA* 63: 200–201.

2000b   A Trading City: Ugarit and the West. *NEA* 63: 192–93.

2000c   Ugarit: 6000 Years of History. *NEA* 63: 186–90.

2006   *The City of Ugarit at Tell Ras Shamra*. Winona Lake, IN: Eisenbrauns.

Yon, M., et al.

1987   *Ras Shamra–Ougarit IV: Le centre de la ville, 38e–44e campagnes (1978–1984)*. Paris: Editions Rechereche sur les civilisations.

Younker, R. W.

1997   Moabite Social Structure. *BA* 60: 237–48.

Zayadine, F.

1991   Sculpture in Ancient Jordan. Pp. 31–61 in Bienkowski 1991.

1996   Palmyre, Pétra, la mer Erythrée et les routes de le soie. *AAAS* 47: 167–78.

Zayadine, F., and P. Bordreuil

1987   Die Zeit der Königreiche Edom, Moad und Ammon. Pp. 117–69 in Mittmann et al. 1987.

Zertal, A.

1985   Has Joshua's Altar Been Found on Mt. Ebal? *BAR* 11/1: 26–43.

1986   How Can Kempinski Be So Wrong? *BAR* 12/1: 49–53.

1987   An Early IA Cult Site on Mount Ebal: Excavation Seasons 1982–1987. *TA* 13–14: 105–65.

1988 A Cult Center with a Burnt-Offering Altar from the Early Iron Age 1 Period at Mt. Ebal. Pp. 137–53 in *'Wünschet Jerusalem Frieden': The Collected Communciations of the XIIth Congress of the International Organization for the Study of the Old Testament, Jerusalem, 1986*, ed. M. Augustin and K.-D. Schunk. Frankfurt am Main: Peter Lang.

1991 Israel Enters Canaan: Following the Pottery Trail. *BAR* 17/5: 28–49.

1994 'To the Land of the Perizzites and the Giants': On the Israelite Settlement in the Hill Country of Manasseh. Pp. 47–69 in Finkelstein and Naʾaman 1994.

2002 Philistine Kin Found in Early Israel. *BAR* 28/3: 18–31.

Ziffer, I.
1990 *At that Time the Canaanites Were in the Land: Daily Life in Canaan in the Middle Bronze Age 2, 2000–1550 B.C.E.* Tel Aviv: Eretz Israel Museum.

Zimmerli, W.
1965 The Special Form and Traditio-historical Character of Ezekiel's Prophesy. *VT* 15: 515–27.

Zwickel, W.
1999 *Der salomonische Tempel.* Mainz am Rhein: von Zabern.

Maps and Illustrations

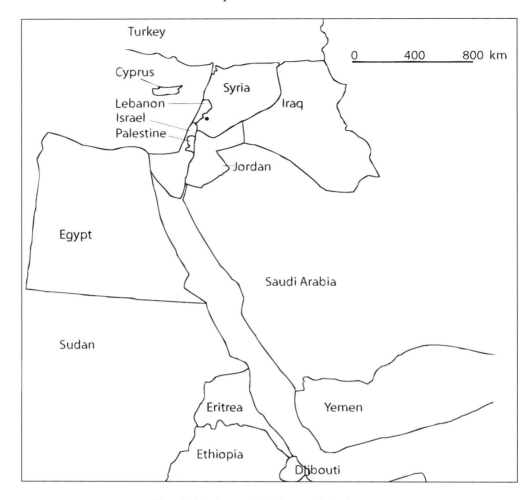

Map I. Modern political map of the Levant.

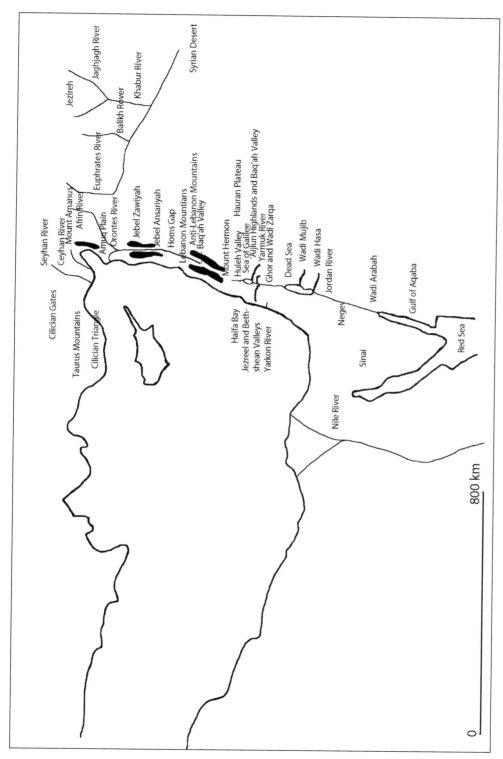

Map 2. Physical geography of the Levant

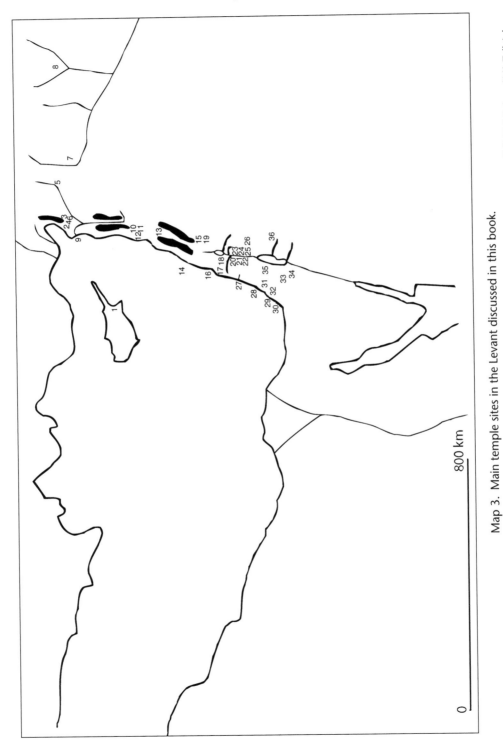

Map 3. Main temple sites in the Levant discussed in this book.

(1) Kition, (2) Alalakh/Tell Taʻyinat, (3) ʻAin Dara, (4) Aleppo, (5) Charchemish, (6) Emar, (7) Ebla, (8) Guzana, (9) Ugarit, (10) Tell Sukas, (11) Tell Arka, (12) Sarepta, (13) Kamid el-Loz, (14) Tyre, (15) Tel Dan, (16) Abu Hawam, (17) Megiddo, (18) Beth-shean, (19) Hazor, (20) Bull Site, (21) Shechem, (22) Mount Ebal, (23) Pella, (24) Tell el Mazar, (25) Deir ʻAlla, (26) Amman, (27) Tel Mevorakh, (28) Tell Qasile, (29) Ashdod, (30) Kuntillet ʻAjrud, (31) Ekron, (32) Lachish, (33) Tell Arad, (34) Horvat Qitmit, (35) Jerusalem, (36) Khirbat al-Mudayna.

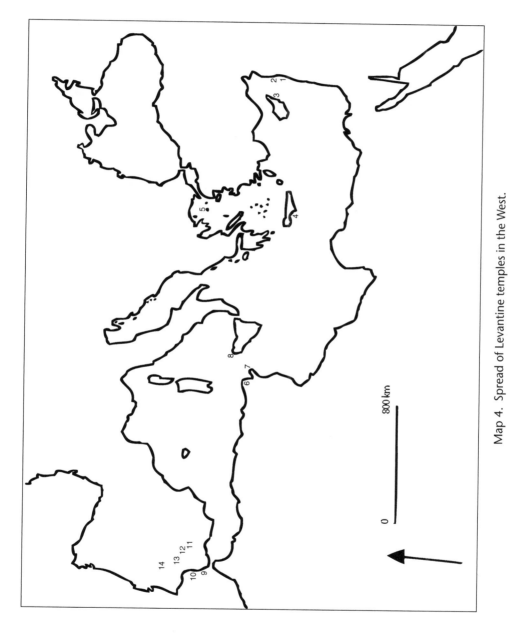

Map 4. Spread of Levantine temples in the West.

(1) Tyre, (2) Sidon, (3) Kition, (4) Kommos, (5) Thasos, (6) Carthage, (7) Kerkouane, (8) Motya, (9) Gadir, (10) El Cerro de San Juan del Rio, (11) Cerro de Montemolin, (12) Carmona, (13) El Carambolo, (14) Cancho Roano.

Fig. 1. ʿAin Dara, sanctuary setting (photo by the author).

Fig. 2. ʿAin Dara, entrance (photo by the author).

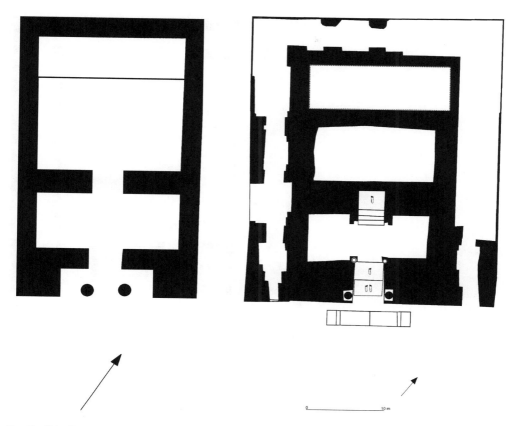

Fig. 3. ʿAin Dara, temple, phase 2
(after Monson 2000: 31).

Fig. 4. ʿAin Dara, structural remains of all three
versions (after Monson 2000: 23).

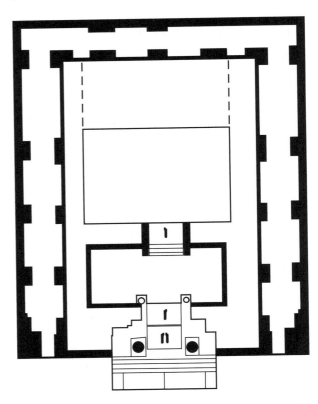

Fig. 5 (right). ʿAin Dara, final
version of the temple, schematic
plan (after Stager 2000: 46).

Fig. 6 (below). ʿAin Dara,
exterior wall (photo by the
author).

Fig. 7. ʿAin Dara, view of the exterior wall (photo by the author).

Fig. 8. ʿAin Dara, claw-footed figures (photo by the author).

Fig. 9. ʿAin Dara, incised footprints (photo by the author).

Fig. 10. Aleppo Citadel, plan of Middle
Bronze Age temple remains (after Kohlmeyer
2000: fig. 6).

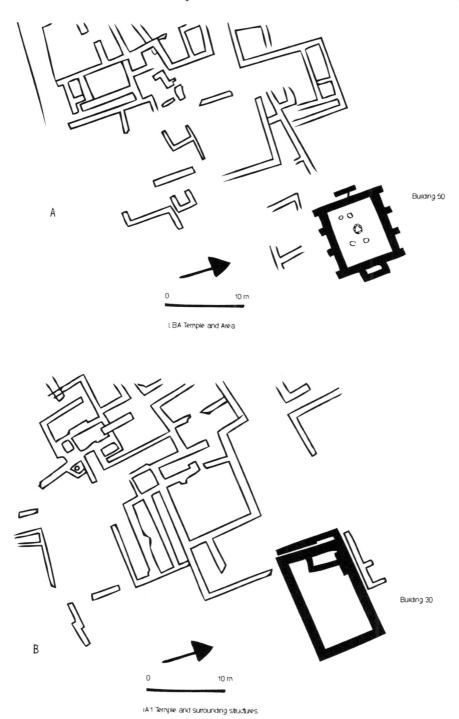

A

Building 50

0   10 m

LBA Temple and Area

B

Building 30

0   10 m

IA1 Temple and surrounding structures

Fig. 11. Abu Hawam, Late Bronze Age and Iron Age I settings (after Hamilton 1934: pls. 4, 11).

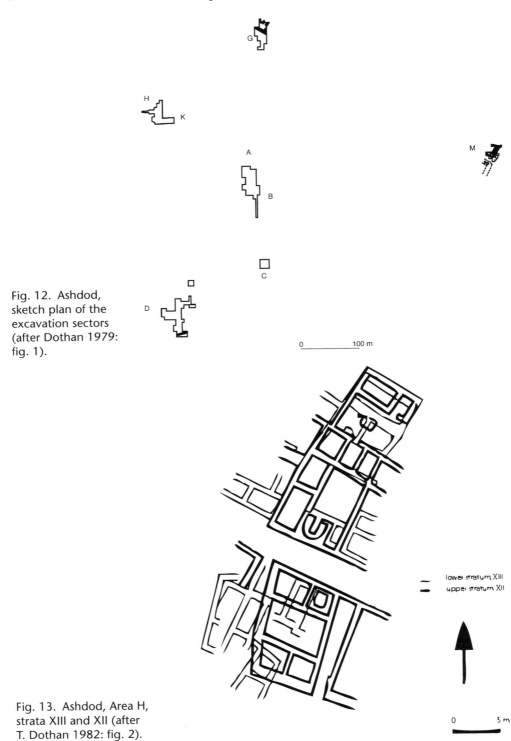

Fig. 12. Ashdod,
sketch plan of the
excavation sectors
(after Dothan 1979:
fig. 1).

0 —————— 100 m

lower stratum XIII
upper stratum XII

Fig. 13. Ashdod, Area H,
strata XIII and XII (after
T. Dothan 1982: fig. 2).

0 ———— 5 m

Fig. 14. Ashdod, "Musicians Stand" (Israel Museum, IAA 1968-1182).

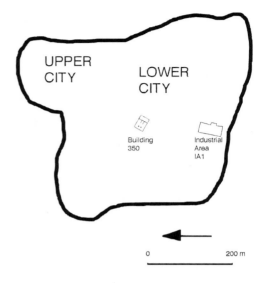

Fig. 15. Ekron, schematic plan of site (after Dothan and Gitin 1990: 23).

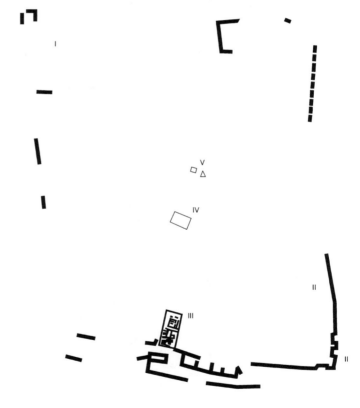

Fig. 16. Ekron, sketch plan of the excavation sectors (after Dothan and Dothan 1992: 240).

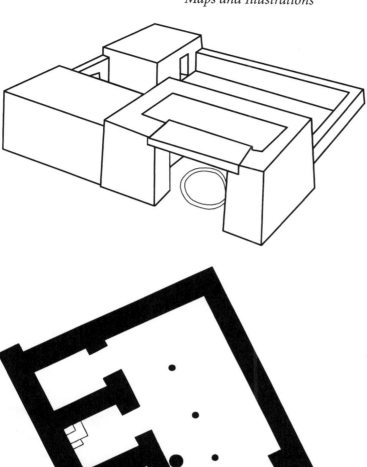

Fig. 17. Ekron, restored view of Building 351, field IV, stratum VIA—"Hearth Sanctuary" twelfth century B.C.E. (after Dothan and Dothan 1992: 244).

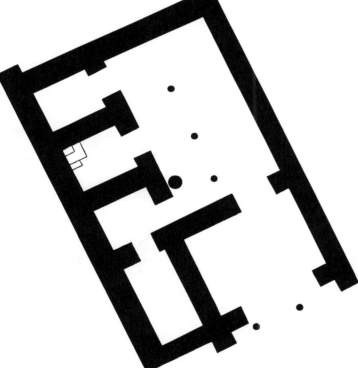

0   5 m

Fig. 18. Ekron, Building 350, field IV, stratum V (eleventh century B.C.E.; after Dothan and Gitin 1997: 32).

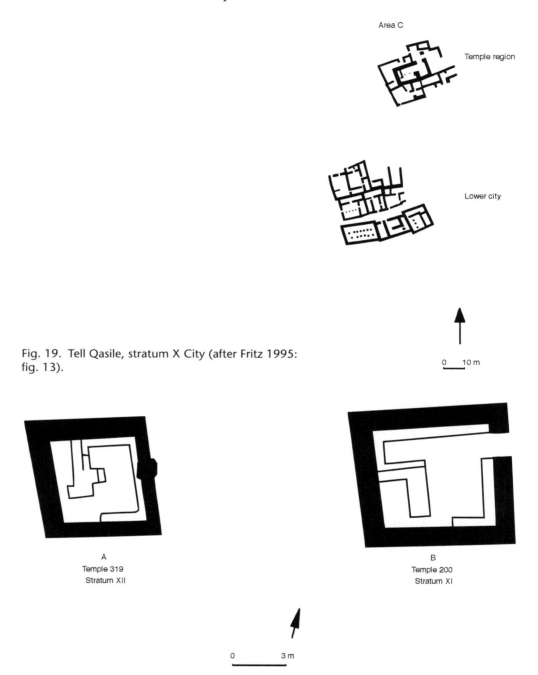

Area C

Temple region

Lower city

Fig. 19. Tell Qasile, stratum X City (after Fritz 1995: fig. 13).

0   10 m

A
Temple 319
Stratum XII

B
Temple 200
Stratum XI

0   3 m

Fig. 20. Tell Qasile, temple plans (after Mazar 1980: fig. 13).

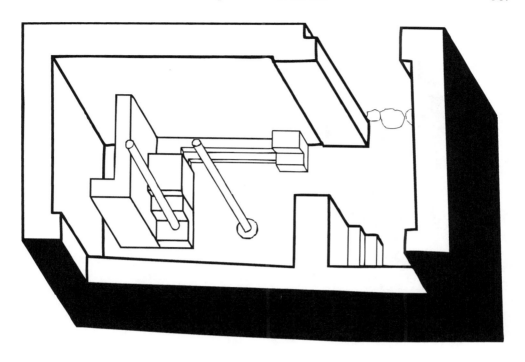

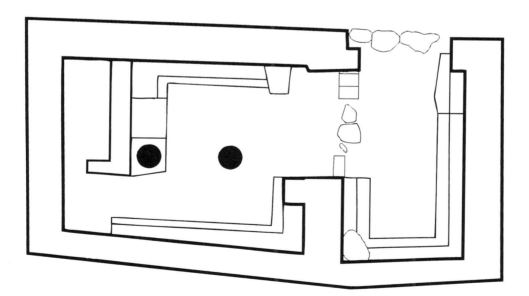

Fig. 21. Tell Qasile, isometric reconstruction and plan of Temple 131 (Stratum X; after Mazar 1980: figs. 10–11).

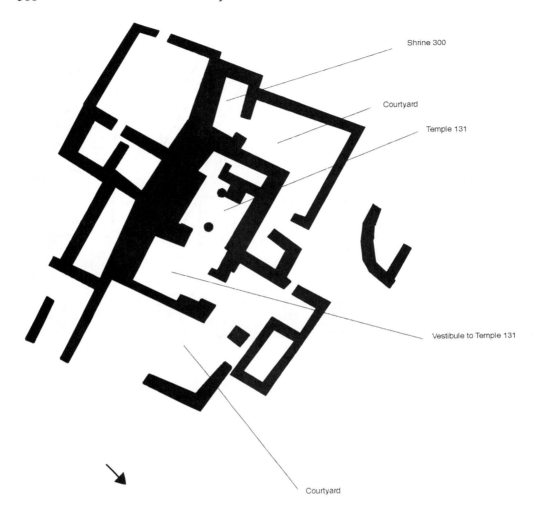

Shrine 300

Courtyard

Temple 131

Vestibule to Temple 131

Courtyard

Fig. 22. Tell Qasile, stratum X sanctuary area (after A. Mazar 1992a: fig. 8.14).

Fig. 23. Tell Qasile, Temple 131 interior (photo by the author).

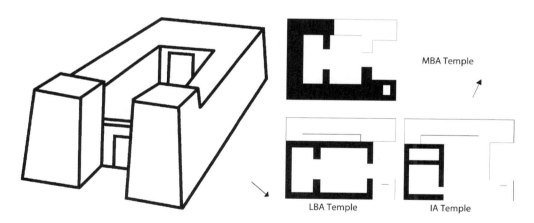

Fig. 24. Pella: A: plans of the Middle Bronze, Late Bronze and Iron Age temples (after Bourke 2005: fig. 3). B: view of the restored Middle Bronze Age temple with only partial roof (after Churcher 2003).

Fig. 25. Beth-shean, acropolis (photo by the author).

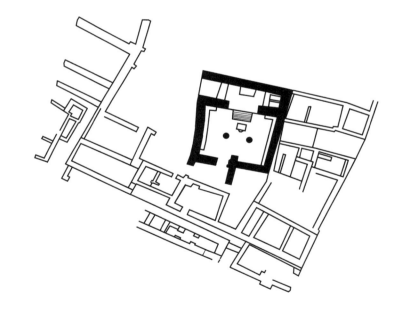

Fig. 26. Beth-
shean,
stratum VI
(twelfth century
B.C.E.; after James
1966: fig. 77).

0   20 m

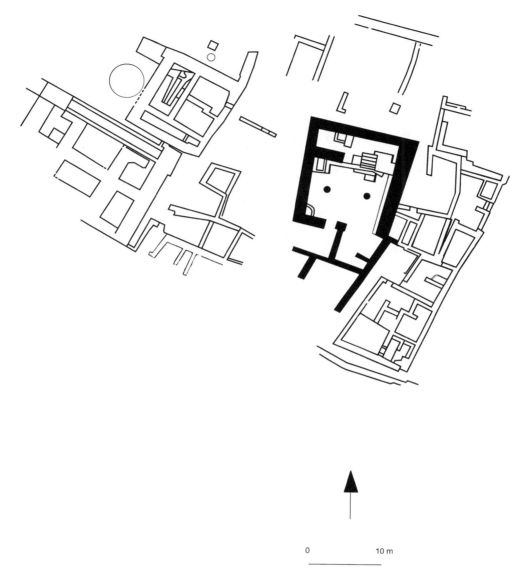

0   10 m

Fig. 27. Beth-shean, stratum VII (thirteenth century B.C.E.; after James and McGovern 1993: map 1).

Fig. 28. Beth-shean, stratum V (1050 B.C.E.; after James 1966: fig. 75; and Fritz 1995: fig. 11).

Fig. 29. Hazor, view from top of the tell (photo by the author).

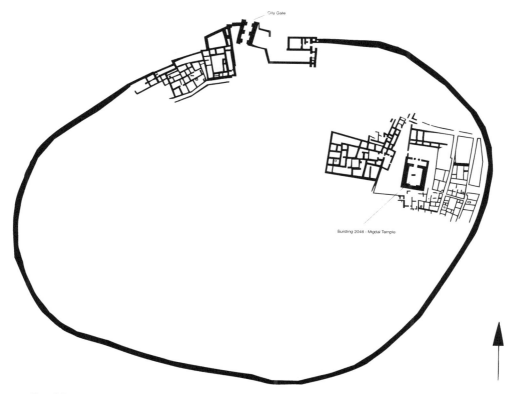

Fig. 30. Megiddo, stratum VIIA (twelfth century B.C.E.; after Kempinski 1989: plan 5).

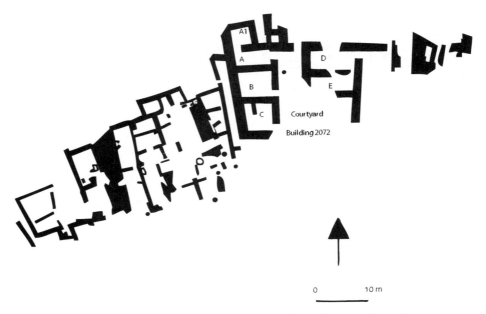

Fig. 31. Megiddo, Cult Building 2072, stratum VI (eleventh or tenth century B.C.E.; after Harrison 2003: 31).

Fig. 32. Megiddo, painted vase in Philistine style, "Orpheus Jug," eleventh century B.C.E. (Israel Museum, IAA 1936-1321).

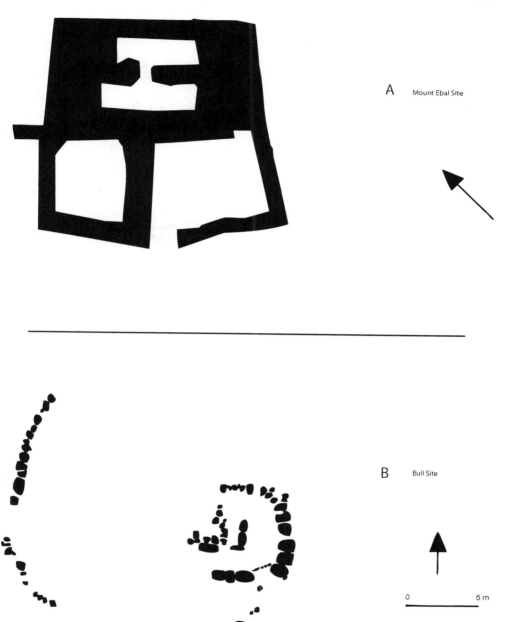

A   Mount Ebal Site

B   Bull Site

0   5 m

Fig. 33. Mount Ebal, altar (after Shanks 1988: 50) and Bull Site in territory of Manasseh (after Bloch-Smith and Nakhai 1999: 77).

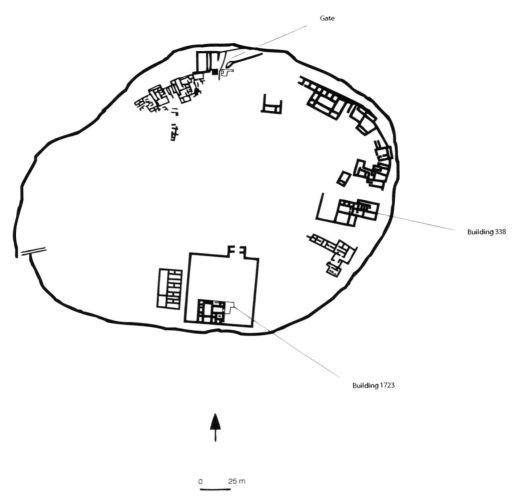

Fig. 34. Megiddo, stratum VA–IVB (tenth century B.C.E.; after Finkelstein and Ussishkin 1994: 39).

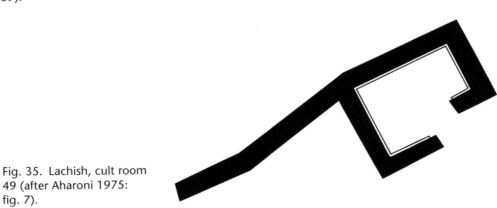

Fig. 35. Lachish, cult room 49 (after Aharoni 1975: fig. 7).

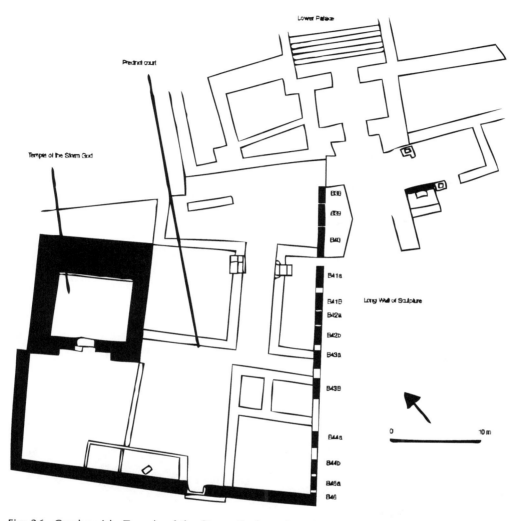

Fig. 36. Carchemish, Temple of the Storm God precinct. Long Wall of sculpture (after Woolley 1952: 29).

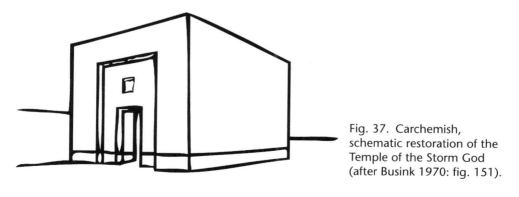

Fig. 37. Carchemish, schematic restoration of the Temple of the Storm God (after Busink 1970: fig. 151).

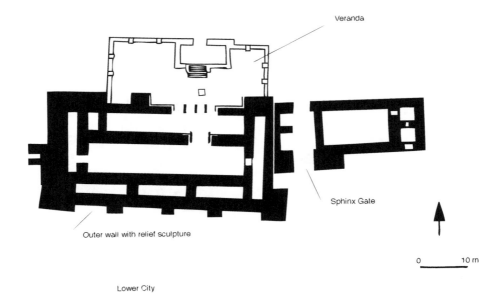

Inner plaza

Veranda

Sphinx Gate

Outer wall with relief sculpture

0   10 m

Lower City

Fig. 38. Guzana, temple-palace complex (after Busink 1970: fig. 164).

Fig. 39. Guzana, façade restored at the archaeological museum in Aleppo (photo by the author).

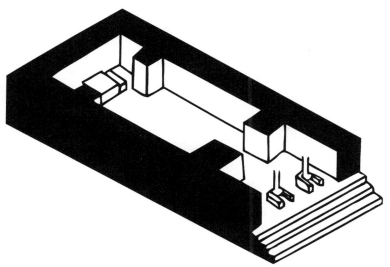

Fig. 40. Tell Taʿyinat, reconstruction (after Fritz 1987b: 42).

Fig. 41. Tell Taʿyinat, lion column bases in the archaeological museum in Hatay (photo by the author).

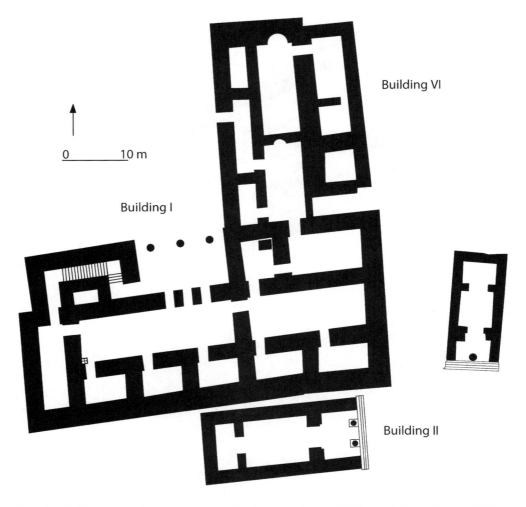

Fig. 42. Tell Ta'yinat, temple and palace (Buildings I, II, and IV) Phase 3 (after Haines 1971: pl. 103; and Harrison 2009: 187).

Fig. 43. Sidon, Crusader castle (photo by the author).

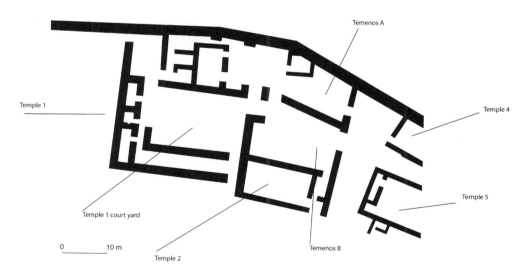

Fig. 44. Kition, temples in Area II (1200–1150 B.C.E.; after Webb and Karageorghis n.d.: plan II).

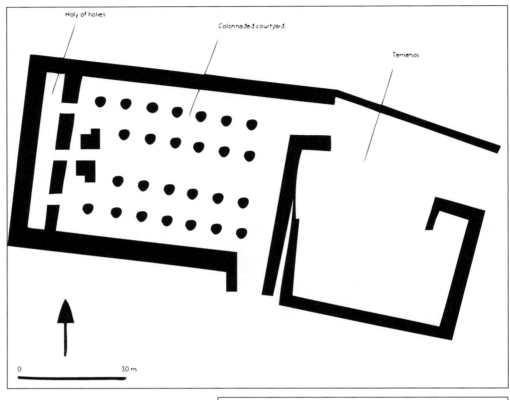

Fig. 45 (above). Kition, Phoenician period Temple of Astarte, first phase (after Karageorghis 1982: fig. 95).

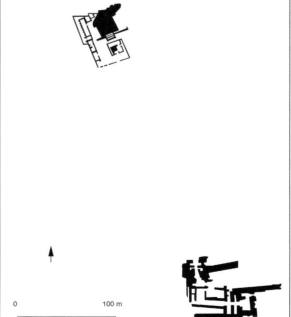

Fig. 46 (right). Tel Dan, schematic plan of site showing lower city, city gate, and High Place complex (after Biran 1994: fig. 4).

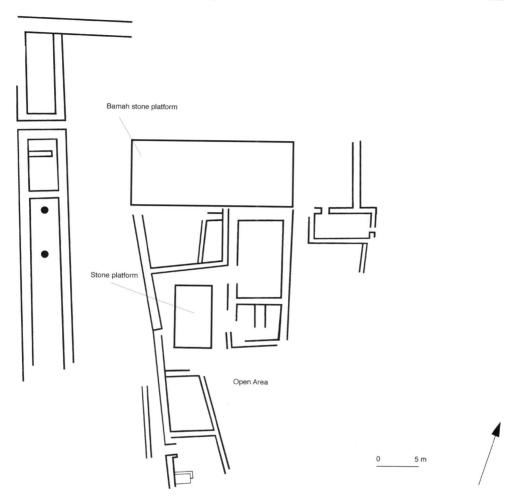

Fig. 47. Tel Dan, High Place complex, stratum IV (tenth century B.C.E., Jeroboam I; after Biran 1994: fig. 143).

Maps and Illustrations

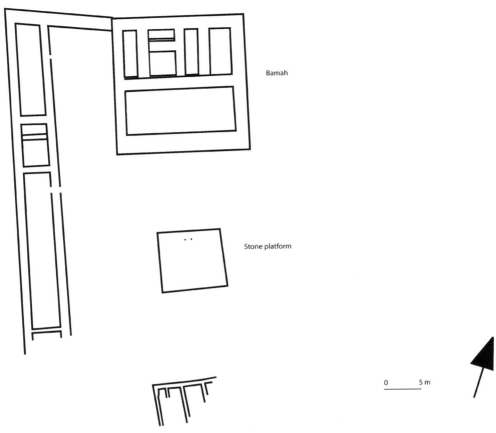

Fig. 48. Tel Dan, High Place complex (ninth century B.C.E., Ahab; after Biran 1994: fig. 149).

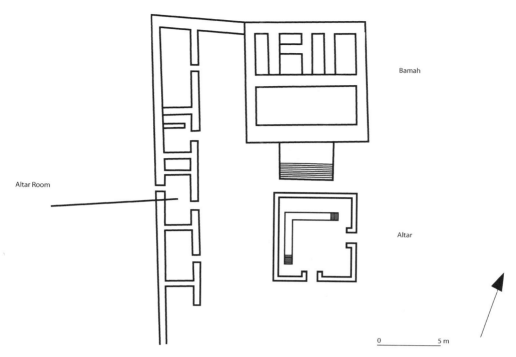

Bamah

Altar Room

Altar

0   5 m

Fig. 49. Tel Dan, High Place complex (eighth century B.C.E., Jeroboam II; after Biran 1994: fig. 163).

Fig. 50. Tel Dan, High Place complex (photo by the author).

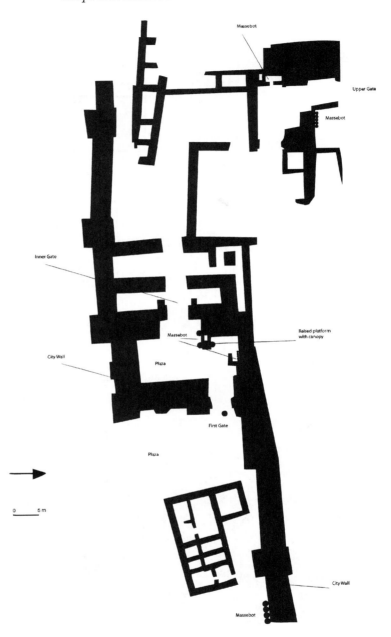

Fig. 51. Tel Dan, gate complexes with *maṣṣēbôt* shrines (after Biran 1998: 42–43).

Fig. 52. Tel Dan, lower city (photo by the author).

Fig. 53. Tell Arad Fortress (photo by the author).

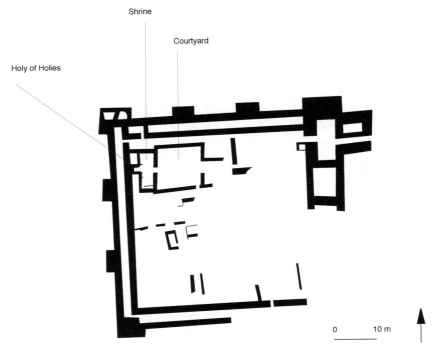

Shrine

Courtyard

Holy of Holies

0   10 m

Fig. 54. Tell Arad, fortress and shrine, stratum X (after Herzog et al. 1984: fig. 6).

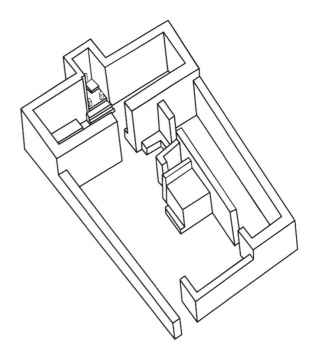

Fig. 55. Tell Arad, shrine in the fortress, stratum X (ninth–eighth century B.C.E.; after Herzog et al. 1987: 31).

Fig. 56. Tell Arad, shrine courtyard, altar, holy of holies (photo by the author).

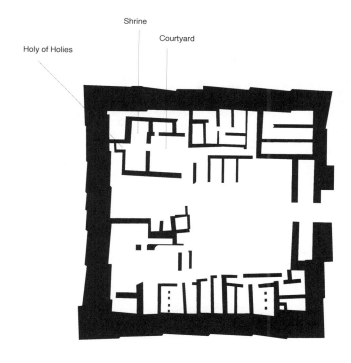

Fig. 57. Tell Arad, fortress and shrine, stratum VIII, late eighth century B.C.E. (Herzog et al. 1984: fig. 21).

Fig. 58. Tell Arad, schematic plan of the final shrine (after Herzog et al. 1984: fig. 8).

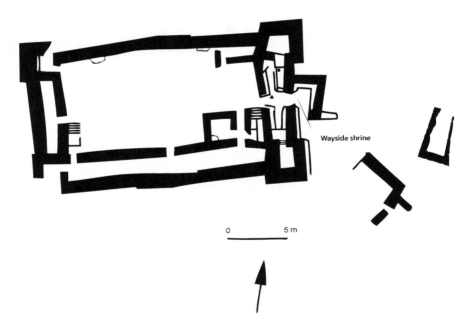

Wayside shrine

0   5 m

Fig. 59. Teman, fortified caravansaray with wayside chapel
(after Isserlin 1998: fig. 56).

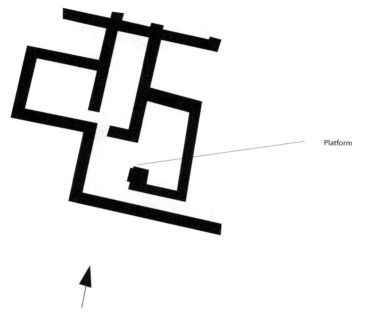

Platform

0   2 m

Fig. 60. Ashdod, Area D, plan, stratum VIII temple (eighth century B.C.E.; after M. Dothan 1993: 99).

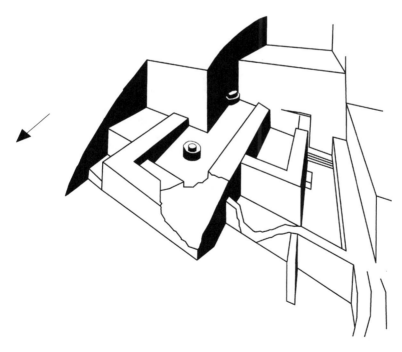

Fig. 61. Deir ʿAlla, Late Bronze Age sanctuary (after Franken 1992).

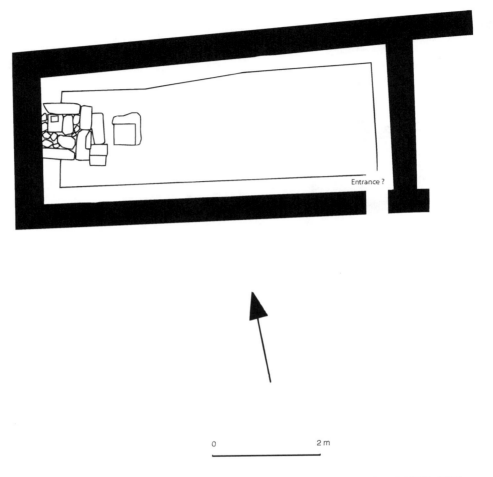

Fig. 62. Sarepta, plan of the Temple of Tanit, phase 1 (after Pritichard 1978: 125).

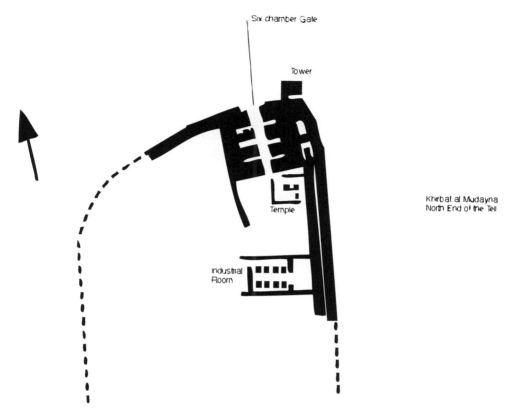

Six chamber Gate

Tower

Khirbat al Mudayna
North End of the Tell

Temple

Industrial
Room

Fig. 63. Khirbat al-Mudayna, site (after Daviau and Dion 2002: 40).

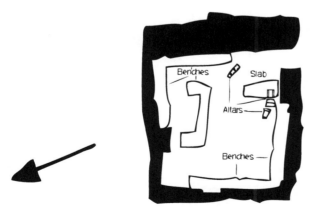

Benches   Slab

Altars

Benches

Fig. 64. Khirbat al-Mudayna
temple plan (after Daviau and
Dion 2002: 42; and Daviau and
Steiner 2000: fig. 2).

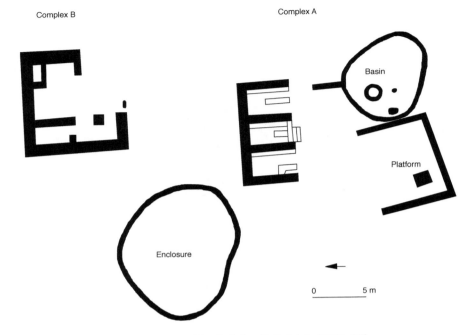

Fig. 65. Horvat Qitmit (after Beit-Arieh 1988: 37).

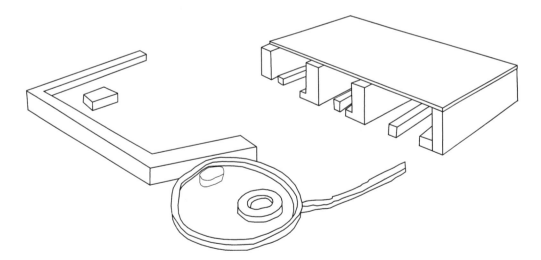

Fig. 66. Horvat Qitmit, complex A reconstruction (after Beit-Arieh and Beck 1995: fig. 9.1).

0   3 m

Fig. 67. Horvat Qitmit, complex B (after Beit-Arieh and Beck 1995: fig. 2.12).

Fig. 68. Horvat Qitmit, complex B reconstruction (after Beit-Arieh and Beck 1995: fig. 9.2).

Fig. 69. Eshmun Sanctuary (photo by the author).

Fig. 70. Amrit,
reconstruction of shrine
(after Jourdain-Annequin
1992: fig. 3).

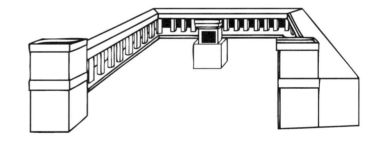

VIII.

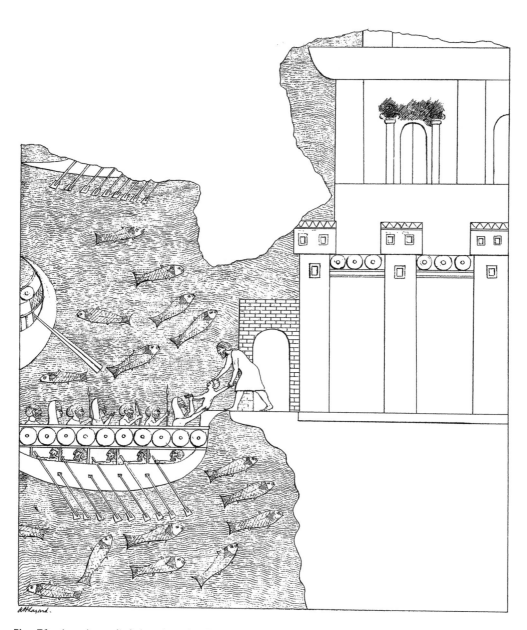

Fig. 71. Assyrian relief showing the flight of Lulu, King of Tyre (British Museum, Layard drawings collection).

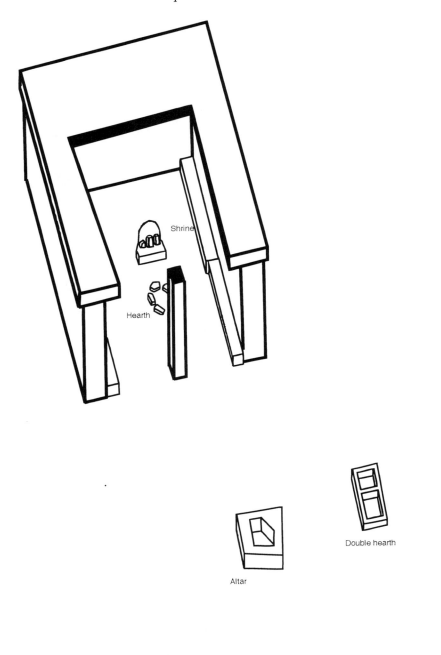

Shrine

Hearth

Altar

Double hearth

0   5 m

Fig. 72. Kommos, temple B, phase 2 (after Shaw 1989: fig. 5).

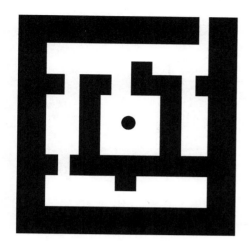

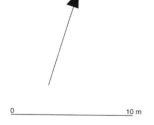

Fig. 73. Amman airport temple (after Herr 1983b: 225).

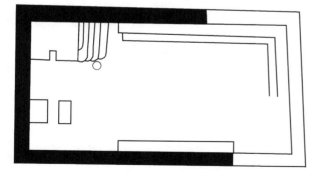

Fig. 74. Tel Mevorakh, Late Bronze Age temple (after Stern 1977: 90).

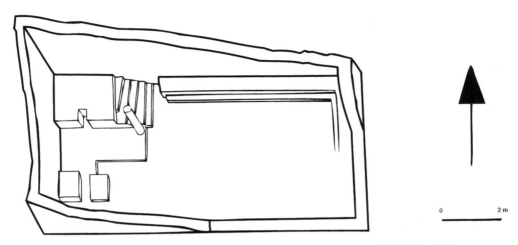

Fig. 75. Tel Mevorakh, Late Bronze Age temple (after Stern 1994: fig. 20).

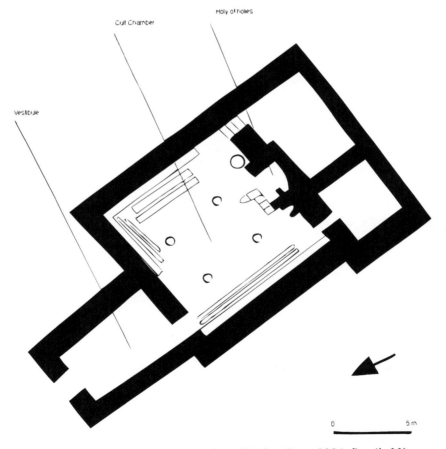

Fig. 76. Lachish, Fosse Temple, phase III (after Stern 1984: fig. 4b.11).

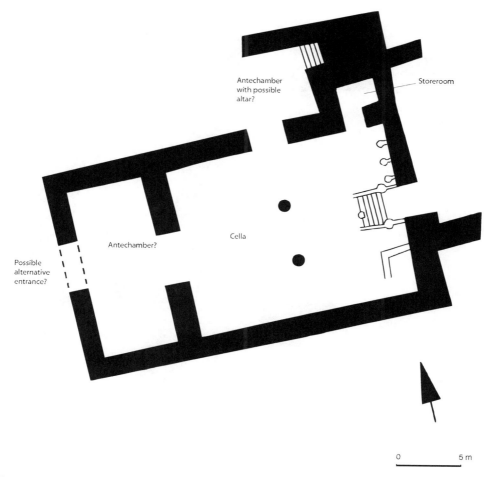

Antechamber
with possible
altar?

Storeroom

Antechamber?

Cella

Possible
alternative
entrance?

0   5 m

Fig. 77. Lachish, Area P, Stratum VI temple—Acropolis Summit Temple (after Ussishkin 1978: fig. 3; and Clamer and Ussishkin 1977: 73).

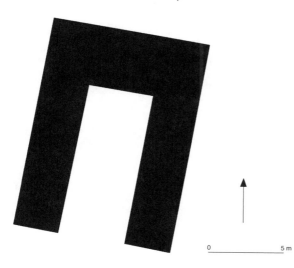

Fig. 78. Ebla, Temple B1, stratum IIIA–B (sector B; after Matthiae 1981: fig. 28).

0   5 m

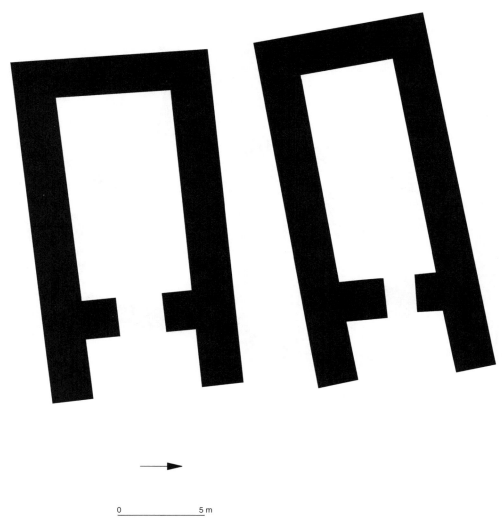

Fig. 79. Emar, temples of Baal and Astarte on the south of the southwest promontory, Late Bronze Age (after Margueron 1983: fig. 3).

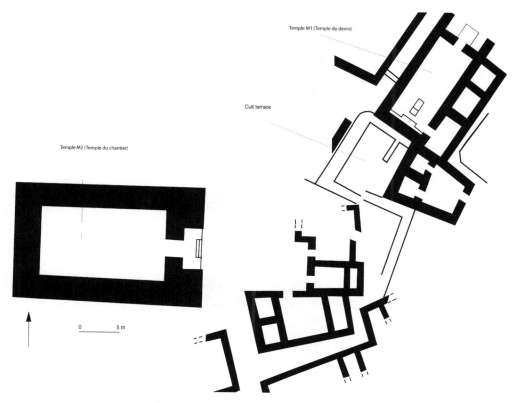

Temple M1 (Temple du devin)

Cult terrace

Temple M2 (Temple du chantier)

0   5 m

Fig. 80. Emar, Area M, cultic region (after Margueron 1983: fig. 4).

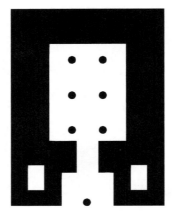

A

Temple 1a plan

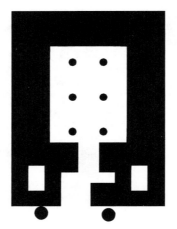

B

Temple 1b plan

Fig. 81. Shechem, Middle Bronze Age *migdāl* temple I (after G. E. Wright 1966: figs. 41, 46, 48).

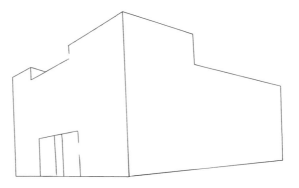

C

Temple 1a reconstruction

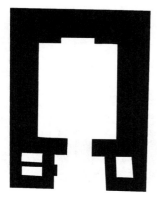

Fig. 82. Megiddo, Temple 2048—*migdāl* temple plan. Stratum VIII early phase (seventeenth century B.C.E., Middle Bronze Age; after G. E. Wright 1965: fig. 51; and Finkelstein and Ussishkin 1994: 31).

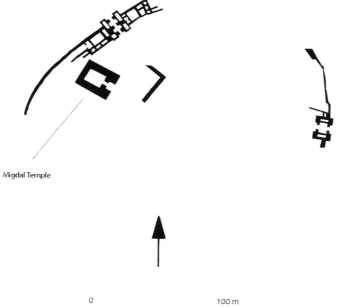

Migdal Temple

0   100 m

Fig. 83. Shechem, sketch plan of the site (after G. E. Wright 1965: fig. 13).

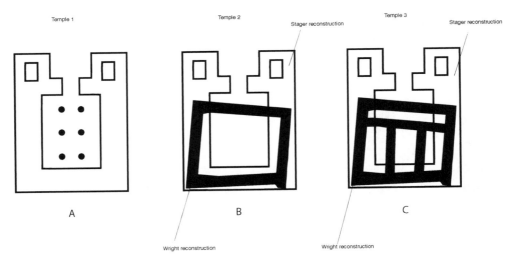

Fig. 84. Shechem, G. E. Wright and Stager *migdāl* temple plans (after G. E. Wright 1965; and Stager 2003: 30).

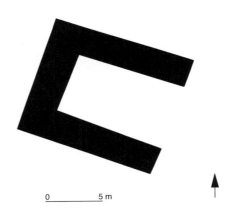

Fig. 85. Ebla, Temple N, Stratum III A–B (sector B; after Matthiae 1981: fig. 27).

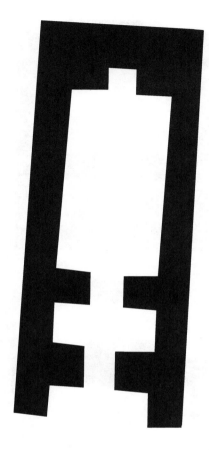

0   5 m

Fig. 86. Ebla, Temple D, stratum III A–B (sector B; after Matthiae 1981: fig. 30).

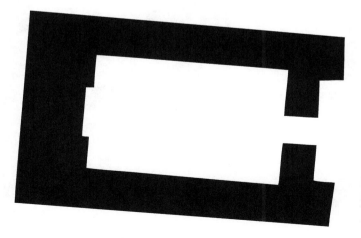

Fig. 87. Ebla, reconstructed plan for Temple P2 (after Bonfil 1997: plan II.9).

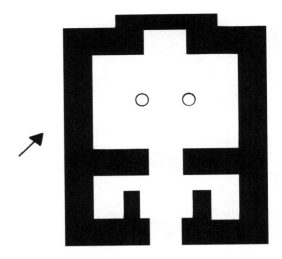

Fig. 88. Hazor, Area H, Middle Bronze
Age temple (after Mazar 1992a:
fig. 6.61C).

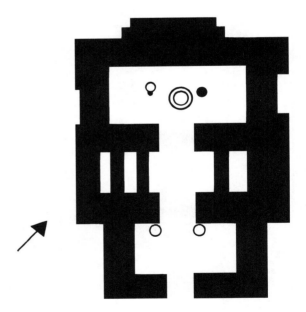

Fig. 89. Hazor, Area H, Late Bronze
Age temple, stratum XIII (thirteenth
century B.C.E.; after A. Mazar 1992a:
fig. 7.6; 1992b: fig. 4).

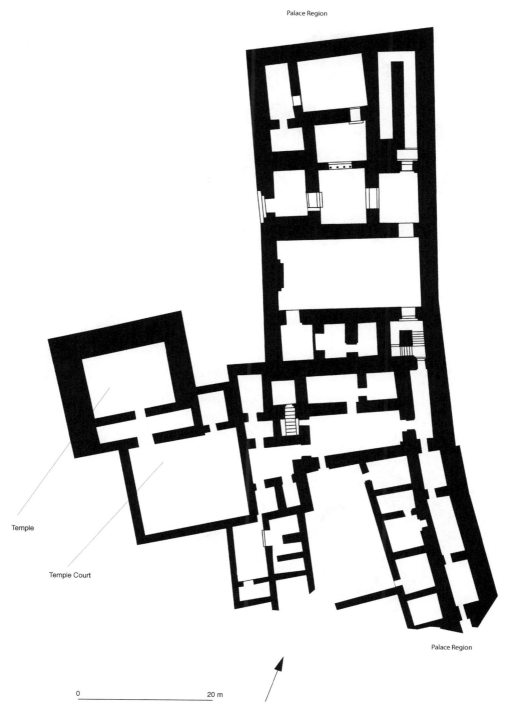

Palace Region

Temple

Temple Court

Palace Region

0 ——————————— 20 m

Fig. 90. Alalakh, temple and palace complex, stratum VII, Middle Bronze Age (after Woolley 1955: fig. 35).

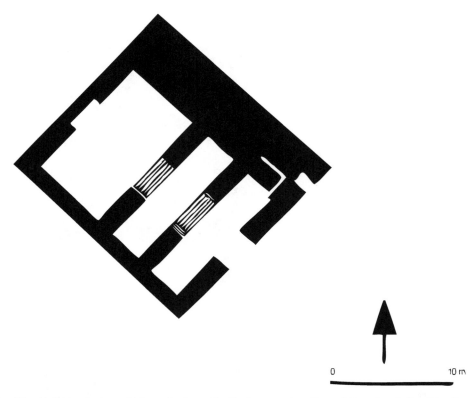

Fig. 91. Alalakh, stratum IV temple, hypothetical reconstruction of the plan (after Woolley 1958: fig. 16).

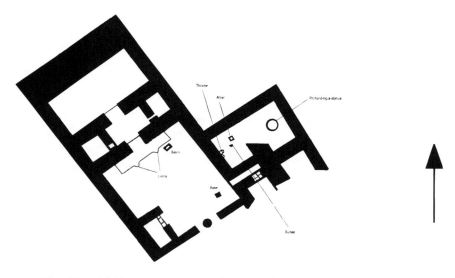

Fig. 92. Alalakh, stratum IB temple plan (after Woolley 1953: fig. 25).

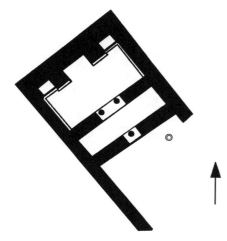

Fig. 93. Alalakh, stratum IA temple plan (after Woolley 1953: fig. 24).

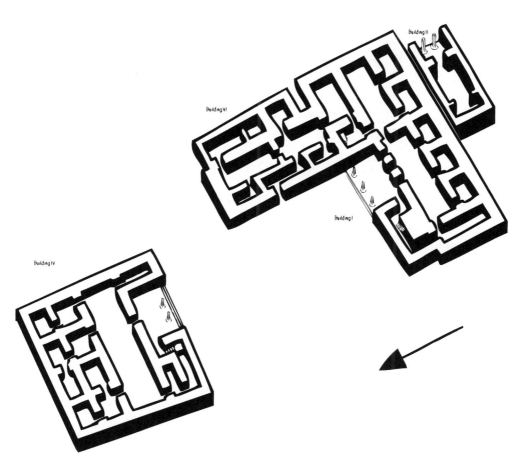

Fig. 94. Tell Taʿyinat, temple and palaces, phase II (after Haines 1971: pl. 106).

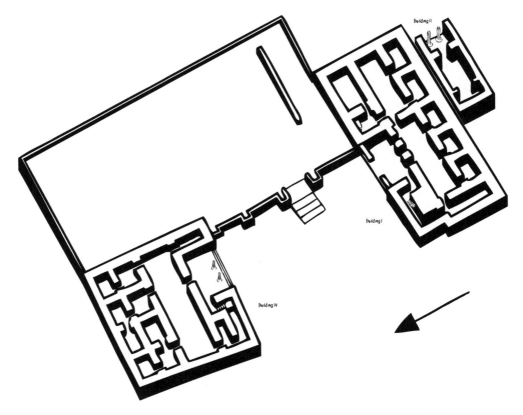

Fig. 95. Tell Taʿyinat, temple and palaces, phase III (after Haines 1971: pl. 107).

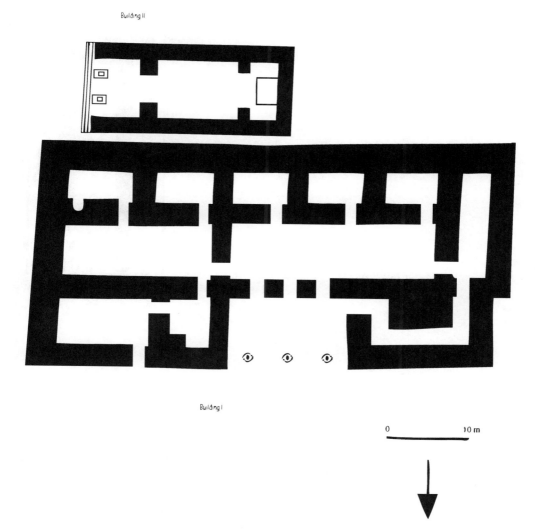

Fig. 96. Tell Taʿyinat, plan of the temple and the palace, phase II (after Busink 1970: fig. 166).

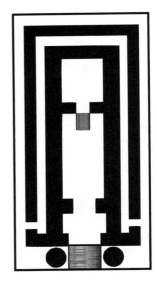

Fig. 97. Temple of Solomon, Reconstruction based on Watzinger and Mazar (after A. Mazar 1992a: fig. 9.4).

Fig. 98. Ugarit, acropolis temples (photo by the author).

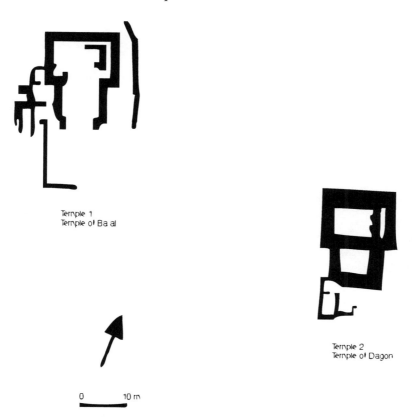

Temple 1
Temple of Ba al

Temple 2
Temple of Dagon

0   10 m

Fig. 99. Ugarit, sketch plan of the acropolis showing placement of the temples (after Yon 1984: fig. 2).

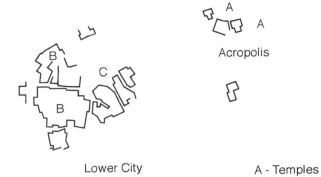

Acropolis

Lower City

A - Temples
B - Palaces
C - Houses

Fig. 100. Ugarit, sketch
plan of the major regions
of the site (after Mission
Archéologique de Ras Shamra
1979: fig. 2).

0   50 m

Fig. 101. Ugarit, acropolis temple 1 (photo by the author).

Fig. 102. Ugarit, palace (photo by the author).

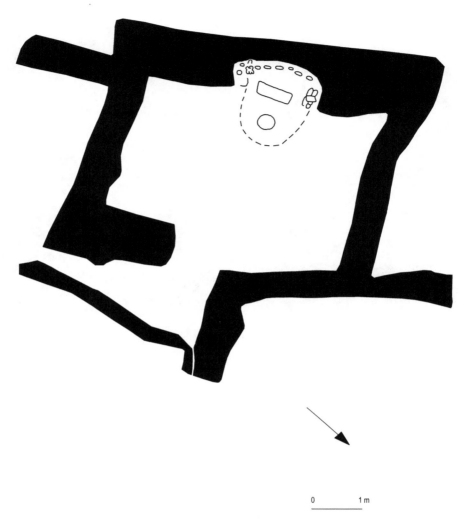

0 _____ 1 m

Fig. 103. Hazor, Area C temple, Iron Age (LBA III; after Yadin 1972: fig. 16).

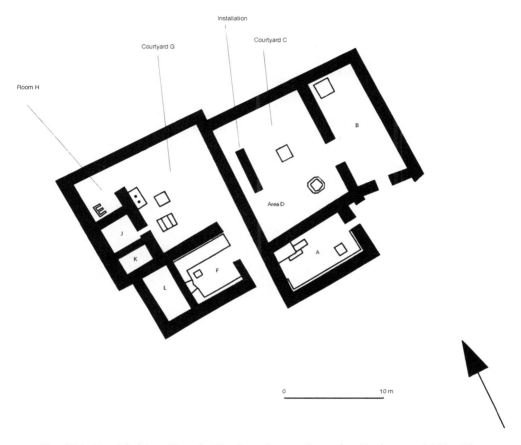

Fig. 104. Kamid el-Loz, Temple T2c (Late Bronze Age; after Hachmann 1983: 67).

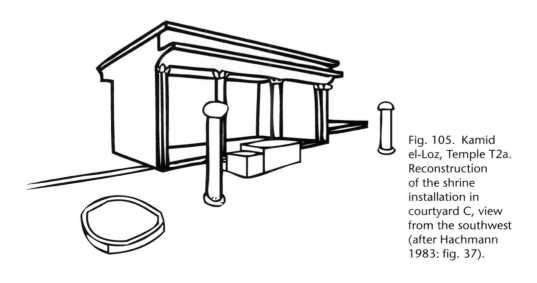

Fig. 105. Kamid el-Loz, Temple T2a. Reconstruction of the shrine installation in courtyard C, view from the southwest (after Hachmann 1983: fig. 37).

Fig. 106. Tel Dan, lower city roadway (photo by the author).

Fig. 107. Byblos, Temple of the Obelisks (photo by the author).

Fig. 108. Kition, Temple of Astarte (photo by the author).

Fig. 109. Palaepaphos, Temple of Aphrodite (photo by the author).

Fig. 110. ʿAin Dara, ashlar masonry (photo by the author).

Fig. 111. Wood-crib construction technique: based on findings from Zincirli (after Frankfort 1985: fig. 333).

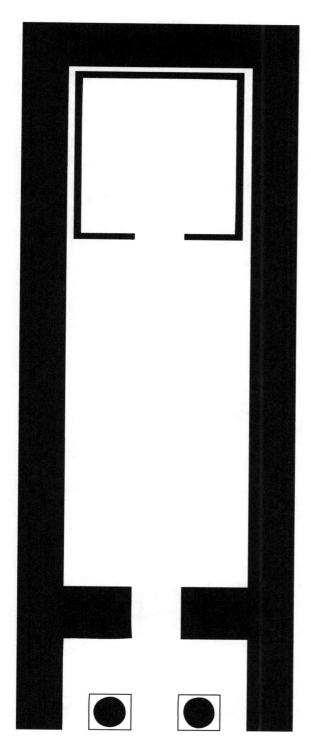

Fig. 112. Temple of Solomon, reconstruction based on Fritz 1987b: 41.

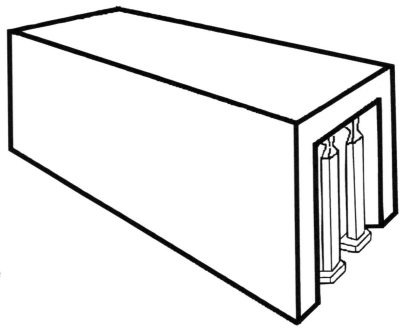

Fig. 113. Temple
of Solomon,
reconstruction
based on Fritz
1987b: 41.

Fig. 114. Temple
of Solomon,
reconstruction
based on Busink
(after Busink in
Meyers 1991: 39).

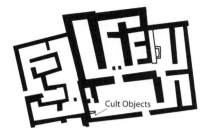

Cult Objects

Fig. 115. Megiddo, stratum VA complex with cult room (Building 2081; after Wright 1985: vol. 2, fig. 182).

0   10 m

Fig. 116a (left). Tell El-Farʿah North, terra-cotta shrine model (Israel Museum, IAA 1940–286); Fig. 116b (below). Ramat Rahel, Balustrade, eighth–seventh century B.C.E. (Israel Museum, IAA 1964-1287).

Fig. 117. "Woman at the Window," from Nimrud ivories (British Museum ME 118159).

Fig. 118. Yazılıkaya
(photo by the
author).

Fig. 119. Hattuša, Great Temple (photo by the author).

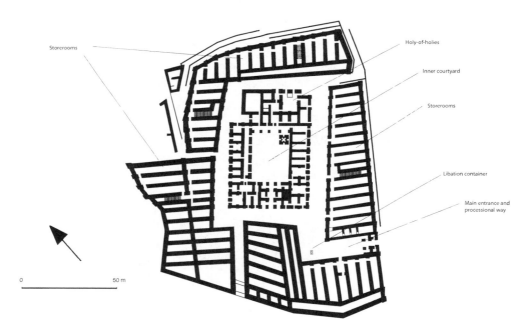

Fig. 120. Hattuša, Great Temple (Temple I) plan (after MacQueen 1986: fig. 108).

Fig. 121. Guzana, Metope (Walters Museum).

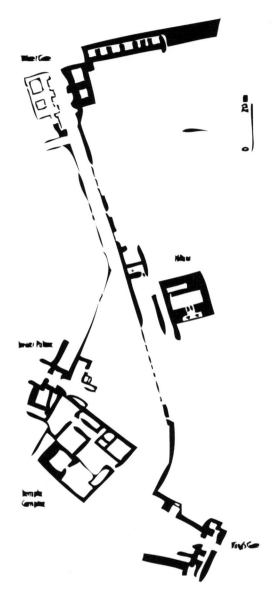

Fig. 122. Carchemish, processional route
(after Woolley 1952: pl. 41a).

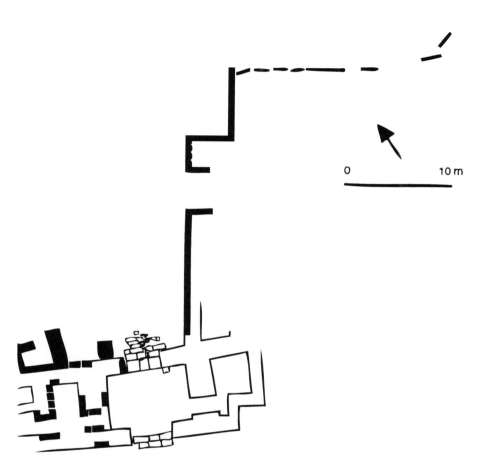

Fig. 123: Carchemish, King's Gate (after Woolley 1952: pl. 43a).

Fig. 124. Guzana, reconstruction of the griffin statue in the entrance of the temple-palace, Aleppo Archaeological Museum (photo by the author).

Fig. 125. Tell Ta'yinat, base (photo by the author).

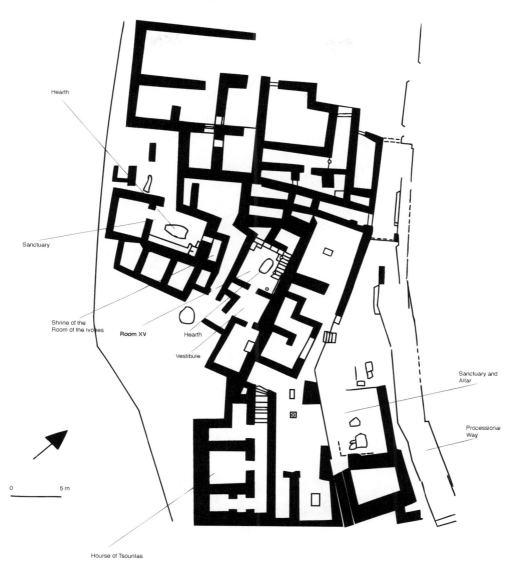

Fig. 126. Mycenae, sacred area with temple and sanctuaries (after Rutkowski 1986: fig. 255).

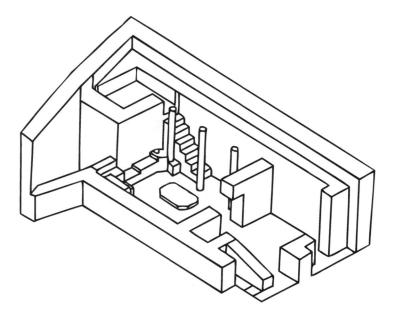

Fig. 127. Mycenae, isodomic reconstruction of the sanctuary (Room XV) from the sacred area of the site (after Rutkowski 1986: fig. 258).

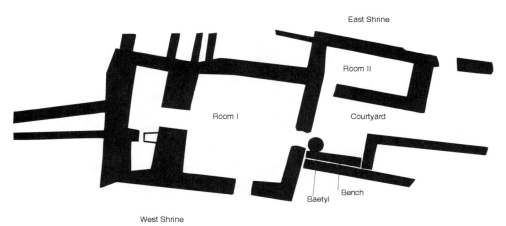

Fig. 128. Philakopi, plan of the sanctuary, phase IIa (Late Bronze Age, LH IIIBI; after Rutkowski 1986: fig. 263).

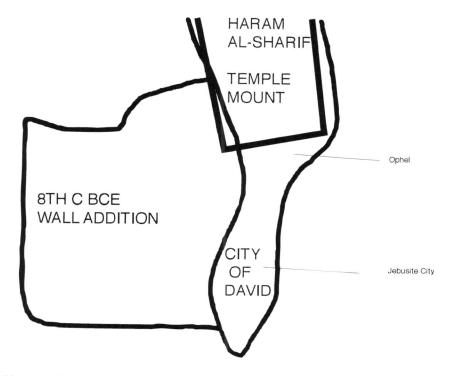

Fig. 129. Jerusalem, schematic plan of the spread of the Iron Age City (after Shanks 2000: 40).

Fig. 130. Carchemish, *ḫilani* plan (after Woolley 1953: pl. 38).

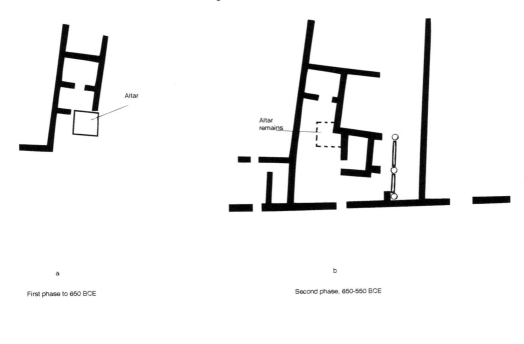

a

First phase to 650 BCE

b

Second phase, 650-550 BCE

0   5 m

Fig. 131. Kition-Bamboula, Archaic-period sanctuary phases a and b (after Caubet 1984: figs. 1, 2, 4).

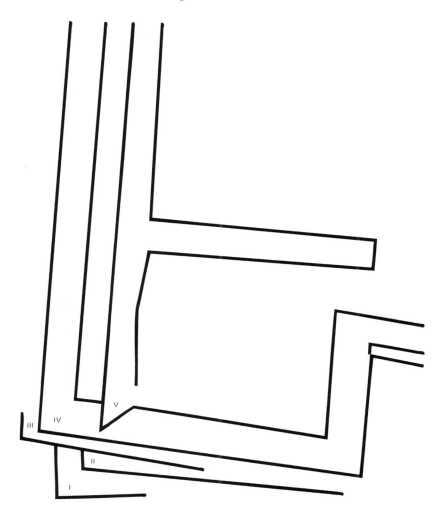

Fig. 132. El Cerro de San Juan del Río, plan showing the remains of the superimposed temples (after Escacena Carrasco and de Montes 1998: fig. 3).

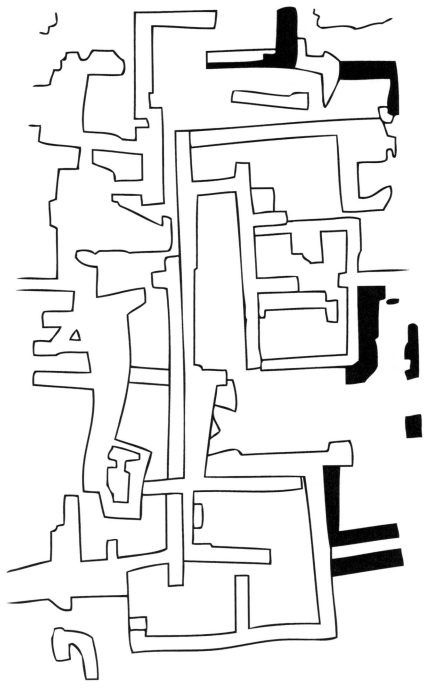

Fig. 133. El Carambolo, remains of the major structure in level IV, possibly a temple (in solid black lines), shown in relation to the later walls on the site (after Belén Deamos 2001: fig. 2).

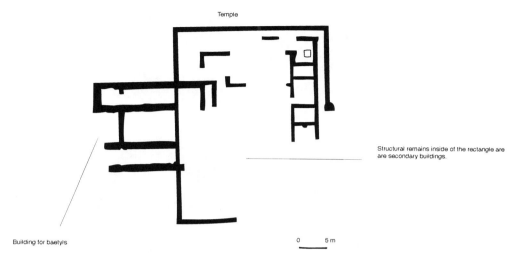

Temple

Structural remains inside of the rectangle are
are secondary buildings.

Building for baetyls

0   5 m

Fig. 134. Motya, temple at Cappidazzu plan (after Isserlin 1982: fig. 7).

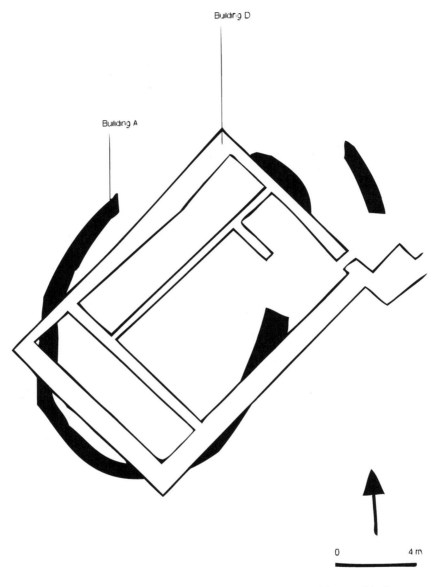

Fig. 135. El Cerro de Montemolín (Marchena), acropolis with Building D (sixth century B.C.E.) superimposed atop Building A (eighth–seventh centuries B.C.E.; after Belén Deamos 2001: fig. 8).

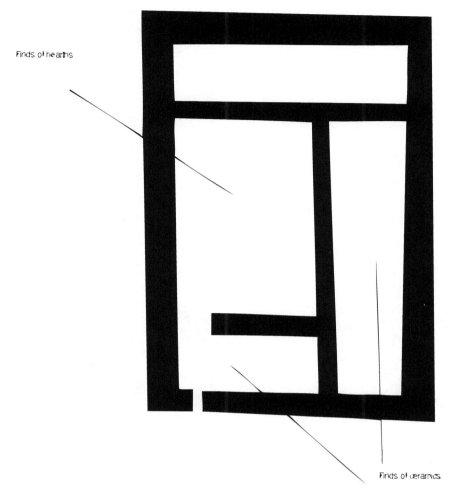

Finds of hearths

Finds of ceramics

Fig. 136. El Cerro de Montemolín (Marchena), Building D with internal walls and types of finds marked (after Belén Deamos 2001: fig. 9).

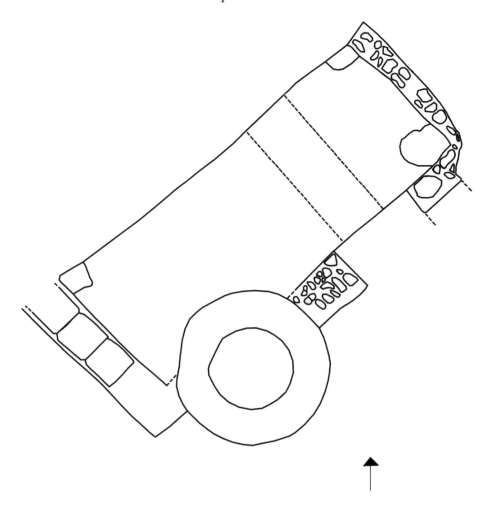

Fig. 137. Carmona, Cult Building (after Neville 2007: fig. 4.5).

Index of Authors

Wright, G. E.   166, 168, 169,
    170, 173, 184, 188, 225,
    253
Wright, G. R. H.   2, 12, 13, 93,
    101, 134, 155, 157, 158,
    159, 164, 167, 181, 182,
    185, 186, 187, 188, 190,
    193, 194, 196, 197, 198

Xella, P.   243

Yadin, Y.   3, 8, 32, 90, 91, 98,
    103, 172, 184, 188, 195,
    205, 212, 237, 254
Yassine, K.   105
Yasur-Landau, T.   38, 39, 51,
    52, 73, 216, 218, 219
Yeivin, S.   185
Yener, A.   21, 98, 113
Yisrael, Y.   141
Yoffee, N.   304
Yon, M.   109, 181, 182

Younger, J. G.   199

Zarzecki-Peleg, A.   178, 179
Zayadine, F.   44, 54, 278
Zertal, A.   42, 43, 94, 95, 96,
    97, 193, 238
Ziffer, I.   172
Zimansky, P.   63
Zimmerli, W.   12
Zukerman, A.   39, 40, 49, 60
Zwickel, W.   2, 4, 250, 252, 253

Index of Ancient Sources

Classical Sources
Avienus
  Ora Maritima
    255   290
Clement of Alexandria
  Stromata
    1.114   244
Herodotus
  Histories
    1.83   16
    2.44   117, 284
    2.44–45   245
    2.45   206
    2.115   287
    6.19   16
Homer
  Iliad
    1.39   15
Josephus
  Against Apion
    1.113   272
    1.118–19   246
    17.18.116–17   244
    17.106–8   244
    17.113   146
    17.113–16   244

Josephus *(cont.)*
  Antiquities
    1.6.2.130–38   47
    1.6.4.143–45   47
    1.12.4.22–221   47
    8.144–47   244
    8.146–47   246
  Jewish War
    5.5.7   14
    15.184   253
Justin
  Epitoma
    18.3.2–5   32
Nonnios
  Dionysiaca
    40.465–500   247
Philostratus
  Vita Apollonii
    5.5   288, 290
Ptolemy
  Geographia
    4.3.13   286
Silius Italicus
  Punicia
    3.14–60   288

Strabo
  3.5.5   287, 290
  3.5.5–9   288
  5.25.12   284
Thucydides
  History
    6.2   293
Verres
  In Verrem
    2.4.46.104   286
Xenophon
  Apology
    15   16

Ancient Near Eastern Sources
CTA
  4.5.116–19   56
KAI
  47:1   243
KTU
  1.24:14   181
  1.100:15   181
  6.13   181
  6.14   181
KUB
  55.43 iv 31   209
RS
  1[089] + 2[033] + 5183   182
  4.427   182

Index of Biblical Sources

Index of Ancient Sites

Index of Topics

The Index of Topics, in addition to general subjects, also includes modern geographic names cited in the text.

473